Todd & Wilson's
Textbook on Trusts

Todd & Wilson's

Textbook on

Trusts

....

Ninth edition

Sarah Wilson
LLB, MA, PhD

OXFORD
UNIVERSITY PRESS

OXFORD
UNIVERSITY PRESS

Great Clarendon Street, Oxford OX2 6DP

Oxford University Press is a department of the University of Oxford.
It furthers the University's objective of excellence in research, scholarship,
and education by publishing worldwide in

Oxford New York

Auckland Cape Town Dar es Salaam Hong Kong Karachi
Kuala Lumpur Madrid Melbourne Mexico City Nairobi
New Delhi Shanghai Taipei Toronto

With offices in

Argentina Austria Brazil Chile Czech Republic France Greece
Guatemala Hungary Italy Japan Poland Portugal Singapore
South Korea Switzerland Thailand Turkey Ukraine Vietnam

Oxford is a registered trade mark of Oxford University Press
in the UK and in certain other countries

Published in the United States
by Oxford University Press Inc., New York

© Sarah Wilson, 2009

British Library Cataloguing in Publication Data

Data available

Library of Congress Cataloging in Publication Data

Data available

Typeset by Newgen Imaging Systems (P) Ltd., Chennai, India
Printed in Great Britain
on acid-free paper by
Ashford Colour Press Ltd, Gosport, Hampshire

ISBN 978–0–19–955308–2

1 3 5 7 9 10 8 6 4 2

OUTLINE CONTENTS

DETAILED CONTENTS

5   Formalities and other requirements for validity   116

6   Perpetuities   133

7 Introduction to resulting and constructive trusts 149

8 Resulting trusts, gifts to non-charitable unincorporated associations, and pension funds 174

9 Beneficial interests in the family home: a case study 193

10 Secret and half-secret trusts (and constructive and resulting trusts)   249

11 Equitable fraud and the constructive trust   269

14   Cy près   346

15   The office of trustee: commencement and termination   360

---

16 Powers, discretions, and duties of trustees   392

---

17 Variation of trusts   409

18 Breach of trust 424

19 Remedies 457

PREFACE

This book continues the tradition begun by Paul Todd in being aimed primarily at law students in their second or third year of undergraduate study at university. It is an introductory text, and therefore it is shorter than many traditional textbooks on trusts available today. Like its predecessors it aims to present the law as briefly as possible without sacrificing clarity in the more complex areas, and in this spirit, I have always been mindful to concentrate on principle rather than detail. In terms of scope, the book continues to prioritize areas commonly taught on trusts courses rather than attempting to encompass everything about equity and trusts, and thus it continues to give less coverage to those aspects of equity and trusts usually covered elsewhere in undergraduate law programmes (notably land law, contract, commercial law and English legal system). This edition continues this emphasis, but it also has a number of matters which need specific reference in this introduction.

Although it is the case that the text has always concentrated on providing comprehensive coverage within areas commonly taught, rather than across the entire sphere of equitable jurisdiction and even the entire operations of trusts law, there has been a slight increase in its size overall. This reflects the way that even if 'the subject' of trusts law is not actually increasing in size, then the materials which are required for understanding it are increasing in volume. This can be seen, for example, in the areas of charity law, remedies following breach of trust, and also trusts arising from cohabitation where there have been rapid developments in recent times, but also ones characteristically of a nature which requires understanding of past approaches, and even significant integration of past and new approaches. This has led to the need for slightly increased coverage overall, but it has also precipitated new thinking on how the text is presented and how its guide through trusts law is actually approached. This has set in motion a much more comprehensive use made, in the preparation of this text, of its companion Online Resource Centre.

It was always likely in any case that the ORC was going to be very important for areas experiencing rapid and extensive development, and here it provides a mechanism for very quick communication of key developments in law, or policy movements, which occur between editions. However, it is also the case that the nature of developments has meant that the ORC's use is gradually being extended beyond this, and even beyond the further rationale highlighted in the 2007 edition which is illuminated further below. The sheer volume of materials required for understanding key aspects of trusts in the twenty-first century has resulted in two new developments in the use made of the ORC in this edition, both of which are likely to be extended still further subsequently. The first 'new use' of the ORC is that some areas which are becoming less significant in the way trusts courses are commonly taught are being relocated on the ORC to allow maximum 'text space' for ones which are currently most important. In this edition this can be seen in materials from the last edition, providing a brief companion to the Land Registration Act 2002, which have now been relocated to the ORC. The same has happened to materials concerning covenants to settle property on trust, which have been removed from their traditional location in the chapter concerning the constituting of trusts. The second innovation in the use of the ORC also follows on from the need to provide maximum text space for central materials, but it also reflects the way in which this text has always sought to provide consideration and critical appraisal of, and insight into, legal developments as part of its analysis of how trusts law is composed and how it operates. Thus, while the text would consider 'wider perspectives' as part of its core analysis of trusts law, the growing volume of 'key materials' means that it no longer always possible to locate them alongside the main text materials which they accompany. For this reason the ORC is likely, increasingly, to be the place for 'wider perspectives' or 'further reflections' on a particular matter. In this particular edition this can be seen with some of the 'older' materials on charity law, and also in relation to materials on the way in which it is possible for the Fraud Act 2006 to impact on trustees and even the office of trusteeship itself.

As suggested immediately above, the ORC is considered a very important development for this text for an additional reason. This is because in the 2005 edition I commenced a concerted effort to integrate more closely the law of trusts with the scholarship which has grown up around it. And in this regard, the limitations of space within the actual text have always been a rationale for a well developed companion online resource centre. And in this edition I am wishing to reaffirm the way in which I believe that the study of trusts can be enriched greatly by reference to the work of academics. I am also reiterating that the ORC represents a very effective way of squaring this very real advantage for study with the very real constraints in space which are present to ensure that the text does not grow any more than is necessary. This is because allowing it to do so could compromise one of this text's signature features—that of providing an introductory text which concentrates on explaining key principles clearly, and in the most comprehensive way possible, without appearing to be intimidating.

Thus, this edition remains more or less the size it has always been, but it is supported by an increasingly comprehensive external learning resource in the form of the ORC, which also aims to deliver important changes quickly and effectively in-between editions. And in this vein, the book continues to emphasize—either in the text or in the ORC—that trusts is not only a highly dynamic area, but one of monumental importance across social and economic spheres, and also domestic and commercial environs. Thus, trusts lawyers are required to focus critically on new developments, and increasingly to do so by engaging with writings beyond this edition, in studies of economy and society, regulation, sociology, and critical approaches to professional practise and cultures.

In terms of the actual *content* of this current edition, as suggested above, greatest coverage continues to be given to areas most squarely within the ambit of equity and trusts, and which students are unlikely to know much about prior to undertaking the study of equity and trusts. However there is much that is new in this edition, and no fewer than six of its chapters have been completely, or at least very substantially, rewritten on account of two factors. Most obviously, much change in the content of the book reflects actual developments which have occurred in spheres of law-making or policy. However it is also the case that two chapters have been entirely rewritten in order to take a fresh look at fundamental considerations in introducing trusts law to students.

This latter proposition can be seen in the new chapters which seek actually to introduce trusts and trusts law, and the wider underpinnings of both in English law's distinctive equitable jurisdiction which subsists alongside legal rights and remedies, which are altogether more familiar to students of law when they start to undertake a study of trusts. Accordingly the new chapter 1 is very much oriented towards trying to explain the phenomena of equity and equitable jurisdiction, as well as introducing students to the idea of a 'trust device', and why anyone might wish to create a trust, and for what purposes. The point is also made at this stage that in the twenty-first century, the trust can be found being used across a number of different social and economic situations, and reflecting relationships between people which are domestic and commercial and 'professional' alike. This latter theme is developed more comprehensively in chapter 2, but the new chapter 1 provides a better companion to this than its predecessor, and does, I think, address at a more basic and helpful level key questions of 'what are trusts?' 'why use a trust?'. It is here that materials which have traditionally been located here remain, such as ones relating to the origins of equity and the nature of equitable jurisdiction and the way in which some equitable interests are regarded as 'real' rights relating to property. But it is equally focused on identifying the key features of a trust, and the different 'parties' found within the trust setting, and especially on indicating why trusts are to be found so widely used.

A similar, although not identical, approach can be found in a newly written chapter 3 which has traditionally been entitled 'Constitution of Trusts and Covenants to Settle'. As indicated above, materials relating to covenants to settle property on trust have been relocated from the main text into the ORC, but the new chapter 3 also reflects more fundamental rethinking of the traditional content and presentation of the subject matter of the requirement that in order to be valid a trust must be constituted. Although the way in which this is strongly oriented towards the legal requirements of transferring property from one person to another has always been reflected in the materials, the complexities arising here are now given much greater emphasis. Thus the new chapter tackles directly the ways in which determining 'what is required' does not always easily distinguish the creation of a trust from other dealings relating to property where *title* to it is being passed from one person to another. Thus the new chapter is actually called 'Constitution of trusts and equity's "perfection" of transfers of property' to try to address this, and to make more explicit the legal requirements and the role of equity in transfers of property from one person to another generally. It is hoped that this approach will help to clarify an area where students can experience difficulties on account of having to grasp principles of equity which apply to the creation of trusts but also beyond this, and where key case law is characterized by unhelpful and often unclear references to transfers of property which are in furtherance of creating 'trusts' and making 'gifts'.

As indicated above there have also been a number of chapters re-written on account of actual changes in law, or key policy development—and in several cases a combination of the two. In many respects, the least radical rewriting has occurred in chapter 7's 'Introduction to Resulting and Constructive Trusts', but even here some vital reworking in this location has arisen on account of developments in relation to the family home and also in the sphere of remedies. In relation to the former, this is on account of changing emphasis on the similarities and differences between constructive trusts and proprietary estoppel; and also a rethinking of the relative importance of resulting trusts as well as ones which are constructive in light of the key House of Lords' decision in *Stack v Dowden* in 2007 (on which more follows shortly). In relation to the latter, in the study of remedies (explored further in chapter 19), the spotlight very much continues to be on constructive trusteeship in developments relating to liability for 'strangers' to a trust arising from 'knowing receipt' of trust property or 'dishonest assistance' of a breach of trust. These have been noted in the introduction to constructive trusts in chapter 7. This facilitates extensive discussion in chapter 19, which includes an examination of views suggesting that stranger liability might be more effectively and comprehensively achieved by attaching it not to constructive trusteeship, but instead to restitutionary principles of unjust enrichment.

On account of the text immediately preceding, in terms of identifying chapters which have been completely rewritten for this edition, perhaps it is appropriate at this point to introduce chapter 19. In this edition chapter 19 has been almost entirely rewritten for a number of purposes, including the reflection of developments in the sphere of constructive trusteeship, as part of the 'sum' of actions which are available to a beneficiary in circumstances where trust property 'disappears' following a trustee's breach of trust. However, it is also the case that the section on the nature of equity's remedies which opens chapter 19 has been extended to provide greater coverage on injunctions. But most space within the chapter continues to be devoted to the principles which are guiding proprietary tracing claims, constructive trusteeship, and restitutionary actions, and current thought on their interrelationships with one another. Here most emphasis continues to be given to actions which are available to a beneficiary under a trust (and thus remedies available in equity rather than at common law), with the key case of *Foskett v McKeown* [2000] 3 All ER 97 pointing also to the continuing prominence within 'tracing' claims of principles of proprietary entitlement, and less emphasis on alternative approaches in restitution.

However this edition also seeks to explore—tentatively at least—the way in which *Foskett v McKeown* also appears to be authority for a further emerging trend of utmost significance. In standing as authority for the prominence of 'proprietary entitlement', *Foskett* appears also to be an important statement on the *nature of* proprietary entitlement in the twenty-first century, suggesting that increasingly less distinction should be drawn (than is currently the case) between actions available to those who own property at law and those who own proprietary interests in equity, such as a beneficiary under a trust. Thus, some tentative consideration is given to the likelihood that an increasingly universal approach to tracing actions might emerge over time. Alongside this, attention is also paid to 'personal' remedies following breach of trust, and continuing debate about the legal basis for actions currently pursued as 'knowing receipt', and also recent developments in 'dishonest assistance' embodied in the Court of Appeal decision in *Adnan Shaaban Abou-Rahmah v Al-Haji Abdul Kadir Abacha* [2006] EWCA Civ 1492, and its relationship with that of the Privy Council in *Barlow Clowes International Ltd (in liquidation) v Eurotrust International Ltd* [2006] 1 All ER 333 which was given extensive treatment in the 2007 edition.

The 2007 edition 'flagged up' the way in which this text is seeking to provide a continuing focus on highly dynamic aspects of trusts law, such as remedies, and ones which are found increasingly in 'everyday-life', such as 'commercial dimensions' of trusts, and the role of trusts in respect of personal asset management and in ownership of the family home. It also noted a commitment to continue to include areas such as perpetuity requirements for private trusts, which are considerably less dynamic and are no longer even widely taught, on account that they do remain a fundamental part of trusts law, and students of trusts do need to have some appreciation that they exist and what purpose they might serve. In respect of those areas which *are* dynamic, it has not been possible to work on them with equal diligence in this edition, and priority has had to be given to materials relating to charity, and also the study of trusts and the family home, with the impetus for both arising from changes in law.

Taking the former first, the Charities Act 2006 which received Royal Assent in November 2006 has required chapter 12—introducing charity law—to be extensively reworked, and chapter 13 on the legal definition of charity to be almost entirely rewritten. This is so as to explain the relationships subsisting between 'traditional' approaches to accommodating charity in English law and the statutory provisions of the 2006 Act. Thus, key changes in the administration of charitable organizations—especially the creation of the Charity Commission as a statutory *body*, and also the creation of the Charitable Incorporated Organization (CIO) as a new 'choice of form' for charitable organizations are considered in chapter 12, whilst extensive consideration is given to the legal definition of charity itself in chapter 13. Thus as the materials above suggest, chapter 13 remains strongly focused on explaining traditional approaches to defining charity in English law, but this is now strongly oriented towards explaining the interactions between traditional approaches and the new ones in furtherance of the new statutory provisions. In continuing to make reference to the way in which the new regime under the 2006 Act is coming into force incrementally through a number of commencement orders, it has been duly noted that the provisions relating to the definition of charity, including ones relating to public benefit, came into force in April 2008. And in respect of the latter—public benefit—there is an extensive consideration of the Charity Commission's Guidance on Public Benefit which was published in January 2008.

In respect of the latter, developments relating to the family home, it is the case that chapter 9 has been almost entirely re-written to reflect developments which commenced in earnest a very short time after publication of the 2007 edition. This chapter had actually been extensively reworked in the 2007 edition to provide an analysis reflecting three key considerations. The first two concerned the Court of Appeal decision in *Oxley* v *Hiscock* [2004] 3 All ER 703: firstly, considering it as the leading case on *quantifying* equitable interests in family homes, and also secondly, observing that it stood as a 'high watermark' authority for the courts' use of proprietary estoppel principles in making determinations of ownership. Thirdly, the chapter also gave extensive consideration to policy movements in this sphere beyond the work of the courts, and embodied in the work of the Law Commission. Although the Law Commission has made a number of contributions to the 'sharing homes' question, the 2007 edition of the *Textbook* gave a lengthy reportage on the progress of Cohabitation Project announced in 2005. Building on the coverage given then to the publication of the Consultation Paper No. 179 *Cohabitation: The Financial Consequences of Relationship Breakdown*, this new edition integrates the 2007 *Report on Cohabitation* published in July 2007.

However, the biggest impetus for the changes made to this chapter in this new edition has arisen from the House of Lords' decision in *Stack* v *Dowden* [2007] UKHL 17. From this it is clear that *Oxley* is no longer the leading case on quantification of beneficial shares, and albeit that *Stack* endorsed much of *Oxley*'s spirit and direction in this regard, there are also some marked differences between the two cases. The new chapter seeks to explain the interplay between these two key decisions in making a clear statement on the current state of the law. And furthermore the materials also explore the way in which *Stack* has added a number of very important considerations to the sphere of shared home ownership (and especially introducing a new type of case of disputed home ownership), as well as providing some much needed clarity in certain respects. Read alongside newer cases still (and especially *Abbot* v *Abbott* [2007] UKPC 53; *Fowler* v *Barron* [2008] EWCA 377; and *James* v *Thomas* [2007] EWCA Civ 1212) the analysis of *Stack* also seeks to explore the proposition that although parts of the House of Lords' decision were very critical of the landmark decision of the House in *Lloyds Bank* v *Rosset* [1991] 1 AC 107 (HL), actually establishing a proprietary interest in a shared property does remain governed by the criteria of this earlier House of Lords' decision.

Elsewhere in the text, changes of a more incremental nature have been made in this new edition, alongside the constant tasks associated with updating. For example, brief reference is made to the way in which the Law Commission has now resumed work on considerations relating to capital and income in the context of (powers and duties arising from) investment: following publication in 2004 of Consultation Paper No. 175 on *Capital and Income in Trusts: Classification and Apportionment*, work on this project was suspended in 2006 to allow for the completion of the Cohabitation project. And still within the broad sphere of trustees' activities, fleeting reference has been made to the Companies Act 2006, which was (like the Charities Act 2006 which received Royal Assent at the same time) only starting to come into force when the 2007 edition was being prepared. Although extensive reflection on the Companies Act 2006 is not required for this text, it does influence the coverage which has traditionally been given to fiduciary relationships and liability in equity flowing from 'fiduciary office'. In this edition, thus, reference is made to the approach taken in the legislation to *special* rules for corporate fiduciaries which do mark a departure from traditional equitable rules concerning fiduciaries *generally*.

When commencing your study of trusts it is worth appreciating that concepts in trusts law are very difficult, and this is not helped by the way in which many appear to be 'abstract' rather than tangible, and the way in which the accompanying terminology can on occasion be very confusing. And to assist this, as a matter of presentation, the text makes reference only to words 'he' and 'his', that are used interchangably for both genders. In recognition of this, every effort has been made to make the materials as accessible as possible, while trying to explain the concepts as fully as possible. And it is also worth remembering that although you will find things difficult at times, trusts is a really fascinating subject which is *definitely* worth the effort which it will take trying to get to grips with.

This was my impression as a student, and it certainly remains so now that I am a teacher myself. It is also the case that my own experiences as a student, as well as a teacher, strongly suggest that the best law students are not those who necessarily do the most work, but those who think hardest about the subject. I encourage my own students to email me, and each other, since this is a good way of discussing things. It also gives insight into areas of difficulty, and often encourages me to consider things I might have missed.

In terms of those to whom thanks are owed as a new edition of this text is published, I would like to thank Anna Lawson, Michael Cardwell and Sarah Blandy for inspiration and friendship. And at the University of Manchester special thanks are due to my friend Gillian Ulph for the stimulation and support she provides tirelessly, and also Margot Brazier for her support on a more general level. As always special thanks are due to my husband and colleague Gary Wilson for all the support he provides, all the time, and especially for his thoughtful and extremely valuable insights into trusts law.

And lastly (but certainly not least), I would also like to thank the editorial and production staff at OUP for all their hard work in helping to prepare this edition, and for their support and expertise, from which as an author I continue to benefit considerably.

It remains only for me to encourage you to enjoy your study of trusts.

The law is, as far as possible, stated as it stood 31 January 2009.

Sarah Wilson
sarah.wilson@manchester.ac.uk

TABLE OF CASES

TABLE OF STATUTES

STATUTORY INSTRUMENTS

1

Law and equity and an introduction
to the trust

A trust is a device where there are two types of 'ownership' of property simultaneously in existence. In a trust situation, ownership of property is divided into two types of ownership in or title to property: legal title, and equitable title, and in this arrangement these distinctive titles will exist at the same time. The reasons for this will become more apparent, as will the consequences for this being the case, and also the way in which this is actually possible. Thus the purpose of this chapter is to explore fundamentally what is meant by a 'trust' and why trusts arise and what purposes they serve. The chapter is also concerned to explain that this extremely useful, flexible, and highly adaptable device, which has a number of uses in everyday life across commercial dealings and in the context of interpersonal relationships, is capable of existing on account of a distinctive jurisdiction found within English law. The basis for the trust instrument to subsist in English law is equity and the equitable jurisdiction subsisting in English law.

The jurisdictional basis for the trust instrument, and indeed the characteristics of this jurisdiction itself will become more clear in due course, and these very first materials concern why equity might have evolved the trust instrument at all. It will be explained how equity actually developed the trust, and how this was even possible on account of equity's own origins and lasting significance. In terms of fundamental questions of why equity has developed the trust, the key to understanding this lies in relation to appreciating the significance of 'property' in English law, and particularly the significance of ownership of property.

Thus, in the trust scenario there are two types of ownership of property simultaneously in existence, and the rationale for this is located in appreciating the significance of property and its ownership in English law.

1.1 English law and two types of ownership

It is not really the place of this particular textbook to provide an account of property and ownership in English law. There are other texts which are dedicated to this and which have been written for this very purpose, and which will provide very detailed discussion of English law and 'property' itself and of the concept of ownership, in terms of the nature of ownership, and its rootings in 'property', its nature of entitlements and rights, and how it might differ for example from possession. However, understanding why equity has evolved the trust, and what uses and purposes it serves does require some appreciation of how important property is in English law and particularly in relation to rights arising within the context of private law.

In this manner, understanding the trust involves some appreciation of the way in which in English law distinction is drawn between ownership at law and that which subsists in equity. It will very shortly become apparent that these types of ownership as they operate in English law are very different, but that nevertheless they are capable of simultaneous existence, and will often arise simultaneously in respect of property. Indeed, this book is all about the consequences of the simultaneous occurrence of these two types of ownership. And this itself stems from the significance of ownership of property which is ownership of property at law.

1.1.1 The significance of ownership of property in English law

In the course of everyday dealings it is very clear that property is owned by a given individual. Much of the property which is encountered in everyday life is identifiable with 'an owner' (although note the observation which is made in respect of land shortly). And in this usual scenario of ownership, all the rights and interests relating to that property are those of the owner of property, and this is reflected in the owner holding legal title to the property. In this scenario ownership is not in any way split.

In English law, legal title represents rights of the owner which are 'good against the world', and holding legal title represents the right which the owner of property has to deal freely with his property. Holding legal title entitles an owner of property to sell it (where legal title will be transferred to a new owner); or to use the property to raise security. Both these benefits of holding legal title indicate that this is capable of having considerable value, and thus title to property facilitates free dealings and dealings with confidence, because ascertaining someone has legal title to property is crucial to knowing it is theirs to sell or to use to raise security. Notwithstanding that title to property is the basis for these transactions, and that legal title is extremely valuable, one of the rights that an owner of property enjoys by virtue of being its owner is that he is entitled to give it to another.

In this situation, where a gift is made, legal title to the property is transferred to the recipient because this is what its original owner wishes to happen. In this latter situation the owner is not wishing the transfer to be one for consideration. Making gifts is something which happens so commonly that few will give any thought to how this happens, and what this amounts to. Legal title to (and thus ownership of) property is transferred to another because the donor wishes this to happen.

1.2 Understanding the trust: appreciating the nature of equitable and legal title: *Westdeutsche Landesbank Girozentrale* v *Islington LBC*

Unlike in the case of absolute ownership, in the simplest variety of trust, there will be two people simultaneously owning the property in question. However, the relationship each person will have to the property will be quite different from that of the other. In this situation, where property is held on trust, there is a legal owner, who is called a trustee. He has essentially a management role, and is subject to duties in respect of the property and the administration of the trust. There is also an equitable owner, who is called a *cestui que trust*, or beneficiary. It is the beneficiary who is entitled to enjoy the property, and whose position is therefore closest to being what a layman might consider to be an owner. It is in respect of the beneficiary that the trustee's duties are owed, and he can enforce them against the trustee.

The introduction made to what happens in the situation in which property is conferred by way of a gift helps to introduce the trust, and what it actually is. This is because making a gift and declaring a trust have important points of commonality, and also fundamental points of difference which are set out in the following points:

- A trust is very like a gift because both will arise where the owner of property wishes for another to be able to enjoy it and have benefits from it.
- A trust is different from a gift because although conferring a benefit to another is at the heart of both, the trust achieves this in quite a different way.
- While a gift in favour of another is achieved through an outright transfer of title to the intended recipient, enjoyment of property subject to a trust is achieved by the existence of two distinct types of ownership.
- When property owned by someone is settled on trust, ownership separates into two distinctive 'titles' to the property.
- The person(s) intended to benefit from the property acquires 'equitable title' to it, while the person(s) responsible for ensuring this happens are vested with 'legal title'.

Most of these points can illustrated by reference to figure 1.1 which is a diagrammatic representation of the creation of a trust.

As the diagrammatic representation in figure 1.1 illustrates, it is the separation of ownership into equitable and legal estates which is fundamental to the law of trusts. It is this which provides the key to the whole thing, and the foundation for the remainder of this book on the law of trusts. In this book devoted to the law of trusts, the importance of equitable ownership will be emphasised throughout. This is unsurprising at one level, given the subject matter of the book, but this is

	Before	After
Legal title—burdensome (managerial in nature)	Settlor	Trustee
Equitable title (beneficial: provides enjoyment)	None	Beneficiary or *cestui que trust* Note: either trustee or beneficiary may also be settlor

Figure 1.1 The creation of a trust

itself premised on the way in which understanding equitable ownership is very important. It will become clear just how valuable equitable rights are, both in terms of the benefits which equitable ownership confers upon those who are so entitled, but also in terms of the ways in which it defines concomitant responsibilities and duties for those who are trustees of the property.

Before any substantive consideration of equitable ownership can be made, some attention must be given to the way in which the trust, and distinct legal and equitable titles, actually arise. There are important introductory considerations to be made of how these very valuable rights (and the formidable duties which accompany them) are created, and how the law knows when such an arrangement has come into being. The starting point for understanding how the trust and the distinct forms of ownership which characterise it come into being is the decision in *Westdeutsche Landesbank Girozentrale* v *Islington London Borough Council* [1996] AC 669, and particularly the now very famous passage from the judgment of Lord Browne-Wilkinson. That judgment insisted, probably as part of the *ratio* of the case, that the owner of any property is vested with legal title alone. It is only when separation of title is sought that distinct equitable ownership will arise. Indeed, it is clear in light of *Westdeutsche* that distinct equitable title is not recognised as being vested with separate existence unless and until title is separated into legal and equitable estates:

A person solely entitled to the full beneficial ownership of money or property, both at law and in equity, does not enjoy an equitable interest in that property. The legal title carries with it all rights. Unless and until there is a separation of the legal and equitable estates, there is no separate equitable title.

This analysis suggests that, in absence of a trust, equitable ownership would appear to have no intrinsic value. This does of course require some thought given that already equitable title is being associated with 'value' through its associations with entitlement, benefit, and enjoyment, while legal title more readily connotes responsibility and burden. Moreover, bare legal title is usually regarded as having no value (see for example some of the cases considered in chapter 5). However it is also the case that in absence of a trust, people who are legal owners of property believe, entirely correctly, that their ownership gives them valuable rights. An explanation for this apparent paradox is to suggest that in absence of a trust, owners at law hold equitable title as well, and that it is the equitable interest in the property rather than the legal title to it which carries with it the valuable rights of ownership. And in this context, while the duties of legal ownership are not any different in character, they cease to be burdensome—or even that obvious—when owed by one person to himself rather than to another.

1.2.1 Title to property: legal and equitable interests

In earlier editions of this book, depictions of figure 1.1 had shown the settlor, as the original owner, as being vested with legal and equitable title 'before' a trust came into existence. However, the true position, as set out by Lord Browne-Wilkinson above, is that all rights are subsumed under the legal title; that is, in the absence of a trust it is legal title itself which is valuable. For present purposes it probably does not matter a great deal—the difference is no more than semantic. Lord Browne-Wilkinson's approach does however significantly affect resulting trusts (which are considered in chapter 7) and tracing in equity (chapter 19), where arguments based on the idea that settlors might simply be able to keep the equitable title they have always had, parting only with their legal title, have had to be abandoned.

1.2.2 Separation of title into distinct ownership: the trust and requirement of 'something more'

The most common scenario for a trust to arise is where the legal owner of property makes a declaration that the property is to be held on trust for the benefit of a person or persons. This will most commonly involve transferring legal title to a trustee, upon which the trust is said to be constituted. However, this is not tantamount to saying that a trust will automatically arise where ownership becomes separated into distinctive legal and equitable title. Although the existence of separate titles is unusual outside the context of a trust, there is something further in addition which must be present before a trust is said to arise. A trust will only arise where the original owner of the trust intends for the property to become subject to a trust, and thus intends for a trust to arise.

The significance of an *intention to create* a trust will remain visible throughout this study of trusts. And closely alongside intention to create a trust, is the role of conscience in bringing a trust into existence. From Lord Browne-Wilkinson's judgment in *Westdeutsche* it is clear that the basis for all trusts is *conscience*. Just as it is so that it is the appearance of distinct equitable title upon separation of ownership which is of essence to, and actually forms the basis of the law of trusts, it is also vital to understand that a trust will not automatically arise upon separation of ownership. This is considered in more depth in chapters 7 and 19, and also in chapter 3, but for the moment, further explanation can be gleaned from the case of *Westdeutsche*. Again, Lord Browne-Wilkinson insisted that it is not separation of ownership into distinct equitable and legal titles which gives rise to a trust, and something more is required. This 'something more' is that the basis of all trusts is *conscience*.

Accordingly, when legal title to property is transferred to another in the presence of an intention to create a trust, this reasoning proposes that a trust actually arises by virtue of, and precisely because the conscience of the legal owner is affected. This requires him to hold property as owner at law on behalf of the owner of the property in equity. Thus, this type of legal ownership is quite different from that which is unencumbered by obligations to another, and which normally (as illustrated above) entitles the holder to deal freely with the property. Usually, the conscience of the legal owner is 'affected' in this way from his undertaking of trusteeship (and its attendant duties) which is voluntary in nature (although as chapter 3 reveals, there can be some difficulty with this in circumstances where the settlor is found to have declared himself trustee). However, it is also the case that actual imposition upon the conscience of an individual can arise where legal title and thus (initially in absence of a trust) ownership of property has been acquired through inequitable conduct on his part (greater explanation is given of this latter type of situation in chapters 7, 9, and 11).

1.2.3 **The parties which can be identified in a trust arrangement**

Some of this description is now getting very technical because parties who arise in a trust arrangement are starting to be identified, and so the next step is for this to be explained properly. In turn this will be followed by explaining *why* an owner of property would choose to make it subject to a trust, rather than just give it as a gift to another, and some consideration of *how* this is actually possible on account of equity and equitable jurisdiction. The owner of property who decides to settle it on trust rather than to make an outright gift of it to another becomes a *settlor* of trust property when he does this in order to confer some kind of enjoyment for another.

The person who is the recipient of this generosity is the *beneficiary*, who is the person entitled to the benefit of trust property. When a trust arises and ownership is divided into distinct titles, the beneficiary will own the property *in equity*. Crucially, it is only the beneficiary under a private trust who has *locus standi* to enforce it, to ensure that he can accrue the benefits intended by the settlor.

The key to the beneficiary's enjoyment of the trust property is that the *trustee* has responsibility for it. When a trust arises, 'ownership' of the property leaves the settlor, and becomes separated into two components; one is equitable title and the other is legal title. Legal title is title at law, which the trustee holds. But this is a different type of holding title from that normally arising from ownership, because in this arrangement a trustee holds this for the benefit of the beneficiary, and incurs a number of responsibilities and duties in respect of this.

In summary, the settlor is the original owner of property (who holds legal title to the property—according to *Westdeutsche* there is no distinct equitable title to property at this stage) and creates a trust by conveying legal title to it to one or more trustees, manifesting an intention that it is to be held on trust for one or more beneficiaries. Upon this, and in the presence of intention and conscience (*Westdeutsche*) title becomes separated, and a trust will arise. The trustees of property become its owners at common law, and are given control of the property, but also responsibility for it, and thus they hold legal title in furtherance of the entitlements which the beneficiaries are due under the arrangement (the conscience element from *Westdeutsche*), and become subject to a number of duties reflecting this.

The relationship between trustee and beneficiary is one which the law recognises as being fiduciary, and trustees will accordingly owe fiduciary duties to beneficiaries. The nature of such duties will be considered more fully in chapter 15, but for now it is sufficient to clarify that legal ownership arising in the context of the trust can be particularly onerous.

There are a few further basic points which accompany this state of being and the terminology of the parties which arise along with it:

- It is worth noting at this stage that settlors, trustees, and beneficiaries are not necessarily different people.
- Indeed, in a resulting trust scenario (considered in due course) the original owner of property will always become a beneficiary when his property becomes trust property: in other words, settlor and beneficiary are the same person in this situation.

- A settlor can validly constitute a trust by declaring himself trustee of his own property, on behalf of one or more beneficiaries.
- A trustee may be the beneficiary, or one of a number of beneficiaries.
- Settlors can even be trustees and beneficiaries, and this is normal in the case of trusts arising from the family home.
- Once a trust is constituted (which is considered in detail in chapter 3) the settlor ceases to be part of the arrangement: the trustees have the duties which arise in relation to the trust property, and it is only the beneficiary who has the standing to enforce a trust. An original owner may in practice remain within the arrangement, but this is where he becomes a trustee or beneficiary, and thus he acquires a different capacity.

1.2.4 The reasons for creating a trust: the trust as an alternative to making an outright gift

In the materials above it has been suggested that in common with an outright gift (or transfer of property to another—without consideration), a trust has at its heart conferring a benefit for someone whom the owner of property wishes to have a benefit from it. And it is very clear that the beneficiary under a trust is intended to have enjoyment and benefit of property which becomes trust property. Indeed, trustees hold legal title to the property for this very purpose, and become subject to a number of duties in order to ensure this. If this is so, then why go to all the trouble to make a trust arrangement rather than simply give your property to the intended recipient?

Transferring property to another by way of a gift is actually very easy, especially in the context of property other than land, and transfers of personalty (which are physical chattels rather than intangible property) can be effected by either a deed of gift or by manifesting an intention to confer the property to another and 'delivering' it to a recipient (this can be seen in cases discussed in chapters 3 and 5), and ensuring that any formalities requirements are met (this is considered in chapter 5, and in the context of personalty concerns a number of choses in action). With this in mind, immediately below it becomes apparent that there are reasons which are both settlor-oriented, and beneficiary-oriented which suggest in favour of creating a trust rather than making a gift.

From the perspective of an *original owner of property*, declaring a trust (and thus becoming a settlor rather than simply a donor) is a useful device for being able to have a say in how your property is used and applied. This is not the case in an out-and-out gift of property to another, and the trust mechanism will thus allow a settlor to exercise some control over what happens to property which is intended to benefit another. The settlor will provide instructions to this effect in a trust arrangement, and this may well be underpinned by seeking to protect a recipient from their own financial fecklessness, or it may well be motivated by a desire to ensure wealth remains within a family over successive generations rather than being 'lost'.

From the perspective of a *recipient of property*, creating a trust is a useful device where it is the intention of its owner that someone should be able to benefit from property, but who should remain free of the responsibility which attaches to it.

This can be seen in both real property (because houses have to be maintained, and any financial liabilities incurred on them have to be satisfied, etc.), and in relation to personal property, which might for example take the form of investments that must be looked after.

The trust and the creation of enforceable rights for 'third parties'

In addition to giving the intended recipient of property the benefits of property ownership without its responsibilities, the trust arrangement *creates enforceable rights* in relation to the property for the *beneficiary* under a trust. This is very important in the way it contrasts with a contractual arrangement. A beneficiary under a trust is not a party to the trust arrangement: this is brought into being where the owner of property transfers title to it to a trustee, or declares himself trustee of the property.

Under a contractual arrangement the doctrine of privity of contract usually prevents anyone other than the parties themselves being able to enforce the arrangement (NB the Contract (Rights of Third Parties) Act 1999). The creation of a trust gives the third party beneficiary enforceable rights, and indeed it is only the beneficiary who can enforce a trust. So in this respect the innovation of the trust can be seen as one which has traditionally had important functions in getting around the limitations of the doctrine of privity. This is considered further in chapter 2.

1.2.5 What does the trust owe to equitable jurisdiction, and *what is* equitable jurisdiction?

It was suggested above that legal title is good against the world and it forms the basis of free-dealings with property. In this respect, legal title is a highly visible indicator of property 'belonging' to another. Equitable interests are more complicated: their existence suggests that a holder of legal title does not enjoy all the rights of ownership, and this is the key to understanding both the reasons for the existence of equitable title, and also the difficulties to which holding equitable title can give rise. Essentially equitable title to property emerged as a response to the complexities of owning property, and the injustices which can be caused by recognising legal title alone. This was in turn possible on account of the historical emergence of equitable jurisdiction from medieval times onwards. Over time this would give rise to the Court of Chancery, which has historically been administered entirely separately from the courts of common law, and these jurisdictions were only actually fused in the late nineteenth century (in the Judicature Acts of 1873–5).

Almost immediately below there is a brief account of equity's emergence and its historical development, and the emergence of the Court of Chancery. This is focused on the dominance of the common law which had been characteristic of the law of England since the Norman Conquest, and which had emerged as a jurisdiction which recognised only rights which were rights at law. And in the course of looking at equity's modern significance it will be noted that at one level equitable jurisdiction developed as a complementary jurisdiction which was concerned with supporting the subsistence and enforcement of legal rights; indeed, this can be seen in the equitable maxim that 'equity follows the law'. However, it will also become apparent that equitable jurisdiction is noted most especially for being a jurisdiction which is more flexible than the common law, and which sought to mitigate the harshness that having (or not having) legal rights to property could give rise to, and the somewhat inflexible nature of remedies available at law (illustrated for example in the study of contract and tort).

Before this however, it is now suggested that although equity remains concerned with supporting legal rights, the key to understanding equity's development of the trust instrument lies in why equity recognises title to property which is not legal title at all. Equity is a more flexible jurisdiction than law, but at the heart of this is the way in which equity's jurisdiction is concerned to respond to injustice. The rationale for this is equity's recognition that recognising legal title alone in the context of dealings with property can mean that the interests of those other than the holder of legal title can be overlooked. This might be an appropriate reflection of the circumstances, but it might also lead to injustice, hence equity's desire to intervene and prevent injustice in circumstances where this is called for.

This led to equity developing its own remedies, which were not available at common law, and were focused on preventing injustices. Indeed, although equity's recognition that interests in property other than legal title can subsist and can be valuable, it is also the case that the existence of equitable interests is much harder to detect, and much less visible than legal title. Thus, equity's development of remedies not available at common law and its jurisdiction more broadly sought to protect the interests of those who should have an interest in property which was not reflected in legal title. This jurisdiction started off being *ad hoc* in nature, gradually becoming more formalised, and although the jurisdiction of courts of equity and common law is now fused the principles governing the granting of equitable remedies remains unaltered. But firstly, how did all this begin?

Looking at numerous points in time, beginning with the feudal system put in place following the Norman Conquest, is essential for understanding the dual ownership which underpins the law of trusts. It is from these origins that it becomes clear why the English legal system divides into common law and equity; why there are two different systems, and why, until recently, there have been two separate jurisdictions. Fundamentally this brief history explains why it is that equity is able to confer property rights at all.

Equity and trusts are found exclusively in England and other non-Roman legal systems, and neither has any place, for example, on the Continent. That a legal system should develop two different concepts of ownership, both of which can apply simultaneously to the same property, and effectively create two separate legal systems, is by no means self-evident. The reason lies in historical differences between England and Continental countries, dating from the feudal era, and in particular the Norman Conquest.

1.3 Equity and its origins in feudalism

Although equity is English in origin, it developed as an incidental result of feudalism. In pre-feudal times land was owned absolutely. The essence of the feudal system was that, in relatively lawless times, landowners collectively and for their mutual protection, bound themselves to an overlord, who was often a military expert, offering service (often of a military nature) or produce to the overlord in exchange for protection. Eventually land became held on condition that services or produce were provided, and tenure of land became the exclusive bond between overlord and tenant.

Although feudalism became universal, it was not centralised; each great estate or manor had its own overlord and its own law and customs. It is true that the Crown granted some of its own land to lords in exchange for money or military services, so the Crown became supreme lord of some, but not all, of the land. But the system was essentially *ad hoc*, and indeed came into being *because* of the lawlessness resulting from the lack of a strong central government.

The character of English feudalism after 1066 came about because the chief landowners forcibly resisted the attempt of William I to assert supremacy over them. William therefore confiscated all land following his successful conquest, and subsequently allowed it to be held (or often redeemed) only from the Crown (directly by overlords), in exchange for money or services. So *all* land came to be held from the Crown, in exchange for money or services. It is still technically so held, though the services have usually not been collected for so long that they are barred by limitation (time-barred). Thus in England alone feudal land tenure became centralised, and was imposed from above with the Crown as supreme landlord.

The large landowners or overlords, holding title directly (or immediately) from the Crown, allowed others to hold from them, also as tenants in exchange for personal services. These tenants thus held *immediately* from their lords, and *mediately* from the Crown. They allowed yet others to hold some of their land from them on similar bases, and so on, so large tenurial chains developed.

Eventually the system became so complex that it created problems for the overlords in collecting their feudal dues, and subinfeudation was therefore abolished (except for the Crown) by the statute *Quia Emptores* 1290. This statute is still in force, having survived an attempt to repeal it in 1967, and is often regarded as being a pillar of the law of real property. The result is that today nearly all land is held directly from the Crown.

The original services were personal in nature; tenure was therefore for life only, and was inalienable. It soon became clear, however, that it was more efficient to allow families to remain in possession of land over successive generations if they so wished, or if they did not, to allow them to alienate (e.g., sell) the land, and to convert the services into money payments. Unfortunately (for the lords at any rate), as soon as services became converted into money payments, their value was quickly lost through inflation. However, this also meant that lords increasingly kept and managed their own demesne lands and hired labour to work them, and demesne land itself was able to become a valuable economic asset. Further, this also provided important opportunities for the rising professional classes, as stewards, administrators, and lawyers became central through their employ for a fee under a contract and not by vassalage and land. This development of contractual relationships, while not strictly central, is important for our study of the emergence of modern equity through its enablement of continued domination of the landed elite within feudal social hierarchy.

1.3.1 **Devaluation of dues and the demise of feudalism**

The devaluation of dues meant that many fell obsolete and remained uncollected when they eventually became statute-barred. Many which remained were abolished after the Civil War by the Tenures Abolition Act 1660. The Crown was the main beneficiary by then, as supreme landlord, of the remaining feudal incidents; they were abolished because they effectively constituted extra-Parliamentary revenue for the Crown, and military tenures promoted the creation of private armies.

1.3.2 **Emergence of a more recognisable pattern of land ownership and system of interests**

Nevertheless, though the value of the services themselves diminished, important feudal incidents remained long after 1150. For example, the lord was entitled to payment on succession of land to an heir, and to the right of escheat if a tenant died without an heir, which meant that the land reverted to him. He was also entitled to various rights when the land was held by a minor. As long as any feudal dues remained valuable the lords desired to protect them, and rules about title to land at common law were developed to aid this process. Many of the rights arose on the death of a tenant, especially if there was no heir or the heir was a minor, and could have been avoided by conveying the land to younger adult members of the family, or leaving the land by will. For this reason taxes were imposed on conveyances, and until 1540 freehold estates could not be left by will. It was also important to be able to ascertain who held the land, so until at least 1535 transfers of land at common law had to be open and notorious, whereas many people preferred secret transfers. For similar reasons it was necessary for all conveyances to take immediate effect, so future interests (and therefore settlements) could not be created at common law until 1540.

1.3.3 **Earliest recognition of modern equitable jurisdiction**

Equity's flexibility and its orientation towards achieving justice will become ever-more apparent in reading this text. What will also become very plain is its capacity to evolve and develop to meet new perceived inflexibilities and new needs.

Important foundations for this were laid by the medieval Chancellor's work in relation to the rigidity of the common law of the time. The Chancellor of the King's Court was usually an ecclesiastic who had the power to issue royal writs. This function became discretionary, and came to be based on notions of conscience and justice, while his powers to act against individuals were enforceable by him with the use of imprisonment. It was upon these foundations that the Chancellor's office started to take on many of the features of a court and eventually, probably during the fifteenth century, the Court of Chancery was born.

However, although this is a simple and uncomplicated way of looking at equity and its origins, again it has to be said that equity is far from straightforward. Indeed, the very idea that equity was not originally a substantive system to be contrasted with the law must be considered on account that equity only truly started to exist as such from the sixteenth century, *and also the state of the common law at this time*. According to the legal historian Milsom, 'There was no common law, no body of substantive rules from which equity could be different. And the idea that the law could be unjust, if comprehensible at all, would have been abhorrent. Failures were mechanical.'

But it is nevertheless true that forms of action had ceased to be flexible by the mid-fourteenth century. Milsom suggests that it was during the sixteenth century that the common law started to become liberated from medieval procedural constraints and began to be viewed as a substantive set of rules. In contrast, equity remains highly individual and is based on individual decisions, so much so that in 1670 Vaughan CJ maintained that 'Equity is a universal truth and there can be no precedent in it'.

1.3.4 Equity, the common law, and originality in approach

Thus, there is undoubtedly more to equity's original development than the avoidance of restrictions placed on transfers by the common law and avoidance of feudal dues, but nevertheless equity retains its original character in this regard. It will become apparent how equitable doctrines still develop where doctrines at common law are regarded as inflexible: for example, illustrations can be found in the development of the doctrine of promissory estoppel and the ways in which the trust has traditionally sought to mitigate harshness of the privity doctrine. There is also the estoppel licence and possibly a new variety of the constructive trust. Equity's early role in seeking to avoid feudal dues is also illustrative of the trust's long-standing function as a tax avoidance device. Moreover, it should be becoming clear that surrounding the emergence of the common law as a set of cogent rules, and certainly prior to it, equity's role appeared to be seen as remedying failures of process. Chancellors would see themselves as perfecting the human defects of process which could arise at common law, by focusing on a person's conscience to achieve an outcome which was just. Here, equity's focus on the conscience of an individual ensured that there was no need for the formalism and technicality characteristic of the common law; it was also responsive to individual circumstances and, moreover, a chancery decree would bind only parties to the suit.

Although the thrust of the Chancellor's power could in principle be exercised without altering the substance of the common law in question, the practical result of his jurisdiction was that the exercise of common law rights was affected significantly. Indeed, it may be that in light of the Chancellor's ability to refuse to issue a writ to a claimant at common law, or to compel conveyance of property by its owner to someone else, conflict between the two systems was inevitable. Indeed, conflict did arise, but not until much later. As has already been suggested, at this early stage the common law was itself not very clearly defined, and the conflict which did occur much later was not altogether apparent from the King's (through his Chancellor) exercise of residual discretion.

1.4 The emergence of modern equitable jurisdiction

In its early days, equitable jurisdiction was exercised on an *ad hoc* basis, and its transformation into a modern system did not come about until after around 1700, by which time Chancellors tended to be lawyers rather than ecclesiastics and a system of precedent was beginning to develop. Yet many features of these early days remain visible in equity's modern operation.

One of the key reasons why equity remains very faithful to its historical origins in terms of operation as well as purpose is because retaining these early features has been necessary for equity to avoid conflict with the common law. It is one thing for equity to seek to mitigate the harshness caused by recognising legal rights only and having available only remedies which are ones 'at law', but equity had to evolve in the context that legal rights were at the heart of ownership of property, and they remain so. Modern equitable jurisdiction is premised on twelve key 'maxims' of equity, and a number of principles which have emerged from them. These are central to the nature of equitable jurisdiction today, and are central to *how* this is exercised and *what* equity can actually do *to whom* in the face of an injustice. The maxims emerged as equity's jurisdiction became more formalised and less *ad hoc*, and are as follows:

(1) Equity will not suffer a wrong without a remedy.

(2) Equity follows the law.

(3) Where there is equal equity, the law shall prevail.

(4) Where the equities are equal, the first in time shall prevail.

(5) He who seeks equity must do equity.

(6) He who comes to equity must come with clean hands.

(7) Delay defeats equities.

(8) Equality is equity.

(9) Equity looks to the intent rather than the form.

(10) Equity looks on that as done which ought to be done.

(11) Equity imputes an intention to fulfil an obligation.

(12) Equity acts *in personam*.

Though only the above twelve are usually regarded as the definitive equitable maxims, equity has developed additional principles which may be treated to all intents and purposes as if they were among the maxims. The following may not be an exhaustive list, but all these principles will appear again in the book, bearing in mind that the language of these maxims and principles appears to vary slightly between different authorities.

(i) The principle that *'equity will not assist a volunteer'* is fundamental to the discussion in chapter 3 which relates to the constitution of trusts and the effecting of gifts.

(ii) Also at the heart of chapter 3 is the mantra that *'equity will not perfect an imperfect gift'*.

(iii) The way in which *'equity will not construe a valid power out of an invalid trust'* has very strong references to materials in chapters 2 and 4 which reveal the nature of the trust, and also the conditions which must be satisfied in order for a valid trust to exist.

(iv) That *'equity will not permit the provisions of a statute intended to prevent fraud to be used as an instrument for fraud'* will be explained in materials relating to formality requirements for trusts, in chapters 5 and 11, and this accommodates the need for a trust to operate in certain situations where this might be difficult to achieve, as illustrated in chapters 9 and 10.

(v) The way in which *'equity will not permit a trust to fail for want of a trustee'* is a theme which runs throughout this text in some form or another.

1.4.1 The nature of modern equitable jurisdiction and the frameworks for its operations

One feature of equitable jurisdiction has always been that it is exercised against specific persons—equity acts *in personam*. This can be seen in one of the Chancellor's earliest instruments, the 'Use', which is considered shortly, and today it is an important maxim of equity. In the case of the Use the remedy was personal against the feoffee to Uses, who held the legal estate in the land, and this can be seen today in the modern trust in the nature of an action against the owner of a legal estate in land, or the legal owner of money or goods: this means that as long as a legal owner or trustee can be found, the precise location of the property (for example abroad) does not matter.

Nevertheless, as equity developed it acted not only against the original legal owner of the property, but also against subsequent owners in certain circumstances, and this led to gradual appreciation that some equitable rights were capable of being amounting to property rights. And this has been reflected in numerous statutory provisions and especially the 1925 property legislation. The famous 1925 property legislation—which is otherwise largely beyond the scope of this text—has influenced the development of equity by reducing the number of legal estates in land, thus having a knock-on effect on the equitable interests which can arise in respect of them, but at the same time does give important recognition to equitable interests alongside legal rights. This can also be seen in some taxation legislation (considered in chapter 5) which treats equitable interests as property interests. So although it is still accurate to say that equity acts *in personam*, some equitable rights also have the characteristics of rights *in rem*, but it is of course the case that there are significant differences between legal and equitable title or ownership.

1.4.1.1 *The nature of legal and equitable ownership*

The description of one of equity's earliest innovations, the Use, alongside the introduction to the modern trust (following below) shows that in terms of locating the trust within equity's jurisdiction it was equitable ownership which has always been associated with enjoyment, and in the modern trust legal ownership manifested in trusteeship represents capacity for responsibility and management of property for the benefit of another. Thus a trustee undertakes onerous duties (considered in chapters 15 and 16, and also 18), and is often paid for undertaking trusteeship (e.g., banks and solicitors), while the beneficiary owns the property in equity. And as already considered, in absence of a trust, most legal owners of property would not see holding legal title as burdensome or onerous. And like legal ownership in property, equitable ownership is also transferable, which is a fundamental attraction of any property right (the mechanics and requirements of disposition of equitable interests are considered in chapter 5).

1.4.1.2 *Other equitable interests*

The equitable principles discussed in this section do not apply only to full equitable ownership of chattels or estates in land, and equity also recognises other interests in property which are less than full ownership, and some of the following cases and examples concern equitable interests, rather than full equitable ownership.

For example, suppose A has freehold legal title to land, and contracts to lease the land to B for seven years. Under the contract, B is entitled to possession and enjoyment of the land for that period. The contract is enforceable at common law, just like any other contract, and if a lease is not executed, or B is denied possession or enjoyment of the land, he can claim damages. However, the common law will not actually recognise B as lessee until the lease is executed in the prescribed formal manner. But unlike many contracts, this arrangement is also enforceable in equity, allowing B to claim the equitable remedies of specific performance, which forces A to execute the lease, and injunction, which stops A acting in a manner inconsistent with the grant of the lease. Furthermore, because 'equity looks on that as done which ought to be done' *Walsh* v *Lonsdale* (1882) 20 Ch D is authority that B is treated as if he were *already* a lessee in equity, even if no formal lease has yet been executed. So a contract for a lease can create an immediate equitable interest in land, called an estate contract (a lease being an estate in land), to which the equitable principles discussed below apply, with the same principles applying to contracts for lesser interests in land (such as a contract to create a legal easement, which is essentially a right of way and thus much less extensive than legal ownership).

Terminologically, so far as land is concerned, an *estate*, whether legal or equitable, connotes an interest akin to ownership; an *interest in land* can include an estate, but also includes rights that are much less extensive than ownership.

1.4.2 Equitable remedies

Some specific applications of equitable remedies are discussed in chapter 19, but it is necessary even at this stage to introduce the equitable remedies, and consider the general principles applicable to them.

Originally equity developed its own remedies, which were not available to the common law, and nor did equity administer common law remedies. This position was to some extent altered by the Common Law Procedure Act 1854, which gave the common law courts some jurisdiction to give equitable remedies, and the Chancery Amendment Act 1858, which allowed the Court of Chancery to award the common law derived remedy of damages, but only in addition to, or in substitution for an equitable remedy. As will be explained shortly, in 1873–5 the courts were fused, but the principles governing the grant of equitable remedies were not changed by that legislation, and are still applicable to actions to protect equitable interests or estates, and other rights having an equitable origin. Thus, it is still necessary to consider the equitable remedies separately from the common law remedies.

The main general equitable remedies are the injunction and specific performance. For the ones which apply more specifically in breaches occurring in the context of trusteeship, there is discussion of breach of fiduciary duty and the remedy of account (in chapters 15 and 18), and sometimes equity imposes a constructive trust (see chapters 7, 9, 10, 11, and 19). Damages could not originally be awarded by the Court of Chancery, and can be now only on the basis of the 1858 Act, and in any event the quantum of equitable damages may differ from that appropriate in a common law action.

Equitable remedies are available for breaches of equitable obligations, such as those considered in chapters 11, 15, and 18, but in addition injunctions can be used to prevent commissions of torts. For some torts, such as negligence claims arising out of road accident cases, the remedy is obviously inappropriate, but it can be useful for continuing torts, such as trespass or nuisance. As will be seen in chapter 15, injunctions can also be used to prevent abuses of confidential information.

1.4.2.1 *The discretionary nature of equitable remedies*

The major difference between the two systems is that whereas common law remedies are available as of right, equitable remedies retain the discretionary nature of early equitable jurisdiction. Although the creation of wholly new equitable rights and principles has been curtailed over the last two centuries on account of equity becoming more of a defined system, and one increasingly defined by precedent, its remedies remain discretionary, notwithstanding that discretion is exercised according to fairly clear and even rigid principles. The discretionary nature of the remedies can lead to dire consequences, because if an equitable estate or interest depends on the award of an equitable remedy, a refusal to grant the remedy effectively destroys the interest.

1.4.2.2 *Equity's exercise of its discretion*

A common ground for refusal of a remedy is the behaviour of the party claiming the equitable remedy, because 'he who comes into equity must come with clean hands'. This can be seen in *Coatsworth v Johnson* (1886) 54 LT 520, CA where the claimant was in possession of land under a contract for a lease, where no lease that would be recognised at common law had been executed. The landlord in fact turned the claimant out, and the claimant sued for trespass. He would have won the action had he been regarded as a lessee, either at common law or in equity. Indeed, according to *Walsh v Lonsdale* equity would normally regard the claimant as being an equitable lessee, but this particular tenant was already in breach of various covenants under the agreement. Thus, the Court of Appeal refused to grant the equitable remedy and the claimant actually *lost his interest*. This then forced him to pursue the common law, which because he had no lease at common law meant he lost altogether. This case thus illustrates the discretionary nature of equity's jurisdiction and remedies, while emphasising the need to treat common law and equitable rights and remedies separately. It also shows that an entire interest can be lost where an equitable remedy is refused.

1.4.2.3 *Equity, discretion, and the importance of conduct*

There are factors other than conduct of the party seeking a remedy which can cause a claimant to lose his remedy, and actually even innocent parties are capable of losing out in this way. In chapter 19 it is shown that a remedy can be lost where granting it would put another party in breach of their own legal obligations, or where its imposition would cause the defendant hardship. And it is also the case that authorities such as *Mountford v Scott* [1975] Ch 258 show that even where it is granted, equity's discretion is not unlimited.

1.4.3 **Equitable rights and third parties**

Up to this point this discussion of equitable interests and equitable remedies has only been considered in relation to the parties who are immediately affected by them: the position of the beneficiary under a trust and the obligations which trusteeship imposes as a result of this; and in the case of a contract which is enforceable in equity (by virtue of being one for land or for an interest in land, which is considered further in chapter 19) as between the actual contracting parties. What follows now is a consideration of the way in which for equitable rights to be regarded in any sense as property rights, it is necessary also to consider the extent to which they can bind third parties.

1.4.3.1 *Legal title as title which is 'good against the world': what about equitable title?*

The position of legal rights arising from title at law is that they are enforceable against anyone, and they are said to 'bind the world'. Equitable rights on the other hand do not do so, and they might in this respect be perceived as lesser rights on account of the impact they can have on third parties. Illustration of this position and the issues it raises can be made through the very simple example provided by a trustee who tries to sell property to which he has ostensible ownership: he has legal title, and he is attempting to dispose of the property on the basis that ownership is unencumbered. He does not declare that he holds the property on trust for the benefit of another. The maxim that legal title is good against the world is coupled by the somewhat weaker sounding position that 'equitable title binds all except for the *bona fide* purchaser of the legal estate for value, without notice of the equitable title or interest'.

This position ensures that parties will only be bound by equitable interests where their consciences have been affected, and according to the position above, the conscience of such a person will be affected where he is not a good faith purchaser for value without notice of the equitable interest. In this situation, where property is passed to a third party, he will take it subject to any equitable entitlement to it. A person who *is* such a *bona fide* purchaser for value and without notice is known as 'equity's darling' and will take a legal estate free from any equitable rights. The rationale for this is that 'equity's darling' will be, like an equitable owner himself, an innocent victim of a breach of trust, and 'where there is equal equity, the law shall prevail'. This is the basis of the equitable notice doctrine, the operation of which, whereby the interests of equitable owners can be defeated can be seen in *Cave* v *Cave*.

1.4.3.2 *Equity and law:* Cave *v* Cave

In *Cave* v *Cave* (1880) 15 Ch D 639, Charles Cave, as sole trustee and family solicitor, stole trust money and purchased a house with it. As a result of this transaction, the moneys in the trust fund were converted into land, so that the beneficiaries of the fund became beneficiaries of the land. The fraudulent trustee/solicitor then raised money by way of legal mortgage at a time when a legal mortgage took effect by way of a conveyance of the entire freehold estate to the mortgagee, with a covenant to re-convey the property to the mortgagor if the money loaned, plus interest and administration charges, was repaid to the mortgagee on a fixed date. When these conditions were met, equity enforced this covenant and also allowed the mortgagor to demand a later re-conveyance, subject to repayment of the capital loaned, plus interest and administration charges. Here, the mortgagee obtained legal title, and he also provided value, in the form of the money advanced. Accordingly, Fry J held that he had no notice of the beneficiaries' interest. There was no suggestion that the mortgagee was acting in bad faith, and he was therefore a *bona fide* purchaser of the legal estate for value without notice of the beneficiaries' equitable interests, so legal title passed to the mortgagee free of encumbrance.

1.4.3.3 *Conditions attached to the doctrine of notice: equity and the 'purchaser for value'*

For a third party to take free of an equitable interest in property, the purchase must be one for value. Value includes not only consideration recognised at common law, but also equitable consideration. Thus, for example, as well as value in terms of money or money's worth (recognised as consideration by both systems), equity also recognises a future marriage as consideration, and so it constitutes value for the purposes of the *bona fide* purchaser rule. On the other hand, the common law allows contracts under seal to be enforced even in the absence of consideration; equity does not take the same view, and such contracts do not provide value for the purposes of this rule (nor incidentally can such contracts be enforced using equitable remedies). Where the value is money, the purchaser must pay all the money before receiving notice of the equitable interest.

Notice itself includes not only actual, but also constructive notice. For dealings in land this has traditionally meant that the purchaser must inquire about equitable interests with no less diligence than he would inquire of legal interests, and these standards are determined by ordinary conveyancing practice. Thus a careless purchaser is not protected; nor is one who could have discovered the existence of an interest by inspecting the land. Additionally, knowledge of an agent (e.g., solicitor) is imputed, so that the purchaser is treated as having any knowledge that his agent acquires. In *Cave* v *Cave*, however, Charles Cave acted as solicitor for both the mortgagor and the mortgagee, and obviously he knew the truth, but Fry J held that his notice would not be imputed to the mortgagee since he was party to a fraud.

The details of precisely what constitutes notice is covered in land law textbooks and is beyond the scope of this book, but it is worth observing that the notice doctrine developed from land transactions, which are characterised by their thoroughness and lack of haste. For this reason, the notice doctrine works strictly against purchasers. The courts have shown a marked reluctance to apply quite so rigorous a doctrine in ordinary commercial transactions, which are characterised by their informality and speed (see further chapter 19).

1.4.3.4 *Equitable interests, third party rights, and the doctrine of notice*

It is clear that equity further recognises a category of entitlements described as 'equities' or 'mere equities'. This terminology is intended to distinguish them from full equitable proprietary interests. These have been determined to include the deserted wife's equity (as in *National Provincial Bank Ltd* v *Ainsworth* [1965] AC 1175), and the right to have a transaction set aside on grounds of fraud or undue influence (e.g., in *Barclays Bank* v *O'Brien* considered below). Where these mere equities relate to property (as in both the cases above, but for different reasons) they have a limited ability to affect third parties who acquire ownership of it, but it must be appreciated that they are not true interests in property itself. And, the notice doctrine applies not only to full equitable ownership or title but also to these lesser forms of equitable interest in property.

1.4.4 Equities, unconscionable bargains, and the doctrine of undue influence

There has been a hub of activity in the area of undue influence in recent years. The doctrine of undue influence has developed in relation to the law of contract, and it has done so to allow a contract to be set aside where the circumstances are such that a person benefiting from the transaction was aware of circumstances in which the other party may have been acting under the influence of another. As the law has developed it has become apparent that a strong contextual setting for such situations has arisen in respect of financial guarantee transactions, as in the paradigm case of *Barclays Bank* v *O'Brien* [1994] 1 AC 80. In *O'Brien* the House of Lords held that the wife had signed mortgage documentation under the undue influence of her husband, and, that because the mortgagee (the bank) had not taken reasonable steps to ensure that the transaction had been entered into freely, it had constructive notice of the undue influence. As a result, the wife was able to have the transaction set aside.

1.4.4.1 *Undue influence, relationships, notice, and enquiries: the new law*

In *O'Brien* the undue influence was relationship based, and arose on account of the relationship between the wife and the influencing party, her spouse. Following *O'Brien* and another case decided at the same time, *CIBC Mortgages Plc* v *Pitt* [1994] 1 AC 200, the House of Lords in *Royal Bank of Scotland* v *Etridge (No. 2)* [2001] 4 All ER 449 widened the types of relationship which would put creditors on enquiry. Lord Nicholls argued that there was no reason to single out sexual relationships for special protection, referring in his judgment to the decision of the Court of Appeal in *Credit Lyonnais Bank Nederland* v *Burch* [1997] 1 All ER 144 as an example of a case where the relationship between guarantor and debtor had been that of employee and employer in which the *O'Brien* principles were relevant and had been appropriately applied. The types of relationship attracting protection under *O'Brien*, he considered, should not be narrowly prescribed and should not require creditors to assess the degree of trust and confidence existing in any particular relationship. On this basis, protection should extend to all cases where the relationship between guarantor and debtor was non-commercial.

In *Etridge*, the House of Lords confirmed the distinction made in *O'Brien* and *Pitt* between surety and joint loan cases. Lord Nicholls went on to suggest that cases in which a spouse was agreeing to guarantee the debts of their spouse's company should be treated in the same way as surety cases. This should be so even if the guarantor spouse was him/herself a shareholder, a secretary, or director in that company as the holding of any of these positions did not necessarily reflect ability to control the company's affairs. Lord Nicholls declared that creditors were not required to ensure that the surety's consent was free from undue influence nor were they required to instruct solicitors to do this. He affirmed the general *O'Brien* approach and stated that:

The furthest a bank can be expected to go is to take reasonable steps to satisfy itself that the wife has had brought home to her, in a meaningful way, the practical implications of the proposed transaction. This does not wholly eliminate the risk of undue influence or misrepresentation. But it does mean that a wife enters into a transaction with her eyes open so far as the basic elements of the transaction are concerned.

1.4.5 Priorities between successive equitable interests

The equitable maxim 'Where there is equal equity, the law shall prevail' applies only where the purchase made is in respect of a legal estate or title. A purchaser of an *equitable* estate or interest will not generally, therefore, take priority over a prior equitable interest. Another maxim applies: 'Where the equities are equal, the first in time shall prevail.' In other words, priorities of equitable interests generally rank according to the order of time in which they have been created (there are a limited number of exceptions concerning mortgages, which are outside the scope of this book).

In *Cave v Cave*, the value of the property was greater than the amount raised on the first mortgage, so Charles Cave raised further money on a second mortgage. The second mortgagee, like the first, had no notice of the beneficiaries' interests. However, he could not obtain a legal estate, since that had already been conveyed to the first mortgagee (the usual position prior to the 1925 legislation), and so this second mortgage took effect as a mortgage in equity only. Even though he had acted *bona fide*, therefore, had given value and had no notice of the prior equitable interests of the beneficiaries, he was not a *bona fide* purchaser of the *legal* estate for value without notice. He therefore took subject to the claimants' prior equitable interest, Fry J observing 'As between persons having only equitable interests, if their equities are in all other respects equal, priority of time gives the better equity, or, "*Qui prior est tempore potior est jure*"'.

1.4.5.1 *'Notice' of equitable interests, and its application to property other than land*

The notice doctrine originally developed from land transactions, but has been extended to all other forms of property. Indeed, today it is far more important in relation to other forms of property than it is to land on account of property legislation dating from 1925 and more recently the Land Registration Act 2002.

Thus, the same fundamental distinction between legal title and equitable ownership applies to property which is not land, and is thus legally classified as personal property. In the case of goods, common law ownership can be enforced against anyone at all (subject, in the case of sale of goods, to the exceptions contained in the Factors Act 1889, ss. 2, 8, and 9, and the Sale of Goods Act 1979, ss. 21–6, which are discussed in detail in works on sale of goods). Equitable ownership, by contrast, can be lost to a *bona fide* purchaser for value who does not know of the equitable ownership. The different wording is deliberate on account that it seems that many of the detailed workings of the notice doctrine (e.g., constructive and imputed notice considered above) may well apply only to land. The position with personal property is similar, but probably not identical, since this will involve transactions which are less lengthy and quicker, and not subject to the same level of enquiry and process.

Although the doctrine theoretically applies to goods as well as land, in practice buyers of goods are rarely bound by equitable interests in them, as they generally have no reason to suspect that the seller, if he has legal title, does not also have equitable title. In the first place, the vast majority of goods are not held in trust. Also, transfers of goods do not normally involve the degree of investigation and documentation that would be appropriate in the case of land, so an assumption of absolute ownership is normally reasonable.

If the seller does not have legal title, such title can nevertheless pass to the buyer in certain circumstances (under the Factors Act and Sale of Goods Act provisions), but these circumstances are drawn up in such a way that it is almost inconceivable that a buyer who acquires title in this way would be acting in bad faith, or have any notice of an equitable interest. On the other hand, if the seller has no title, and the buyer also acquires no title, because the Factors Act, etc. provisions do not apply in his favour, he will necessarily be bound by any prior equitable interests. This will be so whether or not he acts in good faith, and whether or not he has notice, because he does not acquire any legal title.

It is possible to conclude in the case of goods, that in practice the determining factor will be whether the buyer acquires legal title to the goods, rather than the presence or absence of good faith or notice. However the position in relation to personal property which is *currency* is quite different.

As will become clear in chapter 19, where money is stolen, or a cheque forged by altering the name of the payee, the thief can pass legal title in the money, even though he has no title to it himself, because of an exception to the common law principle that a man cannot pass a title that he does not have (*nemo dat quod non habet*). Money stolen in this way may (for example) be laundered through bank accounts, given to friends, spent at gambling clubs, or used to purchase tangible property. The legal title will be passed on by the thief, and in general, the thief will disappear or not be worth suing. The victim of the theft may in certain circumstances be able to assert equitable title in the money against the recipients, however, and the precise circumstances under which this can be done are considered in chapter 19, where again the distinction between legal and equitable ownership is of fundamental importance. One of the main issues considered there is the state of knowledge required to bind the recipient, which probably differs in some respects from the way the notice doctrine has traditionally applied to land.

1.5 Equitable rights as rights *in rem*

To conclude this discussion, equity began by acting *in personam*, without affecting common law title or ownership, and while this is the case in a number of situations where rights are merely rights *in personam* (classified as mere equities), others do have properties of rights *in rem*, and it is not unreasonable to describe these as additionally giving rights of ownership. This is why it is common to see certain equitable rights described as property rights, and reference made to equitable title to land, and equitable ownership of goods. A number of statutory provisions also treat equitable interests as property interests. This can be seen in s. 53(1)(c) of the Law of Property Act 1925 (considered in depth in chapter 5) which provides that:

[A] disposition of an equitable interest or trust subsisting at the time of the disposition must be in writing signed by the person disposing of the same, or by his agent thereunto lawfully authorised by writing or by will.

This clearly suggests the existence of equitable interests, which are presumably property interests, and which therefore have the characteristics of rights *in rem*. The courts have also accepted that at any rate some equitable rights can have the characteristics of rights *in rem*. In *Baker* v *Archer-Shee* [1927] AC 844, a beneficiary was considered to be the owner of dividends for tax purposes. In *National Provincial Bank Ltd* v *Ainsworth* [1965] AC 1175, the House of Lords distinguished between equitable interests in land, which were full property rights capable of binding third parties as overriding interests under s. 70(1)(g) of the Land Registration Act 1925, and 'mere equities', which were not capable of binding third parties at all.

1.5.1 Rights in law, equity, and illegality: *Tinsley* v *Milligan* and *Rowan* v *Dann*

In *Tinsley* v *Milligan* [1994] 1 AC 340, Stella Tinsley and Kathleen Milligan jointly purchased a home which was registered in Tinsley's name alone. On the principles set out in chapters 7 and 9, the beneficial interest would have been shared between Tinsley and Milligan in equal shares; but to both Tinsley's and Milligan's knowledge, the home was registered in Tinsley's name alone to enable Milligan to make false claims to the Department of Social Security for benefits. After a quarrel Tinsley moved out, and claimed possession from Milligan. Milligan counterclaimed, seeking a declaration that the house was held by Tinsley on trust for both of them in equal shares. Tinsley argued that Milligan's claim was barred by the common law doctrine *ex turpi causa non oritur actio* and by the principle that 'he who comes to equity must come with clean hands'.

The House of Lords held (Lord Keith and Lord Goff dissenting) that because the presumption of resulting trust applied (see chapter 7), Milligan could establish her equitable interest without relying on the illegal transaction, and was therefore entitled to succeed. The case supports the argument, it is suggested, that Milligan's resulting trust interest was a property interest in its own right, which had an existence that was independent of the precise arrangement between the couple. Had it been no more than merely a collection of personal rights against Tinsley, Milligan would surely have failed, since she would have been unable to assert those rights without disclosing the fraud. Lord Browne-Wilkinson went so far as to say:

More than 100 years have elapsed since the fusion of the administration of law and equity. The reality of the matter is that, in 1993, English law has one single law of property made up of legal and equitable interests. Although for historical reasons legal estates and equitable estates have differing incidents, the person owning either type of estate has a right of property, a right *in rem* not merely a right *in personam*. If the law is that a party is entitled to enforce a property right acquired under an illegal transaction, in my judgment the same rule ought to apply to any property right so acquired, whether such right is legal or equitable.

Even if (as the authors would suggest) this statement goes too far, it is clear at the very least that some equitable rights also have the characteristics of rights *in rem*, and similar principles were applied by the Court of Appeal in *Rowan* v *Dann* (1992) P & CR 202.

1.5.2 Equitable rights as rights *in personam*

It is also still true to say, however, that equitable rights have some of the characteristics of rights *in personam*. Indeed, some equitable rights, such as the 'mere equities' considered by the House of Lords in *National Provincial Bank Ltd* v *Ainsworth* [1965], do not have the characteristics of rights *in rem* at all. In *Richard West and Partners (Inverness) Ltd* v *Dick* [1969] 2 Ch 424, the Court of Appeal held that the English courts had jurisdiction to grant a decree of specific performance of a contract for the sale of land abroad (in Scotland). The defendant was within the jurisdiction, and Harman LJ observed: 'that the Court of Chancery, acting as it does *in personam*, is well able to grant specific performance of a contract to buy or sell foreign land, provided the defendant is domiciled within its jurisdiction'.

1.5.3 Equity, property, and ability of equity to act *in personam*

The ability of equity to act *in personam* can be useful in any case where the property is situated abroad. The worldwide *Mareva* injunction (see chapter 19) depends on equity acting *in personam*, as does equity's ability to trace property through civil law jurisdictions (see chapter 19). In these cases, however, the personal rights are presumably additional to any real rights created. If the land or other property were in England, beneficial interests in it would surely not be defeated merely because the trustee was abroad.

However, there may be situations where the beneficiary's rights are limited by the personal nature of the action. It is also often the trustee, not the beneficiary, who takes action against a third party in respect of the trust property. For example, where property is leased it is the trustee who sues for rent: *Shalit* v *Joseph Nadler Ltd* [1933] 2 KB 79. Of course, the trustee is accountable to the beneficiary, and can be required by the beneficiary to sue, but the beneficiary cannot sue the third party directly. This really is a case where the trustee's rights are rights *in rem*, whereas those of the beneficiary are limited to a personal action against the trustee.

1.5.4 Equitable ownership and negligence suits

Generally speaking, only the owner of property at the time that it is damaged can sue in negligence. It is probable that an equitable owner does not count for these purposes, and that only the legal owner can sue. Again, of course, the equitable owner can require the legal owner to sue, but *Leigh & Sillivan Ltd* v *Aliakmon Shipping Co. Ltd, The Aliakmon* [1986] AC 785 is authority that equitable ownership does not give rise to the right to sue in negligence. This view was adopted by the Court of Appeal in *MCC Proceeds Inc.* v *Lehman Brothers International (Europe)* (*The Independent*, 19 January 1998), on account of difficulties arising from allowing multiplicity of actions. These cases can be contrasted with the 'disappointed beneficiary' cases of *White* v *Jones* [1995] 2 AC 207 and *Ross* v *Caunters* [1980] Ch 297.

In these cases intended beneficiaries excluded from a will by a solicitor's negligent drafting successfully sued but these cases are regarded as being exceptional, in that there was nobody apart from the intended beneficiary who was in any position to bring an action.

1.5.5 Purely personal rights

Thus although for many purposes equitable rights have the characteristics of rights *in rem*, vestiges of their personal origins still remain, and some rights in equity are quite clearly ones which are purely personal. This can be seen in *National Provincial Bank Ltd* v *Ainsworth* [1965] AC 1175, where the House of Lords distinguished between equitable interests in land, which were full property rights capable of binding third parties as overriding interests under s. 70(1)(g) of the Land Registration Act 1925, and 'mere equities', which were not capable of binding third parties at all. The right at issue in *Ainsworth* was the so-called 'deserted wives' equity', or the right, enforceable as against her husband, to occupy the matrimonial home. Although equitable remedies were available to enforce the right, the reasoning was that no equitable interest in land had been created. Therefore, the right was not enforceable against a mortgagee where the husband had defaulted on the mortgage. The actual decision in *Ainsworth* has since been affected by statute, currently the Matrimonial Homes Act 1983, however much of the rationale behind the interesting discussion in Todd [1981] Conv 347 (which suggests that while it is clear is that there is a category of equitable rights which is purely personal, it is not clear what rights fall into that category) still stands.

1.6 The impact of the Judicature Acts 1873–5 upon the emergence of modern equitable jurisdiction

One of the main defects of the English system of justice up until the mid-nineteenth century was that common law and equity were administered in separate courts. The Court of Chancery had no power to grant common law remedies, nor did the common law courts have power to grant equitable remedies. This meant that litigants might have to commence two separate actions in order to obtain justice. Notwithstanding some improvements brought about by the Common Law Procedure Act 1854 (which gave the common law courts the power to award certain equitable remedies) and the Chancery Amendment Act 1858 (Lord Cairns' Act) which gave the Court of Chancery a discretion to award 'equitable' damages where no other remedy was appropriate, this system of civil justice would remain very inefficient, because the courts continued to be administered separately until 1873.

The legislation of 1873–5 provided that subsequently the High Court, though divided for convenience into divisions, would administer both systems. Section 25 of the 1873 Act, now replaced by s. 49 Supreme Court Act 1981, provided that in a case of conflict the rules of equity were to prevail: this was effectively also the position before 1873. The 1873–5 Acts were almost certainly intended to be procedural only, and that was probably their only effect—the generally held view is that they did not alter the substantive law.

Argument is often made that this procedural fusion has constricted equity's freedom to develop, and in many respects, modern equitable jurisdiction is almost as rigid and rule-bound as the common law. Of course it *does* continue to develop, as will become apparent in the chapters which consider equity's development of the implied trust and its application of resulting and constructive trusts to new situations (considered in chapters 7 *et seq.*). Equity has also developed the doctrine of estoppel, and subsequent discussion in chapter 9 will explain how proprietary estoppel has been highly influential in the context of family homes in the past decade. The pace of equitable development today, however, is little (if any) faster than that of the common law.

1.6.1 Equity, freedom, autonomy, and the implications of fusion

At least three observations can be made about equity's continuing evolution and its relationship with law. First, it is probable that legislation, whose role and extent have increased greatly since 1875, today takes on many of the functions once taken on by equity; where the law appears rigid and unjust, legislation is now a possible and realistic answer. It may well be better suited to modern democratic conditions than the exercise of discretionary power by a court. Megaw LJ, for example, expressed this view in *Western Fish Products Ltd* v *Penwith District Council* [1981] 2 All ER 204, 218. Additionally, the nature of case law makes it inevitably uncertain as a method of law reform.

The second observation is that the curtailment of equitable discretion is explicable as a simple consequence of the development of effective law reporting inevitably leading to precedents coming to be regarded as binding, and thus probably owes little to the 1873–5 legislation itself.

The third observation is that unfettered judicial discretion may nowadays be a bad thing; it is arguably better in a society in which expectations are relied upon to promote certainty, rather than discretion. Not only is the latter quality inherently unpredictable, but if administered by a court it is also retroactive. Its exercise can therefore cause considerable injustices, especially where commercial and property transactions are concerned.

1.6.2 Distinctiveness beyond fusion: equity and the forging of a separate identity

It was suggested by Lord Diplock in *United Scientific Holdings Ltd* v *Burnley Borough Council* [1978] AC 904, that since 1875 law and equity should themselves be considered as being fused, and that it is no longer meaningful to speak as though rules of equity still retain a separate identity. Whether or not this is correct (and it is difficult to see it as being more than a semantic argument), there are practical reasons for continuing to treat the two systems separately. Rights which owe their derivation to equitable principles differ, as we saw in 1.5, from those which derive from the common law. Both types of right can exist simultaneously in a given situation, and it is without doubt more convenient to continue to subject them to a separate analysis.

In *Walsh* v *Lonsdale* (1882) 20 Ch D 9, for example, the tenant had a periodic tenancy at common law, and a 17-year equitable lease. If the landlord had sold the land to a third party, the common law tenancy, as a right *in rem*, would certainly have bound the purchaser, whereas the equitable lease would only have done so on the basis of the notice doctrine discussed above. It is thus suggested that it is still sensible to consider common law and equity separately, even after both doctrines have now been administered in the same court for 120 years.

An account of the historic relationship between the nature of equitable rights and legislation affecting property—principally that dating from 1925—can be found in the Online Resource Centre (ORC).

1.7 Equity's emerging jurisdiction and its invention of the earliest trust instrument

Following this account of equity's emerging jurisdiction helps to explain and account for the way in which equity was actually able to develop the trust, in a jurisdiction which has become formalised from discretions which were vested in the medieval office of Chancellor. What follows now is an account of why the Chancellor's efforts were focused on actually developing the trust in this context. Keeping in mind the central association of equity with response to injustice, this will be explained firstly by reference to equity's development of the earliest form of the trust instrument which was called the 'Use'.

The Use has its earliest modern origins in the fifteenth century, but as an instrument and device the Use itself actually developed much earlier and from around 1230. The Use was designed to try to separate out ownership of land from benefit of ownership of land in response to strict rules of succession which meant that it was actually very difficult to make provision for children other than an eldest child. These rules were themselves premised on preserving intact large estates in land, which were subject to certain entitlements and significantly also made subject to payments of 'duties' to the Crown. But this meant that harshness could be experienced by a surviving spouse and other children. At the heart of mitigating this harshness, and addressing the injustices arising, was the King's Chancellor, who had a number of powers and discretions, which provided the foundations of equity, and led to the setting up of the distinctive 'Court of Chancery'.

At its simplest, the mechanics of the Use ensured that a conveyance would be made to one party, usually a lawyer or cleric, but subject to instructions relating to the use of land for the benefit of the *cestui que use*. The real problem was that legal title would not be vested in the party intended to enjoy the property. There was a great deal of contemporary concern that those intended to benefit (according to an anonymous writing from 1502) actually had no protection and 'no more to do with the land than the greatest stranger in the world'. Thus from around 1400 the Chancellor ensured that land for this type of benefit was directed in this way by acting on the conscience of the legal owner. Because he still retained legal title, the common law was theoretically unaffected by this, while the *cestui que use* came to be regarded as the equitable owner.

However, this was not the 'triumph' of the trust, and Henry VII passed anti-avoidance (of feudal dues) legislation in 1490 and 1504. The Use and its ability to create estates and interests in land was actually having the result that payment of dues upon death were being avoided, because legal estates needed only rarely to be transferred, and the Crown was not pleased to see this decline in revenue. Nevertheless, when the Chancellor created the Use it was necessary to decide which equitable estates would be protected.

Given that one of the most important consequences of the Use was the avoidance of feudal dues, and that soon a great proportion of land was held to Uses, the combination of legal and equitable title was achieved through execution of the Use by conveying the legal estate to the *cestui que use*. The Crown as supreme landlord was affected significantly by its growth, and Henry VIII enacted the Statute of Uses in 1535 to check its creativity, and to try to liberalise duties due. But instead of curbing its application, the Statute actually fostered greater creativity through the invention of the 'Use upon a Use'. This is what eventually became called a trust by 1700, and accordingly the person intended to benefit became known as the *cestui que trust*. The basic rationale of the instrument remains the same—to separate out enjoyment of property from its ownership, and to ensure this happens by imposing duties upon the owner of legal title to the property.

1.7.1 The trust today, and a preamble to understanding how it is used and where it is encountered

The 1700s marked the beginnings of the modern trust, and as it has been suggested above, a system of precedent was also starting to develop around this time. Many of equity's earliest features would continue to remain in this setting, as would the way in which during the eighteenth century the use made of the trust instrument was still very much oriented towards land and creating different interests in land. It will become clear shortly that trusts today can be found in a vast array of different social and economic contexts, and relating to personal property (both tangible and intangible) as well as to land. However, the eighteenth century origins of modern trusts law remain highly significant because they explain the way in which modern trusts law evolved very much in light of the family settlement type trusts relating to land. These are considered in more detail in chapter 2, but for present purposes, reference to them is made to suggest that these origins are at the heart of the considerable debate which currently relates to the continuing relevance of rules underpinning trusts arrangements and trusteeship in the twenty-first century.

It was suggested above that some of the earliest features of the earliest Use actually remain in modern approaches to regulating the trust, and particularly those who are trustees under a trust arrangement. And today there is criticism that principles which developed at this time, and certainly during the eighteenth century, may have undesirable consequences for modern ways of 'doing things'. The eighteenth century was a time, after all, before modern banking practices and limited liability companies (as presently constituted) existed. Thus, even if principles developed in the context of family settlement trusts were well suited to this type of arrangement, it does not necessarily mean they are equipped to meet the challenges of trusts administration in the twenty-first century, or even that they are appropriate to doing so. This will become clearer in subsequent parts of the text, for example in chapter 4, which shows how assumptions based on family type trusts until very recently impeded the development of the law relating to certainties. Further on, chapters 15 and 18 consider whether trustees' duties are too onerous for similar reasons. The heart of these difficulties lies in the way in which family trusts are not in their nature intended as risky ventures, and a significant 'focal point' of them is in guarding against fraud of the trustees. This suggests that applying similar principles to professional trustees, who may well be expected to take business risks, is arguably inappropriate.

What follows in the next chapter is a more thorough examination of the modern trust itself, looking at the different types of trust which are encountered, and the key terminology associated with different types of trust. Following on from that it will become apparent that today's trust instrument still has very strong applications in property which is land, but applies equally to goods, and that many modern applications of the trust concern personal property rather than land, and can be found to be present within a number of social and economic spheres.

 online resource centre

FURTHER READING

Hayton 'Developing the Obligation Characteristic of the Trust' (2001) Law Quarterly Review 96.

Parkinson 'Reconceptualising the Express Trust' (2002) Cambridge Law Journal 657.

Todd 'Estoppel Licences and Third Party Rights' (1981) Conveyancer 347.

2

··

The nature of the trust: its operation
and applications in society and economy

It will become apparent shortly that the trust is put to a variety of uses in English law. This is on account of its special feature of dividing ownership of property into distinct legal and equitable title. Just by way of reiteration of the key point made in chapter 1, a trust involves a division of the ownership of property. The settlor is the original owner of property and creates a trust by conveying legal title to it to one or more trustees, manifesting an intention that it is to be held on trust for one or more beneficiaries. The trustees of property become its owners at common law, and are given control of the property, but also responsibility for it.

What will become clear in due course is that this is the scenario which arises in what is known as an express trust. This is a trust which is expressly created by the settlor. It is important to understand this at this stage because trusts which are not expressly created by a settlor in this way can nevertheless still arise, and indeed they do. This is explained by reference to trusts which are constructive and ones which are resulting (and which are often associated with trusts which are 'implied' or arise from operation of law).

It is also important to understand that no trust is created unless legal title is actually vested in (i.e., given to) the trustee (as explained in chapter 3). This is so regardless of even very clear intentions of a settlor to create a trust. Vesting legal title in the trustee is known as 'constituting' the trust, and there upon trustees come under equitable obligations enforceable by the beneficiaries.

2.1 An introduction to the basic nature of the trust and some key features

Through this basic model of an express trust, and by reference to the process of constituting the trust, it is possible to glean the essence of a trust. This will become even more apparent in the text below, in which the trust is compared with the features and operation of other civil law concepts arising from contract. For present purposes, it is sufficient to note that:

- It is not necessary for settlors, trustees and beneficiaries to be different people.

A settlor can validly constitute a trust by declaring *himself* trustee of his own property, on behalf of one or more beneficiaries. This is discussed in detail in chapter 3. The settlor may be a beneficiary, and will always be in the case of a resulting trust (see chapter 7). A trustee may be the beneficiary, or one of a number of beneficiaries. Settlors can even be trustees *and* beneficiaries, as illustrated in the case study of the family home.

- The property subject to, and thus settled *on trust* can include an equitable interest.

In other words a beneficiary under a trust may constitute a further trust of his equitable interest, thereby creating a sub-trust. Sub-trusts are common in tax-avoiding settlements. The beneficiary under the sub-trust can himself repeat the process, creating a further sub-trust, and there is no limit to the number of times this process may be repeated.

- The application of the trust to purposes which are charitable.

The illustrations and points which have been made up to now in this chapter relate to trusts which are known as 'private' trusts. This means that they are privately created trusts, the defining term for which is trusts which are 'non-charitable'. It will become apparent that charitable trusts are created alongside private trusts, but they have different features and are subject to different rules. A brief reference will be made to this below in this chapter, but the substantive law relating to charitable trusts is examined once this text's coverage of the essential features and operation of *non-charitable private* trusts is completed. Prior to the consideration given to charitable trusts (which is located in chapters 12–14), it is sufficient to say that in a charitable trust there may be no true beneficiaries at all. Instead, these arrangements are enforced by the Attorney-General, and their validity *as* charitable trusts is determined by special rules which apply only to charitable trusts (all of which will be explained in chapters 12–14).

- The creation of private trusts for purposes rather than beneficiaries.

The example of the private trust provided up to this point, where property is settled on trust for a beneficiary, assumes that the beneficiary has a full equitable interest in the property concerned and there are no restrictions on the use which can be made of this property. However, it will become clear in chapter 4 that it may be possible to create what are known as private (i.e., non-charitable) *purpose* trusts, benefiting a defined group of people. Arguably, these people are not true beneficiaries, because they are constrained to use the property for a particular purpose. An example might be a conveyance of land to A and B, in trust to be used as a football pitch for the employees of X Ltd. The employees are arguably not true beneficiaries, because they cannot use the land in any way they wish. Nevertheless, the trust is probably valid, because in spite of this they have sufficient interest in the property to be able to enforce the equitable obligations owed by the trustees. In this broad 'alternative' non-charitable trust scenario there may also be an anomalous category of unenforceable trusts, which do, nevertheless, share other characteristics of ordinary trusts. These arrangements, which are also considered in chapter 4, seem to be limited to trusts for the benefit of animals and the maintenance of tombs, and should be regarded as exceptional.

Before proceeding with the substantive analysis of the law relating to trusts—both non-charitable and also charitable—there is now the opportunity to check understanding of these core ideas by taking a closer look at *why* trusts are created and *who* creates them.

2.2 Introducing different types of trust: express, implied, resulting, and constructive trusts explained

It was suggested above that many of the trusts which will be encountered in this text will be express trusts. This type of arrangement—where a trust arises from the express wishes of a settlor to settle property on trust—is easiest to understand, and it is used as a starting point to explain and illustrate the creation and operation of trusts more generally. The 'express trust' scenario is where the settlor has expressed an intention to set up a trust, but reference was also made to the fact that there are other types of trust which need explaining and illuminating. In one respect this is key to understanding the vast number of different uses to which the trust is being put in current times, and to which it could also be potentially applied, because this does require appreciation of trusts which are resulting and constructive. It is also the case that, as will become apparent in chapter 5, more technically, these latter types of trust are not subject to the same formality requirements which express trusts must meet in order to be valid. In other words, it is important to understand that there are different types of trust to consider. Thus, in addition to the way in which a trust can be created expressly by a settlor, note must be made of the way in which private (i.e., non-charitable trusts) can also be:

(1) *Constructive.* A *constructive trust* will arise in a number of different factual situations which will often appear to be diverse. However, all constructive trusts have in common that they will arise where a trust is imposed by the courts irrespective of the intention of the owner (of what becomes the 'trust property'), and in this respect they can be said to arise from the operation of law.

(2) *Resulting trusts* are also found in a diverse variety of factual situations, but are more difficult to pin down than constructive trusts which are essentially (with limited exception) impositions of trusteeship in unconscionable situations. In seeking to understand resulting trusts, it is helpful to remember that all resulting trusts do have one element in common. Although legal title is vested in a trustee, the settlor and the beneficiary are actually the same person. In understanding how this transpires, it will do so for two reasons: for present purposes, this is explained in a very simple manner, in anticipation of fuller consideration given in chapters 7 *et seq.* Broadly (and with emphasis on simplicity at this introductory stage), this will occur because the settlor has tried to create a trust in favour of a third-party beneficiary, and although legal title has been transferred from him, he has failed to divest himself of equitable interest in the property. Here, equitable title never leaves him. Alternatively, a resulting trust will arise where property has been divested from him, but it is for some reason later returned back to him.

Both constructive and resulting trusts require far more consideration than this very basic introduction is intended to give. Chapter 7 offers an introduction to constructive and resulting trusts by way of introducing these less 'formal' (in terms of creation) trusts, and thereafter their essential characteristics and operational features. Thereafter, through chapters 8, 9, 10, and 11, the workings of resulting and constructive trusts will be explored through discussions of: the ways in which associations without legal personality can hold property; pension funds; trusts arising from cohabitation; secret trusts; and equitable fraud. Thereafter, chapters 15, 18, and 19 include discussions of the application of constructive trusts to liabilities which arise both for fiduciaries, and also strangers, to a trust for unauthorised profits which are made from trust property, or the receipt of trust property which has been applied in breach of trust.

2.2.1 Other terminology used in explaining classifications of trusts

It will also become apparent from examining sources of trusts law itself and especially academic writings, that a vast array of terminology can be used to help in the classification of trusts.

- References made to *express* trusts as being *executed* or *executory*.

Following on from the way in which, much as it sounds, an express trust arises where a settlor expressly settles property on trust for a beneficiary or beneficiaries, in some cases and commentaries of academics reference will be made to trusts which are 'executed' and ones which are 'executory'. This book does not attach any significance to this terminology beyond initially explaining it at this introductory point. Essentially the difference between these terms is that while in an executed trust the settlor has made clear the interests which are to be taken by the beneficiaries, in an executory trust scenario defining the beneficial interests under the trust does not become clear until a further document is executed. In this latter situation, a valid trust is created, but it remains executory until the further 'instructions' are executed. This distinction does not really impact on this text's analysis at all, and it remains only to note that stricter rules of construction apply to executed trusts than to ones which are executory: this is because in the latter scenario the courts are concerned with more 'open' questions relating to ascertaining a settlor's true intentions, in absence of specific directions on the application of property to beneficiaries.

- References to trusts which are *implied* trusts.

Reference is made by a number of writers to *implied* trusts to explain the arrangement which arises where the settlor's intention to create a trust is not expressed as such but can instead be inferred either from his words, or even conduct. Opinion is divided on whether this categorisation serves useful purpose. At one level it is a convenient and accurate term for trusts which are not created with express words, but equally it will become apparent that words (which do not actually say 'I declare that') are capable of amounting to an express trust on account that this is what settlers intended to do. In this manner, reference to an 'implied trust' might be seen as more appropriate where express words are not used, but it is not obvious that this serves a purpose which could not be achieved by using the terminology of resulting or constructive trust.

- References made to trusts which are '*bare* trusts'.

Bare or 'simple' trusts are said to arise when property is held by a trustee, in trust for an adult beneficiary with an interest in property which is described as *absolute*. This pertains to situations where, essentially, the beneficiary may at any time request that legal title is conveyed to him, and upon receiving this request the trustee must comply. In circumstances where a trustee must convey legal title to the beneficiary upon his request, it is perhaps not surprising that the trustee of a 'bare' trust is not subjected to the duties relating to trusteeship which pertain to other 'special' trusts. A common illustration of this scenario is where a solicitor acts on behalf of a client. In a number of transactions, most commonly the purchase of a domestic dwelling house, a solicitor will hold money on behalf of a client in anticipation of completion; and upon completion the client will instruct the solicitor to pay over moneys falling due, and the solicitor must do so. In this scenario, a bare trust arises *ab initio* on account that property is given to a trustee to hold on behalf of its original owner. It can also arise when at some time after its creation a trust *becomes* a bare one. This can be illustrated by a trust which confers a life interest in property to A and, upon A's death, passes to B absolutely: upon A's death, B becomes entitled to the property *absolutely*, and the trustee must convey legal title to B upon his request.

2.3 Circumstances in which trusts are created

Trusts arise in many everyday situations, which cover widely differing circumstances. What will become clear is that the basic nature of the trust is thus widely adaptable to a number of different social and economic scenarios. Although principles which apply to each variety of trust are similar rather than identical, in many respects it is remarkable just how much variety can be derived from the same basic concept.

2.3.1 Trusts relating to family arrangements

2.3.1.1 *Family settlement arrangements*

The purpose of many express trusts (i.e., those which are deliberately created by a settlor) is the retention of wealth by the wealthy. This is what will be seen to underpin many of the private trusts which are encountered in this text which arise today, and it was ever thus. The modern trust and the concomitant entitlements of beneficiaries and duties of trustees, have grown up around family settlements which have over centuries sought to tie up wealth within a family, and were drafted to minimise both free disposal within the family itself and also to minimise exposure to taxation. These arrangements can be made by will, but it can be advantageous from a taxation viewpoint for them to be constituted during the life of the settlor (i.e., *inter vivos*). Although they were more important historically than they are today, family settlements are still common, and frequently give rise to litigation. It is not, of course, the function of this book to comment on the desirability or otherwise of these schemes. This is a political question, on which views may validly differ. Only the legal consequences are appropriate for discussion here.

Administration of family trusts

The trustees may be members of the family, and in the early days of such set-tlements often were. They may be solicitors who are familiar with the family business. Neither of these appointments is considered by the courts to be very desirable, however, because of the likelihood of conflict of interest where the trus-tee is too closely connected to, or involved with, the beneficiaries. It was probably because the modern law of trusts largely developed at a time when this sort of trust was exceedingly common, and when the trustees were normally family members, that the nature of trustees' duties (on which, see chapters 15, 16, and 18) is so stringent.

Family trusts may also be administered by the trustee and executor departments of banks. Proper professional administration can be of the greatest importance if tax benefits are to be maximised. Banks charge quite heavily for taking on these duties, by way of a charging clause that they insist on putting into the trust instru-ment. The charges are therefore usually fixed at the outset, and do not depend on how the trust is administered. It will become clear that this is very important when conflicts of interest and duty arising in the office of trustee are considered in chapter 15.

The terminology relating to settlements will arise again throughout the book. All settlements involve the creation of successions of interests, and the simplest form would be where A leaves property to B for life and thereafter for C. B is the *life tenant*, and is usually entitled to the immediate income from the property. He is sometimes referred to as an income beneficiary. C is entitled in remainder. He is the *remainder-man*, sometimes referred to as a capital beneficiary.

In this case the extent of C's interest is known at the outset, and so it is a *vested* interest. Suppose, on the other hand, the gift is to B for life and then to the first of C, D, and E to marry. It is unknown yet which will marry first, and the inter-ests of C, D, and E are said to be contingent. More is made of this distinction in chapter 6.

In citations of cases 'ST' indicates a settlement trust and 'WT' a will trust.

2.3.1.2 *Trusts arising from marriage or cohabitation*

Also located within the broad setting of 'family property' are trusts arising from marriage, or from cohabitation of a family home. However, these arrangements are perhaps less overtly concerned with wealth and more with determining issues of ownership of a family home, either because the relationship between the parties has broken down, or a third party acquires an interest in the property (e.g., the position of a financial lender who has a charge over the property). It is also the case that the nature of the trust arrangement itself in these scenarios can be quite dif-ferent from the express creation of a trust as illuminated above. While some trusts relating to family homes will be expressly created, trusts which are resulting and constructive trusts will often arise in these (often) informal family arrangements. A common example of such a situation, and the operation of a trust within it is where a wife or female cohabitee (X) provides money towards the purchase of a home, which, though intended to be jointly occupied, is conveyed into the name of the man alone (Y). Y holds X's interest in the home on resulting trust, so that both parties share equitable title. Or in circumstances where property is legally vested in Y alone, but Y makes a representation to X that the home is 'both of theirs', then Y can be deemed to hold legal title as a constructive trustee on trust for both himself and X. The 'workings' of such an arrangement are explored fully in chapter 9's consideration of the family home. This will also explain the way in which although proprietary estoppel has been very significant in disputes relating to shared homes over much of the last decade that the House of Lords very recently restated the importance of the trust.

2.3.1.3 *Trusts and succession*

Closely related to maintaining familial wealth, and determinations of the ownership of a family home are questions relating to succession. Trusts do have a limited role to play in succession, but the main function of this section is to explain terms which will be used later in various parts of the book.

When a person dies, the legal and beneficial entitlement to all his property passes to his 'personal representatives'. If he made a will in which he appointed specific persons to be his personal representatives, they are known as his 'executors', and their first task is to obtain probate of the will (i.e., have the will registered by the registrar). Thereafter, their duty is to meet the debts and funeral expenses of the deceased out of his property, and then to distribute the rest in accordance with the instructions given in the will.

Trusts, succession and intestacy

When a person dies intestate (i.e., without making a will), a statutory scheme provided by the Administration of Estates Act 1925 comes into play. This attempts to give effect to what most people are assumed to intend to happen to their property after their deaths, by providing first for any widow or widower, then for children and so on, so that the closest relations obtain the benefits which the deceased would probably have wished for them. The scheme extends outwards, so that if the deceased has no close relatives, his more distant relations will benefit. If he has no relations at all, the property passes to the Crown.

Since there is no will, his personal representatives will not be executors, but 'administrators' (i.e., the persons who have obtained a grant entitling them to administer the estate). These will usually be the persons who are entitled to the property. If the deceased left a widow, she is entitled to a grant of administration, permitting her to distribute the property; if there is no widow, the right passes to the children, and so on.

The distinction between executors and administrators was material to the discussion in *Re Gonin* [1979] Ch 16 (see chapter 3).

Trustees, executors and personal representatives

Whether the personal representatives are executors of a will or administrators on intestacy, their duties are the same, and many of the rules which apply to trustees (see chapters 14–16) apply also to them. They hold their office for life, but the active duties are usually completed within one or two years. They must collect in all the deceased's assets, pay all debts and expenses, and then distribute the property either in accordance with the terms of the will or the statutory scheme, as the case may be.

Gifts, property, and the 'residuary legatee'

Wills commonly provide for specific gifts to relatives or friends. A gift of land is called a 'devise', and its recipient a 'devisee'; a gift of personal property, including money, is a 'legacy', and its recipient a 'legatee'. Property which is not specifically disposed of by will is called 'the residue', and the entitled person(s) the 'residuary legatee(s)'. If a specific gift fails for any reason (possible reasons appear in chapter 4), it is added to the residue. In practice, this often comprises the bulk of the property, as it is usual to provide small specific gifts to selected friends and relatives, and simply leave the rest to the person whom one most desires to benefit.

Trusts arising on death

Trusts may arise on a death, either because the will specifies that some property is to be held on trust, or because the intended recipient is under the age of 18, so that the legal title must be held for him until he reaches that age. Where trusts are deliberately created, it is usual to name the persons who are to act as trustees, and when the executors have completed their administration, they must transfer that property to the trustees. Often, the same persons will be named as both executors and trustees, and will continue to hold the legal title in their new capacity.

Death, the administration of property, and the role of executors

It is important to appreciate that the legatees, devisees, and beneficiaries under any trust created by the will have no beneficial interest in that property until such time as the executors appropriate (i.e., earmark) property to meet the gifts or trusts created by the will. What they have is merely a right to demand the proper administration of the estate by the executors. Similarly, persons entitled under an intestacy have no beneficial interest in the property until the administrators have paid off all the liabilities affecting the deceased's property and prepared their accounts, showing what is available for those persons. For the sake of convenience, the persons entitled under an intestacy are referred to as the 'next of kin' rather than legatees, etc.

It is possible for a partial intestacy to occur, for example, where the deceased failed to specify in his will who the residuary legatee is to be, or where the residuary gift fails. In such a case, the property will pass to the next of kin, as provided by the statutory scheme.

2.3.2 Trusts arising in personal asset maintenance and management

There are also a number of other trusts which are associated with personal asset *maintenance* but which signal their application outside the context of family wealth and even the family home. These include:

- Trusts relating to share holdings.

Shares are often owned out-and-out by the shareholder, but they may also be held by nominees. This practice is most common in holdings of shares in public, rather than private, companies, and in this scenario, the nominee is often a bank. In that case the legal estate is held by the nominee in trust for the shareholder. One reason for this might be if it is intended that the trustee should manage the portfolio, as would be the case, for example, with a unit trust.

- Trusts arising from pensions provision.

The rise of pension funds and the need to create a workable legal framework for the operation and safe-guarding of pension assets has brought the trust into prominence in respect of one of the biggest socio-economic issues of current times. The attractiveness of the trust arrangement was crucially recognised in the Report of Sir Roy Goode's *Pension Law Review Committee* (1993, Cmnd 2342). The Committee's recommendations resulted in the passage of the Pensions Act 1995. The 1995 Act sought to reflect the importance of rigorous regulation and supervision of pension schemes, and one of its principal tenets was its accommodation of the reality that the beneficiaries under a pension scheme differed from under the normal trust arrangement; indeed, the entitlement of beneficiaries under a pension scheme could be seen to arise from contractual origins (provided by their contracts of employment). This aside, the trust was deemed best able to promote the expedient and safe use of such schemes, subject to some modification of its 'normal' operations from specific pensions legislation.

The issue of pensions and their operation in contemporary society is one of the most important socio-economic issues of today. With the combination of declining birth rate, longer life expectancy, and a broader global context signalling the dismantling of the welfare state, the focus on privately funded pensions outside state provision has increased. Today's issues arise very strongly from the need to plan for tomorrow, and private pension schemes (occupational and otherwise) are very much concerned with planned long-term personal asset management. In this respect, while the trust's traditional associations are strongly with wealth and its preservation, it is nevertheless significant that it is these age-old principles which are envisioned as the blueprint for this personal asset management into the twenty-first century. This is a testament to the trust's versatility, adaptability, and also to its endurance. This is so notwithstanding that demonstrating how pension funds are modelled on the trust instrument will reveal some crucial departures from 'ordinary' trust principles, as will become clear in chapter 8.

- Trusts arising from personal insolvency.

The protective trust is a special type of trust that was developed as a method of protecting family property against the consequences of the family falling into debt. Generally speaking, any property owned by a debtor can be taken to satisfy his creditors, and in the extreme event of bankruptcy, all of the debtor's property becomes vested in his trustee in bankruptcy, including of course any interest under a family settlement.

2.3.2.1 *Trusts for protection and bankruptcy, and the significance of the nineteenth century*

In the nineteenth century, when family settlements were more common than today, such an interest would usually be a life interest, and where improvidence was feared, this interest might be made determinable upon the bankruptcy or attempted alienation of the interest on the part of its owner. At first, the practice was to provide for a gift over to some other member of the family if the life interest was thus brought to an end, but by the latter part of the nineteenth century a more satisfactory solution was discovered, and today a protective trust consists of a determinable life interest, the determination of which brings into play a discretionary trust in favour of the former life tenant, his spouse, and children (if any), and ultimately his next of kin who would inherit in the event of his death.

2.3.2.2 *The protective trust and its operation in bankruptcy*

The obvious advantages are that on the bankruptcy or alienation of the debtor's property the interest in the trust property simply ceases to exist, and cannot be claimed by creditors or the trustees in bankruptcy. The property itself remains in the hands of the trustees who can distribute the income as they see fit in the circumstances. If the reason for the determination is the actual indebtedness of the former life tenant, it would clearly be pointless to make payments to him, as the creditors could then seize the money, but the lifestyle of the family can be maintained by paying the income instead to the wife, or directly to those who supply his needs, since they can apply it for the 'use and benefit' of the former life tenant without placing money directly into his hands. It is not even necessary to set out in express terms the nature of the trusts, since s. 33 of the Trustee Act 1925 provides a model form which can be invoked simply by directing that the property shall be held on 'protective trusts' for the benefit of the person who is to be the life tenant (called 'the principal beneficiary' in the section).

2.3.2.3 *Limitations of the protective trust*

There are two main limitations. First, it is not possible to settle property upon oneself via such trusts, and protective trusts would usually be created by the parent of the principal beneficiary on his behalf. Second, the life interest must be made *determinable* upon the relevant event—that is, so defined that it ends naturally on the happening of the event. If, on the other hand, it is made subject to a *condition subsequent*, that condition may be void as a device to defeat one's creditors. The difference is purely one of language, and is devoid of moral principle.

2.3.2.4 *Bankruptcy and the assets available to creditors: the significance of the family home*

The references made to the family home in this context do of course relate to the strong possibility that in the event of bankruptcy, a trustee in bankruptcy is likely to want to seek the sale of the family home in order to satisfy the claims of creditors. And in this light, traditionally, it was the position that if a trustee in bankruptcy wishes to pursue this, it is only in exceptional circumstances (see, for example, *Re Solomon* [1967] Ch 573 *and Re Lowrie* [1981] 3 All ER 353) that he will not be able to do so. It is of course possible to analyse this contentious position of the family home as a reflection of deeply entrenched retributionist ideas which have associated bankruptcy with misconduct, or at the very least irresponsibility and improvidence, rather than *misfortune* since Victorian times. It might instead be seen more simply as part of the 'economic reality' of creditor entitlement to be paid for the money he has advanced to the debtor.

In some respects, the Insolvency Act 1986—where the law relating to personal insolvency is largely located, alongside that of corporate insolvency—entrenched further associations of indebtedness with irresponsibility, through contending that for some bankruptcy might represent 'an easy solution for those who can bear with equanimity the stigma of their own failure' (Sir Kenneth Cork, see below). However, the provisions of s. 335A state that where an application for sale of a home is made, the court shall make an order which it considers just and reasonable, having regard to a number of factors relating to the family home's 'own claim to protection', as alluded to in the judgment of Megarry V-C in *Re Bailey* [1977] 1 WLR 278.

Predictably, the provisions focus on the interests of the bankrupt's creditors, who are identified in s. 335A(a). In addition, where the proposed sale includes a dwelling house which 'is or has been the home of the bankrupt or the bankrupt's spouse or former spouse', the provisions of s. 335A(b) determine that the court's calculus of just and reasonable involves it having regard to a number of factors. These factors located in s. 335A(b) relate to (i) the *conduct* of the spouse or former spouse, so far as contributing to the bankruptcy; (ii) the *needs and financial resources* of the spouse or former spouse; and (iii) the *needs of any children*. In these circumstances, the court will also have regard to (c) all the circumstances of the case *other than the needs of the bankrupt*.

This is hardly a protection charter, though, because where an application for sale is made after one year following the vesting of a bankrupt's property in the trustee in bankruptcy, the assumption will be made that the interests of creditors do outweigh all other 'competing' considerations, apart from those which reflect 'exceptional circumstances' (which itself appears to reflect the position prior to the 1986 Act). Thus this is a mechanism for *delay* rather than *protection* in many respects, but greater *delay* (and arguably also even *protection*) of a bankrupt's property does appear to flow from the Enterprise Act 2002. In spirit and intendment, this enactment signalled a strongly changed emphasis across bankruptcy law, by seeking to align the consequences of bankruptcy (essentially, disqualification as a bankrupt and attendant impotencies) and prospects for rehabilitation to degrees to which a bankrupt could be deemed to have contributed to his bankruptcy (see Wilson and Wilson, 2001). In relation to a bankrupt's family home, the Enterprise Act (which amends the Insolvency Act 1986) provides that where the trustee in bankruptcy has not sold the property or applied for an order of possession within three years of the date of the bankruptcy, the property reverts to the bankrupt, and is thus not part of the estate which can be applied to creditors' claims.

2.3.3 Trusts arising in commercial arrangements

In one respect, the growing significance of trusts law outside its traditional roots in family arrangements, and its increasing applications in commerce and business activity and practice is alluded to later in this chapter, by looking at trusts and loan arrangements which derive from the law of contract. On another level, the way in which entrepreneurial activity is politically at centre-stage is evident from the attention paid to the new Companies Act 2006, whilst it was before Parliament. Along with changes in law which have already been made to e-commerce and corporate insolvency, and the emphasis given to business fraud within the genesis of the Fraud Act 2006, the reforms in company law point to the New Labour Government's political economy being strongly oriented towards promoting— in the words of Gordon Brown MP, Chancellor of the Exchequer, in 1999—a 'pro-enterprise and pro-opportunity Britain'.

The current discourses on company law, along with those underpinning the Enterprise Act's new provisions for personal and corporate insolvency, is that entrepreneurial activity is itself defined by taking risks. Risk-taking is at the heart of a healthy wealth-creating economy, but even legitimate and appropriate risk-taking may not 'pay off', and in these circumstances business failure is a possibility. In the event of a corporate insolvency (the legal term given to an incorporated business's inability to pay its debts), all business assets will become available for satisfying the claims of its creditors. In a context where there is likely to be a disparity between assets which are available and claims made in respect of them, the priority of claims will be determined by statute. Indeed, in 1982 the Report of Sir Kenneth Cork's *Committee on Insolvency Law and Practice* (Cmnd 8558) proposed that one of the core aims of modern insolvency law must be to ensure a 'workable system of clear priorities and ranking amongst creditors'. Accordingly, this system is now found in the Insolvency Act 1986 as amended by the Enterprise Act 2002, and all assets of a business will become subject to this statutory system of priorities.

2.3.3.1 *Loans, security and the ordinary consequences of corporate insolvency*

This position of business assets and business creditors in the event of an insolvency illustrates one very clear importation of trust principles into commercial dealings. The discussion on *Quistclose* trusts which occurs shortly, shows how by this mechanism money is advanced by a creditor to a borrower, but is so subject to a trust. This means that the property never becomes part of a business's assets, and thus it will not form part of what becomes available for creditors *generally* in the event of insolvency. Thus, this is a mechanism by which a *particular* creditor can protect his own position viz. what would otherwise be competing claims.

Thus, the protection of credit advanced, which can be achieved through making it subject to a trust, might in many respects be regarded as a most suitable response to the inevitable exigencies of business: businesses do fail, even where practices are sound and responsible, and in these circumstances ordinary unsecured creditors (i.e., those who make advances without taking security) will often lose out. This general attractiveness of a trust arrangement might increase still further in light of changes which have been made to the position of certain creditors in the Enterprise Act 2002, and especially that of a *secured* creditor known as a 'floating charge' holder.

2.3.3.2 *Loans, trusts and insolvency: the significance of the Enterprise Act 2002*

In the operation of such a charge, a creditor will take as security for his loan what is known as a 'floating charge' over a company's more 'fluid' assets, such as 'stock-in-trade'. This can be a very attractive arrangement for companies because it allows them to deal freely with their 'fluid' assets, until they become fixed by 'crystallisation', which will be triggered by a number of possible events, including actual or imminent insolvency. Upon crystallisation, the holder of such a charge would then commonly appoint an administrative receiver for the purposes of realising his security. However, the Enterprise Act's provisions have now made the traditional position of a floating charge holder less attractive in two distinct ways. This is on account of the Act's primary 'twin' objectives: first, to try to promote the rescue of struggling companies where this is possible, and second, to improve the position of unsecured creditors where this is not.

The Act now prevents the holder of a floating charge from appointing an administrative receiver, whom (by way of recap) he would engage in order to realise his own security. This is so as to enhance a failing company's prospects of being rescued; either through a voluntary arrangement (with creditors) or administration (in which an appointed administrator puts together a 'rescue package' to try to save the company from insolvent liquidation). It is also the case that the floating charge holder's traditional position in the statutory ranking of creditors upon insolvency (as determined in the Insolvency Act 1986) has changed on account of the 2002 Act. While holders of floating charges still rank above 'general creditors of the company', it is also the case that prior to being paid under the new statutory scheme, a 'prescribed proportion' is now taken from them, and applied to helping to meet the claims of unsecured creditors. According to s. 176A of the Insolvency Act 1986 (inserted by the Enterprise Act) floating charge holders will only be paid the amount which 'exceeds the amount required for the satisfaction of unsecured creditors', which is effectively the amount remaining after the 'prescribed proportion' has been removed.

2.3.3.3 *The trust as the new security in commercial transactions?*

From the documentation which accompanied the Enterprise Act, this is actually quite a complex calculation process, and certainly beyond the scope of this text. But it is worth noting that the *Enterprise Act Evaluation Planning Paper* (published in 2003 by the Insolvency Service) does suggest that the amount set aside for unsecured creditors in this manner can be up to £600,000. This measure operates unless it is felt that 'the cost of making a distribution to unsecured creditors would be disproportionate to the benefits', which is recognition that notwithstanding the *spirit* of these reforms, pursuing this method of redistribution in favour of unsecured creditors may be uneconomic in some circumstances. However, the *Evaluation's* invitation for consultation on the proposed operation of these 'prescribed part' provisions does intimate recognition of inherent difficulties, and especially ones relating to potential scope of operation. Although it does not express this quite so directly, the *Evaluation* is concerned to determine whether these provisions may be going too far, and may operate beyond helping to protect unsecured creditors.

It is not difficult to see these provisions as ones which are helping to convert unsecured creditors into secured creditors at the expense of those who *do* seek to protect themselves by security for their loans. The outcomes of this 'evaluation' remain to be seen, but it is not difficult to imagine that floating charges might well become far less attractive for lenders. In one respect this might well diminish what is an important 'life-line' for struggling businesses, but from the perspective of lenders *themselves*, they are likely to be looking at other possibilities for securing their advances. In these conditions, it may be that creditors will increasingly look towards the trust as a mechanism which provides security through its protection of assets from the consequences of a debtor's insolvency.

2.3.3.4 *Commercial trusts and ordinary trust principles?*

It is clear at one level that trusts which protect loans made to businesses do so on account of the features which underpin the operation of all trusts; these are, of course, the division of title to property into legal and beneficial ownership, coupled with the intention of the owner of property that it should be subject to the trust. And even prior to the changes introduced by the Enterprise Act 2002 which, it is suggested, might well heighten the trust's attractiveness in commercial transactions, a number of academic commentators have observed the growing 'commercial applications of trusts'. It is also the case that the Law Commission has commented on the growing use of trusts in the sphere of commercial deal-ings, in its recent *Report on Trustee Exemption Clauses* (considered in chapter 18; for this point, see especially para. 6.80). However, in making this observation, the Law Commission also highlighted some important features which distinguish so-called 'commercial trusts' from those arrangements otherwise made outside the domain of commercial dealings. The Law Commission remarked that set-tlors in such arrangements tend to be market equals of trustees, and are thus well versed in the needs of business and the risks which pertain to commercial trans-actions, and the technical operation of trusts (para. 6.81). It was also observed (in para. 6.82) that where the settlor acts in the course of a business (which would cover the majority of corporate settlors and some individuals) it will only be in very unusual circumstances that the transaction being entered into is of a type with which his is not familiar.

2.3.4 Charities, trade unions and unincorporated associations

Trusts can also be used to enable property to be held for the benefit of people who for some reason cannot hold it themselves. Interestingly, some of the earli-est uses made of the trust instrument were for Franciscan friars for this very pur-pose. Incorporated bodies, such as companies, which are incorporated under the Companies Acts, and universities, which are incorporated by charter, have legal personality, and can therefore hold property themselves. So there is no need, for example, for treasurers or directors to hold the property on their behalf as trustees, and normally they do not. It will become apparent that they may owe fiduciary duties, which are akin to those of trustees.

Charities (on which see chapters 12, 13, and 14) can also be incorporated, in which case they too may hold property in their own right. If they do so, the courts are undecided whether they hold absolutely, subject to the articles of association under the Companies Acts, or whether they are held on trust for charitable pur-poses. Purpose trusts will be encountered again in chapter 4, when it will become apparent that they are rather unusual in that there are no true beneficiaries.

Not all charities are incorporated, however. Unincorporated bodies have no legal personality, and cannot hold property themselves. In the case of unincor-porated charities, the property is held by trustees, who are often individuals, for the purposes of the charity. Donations to charity therefore commonly give rise to trusts.

2.3.4.1 *Trusts and non-charitable associations*

A trust can also, in theory, be a method of enabling property to be held by members' clubs, which are also unincorporated. Nominated trustees (who would usually be officers of the club) could hold the property on trust for the members. This gives rise to no difficulties as long as the membership is fixed, or the club is of short duration (e.g., a club which is geared to a specific, one-off event). Most clubs have a fluctuating membership, however, and in this case, as will become appar-ent, the trust solution can give rise to perpetuity problems, because the interests of future members may not vest until outside the perpetuity period (on which, see further chapter 6). This is not a problem that arises in the case of charities, because they are exempt from the perpetuity rules.

Unincorporated societies: the significance of the trust (and the contract)
The usual analysis for members' clubs is not based on the trust, therefore. The usual analysis is that the present members hold the club property absolutely, subject to their *contractual* rights and duties arising from membership. These may, for example, prevent them taking their share of the club property for themselves on resignation, or at any other time. They may allow the officers to decide how the property is to be used. If property is held by officers, they will hold it as agents of the members, not as trustees. Trade unions are in a peculiar (and unique) position, being regarded as unincorporated for most purposes, though sharing some of the features of corporate bodies.

2.4 Trusts distinguished from similar common law concepts

Working from the peculiarities of two different types of ownership, it can be seen quite clearly that the trust, where ownership is separated into ownership at law and that which subsists in equity, interfaces the twin systems (and until recently jurisdictions) of equity and law. However, this is a long way from being able to point to exactly what a trust is and indeed what it does. It is true that the trust will give a non-legal owner enforceable rights in respect of the trust property, but while its function is clear enough and perhaps easy to understand, a trust isn't always easy to define. Part of the reason for this is that the trust is an extremely flexible instrument, as the examples in figure 2.1 (on p. 46) illustrate.

This is, of course, connected directly to the attention which has already been drawn to the use which is made of trusts, across widely differing social and economic situations, of which the examples given above are *illustrative* but by no means exhaustive. It is of course the case that understanding *what* a trust *is* is in many ways a prelude to understanding how it is used, and in many respects it would be appropriate to have considered this more fully before looking at common uses made of the trust. However, it is also the case that appreciating how trusts are used might help us to understand more about what, fundamentally, a trust *is*. The trust is not easy to 'pin down' in many respects, and this is complicated further by the way in which other wholly different legal devices are applied to situations similar to those where trusts are to be found. For example, it has already been suggested that members' clubs are normally based on contract, not trust, but that the property of charities which are unincorporated is held by trustees. It is also the case that while banks may be trustees if they are specifically constituted as such, ordinary accounts create only a debtor–creditor relationship. In the commercial–corporate sphere, company directors are not usually trustees, but it will become apparent (in chapter 15) that they share many trustees' duties.

In light of these difficulties this book has traditionally looked at concepts found within the common law to try to explain what a trust *is* by looking at what it *is not*. Indeed, by looking at what is special about a trust (and what is not a characteristic of a number of common law concepts), this approach can help foster appreciation of *what* a trust is, and *why* it is able to do the things it can. In this edition, exploring what a trust can do that other legal devices cannot has been pursued through considering the common law contract arrangement itself, and also the loan which is based on principles of ordinary contract law.

2.4.1 The trust in light of the contract

A private trust, then, is created either by a declaration of trust by the settlor, in which case he becomes trustee himself, or by his arranging for someone else to act as trustee. The beneficiary (or if a purpose trust, the person who can enforce it) need not be a party to the arrangement at all. Yet it is the *beneficiary*, and not the settlor, who can enforce the trust, because the settlor retains no interest in the property (in his capacity *as* settlor—he can of course be a beneficiary). This is so whether or not the beneficiary has given any consideration, because he is in effect the recipient of a gift. So it is only the third party to the arrangement who can enforce it.

2.4.1.1 *Trusts, contracts, enforceability, and the doctrine of privity*

Earlier editions of this book have explained that while a third party (i.e., not one of the original contracting parties) can benefit from a contract, they cannot generally enforce it themselves by legal action, by virtue of the privity of contract doctrine. This is the essence of ways in which the trust has interfaced with the law of contract historically. Here, the trust was able to provide a means by which enforceable legal rights could be made in favour of a third party without having to use the law of contract, and thus without falling foul of the doctrine of privity. Indeed, the creation of a trust in favour of a recipient is very similar to making him a gift: he need do nothing in return, the gift gives him enforceable rights and, once made, the gift cannot be revoked. Traditionally, this was in contrast with the position of the contract, which was always revocable by the parties to it, but this must now be reviewed in light of reforms to the law of contract brought about by the Contracts (Rights of Third Parties) Act 1999.

2.4.1.2 *Contract law and criticism of the doctrine of privity*

The privity of contract doctrine has long attracted criticism, especially in relation to contracts which were clearly intended to provide a third party with a benefit, and the very famous case of *Beswick v Beswick* [1968] AC 58 (considered below) is an illustration of its capability to produce some very harsh results. Indeed, Mrs Beswick's fortune turned solely on her ability to enforce the contract as administratrix of her husband's estate. In 1998 the Law Commission published its recommendations for reform of this branch of contract law in *Privity of Contract: Contracts for the Benefit of Third Parties* (Law Com. 242), and this was followed by the 1999 Act. It is now possible for a person who is not party to a contract to enforce it where, according to s. 1, his right to enforce a term of the contract has been expressly provided for by the contract or (subject to s. 1(2) where this will not apply where on proper construction of the contract it appears that the parties did not intend the term to be enforceable by the third party) the term purports to confer a benefit for him.

2.4.1.3 *The 1999 Act and contracting out*

Because the main focus of this chapter, and indeed the text overall is the trust, much can be understood about the trust by looking at its features and operations alongside those of the contract. And at this point some brief consideration must be given to the significance of the 1999 Act. This relates of course to the traditional position of the contract, and the way in which the Act allows the parties to 'contract out' of the general position (namely by giving the third party enforceable rights, and thus effectively making the arrangement revocable) by virtue of s. 1(2). Recommendations of the Law Commission were also mindful of the need to give careful consideration to the rights of the contracting parties to vary or cancel, and that this should be lost once the third party (X) had relied on it and accepted it; while the Law Commission's recommendation that the contracting parties may expressly reserve the right to vary or cancel the third party's reliance or acceptance is provided for by s. 2.

2.4.1.4 *Contract and the trust: complementarity and historical association*

While the traditional position of a contract was that (outside the narrow and well-established exceptions to the privity doctrine) it could not be enforced by anyone who was not a party to it, trusts are enforceable by beneficiaries who need not be party to the arrangement. Furthermore, the contract and trust have traditionally operated in actual reverse of one another in this respect, in that it is the beneficiary and no one else who can enforce the trust—and this includes the settlor, who while always being part of the arrangement is unable to enforce it. Moreover, concepts of irrevocability and permanence also marked the contract as something quite distinct from the trust. In examining these related concepts of enforceability and revocability, it thus follows that the main distinction between the trust and the contract has now ceased to exist, and that in the law of contract itself facility can now be found for both types of transaction.

Of course traditionally, if the trustee was acting by virtue of a contract with the settlor, for example if he was acting as his solicitor or banker, then the settlor could enforce the contract. It may also be that a settlement of property by A on B, subject to a condition that B holds it for the benefit of X, always leads to the implication of a contract between A and B. A's remedies are in contract, however, and these are quite different from those available to a beneficiary for breach of trust.

However, in spite of recent reforms, it would be a mistake not still to consider the significance of the trust alongside contract law. To fail to explore just why the trust has been such a useful device in light of the rules of contract in English law on account of relatively recent changes would be grossly to undersell its role in modern society hitherto.

2.4.1.5 *A traditional contract example*

Suppose, for example, A contracts with B that, in consideration of a payment by A to B of a sum of money, B pays X an annuity for his (X's) life. No trust is constituted, however. Assume also that X does not provide consideration for this benefit, and is not party to the arrangement. X is therefore unable to enforce the contract in his own right. This is shown diagrammatically in figure 2.1.

A can enforce the contract, but often such arrangements are made in favour of wives, sons, or daughters, in which case A may well predecease them. In that event,

By contract with B, A agrees to confer a benefit on X

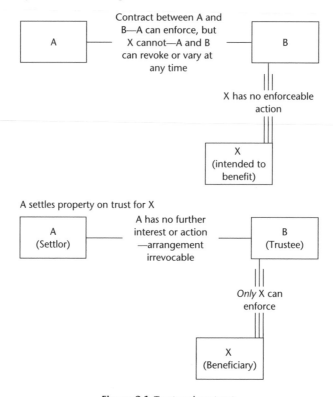

Figure 2.1 Trust and contract

after A's death A's personal representatives will be able to enforce the contract on A's behalf. As a third party, X cannot force them to do so, however, and cannot sue B directly. Of course, if X is A's personal representative, X can sue in that capacity, but not as a third party.

The leading authority is the House of Lords' decision in *Beswick v Beswick* [1968] AC 58. A coal merchant (Peter Beswick), who was over 70 years old, transferred his business to his nephew, who in return agreed, among other things, that he would, after Peter Beswick's death, pay £5 a week to his widow. (This may not sound like a great deal of money, but the agreement was made almost 30 years ago. It would be the equivalent of some £50–£60 a week today, or enough to make a substantial difference to Mrs Beswick's lifestyle.) Peter Beswick died about 18 months later, and his widow took out letters of administration to his estate (i.e., she became his administratrix: see further below).

Beswick v Beswick
The traditional contract approach Mrs Beswick sued to enforce the contract against the nephew. The House of Lords held that she was not able to sue in her own right (i.e., she could not sue as X), but that she could sue as administratrix of her late husband's estate (i.e., as A, one of the contracting parties). Here, she was literally stepping into the shoes of her late husband. She was also able to

obtain specific performance of payment of the annuity to herself (in her personal capacity).

2.4.1.6 *Enforcement of the contract by the other contracting party (A)*

Here, Mrs Beswick was suing as a party to the contract, and the reforms introduced by the Contracts (Rights of Third Parties) Act 1999 Act do not affect remedies available to the promisee. Although this was considered by the Law Commission, no changes to the law were recommended, and it is clear that if X is capable of enforcing directly, this is actually now far less important than it used to be. Where specific performance is available to A (or his personal representatives), he can ensure that the third party X can obtain the benefit of the contract, as was envisaged by the parties at the time of its making. Indeed, here, A can ensure that X obtains the benefit he has bargained for.

The contract's limitations

However, the case of *Beswick* is itself illustrative of the difficulties which can be characteristic of the operation of specific performance, and its availability in the case itself depended upon, among other things, the fact that B, the Beswicks' nephew, had received all the consideration (the transfer to him of the goodwill in Mr Beswick senior's business). Moreover, the availability of specific performance generally depends on mutuality of enforcement. This will be considered in some detail in chapter 19, but in essence this means that it will be available as a remedy only where the contract would also be specifically enforceable in the other direction (here, by B against A). This was the case in *Beswick* itself because Mr Beswick senior (A) had promised to transfer the goodwill of a business, but it will by no means always be the case that this requirement will be met. Indeed, while the more modern approach to specific performance focuses on the most appropriate remedy (see further chapter 19), it is also the case that it is unlikely to be ordered where consideration moving from A to B is money alone.

'Compensatory' nature of contractual damages

In situations where A or his personal representatives cannot obtain specific performance, but where B does not perform the bargain at all, A can get his property back on grounds of total failure of consideration. This may be of no benefit to X, of course, unless A chooses to make another similar arrangement for his benefit. Where B has partially performed the bargain, the return of property on the grounds of total failure of consideration will not be available to A, who is now forced to rely on contractual damages.

The problem here lies in the fact that contractual damages are compensatory, and where the contract is intended to provide a benefit for a third party, it is easy to see that A has actually suffered no loss himself. Thus, in most cases, A will be limited to the recovery of nominal damages. While there is limited authority that A can recover all that X could have recovered had he been a contracting party himself—particularly in the *dicta* of Lush LJ in *Lloyd's* v *Harper* (1880) 16 Ch D 290, and of Lord Denning MR in *Jackson* v *Horizon Holidays Ltd* [1975] 1 WLR 1468, it is almost certain that these views are wrong. In *Beswick* v *Beswick* itself, all Their Lordships apart from Lord Pearce thought that, had specific performance not been available, the administratrix would have been entitled to nominal damages only, as Mr Beswick's estate had suffered no loss. A similar view was taken by all members of the House of Lords in *Woodar Investment Developments Ltd* v *Wimpey Contractors (UK) Ltd* [1980] 1 WLR 277, where the *dicta* referred to above in *Lloyd's* v *Harper* and *Jackson* v *Horizon Holidays Ltd* were disapproved.

Thus, *Woodar Investment Developments Ltd* v *Wimpey Contractors (UK) Ltd* stands as authority for the proposition that where specific performance is not available, in most other cases damages recoverable by A will be nominal. The view was also expressed in *Woodar* (particularly by Lords Salmon, Keith, and Scarman) that the law was very unsatisfactory, but could only be altered by statute. Any such attestation would now seem unlikely in light of the Law Commission's recommendation and resulting legislation, but there are however exceptions to the *Woodar* principle, including the one which can be found in *Lloyd's* v *Harper*, where one party contracts as trustee for another. Here, where A contracts as X's trustee, the contracting party's damages will be calculated on the beneficiary's loss. However, the beneficiary will not be able to sue directly, but he must require the trustee to sue on his behalf.

2.4.1.7 *A trust example*

Traditionally, this was very different in a trust example, where instead of B being a contracting party, he was instead constituted trustee for X. Not only was X capable of suing B in his own right, but once constituted, the trust represented a permanent and irrevocable arrangement whereby A and B were no longer free to vary the arrangement to X's detriment, on the basis that this would be akin to making a gift to X, and then taking it back again. It was for this reason that the creation of a trust was able to avoid the privity of contract rules. This is perfectly in order, of course, so long as this is what A and B intend. Now the Contracts (Rights of Third Parties) Act 1999 removes this crucial distinction between the contract and the trust.

2.4.2 **Trusts and loans**

When you lend money to a friend or business partner, or deposit money in a bank account, your friend, business partner, or bank becomes a debtor, not a trustee, and you become a creditor, not a beneficiary. It should be clear from the above that a debtor will be in a very different position from a trustee. A debtor's liability to repay a loan is contractual, and therefore strict, subject to the terms of the loan. In other words, it does not require proof of negligence or bad faith. It is not avoided, for example, by the theft by a third person either of the money loaned, or of any property purchased with the money, however innocent the debtor may be. On the other hand, the property the creditor has loaned passes to the debtor, so if the debtor goes bankrupt, the creditor takes his place as one among many unsecured creditors, and is unlikely to see the return of any or all his money.

2.4.2.1 *Beneficiary's position contrasted with creditor's*

A trustee's duties are less strict (see chapters 15, 16, and 18), but in the event of a trustee's bankruptcy, a beneficiary is in the position of a secured creditor, because he has retained equitable property, which will be protected from the claims of the general creditors. In effect, the property never becomes part of the debtor's estate.

Both legal and equitable obligations can coexist, however, so that a loan can also constitute a trust. Thus, a creditor can also be a beneficiary, and this protects him in the event of the debtor's bankruptcy.

2.4.2.2 *Express declaration of trusteeship by debtor*

The most certain method of making a loan to a debtor which will also give rise to a trust in favour of the creditor, is to require the debtor to declare himself trustee on behalf of the creditor. A common commercial transaction where this is routinely done is the bankers' documentary credit, where the bank, on releasing to its customer shipping documents, which are its security, to enable the customer to re-sell goods (and hence obtain money to repay the bank), protects itself against the bankruptcy of its customer by taking a trust receipt, under which the customer (typically) declares himself trustee for the bank of the goods until they are sold, and trustee of the proceeds of sale once the goods are sold. Thus the bank becomes both creditor and beneficiary under the trust, and hence retains equitable title in the goods and (if sold) the proceeds of sale. Since the customer obtains the goods only as trustee, if he goes bankrupt, whether before or after the goods are sold, the bank will be able to claim the goods or the proceeds of sale (so long as they are traceable under the equitable rules described in chapter 19) in preference to the general creditors.

Other examples of the use of trusts to protect against bankruptcy are considered in chapter 3.

2.4.2.3 *No express declaration of trusteeship by debtor*

Even where words of trust are not expressly used, the courts have held, in a line of authorities going back at least 150 years, that where A advances to B an identifiable sum of money for a particular purpose, the obligations of trusteeship are imposed upon B.

The leading authority is the House of Lords decision in *Barclays Bank Ltd* v *Quistclose Investments Ltd* [1970] AC 567. The case revolved around Rolls Razor Ltd, who were in serious financial difficulties and had an overdraft with Barclays Bank of some £484,000, against a permitted limit of £250,000. If Rolls Razor were to stay in business, it was essential for them to obtain a loan of around £210,000 in order to pay dividends which they had declared on their ordinary shares, and which in the absence of such a loan they were unable to pay. They succeeded in obtaining the loan from Quistclose Investments Ltd, who agreed to make the loan on the condition 'that it is used to pay the forthcoming dividend due on July 24, next'. The sum was paid into a special account with Barclays Bank, on the condition (agreed with the bank) that the account would 'only be used to meet the dividend due on July 24, 1964'.

The House of Lords judgment and the finding of a trust

Rolls Razor went into voluntary liquidation on 27 August, without having paid the dividend. Barclays wanted to count the money in the special account against Rolls Razor's overdraft, but the House of Lords held that Barclays held the money on trust for Quistclose, so that Quistclose was able to claim back the entire sum. Lord Wilberforce stated (at p. 580):

The mutual intention of the respondents [Quistclose] and of Rolls Razor Ltd, and the essence of the bargain, was that the sum advanced should not become part of the assets of Rolls Razor Ltd, but should be used exclusively for payment of a particular class of creditors, namely, those entitled to the dividend. A necessary consequence from this, by process simply of interpretation, must be that if, for any reason, the dividend could not be paid, the money was to be returned to the respondents: the word 'only' or 'exclusively' can have no other meaning or effect.

That arrangements of this character for the payment of a person's creditors by a third person give rise to a relationship of a fiduciary character or trust, in favour, as a primary trust, of the creditors, and secondarily, if the primary trust fails, of the third person, has been recognised in a series of cases over some 150 years.

Quistclose

The effect of the decision, of course, was that the money loaned by Quistclose was secured from the consequences of Rolls Razor's bankruptcy, since it never became part of Rolls Razor's general assets.

Note that it was Barclays, who as bankers had legal title to the money, who were held to be trustees. This raised the issue of the bank's notice of the trust since, on the principles in chapter 1, they would have taken free of Quistclose's interest in the absence of notice. Lord Wilberforce commented (at p. 582):

It is common ground, and I think right, that a mere request to put the money into a separate account is not sufficient to constitute notice. But [in this case]...there is no doubt that the bank was told that the money had been provided on loan by a third person and was to be used only for the purpose of paying the dividend. This was sufficient to give them notice that it was trust money and not assets of Rolls Razor Ltd: the fact, if it be so, that they were unaware of the lender's identity (though the respondent's name as drawer was on the cheque) is of no significance.

He went on to say that the bank was also aware that Rolls Razor could not itself, without a loan from an outside source, provide the money to pay the dividend, and that the bank never contemplated that the money so provided could be used to reduce the existing overdraft.

2.4.2.4 *Money must be for a specific purpose*

The decision in *Quistclose* seems to depend on the fact that the money was to be used for a specific purpose, that that purpose was known to the recipient, and that the money was paid into a special account, which could be used for no other purpose. The last requirement, for a special account, may not be absolutely rigid, but at the very least the money must be earmarked for the particular purpose *and no other*, in order to negative the inference that the payments are to be included in the general assets of the company. In the absence of such a requirement, a prospective purchaser through a car import company, for example, who pays a deposit of £1,000 for the purpose of importing a car, would be able to reclaim that £1,000 in the event of the car import company going into liquidation before the car is obtained. The payment, after all, is made for a particular purpose, which is known to the recipient (the company), but except in the unlikely event that the company can use that money for *no purpose other* than obtaining the car, the prospective purchaser is not protected on *Quistclose* principles. The position is somewhat similar to cases where money has been paid to a company for the purpose of obtaining an allotment of shares, but no trust has been held to have been created. Commenting on those cases, Lord Wilberforce said (at p. 581):

I do not think it necessary to examine these cases in detail, nor to comment on them, for I am satisfied that they do not affect the principle on which this appeal should be decided. They are merely examples which show that, in the absence of some special arrangement creating a trust..., payments of this kind are made upon the basis that they are to be included in the company's assets. They do not negative the proposition that a trust may exist where the mutual intention is that they should not.

The significance of the separate account

The setting up of a special fund negates the inference that the payments are to be included in the company's assets, but so long as that inference is negated, it may be that a special fund is not absolutely necessary. In *Re EVTR* [1987] BCLC 646, for example, the appellant, Barber, who had just won £240,000 on premium bonds, agreed to assist a company for whom he had worked in purchasing new equipment. He accordingly deposited £60,000 with the solicitors to the company, and authorised them to release it 'for the sole purpose of buying new equipment'. The money was not paid into a special fund, but was paid out by the company in pursuit of the purpose. Before the new equipment was delivered EVTR went into receivership. The Court of Appeal held that Barber was entitled to recover his money (or at any rate, the balance of £48,536, after agreed deductions) on *Quistclose* principles. Dillon LJ also thought (at p. 649):

> in the light of *Quistclose*, that if the company had gone into liquidation, or the receivers had been appointed, and the scheme had become abortive before the £60,000 had been disbursed by the company, the appellant would have been entitled to recover his full £60,000, as between himself and the company, on the footing that it was impliedly held by the company on a resulting trust for him as the particular purpose of the loan had failed.

Something less than a separate account

At this stage, however, the money would not have been held in a special account, but the inference that it was intended to be included as part of the general assets would have been negated by other factors. The existence of a special account does not appear, then, to be absolutely essential, so long as the inference that the payments are to be included in the company's assets is negated.

A *Quistclose* argument failed in *Anglo Corporation* v *Peacock AG*, CA (unreported), 12 February 1997, where the recipient clearly did not take the money on the understanding that it was to be separated from his general assets and used for a specific purpose. Referring to the House of Lords decision in *Westdeutsche* v *Islington BC* [1996] AC 669 (see chapters 7 and 19), the Court of Appeal placed greater emphasis on the state of mind of the recipient, whereas previous cases had tended to concentrate on the state of mind of the lender. The decision was that the *Quistclose* claim failed because the recipient of the money (AG) 'did not believe it had reached any agreement about the basis on which it would accept the money, and unlike *Quistclose* and *Re Kayford* [below] there was no identifiable trust property, such as money in a special account, on which the trust could be imposed'. This appears at first sight to suggest the necessity for a special account, but is equally consistent with the absence of a special account being a factor, but not necessarily a conclusive factor, against the existence of an agreement; by contrast, obviously the existence of a special account is strong evidence in favour of an agreement.

Quistclose trusts and commercial reality

The reality is, however, that *Quistclose* trusts are often used when the trustee is in liquidation. Merely to have a personal action against the trustee is therefore useless; it is essential for the lender to be able to point to a fund of money held by the trustee and say 'that money is my property'. To be able to do this it is necessary to be able to identify the money, and this is clearly easiest where the money has been paid into a special account. It is not essential, however, so long as the money can be traced on the principles discussed in chapter 19. In *Re Kayford Ltd* [1975] 1 WLR 279 (chapter 3), where it was held that a trust fund had been set up for customers of an insolvent company, Megarry J did not think it fatal that the money had been mixed with small amounts of other money. The case was not decided on *Quistclose* principles, but it was essential to be able to establish that the money belonged in equity to the customers; a personal action against the company would have availed them nothing. The money in *Kayford* was clearly traceable, however, so there was no problem even though there were other small sums in the account.

2.4.2.5 *Money already owed to trustee*

For the purposes of *Quistclose* type trusts, it does not seem to matter where the money comes from. In *Quistclose* itself it was a loan made voluntarily by a third party. *EVTR* also involved a voluntary disposition. In *Carreras Rothmans Ltd v Freeman Mathews Treasure Ltd* [1985] Ch 207, on the other hand, the money paid into the special account was money that Carreras Rothmans (CR) were contractually obliged to pay to Freeman Mathews Treasure (FMT) in any event. Applying *Quistclose*, however, Peter Gibson J held that the money in the special account was held on trust.

The plaintiff (cigarette manufacturers) engaged the defendant advertising agency. The defendant contracted as principal with production agencies and advertising media. The arrangement was that CR paid a monthly fee to FMT, which was used:

(1) as payment in arrears for FMT's services, and

(2) To enable FMT to pay debts incurred to agency and media creditors.

The defendant (FMT) got into financial difficulties, but needed funds to pay its production agencies and advertising media if it was to carry on acting for the claimant.

Carreras Rothmans also knew that if FMT went into liquidation still owing money to media creditors, the media creditors would have sufficient commercial power to compel CR to pay, and therefore (although they were not legally obliged to do so) they would in practice have to pay twice over. An agreement was therefore made between CR and FMT whereby the claimants would pay a monthly sum into a special account at the defendant's bank, the money to be used: 'only for the purposes of meeting the accounts of the media and production fees of third parties directly attributable to CR's involvement with the agency'.

Payments, action, and timing of liquidation
The first payment (of just under £600,000) was made at the end of July, covering debts incurred in June. Unlike the position in the cases discussed above, however, this was money which CR owed to FMT in any event.

The defendant went into liquidation before the debts were cleared. CR immediately found another advertising agency, and to avoid jeopardising its advertising campaign, paid the debts of the media creditors, taking assignments of those debts. Of the money in the special account, Peter Gibson J held that it was held by FMT (and hence by the liquidator) on trust, since it had been paid for a specific purpose, and he made an order requiring the liquidator to carry out that purpose (i.e., payment to the third parties). He did not think it relevant (at pp. 221–2) that

CR was under a contractual obligation to pay the money to FMT in any event, noting (at p. 222C–E) that:

if the common intention is that property is transferred for a specific purpose and not so as to become the property of the transferee, the transferee cannot keep the property if for any reason that purpose cannot be fulfilled. I am left in no doubt that the provider of the moneys in the present case was the plaintiff. True it is that its own witnesses said that if the defendant had not agreed to the terms of the contract letter, the plaintiff would not have broken its contract but would have paid its debt to the defendant, but the fact remains that the plaintiff made its payment on the terms of that letter and the defendant received the moneys only for the stipulated purpose. That purpose was expressed to relate only to the moneys in the account. In my judgment therefore the plaintiff can be equated with the lender in *Quistclose* as having an enforceable right to compel the carrying out of the primary trust.

2.4.2.6 *Enforcement of Quistclose trusts*

Lord Wilberforce's view (at p. 580) was that there was a primary trust in favour of the creditors, who in *Quistclose* were the shareholders, and then on the failure of the primary trust a secondary trust in favour of 'the third person', who is earlier identified as the provider of the money. Since the provider of the money was able to claim it back, it must be assumed that in Lord Wilberforce's view, the primary trust had failed. Similarly, in *EVTR*, the provider of the money was able to claim it back, the primary purpose of the trust having failed. In both cases the secondary trust was enforced, and since the settlor was also beneficiary, these must have been resulting trusts (see further chapter 7).

In *Carreras Rothmans* the primary trust, to pay the media advertisers, could still be carried out, and the order made was to that effect. Peter Gibson J even thought (at p. 223) that the third-party creditors might themselves have had enforceable rights, although the order was applied for by CR. Since enforceable rights are given only to beneficiaries under trusts, the clear implication is that whereas the beneficiary is the provider of the money once the primary trust has failed, the beneficiary under the primary trust is the person to whom payment is to be made.

Difficulties with Carreras Rothmans

There are, however, a number of difficulties with this view, as P.J. Millett QC (as he then was), counsel for CR, pointed out in his article based on the case at (1985) 101 LQR 269. First, it is by no means obvious why the primary trust had failed in *Quistclose* itself, since payment of the dividends could still be carried out. Only Harman LJ in the Court of Appeal ([1968] 1 Ch 540) really addressed this issue, commenting (at p. 548) that:

The money was deposited with the respondent bank, and accepted on the footing that it should only be used for payment of the dividend. That purpose was, however, frustrated by the liquidation of Rolls Razor on the following August 27 before the dividend had been paid, thus making its payment illegal.

It is illegal for a company which is in liquidation to pay dividends to its shareholders, at any rate using its own money, but as Millett pointed out, the money did not belong beneficially to Rolls Razor. Indeed, there was no theoretical reason why Rolls Razor needed to be involved at all; the identity of the trustee was immaterial. Since the money was not theirs, and there was no reason why anybody *apart from*

Rolls Razor could not pay the amount of the dividends, it is difficult to see why the payment became illegal on the liquidation of Rolls Razor.

A resolution—or the creation of additional difficulties?

A possible answer to this is that in determining whether the primary purpose has failed, you look not at whether it has become impossible to achieve, but at whether the settlor's motive has been frustrated. Clearly, it had been in *Quistclose*, since the whole point was to keep Rolls going, and although payment to the shareholders could still theoretically be made, there would obviously be no point in doing this, at any rate from Quistclose's viewpoint.

Although this might appear to be the obvious explanation, there are a number of difficulties with it. First, there were no words of trust in *Quistclose*, and the only reason for inferring a trust was that the money had been lent for a specific purpose. Had it been lent 'to keep Rolls Razor afloat', there would have been no trust. It seems strange, therefore, in deciding whether the trust has failed, to ignore the specific purpose, which can still be carried out, in favour of the purpose of keeping Rolls Razor afloat, which cannot. Second, as Millett observed, nowhere else in the law does a trust fail because it no longer accords with the settlor's wishes; it fails only when performance becomes impossible or illegal, and that had not happened here.

Implied trusts and no expression

Nevertheless, this does feel like the correct explanation of *Quistclose*. There were no words of trust, and it was therefore necessary to imply a trust. In determining the terms of an implied trust, all relevant factors are taken into account, including, but not necessarily limited to, the words that were used. In other words, there is no reason why the terms of the trust should necessarily correspond with the specific purpose. An implied trust, even of land, does not require writing (see chapters 5 and 10), and it is interesting that in *Rowan v Dann* [1992] P & CR 202 (discussed in chapter 1), the Court of Appeal enforced what was effectively an oral *Quistclose* trust of land; it is true that they enforced the secondary trust, which as a resulting trust would not have required writing either, but no doubt was cast on the validity of the primary trust, which had failed.

Options in Carreras Rothmans

Millett was constrained in *Carreras Rothmans* to arrive at a different analysis, however. On the above view, it might have been possible to argue that the primary trust had failed (although that would depend on CR's motive being to keep FMT afloat, whereas arguably CR was concerned only with its own advertising campaign, and had no interest in FMT), but then CR would have obtained the £600,000 back. Since, however, it was contractually bound to pay the £600,000, Millett presumably thought that FMT's liquidators would simply have been able to sue in contract if this were the result, as indeed they did regarding the next month's payment (of £780,000) which had not, by the time of FMT's liquidation, even been paid into the special account. So an argument based on the failure of the primary trust (even assuming it was possible on the facts) would not have appealed to Millett.

So it was assumed that the primary trust had not failed in *Carreras Rothmans*, and on Lord Wilberforce's analysis, and as indeed Peter Gibson J thought in *Carreras Rothmans*, the media advertisers were therefore the beneficiaries. But the media advertisers did not sue; Carreras Rothmans did. Millett got the result that he wanted in *Carreras Rothmans*, an order to pay the money to the media advertisers not to CR (to avoid the potential contractual liability discussed in the previous paragraph), but an order obtained not by the media advertisers but by CR.

Implications if Carreras Rothmans is correct

Assuming that *Carreras Rothmans* is correct, therefore (by no means a certainty given that it is a first instance decision which has not been followed) where (as will become clear) the decision appears inconsistent with the reasoning in the judgment, the question is, on what basis could CR enforce the trust? It is not sufficient that CR had taken assignments of the media advertiser's rights, partly because for tactical reasons CR expressly disclaimed reliance on assignment and partly because that would have led to payment back to CR and not to the media advertisers. It is also unclear from the report exactly what assignments they had taken; debt actions against a company which is in liquidation are valueless, and (at least as far as it is possible to tell from the report), CR had not taken assignments of any other rights the third party creditors might have.

Millett's explanation was that the reason CR could enforce the trust was that they were the beneficiaries all along, under both the primary and the secondary trusts. (In passing, it is worth observing that both primary and secondary trusts therefore become resulting trusts, which also allows for an oral *Quistclose* trust of land.) It is possible to find support for the view that the provider of the money can enforce the trust from *Quistclose* itself, where Lord Wilberforce observes (at p. 581) that:

the lender acquires an equitable right to see that [the money advanced] is applied for the primary designated purpose...if the primary purpose cannot be carried out, the question arises if a secondary purpose (i.e., repayment to the lender) has been agreed, expressly or by implication: if it has, the remedies of equity may be invoked to give effect to it...

Merits of Millett's views

In a number of respects this passage is not very convincing, since all it appears to support is the view that if the primary trust is not carried out, the lender acquires an equitable right to enforce the *secondary* trust.

Millett then had to argue that, even though CR were beneficiaries, the order should be to pay the media advertisers, not CR themselves (for the reasons already set out). He therefore argued that they had a power to direct the trustees to carry out the stated purpose. The problem with this argument is that directions to trustees are in principle revocable, and on this view, therefore, the lender can revoke any directions and claim the money back at any time, as beneficiary.

Quistclose would not have to wait for Rolls Razor to go into liquidation, should they choose to claim the money back earlier. Millett's general position on revocation is not, in the author's view, the most convincing part of his article, but in cases such as *Quistclose* and *Carreras Rothmans*, it is certainly possible to imply a contractual term between settlor and trustee (who are clearly in a contractual relationship with each other), that the settlor will not revoke his directions unless the purpose of the *directions* is frustrated. The purpose of the directions had clearly been frustrated in *Quistclose*, but arguably not in *Carreras Rothmans*, if CR's main concern was merely to ensure the continuation of their advertising campaign.

To conclude, Lord Wilberforce's analysis in *Quistclose* can probably be justified in spite of difficulties over why the primary trust had failed. However, if *Quistclose* is correct, the decision in *Carreras Rothmans* is not, since CR should have had no right to enforce the order. Millett's analysis is inconsistent with Lord Wilberforce's, and lacks the beauty of simplicity, but (unsurprisingly in the circumstances) is consistent with the *decision* in all the cases, including *Carreras Rothmans*. It also avoids the problems of failure of primary purpose in *Quistclose*.

Another possible view is that the primary trust in *Quistclose* cases is a pure purpose trust without true beneficiaries at all. This view was taken by Megarry J in *Re Northern Developments (Holdings) Ltd* (unreported) 6 October 1978, but considered in *Carreras Rothmans* and discussed by P.J. Millett QC in the article referred to above.

Quistclose trusts and the significance of Twinsectra v Yardley

The most significant consideration which has been given to *Quistclose* trusts in recent times is that of the House of Lords, in the very important decision in *Twinsectra* v *Yardley* [2002] 2 All ER 377. The case is a very important decision on the liability which can be incurred by a third party to a trust where there has been a breach of that trust committed by a trustee to it. In the parlance of equity and trusts, the issues raised by 'assisting' a breach of trust, or being an 'accessory' in the breach of a trust will be considered later in chapter 19. This decision is also an important point of reference for this chapter's consideration of the nature of the trust, and its central features, at this point, through discussion of the *Quistclose* trust.

Twinsectra: *the Quistclose trust explored through its facts*

In a case involving two solicitors, *Twinsectra* arose initially through the involvement of one (Leach) with the purchase of land for a client. To complete the purchase the client needed to borrow £1 million. A lender, Twinsectra, was found but was only willing to make the loan if repayment was secured by a solicitor's personal undertaking. The first solicitor was unwilling to give such an undertaking so the client approached the second solicitor (Sims) who represented himself as acting for the client. The second solicitor then received the loan money after his firm gave an undertaking to the lender *inter alia* that the loan moneys were to be retained until such time as they were applied to the client's purchase; that the loan moneys would be utilised solely for the acquisition of property on behalf of the client and for no other purposes; and that the loan would be repaid together with interest.

The second solicitor sought assurances from the client that the money would be used in the acquisition of property and received them through the first solicitor. The money was then released to the first solicitor as instructed by the client. The first solicitor considered the money as held on account for the client and paid it out on the client's instructions, and took no steps to ensure that the money was only applied in the acquisition of property. In the event, the client used a substantial part of it for other purposes. The second solicitor became bankrupt and the loan was not repaid. The lender commenced proceedings against the borrower and both solicitors. The action against the first solicitor, Leach, alleged that he had dishonestly assisted in the second solicitor's breach of trust. The matters of concern here hinged on whether a trust did exist in respect of the loan: this would form the basis for establishing that there had been a breach of trust in the (second) solicitor's conduct. This in turn would affect the liability of the other solicitor. It would also allow for the recovery of the sums which had not been applied in accordance with the lender's instructions.

A Quistclose trust arising through a loan for specific purposes?
The crucial consequence of the loan found to be subject to a trust would be that property subject to a trust remains distinctive from other assets which might be the subject of competing claims. On *Quistclose* this can be achieved on there being a resulting trust in favour of the provider of the property. The ability to determine that the loan was held by Sims subject to a trust in favour of Twinsectra was crucial to being able to establish that a breach of trust had arisen where the loan had been applied in contravention with the undertaking to apply it to the purchase of property for which it had been advanced. Problems in establishing this arose in the way in which it was argued that there was no intention to create a trust, and that there was an absence of obvious 'specific purpose' on account of the way in which the money was to be applied to an unspecified purchase of property.

The House of Lords held that intention to create a trust (of the property held by Sims) could be found on the construction of the undertaking that the money was to be used for the acquisition of property and for no other purpose. This gave rise to an obligation on Sims' part to release the money to Leach only for the acquisition of property—an obligation which was fiduciary rather than contractual in nature. At first instance no trust had been found on account of lack of certainty of objects, because the proposed acquisition related to property which was unspecified, the Court of Appeal concluding there was a trust in which beneficial interest was either in suspense or held by the borrower (subject to the lender's contractual right to determine the application of the property).

In the House of Lords, Lord Millett, who provided the analysis of the *Quistclose* trust for his Brethren considered the most appropriate location of beneficial interests underlying a trust invoked by advancing money for a specific purpose. His conclusion ultimately was that beneficial interest in advancements of this nature, in these circumstances, is held on resulting trust for the lender. But other possibilities were considered; for example, that the trust is in favour of those (people or purposes) intended to benefit from the trust; that beneficial interest is held by the borrower, and that it is held in 'suspense'.

What is interesting about this case is the way in which it gives lengthy and extensive consideration to the other views considered and advanced, and ultimately to why the resulting trust in favour of the lender was the one ultimately to be preferred. The conclusion that a resulting trust arose in favour of the lender, and that this operated subject to the mandate of the borrower to apply the sums advanced to the specified purposes, ensured that Sims did hold the money on (resulting) trust for Twinsectra. At that point, it did not matter that the money was advanced to be applied to a purpose rather than to benefit an identifiable individual.

2.5 Trusts and restitution: beyond *quasi*-contract?

Restitution leads on from the discussions above on account of its conceptual location alongside the law of contract. Often classified as *'quasi*-contract', there is a basic consensus that restitution is concerned with reversing an unjust enrichment which one has received at the expense of another. Writers on the law of obligations point to the significance of features of contract and also tort which have shaped restitution's unique nature, while also noting that it is actually a ubiquitous doctrine which is found almost universally across different systems of law, in some form.

The crucial question here is how restitution might apply in the context of this study of equity and the law of trusts, given that its strongest traditional associations are to be found in *quasi*-contract. It will become clear that questions of restitution are currently never far away from what is at the heart of this text: this is the determination of rights and interests relating to property within the trust arrangement, on account of the way in which ownership is vested in one party for the benefit of another. Where trust property falls into the hands of those who are not entitled to it, it is clear that there should be a remedy of some sort, but on what basis should this arise? These issues are discussed in chapter 19. It will become clear within chapter 19 that in the context of remedies pertaining to misapplied trust property, the principles which govern remedies based on proprietary entitlement, and which involve 'tracing' trust property into the hands of another, are not entirely clear in respect of their availability or operation and effect. But equally there is concern that despite the enthusiasm for restitution among judges and particularly academic commentators, there is also concern that, in the words of Lord Woolf in *Westdeutsche* v *London Islington Borough Council* [1996] AC 669:

[t]hose concerned with developing the law of restitution are anxious to ensure that, in certain circumstances, the plaintiff should have the right to recover property which he has unjustly lost...in my view such development is not based on sound principle and in the name of unjust enrichment is capable of producing most unjust results [and even that] [t]he search for a perceived need to strengthen the remedies of a plaintiff claiming in restitution involves, to my mind, a distortion of trust principles.

That having been said, since *Westdeutsche*, more recent cases like *Foskett* v *McKowen* [2000] 2 WLR 1299 and *BCCI* v *Akindele* [2001] Ch 437 are suggesting a move away from restitution. Thus, it may well be the case that this is signalling that a more coherent approach to remedies based on proprietary entitlement will in due course transpire.

2.6 Trusts and powers

2.6.1 Fixed and discretionary trusts

So far the assumption has been made that the extent of the beneficial interests under a trust has been known at the outset, and indeed many trusts are of this nature. An example might be property divided equally among the sons of the settlor. Each son has an interest which is fixed and ascertainable from the outset. Trusts arising from undivided shares in land, for example, are normally fixed trusts because each co-owner will have a defined share from the start.

This situation is by no means universal, however. With many trusts, the trustees are given a discretion as to how the property is to be distributed, usually within a defined class of possible beneficiary. This type of trust is usually termed a discretionary trust, although the term 'trust power' is also sometimes used. Obviously, nobody within the class of possible beneficiaries (such people are referred to as 'objects', as will become apparent in chapter 4), can claim a defined interest, or indeed any interest at all, unless and until the trustees' discretion is exercised in their favour. Yet though the trustees have a discretion as to how the property is distributed, that discretion does not extend to a refusal to distribute it at all. The trustees *must* administer the trust. They *must* appoint (i.e., decide who from within the class will benefit, and also the size of each beneficial interest). But whom they appoint, and in what proportions, is up to them.

Family trusts used often to be of this nature for tax reasons. There were a number of advantages in giving discretion to the trustees. One was to enable them to alter the beneficial interests to take advantage of changing tax circumstances. Another was that tax liability attached in some circumstances only where rights were created, and none of the beneficiaries has any right to the property at all unless and until the discretion is exercised in their favour. Discretionary trusts have been hard hit by recent tax legislation, however, and are probably less common today.

As it will become apparent in chapter 4, the distinction between fixed and discretionary trusts is important, as the orthodox view is that different requirements of certainty of object apply.

2.6.2 Nature of powers

A power (sometimes called a 'mere power') differs from a discretionary trust in the following respects. First, the legal title is given, not to trustees, but to donees of the power. They have a discretion not only as to *how* to distribute the property, but also as to *whether* to distribute it. They are under no obligation to appoint at all. In other words, whereas a trust is imperative, because the trustees must appoint, a power is discretionary, because the donees of a power need not appoint at all—the choice is theirs.

There may be limited exceptions to this position. In *Klug v Klug* [1918] 2 Ch 67, a mother who disapproved of her daughter's marriage without her consent capriciously refused to exercise a power in her favour. On application by the public trustee, the court ordered that the power should be exercised. This case was relied on in *Mettoy Pension Trustees v Evans* [1991] 2 All ER 513, noted at [1991] Conv 364, where Warner J held that the court could enforce a fiduciary power in the same manner as a discretionary trust. The case is unusual, however, in that there was nobody else who was capable of exercising the power. Assuming that these cases are correct, they create limited exceptions where non-exercise of a power is capricious, and where there is nobody available to exercise a power. The cases do not affect the general principle that where donees of a power make a *bona fide* decision not to exercise it, the courts will not compel them to do so.

2.6.2.1 *What happens where a power is not exercised?*
If the donees of a power do not appoint, a gift or trust over may have been provided for in default of appointment. A gift or trust over is a gift or trust which takes effect where the property has not otherwise been fully disposed of. It must be provided for in the original trust instrument, and if it has, it will take effect. If not, the property goes on resulting trust to the settlor (see further chapter 7).

2.6.2.2 *A special power of appointment*

A power to distribute property to a limited class of persons (either specified persons, or specified groups or 'classes' of people called the 'objects' of the power) is called a 'special power of appointment'. If no particular instructions are given to the donee of a power, or restrictions as to whom property might be given, the power conferred is known as a 'general power of appointment'. There is also a category of intermediate, or hybrid powers, where a donee is given power to appoint to anyone except those within a particular class. In each case a donee may also be an object of the power. Obviously, a donee under a general power of appointment is in a position akin to that of an absolute owner. The distinction between general and special powers of appointment is of importance when considering perpetuities (chapter 6).

2.6.2.3 *Understanding the purpose of powers: a hangover from the past*

The purpose of mere powers is not immediately apparent. Probably they are a hangover from days when testators did not trust wives and eldest sons to administer family property in the manner that they regarded as sensible. So, although the settlor in general terms wished to benefit his wife or eldest son, he did not wish to give them enforceable rights. Therefore the property was settled on somebody else, who had the power to appoint to the wife or eldest son, but need not do so if such appointment appeared unwise.

In recent years the practice has arisen of creating powers with discretionary trusts over, in default of appointment, where the donees under the power are the same people as the trustees under the discretionary trust. In most respects this has an identical effect to a discretionary trust. For example, if A is given power to appoint to B, C, or D, with a trust over in default in favour of E and F, A cannot avoid appointing altogether, and this is no different from a discretionary trust in favour of B, C, D, E, and F. The only exception might be where A refuses to carry out his duties at all, and the court is required ultimately to distribute the property. In the case of a power with trust over, B, C, and D would have no claim. If the instrument was in the form of a single trust, they would. But it is unlikely that settlors have frequent regard to this extreme and pathological situation.

2.6.2.4 *Trust/power distinction and a modern significance*

So why use a power and trust over in default? As the materials in chapter 4 will explain, between 1955 and 1971 the certainty of object test for powers was thought to be less stringent than that for discretionary trusts. In other words, an instrument which was valid as a power might be invalid as a discretionary trust, if there was a wide range of objects. It therefore became common practice to draft powers with a wide range of objects, which were valid, while confining the trust over to a narrow range of objects. Such an instrument could be valid, whereas if drafted as a trust alone it would fall foul of the certainty of object requirements. If this is indeed the explanation for such instruments, one might expect that they will become less common now that, since 1971, the certainty tests for trusts and powers have been regarded as being practically the same.

As with discretionary trusts, the objects of the power have no definable interest in the property unless that power is exercised in their favour. The objects can come to court to enforce the power, however, to the very limited extent that the court will restrain disposal of the property otherwise than in accordance with the terms of the power.

2.6.3 The extent of the discretion and the nature of enforcement

For mere powers, the donee's discretion seems to be unfettered except to the extent that he must not dispose of the property otherwise than in accordance with the terms of the power.

So far as discretionary trusts are concerned, though members of the class of possible beneficiaries have no defined interest in the property unless and until the trustees' discretion is exercised in their favour, nevertheless, they have sufficient *locus standi* to come to court to enforce the trust. Clearly the degree to which enforcement is possible is limited by the discretionary nature of the arrangement, but the courts will restrain the trustees from acting contrary to the terms of the trust instrument. And if they refuse to distribute at all, a court can remove them and appoint new trustees, or in the final analysis distribute the property itself. Furthermore, unlike donees of mere powers, the trustees' discretion is not absolute. In considering its exercise, they must make a survey of the entire field of objects, and consider each individual case responsibly, on its merits: *per* Lord Wilberforce in *Re Baden's Deed Trusts, McPhail v Doulton* [1971] AC 424. The requirement that discretion must be properly exercised is not merely academic. In *Turner v Turner* [1984] Ch 100, the trustees (who were relatives of the settlor, without any previous experience or understanding of trusts) simply acted on the instructions of the settlor (i.e., did not exercise their own discretion at all, but effectively delegated it to him). Mervyn Davies J held that the appointments they made were invalid.

2.6.3.1 *Trusts and powers: explaining the duties of trustees and donees of a power*

Where a power with discretionary trust over is created, where the donees of the power and the trustees are the same people, it was suggested above that this is very like a discretionary trust. On principle, therefore, the exercise of the power should be controlled in the same way as that of a discretionary trust, rather than a mere power. Sir Robert Megarry V-C provides some support for this view in *Re Hay's ST* [1982] 1 WLR 1202, holding that the extent of the duty to consider both whether or not a power should be exercised, and how it should be exercised, is stronger when the power is given to someone who is also a trustee, than when a mere power is exercised. For example, it is not sufficient simply to appoint property to the objects who happen to be at hand, whereas the donee of a mere power can do this. It seems that it is necessary periodically to consider whether or not to exercise the power, and at least to appreciate the width of the field of objects, even if it is not possible to compile a list of all the objects or ascertain accurately their number. Also, individual appointments need to be considered on their merits. It is not clear whether Sir Robert Megarry V-C regarded this duty as the same as in the case of discretionary trusts, or a lesser duty, though still more stringent than in the case of a mere power.

The extent of the duty is important, at least on the orthodox view, when considering certainty of objects, and we shall return to it in chapter 4.

2.6.4 **Distinguishing between trusts and powers**

The distinction between discretionary trusts and powers is often extremely fine. It is a matter of construing the settlor's intention, and therefore no precise criteria can be laid down. The courts have no particular presumption one way or the other, and in the days when certainty requirements used to be much stricter for discretionary trusts than powers, the courts refused to spell valid powers out of invalid trusts (see the equitable maxims referred to in chapter 1).

If the settlor provides for a gift over or trust over in default of appointment, or has otherwise provided for this contingency, a power must be intended. This is because a trustee *must* appoint. The converse statement does not follow, however, and the courts will by no means presume a trust because there is no gift over in default. If in this case a power is construed, a failure to appoint leads to a resulting trust in favour of the settlor.

2.6.4.1 *Reasons to distinguish from a power*

There are a number of reasons why it is necessary to distinguish between trusts and powers:

- The duties of donees and trustees and method of enforcement are different (see above).
- The certainty of object rules used to be different, and may still be in detailed respects (see chapter 4).
- Suppose an appointment has become impossible, perhaps because the donee or trustee has died. In default of appointment under a power, either the instrument will provide for a gift over, or there will be a resulting trust back to the settlor. The objects have no claim. In the case of a discretionary trust, however, the property will ultimately be distributed among the objects. If the discretion is given to one person in particular, say a particular member of a family, and he dies without exercising that discretion, the court itself must do so, and in *Burrough v Philcox* (1840) 5 My & Cr 72, Lord Cottenham held that the property should be divided equally among the objects. This solution will not always be sensible except in family-type trusts, however, and where it is not the courts will not adopt it (*Re Baden's Deed Trusts, McPhail v Doulton* [1971] AC 424, see chapter 4).

 online resource centre

FURTHER READING

Bridge 'The *Quistclose* Trust in a World of Secured Transactions' (1992) Oxford Journal of Legal Studies 333.

Conaglen 'The Nature and Function of Fiduciary Loyalty' (2005) Law Quarterly Review 452.

Emery 'The Most Hallowed Principle: Certainty of Beneficiaries of Trusts and Powers of Appointment' (1982) Law Quarterly Review 551.

Harris 'Trust, Power and Duty' (1971)Law Quarterly Review 31.

Hopkins 'Certain Uncertainties of Trusts and Powers' (1971) Cambridge Law Journal 68.

Millett 'The *Quistclose* Trust: Who Can Enforce It?' (1985) Law Quarterly Review 269.

Thompson 'Criminal Law and Property Law: An Unhappy Combination' (2002) Conveyancer 387.

Wilson and Wilson '"Responsible risk-takers": Notions of Directorial Responsibility Past, Present and Future' (2001) Journal of Corporate Law Studies 211.

3

....

Constitution of trusts and equity's 'perfection' of transfers of property

The significance of this chapter follows from the introduction made in chapter 1 to the significance of property in the creation of trusts, and to the similarities and differences subsisting between the trust and the gift as mechanisms by which an owner of property can ensure that another can benefit and receive enjoyment from property belonging to the former. It was explained at that point that in the case of a gift this gesture of generosity by an owner of property would be achieved by an outright transfer of ownership (manifested in legal title) to the intended recipient, and this exposed the key difference between a trust and a gift. Whereas a gift is achieved by outright transfer of ownership from the owner of property to the intended recipient, when property is settled on trust, enjoyment for the latter is achieved through the simultaneous existence of two types of ownership of what becomes 'trust property'.

The materials in this chapter are focused on the requirements of a valid trust, and particularly the requirement that the trust must be constituted. This is the requirement that legal title to the property is vested in the trustee. A trust cannot come into being without this happening, and the general position is where this has been attempted and has not been effectively executed, the trust will not be constituted and the arrangement cannot come into being. It will become apparent that this is very much a consequence of the principle that equity will not *perfect* or 'complete' an imperfect (or incomplete) gift or trust, and this is itself very closely tied in with formalities requirements which accompany transfers of property generally, including in situations where legal title is being vested in a trustee. The significance and actual requirements pertaining to so-called 'transfer formalities'—formalities associated with actual transfers of legal title to property from one person to another is considered (along with other types of formality arising from declarations of trust and disposition of equitable interests) in greater detail in chapter 5. For present purposes, formality considerations will arise, but it would be helpful to remember that 'transfer formalities' arise in considering constituting a trust where it is intended that someone other than the original owner of property is to act as trustee. In order for the trustee to have control of the property and to undertake the responsibilities for it which reflect his duties to ensure the beneficiary can enjoy the benefits of the property, he must have the legal capacity to deal with the property. This means he must hold legal title to it, and in order for this to happen, legal title must be transferred from the owner to the trustee.

3.1 A general overview of the requirement that the trust must be constituted

In general, the legal title to trust property must be transferred to trustees for a valid trust to be constituted. The trustees must have control of the property. If formalities are required for this transfer, for example in the case of land or shares, then they must be complied with, otherwise the trustees will not be able to deal with the property.

In terms of linking the *requirement* that the trust must be constituted in order for the arrangement to be valid at all with the *consequences* of the process of constituting the trust, the effect of constituting a trust is:

- The arrangement becomes irreversible by the settlor, and it cannot be revoked (unless the settlor has, by the terms of the trust, specifically granted himself or someone else a power to revoke the settlement).
- In the case of a private trust this confers to the beneficiaries enforceable rights in relation to the property, whether or not they have provided any consideration (see for example *Paul* v *Paul* (1882) 20 Ch D 742). Indeed, it is only the beneficiaries, and not the settlor, who can enforce the trust, because the settlor retains no interest in the property (assuming he is not also a trustee or beneficiary).
- It confers to the beneficiaries an equitable interest in the property which forms the subject matter of the trust.

3.1.1 Vesting of property in trustees

For a valid private trust to come into existence, there are two elements which are at the heart of this. In many respects they can be described as 'both necessary and also sufficient' (noting formalities requirements) for this to happen:

- There must be a manifest intention on the part of the settlor to create a trust.

This reflects the way in which the owner of property must intend for it to become trust property, and that he must not actually be seeking to effect some other kind of transaction, such as making an outright gift or loan. The intention must be expressed in a way which complies with the certainty requirements (see chapter 4).

- The trust property must be properly vested in trustees who hold it in that capacity on behalf of the beneficiaries.

As chapter 1 explained, a trust involves a division of the ownership of property, and the trustees become owners at common law, and are given control of the property. The beneficiaries become owners in equity, and in effect it is they who are to enjoy the property. This is at the heart of the way in which chapter 1 also explained that, according to *Westdeutsche Landesbank Girozentrale* v *Islington London Borough Council* [1966] AC 669, for a trust to arise, when a trustee is vested with legal title, his conscience must be affected. This requirement is essentially that the trustee must understand that he is receiving legal title not in order to enjoy all the benefits of ownership, but is doing so in furtherance of delivering benefit and enjoyment of the property to the beneficiary.

3.1.1.1 *Constituting a trust: it can be constituted 'by accident'*

Notwithstanding what has been said above about what is required on the part of the owner of property who becomes a settlor in the creation of the trust, it is nevertheless possible for property actually to be transferred from its owner and vested in the trustee in a *manner* which was not intended by the settler. Indeed, *Re Ralli's WT* [1964] Ch 288 and also *Strong v Bird* (1874) LR 18 Eq 315 are authority that property can actually be conveyed to trustees in any manner, even accidentally, and that this *is* sufficient to constitute the trust.

The most usual scenario arising in a trust arrangement is that whereby someone is selected by the owner of property who wishes to settle it on trust to perform this role. However it is also the case that it is perfectly possible for an owner of property to elect to undertake the responsibilities of trusteeship himself in the course of settling property on trust. In the former more usual situation, the intended trustee will need to have legal title to the property vested in him, and this means that any 'transfer formalities' required (which will be determined by the nature of the property) must be complied with. This will be seen shortly in the discussion of *Milroy v Lord* (1862) below.

3.2 *Milroy v Lord* (1862) and the principle that 'equity will not perfect an imperfect gift'

If the trust property is not properly vested in trustees, then there is no trust. This reflects the equitable principle that equity will not perfect an imperfect 'transfer'. *Milroy v Lord* (1862) 4 De GF & J 264 is the leading authority.

The settlor had executed a voluntary deed, purporting to transfer shares to a trustee on trust for the claimants. The voluntary deed was incapable of transferring legal title, however, since that could only be achieved by registering the name of the transferee in the books of the bank. The Court of Appeal in Chancery held that no trust had been constituted, with Turner LJ stating that there is no equity to perfect an imperfect gift:

in order to render a voluntary settlement valid and effectual, the settlor must have done everything which, according to the nature of the property comprised in the settlement, was necessary to be done in order to transfer the property and render the settlement binding upon him. He may of course do this by actually transferring the property to the persons for whom he intends to provide, and the provision will then be effectual, and it will be equally effectual if he transfers the property to a trustee for the purposes of the settlement, or declares that he himself holds it on trust for those purposes; ... but, in order to render the settlement binding, one or other of these modes must ... be resorted to, for there is no equity in this Court to perfect an imperfect gift. The cases I think go further to this extent, that if the settlement is intended to be effectuated by one of the modes to which I have referred, the Court will not give effect to it by applying another of those modes. If it is intended to take effect by transfer, the Court will not hold the intended transfer to operate as a declaration of trust, for then every imperfect instrument would be made effectual by being converted into a perfect trust.

Although *Milroy* is most often cited as authority for what is required for constituting a trust, actually the case has much broader significance for what is required for transfers of property generally. For voluntary transfers of property (that is transfers which are *gifts* and are not transfers for consideration) to be effective, *Milroy* requires that there is either:

- An outright transfer to a recipient of property.

This is an absolute gift, and this is achieved by an outright transfer of ownership from the original owner to the recipient, and requires that any 'transfer formalities' requirements have been met in order to be effective.

- A trust for the benefit of the recipient may be declared, and can be constituted by one of two methods.

In declaring a trust in favour of an intended recipient of the benefit of property, the trust must be constituted and legal title vested in the trustee, which can be achieved in one of two ways. The settlor must have ***done all in his power*** to transfer legal title to the person intended to act as trustee **or** the settlor must have ***declared himself to be trustee*** of the property.

3.2.1 Focusing on the trust and satisfying *Milroy* v *Lord*

According to Turner LJ there are two methods which subsist for constituting a trust: that property is transferred to another for the purposes of acting as trustee, or the owner of property can undertake these responsibilities himself when property is settled on trust by him. The remainder of the materials will consider the issues which are raised in the course of understanding what is required in both scenarios whereby a trust is constituted. It is important to stress this because although *Milroy* is authority that both methods are capable of bringing into being a valid trust, it is also the case that *different* considerations arise in respect of the two mechanisms, in terms of determining whether the requirements laid down by *Milroy* have been met and complied with. This is very important because failure to comply with *Milroy*'s requirements will mean that no trust will come into being, whichever of the two methods is actually being used, but the requirements of each *are* distinct and will now be considered in turn.

3.3 Transferring property to another: the extent of the requirement under *Milroy* v *Lord*

Taking the more usual situation first, that whereby an owner of property wishes for someone other than himself to act as trustee, the requirements of *Milroy* are focused strongly on the requirements to transfer legal title to property more generally. This is very strongly bound in with 'transfer formalities' requirements which must be complied with, and if they are not, then the transfer will fail because equity will not be prepared to 'complete' it; hence the principle 'equity will not perfect an imperfect gift'.

However, the heading also quite deliberately refers to the 'extent of the requirement' of *Milroy v Lord* because it is clear from Turner LJ's judgment that the requirement which must actually be met is that the settlor has done all in his power to ensure that the transfer to the trustee has taken place. Thus, the requirement for successful constitution is *not* that the transfer has actually necessarily succeeded (which is where formality requirements become very prominent, as the cases considered below will reveal). So while *Milroy v Lord* is authority that equity will not complete incomplete transfers of property, the case is also authority that a transfer of legal title to property to a trustee can still be effective where it can be established that the transferor has done all in his power to effect the transfer. The import of this is that a trust is capable of being fully constituted even in situations where there are 'matters outstanding'.

It will become apparent that this approach is very strongly connected with equity's characteristically flexible nature, and its interest in substance rather than form, and there is now some detailed consideration of actually applying this rule that the owner of property has done all in his power to effect the transfer.

3.3.1 The last act of the settlor and the 'Rule in *Re Rose*'

Where the settlor does not constitute himself trustee (on which, see below), generally speaking, the legal title has actually to be transferred to the trustees, but *Milroy v Lord* requires only that the settlor must have done everything which was necessary to be done in order to transfer the property. It is possible, therefore, for a trust to be constituted where the settlor has done all that is within his power to constitute the trust by transferring the property to a trustee, but has been thwarted by formalities which are outside his control. In these circumstances equity regards the trust as constituted by the last act of the settlor.

3.3.1.1 *Equity 'perfection' and the 'last act [of the settlor]'*

This principle was applied in *Re Rose* [1952] Ch 499, CA, where the settlor intended to transfer shares, but where the directors of the company had an effective veto over any transfer. Rose executed transfers in shares in the required form in March 1943, but they could not take effect (at any rate at common law) until the directors of the company had registered them. They did this in June 1943. Rose died more than five years after executing the transfers, but less than five years after they were registered. If the effective date of the transfer was June 1943 then estate duty was payable, whereas if the transfer took effect in March it was not.

The Court of Appeal held that the date of constitution of the trust was when the settlor had done all he could, rather than when the directors consented to, and registered, the transfer. Equity regarded the property as transferred by Rose's last act. Evershed MR said (at pp. 511–12) that he adopted in full the words of Jenkins J in *Re Rose* [1949] 1 Ch 78:

I was referred on that to the well known case of *Milroy v Lord*, and also to the recent case of *In re Fry* [see below]. Those cases, as I understand them, turn on the fact that the deceased donor had not done all in his power, according to the nature of the property given, to vest the legal interest in the property in the donee. In such circumstances it is, of course, well settled that there is no equity to complete the imperfect gift.... In *Milroy v Lord* the...document was not the appropriate document to pass any interest in the property at all. In this case, as

I understand it, the testator had done everything in his power to divest himself of the shares in question...

3.3.2 **The application of the 'last act' doctrine and the difficulties it has exposed**

It was suggested above in the introduction to the 'last act' doctrine that it was easy to relate such an approach to equity's flexible nature and to equity's interest in substance rather than form, and *Re Rose; Rose* v *IRC* is in many respects a textbook illustration of this. However, the application of the 'last act' doctrine has also given rise to some difficulties. These can be seen to cluster determining *when* and indeed *if* the owner of property really has done all he can, and *has* performed the last act. This has crucial consequences. Where a settlor is found to have performed the last act, a valid trust will come into being. *Rose* is authority that the doctrine applies to donors in outright 'gift' transfers, as well as to trusts. If it is found that a settlor has not performed the last act, then the potential recipient (an intended beneficiary under a trust, or recipient of an intended gift) will lose out because equity does not complete incomplete gifts and it will not complete incomplete trusts.

Thus the consequences of being found on the right/wrong side of a settlor doing/ not doing all in his power to effect a transfer of property are considerable. In this context, it is significant that the application of this principle can be seen in cases where some very fine distinctions appear to have been drawn.

3.3.2.1 *The 'rule in* Re Rose' *and the significance of* Re Fry

In *Re Fry* [1946] 1 Ch 312, by contrast, more may have been required from the testator effectively to transfer legal title to the shares. The reason in this case that the shares could not be registered was because Treasury consent had not been obtained, as required by the Defence (Finance) Regulations 1939, under which shares could not be registered until Treasury consent was obtained. Although all the requisite forms had been filled in by the donor, the required Treasury consent had not been obtained before he died. This appears at first sight to be similar to *Rose*, but as Romer J explained (at pp. 317–18):

Now I should have thought it was difficult to say that the testator had done everything that was required to be done by him at the time of his death, for it was necessary for him to obtain permission from the Treasury for the assignment and he had not obtained it. Moreover, the Treasury might in any case have required further information of the kind referred to in the questionnaire submitted to him, or answers supplemental to those which he had given in reply to it; and, if so approached, he might have refused to concern himself with the matter further, in which case I do not know how anyone else could have compelled him to do so.

In this case, therefore, the testator may not have done all that was required, so the principles later elaborated in *Re Rose* could not apply.

3.3.2.2 *In search of guiding principles*

It is not entirely clear what mechanism is operating in *Re Rose*, and the case is not without its difficulties. Some of these issues were explored in '*Re Rose*: Revisited'

[1998] CLJ 57, 46–54. One possibility is that once the settlor has done all that he needs to do to constitute the trust (or effect an out-and-out transfer) he is treated as if he has declared himself trustee of the property until legal title is actually transferred to the trustees (or, in the case of an out-and-out transfer, to the transferee). This is problematic however, as it would appear to conflict with the principles discussed below. The forthcoming section will reveal a long line of authorities which are testament to the courts' reluctance to infer declaration of trusteeship by the settlor in absence of clear intention on his part to become a trustee. On the contrary, in one transfer Rose clearly intended to make a gift of the shares to his wife, and not to become trustee of them, which is itself very difficult to square with a declaration of trust analysis.

3.3.2.3 The 'last act' and the imposition of a trust

Another possibility is that equity imposes a constructive trust over the intervening period. It will not normally matter which of these approaches is correct, but arguably declarations of trust of land must be in writing unless they can be categorised as implied, resulting, or constructive trusts (see chapters 5, 7, and 9). In *Mascall* v *Mascall* [1984] 50 P & CR 119, the Court of Appeal applied *Re Rose* to registered land, but since the requisite writing was present the categorisation argument was not further advanced. The transferor had executed a transfer and sent it to the Inland Revenue, and also handed the land certificate to the transferee. At this stage, before the transfer and land certificate had been sent to the Land Registry for registration of the transferee as proprietor, the transferor changed his mind, after a quarrel with the transferee. The Court of Appeal held the transfer effective, since it was for the transferee to apply to the Land Registry for registration as proprietor, and the transferor had done everything he had to do to complete the transfer.

3.3.2.4 Re Rose *and entrenchment of* Mascall v Mascall

Although *Mascall v Mascall* is silent on whether the trust in *Re Rose* is express or constructive, it is difficult to see what resemblance, in any way, the testator in *Rose* bears to those whose conduct has become the basis of the cases considered in chapter 11 (or in chapters 10 or 19). Indeed in 'Revisited' it was suggested that far from there being reasons why equity would wish to impose a constructive trust on Rose and people like him, there were sound reasons of policy why equity would wish to look kindly on those who wished to dispose of their property in favour of others. Moreover, the alternative solution, that the donor is taken to have declared himself trustee for the intervening period, also looks wrong in principle given that he had intended a gift, and equity will not normally infer a declaration of trusteeship from an incomplete gift (see next section). Furthermore, on closer examination, *Re Rose* is very difficult to distinguish from *Re Fry* since the directors in *Rose* were not under any obligation to register the transfer (although they may well have routinely done so in practice), and so could presumably, had they felt so inclined, have refused to do so, or have required further particulars from the donor. It is here that both cases (*Fry* and *Rose*) contrast with the position in *Mascall* where the Land Registry was under a statutory duty to register the title.

3.3.2.5 'Hard case' and 'right result'

While it is the case that *Re Rose* has the feel of a 'right result' for the family in question in relation to liability for estates duty, the article draws attention to the fact that any analysis which is based on trusteeship would also entail Rose being liable as trustee, and thus charged with the obligation of looking after the shares on the beneficiary's behalf, and also open to attendant liability. Happily, this was for a short time only, and the directors (of whom the testator was one) were unlikely not to effect the transfer in favour of his wife (also a director). Nevertheless, it is not difficult to envisage that on different facts, the outcome might not have been so positive. However, much as *Re Rose* might appear to be wrong in principle, it must be regarded as good authority, not only because it was applied in *Mascall* v *Mascall* (notwithstanding express argument that *Rose* was wrong), but also because it was approved by the House of Lords in *Vandervell* v *IRC* [1967] 2 AC 691 (see chapter 5).

While the CLJ article considers in some detail the difficulties raised by *Re Rose*, it does also suggest that in light of *Westdeutsche* (considered in chapter 1 and also briefly in chapter 7 in this context) there is now the opportunity to explain the case in such a way which avoids the difficulties of articulating it around a trust analysis. Equally continuing to use a trusts analysis does raise a number of difficulties, some of which are acknowledged in more recent cases (considered below in 3.5) but a fuller and more considered explanation within the case law would be extremely timely and welcome.

3.4 Satisfying *Milroy* v *Lord* through declarations of self as trustee

In *Milroy* v *Lord*, Turner LJ also allows for the settlor to declare himself trustee in order to meet the requirement that the trust is constituted. It will become clear that this is regarded as being perfectly acceptable when reference is made to the leading authority here, which is *Richards* v *Delbridge* (1874) LR Eq 11, and *Milroy* itself.

Ahead of this some reference is made to the proposition made earlier that, although a declaration of trusteeship by an owner of property like the 'last act' rule derives its authority from *Milroy* v *Lord*, there are different considerations found reflected in the case law surrounding these two ways of constituting a trust. In the 'last act' cases, it was clear that issues arising in the cases clustered questions of when and indeed whether the 'last act' had been performed, bearing in mind the implications of a last act being found present or absent.

The broad parameters for declarations of trust by the settlor are the same as those found in the 'last act' cases inasmuch as the consequences of a valid declaration of trusteeship by the settlor being found/being absent will be crucial to the validity of the trust, and in the latter situation (like in the former mechanism) no trust can arise. However, the issues surrounding and actually determining validity are quite different. In the 'last act' cases, the context was the transfer of property, while in the case of declarations of trusteeship by the settlor, the courts are looking for evidence that an owner of property is seeking to undertake the obligations of trusteeship himself, and not at whether he has tried to transfer legal title to another for these purposes.

Ahead of considering what the court is looking for in determining whether a settlor has declared himself to be trustee, and linking this with the previous materials considering the 'last act' doctrine in transfers of legal title to a trustee, it is worth clarifying that in the materials considered at this point the focus of attention—declarations of trust by a settlor—there are no 'transfer formalities' to be complied with. This is because the person who must have legal title for the purposes of dealing with it on behalf of the beneficiaries is already in possession of it: this is an absolute owner who is seeking to settle the property on trust. Here, the person who becomes a settlor on account of his intention to do this will keep hold of legal title himself, but because a trust has come into existence, equitable ownership also now subsists. This is held by the beneficiary, and this means that the legal title now in existence is nominal legal title which is held by a trustee in furtherance of obligations to the beneficiary. It is still being held by the same person, but it is a different type of legal title from that found in absolute ownership.

However, for clarity, it should be stated that this is the case as far as so-called 'transfer' formalities are concerned, and there may still be formalities relating to the actual *declaration* of trust itself. As will become clear in chapter 5, so-called 'declaration formalities' will be required where a trust is being declared of property which is land, which must according to s. 53(1)(b) of the Law of Property Act 1925 be manifested and evidenced in signed writing in order to be valid. There are no formalities required for declaring trusts of personalty but such are often in practice made in writing for tax planning purposes.

3.4.1 Satisfying *Milroy* v *Lord*: declarations of self as trustee and 'failed gifts'

What will become apparent shortly is that courts are not keen except in the clearest cases, to infer on the part of a settlor an intention to declare himself trustee. It will become clear that an intention must be shown to create a trust, rather than to effect some other transaction, such as an outright gift. Indeed in contrast, an intention to make an outright gift will more easily be inferred from what is said and done in absence of the clearest evidence of an intention to create a trust.

Thus, in *Jones* v *Lock* (1865) LR 1 Ch App 25, the father of a baby boy handed a cheque to his nine-month old son, uttering words which made it clear that he meant the child to have the sum represented by the cheque, although he immediately removed the cheque from the baby for safe-keeping. He died some days later, without having endorsed (signed) the cheque, which would have been necessary to pass title in it to the child. The court refused to construe his actions as amounting to a declaration of trust, with himself as trustee, in favour of the child.

Lord Cranworth LC did not think that an irrevocable intention to create a *trust* of the property had been manifested. There was an intention to make an outright gift, but no gift had actually been made. It was not, therefore, a declaration of trust.

A similar result obtained in *Richards* v *Delbridge* (1874) LR Eq 11. Delbridge wished to give his infant grandson, Richards, the lease he had on his place of business as a bone manure merchant. He endorsed on the lease: 'This deed and all thereto belonging I give to Edward Benetto Richards from this time forth, with all the stock-in-trade.' He gave the lease to Richards' mother to hold for Richards, but died before the lease was actually delivered to Richards himself. It was held that there had been no transfer of the lease to Richards, nor a declaration of trust in his favour. Sir George Jessel MR refused to infer a declaration of trust from the failed gift.

It is this latter sentence which is central for appreciating *why* it is very important to clarify that *Milroy* is authority for the position of what is required for voluntary transfers generally. This is because while these cases are concerned to explore what is required in order to validly constitute a trust (and in this immediate context, what is required to achieve this through a declaration of trusteeship by a settlor), they commonly raise issues of making gifts, and particularly failed attempts to transfer property outright to an intended recipient (which because it is one without consideration is deemed to be one which is *voluntary*, and thus one by way of a gift).

As can be seen from both *Jones* v *Lock* and *Richards* v *Delbridge*, the courts will more readily find that an owner of property intended to make a gift of his property (by way of an outright transfer) in favour of another, rather than that he intended to declare a trust of the property, and also that such gifts often fail for want of the appropriate formalities to transfer the property. This is often the very reason why their status and validity has come into question: these failed transfers are incapable of amounting to gifts, and so the only way they can be 'saved' (by satisfying *Milroy* v *Lord*) is by 'finding' an intention to create a trust.

3.4.2 *Richards* v *Delbridge*: what is required for satisfying *Milroy* v *Lord*?

To reiterate, a declaration of trusteeship by a settlor is what is said to subsist in situations where it is found that an owner of property who settles it on trust is actually intending to undertake the obligations of trusteeship himself. In these circumstances there are no transfer formality requirements and declaration formalities will only be required if the 'trust property' is land. What follows now is an examination of *what* it required for a person to be found to have undertaken trusteeship responsibilities himself, and *why* the courts might be looking for the elements which the cases indicate are regarded as important. And at this stage remember that the consequences of failing to find that an owner of property has not intended to undertake the responsibilities of trusteeship himself is that the trust will fail because, according to *Milroy v Lord*, equity will not perfect an imperfect trust.

In the introduction to *Richards v Delbridge* (1874) LR Eq 11 above it was explained that on the facts of the case there had been no transfer of the lease to Richards, nor a declaration of trust in his favour. The outcome of this case was that Sir George Jessel MR refused to infer a declaration of trust from the failed gift, but his judgment is important authority for what is required to infer a declaration of trust. Sir George Jessel's judgment is the starting point for explaining what is required for it to be found that an owner of property has declared himself a trustee of it, and what can be permitted in order that this can be found on the part of an owner of property who settles it on trust. According to Sir George Jessel in *Richards*:

The principle is a very simple one. A man may transfer his property...in one of two ways: he may do such acts as amount in law to a conveyance or assignment of the property, and thus completely divest himself of the legal ownership, in which case the person who by those acts acquires the property takes it beneficially, or on trust, as the case may be; or the legal owner of the property may, by one or other of the modes recognised as amounting to a valid declaration of trust, constitute himself a trustee, and, without an actual transfer of the legal title, may so deal with the property as to deprive himself of its beneficial ownership, and declare that he will hold it from that time forward on trust for the other person. It is true that he need not use the words, 'I declare myself a trustee', but he must do something which is equivalent to it, and use expressions which have that meaning... for a man to make himself trustee there must be an expression of intention to become a trustee, whereas words of present gift shew an intention to give over property to another, and not to retain it in the donor's own hands for any purpose, fiduciary or otherwise.

3.4.3 Applying *Richards* v *Delbridge*: what is required and can be permitted to satisfy *Milroy* v *Lord*?

The first point to make about this very famous passage is that it emphasises the fundamental difference between a gift and the trust. It is the case that a gift is achieved by an outright transfer of ownership whereas a trust is premised on the co-existence of two very different types of ownership, and fundamentally this means that the donor of a gift retains no interest after the property has been transferred, whereas a trustee's fiduciary obligations continue. When this is borne in mind it should come as no surprise thus that the courts will refuse to infer a declaration of trusteeship from a failed gift.

However, in focusing the judgment on how it can be shown that an owner of property has intended to undertake the responsibilities of trusteeship, Sir George Jessel observed that showing this does not actually require the settlor to use the words 'I declare myself a trustee'. However, Jessel MR was insistent that for a settlor to be taken to intend such, he must do something which is equivalent with saying 'I declare myself trustee.' In many respects in taking this as the starting point, Jessel MR is suggesting that the best way to make it clear that these obligations are being undertaken is actually to say 'I declare myself trustee'. But not stipulating this as a requirement acknowledges that in 'real life' declarations of trust will often arise in circumstances where such an expression is not actually uttered.

However, Sir George Jessel did insist that something must be done which is equivalent to saying 'I declare myself trustee.' And it is clear from the cases where *Richards* v *Delbridge* has been applied that the issues raised in this context concern what will be regarded as equivalent to saying 'I declare myself trustee' and what will not be regarded as equivalent to it, given that in the latter scenario, no trust can come into being, because the trust cannot be said to have been constituted.

3.4.3.1 *Applying* Richards *v* Delbridge: *the scope of the requirement*

From the case law it can be ascertained that it is possible to infer a declaration of trusteeship from conduct, or from words which can be construed as equivalent to a declaration of trusteeship, or from a mixture of the two. In *Paul* v *Constance* [1977] 1 WLR 527, Constance was injured at work, and obtained £950 in damages, which he put into a bank account in his name alone. The evidence suggested, however, that the money was intended for himself and Mrs Paul, with whom he was living. However, he was not married to Mrs Paul, and the reason for not opening a joint account was to avoid embarrassment for her, and this was apparently on the instigation of the bank manager.

3.4.3.2 Paul v Constance *as an illustration of the scope of* Richards v Delbridge

After the account was opened, subsequent additions were made to the account, in particular from bingo winnings which Constance and Paul played as a joint venture. One withdrawal of £150 was also made, which was divided equally between them. Constance then died, and the question at issue was whether Mrs Paul could claim any share of the fund. If the money in the account had belonged solely to Constance, then his wife, Mrs Constance, from whom he had parted, would be entitled to it on his death.

The Court of Appeal held that Constance held the money on trust for Mrs Paul. No words of trust were used, but regard was had to the unsophisticated character of Constance, and the nature of his relationship with Mrs Paul. Scarman LJ said:

> there must be clear evidence from what is said or done of an intention to create a trust...'an intention to dispose of property or a fund so that somebody else to the exclusion of the disponent acquires a beneficial interest in it.'...
> When one looks at the detailed evidence to see whether it goes as far as that—and I think that the evidence does go as far as that—one finds that from the time that the deceased received his damages right up to his death he was saying, on occasions, that the money was as much the plaintiff's as his. When they discussed the damages, how to invest them or what to do with them and when they discussed the bank account, he would say to her: 'The money is as much yours as mine'... .
> It might, however, be thought that this was a borderline case, since it is not easy to pinpoint a specific moment of declaration...

3.4.3.3 *Declarations, requirements, and a 'borderline' case*

There are two further points to make regarding *Paul* v *Constance*. First, in addition to Constance's conduct, there are also his actual words that 'the money is as much yours as mine'. These may not obviously seem equivalent to a declaration of trusteeship, but surely what he is really saying is that although (because the bank manager advised it) legal title to the money would be vested in Constance, the money in fact belonged to both of them. Since Constance had legal title, it could only be the equitable title that was shared, so, in fact, these words are exactly appropriate for a declaration of trusteeship. There is a more extensive discussion of similar informal words of declaration in chapter 9.

The second point is that Scarman LJ thought it difficult to pinpoint a specific moment of declaration. If it had been impossible to do so, then this is strongly suggestive that there ought to have been no trust. Trusts are, in principle, irrevocable, and there must be a moment at which the irrevocable commitment is made. *Before* that moment, Constance could have changed his mind, but *afterwards* he could not. That is essential to the nature of a trust, although in the case itself it was difficult to pinpoint exactly which moment this was.

This case is authority that words and/or conduct of a simple and unsophisticated nature will, in appropriate circumstances, be regarded as being equivalent to saying 'I declare myself trustee'. While these situations are very 'fact dependent' and *Paul* v *Constance* was considered a borderline case, and making more generalised observations on what is required is difficult, much of its import *can* be seen replicated in *Rowe v France* [1999] 2 FLR 787.

3.4.3.4 *Declarations of trust and financial distress*

There are also a number of cases where companies in financial trouble have been held to have declared themselves trustee of various moneys for their customers, or others with whom they deal. The result has been that the beneficiaries have taken in preference to the general creditors. And in making reference back to meeting the requirements of *Richards v Delbridge*, these cases can be seen as authority that conduct alone (in absence of any words) can be regarded as being equivalent to saying 'I declare myself trustee'. It will become apparent that in some cases equivalence will be found, and in others it will not be so, but as a general observation, conduct alone is in principle capable of being equivalent with saying 'I declare myself trustee.'

In *Re Kayford Ltd* [1975] 1 WLR 279, a mail order company was in financial difficulties. In order to protect customers in the event of insolvency, the company considered setting up a separate bank account, called the 'Customers' Trust Deposit Account' to hold the customers' deposits and payments until their goods were delivered, the intention of the company being that this money should be kept separate from the company's general funds. But the company took the advice of the bank, and instead of opening a new account, used a dormant account (with a small credit balance) in the company's name. On the winding up of the company Megarry J held that the money in the account (apart from a small credit balance) was held on trust for the customers.

Hence, the customers were not mere creditors of the company but beneficial owners of the moneys which they had paid until such time as their goods were delivered. Megarry J observed that 'it is well settled that a trust can be created without using the words "trust" or "confidence" or the like: the question is whether a sufficient intention to create a trust has been manifested'.

Nor did he consider it fatal that the money had not been put into a separate account, but mixed with other moneys:

In *Re Nanwa Gold Mines Ltd* [1955] 1 WLR 1080 the money was sent on the faith of a promise to keep it in a separate account, but there is nothing in that case or in any other authority that I know of to suggest that this is essential. I feel no doubt that here a trust was created. From the outset the advice (which was accepted) was to establish a trust account at the bank. The whole purpose of what was done was to ensure that the moneys remained in the beneficial ownership of those who sent them, and a trust is the obvious means of achieving this. No doubt the general rule is that if you send money to a company for goods which are not yet delivered, you are merely a creditor of the company unless a trust is created. The sender may create a trust by using appropriate words when he sends the money (though I wonder how many do this, even if they are equity lawyers), or the company may do it by taking suitable steps on or before receiving the money. If either is done, the obligations in respect of the money are transformed from contract to property, from debt to trust. Payment into a separate bank account is a useful (though by no means conclusive) indication of an intention to create a trust, but of course there is nothing to prevent the company from binding itself by a trust even if there are no effective banking arrangements...I should, however, add one thing. Different considerations may perhaps arise in relation to trade creditors; but here I am concerned only with members of the public, some of whom can ill afford to exchange their money for a claim to a dividend in the liquidation, and all of whom are likely to be anxious to avoid this.

However, the context of *Kayford* does now seem dated in light of modern consumer protection legislation, and Megarry J's judgment on the requirements of declarations of trust must, on one level, be read in light of this. Nevertheless, the commentary about the circumstances which can give rise to declarations of trust is still of utmost importance for trusts lawyers, who must be able to appreciate and understand a number of fundamental values, and how they have developed: there will always be a need to consider how these values might be applied in novel situations. *Re Nanwa Gold Mines Ltd* was an early *Quistclose*-type trust (for the requirements of which see chapter 2). As in the *Quistclose* situation, however, it is essential to be able to establish that the money belongs in equity to the customers; a personal action by them against the company after it had been wound up would clearly have availed them nothing. Therefore the money must be traceable on the principles in chapter 19. It was in *Kayford*, since the amount in the account never dropped below the amount of the small initial deposit, so that the excess could be clearly identified as trust property. Obviously, where the money is kept entirely separate, in a separate account, no difficulties of identification arise.

Re Kayford was applied by the Court of Appeal in *Re Chelsea Cloisters Ltd* [1980] 41 P & CR 98, where a 'tenants' deposit account' was set up to hold deposits against damage and breakages. Even in the absence of words of trust, however, there has to be evidence of an intention to create a trust, which is an irrevocable step, depriving the company of all beneficial interest in the money. It is not enough merely to put the money into a separate account. The requisite intention was not present in *Re Multi Guarantee Co. Ltd* [1987] BCLC 257, where the Court of Appeal distinguished the two previous cases. It had not been finally decided what to do with the money in the account, so an irrevocable intention was not established.

These cases have been criticised by Professor Michael Bridge [1992] 12 OJLS 333, and one must wonder whether they actually take us any nearer to understanding what the courts will regard as being equivalent to the words 'I declare myself trustee.'

3.4.3.5 *Donors' intentions: distinguishing gifts and trusts, and the significance attached by the courts to the nature of the trust*

Although it was suggested a little earlier that it is actually very difficult to make generalisations on what will be regarded as equivalent to saying 'I declare myself trustee' and what will fall short of this (bearing in mind that a trust cannot come into existence in the latter situation), the cases *do* all point to a consistent approach taken by the courts in one important respect. These cases all stand as authority that the courts *are* mindful of the *nature* of the trust when considering whether what is said and done can actually be equated with saying 'I declare myself trustee'. This is manifested in the extensive references which can be found to the trust as an arrangement which once put in place is permanent and irrevocable. And this is very important for proposing that the courts will infer this far less readily on the part of an owner of property than that he intended an out-and-out gift.

This does also of course chime in with the highly onerous and burdensome nature of trusteeship itself, which would also explain why the courts are happier to infer an owner of property is seeking to give it away, rather than make it subject to a trust. In this regard, although the nuances of trusteeship are evident in the cases, more direct reference to the *nature of trusteeship* is something which the courts *should* be emphasising much more explicitly alongside the emphasis which *is* being given to the *nature of the trust* itself.

3.5 Constitution of trusts and perfection of transfers by equity: some recent developments and emerging new approaches

There are three important cases dating from the early years of the twenty-first century which are relevant to this chapter's consideration of incomplete gifts and the constitution of trusts. These are especially *Choitram (T) International SA v Pagarani* [2001] 2 All ER 492 and *Pennington v Waine* [2002] 1 WLR 2075, with reference also being made to *Pehrsson v von Greyerz* (unreported). These cases are very significant in this discussion about the role played by constituting the trust in bringing into being a valid trust, and the way in which what must be done in these circumstances reflects the requirements of *Milroy v Lord* (1862). These cases also provide important reflection on the more general import of *Milroy v Lord* as authority that where requirements pertaining to constituting a trust (and voluntary transfers of property more generally) are not complied with, equity will not complete an incomplete gift and nor will equity complete an incomplete trust.

What these more recent cases suggest is that the courts may be moving away from *Milroy v Lord* both in terms of its requirements and possibly even from the cardinal principles of equity which for almost two hundred years *Milroy* was regarded as embodying. An explanation of this proposition, and also some indication of its implications will be pursued by a more detailed look at each of these three cases.

3.5.1 *Milroy v Lord* and the constitution of trusts: the significance of *Choitram v Pagarani*

Dealing firstly with *Choitram v Pagarani* (before considering how the cases can be seen to raise some important considerations in common) the starting point for considering its significance is the criteria for the constitution of a trust as laid out in *Milroy v Lord*. *Choitram v Pagarani*'s significance lies in the manner in which its facts presented the courts with circumstances which did not demonstrate direct fit with the two methods for the creation of a fully constituted trust as laid down by the authority provided by *Milroy v Lord*. *Choitram v Pagarani* involved a wealthy Indian businessman who wished for a charitable foundation to be set up to receive a large portion of his wealth after his death. The source of the charitable foundation's benefit was to come from the shares and deposit and credit balances in companies which the businessman owned. To this end, and knowing he was in his last illness in 1992, a trust deed establishing the charitable foundation was drafted and signed by the donor, with the deed stating that he was the settlor, and appointing seven trustees of whom he was one. Upon his death shortly afterwards, no share transfers had been executed in favour of the foundation, and nor had a formal declaration of trust been executed. The decision at first instance found that there was no trust in favour of the foundation because there was no effective transfer of property, and neither had there been an effective declaration of trust. This was upheld on appeal to the Court of Appeal of the British Virgin Islands. In the Privy Council the appeal was allowed on grounds that it was found that the settlor had constituted the trust, and that the language and articulation of 'gift' by the donor in the context of the charitable foundation could only be interpreted as intending the creation of a trust. In this manner, according Lord Browne-Wilkinson, the case was consistent with, and did not breach the requirements of *Milroy v Lord*. As his Lordship explained:

> Although the words used by [the donor] are normally appropriate to an outright gift—'I give to X'—in the present context there is no breach of the principle in *Milroy* v *Lord* if the words of [the] gift (to the foundation) are given their only possible meaning in this context. The foundation has no legal existence apart from the trust declared by the foundation trust deed. Therefore the words 'I give to the foundation' can only mean 'I give to the Trustees of the Foundation trust deed to be held by them on trusts of the Foundation trust deed'. Although the words are apparently words of outright gift they are essentially words of gift on trust.

The conclusion drawn here was, according to Lord Browne-Wilkinson that 'although equity will not aid a volunteer, it will not strive officiously to defeat a gift'. And, significantly, on the facts of the case, the declaration to one of a number of trustees was such that it would be unconscionable for the donor to resile from his gift (see criticisms of Rickett [2001] Conv 515).

3.5.2 *Milroy v Lord*, the 'rule in *Re Rose*' and questions of constitution

The first case being considered here is that of *the Trustees of the Property of Pehrsson v von Greyerz* (unreported) (Privy Council, 16 June 1999), and it forms part of a discussion of the 'last act' doctrine which will progress to considering *Pennington v Waine* [2002]. Like a number of these cases, this was another case involving shares as trust property and in considering whether the purported arrangement had become constituted as a valid trust, the Privy Council had to consider whether the status and the significance of the appointment of trustees of shares alone had the effect of constituting the trust. This question arose in light of a purported transfer by Pehrsson to von Greyerz of shares in a company, and the execution of documentation which was not appropriate for doing this. Presiding Lord Hoffman found that there was no evidence that a transfer of the beneficial interest in the shares to the respondent had occurred, and all the dealings which the appellant had with her were concerned only with procuring the registration of shares in the former's name. On this basis it was impossible to construe a gift as having taken place before the transfer had been registered, a gift which if this had been the case, would have concerned a gift and transfer of the shares' beneficial interest. It was held in the Privy Council that the intended recipient (von Greyerz) could not rely on the rule in *Re Rose* until transfers for the shares had been executed in her favour by the nominee shareholders, and the latter had either delivered the transfers to her or constituted themselves as agents for her. Until one of these courses of action had taken place, the nominee shareholders remained nominees for the appellant, Mr Pehrsson. The transfers were in fact not executed until the same day as registration, and up until the time of delivery or constitution of agency, it remained open for the donor to countermand the gift.

Subsequently, in 2002 the Court of Appeal considered the case of *Pennington v Waine* [2002] 1 WLR 2075, which like many others in this area concerned transfers of shares. In addition, very significantly like *Pehrsson* v *von Greyerz*, this decision very clearly attached significance to the ability or otherwise of a donor to change his mind about an intended transfer to the recipient. This latter point will become very prominent when in due course the implications of some common threads which can be identified between these cases will be explored. For present purposes, some background to *Pennington* v *Waine* will help to clarify what the case was actually about, because the facts are quite complicated.

3.5.2.1 *Equity, incomplete gifts, and the 'rule in* Re Rose' *and* Pennington v Waine

This is in essence a consideration of the *Rose* v *IRC* litigation, and particularly the principle of the donor having done everything in his power to effect the transfer which it embodies. The Court of Appeal judgment in *Pennington* v *Waine* suggests that it is now possible for mere completion of the relevant documents of transfer to give rise to an assignment in equity of the property concerned to the intended recipient, in circumstances where the donor cannot be said to have done everything in his power to effect the transfer of the property. The principle of 'everything in his power' is, of course, a development of the rule in *Milroy* v *Lord*, and has become known as the 'rule in *Re Rose*'.

The case of *Pennington* v *Waine* raises some very interesting issues about the 'rule in *Re Rose*', and provides an updated context for a reiteration of a number of concerns about *Re Rose* which were discussed in [1998] CLJ 46. While accepting that a sound policy in favour of the 'last act' can be found in principle, a number of commentators have expressed misgivings about the rule itself, and especially about regarding *Re Rose; Rose* v *IRC* as authority for its application (which was upheld in *Mascall* v *Mascall* [1984]). It would now appear that the 'rule in *Re Rose*' has actually been extended with *Pennington* v *Waine* suggesting that it can now be applied in situations where a transfer can fall considerably short of the donor having done everything in his power. This is because *Pennington* suggests that the courts are becoming increasingly interested in determining whether it would be unconscionable for the gift not to be 'completed' in favour of the intended recipient. As with *Re Rose* and a number of these cases, the disputation concerned the gift of company shares, the formalities of transfer requiring the registration of the new owner on the company's register of shareholders under s. 182 of the Companies Act 1985 (with these provisions now being located in s. 770 of the Companies Act 2006). This ensures that the possession of share certificates provides evidence of share ownership but does not constitute it, and thus mere delivery will not alone constitute transfer of ownership.

The facts of *Pennington* v *Waine* are briefly as follows. In 1998 the donor, Ada Crampton, executed a form for the transfer of 400 shares held in a family company in favour of her nephew Harold Crampton. The transfer had been drawn up by the company's auditors, and in due course it was signed by her and returned to the auditors and placed on the company's file. Ada's wish was also that her nephew should become a director of the company. Thus, the auditor wrote to Harold informing him of Ada's instructions in respect of the transfer of the shares, stating in respect of this, that no action on Harold's part was required. However, Harold's consent to act as a director was required, and he was asked to complete a prescribed form for this purpose. The auditor took no further action to transfer the shares and Ada died in November of that year without the transfer having been sent to the company for Harold's registration as the shares' new owner. It was held in the Court of Appeal that the gift of the shares to Harold was effective in equity notwithstanding that Ada had not done everything in her power to effect the transfer. Clarke LJ regarded the execution of the share transfer form as constituting the transfer in equity of the shares. This in turn generated a bare trust upon Ada, under which she could have been compelled to procure the process of registration of the shares into Harold's name, thus completing the transfer at law.

What is particularly interesting about this judgment is the view of Arden and Schiemann LJJ of the role of conscionability in the determination of equitable assignment in circumstances where the donor had not done everything in his power to *effect* the transfer. This approach suggests that the test originating in *Milroy* v *Lord* of the last act of the settlor might be being replaced by a different test based not on the donor's actions but on his hypothetical state of mind. This alternative test is constructed around the conscionability or otherwise of a donor's (often hypothetical) ability to revoke an incompleted gift in certain circumstances. *When* such an alternative test (to the donor's actions) would be invoked is not very clear, but the essence of the conscionability test was to be a matter for the courts to determine having regard to all the circumstances of the case. And, although there could not be any comprehensive list of factors which define and constitute unconscionability, according to Arden LJ, on the facts of the case actually before the court the relevant factors could be ascertained as:

Ada made the gift of her own free will: there is no finding that she was not competent to do this. She not only told Harold about the gift and signed a form of transfer which she delivered to Mr Pennington for him to secure registration; her agent also told Harold that he need take no action. In addition, Harold agreed to become a director of the Company without limit of time, which he could not do without shares being transferred to him. If Ada had changed her mind on (say) 10 November 1998, in my judgment the court could properly have concluded that it was too late for her to do this as by that date Harold signed the form 288A (his consent to becoming a director).

The last act of the settlor: is there really a point at which donors can do no more?
In considering *why* it might be that the court's attention became focused on the donor's conscience rather than his actions in this case, it is interesting to note Clarke LJ's commentary on the requirement (of *Re Rose*) that the donor must have done everything in his power for a transfer of interest to be regarded as having taken place in equity. This arose because it had been submitted by counsel for the appellant that the principle that equity will only intervene (to 'complete' the transfer) where the donor has done all in his power to perfect the gift cannot literally be true 'because there is almost always something more which the donor could have done'. Clarke LJ accepted that there was 'some force' in the argument, and indeed later appeared to accept that equity could not be regarded as intervening only where the donor has done all that he can because there are seldom situations in which the donor could not possibly do anything further. Hence, it was held sufficient for equitable assignment that the stock transfer form had been executed in circumstances where there was no intention of revoking it in the future.

The judgment of Arden LJ (with whom Clarke and Schiemann LJJ agreed on this point) considered the role of conscionability in the determination of an equitable assignment in circumstances where the donor had not done everything in his power to effect the transfer. Hence the suggestion that the 'last act' test originating in *Milroy* v *Lord* is being replaced by an altogether different approach, which is causing concern.

It would thus appear at some levels that some of the concerns which have been expressed by academic commentators about *Re Rose* were addressed in *Pennington*. This can be seen in respect of circumstances whereby after the purported transfer in equity there was actually still room for discretion in decision-making in regard to it, and situations whereby what remained outstanding could not be confined to formality requirements regarding the transfer in law. However, this advancement by Clarke LJ of the 'fallacy' of the last act of the settlor does not appear remotely to be concerned with arguments which counsel caution in its application. It appears instead to have been advanced as an endorsement of and even as justification for actually extending the circumstances in which equity is prepared to regard a gift as one which is perfect or easily perfected, and this has caused concern amongst academic commentators.

'Re Rose revisited' revisited: donors, giving, certainty, and conscionability
While *Choitram* v *Pagarani* makes it clear that while equity will not come to aid a volunteer 'it will not strive officiously to defeat a gift', *Pennington* v *Waine* suggests that far too much accommodation might be being given to the position of would-be donees. It is difficult to see the very premise of a gift as not being inextricably connected with the intention of the donor, and the rules surrounding equity's strictness in not perfecting those gifts which are not perfectly made reflects this, and allows for the donor to revoke the gift before the point at which it is irrevocably made. It appears from the facts of the case, and the convincing representation of them in the passage from Arden LJ's judgment above, that the gift to Harold was intended. And, in this respect *Pennington* v *Waine* appears to be directly analogous with *Rose* v *IRC*, inasmuch as both point to situations whereby on their facts, each donor was extremely unlikely to have changed his mind. Although there is much to suggest that this *was* the intention both in *Rose* v *IRC* and *Pennington* v *Waine*, it is easy to envisage situations where the issues surrounding intention are more equivocal and far less clear cut. The Court of Appeal has demonstrated a cavalier attitude towards the principle of *Milroy* v *Lord* which is founded upon the interests of certainty when ascertaining the wishes of the donor, and which is a cornerstone of the rules surrounding making gifts: a gift will be construed as such if a gift is intended. It appears to be putting in its place a test which subjects donors, their actions, and their intentions to a test of conscionability.

Milroy v *Lord* and the case law which followed it (notably *Jones* v *Lock* and *Richards* v *Delbridge*) might be seen to have produced some harsh results, and indeed the rule against imperfectly constituted gifts has led to harsh and seemingly paradoxical results. At one point Arden LJ made clear her views that an alternative test based in conscionability provides a less paternalistic framework for the consideration of gifts and giving, and one which leads to a 'benevolent construction' of gifts which gives effects to the clear wishes of the donor.

There is much which is intelligent and considered in this alternative construction of gifts, and it is of course the case that Arden LJ positioned paternalism alongside its ideological opposite; that is autonomy and respect for individuals. Thus, she framed her alternative test as a mechanism for ensuring that respect is given to the original intentions of the donor, asserting that approaches which (often hypo-thetically) permit donors to change their minds could be regarded as paternalistic. Although there is strength in this argument, there is also one central objective which *must* inform the courts' approach to the status of imperfect gifts and the position of the parties involved which should counsel caution, and which is pre-sent in the very next sentence of Arden LJ's judgment. This is, of course, the need to safeguard the position of the donor. At this point, perhaps it is worth remembering that the donor is central to the process of giving, and must necessarily remain so. *Pennington* v *Waine* suggests that there is a danger that the balance may be becom-ing tipped in a direction which might actually work against the donor's interests (albeit mainly hypothetically), and could operate to position the potential donee at the former's expense.

3.5.2.2 *Gifts and the creation of trusts:* Pennington v Waine, *donors, and their wishes*

It is the case that both *Rose* and, more recently, *Pennington* concerned transfers which were intended as outright gifts as distinct from property intended to become subject to a trust. However the difficulties raised by *Pennington* do have important application in situations where the donor (at the outset at least) does intend to divest himself of all interest in the property, but this time in favour of a third party who is intended to hold the property on trust for an intended beneficiary, as was the case in one of the transfers in *Rose*. *Pennington* v *Waine* does suggest (des-pite Arden LJ's insistence to the contrary) that rather serious inroads might also be made into the closely related principle that equity will not infer perfect trust from an imperfect gift. Trusts law is constructed around the essence of the trust as an arrangement which is irrevocable, and this quite rightly attaches considerable import to the intention of the donor (although it was remarked in the case itself that perhaps too little attention was paid to this by the courts when ascertaining declarations of trust by settlors). While it is the case that once the trust is in place, its enforcement is at the hands of the beneficiary, ordinarily to the exclusion of the donor (unless he is a party to the trust or becomes a beneficiary under it), this position arises once and *only* once the trust is fully constituted. Equally a gift once given is irrevocable, but again this only happens once a gift has been made and correct 'transfer' formalities have been complied with.

The traditional approach, as enumerated in *Richards* v *Delbridge* (1874) LR 11 Eq, has propounded that the finding of a trust should only be made subject to a very high standard of proof. And in having its own roots in *Milroy* v *Lord*, *Richards* is of course itself an embodiment of the way in which *Milroy* v *Lord* is seeking to ensure that what happens to a person's property is what was intended, and that this com-plies with what the law requires. In turn this is of course premised on the way in which what is at stake here are the valuable property rights and entitlements for recipients which follow from making a gift or declaring a trust.

It is thus suggested that, instead of focusing on the role of transfer formalities in outright transfers of property and certainty of intention and the irrevocability of the trust arrangement which is consistent with the nature of the gift and of the trust respectively, the doctrine of conscionability in conception might undermine the way in which making gifts and creating beneficiaries from recipients of trust property are and *should be* at the behest of the donor. Given that Clarke LJ was himself moved to remark in *Pennington* v *Waine* that hard cases make bad law, it is a great pity that the Court of Appeal seems to have taken an approach which appears to be less interested in the wishes of the donor than it should be. And instead of favouring certainty (even if this produces harsh results) which follows from looking at what is actually said and what is actually done, the courts appear to be making a move towards the much more vague notion of subjecting the donor, his actions and his intentions, to far more nebulous notions of conscionability and even paternalism.

3.6 'Exceptions' to the principle that equity will not assist volunteers

The recent developments considered above suggest that the courts are becoming altogether more relaxed in their approaches to assisting volunteers and completing incomplete transfers. Although it is not entirely clear how this trend will develop henceforth, a number of commentators have noted it is not necessarily a welcome one (see, for example, Halliwell [2003] Conv 192), and it will be interesting to see what does actually happen in subsequent cases. Meanwhile, there *is* still strong authority in favour of the principle that equity will not assist a volunteer (even if *Choithram* v *Pagarani* [2001] suggests that this requires distinguishing such a situation from equity striving 'officiously to defeat a gift') and also that equity will not complete an imperfect gift (whatever the implications of adopting the *Pennington* v *Waine* approach might actually be).

   This section closes this discussion of equity's approach to incomplete transfers arising in the context of outright transfers of property (by way of a gift) and constituting trusts by considering two established exceptions to the principle that equity will not assist a volunteer. It can be argued that they are not genuine exceptions, but merely additional methods by which a trust can be fully constituted or a gift effected, but whether or not this is the case, they operate as if they were exceptions to the general rule.

   It should also perhaps be mentioned that it would be very rare for either of the exceptions considered below to occur. This is because no settlor would actually deliberately invoke them, and where problems do actually occur in this area they will arise *ex post* facto and on account of competing claims to a deceased person's property.

3.6.1 Gifts which are made *donatio mortis causa*

A *donatio mortis causa* (which, translated from Latin, broadly means 'gift by reason of death') is a gift made in contemplation of, and conditional upon, the death of the donor. It is different from an ordinary, immediate gift, for the donee's title does not come into existence until the death occurs: until such time, the donor may revoke. Nor is it a testamentary gift taking effect under the terms of a properly attested will. Suppose, for example, that A is terminally ill, or about to engage in a dangerous activity and, realising that death is a possibility, entrusts some of his property to B, telling him that if he (A that is) should die, B may keep the property as his own. Although B has custody of the property he will not own it unless and until A dies.

If that happens, equity regards B's title as perfected, and he may claim the property in preference to anyone to whom A may have chosen to bequeath it in his will. So if A has already made a will in which all his personal property, which would otherwise include the property entrusted to B, is left to X, B has a better claim by virtue of the conditional gift made ***donatio mortis causa***.

Historically *donationes mortis causa* (plural) were most likely when A wished to benefit his mistress (B) on his death but, not wanting to disclose her to his 'legitimate' family, is reluctant to use his will or make an *inter viros* transfer to her. Here the *donatio mortis causa* will assist, but it has applications more generally for situations where the prospect of imminent death does not permit 'proper' arrangements.

3.6.1.1 *Equity's stringent conditions*

To permit the making of a disposition which is neither an immediate perfect gift nor a formal testamentary disposition is to invite fraudulent claims intended to defeat the expectations of legatees, and thus equity hedges a *donatio mortis causa* with stringent conditions. The necessary conditions for a *donatio mortis causa* to be upheld were set out by Farwell J in *Re Craven's Estate* [1937] Ch 423:

The transfer must be with the intention of giving, and not simply of securing, the goods. There is no *donatio mortis causa* if A simply wants B to look after his property.

1. It must be clear that the property was handed over in contemplation of a real possibility of death, and some specific focus on the possibility of death must be shown. The donor must anticipate some hazard to life. This is usually a serious illness, but extreme hazard (such as motor racing) is also probably covered, but not normal, everyday risks, such as that associated with air travel.

2. The gift must be conditional upon death occurring, and otherwise revocable. This means that the 'donor' must intend to keep the property himself if he survives. This requirement is superfluous where the property is a chattel which could be transferred by simple delivery, since because its owner could obviously have made a valid immediate gift if he chose, but it is relevant where some further formal step is required to perfect the title, as for example in the case of land (which is considered below).

3. The donor must have effectively parted with dominion over the subject matter of the gift. In other words, the property must have been handed over, or the means of access to it transferred. For example, this can be shown by giving to the recipient the key to the bank deposit box where the property is lodged. The test is whether the donor has put it out of his power between the dates of gift and death to alter the subject matter of gift and substitute other property for it: see also *Re Lillingston* [1952] 2 All ER 184, at p. 191. In *Woodard* v *Woodard* [1995] 3 All ER 980, the Court of Appeal inferred a *donatio mortis causa* of a car from the handing over of its keys, where the donor had also said 'You can keep the keys, I won't be driving it any more.' It was immaterial that the car was already in the donee's possession as bailee, or that another set of keys (which the donor was in any case in no position to use) might have existed.

   It is also possible to transfer property which is not capable of physical delivery, by handing over *indicia* of title, such as a savings bank book, or (presumably) a bill of lading covering a consignment of cargo aboard a ship. The test is whether handing over the document 'amounted to a transfer', in which case possession or production of the document would entitle the possessor to the money in the account.

3.6.1.2 Donatio mortis causa *and land*

Long after most students of the law of trusts must have thought that *donatio mortis causa* cases were ancient history, a *donatio mortis causa* was successfully argued before the Court of Appeal in *Sen* v *Headley* [1991] Ch 425. It had long been thought that it was impossible to have a *donatio mortis causa* of land, because the third of Farwell J's conditions cannot be satisfied, even by delivery of the title deeds; but on the assumption that *Sen* v *Headley* is correct, this view must now be regarded as wrong. In this case Mr Hewett, who was, at the age of 86, on his death-bed, gave the claimant, Mrs Sen, the keys to a steel box with the title deeds to his house inside, saying to her 'The house is yours, Margaret. You have the keys. They are in your bag. The deeds are in the steel box.' It appeared that Mr Hewett and Mrs Sen had, for some thirty years, lived together as if married. Title to the house was unregistered.

After Hewett's death, the gift was challenged by his next of kin. There were no difficulties over Farwell J's first two criteria set out above, but at first instance ([1990] Ch 728), Mummery J thought that the third was not satisfied: Hewett had not parted with dominion over the house, and it was concluded in effect, that land cannot form the subject matter of a *donatio mortis causa*.

Clearly, the transfer of title deeds could not amount to a transfer of the land itself during Hewett's lifetime, since no deed was executed, and a declaration of trust would require writing. This is because it would have to be a declaration of trust of land (see chapter 5). Here there was no documentation at all, and Margaret could at most acquire a 'mere *spes*' (hope or expectation) of obtaining the property. Mummery J's view was that the entire doctrine was anomalous, and that judicial caution should be exercised before extending it, that the policy of the law required formality for dispositions of land and interests in land, and that, accordingly, the *donatio mortis causa* doctrine would not be extended so as to allow an attempt at disposition on death which avoided the Wills Act formalities (on which, see chapter 10), or the perfection of an imperfect *inter vivos* gift.

The clear inference from Mummery J's judgment was that *donatio mortis causa* could *never* apply to land, and this view was in line with the orthodox views that had been long held. However, Mummery J was reversed in the Court of Appeal, however, on analogy with extensions of the doctrine in previous cases. In *Snellgrove* v *Bailey* [1744] 3 Atk 213, the doctrine had been applied to a gift of money secured by a bond, by delivery of the bond; in *Duffield* v *Elwes* (1827) 1 Bli (NS) 497, the House of Lords had applied the doctrine to a gift of money secured by a mortgage of land, by delivery of the mortgage deed. In each case, transfer of *indicia* of title was all that was required, but one problem with this reasoning was that in *Duffield* v *Elwes*, Lord Eldon thought the doctrine would not apply to a gift of land by delivery of the title deeds.

No doubt the doctrine was anomalous, but in the view of Nourse LJ, that did not justify creating anomalous exceptions to the admittedly anomalous doctrine. The only reason why, with unregistered land, transfer of the title deeds did not transfer title to the property was because of a formality statute. All *donationes mortis causa* avoid formality provisions, usually ones pertaining to wills. There was no reason why the formality provisions relating to land should be regarded as presenting any greater obstacle than any other formality provisions, and no reason why this case should be treated differently from other gifts made *donationes mortis causa* which had been upheld.

It does not necessarily follow that this will necessarily work with all species of property. For example, there are difficulties with shares in private companies, which cannot be physically transferred, because registration of a new owner may be refused. This situation would not thus be regarded as directly analogous to land.

Death sooner than expected
It seems on the basis of *Wilkes* v *Allington* [1931] 2 Ch 104 that the gift is valid even if the donor dies sooner than expected, and even if from a different cause. The donor was suffering from an incurable disease, and made the gift knowing that he had not long to live. In fact he died even earlier than expected of pneumonia, but the gift was held to be valid. Whether the same principle would apply even if the death were completely different from the donor's expectation, for example if he actually dies of food poisoning, is less clear.

3.6.2 The rule in *Strong* v *Bird*

The other exception to the principle that equity will not assist a volunteer (and an example of the presumption that equitable title follows legal, which is considered in chapter 7) is the rule in *Strong* v *Bird* (1874) LR 18 Eq 315. This rule can be invoked in circumstances such as are given by way of illustration. Person A hands his share certificates to person B but fails to procure the transfer and registration of B as owner. A then dies, leaving a will which appoints B as his executor but makes another person C the legatee of all his personal property. Again, equity treats the gift as perfected, this time by the vesting of A's property in B in his capacity as executor, and the claims of the beneficiaries under the will, here C, are overridden.

The same principle operates if B owes A money, but A makes no effort to collect his debt and appoints B his executor: these were the facts of *Strong* v *Bird* itself. The appointment is, as it were, a conclusive release of the debt. But it must be clear that there was an intention to make the gift or release the debt, and that this intention continued until death.

3.6.2.1 *Facts and central issue of law*

In *Strong* v *Bird*, the defendant borrowed £1,100 from his stepmother. His stepmother lived in his house and paid rent at £212 quarterly. The money borrowed by the defendant was to be repaid by eleven deductions of £100 from quarterly rent. The stepmother made two deductions, but after that made no more, and continued to pay the full £212 until her death. Verbally, she forgave the defendant the remainder of debt (but this was ineffective as a release at law). The defendant was appointed executor under her will. The residuary legatees claimed the remainder of the debt, but Sir George Jessel MR held the defendant not liable. His appointment as an executor extinguished the debt at common law since it is impossible for an executor to sue himself. It seems that equity acquiesces with the common law position, subject to the other requirements of doctrine.

In *Re Stewart* [1908] 2 Ch 251, Neville J applied the same principle to perfect an imperfect *inter vivos* gift of bonds by appointment of the intended donee as executor. Equity would not interfere with the common law transfer of title. The doctrine depends on an attempt to make an immediate *inter vivos* gift of specific property, a continuing intent to make the gift until death, and the vesting of legal title in the donee.

One might argue that the logic of the rule in *Strong v Bird* requires that B be *voluntarily* appointed executor by A, but there is some authority that the rule operates if B becomes A's administrator, instead of his executor. This was the view of Farwell J in *Re James* [1935] Ch 449, where a housekeeper had herself appointed one of two administratrices of the testator's estate.

In *Re Gonin* [1979] Ch 16, Walton J cast doubt on *Re James*. In *Re Gonin*, the claimant alleged that, in return for her returning home after being called away during the Second World War, and going to live with and look after her parents, her parents had verbally agreed that the parental home and its contents should become hers on their deaths. The claimant's father died in 1957, leaving no estate. After the death of the claimant's mother in 1968, the claimant took out letters of administration to her estate, and began an action to determine whether she was entitled, as administratrix, to vest the freehold in the property in herself.

Executors and administrators

She claimed both land and contents (furniture) under the rule in *Strong v Bird*, on the basis that the claimant's mother intended to give the claimant the house on her death, and the gift was perfected by the claimant taking out letters of administration.

Walton J took the view that the appointment of an administrator was quite different to the appointment of an executor, since it is not a voluntary act of the deceased, but of the law. It was also often a matter of pure chance which of many persons entitled to a grant of letters of administration actually took them out:

Why, then, should any special tenderness be shown to a person so selected by law and not the will of the testator, and often indifferently selected among many with an equal claim? It would seem an astonishing doctrine of equity that if the person who wishes to take the benefit of the rule in *Strong v Bird* manages to be the person to obtain a grant then he will be able to do so, but if a person equally entitled manages to obtain a prior grant, then he will not be able to do so.

Re Gonin *and questions remaining*

Walton J did not need actually to decide whether the earlier authority was correct, however, since he also held that even if the rule in *Strong v Bird* applied to administrators, the evidence did not point to a continuing intention on the part of the claimant's mother to give the house to the claimant.

It is nevertheless possible to defend *Re James*. Kodilinye argues ([1982] Conv 14, at p. 17) that the criticisms of *Re James* by Walton J cannot stand, for a number of reasons. He argues that the crux of Jessel MR's principle is that the gift (or release in *Strong v Bird* itself) is perfected by the vesting of the legal title in the donee, and it is immaterial whether that vesting is brought about by the act of the donor or by the operation of law. He also points out that the need to give effect to the will of the testator is already satisfied by the requirement that the donor must have shown an intention to give *inter vivos* until his death. Therefore, there is no need for any *additional* voluntary act by the testator, such as appointing the donee executor. It must be admitted that there is some force in these arguments.

Re James was applied in *Re Ralli's WT*, but the situation there was different because no intention at all was needed on the part of the transferor. It is easier to support Farwell J's views in *Re James* than those of Buckley J in *Re Ralli's WT*.

3.7 Sub-trusts

A further point to note is that the property settled can include an equitable interest. In other words, a beneficiary under a trust may constitute a further trust of his equitable interest, thereby creating a sub-trust. Sub-trusts are common in tax avoiding settlements. The beneficiary under the sub-trust can himself repeat the process, creating a further sub-trust, and there is no limit to the number of times this process may be repeated.

3.7.1 Covenants to settle (property on trust)

A discussion of covenants to settle (property on trust) can be found on the Online Resource Centre (ORC). These materials relate to situations which are not common today, but which were very much so historically, and particularly during the nineteenth century. While much of their context and background has ceased to be of much relevance today, the issues raised are interesting, and especially so for considering some of the similarities and differences between the common law contract and the trust, and also the interplay which has historically subsisted between the two legal devices.

 online resource centre

FURTHER READING

Garton 'The Role of the Trust Mechanism in the Rule in *Re Rose*' (2003) Conveyancer 364.

Halliwell 'Perfecting Imperfect Gifts and Trusts: Have We Reached the End of the Chancellor's Foot?' (2003) Conveyancer 192.

Lowrie and Todd '*Re Rose* revisited' (1998) 57 Cambridge Law Journal 46.

Millett 'The *Quistclose* Trust: Who Can Enforce It?' (1985) Law Quarterly Review 269.

Rickett 'Completely Constituting an *inter vivos* Trust: Property Rules?' (2001) Conveyancer 515.

Tham 'Careless Share Giving' (2006) Conveyancer 411.

4

The three certainties and the significance of the 'beneficiary principle'

Chapter 3 was about the vesting of property in trustees, a prerequisite to the existence of any trust. Chapters 4 to 6 are about further requirements for validity, assuming the property is so vested. This chapter deals with the requirement for certainty, and the significance of trusts law's cardinal 'beneficiary principle'.

The requirements considered in this chapter apply not only to trusts which are expressly created, but also to resulting and constructive trusts. Charitable trusts are exempt from certainty of object requirements, and they are also incidentally largely exempt from the perpetuity rules (see chapter 6). For convenience, certainty of objects requirements for powers are also included in this chapter, by way of comparison with those for discretionary trusts.

4.1 Certainty

4.1.1 Reasons for certainty requirements

There are two main reasons for certainty requirements. The first and obvious reason is to ensure that the property is correctly identified and is dealt with in accordance with the wishes of the settlor. Thus, a doubt as to those wishes leads the courts to play safe rather than risk an unauthorised disposition of a person's property. Additionally, it must be clear to the trustees themselves exactly what their duties are. The difficulty is most acute in the case of testamentary trusts, where those who have the duty of administering the estate have to rely for guidance upon whatever terms the testator may have chosen to express his desires, since obviously it is not possible to ask him.

The second reason is less obvious. Whereas today trustees usually act in a professional capacity, the typical trust of 200 years ago was very different in nature, and the rules originally developed around the older type of trust. These were often family arrangements, and one of the main concerns of the courts was that the trustees might be fraudulent and keep the trust property themselves. Equity has been criticised for making essentially the same assumptions about, for example, banks and company directors today; the problem stems from adapting to a modern situation a set of principles which were originally developed for quite a different purpose. Certainly, a limited degree of successful adaptation has occurred, but the same basic assumption remains, namely that trustees are likely to be fraudulent.

At least until very recently, the courts have tended to over-emphasise the patho-logical situation, in which the trustees refuse to carry out the trust. The courts have insisted that there must exist someone with sufficient interest in the trust property to be able to come to court to compel the trustees to carry out the trust and in the final analysis the courts must be able to administer the trust themselves. This emphasis has led (at least until recently) to much more rigid certainty require-ments than might otherwise have been the case.

4.1.2 **The three certainties**

The classification for certainty usually cited is that of Lord Langdale in *Knight* v *Knight* (1840) 3 Beav 148, 173: while the classification has been criticised, there is no doubt that it is the one adopted by the courts. The essential prerequisites of a valid private express trust are certainty as to the intention of the settlor to create a trust of property (sometimes misleadingly termed certainty of words), certainty as to the property to which the trust is to attach (also referred to as certainty of subject matter), and certainty as to the persons or 'objects' who are to benefit (certainty of object).

4.1.3 **Effect of absence of certainty**

If any of the certainties is absent then no valid express trust will be created, but the precise consequences will depend upon the circumstances. If the settlor attempts to declare himself trustee, the declaration will be invalid whichever certainty is not satisfied. If legal title has been transferred but there is uncertainty as to the intention to create a trust (i.e. to separate the legal and equitable titles) then the transferee will hold it free of any trust. If either of the other certainties is absent, there will be a resulting trust to the settlor (or residuary legatees, in the case of an attempt to establish a trust by will), subject to one exception: *Hancock* v *Watson* [1902] AC 14 establishes that where there is an absolute gift of property in the first instance and trusts are subsequently imposed on that property, if the trusts fail for any reason the property is not held on a resulting trust for the settlor or his estate but will vest absolutely in the person to whom the property was given. This can be seen for example in *Palmer* v *Simmonds* (1854) 2 Drew 221 (below).

4.2 **Certainty of intention**

4.2.1 **Words or intention?**

Although Lord Langdale spoke of certainty in relation to the words alleged to establish the settlor's intention, this is misleading in two respects. First, it is pos-sible to establish a trust without any writing whatever, except where the statu-tory formality requirements obtain (see chapter 5). A trust need not even be orally declared, as it is possible to establish an intention of a settlor to create a trust (i.e. to separate legal and equitable titles) from words or conduct; this may be inferred from the nature of the gift as a whole. No doubt *in fact* most express trusts are created by means of written documents, since they arise either by will or in a formal settlement, carefully documented to meet the settlor's tax-planning needs. A modern trust precedent will be highly intricate and will attempt to provide for almost all conceivable contingencies. In this context—where there *is* a formal document—*Harrison v Gibson* [2006] 1 All ER 858 is authority that the entire document must be construed, giving the words used their natural meaning according to the context in which they appear. But in principle technical words are not necessary, since equity looks to the intention rather than the form of the transaction. It is not even necessary that the word 'trust' should have been employed, if the intention to create a trust is clear.

The second reason why Lord Langdale's statement is misleading is that even where words are present, the courts do not have regard to them alone, though they are important in construing the intention of the would-be settlor. Indeed, to rely on words alone as binding precedent would be dangerous, as the attitude of the courts has changed considerably over the last 150 years or so, especially regarding precatory words (i.e. words expressing a wish, hope or request, rather than being imperative).

4.2.2 History of precatory words

So far as testamentary gifts are concerned, up to about the middle of the nineteenth century the courts were disposed to find that almost any expression of desire by a testator that his property should be used in a given manner was intended to create a binding trust of that property in the hands of an executor or legatee. The reasons historically can be traced to the fact that the administration of estates lay formerly with the ecclesiastical courts, which permitted the executor to keep for himself any undisposed-of residue of property left after the specific bequests had been satisfied. When this jurisdiction was taken over by the Court of Chancery, it preferred to treat the executor as trustee of such residue for the testator's family. Almost any expression of desire or hope would be seized upon to effect this policy. Even this solution was not entirely satisfactory. Widows and eldest sons of gentry were often provided for in any event by a marriage settlement, or entail of the estate, and the courts were suspicious of their ability to manage the family property in prudent fashion (that is to say, keeping it in the family). Therefore a similar principle was applied to legatees as had formerly been applied to executors. The outcome was that precatory words like 'wish', 'hope', or even 'in confidence' that the legatee would use the gift to benefit others, were taken to create binding trusts.

4.2.2.1 *Precatory words and the courts' new approach from 1830*

The rationale for the lenient view taken of precatory words largely disappeared with the Executors Act of 1830, which specifically required executors to hold property in an appropriate manner. Since 1830, therefore, the courts have felt able to tighten up their attitude, the modern view being derived from the judgment of Cotton LJ in *Re Adams and the Kensington Vestry* (1884) 27 Ch D 394, 410, where it was established that beneficiaries were no longer to be made trustees unless this was the testator's clear intention, and a gift to the widow 'in full confidence that she would do what was right as to the disposal thereof between my children, either in her lifetime or by will after her decease' was treated as giving the widow an absolute interest unfettered by any trust in favour of the children. Cotton LJ thought that many of the older authorities had gone too far; he also thought that one should consider the total effect of the instrument (not only the particular words) to ascertain the testator's intention. Other cases around the same time made it clear that the attitude of the courts towards precatory words had changed.

4.2.3 **Law relating to precatory words**

Since intention is all important, however, a trust may still be created by precatory words, if such intention appears from the document (or settlor's conduct) as a whole. See, for example, the cases considered in chapter 3.

Because the whole document or transaction is to be considered, it does not follow that the same precatory words will always have the same effect. Thus, in *Re Hamilton* [1895] 2 Ch 370, 373, Lindley LJ said (of a testamentary gift):

You must take the will which you have to construe and see what it means, and if you come to the conclusion that no trust was intended, you say so, although previous judges have said the contrary on some wills more or less similar to the one you have to construe.

In *Cominsky v Bowring-Hanbury* [1905] AC 84, the House of Lords found a trust on the basis of words very similar to those employed in *Re Adams and the Kensington Vestry*: 'absolutely in full confidence that she [the widow] will make such use of [the property] as I would have made myself and that at her death she will devise it to such one or more of my nieces as she may think fit'.

4.2.3.1 *A testator's reproduction of exact language*

If on the other hand, a testator reproduces the exact language of an earlier will which has previously been held to create a trust, it may be possible to infer that he intended to use the earlier will as a precedent. If so, there is authority that the court in construing the later will should follow the earlier decision, at least unless that decision was clearly wrong (*Re Steele's WT* [1948] Ch 603). Though this case attaches great significance to the actual precatory words used, it is not really an exception to the flexible approach described above, because all the circumstances do indeed point to an intention to create a trust. It follows that draftsmen should make clear beyond doubt that precatory words are intended to indicate desire alone, unless of course a trust is indeed intended.

A further, somewhat technical, consideration is that the creation of a gift in a will, followed by the inclusion of a precatory expression in a codicil, raises a stronger inference of intention to create a trust than would be the case were both gift and precatory words to appear in the same instrument (*Re Burley* [1910] 1 Ch 215). Lastly, it should not be forgotten that the testator, while not intending to create a trust, may have subjected the property to a power of appointment (on which, see chapter 2) instead of making an outright gift to the legatee. In any case, the decision as to the testator's intention is a matter of construction of the document, and no hard and fast rule can be laid down for determining when this intention is present.

4.3 **Certainty of subject matter**

To satisfy the test it appears to be necessary that the trust property be defined in objective rather than subjective terms, or, in other words, so as not to be a matter on which opinions may reasonably differ. In *Palmer* v *Simmonds* (1854) 2 Drew 221, a testatrix left on trust 'the bulk' of her residuary estate, and Kindersley V-C, after consulting a dictionary, concluded that the word 'bulk' was inadequate to specify any portion of the property as trust property:

What is the meaning then of bulk? The appropriate meaning, according to its derivation, is something which bulges out…Its popular meaning we all know. When a person is said to have given the bulk of his property, what is meant is not the whole but the greater part, and that is in fact consistent with its classical meaning. When, therefore, the testatrix uses that term, can I say that she has used a term expressing a definite, clear, certain part of her estate, or the whole of her estate? I am bound to say that she has not designated the subject as to which she expresses her confidence; and I am therefore of opinion that there is no trust created; that [the residuary legatee] took absolutely, and those claiming under him now take.

Since it was not possible to carve out from the residue that portion which was to be held on trust, the trust failed and the residuary legatee took the whole absolutely. This is an application of what later became the rule in *Hancock* v *Watson* [1902] AC 14.

The same result was reached in *Curtis* v *Rippon* (1820) 5 Madd 434, where not only was there uncertainty as to the property to be subject to the trust, but also as to the identity of the beneficiaries themselves. The widow received all her husband's property under his will, subject to an exhortation (using precatory words that were valid at the time) that she should use the property for the spiritual and temporal good of herself and the children, 'remembering always, according to circumstances, the Church of God and the poor'. The clause rendered uncertain even who was to benefit.

4.3.1 **No certainty in absence of technical or objective meaning**

An approach similar to that in *Palmer* v *Simmonds* was taken in *Re Kolb's WT* [1962] Ch 531, where the testator referred, in an investment clause in his will, to 'blue-chip' securities, a term generally used to designate shares in large public companies which are considered an entirely safe investment. The term has no technical or objective meaning, however, and Cross J held that its meaning in the context must depend on the standard applied by the testator, which could not be determined with sufficient certainty to enable the clause to be upheld. The case was considered in a different context in *Trustees of the British Museum* v *Attorney-General* [1984] 1 WLR 418, which is discussed in chapter 17.

4.3.2 *Re Golay*: **a rogue decision or one which can be made sense of?**

In *Re Golay's WT* [1965] 1 WLR 969, the testator had directed his trustees to allow 'Totty' to 'enjoy one of my flats during her lifetime and to receive a reasonable income from my other properties'. Ungoed-Thomas J felt able to uphold the gift, as the trustees could select a flat, and the income to be received by Totty could be quantified objectively by the court. If, on the other hand, Totty had been entitled to receive what the testator or a specified person considered to be reasonable, then the trust would fail, since the test would be subjective.

The judgment in *Re Golay's WT* is very short, and the case appears to be out of line with the others considered. The test cannot simply be whether the income could be objectively quantified by the court, since a court could equally well quantify 'the bulk' or 'blue-chip securities'. Can it really be supposed that a court, faced with a statutory provision which applied to 'blue-chip securities' would be unable to apply the provision? The courts can define the reasonable man. Surely they would not be defeated by 'blue-chip securities'.

In *Re Golay's WT* it would appear that Ungoed-Thomas J misunderstood the function of a certainty test. The basis for the test seems not to be to make life easier for courts, but to ensure that the trustees can administer the trust. That is why precise objective definitions are required, so that the trustees know exactly which property is subject to the trust, and which property is not. A 'reasonable income' would not seem sufficiently certain to satisfy that criterion, unless the view were taken that the trustees should forever be coming to court to obtain directions.

4.3.3 *Hunter v Moss*: beautifully simple or fraught with difficulty?

In *Hunter v Moss* [1994] 1 WLR 452 (followed in *Re Lewis's of Leicester Ltd* [1995] 1 BCLC 428), an oral declaration of trusteeship of 50 shares of a company's issued share capital of 1,000 shares succeeded, even though the particular shares were not ascertained or identified. However, the company was precisely identified, all the shares in that company were identical, and the quantification (50 shares) was obviously precise. Moreover, as long as the trustee retained all 1,000 shares there would be no point in identifying which 50 shares were subject to the trust.

Difficulties in a case like *Hunter v Moss* could arise if the trustee later split up the fund, sold the shares, and invested some of the proceeds in fund A and some in fund B, one of which funds would then have performed better than the other. It would appear that this problem would not arise if the settlement had been of 5 per cent of the issued share capital, since then it would be clear that the trust owned 5 per cent of fund A and 5 per cent of fund B.

On the assumption that the case is correct, then the applicable principles ought to be those considered in chapter 19. The trustee is mixing trust funds with his own, and the decision in *Re Hallett's Estate* (1880) 13 Ch D 696 suggests that the beneficiaries could choose which fund held their share of the proceeds. If, however, the trustee had declared other trusts of the remaining shares, the contest would be between competing beneficiaries, and there would be no reason to apply *Hallett's Estate*. *Re Diplock* [1948] Ch 465 suggests that in such circumstances, a *pari passu* distribution would be appropriate.

4.3.4 *Hunter v Moss* criticised

All this presupposes that the decision in *Hunter v Moss* is correct, but it has come under fairly heavy academic criticism, e.g., Hayton [1994] 110 LQR 335, and has been regarded as inconsistent with the Privy Council decision in *Re Goldcorp*

Exchange [1995] 1 AC 74 (see also chapters 15 and 19), where an argument was unsuccessfully advanced that a seller of gold bullion (who had gone into liquidation having taken money from the purchasers) had become a trustee of an undivided share in his stocks. Peter Birks ([1995] RLR 83, 87) even went so far as to argue that from the reasoning of the Privy Council in *Re Goldcorp Exchange Ltd*: 'One inference is that the Court of Appeal's decision in *Hunter v Moss* [1994] 1 WLR 452 must be wrong.' In fact, neither case mentions the other, possibly because they were decided at virtually the same time, and there are quite significant differences between the two cases. In *Goldcorp*, there was no declaration of trusteeship by the vendor, so there is a certainty of intention problem; the trust property was not constant, since the vendor's gold stocks were being traded all the time; there is also much authority, for example in *Re Wait* [1927] 1 Ch 606, followed in *Re London Wine Co. (Shippers) Ltd* [1986] PCC 121, and *The Aliakmon* [1986] AC 785, for the reluctance of the courts to import notions of equitable property into commercial sales of goods, primarily for reasons connected with certainty. Any of these would have been quite convincing grounds, in my view, for distinguishing between *Hunter* and *Goldcorp*, even on the assumption that both cases are correct. A different distinction was, however, drawn by Neuberger J in *Re Harvard Securities* [1997] 2 BCLC 369; he took the view that if he was forced to choose between *Hunter* and *Goldcorp*, he was bound to follow the decision of the Court of Appeal in preference to that of the Privy Council, but also took the view that at any rate, for dealings in shares, Hunter was a correct statement of the law. The distinction between shares and other property seems difficult to justify in principle, however, and I cannot see the difficulty with *Hunter v Moss*, while recognising that *Goldcorp* is different, for all of the other three reasons stated above.

4.4 Certainty of objects

Certainty of objects rules serve two main functions. First, if a trustee, or donee of a power, fails to carry out his duties, or exercises his discretion in an improper manner, it is important to be able to ascertain who has *locus standi* to come to court to remedy the situation. Second, a trustee, or donee of a power, has to be able to ascertain who are the objects in order to be able to exercise his discretion in a proper manner.

4.4.1 Rationale of the rules: enforcement

Once a settlement has been made, whether it creates a trust or a power, the settlor ceases to have any interest in the property. Indeed, in the common case of a settlement by will he will naturally be unable to have any further personal say. The question then arises as to what happens if the trustee, or the donee of the power, does not carry out the trust or power. Sometimes a trustee will have agreed to act for consideration (e.g., a bank acting under a remuneration clause). In that case the settlor, or his personal representatives can sue at common law in contract. It is not an altogether satisfactory action, however, because unless he can obtain specific performance, he will be limited to claiming damages for his own loss, which will probably be nominal only. Therefore the courts have always been very concerned that someone who benefits in equity is able to enforce the trust.

The certainty requirements to achieve this end depend on the nature of enforcement by the courts. They have taken a more realistic and less rigid view in recent years of the manner in which trusts are to be ultimately enforced. This has led to a relaxation of certainty rules, which in most respects is to be welcomed.

Generally speaking, all that is now required for this purpose is for it to be possible to tell, with certainty, whether any individual coming to court to enforce a trust or power has sufficient interest to do so: in other words whether or not he is within the class of objects. This test is called the 'individual ascertainability test'. It is not necessary to be able to draw up a list of all the objects, a much more stringent requirement called the 'class ascertainability test'. Further, in applying the individual ascertainability test, it is necessary only that definitions in the settlement be conceptually certain. The court itself can deal with evidential difficulties when an application for enforcement arises. This is considered more fully shortly.

4.4.2 Rationale of the rules: administering the trust

Some writers argue (e.g., Matthews [1984] Conv 22) that this is not a proper function of certainty of objects rules at all, but the orthodox view is otherwise (see, e.g., Jill Martin in her reply in [1984] Conv 304). The certainty test required to enable trustees, or donees of powers, to discover all that is necessary for them to be able to carry out the trust depends on the nature of their discretion. Generally speaking, however, if a trustee, or donee, has to get any impression of the size or composition of the entire class in order to carry out his duties, a more stringent test is required than individual ascertainability.

4.4.3 Operation of the rules

The manner in which a settlement is ultimately enforced, and the nature of the discretion given to trustees or donees of powers, depends on whether a fixed trust, discretionary trust, or power has been created (see chapter 2 for the distinctions). The certainty of objects requirements vary accordingly, so it is necessary to consider separately the certainty requirements for each of these categories.

4.4.4 Powers

The nature of mere powers has been considered in chapter 2. Donees of a power (unlike discretionary trustees) have a discretion not only as to *how* to distribute the property, but also as to *whether* to distribute it. They are under no obligation to appoint at all, subject to limited exceptions. In other words, whereas a trust is imperative, because the trustees have to appoint, a power is discretionary, because the donees of a power need not appoint at all—the choice is theirs.

If there is a gift over in default of appointment, the disposition must take effect as a power, not a trust, since the existence of the gift over is obviously inconsistent with an imperative duty to appoint. The absence of a gift over in default is not necessarily indicative of a trust, however, since the alternative construction, of a power with a resulting trust in favour of the settlor in the absence of appointment, is also possible. It will all depend on the words used in the instrument.

4.4.4.1 *Certainty tests and powers of appointment*

In the case of mere powers (i.e. a power not given to a fiduciary), the donee's discretion seems to be unfettered except in so far that he must not dispose of the property otherwise than in accordance with the terms of the power. The objects can come to court to enforce the power, therefore, only to the limited extent that the court will restrain disposal of the property otherwise than in accordance with the terms of the power.

This limited negative duty can be carried out and enforced so long as 'it can be said with certainty that any given individual is or is not a member of the class'. No more stringent test of certainty than the individual ascertainability test is required.

It is probably more common for powers of appointment to be given to trustees, in which case the donees of the power will not enjoy an unfettered discretion. Sir Robert Megarry V-C took the view in *Re Hay's ST* [1982] 1 WLR 1202, that the extent of the duty to consider both whether or not a power should be exercised, and how it should be exercised, is stronger when the power is given to someone who is also a trustee, than when a mere power is exercised. For example, it is not sufficient simply to appoint to the objects who happen to be at hand, whereas the donee of a mere power can do this. It seems that it is necessary periodically to consider whether or not to exercise the power, and at least to appreciate the width of the field of objects, even if it is not possible to compile a list of all the objects, or ascertain accurately their number. Also, individual appointments need to be considered on their merits:

The trustee must not simply proceed to exercise the power in favour of such of the objects as happen to be at hand or claim his attention. He must first consider what persons or classes of persons are objects of the power within the definition in the settlement or will. In doing this, there is no need to compile a complete list of the objects, or even to make an accurate assessment of the number of them: what is needed is an appreciation of the width of the field, and thus whether a selection is to be made merely from a dozen, or, instead, from thousands or millions...

4.4.4.2 *Tests for certainty: the significance of (distinguishing) trusts and powers*

Nevertheless, if, at the end of the day, the donees of the power refuse to exercise it, that is a choice that they are entitled to make, and there is no reason why the courts should be required to distribute on their behalf. It is still necessary to be able to ascertain of any given individual whether or not he is an object of the power, since only objects of the power will have *locus standi* to enforce it, even to the limited extent of preventing the donees acting otherwise than in accordance with its terms. It is also necessary for the objects to be defined so that the donees can, as required by Sir Robert Megarry V-C above, get a feel for the width of the class.

Despite this, the duty to consider is not so stringent as to require the donees, in order to carry it out, to draw up a list of the entire class of potential beneficiaries, and there is therefore no reason in principle to apply the class ascertainability test to powers.

In *Re Gestetner's Settlement* [1953] 1 Ch 672, Harman J had to consider the validity of a power given to trustees to distribute among a very wide class, including directors and employees or former employees of a large number of companies, with a gift over in default. Since membership of the class constantly fluctuated, it was impossible to draw up a list of the entire class at any one time. He held that it was not necessary to know all the objects in order to appoint, and that it was not fatal that the entire class could not be ascertained.

In *Re Gulbenkian's Settlements* [1970] AC 508, trustees were given a power to apply income from the trust fund to maintain, among others, any person in whose house or in whose company or in whose care Gulbenkian may from time to time be residing, and there was a gift over in default of appointment. In upholding the power, the House of Lords held that the individual ascertainability test was the applicable test for powers: a power would be valid if it could be said with certainty whether any given individual was *or was not* a member of the class, and would not fail simply because it was impossible to ascertain every member of the class.

Note that the dispositions in both *Gestetner* and *Gulbenkian* must have been powers, as in each case there was a gift over in default of appointment. A gift over would be inappropriate in a discretionary trust, since the trustees are obliged to appoint.

4.4.4.3 *The significance of the Gulbenkian test*

There are two points specifically to note about the *Gulbenkian* test. First, the italicised words, *or was not*, are important. Second, the House of Lords expressly rejected Lord Denning MR's test in the Court of Appeal in *Gulbenkian* [1968] Ch 126, at pp. 132–34. On the basis that a power would only be held void for uncertainty if it was impossible to carry it out, he had taken the view that it should be necessary only to be able to identify one single beneficiary as being clearly within the class. The House of Lords disagreed, primarily because this test took no account of the trustees' duty to carry out the power in a fiduciary manner. The Denning test would only really be appropriate were the trustees at liberty to distribute to the first person who came to hand, and it has been shown that this is not the case. The Denning test is in any case no good for enforcement purposes, where the donees of the power propose to appoint somebody who is not the object of the power. Anybody coming to court for an injunction will have to show that he is an object, and also that the person in whose favour it is proposed to appoint is not. That requires the ability to determine of anybody whether or not he is within the class. It is not sufficient to be able to say of one person alone.

The importance of these two points will become apparent later in the chapter.

4.4.5 **Discretionary trusts**

The nature of discretionary trusts (sometimes called 'trust powers'), and the reasons for using them, were considered in chapter 2. As with mere powers, nobody who is an object can claim a defined interest, or indeed any interest at all, unless and until the trustees' discretion is exercised in his favour. But they differ from mere powers and fixed trusts in that the trustees are under an obligation to distribute the property.

Clearly, the extent to which a discretionary trust can be enforced is limited by its discretionary nature. The courts will, however, restrain the trustees from acting contrary to the terms of the trust instrument. And if they refuse to distribute at all, a court can remove them and appoint new trustees, or in the final analysis distribute the property itself. There are also ancillary rights enjoyed by potential beneficiaries under a discretionary trust: for example, in *Re Murphy's Settlements* [1998] 3 All ER 1, an order was obtained against the settlor to identify the trustees to enable the potential beneficiary to assert his rights against them.

Since 1971 the test for discretionary trusts has been assimilated to that for powers (i.e. individual ascertainability). However, the test is still slightly more stringent than that for powers because the trustees must distribute, and in order to exercise their discretion must have at least some idea of the range of objects. Also, at the end of the day, if they refuse to distribute, the court must be able to distribute in their place.

4.4.5.1 *The pre-1971 approach*

Before 1971 the approach of the courts was dictated by their view of ultimate enforcement. They took the view that if the trustees refused to distribute, the court could not itself exercise any discretion on their behalf (see, e.g., the view of Jenkins LJ in *IRC* v *Broadway Cottages Trust* [1955] Ch 20). The court could remove the trustees and appoint others in their place, but in theory it could be impossible to find any other trustees prepared to execute the trust. It followed that, however unlikely this eventuality might be, ultimately a court had to be prepared to carry out the trust itself. Since it refused to exercise any discretion it could only divide the property equally among all the objects.

'Ultimate enforcement': a matter of logic

Although there is a logic to this conclusion, given the premises, equality of distribution will often not implement the intentions of the settlor, and indeed is quite likely to frustrate them. It seems that the equality principle originated in nineteenth-century family settlements (e.g., *Burrough* v *Philcox* (1840) 5 My & Cr 72), where it may have been the most reliable method of carrying out the settlor's intention. It is much less likely to be appropriate, however, in modern settlements, for example, dividing proceeds among employees of a company.

Nevertheless, equality of distribution was the rule, and of course it could only be done if it was possible to draw up a list of all the objects. For this reason, *Broadway* applied the class ascertainability test to discretionary trusts.

The class in *Broadway* was undoubtedly extremely wide, consisting mostly of remote issue, as well as a number of charities. Two charities (Broadway Cottages Trust and Sunnylands Trust) had received income under the settlement, and claimed an income tax exemption on it, but in order to do so they had to show that the settlement was valid. The class was never held to be unascertainable, since the charities conceded the point (perhaps unwisely, since it was conceptually certain, and only evidential difficulties prevented drawing up an entire list of objects: see further the discussion on fixed trusts, below). The Crown for its part conceded that the individual ascertainability test was satisfied. On the basis of these concessions, the Court of Appeal held that the trust failed: *Gestetner* did not apply, since here there was no gift over, there was an obligation to distribute, and the whole range of objects had to be ascertainable.

'Ultimate enforcement', class ascertainment, and the only option of the court

Jenkins LJ took the view that if the court was called upon to enforce the trust 'it could not mend the invalidity of the trust by imposing an arbitrary distribution among some only of the whole unascertainable class'. The court could only effect a distribution to all the objects equally. The irony of this is that, given that some of the objects were charities and others people, equality of distribution was probably the last thing the settlor would have wanted.

One result of this case was that the test for certainty was much more stringent for discretionary trusts than for powers (on which, see above). This had two main consequences: first, many perfectly reasonable trusts failed; second, the courts were at pains to construe doubtful dispositions as powers, rather than discretionary trusts.

4.4.5.2 *Re Baden's Deed Trusts (No. 1),* McPhail v Doulton

In *Re Baden's Deed Trusts (No. 1), McPhail* v *Doulton* [1971] AC 424, however, the House of Lords decisively rejected the principle of equality of distribution in a case where equal distribution would have made a nonsense of the settlor's intention. The House accepted that even in the final analysis (in other words even assuming that no trustee can be found who is prepared to execute the trust), the court could exercise the necessary discretion itself. Therefore, the reasoning in the *IRC* v *Broadway Cottages Trust* [1955] Ch 20 was inapplicable (and indeed, *Broadway Cottages* was overruled). All that is required is for it to be possible to tell, with certainty, whether any individual coming to court to enforce a trust or power has sufficient interest to do so: in other words whether or not he is within the class of objects. This requirement is of course satisfied by the individual ascertainability test.

Re Baden: a test for discretionary trusts essentially the same as for powers

The *ratio* of *Re Baden's Deed Trusts (No. 1)* is that the test for certainty for discretionary trusts is essentially the same as that for powers, the individual ascertainability test, not the class ascertainability test.

Lord Wilberforce also made the point that in applying the test the courts are concerned only with conceptual uncertainty. A trust will not fail merely because there are evidential difficulties in ascertaining whether or not someone is within the class, as the court is never defeated by evidential uncertainty, and can deal with problems of proof when an application for enforcement arises:

I desire to emphasise the distinction clearly made...between linguistic or semantic uncertainty which, if unresolved by the court, renders the gift void, and the difficulty of ascertaining the existence or whereabouts of members of the class, a matter with which the court can appropriately deal on an application for directions.

Thus, a trust in favour of the first 20 people who crossed Clifton suspension bridge in 1996 should be enforceable: the class is conceptually certain even though proof may be difficult. A trust in favour of 'all my friends' is different, however. It is conceptually uncertain, because 'all my friends' is not a phrase capable of precise definition. Such a trust ought therefore to fail even on the *McPhail* v *Doulton* test.

4.4.5.3 *Problems of applying the individual ascertainability test*

The outcome in *Re Baden's Deed Trusts (No. 1)* was largely consequential on the court changing its views about the ultimate enforcement of a discretionary trust.

Unfortunately, the relaxation may lead to difficulties over administration. Unlike donees of mere powers, the trustees' discretion is not absolute. In considering its exercise, they must, according to Lord Wilberforce in *McPhail v Doulton* itself, make a survey of the entire field of objects, and consider each individual case responsibly, on its merits. This ought to require a more rigorous certainty test than individual ascertainability. For example, the Clifton suspension bridge example should fail (assuming no central record is kept of people walking over Clifton bridge), because the trustees could not possibly survey the entire field.

A new test and its impact upon trustees
Since under the new test trustees may be unable to discover the identities of all the possible beneficiaries, they will sometimes be unable to carry out their duties. Some discretionary trusts could be very difficult to administer were the trustees unable to survey the entire field of possible beneficiaries. An example might be a discretionary trust to distribute property 'according to the age and ability of the potential beneficiaries'.

Lord Wilberforce himself suggested a way out of the difficulty. He thought that even if a disposition satisfied the individual ascertainability test, it might fail if the class is so widely drawn as to be administratively unworkable. An example he gave was a gift to 'all the residents of Greater London', but the acceptable width of the class presumably depends on the exact nature of the trustees' duties, and whether they must actually survey the entire field (on which, see below).

A 'way out' for trustees: negating sensible intention
Another possible solution is that if the terms of a trust negative any sensible intention on the part of the settlor, it may fail on the grounds of capriciousness. This was suggested *obiter* by Templeman J in *Re Manisty's Settlement* [1974] Ch 17. The same applies, incidentally, to powers, and indeed *Manisty* actually concerned a valid power (see further below).

It is suggested that the real problem is the distinction, drawn by Lord Wilberforce, between, on the one hand, linguistic or semantic uncertainty which, if unresolved by the court, renders the gift void, and on the other hand, evidential difficulties of ascertaining the existence or whereabouts of members of the class (see below). This distinction does not seem rational and it loses sight of the purposes of certainty tests. Indeed, it was suggested earlier that the court (which is happy to apply the reasonable man test when required to do so) is no more defeated by linguistic or semantic uncertainty than it is by evidential difficulties. Trustees administering the trust, on the other hand, will be equally defeated by both types of uncertainty. Unfortunately, there are traces of the distinction in *Gulbenkian*, and it has been adopted by at least one of the judges in *Re Baden's Trusts (No. 2)* [1973] Ch 9 (see below), so it may well become entrenched in the law.

The new test and the doctrine of Saunders v Vautier
Another problem with the new certainty test is how, if at all, the doctrine in *Saunders* v *Vautier* (1841) 10 LJ Ch 354 applies. Under this doctrine (on which, see further, chapter 17), all the beneficiaries, collectively entitled, can (so long as they are adult and *sui juris*) terminate the trust and distribute or resettle the trust property. It is difficult to see how this doctrine can operate if the entire class of beneficiaries cannot be ascertained.

One possible answer is that *Saunders* v *Vautier* applies only to fixed trusts, on the grounds that the objects of a discretionary trust do not have full beneficial interests unless and until the trustees' discretion is exercised in their favour, but Lord Upjohn in *Gulbenkian* suggests otherwise. The other possible answer is that the courts would use a device similar to the *Benjamin* order discussed below (in relation to fixed trusts).

4.4.5.4 *Re Baden's Deed Trusts (No. 2)*

The disposition in *Re Baden's Deed Trusts* was remitted to the Chancery Division so that the House of Lords test could be applied. Eventually it came again to the Court of Appeal, where differing opinions were given: *Re Baden's Deed Trusts (No. 2)* [1973] Ch 9. By this time some twelve years had passed since Mr Baden's death, the fund was still sterilised by litigation, and a considerable proportion had been dissipated in legal costs. Sachs LJ observed that the situation 'lacks attraction'.

Baden No. 2: the Court of Appeal and the search for a workable position
The disposition was 'to or for the benefit of any of the officers and employees or ex-officers or ex-employees of the company or to any relatives or dependants of any such persons'. It was argued by John Vinelott QC, who was challenging the disposition on behalf of the executors, that it could not be shown that any person definitely is or *is not* within the class (as required by the *Gulbenkian* test). Had this ingenious argument been accepted it would have meant virtually returning to the rejected class-ascertainability test, as Megaw LJ observed. The Court of Appeal rejected the argument, but not on identical grounds.

Sachs LJ—a focus on evidential difficulties
Sachs LJ avoided the difficulty by emphasising that the court was concerned only with conceptual certainty, so that it should not be fatal that there might be *evidential* difficulties in drawing up John Vinelott QC's list. This effectively destroys the Vinelott argument, which was addressed primarily towards *evidential* difficulties in drawing up the class. Sachs LJ also took the view that the courts would place the burden of proof, in effect, on someone claiming to be within the class. This seems acceptable if ultimate enforcement is the issue, and the test is of the *locus standi* of the claimant, but it does not help the administration of the trust.

Megaw LJ—a focus on a 'substantial number'
Megaw LJ adopted a different solution requiring that, as regards a substantial number of objects, it can be shown with certainty that they fall within the class. This is rather a vague test—clearly it is not enough to be able to show that *one* person is certainly within the class, as this test was rejected in *Gulbenkian* (see the discussion of powers, above). Presumably, the test requires evidential, as well as conceptual, certainty. Maybe Megaw LJ adopted it simply because he could find no other way of rejecting Mr Vinelott's argument without returning either to the rejected *Broadway* test, or to the Denning test which had been rejected in *Gulbenkian*. Indeed, none of the judges in the Court of Appeal was able to find a satisfactory solution to this difficulty. The test may have the merit, however, of ensuring that the trustees will be able to get a feel for the width of the class, which they need to be able to exercise their discretion.

Stamp LJ—the strictest formulation of the test

Stamp LJ's test is probably the strictest of the three, and he seemed to be quite impressed by the Vinelott argument. He emphasised that it must be possible for the trustees to make a comprehensive survey of the range of objects, but he did not think it would be fatal if at the end of the survey it was impossible to draw up a list of every single beneficiary. He would have taken the view that the trust failed, had he not felt compelled to follow an early House of Lords authority, which had held that a discretionary trust for 'relations' was valid, 'relations' being defined narrowly as 'next-of-kin'.

Of the three tests, that of Sachs LJ will usually be the easiest to satisfy, but it relies heavily on an additional administrative unworkability test, the extent and application of which, as will become clear in the next section, are quite unclear. At this point the following is also suggested:

The Court of Appeal decision: what analysis can follow?

- The distinction drawn by Sachs LJ between conceptual and evidential uncertainty has its origin in Lord Wilberforce's speech in *McPhail* v *Doulton*, and indeed, there are traces of a similar distinction in *Gulbenkian*. The justification is that evidential distinctions can always be resolved by the courts, but, as was explained earlier, the courts can also resolve conceptual uncertainties. But surely, once the *Broadway* equality of distribution principle has been abandoned, the justification for certainty rules is not to assist the courts but rather to assist the trustees in administering the trust. And trustees will be defeated just as easily by evidential as by conceptual difficulties.

- If a class is conceptually certain then the only reason why a list of the entire class cannot be drawn up is evidential. The class ascertainability test, if it was ever meaningful at all, must have been an evidential test: if the test were simply conceptual, then there would be no difference between the individual and class ascertainability tests.

- It is suggested, therefore, that no good basis can be found for the conceptual/ evidential distinction. Proponents of Sachs LJ's view would respond that the test of administrative workability is sufficient to ensure that the trust is workable, but in that case it is reasonable to ask why any test is needed at all apart from administrative workability. In any case, evidential issues would now need to be dealt with by the administrative workability test, and it is not obvious that that is an improvement over dealing with them as part of the individual ascertainability test itself.

- Megaw LJ's test is evidential and addresses the problem of making the trust workable for trustees. It is therefore suggested that this is preferable to Sachs LJ's test.

- Stamp LJ's test is also evidential (indeed, entirely so, since 'next-of-kin' is not itself conceptually certain), but once the *Broadway* equality of distribution principle has been rejected, it is difficult to justify a test as strict as Stamp LJ's, since his test amounts virtually to a return to the class ascertainability test.

This, then, is an argument for preferring Megaw LJ's test, or at any rate a test similar to it.

4.4.5.5 *Administrative unworkability*

The question of administrative unworkability was considered in *Re Manisty's Settlement* [1974] Ch 17, where a power given to trustees was upheld where they were able to appoint anyone in the world apart from a small excepted class (a power where the objects are defined only by reference to an *excepted* class is called an intermediate or hybrid power). A similar decision was reached in *Re Hay's ST* [1982] 1 WLR 1202. These decisions suggest that very rarely will a power fail on grounds of administrative unworkability, simply because of the width of the class.

The courts are not concerned with questions of ultimate enforcement with a power, however, and it is arguable that the decisions in *Kay* and *Manisty* ought not to apply directly where, as here, the instrument is drafted as a trust. Indeed, in *Re Hay's ST* [1982] 1 WLR 1202 itself, Sir Robert Megarry V-C noted that: 'The words of Lord Wilberforce [about administrative unworkability]...are directed towards trusts, not powers.'

'Administrative (un)workability': what happens in the case of a trust?
The problem arose directly in the Divisional Court in *R v District Auditor, ex parte West Yorkshire Metropolitan County Council* [1986] RVR 24. Prior to the abolition of the Metropolitan County Councils, they were prohibited from incurring expenditure under the Local Government Act 1972, s. 137(1):

which in their opinion is in the interests of their area or any part of it or some or all of its inhabitants.

after 1 April 1985.

When West Yorkshire Metropolitan County Council realised that they were going to have a large surplus on 1 April 1985, they sought to find ways of ensuring that this money could still be spent after the 1 April deadline. In their attempt to achieve this aim, they purported to set up a discretionary trust of £400,000, having a duration of eleven months, 'for the benefit of any or all or some of the inhabitants of the County of West Yorkshire'. The trust also directed the trustees to use the fund specifically:

  (a) to assist economic development in the county in order to relieve unemployment and poverty;
  (b) to assist bodies concerned with youth and community problems;
  (c) to assist and encourage ethnic and other minority groups;
  (d) to inform all interested persons of the consequences of the proposed abolition of the Council (and the other Metropolitan County Councils) and of other programmes affecting local government in the county.

West Yorkshire: a case of an administratively unworkable trust?
This was held to be administratively unworkable. The inhabitants of the County of West Yorkshire numbered about two and a half million. The range of objects was held to be so hopelessly wide as to be incapable of forming anything like a class.

There are clear statements in the case that trusts may be treated differently from powers in this regard, since a court may be called upon ultimately to execute a trust, whereas it will not, of course, be required to execute a power.

The second possibility is that the terms of the trust negative any sensible intention on the part of the settlor. Indeed, in *Manisty*, Templeman J thought this was the real problem over 'residents of Greater London':

The settlor neither gives the trustees an unlimited power which they can exercise sensibly, nor a power limited to what may be described as a 'sensible' class, but a power limited to a class, membership of which is accidental and irrelevant to any settled purpose or to any method of limiting or selecting beneficiaries.

In addressing these issues the width of the class is not the only factor, since other factors may make clear what the intention of the settlor was. For example, in *Re Hay's ST* [1982] 1 WLR 1202, Sir Robert Megarry V-C said of this passage:

In *Re Manisty's Settlement* [1974] Ch 17 at 27 Templeman J appears to be suggesting that a power to benefit 'residents in Greater London' is void as being capricious 'because the terms of the power negative any sensible intention on the part of the settlor'. In saying that, I do not think that the judge had in mind a case in which the settlor was, for instance, a former chairman of the Greater London Council, as subsequent words of his on that page indicate.

Alternatively, suppose that trustees were directed to use the fund, in their discretion, to provide library facilities for the residents of Greater London. It might also be perfectly possible to infer a sensible intention on the part of the settlor. On the other hand, fairly precise guidelines were laid down in *R v District Auditor, ex parte West Yorkshire Metropolitan County Council*, but this was still insufficient to save the trust.

Suppose that even the class ascertainability test is satisfied. Then it could not be said that the disposition was administratively unworkable, because clearly the trustees could survey the entire class. Presumably, the disposition could still fail, however, if the terms were such as to negative any sensible intention on the part of the settlor.

4.4.6 Fixed trusts

It is usually argued that, since it is of the essence of a fixed trust that the property is to be divided among all the beneficiaries in fixed proportions (e.g., in equal shares), it can only be workable if the entire class of beneficiaries is known. The conventional view, therefore, is that the test of certainty is the class ascertainability test.

This was certainly the view of Jenkins LJ in *IRC v Broadway Cottages Trust* [1955] Ch 20, at p. 29:

There can be no division in equal shares amongst a class of persons unless all the members of the class are known.

In other words, a complete list of objects must be able to be drawn up. From the fact that in *McPhail v Doulton* [1971] AC 424, the House of Lords was concerned only to assimilate discretionary trusts and powers, the implication usually drawn is that the reasoning was not intended also to apply to fixed trusts.

However, there are fairly convincing contrary arguments (see, e.g., Matthews [1984] Conv 22). The orthodox view presupposes that *Broadway* still stands insofar that later cases have not directly detracted from it, but it is arguable that even when it was decided, *Broadway* was wholly out of line with other authorities, in which case there is no reason for it still to be regarded as authority for anything at all.

It is suggested that the central issue is the basis upon which the trust property is distributed by the trustees, or if the issue becomes one of ultimate enforcement, by the courts. It is often assumed that distribution is impossible unless the entire class can be ascertained, but this need not be the case, and even if it is, application of the class ascertainability test may not necessarily resolve the difficulty.

4.4.6.1 *A fixed trust: how it might work*

Suppose, for example, that in 1986 Michael settled property upon trustees with directions that in 1991 the property was to be sold, and that the proceeds of sale were to be distributed equally, in favour of those of his three sons, Paul, Quentin, and Richard, who are still then living. Assuming that in 1986 all three of the settlor's sons were known to be alive, it is obvious that this is a fixed trust, and that it satisfies the class ascertainability test.

Suppose now that at some time after 1986 Richard went on an Antarctic expedition, from which by 1991 he has not returned. He is thought (but not known definitely) to have perished on the expedition. The trustees sell the property, and wish to distribute it in accordance with their directions. Despite the fact that the class ascertainability test was clearly satisfied, and that the trust did not fail for want of certainty, they clearly have a problem.

If at this point the trustees asked for directions, it is likely that the court would resolve the difficulty by making a *Benjamin* order (based on *Re Benjamin* [1902] 1 Ch 723). The trustees would be directed to distribute on the basis that Richard was dead. If Richard later turned up alive, he would still have an interest in the proceeds of sale, which he would be able to claim from Paul and Quentin if it were still traceable, and assuming that his claim was not barred by limitation. The trustees personally would be protected from any action, however.

It is clear, then, that evidential difficulties, even in the distribution of fixed trusts, can be resolved by the courts. Is there any reason of logic or principle why the position should be any different if, by the time of the settlement in 1986, Richard had already embarked upon the expedition, and it was not known even then whether he was alive or dead? In those circumstances it would not after all, be possible at the date of the settlement, to draw up a list of all the objects, since it would not be possible to say with certainty whether Richard should be included or not. A strong argument can therefore be made that there is no need to apply the class ascertainability test, even to fixed trusts.

As explained earlier, in applying the individual ascertainability test, Lord Wilberforce distinguished between evidential and conceptual uncertainty, on the ground that the courts are never defeated by evidential uncertainty. Does it follow that, if the class ascertainability test does still apply to fixed trusts, the same distinction also applies? If so, it leads to some interesting consequences.

4.4.6.2 *Fixed trusts and the significance of Broadway Cottages*

In *Broadway* (see 4.4.5.1), although the class was very large, it was not conceptually uncertain. There was no problem defining the class conceptually, and *it was conceded* in *Broadway*, rather than concluded from rational argument, that the class could not be ascertained. Perhaps the concession was wrongly made, and in reality, even in *Broadway* itself, the class ascertainability test was satisfied. *Broadway* was indeed criticised in *Re Gulbenkian's Settlements* [1970] AC 508 (in particular, by Lords Reid and Upjohn), and by Lord Wilberforce in *McPhail* v *Doulton* (above), on the grounds that the Court of Appeal had confused conceptual and evidential uncertainty.

If, however, the distinction between conceptual and evidential uncertainty applies equally to the class as to the individual ascertainability test, it is difficult to see any difference between the two tests. If it can be said of any individual that he or she falls outside the class, then there can be no conceptual difficulty in defining the class as a whole. Indeed, there is no *conceptual* difficulty in defining the class in the above example, merely an evidential difficulty in ascertaining whether Richard is a member. In principle, however, evidential difficulties, as in *Broadway* and the example, are capable of resolution by the courts.

4.4.6.3 *Fixed trusts and some concluding thoughts*

It is suggested, however, that the class ascertainability test has always been an evidential test, and that the distinction between conceptual and evidential uncertainty has only ever been applied to the individual ascertainability test. Even there, we have already argued that it is inappropriate. Further, if it is accepted that a function of the certainty of object test is to ensure that the trust is administratively workable, then even if one accepts that there is no need to apply the class ascertainability test to fixed trusts, one can argue for a more rigorous test than for discretionary trusts. One way of achieving this is to apply different tests of administrative workability, since it does not follow that merely because a discretionary trust is administratively workable with a given class of objects, a trust with the same class of objects will necessarily be so if the trustees' discretion is removed. It is

Duties of trustees	Arguments for class ascertainability	Arguments for individual ascertainability
Must distribute according to instrument	*Fixed trusts* Necessary to enable trustees to distribute	Distribution on basis of *Benjamin* order
Must distribute— discretion as to how	*Discretionary trusts* Ultimate enforcement Trustees need to ascertain entire class in order to decide how to exercise their discretion	*Locus standi* Class ascertability test leads to unjust results Administrative unworkability/ capriciousness safeguards sufficient
Need not distribute, but must consider whether to do so and if so how	*Powers* As above, except that ultimate enforcement no longer an issue	As above, except that *locus standi* only to prevent distribution inconsistent with power

Figure 4.1 Fixed trusts, discretionary trusts, and powers

probably more satisfactory, however, to have a stricter certainty test for fixed trusts, albeit perhaps a test not as strict as the class ascertainability test.

4.5 The beneficiary principle and private purpose trusts

The principles relating to private (i.e. non-charitable) purpose trusts follow on naturally from the discussion on certainty of objects and particularly the primacy of the 'beneficiary principle' considered in the previous chapter.

4.5.1 Private purpose trusts

Purpose trusts may either be for a pure purpose (e.g., a trust to advance a cause), where no individual directly benefits, or for the benefit of an ascertainable group of people (e.g., a trust to build a school swimming pool). A private (non-charitable) purpose trust of the first type is usually struck down, because it is not enforceable by anyone. Charitable trusts (which are dealt with in chapters 12–14) are always purpose trusts, and are valid, but problems of enforcement do not arise as the Attorney-General has *locus standi* to sue.

Where an ascertainable group of people is intended to benefit, it appears that the trust is valid.

4.5.2 The beneficiary principle

The materials which have considered certainty requirements emphasised the importance of trusts being enforceable, and in the absence of state enforcement (which occurs only for charities) this means that there must be a person with a sufficient interest to enforce the trust. As long ago as 1804, Sir William Grant MR observed, in *Morice* v *Bishop of Durham* (1804) 9 Ves 405, that 'There must be somebody, in whose favour the court can decree performance'. Who this person might be, and the precise nature of the enforcement, were not made clear in *Morice* v *Bishop of Durham*, but it will be suggested shortly that this has now been taken to mean that there has to be a beneficiary, and this case is often said to be the foundation of the 'beneficiary principle'. Leaving aside these arguments for the present, what is clear is that where the purpose is sufficiently abstract and impersonal as not directly to benefit any identifiable human being, there is nobody to enforce the trust. *Morice* v *Bishop of Durham* implies that dispositions of this nature, unless charitable, should generally therefore be void. Examples of such purposes might be the preservation of peace between nations, or the abolition of vivisection, where no individual clearly has sufficient interest to enforce the trust.

Similar sentiments to those of Sir William Grant MR were echoed by Lord Parker of Waddington in *Bowman* v *Secular Society Ltd* [1917] AC 406 at p. 441:

A trust to be valid must be for the benefit of individuals...or must be in that class of gifts for the benefit of the public which the courts in this country recognise as charitable...

(Note, however, that these views in the House of Lords are *dicta*, since the case actually concerned a valid gift to a company.)

4.5.2.1 *A principle with a respectable pedigree and universal application?*

Yet although the beneficiary principle has a respectable pedigree, it is only relatively recently that it has become regarded as universally applicable. Exceptions developed to it. Trusts to erect or maintain tombs and monuments were upheld, as in *Pirbright* v *Salwey* [1896] WN 86, which was a trust to decorate a family burial enclosure. Also upheld were trusts for the maintenance of specific animals (e.g., *Re Dean* (1889) 41 Ch D 522) and (in *Re Thompson* [1934] Ch 342) a trust for the promotion and furtherance of fox hunting. It was arguable that the exceptions were of sufficient width as to negate the beneficiary principle, or at any rate to limit it to testamentary dispositions.

4.5.2.2 *The modern view:* Re Astor's ST

The tide turned, and the modern view can probably be said to trace its origins to *Re Astor's ST* [1952] Ch 534 (discussed in depth by L.A. Sheridan (1953) 17 LQR 46), where trustees were instructed to hold a fund upon various trusts including 'the maintenance of good relations between nations [and]...the preservation of the independence of newspapers'. The purposes were not charitable, but the settlement was drafted expressly (by limiting its duration) so as to be valid under the perpetuity rules (see chapter 6). The trust was held to be void, because there were no human beneficiaries capable of enforcing it. Roxburgh J held that the exceptions discussed above did not negate the general principle, or limit it to testamentary dispositions, and observed that some of the cases could be explained as trusts which were enforceable by the residuary beneficiary. This is not entirely satisfactory, however, since the residuary beneficiary has no interest in enforcing the trust, and the exception implies that wherever there is a gift over, any purpose trust that does not infringe perpetuity principles will be enforceable. It would be more satisfactory to explain these exceptional cases as incorrect, but presumably Roxburgh J felt unable to do this at first instance.

A similar case to *Astor*, where there were no clearly identifiable human beneficiaries, was *Re Shaw* [1957] 1 WLR 729, where Harman J held void on the same principle a trust to research into the development of a 40-letter alphabet. The case concerned the will of George Bernard Shaw, and although by 1950, when the will was made, Shaw was already 94 years old, Harman J noted its 'youthful exuberance'. Having also commented that the author was an indefatigable reformer, Harman J went on to note the 'marriage of incompatibles' in the will between Shaw's own work and that of a skilled equity draftsman: 'The two styles, as ever, make an unfortunate mixture.' Only copyrights and royalties were settled in the will, but these were far greater than anticipated—hence the litigation.

The purposes included the following:

(1) To institute and finance a series of inquiries to ascertain as far as possible the following statistics
   (a) the number of extant persons who speak the English language and write it by the established and official alphabet of 26 letters (hereinafter called Dr Johnson's alphabet);
   (b) how much time could be saved per individual scribe by the substitution for the said alphabet of an alphabet containing at least 40 letters (hereinafter called the proposed British alphabet)...;

(c) how many of these persons are engaged in writing or printing English at any and every moment in the world;

(d) on these factors to estimate the time and labour wasted by our lack of at least 14 unequivocal single symbols;

(e) to add where possible…estimates of the loss of income in British and American currency…

(2) To employ a phonetic expert to transliterate my play entitled 'Androcles and the Lion' into the proposed British alphabet assuming the pronunciation to resemble that recorded of His Majesty our late King George V, and sometimes described as Northern English…

The purposes having been held non-charitable (on which see further chapter 13), the settlement was struck down on the grounds that there were no identifiable beneficiaries who could enforce it.

4.5.2.3 *Reasons of policy against purpose trusts*

In cases of this type, the courts may have been reluctant to uphold the trusts for other reasons also. For example, Roxburgh J in *Astor* thought that it was against public policy to allow large accumulations of private capital to be dispersed with no administrative state control. These reasons cannot be decisive, however, as they could be applied to all non-charitable trusts, whether or not purpose trusts. The courts in any case disallow trusts for useless or capricious purposes (see further chapter 5).

4.5.2.4 *Explaining cases which do not comply with the beneficiary principle*

There remain the cases, described above, which do not comply with the beneficiary principle. It has been seen that they were regarded as exceptions in *Re Astor's ST*, and similarly in *Re Endacott* [1960] Ch 232, where a gift 'to North Tawton Devon Parish Council for the purpose of providing some useful memorial to myself…' was held void by the Court of Appeal. Cases such as *Re Dean* (1889) 41 Ch D 522 and *Re Thompson* [1934] Ch 342 were regarded as anomalous and not to be extended. It is a pity, however, that the Court of Appeal did not take the opportunity to over-rule them, as it is very difficult to know exactly what they stand for, or on what principle they operate, or the basis upon which they are enforced.

All private trusts are subject to the rule against perpetuities (see chapter 6), and if trusts such as those in *Re Dean* and *Re Thompson* remain valid today, there are no beneficial interests capable of vesting. At common law, therefore, these were subject to the rule against inalienability, which rendered void any such trusts which were capable of lasting beyond 21 years. Moreover, with trusts of this type, neither the alternative 80-year period nor the wait-and-see provisions of the Perpetuities and Accumulations Act 1964 would seem to apply. It therefore follows that if such trusts remain valid at all, they must be limited to a maximum duration of 21 years.

It may also be possible to make provision for a pure purpose indirectly, using a device. One such device is considered in chapter 12. A gift is made to charity A so long as it maintains the testator's grave to the satisfaction of the testator's trustees, with a gift over to charity B. The gift over is exempt from perpetuity rules (see chapter 6), so long as B is a charity. If B is not a charity the gift over will fail for perpetuity unless the gift is appropriately limited in duration: *Re Wightwick* [1950] 1 Ch 260.

There is authority, however, that a trust to pay income to a corporation so long as the corporation maintains the testator's grave to the satisfaction of his trustees is not subject to perpetuity, at any rate at common law. In *Re Chardon* [1928] 1 Ch 464, the will provided:

I give unto my trustees the sum of two hundred pounds free of duty upon trust to invest the same upon any of the investments hereinafter authorised and pay the income thereof to the South Metropolitan Cemetery Company West Norwood during such period as they shall continue to maintain and keep the graves of my great grandfather and the said Priscilla Navone in the said Cemetery in good order and condition with flowers and plants thereon as the same have hitherto been kept by me.

Romer J held the gift valid, and the decision was followed in *Re Chambers* [1950] 1 Ch 267. It depended on the gift of the income being absolute: *Re Wightwick* [1950] 1 Ch 260.

In *Re Chardon*, if the graves were not maintained the cemetery company would have ceased to be entitled to the income; a resulting trust would have arisen and the income fallen into residue. At common law, a resulting trust probably did not attract the perpetuity rules (*Re Chardon* was decided on the common law perpetuity rule). Today, the disposition would be caught under the Perpetuities and Accumulations Act 1964, s. 12, so this device no longer works.

4.5.2.5 *Purpose trusts for benefit of identifiable objects*

Sometimes, on the other hand, identifiable people are intended directly to benefit, but the gift is nevertheless limited for a particular purpose. Here the problem is different. There are people (who must be ascertainable within the certainty of object tests discussed earlier) with an interest in enforcing the trust. It may be possible to regard these people as entitled to a full beneficial interest, subject to a condition (e.g., direction to the trustees to apply the fund only for a particular purpose), in which case these are simply ordinary private trusts.

Re Abbott: *a 'right result' and a plethora of difficulties?*
For example, *Re Abbott* [1900] 2 Ch 326, which concerned a trust for the maintenance of two old ladies, was upheld (see further chapter 8). There was no question of the trust being invalid, even though the fund is clearly intended to be used for a purpose, rather than simply given to the two ladies. Yet the case is probably best analysed as an ordinary trust for the two ladies, with a direction to the trustees to apply the fund only for their maintenance. In other words, this is not, in reality, treated as a purpose trust at all.

Suppose, however, that although objects can be found with an interest in enforcing the trust, none is entitled to a full beneficial interest. Although the contrary view is arguable, it is probable that only where a full beneficial interest is granted to the identifiable objects will the disposition be valid. In *Leahy v Attorney-General for New South Wales* [1959] AC 457, property was to be held on trust for 'such order of nuns of the Catholic Church or the Christian brothers as my executors and trustees shall select'. The trust was not charitable, and Viscount Simonds in the Privy Council thought that it failed as a private trust on the ground that, even though the individual members had an interest in enforcing the trust, they were not granted a full beneficial interest:

If the words 'for the general purposes of the association' were held to import a trust, the question would have to be asked, what is the trust and who are the beneficiaries? A gift can be made to persons (including a corporation) but it cannot be made to a purpose or to an object; so also, a trust may be created for the benefit of persons as *cestuis que trust*, but not for a purpose or object unless the purpose or object be charitable. For a purpose or object cannot sue, but, if it be charitable, the Attorney-General can sue to enforce it.... It is therefore by disregarding the words 'for the general purposes of the association' (which are assumed not to be charitable purposes) and treating the gift as an absolute gift to individuals that it can be sustained.

Leahy: *a gift can be made to a person, but not to an object*

A gift can therefore be made to a person, but not to an object.

Viscount Simonds's views in *Leahy* are technically *obiter dicta*, because the case is also explicable on other grounds. The gift ought also to have failed for perpetuity (although in the event it was validated by the New South Wales Conveyancing Act). Obviously, however, the reasoned views of the Judicial Committee of the Privy Council must be regarded as very strong authority, in the absence of authority to the contrary.

Somewhat inconclusive contrary authority can be found in *Re Denley's Trust Deed* [1969] 1 Ch 373, where Goff J thought that the *Astor/Endacott* principles invalidated only 'abstract or impersonal' purpose trusts:

I think there may be a purpose or object trust, the carrying out of which would benefit an individual or individuals, where that benefit is so indirect or intangible or which is otherwise so framed as not to give those persons any *locus standi* to apply to the court to enforce the trust, in which case the beneficiary principle would, as it seems to me, apply to invalidate the trust, quite apart from any question of uncertainty or perpetuity. Such cases can be considered if and when they arise. The present is not, in my judgment, of that character, and it will be seen that...the trust deed expressly states that, subject to any rules and regulations made by the trustees, the employees of the company shall be entitled to the use and enjoyment of the land. Apart from this possible exception, in my judgment the beneficiary principle of *Re Astor's ST* [1952] Ch 534, which was approved in *Re Endacott* [1960] Ch 232, CA—see particularly by Harman LJ—is confined to purpose or object trusts which are abstract or impersonal. The objection is not that the trust is for a purpose or object *per se*, but that there is no beneficiary or *cestui que trust*.

He went on to say that:

Where, then, the trust, though expressed as a purpose, is directly or indirectly for the benefit of an individual or individuals, it seems to me that it is in general outside the mischief of the beneficiary principle.

Re Denley: *what reasoning is at work?*

These quotations are unfortunately not entirely clear. One view is that the test is not whether a full beneficial interest is granted, but whether individuals who are ascertainable have *locus standi* to sue. They will have so long as the benefit is not too indirect or intangible. The trust (which was upheld by Goff J) was 'for the purpose of a recreation or sports ground primarily for the benefit of the employees of the company', with a gift over at the end of the perpetuity period to the General Hospital, Cheltenham. This view of *Denley* was adopted by Megarry J in *Re Northern Developments (Holdings) Ltd*, unreported, 6 October 1978.

Another view of *Denley*, however, is that Goff J construed it as a trust for individuals, and not as a purpose trust at all. If this view is correct then the case breaks no new ground, and all private purpose trusts remain void, apart from the anomalous exceptions discussed above. This view was taken, for example, by Vinelott J in *Re Grant's WT* [1980] 1 WLR 360 (at p. 370):

That case [*Denley*] on a proper analysis, in my judgment, falls altogether outside the categories of gifts to unincorporated association and purpose trusts. I can see no distinction in principle between a trust to permit a class defined by reference to employment to use and enjoy land in accordance with rules to be made at the discretion of trustees on the one hand, and, on the other hand, a trust to distribute income at the discretion of trustees amongst a class, defined by reference to, for example, relationship to the settlor. In both cases the benefit to be taken by any member of the class is at the discretion of the trustees, but any member of the class can apply to the court to compel the trustees to administer the trust in accordance with its terms.

A similar view can be found in (1985) 101 LQR 269, at pp. 280–82 (P.J. Millett QC).

After Re Denley: *what happens now?*
Given that the trust was enforceable in *Denley*, and that similar trusts will continue to be enforceable, does it matter how the case is analysed? It could certainly affect the applicable perpetuity period. Consider also the question of enforcement. If the trustees decided to use the fund to install a kidney machine for the benefit of the patients, then that can be relatively easily prevented by injunction. Suppose, however, the trustees do nothing, and no trustees can be found to build and/or maintain the sports ground. Specific performance cannot be awarded, as constant supervision would be required, and an injunction is clearly of no use.

At the end of the day, it is difficult to see what solution can be adopted, apart from distribution of the income from the fund directly to the employees of the company (not the capital, because of the gift over). That puts them into exactly the same position as a beneficiary under an ordinary fixed or discretionary trust.

The issue could also arise if the objects of the trust wanted to terminate it on the basis of *Saunders* v *Vautier* (see chapter 17, and the discussion of discretionary trusts earlier). Presumably, only beneficiaries in the conventional sense can invoke this doctrine, and if the objects of a *Denley*-style purpose have a lesser interest, they will be unable to do so.

Whatever *Denley* decides, pure purpose trusts, such as *Re Astor's ST* [1952] Ch 534 (above), are unaffected by it, and are still void. It is also clear that the individuals to whom direct or indirect benefit is given must be ascertainable within the certainty of object requirements: in *R* v *District Auditor, ex parte West Yorkshire Metropolitan County Council* [1986] RVR 24, an alternative argument that the disposition created a valid private purpose trust failed, since whatever *Denley* decided, and indeed even if there were objects with full beneficial interests, they were not ascertainable under the certainty of objects rules.

 online resource centre

FURTHER READING

Bridge 'The *Quistclose* Trust in a World of Secured Transactions' (1992) Oxford Journal of Legal Studies, 333.

Brown 'What Are We to Do with Testamentary Trusts of Imperfect Obligation?' (2007) Conveyancer 148.

Gravells 'Public Purpose Trusts' (1977) Modern Law Review 397.

Hayton 'Uncertainty of Subject Matter of Trusts' (1994) Law Quarterly Review 335.

Martin and Hayton 'Certainty of Objects: What is Heresy?' (1984) Conveyancer 304.

Matthews 'Heresy and a Half in Certainty of Objects' (1984) Conveyancer 22.

Pawlowski and Summers 'Private Purpose Trusts: A Reform Proposal' (2007) Conveyancer 440.

5

Formalities and other requirements for validity

This chapter looks further at requirements for validity not considered in chapter 4. Only express trusts (whether charitable or not) are subject to all the requirements considered in this chapter, implied, resulting, and constructive trusts (see chapters 7 to 11 and 19) being expressly exempted from the statutory formality requirements of the Law of Property Act 1925, s. 53.

5.1 Introduction to the formalities requirements

There are no formality requirements for trusts, except those laid down by statute; these are now contained in the Law of Property Act 1925 s. 53. The important distinctions to bear in mind are between land and other property, and between declarations and dispositions.

Implied, resulting, and constructive trusts are expressly exempted from the statutory requirements, and so, it appears, are variations of trust carried out under the Variation of Trusts Act 1958 (on which see chapter 17). As appears below, however, the distinction between implied, resulting, and constructive trusts, on the one hand, and express trusts, on the other, may be less important than it appears at first sight; it is probable that express trusts can also, in some circumstances, fall outside the operation of s. 53, even though they are not expressly exempted.

5.1.1 Reasons for the rules

Land is subject to special rules because of its value, and also because real property (i.e. land) transactions are sufficiently complex for it to be undesirable for them to be taken lightly. So far as other property is concerned, the purpose of legislation on formalities is twofold. Bear in mind that equitable interests are intangible, and that it may not be possible to trace their movement unless that movement is evidenced by written documents. The primary purpose of a writing requirement is to prevent fraud—indeed the original statute was entitled the Statute of Frauds 1677. The secondary purpose is to enable the trustees to ascertain where the equitable interests lie, to enable them to carry out the trusts.

5.1.2 The tax angle

The litigation has borne little relation to these primary and secondary purposes, however. It will become apparent that whereas declarations of trusts do not (generally) require writing, dispositions of equitable interests do. The question of what amounts to a disposition has received attention from the courts in recent years, due in part to attempts by settlors to avoid payment of *ad valorem* stamp duty (now abolished on *inter vivos* gifts). Stamp duty is imposed, not upon a transaction itself, but upon the written instrument by which property is transferred. All documents under seal, whatever their value, require a nominal 50p stamp, but more important was the additional *ad valorem* duty, whose amount was calculated as a proportion of the value of the interest being transferred. If the value of such interest was nothing, as (for example) where a bare legal estate carrying no right to beneficial enjoyment was transferred, no *ad valorem* duty was payable. It is the beneficial interest which is valuable, and if that was transferred in writing, then substantial *ad valorem* duty was payable on the written instrument. Taxpayers therefore obviously preferred to avoid transferring the valuable beneficial interest in writing if they could, arguing instead that only the legal interest had been transferred by the written instrument, the beneficial interest having been transferred orally.

With the abolition of *ad valorem* stamp duty on *inter vivos* gifts in 1985, the practical implications of much of the discussion in the first part of this chapter have disappeared. The theoretical basis remains, however, and the *Vandervell* litigation (see below shortly) still raises (albeit incidentally) live taxation issues.

5.2 Land

All the formalities which are required in the case of personalty are also needed in the case of land, but there are additional requirements also. Section 53(1)(b) of the Law of Property Act 1925 provides:

A declaration of trust respecting any land or any interest therein must be manifested and proved by some writing signed by some person who is able to declare such trust or by his will.

This provision applies to freehold and leasehold land, and also to a share in the proceeds of sale of land. The trust need not actually be declared in writing, since what is necessary is that the declaration should be evidenced in writing, and no special form of document is needed—indeed, the necessary writing may be supplied by an exchange of correspondence or the like. The writing must, however, bear the signature of the settlor and not merely his agent. Failure to comply with s. 53(1)(b) will probably not render the trust void, but only unenforceable in the absence of evidence in writing.

For further discussion of s. 53(1)(b), see chapter 9.

5.3 Declarations of trust: personalty

As far as personalty is concerned, a settlor (assuming he is *legal* owner) may create a trust merely by manifesting the intention to create it, and no special formalities are required. So, for example, the simple declaration by the owner of, for example, a stamp collection that he holds it in trust for his nephew will be effective to create a trust of the collection. Even personalty of great value may, in theory, be settled with no greater formality than this. This is true only for *inter vivos* gifts, however. If it is desired to create a trust by will, then the will itself must comply with the provisions of s. 9 of the Wills Act 1837, as amended by the Administration of Justice Act 1982, s. 17, which will be dealt with in the chapter on secret and half-secret trusts (chapter 10).

In fact, as a matter of practice, even with *inter vivos* gifts, the intention to create a trust will usually be declared in a written document setting out in detail the terms of the trust: a major motive for the creation of settlements is tax planning, and documentary evidence for this purpose is often highly desirable.

5.4 **Dispositions of equitable interests**

Dispositions of equitable interests are void, whether in land or personalty, unless in writing. Section 53(1)(c) of the Law of Property Act 1925 provides:

> [A] disposition of an equitable interest or trust subsisting at the time of the disposition must be in writing signed by the person disposing of the same, or by his agent thereunto lawfully authorised by writing or by will.

This provision covers both land and personalty, and even in the case of land it is much more stringent than s. 53(1)(b). The disposition must *itself* be in writing, not merely manifested and proved by writing, and failure to comply probably renders the disposition void, not merely unenforceable.

If the law were to accord with the policy discussed above, dispositions would be defined so as to include dealings with the beneficial interest which can be kept secret from the trustees, but to exclude other dealings. After all, the whole reason for treating dispositions of equitable interests differently from other dispositions is precisely because of the difficulties which would ensue were the trustees to be kept unaware of them. The precursor to this section, s. 9 of the Statute of Frauds 1677, caught 'grants and assignments', clearly reflecting this policy, but the term 'disposition' is at least theoretically wider.

Nevertheless, generally speaking the definition of 'dispositions' accords in general with the policy described. The creation of a trust, by declaration, is outside the scope of the section. So, in general, is its extinguishment (by merger with the legal interest). If the purpose of formality rules is to prevent hidden transactions which prevent trustees from ascertaining who the beneficiaries are, there is no reason ever to require them where the legal and equitable interests merge. The same ought also to apply to the extinguishment of equitable interests.

Transfers or assignments of existing equitable interests, on the other hand, normally require writing. They are within the mischief covered by the legislation if the trustees are not party to the arrangement, but not, one would have thought, if the trustees themselves are directed to transfer the interests. Nevertheless, *Grey* v *IRC* [1960] AC 1 suggests that writing is required even in this situation, and it is thus suggested that the decision is not in accord with the policy described above.

The position is not clear for a surrender of an equitable interest. A surrender cannot, of course, be kept secret from the trustees, and on the principles discussed above surrender should probably not be a disposition. The Court of Appeal held in *Re Paradise Motor Co. Ltd* [1968] 1 WLR 1125 that a disclaimer of an equitable interest is not a disposition. Danckwerts LJ commented that 'a disclaimer operates by way of avoidance and not by way of disposition'. A surrender, however, differs from a disclaimer in that surrender requires a transfer of equitable interest, whereas with a disclaimer there is never any movement of the beneficial interest at all. It is suggested that a surrender may well be a disposition, even though this does not accord with the policy described above.

5.4.1 *Grey* v *IRC*

The usual interpretation of the House of Lords case of *Grey* v *IRC* [1960] AC 1 is that a transfer of an equitable interest on its own constitutes a disposition, even if the trustees are directed to make it, and therefore must be in writing. Until recently, therefore, it would have attracted liability for *ad valorem* stamp duty.

Mr Hunter was beneficial owner of 18,000 shares of £1 each, the legal title being held by nominees. In order to transfer his beneficial interest, Mr Hunter orally directed the nominees (one of whom was Grey) to hold the shares on trust for beneficiaries under six settlements (the nominees were also the trustees under these settlements). Later the trustees/nominees executed six deeds of declaration to this effect, which were of course in writing.

In effect the whole scheme was a tax-avoidance device. If the oral direction had transferred the shares, no *ad valorem* stamp duty was payable; if the transfer had been effected by the written declaration, however, it was.

In deciding in favour of the Inland Revenue, the House of Lords held that a direction, by a beneficiary to the trustees, to transfer his interest to someone else constituted a disposition and must therefore be in writing. Lord Radcliffe did not think that s. 53(1) merely consolidated the earlier Statute of Frauds, and thought that this was a disposition, whether or not it was also within the mischief of the old s. 9. While on a literal interpretation this conclusion may well be inevitable, the transfer in *Grey* does not fall within the mischief of the legislation, as a request to trustees can hardly constitute a secret transaction.

5.4.2 **Variations on** *Grey*

Suppose a beneficiary declares that he himself will hold his interest on trust for another (rather than directing the trustees to do so), so creating, in effect, a sub-trust. A commonly held view is that the issue depends on whether the equitable owner effectively gives away the totality of his interest, so that he, like the trustees who hold the legal title, becomes in turn a merely nominal owner. If so, this is in reality a case of substitution of a new beneficiary, for which on policy grounds formality ought to be required.

If, on the other hand, the equitable owner purports to assume the active role of a trustee of his equitable interest, for example by declaring discretionary trusts, the case resembles a straightforward sub-trust, and should arguably be regarded as a declaration of trust, and not a disposition of an equitable interest at all.

Suppose that Mr Hunter had surrendered his interest, and asked the trustees immediately to declare new trusts, these not of course requiring writing. Suppose also that the trustees were happy to comply with Hunter's request. If surrenders of equitable interests do not require writing (on which, see above), this would have allowed for an easy way to achieve a *Grey* disposition without attracting stamp duty. If surrenders do require writing, however, the surrender is caught by the writing requirement, even if the declaration of new trusts is not.

5.4.3 The *Vandervell* litigation

I suggested above that, in principle, the merger of legal and equitable interests, extinguishing rather than disposing of the equitable interest, should not require writing, on the grounds that it is not a hidden transaction of the type which the law would wish to prevent. On the same principle, it should also be possible for an equitable owner orally to direct the trustees to transfer *both* their legal and his equitable interest to a single third party. In this event also, his equitable interest is extinguished, and the transaction cannot be secret from the trustees. The House of Lords came to this conclusion in *Vandervell* v *IRC* [1967] 2 AC 291.

There are two *Vandervell* cases, both arising from a scheme which was originally intended to transfer money to endow a chair without attracting taxation, in this case surtax.

5.4.4 *Vandervell* v *IRC*

Mr Vandervell wished to make a gift of £150,000 to the Royal College of Surgeons in order to endow a chair of pharmacology. He was equitable owner of a substantial number of shares in Vandervell Products Ltd, a private limited liability company which he controlled, and which produced, among other products, the Vanwall racing car which competed in Formula 1 races from 1954 to 1958, and won the Manufacturers' Championship in 1958. The legal interest in Vandervell's shares was held by a bank as nominee.

In order to endow the chair, he arranged with the bank orally (presumably to avoid stamp duty) to transfer both legal and equitable interests in these shares to the Royal College of Surgeons (RCS). It was not Vandervell's intention that the college should receive the shares absolutely, with all the implications that would have had for control of Vandervell Products Ltd. The intention, rather, was that it should receive dividends on the shares large enough to provide £150,000, upon which, as a charity, it was not liable to pay tax.

Vandervell retained an option to repurchase the shares themselves for a nominal amount (£5,000), however. He did not retain it in his own name, for that would have left him liable to pay surtax on the dividends. Instead, he set up a trustee company, Vandervell Trustees Ltd, to whom the option was granted.

The RCS actually received some £266,000 by means of this device.

At this stage, therefore, the legal interest in the shares had been transferred to the RCS. Vandervell Trustees Ltd had the legal interest in the option. If the equitable interest in either remained in Vandervell himself, however, he would be liable to surtax, on the basis of s. 415 of the Income Tax Act 1952. Clearly, Vandervell had to show that he had divested himself of the entire benefit of the shares.

The shares

Figure 5.1 *Vandervell (No. 1)*

Although the particular income tax provision at issue in *Vandervell* has been long since replaced, the principles of using trusts, and in particular charities, as a means of avoiding taxation, still survive. The principle is essentially that liability to income tax can be minimised by ensuring that the income is received by those whose taxation liability is least. The so-called 'granny trust', where the income is paid to infant grandchildren, is a good example of this principle. Further examples of the use of the trust to avoid taxation are considered in chapter 17.

In *Vandervell* itself, as a high earner Mr Vandervell's personal liability to income tax was very high (note that surtax was being claimed, at well over the marginal rates that would have been applicable for standard-rate payers). The RCS as a charity, however, paid no income tax at all. It was important to show, therefore, that it was the charity and not Vandervell himself who was entitled to the income from the shares. The same principle applies today, where trusts are being used as a device to save income tax: the settlor must ensure that he divests himself effectively of all interest in the trust property, since even the most tenuous connection with the trust may result in the income being deemed to be that of the settlor.

That was essentially the issue in *Vandervell* itself. The shares and the option should be considered separately.

5.4.4.1 *The shares*

The Revenue initially claimed surtax from Mr Vandervell on the ground that he remained the equitable owner of the shares (although the legal title had clearly been vested in the RCS), in the absence of a separate disposition, in writing, of his equitable interest. This argument was rejected by the House of Lords, which held that s. 53(1)(c) had no application to the case where a beneficial owner, solely entitled, directs his bare trustees with regard to the legal and equitable estate. This is the most important part of the *Vandervell* litigation for formality purposes, and is in line with the policy discussed. As far as the shares themselves were concerned, therefore, both legal and equitable interests had been validly transferred despite lack of writing.

An interesting aside is that *Re Rose* [1952] Ch 449 was approved (see chapter 3): the transfer was effective as soon as Vandervell had performed his last act.

5.4.4.2 *The option*

Vandervell was liable to surtax, nevertheless, because the House of Lords also held (Lords Reid and Donovan dissenting) that he had not succeeded in divesting himself of the equitable interest in the option (the legal title to which was now in the trustee company), as this was held on resulting trust for him, along with liability to pay surtax on the dividends. Vandervell was not entitled to the benefit of s. 415(1)(d) because the strict requirements of that section had not been satisfied.

This did not raise a formalities point, however, but was the result simply of Vandervell's failure to state where the equitable interest was to go. Lord Wilberforce noted that the trusts upon which the option was supposed to be held were undefined and in the air, possibly to be defined later. The trustee company itself was clearly not a beneficiary, and an equitable interest cannot remain in the air, and so the only possibility was a resulting trust in favour of the settlor. See further, chapters 2 and 7.

5.4.5 *Re Vandervell's Trusts (No. 2)*

In order to avoid further surtax liability, Vandervell in 1961 instructed the trustee company to exercise the option and repurchase the shares, and this gave rise eventually to further litigation (*Re Vandervell's Trusts (No. 2)* [1974] Ch 269) about whether Vandervell had divested himself of the option and the whereabouts of the equitable interest in the shares thereby purchased.

Clearly, the legal interest in the shares was now vested in the trustee company, Vandervell Trustees Ltd, because it had purchased them. They were also trustees under a separate trust for Vandervell's children: the £5,000 purchase money came from the children's settlement and the trustee company regarded themselves as holding the shares on trust for the children under this settlement. In other words, they regarded the equitable interest in the shares as being in the children.

Liability to surtax now depended on the whereabouts of the equitable interest in the shares during that period (although in the event the Inland Revenue was excluded as a party to the action, and the taxation point was not in fact the main issue). It was argued that, as before, it remained with Vandervell. Again, let us consider separately the option and the shares.

5.4.5.1 *The option*

The Court of Appeal held that the option was destroyed when it was exercised by the trustee company in 1961, so Vandervell's equitable interest in it (resulting from the earlier litigation) was extinguished. This was not a disposition within s. 53.

5.4.5.2 *The shares*

The Court of Appeal held that the children had the equitable interest. The shares had been placed by the trustee company on the trusts of the children's settlements, and the Court of Appeal held that Vandervell had now succeeded in divesting

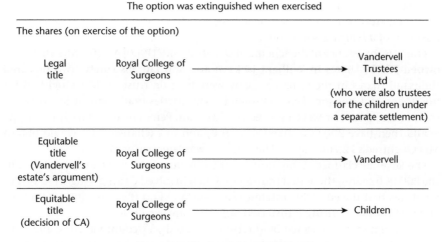

Figure 5.2 *Vandervell (No. 2)* (1961–65)

himself of the entire interest in these shares, there being no longer a resulting trust in his favour. This was because the later trusts were precisely defined, in favour of the children's settlements, so that it was no longer necessary for the equitable interest to remain in the settlor.

Lord Denning analysed the position as a termination of the resulting trust of the option in favour of Vandervell, and a fresh trust of the shares declared (presumably by the trustee company) in favour of the children. He thought that as to the first part, writing is not required to terminate a resulting trust, and that since the new trust was not of land, no formalities were required for its creation.

So far as the formality aspects of the *Vandervell* decisions are concerned, at no stage did s. 53 operate to defeat a transaction in either case. Since none of the transactions could have been kept secret from the trustees this is in accord with the policy of the section.

In 1965 Vandervell, presumably by now justifiably fed up with his scheme, clearly relinquished by deed any interest, legal or equitable, he may still have had in the shares.

5.4.6 *Oughtred* v *IRC*

The point which arose in this third important House of Lords case is logically quite separate from that which arose in the above cases. It is virtually a pure taxation case, and it is difficult to argue either for or against the result from any general policy standpoint on formalities.

Contracts for the sale of personalty do not require writing, but in cases where the equitable remedy of specific performance is available, equity recognises that the buyer has an interest as soon as the contract is made. A possible route round s. 53 (and therefore stamp duty) might therefore be to have an oral contract for the sale of (say) shares, followed later by a formal transfer. The argument is that the oral contract, not the written transfer, conveys the equitable title; the formal transfer merely conveys the bare legal title, which is worth hardly anything for the purposes of *ad valorem* stamp duty.

This was the essence of the scheme in *Oughtred v IRC* [1960] AC 206. Mrs Oughtred owned 72,700 shares in William Jackson and Son Ltd absolutely. Two hundred thousand shares in the same company were held on trust for Mrs Oughtred for life, thence for her son, Peter, absolutely. The parties orally agreed to exchange their interests, so that Mrs Oughtred would obtain Peter's reversionary interest (she would then have 200,000 shares outright), and in exchange Peter would obtain Mrs Oughtred's 72,700 shares. The contract was later performed.

The Revenue claimed stamp duty on the transfer of the reversionary interest in the 200,000 shares, the actual transfer of which involved writing. Oughtred's argument was that the equitable interest was transferred on the oral contract for sale, and that the later writing transferred only the bare legal title.

The argument was rejected by the House of Lords, Viscount Radcliffe and Lord Cohen dissenting. The essence of the majority view was that, although equity in appropriate circumstances can grant specific performance of a contract for the sale of shares (at any rate in a private company, where the shares are unique, but not in a public company, where equivalent shares are freely available on the stock market), and although in that case a constructive trust arises immediately in favour of the purchaser, the buyer does not have a full beneficial interest until the formal transfer. The situation was regarded as analogous to a sale of land, where the deed of conveyance is the effective instrument of transfer (and so liable to stamp duty). The minority view, on the other hand, was that the purchaser obtained a full beneficial interest immediately.

In the case of shares in a limited company, Lord Jenkins observed that:

the title secured by a purchaser by means of an actual transfer is different in kind from, and may well be far superior to, the special form of proprietary interest which equity confers on a purchaser in anticipation of such transfer...Under the contract, the purchaser is, no doubt, entitled in equity as between himself and the vendor to the beneficial interest in the shares, and (subject to due payment of the purchase consideration) to call for a transfer of them from the vendor as trustee for him. But it is only on the execution of the actual transfer that he becomes entitled to be registered as a member, to attend and vote at meetings, to effect transfers on the register, or to receive dividends otherwise than through the vendor as his trustee.

Transfer of legal title definitely confers additional privileges on the purchaser, therefore, and can reasonably be said to confer a superior form of proprietary interest.

In the case of land, between contract and conveyance the vendor is constructive trustee for the purchaser, but there remains a conflict of interest between the two parties (see chapter 7). This therefore differs from a normal trust (see further chapter 15), and it can reasonably be argued that at this stage the purchaser has received less than a full beneficial interest. In *Lloyds Bank plc v Carrick* [1996] 4 All ER 630, however, the purchaser had paid the entire purchase price and gone into occupation, so that all that remained to be done was to transfer the bare legal title. Morritt LJ expressed the view (*obiter*) that in these circumstances the vendor held on bare trust for the purchaser, so that presumably the purchaser had a full beneficial interest even prior to the conveyance.

5.5 Equitable doctrine of part performance

5.5.1 Part performance and the Law of Property (Miscellaneous Provisions) Act 1989

The equitable doctrine of part performance allows for limited avoidance of formality provisions. It developed originally from the principle that equity would not allow a statute to be used as a cloak for fraud (see further chapter 11). In recent years, however, it appeared to be developing away from a purely fraud-based doctrine into an evidential doctrine, with its own detailed rules. These rules were arguably both unsatisfactory and uncertain, and the Law Commission (Law Com. No. 164: 'Formalities for Contracts for Sale, etc. of Land') accordingly recommended the abolition of the doctrine, at any rate in relation to contracts for the sale or other disposition of land, or interests in land. Their proposals were brought into effect by the Law of Property (Miscellaneous Provisions) Act 1989, which also tightened up on formality provisions affecting land.

5.5.1.1 *Formality requirements and the promotion of fraud*

It seems generally to be accepted that in so far as part performance had become a rigid evidential doctrine, it has not survived the 1989 Act. But the question still arises: what if formality provisions are being relied upon to promote a fraud? It seems unlikely that the 1989 Act was ever intended to affect the fundamental principle that equity will not permit a statute to be used as a cloak for fraud. Or suppose the provisions of the 1989 Act itself are used to promote fraud? It must be presumed that the original fraud basis of the doctrine survives the 1989 Act.

It should also be noted that the 1989 Act applies only to formality provisions concerning contracts for the sale of estates and interests in land. In so far that the part performance doctrine applies to other dispositions, and declarations of trust, it has not been affected by the 1989 Act. There are also contracts, apart from those involving land, that require writing. For example, s. 90 of the Copyright, Designs and Patents Act 1988 provides that '[a]n assignment of copyright is not effective unless it is in writing signed by or on behalf of the assignor', and under the Consumer Credit Act 1974 many consumer credit agreements must be in a prescribed written form and signed. No doubt, it would be possible to apply a doctrine based on part performance if these provisions were not complied with. So, although the cases considered in this section concern land, and may therefore not survive the 1989 Act, the principles discussed still apply to other contracts. Thus, for example, an unwritten assignment of copyright may be effective, in spite of the statutory provision to the contrary, if supported by acts of part performance pointing unequivocally to the existence of such an assignment. Also, the payment of money could presumably have the same effect as described here.

5.5.1.2 *Part performance and the avoidance of s. 53 of the Law of Property Act 1925*

Though the doctrine can be used to avoid s. 53 of the Law of Property Act, 1925, by virtue of s. 55(d), the main cases arose from attempts to enforce a contract for a leasehold or freehold estate in land, despite non-compliance with the formalities required by the (now repealed) Law of Property Act 1925, s. 40:

(1) No action may be brought upon any contract for the sale or other disposition of land or any interest in land, unless the agreement upon which such action is brought, or some memorandum or note thereof, is in writing, and signed by the party to be charged or by some other person thereunto by him lawfully authorised.

(2) This section applies to contracts made before or after the commencement of this Act and does not affect the law relating to part performance, or sales by the court.

Like s. 53, s. 40 replaced earlier provisions deriving from the Statute of Frauds 1677, so cases before 1925 were equally authoritative on s. 40.

There are two important points to note about s. 40. First, in the absence of the required formalities it merely prevented an action being brought upon a contract for the sale or other disposition of land or any interest in land, but did not render the contract void. Second, s. 40(2) expressly preserved the old equitable doctrine of part performance.

5.5.1.3 *Formality and certainty: the difficulties with Steadman v Steadman*

Developments in the law of part performance and in particular the House of Lords decision in *Steadman* v *Steadman* [1976] AC 576 clearly worried the Law Commission, not least because it had left the law in an extremely uncertain state. They also took the view (at page 3) that whereas the part performance doctrine was a blunt instrument for doing justice despite non-compliance with statutory formalities, equity had developed more flexible ways of dealing with the position if formalities were not observed. Accordingly, they recommended the abolition of the part performance doctrine.

The recommendations of the Commission led to the enactment of the Law of Property (Miscellaneous Provisions) Act 1989, s. 2 of which provided:

(1) A contract for the sale or other disposition of an interest in land can only be made in writing and only by incorporating all the terms which the parties have expressly agreed in one document or, where contracts are exchanged, in each…

(8) Section 40 of the Law of Property Act 1925 (which is superseded by this section) shall cease to have effect.

5.5.1.4 *The impact of s. 40 of the Law of Property Act 1925*

Apart from the tightening up of the formalities provisions in this section, it differs from its precursor in not making any provision for the part perform-ance doctrine. However, although s. 40 was repealed and s. 40(2) not replaced, the part performance doctrine was not abolished expressly. It should also be remembered that the doctrine did not derive from s. 40(2), but from an earlier, fundamental equitable principle. Since it does not derive from statute, and since it has not been expressly abolished, is it therefore possible to argue that it still survives?

No doubt in interpreting the new statute the courts will take account of the Law Commission's recommendations, which clearly favoured the abolition of the doctrine. It is also worth noting that the section does not merely render unen-forceable any contract which does not comply with its provisions, but that con-tracts failing to comply are void. The Commission took the view (at p. 23) that the doctrine of part performance would cease to have effect in contracts concerning land, presumably because there would be nothing for it to operate on. This was also the view taken by Professor P.H. Pettit ([1989] Conv, at p. 441):

It is an inevitable consequence of section 2 that the doctrine of part-performance no longer has a role to play in contracts concerning land. The simple fact is that under the new law if section 2 is not complied with there is no contract for either party to perform.

It is suggested that, in so far (if at all) as the doctrine had evolved from its fraud-based beginnings, the effect of the 1989 Act is to curtail those developments. Where, however, reliance on the statutory formality provisions could perpetrate a clear fraud, it is surely unlikely that equity will allow that to happen because of a new statute, which does not expressly abolish the doctrine. Nor is it a bar to the operation of the fraud doctrine that the contract is rendered void rather than merely unenforceable, since it is only rendered void by the operation of a formality statute whose provisions are being used as a cloak for fraud. The doctrine that equity will not allow a statute to be used as a cloak for fraud was applied by the Court of Appeal in *Rochefoucauld* v *Boustead* [1897] 1 Ch 196 to avoid s. 7 of the Statute of Frauds 1677 (the precursor to s. 53(1)(b) of the Law of Property Act 1925), which like s. 53(1)(b) and s. 2 of the 1989 Act, rendered non-complying dispositions void. It can thus be suggested , that at any rate to the extent that part performance is based on the equitable fraud doctrine (see chapter 11), it is unaffected by the 1989 Act.

It is arguable, however, that equity has evolved other devices for dealing with the genuinely fraudulent case, and no longer needs to rely on the part performance doctrine. This is what is considered now in the next section.

5.5.2 **Alternatives to part performance**

5.5.2.1 *Proprietary estoppel*

In its report, the Law Commission took the view (at page 18) that if the part performance doctrine were abolished, many of the cases where injustice might be caused by an inability to plead the doctrine could be resolved by the application either of the equitable doctrine of estoppel, or various common law actions. For example, recovery of money paid by a prospective purchaser would normally be recoverable on the grounds of total failure of consideration. If work had been carried out, a *quantum meruit* claim might be made.

So far as estoppel is concerned, the effect of the doctrine (in essence) is that where one party makes a representation upon which another party relies to his detriment, the party making the representation may be estopped from later denying it. Proprietary estoppel, and its potential applications and limitations, are discussed more fully in chapter 9. There is no doubt that it is less effective for the injured party than enforcement of the unwritten contract would have been, but the Commission was of the view (at page 19) that the remedies for proprietary estoppel were sufficient to prevent injustice in most situations where previously the part performance doctrine may have operated. This may be so, in as much as the Law Commission was worried about uncertainty in its criticism of the part performance doctrine. Although it can hardly be said that the equitable estoppel doctrine is a particularly certain alternative, the discussion of shared homes in chapter 9 reveals that the courts are demonstrably showing a leaning towards estoppel-based resolutions to disputed home ownership, in preference to a constructive trust-based approach.

Estoppel reasoning and the position of third parties

There may also be difficulties with estoppel reasoning where third parties are involved. In the part performance cases there was no third party (e.g., purchaser) and the only question was whether the other party to the contract was bound. But estate contracts can also bind third parties (subject to the registration requirements of the Land Charges or Land Registration Acts, the former having been recently considered by the Court of Appeal in *Lloyds Bank plc v Carrick*, CA [1996] 4 All ER 630, whereas estoppels cannot be guaranteed to do so (see further chapter 9).

5.5.2.2 *Constructive trust*

Another possibility, closely related to the discussion in the previous section, is that a constructive trust might protect against any injustice that might arise from the abolition of the part performance doctrine. It seems that constructive trusts *may* arise in similar circumstances to proprietary estoppels, and there is no doubt that a full range of equitable remedies is available to protect a beneficiary under a constructive trust. Constructive trusts also give rise, unlike (probably) proprietary estoppels, to full beneficial interests, and so are capable of binding third parties also.

Constructive trusts arising from inequitable conduct are considered in chapter 7 and in detail in chapter 11, and the constructive trust may well be an alternative to part performance—like equitable estoppel, however, it is no more certain in its operation!

Alternatives to the part performance doctrine are analysed in detail by Lionel Bently and Paul Coughlan in (1990) 10 *Legal Studies*, at p. 325.

5.6 **Capacity**

As a general rule, anyone who has the capacity in law to hold a legal or equitable interest in property also has the capacity to declare a trust of it. The old rules which placed married women in a special position have long been abolished, and the repeal of the Mortmain Acts (by s. 38 of the Charities Act 1960) has removed former restrictions on trusts for corporate bodies. Two special classes of person require consideration, however: minors and persons suffering from mental abnormality.

5.6.1 **Minors**

A minor may hold the legal title to property other than land and can therefore create a trust of such property *inter vivos*. Any such settlement is, however, voidable and the minor may repudiate it during his minority or within a reasonable time of attaining his majority.

Because a minor cannot make a valid will, he cannot therefore create a trust by will. Statutory exceptions are made in the case of soldiers on military service and sailors while at sea.

Since 1925 (Law of Property Act 1925, s. 1(6)) a minor cannot hold a legal estate in land. He therefore cannot settle such an estate, but he may hold an equitable interest in land and can settle this, subject to the possibility of repudiation of the settlement.

Before the passing of the Family Law Reform Act 1969, s. 9 of which reduced the age of majority from 21 to 18 years, the High Court had the power to approve settlements of real and personal property made upon or in contemplation of marriage by males not under 20 and females not under 17 and such approval made the settlement binding. These provisions were repealed by the Family Law Reform Act 1969, s. 11, without, however, affecting anything done before that Act came into force.

5.6.2 **Persons suffering from mental abnormality**

A mentally abnormal person may be unable to effect a valid disposition of his property where his condition can be shown to affect his understanding of the transaction. Some transactions call for a higher degree of understanding than others. In order to make a valid will, the testator must understand not only the nature of the document itself, but be able also to evaluate the claims of all the potential donees in relation to the sum of property to be disposed of. *Inter vivos* transactions may demand a lower degree of understanding, which depends upon the size of the contemplated transfer relative to the total assets of the donor. A low degree of understanding will be sufficient if the amount of the gift is relatively trivial, but if it comprises the donor's only assets of value, so as to pre-empt the devolution of his property after his death, then the same degree of understanding is required as in the case of a will.

5.6.2.1 *Capacity and mental health legislation*

The Mental Health Act 1983, replacing the 1959 Act of the same title, gives the Court of Protection wide powers to manage the affairs of a person whom the judge is satisfied is incapable of managing his property and affairs by reason of mental disorder. A judge may make orders or give directions for the settlement of any property of a patient of full age. These powers may provide for the maintenance or benefit of the patient or members of his family, or for persons or purposes for which the patient might be expected to provide but for his disorder, or otherwise for the management of his affairs. Such a settlement can be varied at any time up to the death of the patient if it appears that any material fact was not disclosed when the settlement was made or that there has been some substantial change of circumstances.

In exercising these powers, the court will be guided by consideration of what the patient would be likely to do if he were not under disability. In *Re TB* [1967] Ch 247 the court approved a revocable settlement of the whole of the patient's property in favour of the patient's illegitimate son and his family, the effect of which was to prevent the property passing to collateral relatives under the rules of intestacy in the anticipated event of the patient's failure to recover testamentary capacity in his lifetime.

Since the Administration of Justice Act 1969 the court has had the power to make a will for a patient of full age whom the judge has reason to believe lacks testamentary capacity.

Applications for approval of schemes to deal with patients' property commonly have the aim of reducing tax liability, although the scheme must be for the benefit of the patient. It is not essential to provide for revocation if the patient should recover: it is sufficient that it is the sort of settlement which he would be likely to make in favour of his family if he were not subject to the abnormality.

5.7 **Public policy: capricious trusts**

5.7.1 **Public policy; void conditions**

Various trusts which would otherwise be valid are held to be void for reasons of public policy, in which case the property will be held on resulting trust for the settlor. Trusts for future-born illegitimate children fell into this category before 1970, because it was supposed that they tended to encourage immorality, and the old law still applies to pre-1970 dispositions. Since that date trusts for future-born illegitimate children have been validated, the present provisions being contained in the Family Law Reform Act 1987.

Conditions affecting dispositions may also be struck down on public policy grounds, in which case the result depends on whether the condition is construed as a condition precedent or a condition subsequent. If the former, the entire gift generally fails (although this statement must be qualified in relation to personal property) and the property results to the settlor. If the latter, the gift, but not the condition, is valid.

5.7.1.1 *Capacity, public policy and illustrations of void trusts*

Examples of invalid conditions are trusts tending to prevent the carrying out of parental duties, trusts in restraint of marriage, and trusts which are fraudulent. Testators sometimes leave property to children subject to a condition subsequent relating to their religious upbringing. In *Blathwayt* v *Lord Cawley* [1976] AC 397, for example, a large estate (valued in 1975 at £2 million) was left in 1936 on various entailed trusts, but such that any person who became entitled was to forfeit his interest if he became a Roman Catholic (or ceased to use the name and arms of Blathwayt). It was argued that with respect to the present children, the religious condition tended to restrain the carrying out of parental duties, and was therefore void on public policy grounds, but the House of Lords held otherwise. The effect of the clause may have been to force the parents to choose between material and spiritual welfare for their offspring, but this was not necessarily contrary to public policy. In the event, however, the House of Lords held by a 3:2 majority (Lords Wilberforce and Fraser of Tullybelton dissenting) that the clause did not apply on its construction.

5.7.1.2 *Void trusts, certainty, and 'conditions subsequent'*

Conditions subsequent can still be struck down on the grounds of uncertainty, as in *Clayton v Ramsden* [1943] AC 320, which concerned a forfeiture on marriage to a person 'not of Jewish parentage and of the Jewish faith'. This was held to be conceptually uncertain. But it seems that so long as a clause is not uncertain the courts will be slow to strike it down on grounds of public policy, and a somewhat similar clause to the above was upheld by the Court of Appeal in *Re Tuck's ST* [1978] Ch 49, where 'an approved wife' of Jewish blood was precisely defined, cases of dispute being dealt with by the Chief Rabbi in London. Names and arms clauses (such as the other clause in *Blathwayt*) have also been upheld (e.g., *Re Neeld* [1962] Ch 643). It may be, though, that such leniency by the courts is misplaced, because social conditions change and clauses of this nature arguably allow the dead too much freedom to interfere in the lives of the living.

5.7.2 Capricious or useless trusts

There is no doubt that the courts can also strike down capricious or useless trusts. An early example is *Brown v Burdett* (1882) 21 Ch D 667, which was an attempt to create a trust to block up windows—surprisingly, this was not an attempt to avoid window tax.

It is to be hoped that the courts tread warily where the validity of a trust is at issue, however. Public policy tests are inherently vague, and in this area in particular there is an acute shortage of judicial definition. Certainty as to the law is important in property transactions, especially for testamentary dispositions, where there is no opportunity for the settlor to correct any mistakes or failures. Public policy is always supposed to be an unruly horse and I would suggest that extensive use of such a jurisdiction would be most inappropriate in this area.

5.7.3 Insolvency Act 1986

The Insolvency Act 1986, replacing earlier complex provisions, empowers the court to set aside certain transactions (called 'transactions at an undervalue') whereby a debtor's property has been placed beyond reach of his creditors. Such transactions include voluntary settlements made by the debtor as well as gifts or sales made for inadequate consideration. Marriage is not regarded as adequate consideration for this purpose.

Section 339 of the Act applies only where a debtor has been adjudged bankrupt. On application by the trustee in bankruptcy, the court may set aside a 'transaction at an undervalue' made by the debtor in the two years preceding the bankruptcy, without need to show that the debtor was already insolvent (i.e. unable to meet his liabilities) at the time of the transaction. Further, a transaction made more than two but less than five years prior to the bankruptcy may be set aside on proof that the debtor was insolvent at the time.

Section 423 applies irrespective of whether the debtor has been adjudged bankrupt. Its effect is to allow any person prejudiced by a transaction at an undervalue (referred to as 'the victim'—usually a creditor) to apply to have the transaction set aside, provided he can establish that the debtor's intention was to place his assets beyond the reach of the victim or otherwise to prejudice the victim's claims against the debtor's property.

In either case, the court has a wide discretion to restore the situation to what it would have been but for the transaction in question.

FURTHER READING

Pettit 'Farewell Section 40' (1989) Conveyancer 441.

6

....

Perpetuities

This chapter follows preceding chapters which introduced the nature of the trust, and thereafter the requirements which must be met in order for a valid express trust to be created. In the former respect the trust was introduced as a highly versatile instrument which in private law operates across domestic and commercial contexts in relation to a number of interests in property. Its central feature is its ability to confer entitlements for those who are intended to benefit from the settlement, whether or not they are party to it, and to confer legal title of property *subject to the trust conferring on its holder responsibility* to manage the property concerned and safeguard the interests of the beneficiary.

Following this, extensive attention across a number of chapters has now been paid to the way in which in order to achieve a valid trust, a number of requirements must be met. The trust must be constituted (i.e. legal title must become vested in the trustee; and certainty must also be manifested in terms of intention to create a trust; the subject matter of the trust; and those who are intended to benefit from it). The previous chapter has examined legal formality requirements, and this one examines the way in which in order to be valid all private trusts must not infringe the rule against perpetuities (although the rule applies only to a much lesser extent to trusts which are charitable). In this respect, it is a logical continuation in the discussion of the requirements of a valid trust. However, it is also an important point of reference for much earlier discussion on the very close relationship which the law of trusts enjoys with other aspects of property law, and increasingly the law relating to commercial transactions. The nature of the perpetuity requirements will very quickly become apparent as restricting the use made of trusts to safeguard property, and over time, a number of transactions relating to proprietary interests and entitlements have accidentally become subject to their provisions.

6.1 Introduction: permanent and irrevocable; reach of the trust

The essence of a trust is to direct that property is to be used, if not in a particular way, then applied for the benefit of a particular beneficiary. And it is in this regard that, in previous chapters it has become apparent that a permanent irrevocable arrangement comes into force when a settlor settles property on trust. There has also been an introduction made to the role of the trustee in this arrangement, and to the way in which the incumbent of such an office holds legal title to the property, and is charged with managing it in such a way as to enable the beneficiary to derive benefit from it. What this chapter seeks to do is explain the trust as a permanent irrevocable arrangement in light of what is known as 'the rule against perpetuities'.

6.1.1 Settling property on trust: the settlor's reach

What the existence of a trust does in reality is restrict use which can be made of the property which is subject to a trust. Although the beneficiary or beneficiaries are the ones in whose favour the trust is made, the recipients of the property, and sometimes even the use they can make of it, are directed by the settlor. The trust property must be applied in accordance with the terms of the trust, and thus the settlor's wishes. At its broadest, the term 'perpetuity' applies to trust lawyers' consideration of the ability of owners of property to restrict the way in which their successors in title are able to utilise it. This is very important because it can involve looking at situations in which subsequent holders of title are not able to deal with property as freely as the person who has imposed the restrictions was once able to do. At the most extreme, this might well involve interference with free applications of property on account of the wishes of generations from beyond the recent past.

6.1.2 Can the dead rule the living?

The rule against perpetuities operates to place limits on the ability of the present generation to tie up property into the future. The reason for this is that property subject to a trust is property which must be applied subject to conditions, and cannot be freely used. The free use of property is prevented, and the law places limits on the way in which restrictions can limit future generations.

6.1.3 Trusts, wealth preservation, and the 'dead hand rule'

Trusts are historically associated with the object of the preservation of wealth, and restrictions on its use will help to encourage this: settling property in such a way is advantageous from this perspective. More detailed explanation of this will follow shortly, but essentially the rule against perpetuities operates in a manner which ensures that there are limits on the time allowed for property actually to vest in its intended beneficial owner. It is from this that limits on the duration which property can be held on trust arise. This, along with the closely related rule against excessive accumulations (which fetters a settlor's ability to direct the accumulation of income generated under a trust) is a reflection of the desirability of wealth preservation and also its limits. As generations pass, the law recognises that there must be limits on the ability of one generation to dictate the preservation (or devolution) of property to generations which follow. The law central to this has evolved into two distinct rules: the rule against perpetuity and the rule against excessive accumulations. The former rule places time limits in which trust property must vest and thus be subject to a trust, and the latter places limits on how long income accumulated under a trust can be 'tied into' such settlements. However, both are premised on recognition by the law of the need to limit the way in which the living can be controlled by the wishes of their ancestors: it limits the operation of what is sometimes known as the 'dead hand rule'. As Ruth Deech has noted, in 'Lives in Being Revisited' (1981) LQR, at 594:

the Rule [against perpetuities] is necessary in order to strike a balance between on the one hand the freedom of the present generation and, on the other, that of future generations to deal as they wish with the property in which they have interests. If a settlor had total liberty to dispose of his property among future beneficiaries, the recipients, being fettered by his wishes, would never enjoy that same freedom in turn.

6.1.4 Striking the balance: *dead hand rule* v *present autonomy*

Given that property held on trust is property which is tied, and its use restricted, the rules against perpetuities and also excessive accumulations can be seen as reflections of the tension between the preservation of wealth and the actual creation of wealth. It can furthermore even be seen as indicative of conflict between private familial wealth and a more public wider economic wellbeing, which can *itself* also cut across the preservation–creation axis. As Ruth Deech continues, in her critique of the dead hand rule (as cited above):

The liberty to make fresh rearrangements of assets is necessary... to be rid of irksome conditions attached by earlier donors to the enjoyment of income but also in order to be able to manoeuvre in the light of new tax laws, changes in the nature of property and in the personal circumstances of the beneficiaries, unforeseeable by the best intentioned and most perspicuous of donors.

6.2 Current law and policy focus on law reform

A more detailed consideration is now given to the rule against perpetuity and the rule against excessive accumulations in turn. The current operation of each will be discussed closely alongside the proposals for their reform which are currently being considered.

6.2.1 Confusion, dissatisfaction, and the Law Commission's work

Notwithstanding the rationale behind the rule against perpetuity and the rule against excessive accumulations of income in respect of property settled subject to a trust, the Law Commission's Report *The Law of Trusts. The Rules against Perpetuities and Excessive Accumulations* (Law Com. No. 251 (1998)) provides some insight into why calls for their modification, and even abolition have been made many times recently. Historically, the view taken by this text has been that historical justifications for the rules, which are very much founded on family settlements and Britain's pre-industrial economy, are not necessarily strong arguments for a law on perpetuities, notwithstanding the eminently sensible limiting rationale they propose. It has consistently been entreated that better ways of achieving control over settlors' desires to control are through wider powers of investment and through mechanisms for the variation of trusts.

Against this backdrop, the rules against perpetuities and excessive accumulations have twice recently been considered by the Law Commission, first in *The Law of Trusts. The Rules against Perpetuities and Excessive Accumulations*, Consultation Paper No. 133 (1993), and following responses to that paper, in the Law Commission Report of the same name, noted above. Commenting on the current regime, a twin system of common law and statutory provisions, both the Consultation and Report reflect the two central issues surrounding the rules' status in modern law. They raise the question of whether some restriction on the ability to tie up property is necessary and, thereafter, whether the current law is the best means of achieving this. The Law Commission did conclude that there was continuing need to prevent property being tied up in a restricted manner, but stopped short of recommending abolition of the rule, notwithstanding extensive criticism levied at the current law. But a considerable overhaul of existing provisions was recommended.

The Law Commission's 1998 Report followed the Consultation dating from 1993, which was delayed by its own admission, and explained (at 2, 1998) on account of staff shortages and 'the pressure to complete more urgent projects'. In this climate, although a draft Bill did follow the Report, it is difficult to predict precisely when the reforms will be given attention in Parliament, and become enacted. Even then, if (and it is more likely a question of when) the Law Commission's proposals for reform are accepted then much of the current state of the law will cease to have any relevance, at any rate prospectively. However, it is not intended that any legislation should have any automatic retroactive effect, so the common law is likely to continue to be relevant at least for one more lifetime. Nevertheless, it is also the case that the attention accorded to perpetuities in teaching undertaken by law schools has diminished in recent times, and especially from the 1990s, in light of the Law Commission's recommendations for reform. For this work too, the decision has been taken to curtail significantly coverage given to perpetuities. Thus, both the current law and also proposals for reform are considered in summary form only. They have also been examined closely alongside the Law Commission documentation (especially the 1998 Report), which is at present a permanent point of reference in this transitional phase. Making such close reference to the policy documentation will bolster understanding. And the Law Commission work does also provide, alongside the proposed direction of reforms, a fairly clear as well as comprehensive account of the current law at common law and under statute—no small thing in this very complicated and often 'clumsy' area of trusts law.

6.3 **Rule against perpetuity and the structure of the law**

6.3.1 **Current law and historical background**

Within the broad introduction above, it is clear that 'perpetuity' is a by-word for restrictions placed on future dealings with property. That desire to restrict free alienation (or use or application) of property historically has its origins in the ownership of land: historically, the desire to restrict freedom to deal freely with property has its origins in land ownership. Land ownership is in many respects still the ultimate expression of property ownership, but as the introductory chapter explained, it was with interests in land that principles of property ownership originally became carved out. As a result of the desire of landowners to preserve their rights in and enjoyment of property, those who became expert in conveyancing developed forms of 'settlements' of property designed to achieve less than unfettered entitlement to land when property passes. And it is in this context that English law has sought to restrict the extent to which these intended restrictions can operate. Just as the term 'perpetuity' is used to illustrate restrictions placed on future dealings with property, 'the rule against perpetuities' has developed to place limits on such restrictions on free dealings with property.

6.3.2 **Rule against perpetuities: an unhelpful term?**

The way the rule against perpetuities works is to operate to restrict the time within which future interests (i.e. ones which do not take effect immediately) in property created by a disposition must vest (or take effect). This is not an easy area of trusts law to comprehend, and as the Law Commission noted in its Report, even the term 'rule against perpetuities' lacks a certain intrinsic helpfulness. Notwithstanding that the term 'perpetuity' fits what has been said about the prevention of present and future generations being tied into the wishes of their ancestors, it is also the case that the rule against perpetuities is actually directly concerned with the commencement of interests, rather than with their actual duration (by restricting the time within which future interests must vest for the disposition to be valid). However, as the Law Commission notes (at 3, 1998), restrictions on the time within which future interests can be created will almost always have the effect of limiting the life of a trust. The Law Commission, in citing Simpson (1979) 'Entails and Perpetuities' 24 Jur Rev 1, 17, also points to ambiguity in use of the term 'against', emphasising instead the permissive effect of the rule:

The rule against perpetuities, to be comprehended, must be understood as permitting them within limits, and most modern discussion of the rule…is distorted by a failure to appreciate that the contemporary oddity of the rule lies not in what it prevents, but in how much it allows.

6.4 **Emergence of 'restrictions on restrictions': development of the common law**

The common law on perpetuities developed in the sixteenth and seventeenth centuries, directed primarily at settlements of land. At that time, equity allowed the creation of future interests, whereas the common law did not. Because Uses (the early form of trust instrument, introduced in chapter 1) were executed, the *common law* was faced with the problem of dealing with future interests in land, which previously had been recognised only in equity. In summary, then, an incidental effect of the Statute of Uses was to enable successive future interests to be created at common law. One consequence of this was that land could more easily be rendered unsaleable, and in particular testators could ensure that large estates remained in the family for many generations, since by creating a succession of limited estates it was possible to ensure that nobody was in a position to convey an entire unencumbered fee simple. The creation of potentially infinite successive future interests was eventually curbed by the development of the common law rule against perpetuities. The rule therefore represented a compromise between the policy of assisting the prudent management of family wealth across generations on the one hand, and the prevention of schemes for tying up property for unaccept-ably long periods on the other.

6.4.1 Perpetuity rules and their modification over time

Since its original inception, however, the policy behind the rule has undergone modification. Although it was originally developed in the context of settlements of land, in the twenty-first century the rule has come to apply in respect of all kinds of interests in property, both real and personal. Since nowadays settlements of land are very rare, mainly for reasons which are unconnected with perpetuities and which are considered in chapter 1, it could be argued that early fears about tying up land for generations should no longer govern modern policy. This is certainly very strongly present as an argument throughout the Law Commission documen-tation from 1993 and 1998.

The chief scope of the rule today is in fact within settlements of personalty (i.e. property which is not land), which are mostly set up with a view to tax saving. But because fiscal law alters fairly rapidly, there is in any case an in-built disincentive to create long-term, immoveable arrangements. The Law Commission recognised this as valid critique of such a rigid prohibition against such settlements, and by the same token therefore, as potentially less of a justification for a stringent rule against perpetuities.

6.4.2 Continuing development in the rule against perpetuity

A closer examination of the Law Commission Report provides insight into why the rule against perpetuities is often characterised as anachronistic, and why there have been frequent calls for its abolition. The Law Commission does concur that the rule against excessive accumulations should go—which it admits has very little purpose, and actually creates a number of practical difficulties. And although the Law Commission insisted that some provisions against perpetuity must remain in force, it did recommend that the law as it is is in need of considerable overhaul. This view in turn rested on a conclusion that the current law was complicated and even inaccessible. Here, the Law Commission accepted (at 2, 1998) that the current law is 'needlessly complicated' and so to the point that it can 'only be understood by specialists' and even that 'In a number of situations it is uncertain whether or how it applies.'

6.4.3 The modern law: how does it apply and how does it 'work'?

The modern law hinges on whether or not the disposition in question came into being before 16 July 1964, the date on which the Perpetuities and Accumulations Act 1964 came into force.

Before looking at the provisions of the common law and of the 1964 Act, generally the thrust of the provisions under the statute and at common law alike concerns what are known as 'future' interests in property. Much complicated discussion could follow around the nature and reach of future interests, but the purpose here is to give a very simple explanation, and to relate them to the law's desire to restrict the dead hand rule at the heart of perpetuities law. An interest which is a future interest is, at this extremely basic level of operation and understanding, an interest in property which is not created and does not take effect immediately. And, following on from this idea of a future interest, as distinct from one which is immediate, the rule against perpetuities operates to restrict the time within which future interests can be created. It is this in turn which has the effect of limiting the life of the trust.

6.4.3.1 *Future interests and their creation: the significance of time*

At common law, the rule against perpetuities operates so that a future interest in any type of property is only valid where there is no possibility that the interest may vest or commence outside the perpetuity period. And where there is the possibility that it may do so outside the perpetuity period, the interest is void from the date that the instrument purporting to create it takes effect. In this respect, the 'perpetuity period' referred to consists of one or more 'lives in being' plus a period of 21 years, and where relevant a period of gestation (as the Law Commission explains in para. 1.7, a child *in utero*, or *en ventre sa mere* is treated as a life in being for the purposes of the rule against perpetuities; explained in para. 4.11). It is from this measure of the 'life in being' that the 'royal lives' clause has become central. This became a favoured device of those drafting settlements since its effect is to terminate the period applicable to the vesting of the gift 21 years after the death of the survivor of all those members of the royal family who are alive at the date of the disposition. Such a clause always validates the gift, since it cannot vest more than 21 years after the death of somebody living at the date of the disposition, and doubtless royal lives clauses became significant because royalty tend to be long-lived!

6.4.3.2 *Understanding the common law: guidance from law reform, and reasoning backwards*

This position is not easy to grasp, and even the Law Commission policy documentation castigating the law's complexity 'explains' its current position with only limited clarity. This itself is in many respects the most appropriate precursor to explain *why* things are going to change. Shortly, it will become apparent how original reforms in 1964 tried to improve on the common law position. Looking at the Act's provisions does in a backward-reasoning way actually explain the common law position better than the act of trying to put it into words alone does. But first, there is the need to consider the idea of an 'interest' to make sense of the central notion of a 'future' interest. In so doing, you will need an appreciation of interests which are 'vesting' and ones which are 'contingent'.

6.4.3.3 *Vesting and contingent interests*

In order for an interest to vest to arise, three factors must be present (see, for example, the similar definition in Law Com. 251, at para. 4.2). First, the person who is to have the interest must be in existence, and identifiable as the person entitled. Second, the size of the interest must be known for certain. Third, nothing further must need to happen before the person in question becomes entitled to the interest. For example, an interest can vest where the person is a living human who is identified by name in the settlement; and the size of his interest is certain (e.g., a fee simple in remainder); and there are no conditions which have to be fulfilled beyond this. It would be different if, for example, the interest could only be obtained if the intended recipient were to marry (since, unlike death, marriage need not occur); or complete study for a degree and graduate from university. Where the obtaining of an interest is dependent on certain conditions coming into play, the interest is known as a *contingent interest*.

6.4.4 Common law: problematic development and calls for reform

The common law provisions are highly complex, and it is difficult even to formulate a basic understanding of them, even in the comparatively clear way in which they are set out in the Law Commission Report. It is also the case that criticism of the common law arose from its harsh operation, as much as its complex nature. A basic appreciation of how the common law can operate harshly can be gleaned by reference to the provision as it was explained above. This requires appreciation of the way in which a future interest in property is rendered void *ab initio* if there is any possibility that it might vest outside the perpetuity period. This meant that a future interest could, and indeed would, be rendered void at the outset if vesting outside the perpetuity period were even a possibility (without establishing when it might actually vest). This has the effect of 'killing' a number of future interests which might not violate the perpetuity rule at all.

Both criticisms of complexity and also undue harshness started to gather momentum in the 1950s and reforms were introduced in 1964 for dispositions taking effect prospectively (after 15 July of that year) by the enactment of the Perpetuities and Accumulations Act 1964.

6.4.5 Statutory perpetuity requirements and the common law position: an outline

This legislation introduced two key changes to the common law. One sought to avoid harshness resulting from a future interest being void from the outset simply on account of the possibility that it might vest outside the perpetuity period. The other substituted a fixed perpetuity period for the common law life in being plus 21 years. The Law Commission Report statutory provisions are summarised as follows (at 4, 1998):

Where an instrument creates a future interest after 15 July 1964—

(1) That instrument will only be void where it (the interest) must vest or take effect (if at all) outside the perpetuity period;
(2) It is therefore necessary to 'wait and see', if need be for the whole perpetuity period, to determine whether the instrument is valid; and
(3) An alternative perpetuity period of up to 80 years may be employed instead of a life in being plus 21 years.

6.4.5.1 *Future interests and 'wait and see'*

The 1964 Act's 'wait and see' principle sought to address the way in which, at common law, a future interest would be void from the outset simply on account of the possibility that it *might* vest outside the perpetuity period. This was perceived as a cause of undue harshness, on account of the 'hardest line' taken on future interests just on the possibility that they might infringe the perpetuity period, and regardless of the way in which many would doubtless not actually do so. 'Wait and see' completely altered the vista by focusing not on the possibility that an interest *may* vest outside the perpetuity period, but by switching emphasis completely to situations where it *must actually* do so. Thus 'wait and see' ensures that an interest will not be void until such time as it becomes apparent that it *must* vest outside the perpetuity period. In addition, the provision of a fixed statutory maximum perpetuity period of (not exceeding) 80 years, replacing the life in being plus 21 years at common law, was extremely radical—not so much because of the apparent extended period of time for vesting, but because it brought to the rules some much needed certainty.

6.4.5.2 *Common law and statutory regimes*

Although the statutory provisions were intended to respond to the complexity and harshness of the common law, the two regimes exist side by side even in dispositions taking effect post-1964. Indeed, the 'wait and see' sections in the 1964 Act apply only to those which are void under the common law rule. The result is therefore a two-stage process, in which the common law rules must be applied first. If the disposition is valid at common law, that is the end of the matter. Only if it would have been void at common law do the provisions of the Act apply, in which case a 'wait and see' operation is triggered. This means that time is allowed to run to see whether the gift does in fact vest within the permitted period.

6.4.6 **Relationship between common law and statutory provisions: more detail**

The interrelationship between the regimes can be quite complicated, however, because if the gift is valid at common law the Act never applies. Under the Act, the donor may expressly stipulate for a period not exceeding 80 years, which it was envisioned would replace the use of 'royal lives' clauses, but this does not actually appear to have occurred. It used to be thought this had to be done expressly and it would not be enough simply to fix a date, so that, for example, a gift 'to be given equally to the issue of X, living on 1 January 2030' would be void even in the case of a 1980 disposition. However, in *Re Green's WT* [1985] 3 All ER 455, Nourse J upheld a similar disposition, made in 1976, for the establishment of a charitable foundation on 1 January 2020 unless an event stated in the gift had occurred before then. A mother believed that her son who, as one of the crew of a bomber, had been killed in the Second World War, was still alive, and the gift to the charity took effect only if he had not claimed the property by the date stipulated. The court held that the gift to charity was not void for perpetuity.

Where the Act applies, the period during which the trustees may wait and see is calculated as follows, assuming that the 80-year period or other express choice has not been made. A list of all those who count as 'lives' by virtue of s. 3(5) is made and, on the death of the last survivor of them all, a further 21 years is added. This gives the maximum time for which wait and see is permitted. If at any time before the expiry of that period it becomes evident that a disposition cannot vest in time, then and only then is it treated as being void. Otherwise, the period is allowed to run its course to see if it will vest in time.

6.5 Proposals for reform and the position of the common law

6.5.1 Mapping common law and statutory provisions: concerns and future directions

If the Law Commission's proposals for reform are accepted (and it is suggested that the issue is more likely to be a case of *when* rather than whether) then the common law will cease to have any relevance, at least in a prospective sense. However, it is not intended that any legislation should have any automatic retro-active effect, so the common law is likely to continue to be relevant at least for one more lifetime.

But the common law *is* very difficult to grasp with much confidence, and by the Law Commission's own admission, it is not simply complicated but actually 'needlessly complicated'. This accusation in the 1998 Report was accompanied by its accusation that the current law is actually out of touch with modern uses of property rights. This is because, as explained above, the rules originated with wills and trusts around family settlements, but their application has not remained so confined. Key difficulties in the current law can be seen in situations where prop-erty interests spring from contexts outside these traditional ones, itself a reflection of the dynamism of property and proprietary interests. It is also in some respects a reflection of changing adaptations of trusts and their applications.

6.5.2 Family settlements and continuing justification of the rule against perpetuities

Family settlement trusts are of course very uncommon today, while commercial transactions and dealings with property much more readily typify use made of interests arising in respect of property. And while the justification for the rule against perpetuities developed around the paradigm of the family trust, what has happened is that, without critical appraisal of the rule and its justifications, it has become applied to interests which are far removed from this model. The Law Commission accepted that the justifications surrounding the family-type trust simply did not extend to these newer manifestations of proprietary interest. And in addition to the fact that its extended reach was created by accident, exporting the rule to a much wider range of interests is actually capable of creating considerable practical difficulties in commercial transactions. To this end, the Law Commission made a series of recommendations in its 1998 Report. These are set out in brief below, considered alongside and against the proposed benefits which such direc-tion in reform can achieve.

6.6 **Conclusions of the Law Commission's enquiries**

The 1998 Report sets out in great detail why reform is due in this sphere, and the way in which the new proposals are envisaged to bring much-needed improvement to the current operation of the rule against perpetuities. These are set out in outline below, but the most appropriate starting point is the fundamental premise on which the reforms are explained. The remit of the Law Commission's 1993 Consultation offered four possible options in light of concerns about the current state of the law. First was the option of no change to existing law, and at the other extreme rested the possibility of abandoning the rule against perpetuities. Other options arose in the shape of replacement of the rule against perpetuities with a new rule, or reforming the rule against perpetuities. Thereafter, the subsequent Report is premised on the need to keep some control over the 'dead hand rule'.

The Law Commission did not think that control over perpetuities should be abolished altogether, and in its assessment of the issues, it concluded that some limits on the power of property owners to dictate its future use should remain. This is a matter which should remain within the law's reach, and this was itself premised on the idea that greater appropriateness had to be built into reform. But the actual reasoning behind the Law Commission's assessment that some form of the rule should remain (and not actually be abolished, or replaced with something completely different) is worthy of attention before an examination is made of the actual direction of the proposals for reform.

6.6.1 **A rule which should remain within the law's reach?**

There are a number of references in the 1998 Report, both direct and indirect, to the way in which some control should be maintained over attempts by one generation to restrict the free application and devolution of property by successive generations. The proposed reformed rule will now only apply to interests in property arising under wills and family settlements, but it is deemed to be necessary and desirable to maintain its reach in such situations. Restricting the rule against perpetuity to 'successive estates and interests in property and to powers of appointment' in this way will, according to the Law Commission, restore the original function of the rule. It removes from the reach of the rule circumstances where 'that justification is absent'. In the outline of the principal recommended reforms, the Law Commission did acknowledge that there was no universal agreement even that the rule should remain at all, even in its original context. According to the Report (at 8, 1998) there was a 'distinguished minority' of respondents to the consultation process calling for the rule to be abolished rather than reformed, on grounds which were grouped by the Law Commission under limitations which were no longer necessary, or which could be achieved by alternative means (e.g., statutory powers of sale; legislation relating to taxation; and legal facilities for the variation of trusts).

6.6.2 **Retention not abolition: scope of reform**

Notwithstanding the arguments against retaining the rule against perpetuities, the Law Commission nevertheless concluded that it should be retained in some form. The case in favour of controlling the 'dead hand rule' outweighed arguments against its continuing application, but the Law Commission acknowledged that this should be framed in reference to an approach which is described as *inclusionary* rather than *exclusionary*. The Law Commission explained this focus as one which defines interests which *should* be subject to the rule against perpetuities, rather than those which should not. This is an approach in which the 'test' is whether there is a need to control the dead hand rule: where there is, the rule will apply; where there is not, the rule shall not.

6.6.2.1 *The 'dead hand rule' and balance in the law's approach*

The question which arises from this new approach (and even 'test') is whether the Law Commission has given sufficient and appropriate consideration to the much-vaunted negativity of the 'dead hand rule'. It is suggested that there is much which points to the affirmative, and that in terms of interests and estates created by trusts and under wills, it is not in the interests of beneficiaries or society in general that the present is ruled by the minds, prejudices, and wisdoms of the past. In terms of making an assessment of the relationship between past and present, and achieving the most appropriate degree of consonance between the two, many historians approach this through use of the principle of historical process. In this framework, 'the present' is regarded as being part of a continuing evolution of societal processes, and part of a trajectory which is still unfolding. Indeed, in a directly applicable manifestation of this, the Law Commission itself acknowledges in the 1998 Report that it is not possible to rule against new kinds of property rights arising in the future. If this is the case, then it must follow that even very well-intentioned ancestral views on the 'best ways' of managing property cannot be accorded equal let alone greater value than current understanding of property and optimising its use.

6.6.3 **New law: a rule with direction, purpose, and rationale**

6.6.3.1 *More limited but more appropriate application*

What remains by adopting such an inclusionary approach is, according to the Law Commission, a rule with more limited application, but with clear purpose. The Law Commission accepted that the rule against perpetuities was being applied to a number of transactions to which it was wholly inappropriate given its origins in familial wealth preservation, and that because of this, it should have a restricted ambit and reach. Here, it should only apply to rights arising under wills and trusts. Pension schemes should be exempt from the rule's applications, and it should not apply to certain rights over property such as options, and rights of first refusal, future easements, etc. created after the enactment of new perpetuities legislation.

To address the current situation whereby there is often uncertainty as to whether the rule applies and the consequent degree of expertise required for advising clients, the Law Commission has proposed that the circumstances in which a transaction is subject to any new rule against perpetuities be set out clearly in statute. This is of course the realisation of the new law's proposed inclusionary approach.

6.6.3.2 *New single statutory perpetuity period to offer certainty and flexibility*

The Law Commission has recommended that there should be one fixed perpetuity period of 125 years. Under the proposed scheme, a future interest or right would only be void for perpetuity when it became clear that it would not take effect within 125 years from the date on which the instrument creating it took effect. This incorporates the virtues of the 1964 Act evident in its 'wait and see' provisions, which acts as a device to prevent future interests being struck out *ab initio* (on grounds of possibility of vesting outside the perpetuity period) as is the case under the common law. The fixed statutory maximum period is more generous than the current statutory provisions, and as such will help to promote flexible and confident dealings with property. The manner in which it is fixed also removes the clumsiness and certainty arising in the common law, and may actually at last sound the death knell of 'royal lives clauses'.

6.6.3.3 *Key perceived benefits of reform*

Following the main body of the document, the Law Commission sets out the intended beneficial effects of the reforms at length. These cluster around promoting greater confidence in dealings with property and thus facilitation of them; encouraging greater flexibility in dealings with property and drafting trusts; provision of greater access to the law and reduction of scope for error in respect of stating the law; and facilitating the production of documents which are simplified and less lengthy, with the result of a reduction of costs incurred for legal and related professional services.

6.7 **Rule against excessive accumulations**

Very much as it sounds, the notion of 'accumulation' of property can be found strongly rooted in ideas of wealth preservation. It is the term given when any profits which are produced by property subject to a trust are added to its original value, rather than being distributed to beneficiaries under the trust. Accumulations are a very common feature of modern trusts, and are premised on the desirability of being able to provide a healthy capital sum for beneficiaries on their coming of age, or other event which reflects their entitlement to the trust (such as marriage), and the facilitation of this. However, the law requires that the time during which accumulation (rather than distribution) is directed to take place is limited to one of the periods permitted. It is another mechanism by which the law places limits on how property can be 'tied up'.

If an accumulation is directed for longer than the common law perpetuity period of a life plus 21 years, the direction is void *ab initio* and no accumulation can be undertaken at all. If, however, the direction does not infringe this rule, it is subject to additional control, and it will only be allowed to take place for a period not exceeding one of the periods specified by statute. Should it overrun, it will be void with regard to the excess, and in this event the surplus accumulated income will pass to the persons who would have been entitled to receive that income if the accumulation had not been directed.

The control of accumulations is statutory, originating in the Accumulations Act 1800, this legislation believed to be an overzealous response to the decision in *Thellusson* v *Woodford* (1799) 4 Ves 227; (1805) 11 Ves 112; 31 ER 117; 32 ER 1030. In this case, a direction to accumulate for what was then the full perpetuity period (thought at that time to be lives in being only) was upheld as lawful at common law. The amount of the moneys to be accumulated was very large, and Parliament considered it undesirable that so large a proportion of the nation's wealth should be tied up for such a long period.

The present statutory periods are contained in the Law of Property Act 1925, ss. 164 to 166, and in the Perpetuities and Accumulations Act 1964, s. 13. In terms of functioning, s. 164 of the 1925 Act sets out four periods and only these can apply to pre-1964 dispositions, while in the case of post-1964 dispositions the additional two periods contained in s. 13 of the 1964 Act are available. Only one period can be used and it is usual in a modern, professionally drafted trust, to specify which it should be. In any other case, the court will determine which period is most appropriate on proper construction of the instrument.

6.7.1 Four possible measures of time determining permitted accumulation of income

The four periods found in the 1964 Act are as follows. First, there is the life of the grantor or settlor; then a period marked as 21 years from the death of the grantor or settlor. The remaining two are: the minority or respective minorities only of any person or persons living or *en ventre sa mère* (unborn) at the death of the grantor, settlor, or testator; and finally the minority or respective minorities only of any person or persons who would, under the limitations of the instrument directing the accumulation, for the time being, if of full age, be entitled to the income directed to be accumulated. In addition (s. 13 of) the Act tries to remedy the peculiarity of s. 164 (which allows periods two and three to run only from the death of the settlor and not from the date of the instrument, and becomes unnecessarily restrictive) by adding 21 years from the making of the disposition the minority or respective minorities only of any person or persons who, under the limitations of the instrument directing the accumulation, would for the time being, if of full age, be entitled to the income directed to be accumulated. In summary, the four periods in s. 164 are:

(i) the life of the grantor or settlor;

(ii) 21 years from the death of the grantor or settlor;

(iii) the minority or respective minorities only of any person or persons living or *en ventre sa mère* at the death of the grantor, settlor, or testator;

(iv) the minority or respective minorities only of any person or persons who, under the limitations of the instrument directing the accumulation, would for the time being, if of full age, be entitled to the income directed to be accumulated.

6.7.2 **Reform proposals: a much restricted application of the rule against excessive accumulations**

The Law Commission in its consideration of the rule against perpetuities and excessive accumulations has recommended that this rule should be abolished except in relation to charitable trusts. It has already been noted (in chapter 1) that charitable trusts can exist perpetually (i.e. they do not infringe the rule against perpetuity), but in reforming the rule against excessive accumulations, charitable trusts which have a power or duty to accumulate income should only be capable of doing so for a period of 21 years. Given their perpetual nature, the ability to accumulate income indefinitely (rather than applying it to its purposes) could operate contrary to benefiting the public. It is very hard to envisage a 'private familial context' *Thellusson* v *Woodford* (1799) situation arising today, but the issues arising in respect of charitable trusts are perhaps more current than ever—the ability of charitable trusts to accumulate assets as distinct from applying them to their purposes is very much a 'live' issue.

6.8 **Rule against inalienability: rule against perpetual trusts**

In the earlier chapter dealing with certainty requirements and the 'beneficiary principle' note was made of the rule against inalienability. This is more commonly known as the rule against perpetual trusts.

6.8.1 **A final point of reference**

In terms of relating the rule against inalienability to the very similar sounding 'rule against perpetuity' it should be clear that while the latter relates to future vesting of interests and estates, the former rule against perpetual trusts does something quite different. Confusion between the two is easier to avoid where reference is made to the rule against perpetuities as the rule against 'remoteness in vesting'. At this point the rule against perpetual trusts sounds quite different, and of course it is. This is even more clear when using its term as the rule against inalienability.

6.8.1.1 *Point of revision*

The rule against perpetual trusts relates to the duration of trusts for non-charitable purposes. These instruments are usually void for want of a beneficiary in a position to enforce the trust, under the authority provided by *Re Astor's ST* [1952]. But even for those dispositions where validity is upheld notwithstanding violation of the beneficiary principle, an additional problem with their validity comes from the way in which they may be perpetual or everlasting. To avoid this, as was explained earlier, they are only valid for the perpetuity period (even dispositions which are valid without a beneficiary).

6.8.1.2 *Difficulties created by perpetual trusts and the need to avoid their operation*

It should have been clear in chapter 4 that the litigation which arises reveals these trusts as highly problematic in terms of enforcement and monitoring performance of them. In this respect, as the Law Commission notes in its 1998 documentation, the rule against inalienability is a device to limit the operation of such trusts in light of these difficulties, and certainly to curtail their development. The materials in chapter 4 did intend to invite a more critical appraisal of the 'private purpose trusts' than the Law Commission actually engages in, although the discussion in the Report does proceed to explain why the rule against inalienability has not been considered within the provinces of the enquiry.

6.8.2 Law Commission's exclusion of the rule against inalienability

This rule has been expressly excluded from the Law Commission's remit because, in the Commission's words, it 'belongs more properly in a review of the law governing non-charitable purpose trusts'.

FURTHER READING

Deech 'Lives in Being Revisited' (1981) Law Quarterly Review 593.

Harpum 'Perpetuities, Pensions and Resulting Trusts' (2000) Conveyancer 170.

7

....

Introduction to resulting
and constructive trusts

The attention given in this text to constructive and resulting trusts arises from the way in which their characteristics and operation necessarily require extensive and thorough treatment. There are two starting points for this discussion.

- The first is the fundamental principle of trusts law which emerged from the principle in *Westdeutsche Landesbank Girozentrale* v *Islington London Borough Council* [1996] AC 669 that the basis for all trusts is conscience.
- The second relates to the way in which up to now, the attention which has been paid to trusts which are *private* (rather than publicly enforceable charitable trusts), has related to trusts which have been termed 'express private trusts'.

This chapter introduces trusts which arise on the basis of conscience but are different from 'express trusts' because they arise from ways other than a settlor's express intention to create a trust. This might seem rather odd given the attention which has been given to the requirements for creating valid private trusts, and especially the ones relating to certainty (of intention) and the constitution of trusts. But what follows in this chapter is an introduction to trusts which arise but are not expressly created.

Following this in chapters 8, 9, and 10 is an extensive exploration of non-express private trusts, pursued through a number of 'case studies'. These 'case studies' are intended to show that non-express private trusts arise in a number of settings in everyday life, and to explain how they work in these individual 'settings' as well as more generally. Before any of this can happen, there must be some appreciation of why—having gone to the trouble to formulate the 'requirements for validity'—equity permits trusts to arise where they have not been expressly created, and indeed has actually 'relaxed' some of the requirements which are otherwise in place for (express) trusts to be valid.

7.1 Introducing trusts which are 'implied': their significance and rationale

It was made clear at the outset that 'property' is at the heart of equity's development of the trust instrument as it has been represented up to now—as one which reflects the express intention of an owner of property to confer a benefit to another. And the central significance of 'property' can also be found in the way in which equity recongises trusts which are implied alongside those which are express.

The term 'implied trust' in English trusts law denotes trusts other than those expressly declared by the settlor. But both are premised on the importance of the concept of property in English law more generally. Earlier parts of this text have touched on the importance of 'ownership' in English law, because this provides the basis for the high levels of autonomy enjoyed by an owner of property in his use and application of property. An owner of property can do more or less anything with it: this includes his rights to enjoy the property, but also includes the right he has to confer it, or *give it*, to another. As the first chapter explained, in English law ownership is manifested in legal title to property, and chapters 1 and 2 pointed to the way in which, in relation to the express private trust, there are both 'settlor-oriented' and 'beneficiary-oriented' attractions to creating a trust.

In the development of 'non-express trusts', equity acknowledges that the implications of the ownership of property can be very complex. And in developing trusts which do not have to be expressly declared by an owner of property in order to be valid, it is clear that equity is seeking to respond to *injustices* which can arise from the ownership of property.

7.1.1 Understanding implied trusts, and 'locating' injustice in the ownership of property

For understanding why equity might have developed trusts which are implied in response to injustices arising from ownership of property, once again reference is made to the very beginnings of this text: chapter 1 considered the way in which 'rights' to or 'interests' in property are characteristically very valuable rights. Here, legal title to property ensures that these rights are sufficiently certain. This is because it is important for the owner of property to be certain he has the capacity to deal freely with his property from his own perspective, and also given that 'dealings' with property are also likely to affect the position of third parties.

The appearance of so-called constructive and resulting trusts is essentially a response to tensions inherent in property and ownership. This is because property rights are extremely valuable and form the basis of many transactional dealings, and this suggests the position on who can deal with property should be *certain*. However, there can be circumstances where this commitment to certainty can cause *injustice* to another party to arise. In other words, recognising only legal title in circumstances where no express trust has been declared can lead to the interests of others (namely, not the legal owner) being 'overlooked'. Equity's response to this has been that distinct equitable interest in property (in favour of someone other than the legal, and apparently only, 'owner') can subsist even in circumstances where no express trust of property has been declared. In short, the study of implied trusts has at its 'core' the tensions between ensuring certainty and achieving justice in relation to property.

7.1.2 Focusing preliminary understanding on the key functions and rationale of implied trusts

What follows shortly is an extended introductory consideration of the two types of implied trust developed by equity. These are trusts which are termed 'resulting trusts' and ones which are called 'constructive trusts'. After that, more detailed consideration is given to the actual 'fact situations' in which they arise. But at this stage, as these two types of implied trust are being introduced, what is being acknowledged is that, in certain circumstances, equity will *imply* that an asset being held by another (evidenced by the location of legal title) is to be held wholly or partly for someone other than the holder of legal title. In these circumstances equity will *imply* a trust where a trust of that property has not been expressly declared. Ahead of this there are a few points which should be noted:

- When working through the materials, it should be borne in mind that when equity implies a trust, this will arise because the interests of justice are greater than prioritising the position of 'certainty' which attaches to legal title.
- It will also become apparent that because these trusts will arise in circumstances where they are not being declared, and parties are often unaware that they have arisen, they are not treated as express trusts in many respects.
- The most important consequence of a trust being implied rather than express is that the former type are exempt from formalities which would otherwise pertain to property in the creation of a trust. This will become very significant in the study made of the family home in chapter 9, in relation to the requirements of 53(1)(b) of the Law of Property Act 1925, which operates subject to provisions of s. 53(2).

7.2 The different types of implied trust

The purpose of the materials above is to identify the concept of a trust which is non-express, and point to the *unifying features* which these trusts which are not expressly declared share in terms of their *basis in conscience* (in common with all trusts); *how they arise* (notably they are not expressly declared); *their rationale* in the context of justice; and how they are not subject to all the requirements which must otherwise be met for a private trust to be valid. What needs to be stressed at this point is that there are actually two different types of implied trust.

While it is the case that, generally, all implied trusts arise in response to equity's concern about justice, the precise nature of response will depend on the circumstances in which the injustice arises, and what is required to address it. This need for different responses to different types of injustice has led to the evolution of the 'resulting trust' and the 'constructive trust'. Both these types of implied trust are now introduced and discussed in some detail, but ahead of this, it is suggested that during this chapter it will become clear that:

- The Resulting Trust is recognition that ownership in property vests in someone other than the apparent owner (the person who holds legal title to property). This will become clear from looking more closely at the circumstances in which a resulting trust arises, and the way in which it is always the case that the beneficiary under a resulting trust is the original owner of property (who, when this trust arises because legal title has been transferred to another, becomes the 'settlor').

- The Constructive Trust arises in a wide variety of circumstances and fact situations. What they have in common is the widely held view that constructive trusts are a response to some kind of 'wrong' which is committed by the holder of legal title to property. Here a trust is imposed because his conscience is affected by his conduct, and as a result he does continue to hold legal title, but he does so as trustee, and this thus makes his 'title' to the property subject to the interests of another.

7.3 An introduction to resulting trusts

It was noted earlier in the brief introduction to resulting trusts (in chapter 2) that they are difficult to pin down, mainly because they can be found in a number of very diverse factual situations. It was also suggested in that introduction that at the heart of all resulting trusts could be found a fundamental characteristic which overarches all the different factual manifestations and applications. This common factor is that the settlor and the beneficiary are the same person.

7.3.1 Settlor and beneficiary are the same person

So what is common to all resulting trusts is that although legal title is vested in a trustee, the settlor and the beneficiary are actually the same person. In the brief introduction in chapter 2 it was suggested that this arose from the occurrence of two broad scenarios. The trust in favour of the settlor-beneficiary might arise where the settlor has tried to create a trust in favour of a third party beneficiary, but failed to do so. This has the consequence that the equitable interest which is created on the transfer of legal title never actually leaves him. It can also arise where property has been divested from the settlor, but for some reason equitable interest in it is at a later date returned to him, on account of an event which has not been foreseen by the donor and hence (or perhaps because of bad drafting) this 'contingency' has not been provided for. This is explained here, alongside a further situation where a resulting trust can arise.

In due course greater attention shall be given to the creation of the resulting trust on account of the *Westdeutsche* determination that unless and until there is separation of titles, while one person holds property absolutely, no distinct equitable title actually exists and equitable ownership is instead encompassed within the legal title which is held. It is the position post-*Westdeutsche* that equitable title is actually created, and this occurs when legal title is transferred to another— because the conscience of its recipient is affected. For the sake of simplicity, at this point it is best to try to keep in mind that equitable interest created in property as a result of the transfer of legal title *remains with* the settlor, or it is *returned to* him. In this manner a resulting trust can be seen to provide the basis of a claim for the recovery of one's own property. Understanding this is vital because what follows is a brief consideration of a number of factual situations to which this 'remains with–or returns to' model can be applied.

7.3.2 **Where and in what situations do resulting trusts arise?**

There is much apparent simplicity in the statement above that the resulting trust is 'recognition that ownership of property vests in someone other than' the person who by holding legal title appears to own it. However, resulting trusts can be difficult to pin down further because they are actually found in numerous 'fact situations' which are actually very diverse. And in this respect they can be more difficult to appreciate than constructive trusts which are (with a possible limited exception that will be considered in due course) impositions of trusteeship in unconscionable situations.

The starting point for understanding resulting trusts, appreciating where they arise and why they do so, is that all resulting trusts do have one element in common. That is that the original owner of property which becomes trust property is actually the beneficiary under a resulting trust. The trust arises because legal title is transferred to another, and so here owner becomes 'settlor', but the circumstances in which this transfer arises will ensure that the settlor will also become the beneficiary under the trust arrangement which now exists. But where do these trusts arise, and how are they recognisable?

In short, legal title is vested in a trustee, while the settlor and the beneficiary are actually the same person. Some reference has already been made to this in respect of certainty requirements and the absence of certainty (considered in chapter 4), and by way of introduction it is important to appreciate at a basic level when the resulting trust can arise.

(1) Situations in which a resulting trust can be implied:

- Where the settlor has tried to create a trust in favour of a third party beneficiary, and although legal title has been transferred from him, he has failed to divest himself of equitable interest in the property. Here, equitable title never leaves him; *OR* property has been divested from him successfully initially, but it is for some reason later returned back to him.

- Where there has been a what is known as a 'voluntary conveyance' of property to another. Here, title to property is transferred to another in circumstances where no consideration is given. A resulting trust being 'implied' is based on the proposition that in circumstances where legal title is transferred to another, it is inappropriate for this to confer upon its new holder all the entitlements of ownership: this will create a distinct equitable interest which will not 'follow' legal title.

(2) Why are the settlor and beneficiary the same person?: applying situations to 'trust actors'.

- Where an owner of property attempts to settle property on trust for a third party beneficiary, but failed to do so, the equitable interest which is created on the transfer of legal title never actually leaves him.

- Where property has been divested from the settlor, but for some reason equitable interest in it is returned back to him at a later date. Here equitable interest is said to result to him on account of an unforeseen event not provided for, or through careless drafting of the trust.

- Where there has been a voluntary conveyance, the owner of that property becomes settlor when he conveys legal title to the new legal owner, and a beneficiary under the trust created because it is inappropriate for the new holder of legal title to have the full entitlements of ownership, because no consideration has been provided.

What needs to happen before this detailed consideration of resulting trust 'fact situations' is for some explanation to be given of the way in which resulting trusts of different types are actually classified. This is the starting point for actually understanding the 'fact situations' which will now follow, and it will also reiterate the very first point made in this chapter. This is that the basis of all trusts is conscience and intention. Authority for this general position is *Westdeutsche*, and in this respect *Westdeutsche* has also had an important impact on the way in which resulting trusts are actually classified. Indeed, *Westdeutsche* precipitated a rethinking of their traditional classification as 'automatic' and 'presumed intention' resulting trusts, which was the approach adopted in *Re Vandervell's Trusts (No. 2)* [1974] Ch 269, where Megarry J distinguished between presumed and automatic resulting trusts.

7.3.3 How resulting trusts are classified

The starting point for understanding how resulting trusts are classified in English law, and the reasons for this is the case of *Re Vandervell's Trusts (No. 2)*. In this case ([1974] Ch 269) Megarry J distinguished between presumed and automatic resulting trusts:

(a) The first class of case is where the transfer to B is not made on any trust...there is a rebuttable presumption that B holds on resulting trust for A. The question is not one of the automatic consequences of a dispositive failure by A, but one of presumption: the property has been carried to B, and from the absence of consideration and any presumption of advancement B is presumed not only to hold the entire interest on trust but also to hold the beneficial interest for A absolutely. The presumption thus establishes both that B is to take on trust and also what that trust is. Such resulting trusts may be called 'presumed resulting trusts'.

(b) The second class of case is where the transfer to B is made on trusts which leave some or all the beneficial interest undisposed of. Here B automatically holds on resulting trust for A to the extent that the beneficial interest has not been carried to him or others. The resulting trust here does not depend on any intentions or presumptions, but is the automatic consequence of A's failure to dispose of what is vested in him. Since *ex hypothesi* the transfer is on trust, the resulting trust does not establish the trust but merely carries back to A the beneficial interest that has not been disposed of. Such resulting trusts may be called 'automatic resulting trusts'.

7.3.3.1 *Resulting trusts and the* Westdeutsche *reclassification*

A similar but not identical categorisation was adopted by Lord Browne-Wilkinson in *Westdeutsche Landesbank Girozentrale v Islington London Borough Council* [1996] AC 669, at p. 708. In what must now be regarded as a reclassification, under existing law, a resulting trust arises in two sets of circumstances:

(A) where A makes a voluntary payment to B or pays (wholly or in part) for the purchase of property which is vested either in B alone or in the joint names of A and B, there is a presumption that A did not intend to make a gift to B: the money or property is held on trust for A (if he is the sole provider of the money) or in the case of a joint purchase by A and B in shares proportionate to their contributions. It is important to stress that this is only a presumption, which presumption is easily rebutted either by the counter-presumption of advancement or by direct evidence of A's intention to make an out-right transfer...

(B) where A transfers property to B on express trusts, but the trusts do not exhaust the whole of the beneficial interest...[and] *Quistclose Investments Ltd* v *Rolls Razor Ltd* [1970] AC 567.

Both types of resulting trust are traditionally regarded as examples of trusts giving effect to the common intention of the parties. A resulting trust is not imposed by law against the intentions of the trustee (as is a constructive trust); but gives effect to his presumed intention. Megarry J in *Re Vandervell's Trusts (No. 2)* suggests that a resulting trust of type (B) does not depend on intention but operates automatically. However, it will become clear that this can be problematic, as indicated in discussion of *Re West Sussex Constabulary's Widows, Children and Benevolent (1930) Fund Trusts* [1971] Ch 1.

7.4 Category (B) resulting trusts: trusts which are implied from failed attempts to create trusts, and from equitable interest being 'returned' at some later date

7.4.1 Incomplete disposal of the equitable interest

The settlor may have made it clear that property is intended to be held on trust and may even have transferred the legal title to the trustee. There may be some reason, however, why the equitable interest is not properly disposed of. Obviously the trustee cannot keep the trust property for himself and so he holds it on resulting trust for the settlor. There is nowhere else for the equitable interest to go. This can be seen in the following situations:

7.4.1.1 *Situations arising from difficulties concerning formalities, certainty, and public policy*

Sometimes this can arise for technical reasons. For example, we saw in chapter 5 that formalities may be required for the disposal of an equitable interest. If these formalities are not complied with, there will be no effective disposal. In that case the equitable interest never leaves the settlor, and there is a resulting trust. *IRC* v *Broadway Cottages Trust* [1955] Ch 20 is authority that this outcome can also be seen where certainty of objects requirements are not complied with. (see chapter 4).

A trust can also fail for public policy reasons, for example where equity has not allowed a person to retain the fruits of criminal activities. In *Cleaver* v *Mutual Reserve Fund Life Association* [1892] 1 QB 147, the executors of a person who had effected an insurance on his life for the benefit of his wife were held by the Court of Appeal to be able to maintain an action on the policy where the wife had murdered the insured; the trust in favour of the wife was unenforceable, for public policy reasons. There are a number of cases where persons guilty of murder or manslaughter have been prevented from obtaining the property of the victim, either through intestacy (*Re Crippen* [1911] P 108), or through the right of survivorship (*Re K (dec'd)* [1985] 2 WLR 262, affirmed on other grounds [1986] Ch 180, although there relief was granted against forfeiture by the Forfeiture Act 1982).

The result in *Cleaver* was that the executors held the insurance money for the estate of the insured. The result is exactly the same as in any other failed trust case; there is a resulting trust, as in the other cases in this section. In short, this is a category (B) *Westdeutsche* resulting trust.

7.4.1.2 *Situations arising where equitable interests are undefined*

Another possibility is where property is settled on trust but details of the trust are left unclear (i.e. the terms of the trust fail to provide for the totality of the beneficial interest). In *Vandervell v IRC* [1967] 2 AC 291 (a case considered in greater detail in chapter 5) Mr Vandervell made arrangements to endow a chair of pharmacology by transferring shares to the Royal College of Surgeons, to enable it to take the dividends declared on those shares. He did not wish to make an out-and-out transfer, however, and so gave an option to purchase (at a nominal cost) to a trustee company which was under his control. He left no clear instructions with the trustee company as to the terms on which the option was to be held by them.

As explained in chapter 5, Vandervell's liability to surtax on the dividends depended on whether he had divested himself of his entire interest in both the shares and the option. The Revenue failed to show that he had not divested himself of the entire interest in the shares. The point that arises in the present context, however, is that they succeeded in showing that he had not divested himself of his equitable interest in the option, the legal title to which was now in the trustee company. The option was therefore held on resulting trust for him along with liability to pay surtax on the dividends.

Lord Wilberforce said that the trusts upon which the option was supposed to be held were undefined and in the air, possibly to be defined later. The trustee company itself was clearly not a beneficiary. An equitable interest cannot remain in the air and so the only possibility was a resulting trust in favour of the settlor. This is an example, then, of the trust being insufficiently defined.

To counter the Revenue's claims to surtax on the dividends declared on the shares, Mr Vandervell in 1961 instructed the trustee company to exercise the option, and repurchase the shares. The shares were then placed by the trustee company on the trusts of the children's settlements. The Court of Appeal held in *Re Vandervell's Trusts (No. 2)* [1974] Ch 269 that Vandervell had now succeeded in divesting himself of the entire interest in these shares, there being no longer a resulting trust in his favour. The later trusts were precisely defined, in favour of the children's settlements, so it was no longer necessary for this reason for the equitable interest to remain in the settlor.

7.4.1.3 *Situations where a so-called 'necessary pre-condition' is absent*

There can be other reasons, apart from a defective trust instrument, for a failure to dispose of an equitable interest. One possibility is that the body on which money or property is settled has never existed or has ceased to exist. If a general or paramount charitable intention is shown on the part of the donor, a cy près scheme may be applied (considered later in the context of charitable trusts). Otherwise the property will be held on resulting trust for the settlor.

Another situation is where money or property is given for a purpose, and the circumstances necessary to achieve the purpose fail to materialise. For example, in *Essery* v *Coulard* (1884) 26 Ch D 191, a trust for the parties to an intended marriage, and the issue of the marriage, could not take effect when the parties decided to live together without marrying, so Pearson J held that the property was to be held on resulting trust for the settlor. The intention of the settlor (the intended wife) had been to provide for all the issue of the relationship, and this was inevitably defeated by failure to marry, even if a marriage were later to take place: children had already been born, and at that time illegitimate children could not benefit from such a trust. Since a subsequent marriage would not legitimate the children who had already been born, the settlor's intention to provide for all the children had been irrevocably defeated by the failure of the parties to marry.

A similar result was reached in *Re Ames' Settlement* [1946] Ch 217. Property was settled expressly on trusts, declared as part of a marriage settlement, which gave the husband an income for life, with remainder to his wife for life or until her remarriage, with remainder to the issue of the intended marriage. However, although Mr Ames and Miss Hamilton went through a ceremony of marriage, and lived together as if married, the Supreme Court of Kenya later declared the marriage void *ab initio*, a decree of nullity having at that time retrospective effect. In other words, the position was as if there had never been a valid marriage. Nor was there any issue. The income was paid to Mr Ames until his death, and the question arose as to what to do with the capital. The settlement had provided for an ultimate trust of the capital, for an artificial class of the husband's next of kin, in the event of failure of issue of the 'intended marriage', but Vaisey J held that the property should be held on resulting trust for the settlor (or rather, his representatives). *Re Ames* was distinguished by the House of Lords in *Westdeutsche* v *Islington BC* [1996] AC 669.

The same result would not obtain on the same facts today: since 31 July 1971, a decree of nullity in respect of a voidable marriage has not had retrospective effect, so the marriage would not be regarded as void *ab initio*.

7.4.1.4 *Situations where there is a partial disposal of equitable interest*

Sometimes the settlor disposes of some, but not all, of the equitable interest. Usually this occurs because some contingency is unprovided for, perhaps because it is unforeseen, or perhaps because of sloppy drafting. In this case also, the undisposed-of residue 'results' to the settlor.

A good example is *Re Cochrane* [1955] Ch 309, which concerned a marriage settlement of funds for the wife:

during her life so long as she shall continue to reside with the said W.J.B. Cochrane...and after [her] decease or the prior determination of the trust in her favour...upon trust to pay the said income to the said W.J.B. Cochrane (if then living) during his life and after the decease of the survivor of them...in trust for such of their issue as they should jointly or as the survivor of them should appoint, and in default of appointment equally at the age of 21, or in the case of daughters, earlier marriage.

The draftsman appears to have assumed that even if Mrs Cochrane ceased to reside with Mr Cochrane, Mr Cochrane would live long enough either for an appointment to be made, or for his children to take in default of appointment. In the event, however, this did not happen, the timing of events being as follows. First, Mrs Cochrane stopped living with Mr Cochrane. Her interest accordingly terminated. Then Mr Cochrane died, before either any appointment in favour of the children had been made, or the default conditions had occurred. The issue before the court was what should happen to the income from the fund between Cochrane's death and the children reaching 21 or, in the case of daughters, their marriage if earlier.

It can be seen that the contingency that occurred had simply not been provided for, so that for a time there was no clear disposition of the equitable interest. Not only had it not been provided for, but the deed gave no guidance to the court as to what could have been intended. Harman J held that for the unprovided for period there was a resulting trust of the income to the settlor.

7.4.1.5 *Situations where a so-called 'Necessary condition' comes to an end*

It may be that the trust presupposes the existence of a condition which does subsist for a time and then comes to an end. In that case, the general position is once again that there will be a resulting trust of any surplus. For example, in *Hussey* v *Palmer* [1972] 1 WLR 1286 a payment of £607, for improvements to property to enable a widow to live with her daughter and son-in-law, was held on resulting trust for her when differences arose and she had to leave the house.

In this situation, however, there will be a resulting trust only if the surplus is undisposed of at the end of the precondition. Another possibility is that the donor made an unconditional gift, and did not intend to retain any interest in the surplus should the necessary conditions for the gift cease.

In *Re the Trusts of the Abbott Fund* [1900] 2 Ch 326, a fund was collected for the relief of two deaf and dumb ladies (who had been defrauded out of their rights under an earlier settlement). No provision was made for disposal of the fund on the death of the survivor. A surplus of some £367 remained when they died, and Stirling J held that this should be held on resulting trust for the contributors to the fund. It can be seen that the case is not unlike *Re Cochrane* [1955] Ch 309 (see chapter 8), in that the contingency of the death of the ladies had not been provided for.

In reaching his decision in *Re the Trusts of the Abbott Fund*, Stirling J held that the ladies themselves never became absolute owners of the fund. Nor did the trustees once the purposes were accomplished. No resulting trust occurs if either beneficiary or trustee is intended to take absolutely, however.

The fund in *Abbott* was subscribed to by various friends of the Abbotts. On the other hand, where the whole of a specific fund is left by a single individual for the maintenance of given individuals, the courts are more likely to construe the transaction as an absolute gift to those individuals, even where the fund is expressed to be left for a particular purpose (although it depends, of course, on the intention of the donor, which is ultimately a question of fact). An example is the Court of Appeal decision in *Re Osoba* [1979] 1 WLR 247, where a testator left the whole of a fund on trust for the education of his daughter up to university level. On completion of the daughter's university education she was held entitled to the surplus beneficially, the educational purpose being regarded merely as a statement of the testator's motive—in other words, there was no resulting trust in favour of the testator's estate.

The other possibility is a gift to the trustee. *Re the Trusts of the Abbott Fund* applies only where the property was intended to be held on trust, and so does not apply where the intention is to make an out-and-out gift subject to trusts (as opposed to a gift 'on trust', which is subject to the *Abbott* principle). In such cases the trustee is clearly intended to keep the surplus. An example is *Re Foord* [1922] 2 Ch 519, where the testator left in his will: 'all my effects including rubber and other shares I leave absolutely to my sister on trust to pay my wife £300 p.a., etc.'.

7.4.1.6 *Situations where there are anonymous subscriptions to funds*

Where money has been given to a fund, say a disaster appeal fund, one might infer the donor's intention from, among other considerations, whether the donation was anonymous (e.g., small change in a street collecting box). If so, and no means of tracing the donor exists, then the contribution might be construed as an out-and-out gift. Clearly the donor cannot have intended that any surplus left over be held on resulting trust for him, when he has left the organisers no means of finding him in the event of there being a surplus. If there is a surplus left over after the fund has fulfilled his purposes, therefore, and the fund is not charitable, that part of the surplus attributable to his donation will have no owner. It therefore goes to the Crown as *bona vacantia*.

Where the purpose of the fund is charitable, there will be a different outcome. In this case a cy près scheme can be invoked so as to allow the property to be applied to purposes 'as near as possible' to the original purpose. The present discussion pertains to the purpose of the fund not being charitable.

In spite of the general principle suggested above, *Re the Trusts of the Abbott Fund* [1900] 2 Ch 326 was followed in *Re Gillingham Bus Disaster Fund* [1958] Ch 300 (upheld on a different issue [1958] 2 All ER 749), and such donations were directed to be held on resulting trust. The case concerned a fund collected to defray funeral and other expenses incurred as a result of a disaster involving the deaths of 24 Royal Marine cadets in Gillingham. The town clerk of Gillingham wrote a letter to *The Daily Telegraph* in the following terms:

Cadets' memorial. To the editor of '*The Daily Telegraph*'. Sir, The mayors of Gillingham, Rochester, and Chatham have decided to promote a Royal Marine Cadet Corps Memorial Fund to be devoted, among other things, to defraying the funeral expenses, caring for the boys who may be disabled, and then to such worthy cause or causes in memory of the boys who lost their lives, as the mayors may determine.

Harman J held that this was not a charitable purpose, and that the last purpose, 'to such worthy cause or causes in memory of the boys who lost their lives, as the mayors may determine', was void for uncertainty (see further chapter 5). The purposes were therefore taken to be defraying the funeral expenses of the boys who lost their lives, and caring for the boys who were disabled.

Far more money (about £9,000) was collected than was necessary for these purposes, especially as there were common law actions available against the bus company. The question therefore was who owned the surplus: was it the donors, represented by the Official Solicitor, or the Crown (represented by the Treasury Solicitor), as *bona vacantia*? Harman J, following *Re the Trusts of the Abbott Fund*, held that the surplus should be held on resulting trust for the donors.

The difficulty was that, although some of the money had been provided by identifiable people, most had been obtained from street collections. So many of the donors were anonymous and the trustees were therefore required to hold the fund on resulting trust for unknown people. Obviously, this is most inconvenient administratively. It will become clear (in chapter 14) that had the gifts been charitable the cy près doctrine could have provided a way of avoiding this difficulty, but the gifts in *Gillingham* were not charitable. As explained above, if people give money in an anonymous collection, surely it can be assumed that they do not intend to see it back again (a view taken, in a slightly different context, by Jenkins LJ in *Re Ulverston and District New Hospital Building Trusts* [1956] Ch 622). In other words, an out-and-out gift seems a more sensible inference than a gift on trust. Had that inference been drawn by Harman J, the surplus would of course have gone to the Crown as *bona vacantia*. He was, however, reluctant to draw the inference that 'the small giver who is anonymous has any wider intention than the large giver who can be named', and in any case observed that the resulting trust 'doctrine does not rest, in my judgment, on any evidence of state of mind of the settlor' but arises automatically by process of law. The last part of this reasoning cannot survive *Westdeutsche*.

Moreover, doubt was also cast by Goff J, in *Re West Sussex Constabulary's Widows, Children and Benevolent (1930) Fund Trusts* [1971] 1 Ch 1, on Harman J's inferences about the donor's actual intention, since in the later case the out-and-out gift construction was adopted. The case concerned a fund for widows and dependants, to which the members contributed, but there were also outside contributions. Reference here is made only to the outside contributions (with the division of the surplus among the members themselves being considered in chapter 4).

The purpose of the fund was to provide allowances for the widows and dependants of deceased members. Some of its revenue was derived from contributions from its own members. Some was also raised from outside sources, by:

(a) entertainments, raffles and sweepstakes;

(b) collecting boxes;

(c) donations, including legacies.

The fund was wound up at the end of 1967, upon the amalgamation of the constabulary with other police forces, and the question arose as to how to divide it up.

Goff J held that the outside contributions raised from category (c) were held on resulting trust for the contributors. Those raised by categories (a) and (b) were clearly intended to take effect as out-and-out gifts to the fund, and therefore the resulting trust doctrine did not apply to them.

So far as identifiable donations and legacies were concerned (category (c)), Goff J thought these indistinguishable from *Re the Trusts of the Abbott Fund*, so the proportion of the surplus attributable to that source was held on resulting trust. But there were also identifiable collections from raffles and sweepstakes (category (a)), which Goff J thought were out-and-out payments subject only to a (contractual) hope of receiving a prize. Third, however, there were the proceeds of street collecting boxes (category (b)), and here Goff J declined to follow Harman J's earlier judgment, again on the grounds that the intention to be inferred was also that of an out-and-out gift. Thus, nobody could lay claim to the proportion of the surplus attributable to the last two categories, so it went to the Crown as *bona vacantia*.

Clearly, the *West Sussex* case is easier to justify in conceptual terms than the earlier case, and of the two *West Sussex* is, we suggest, more likely to be followed in the future. Understandably, however, Harman J was concerned in the earlier case to ensure that the Crown was not the main beneficiary of a fund collected in highly publicised and tragic circumstances.

7.5 Category (A) resulting trusts: trusts implied from a 'voluntary conveyance'

Broadly, this type of trust arises where there is a voluntary transfer of legal title to property (i.e. a transfer which is not one for value). Here, it is provided that *unless* there is a presumption of advancement, the presumption is that equitable title does *not follow* legal title to the transferee, but will instead remain with the transferor. Now there is a trust; legal title has been transferred to another, but because there has not been a transfer for value, equitable title has not passed to the new legal owner of property.

In other words, where there is a transfer of legal title to property, but the transfer has not been one for value, then although legal title has been transferred, equitable title remains with the transferor.

That is, unless there is a presumption of advancement. The presence of a presumption of advancement will alter the outcome significantly, as a presumption of advancement means that equitable title will follow legal title.

7.5.1 Authority for the operation of a resulting trust in voluntary conveyances

The presumption of a resulting trust in such situations goes back at least as far as the late eighteenth century, and its most often cited authoritative basis is the case *Dyer* v *Dyer* (1788) 2 Cox Eq Cas 92. In this case Eyre CB remarked that:

> The trust of a legal estate, whether . . . taken in the names of the purchasers and others jointly, or in the names of others without that of the purchaser; whether in the name of one or several; whether jointly or successive results to the man who advances the purchase money. This is a general proposition supported by all the cases, and there is nothing to contradict it; and it goes on a strict analogy to the rule of common law, that where a feoffment is made without consideration, the use results to the feoffer [the transferor].

In terms of linguistic clarity, the feoffment translates into 'transfer' for immediate purposes and feoffer becomes the 'transferor'. The effect of the presumption of a resulting trust is that equitable title effectively never leaves the transferor.

7.5.1.1 *The presumption of advancement*

The presumption of advancement has already been mentioned in Megarry J's *Vandervell* classification of resulting trusts and also in Lord Brown-Wilkinson's reclassification in *Westdeutsche*. It is alluded to in *Dyer* in Eyre CB's articulation of nothing which might contradict the operation of the resulting trust as a result of the rule of common law whereby if a transfer is made without consideration, it results (remains with/returns to) the transferor.

7.5.1.2 *The presumption of the resulting trust and presumption of advancement compared*

At its most simplistic, the presumption of advancement produces an operation which is the complete opposite to that of a resulting trust. The presumption of a resulting trust is that equitable title will not follow (a) legal (transfer of) title, and will remain with the transferor of the property. The presumption of advancement provides the reverse, and ensures that on the occurrence of a transfer, equitable title will not remain with the transferor, and will actually 'follow' legal title and become vested (like legal title) with the transferee.

7.5.1.3 *When does the presumption that equitable title follows legal title on a transfer arise?*

Once again, this concept is rooted in history and in the ideologies of a society very different from today's. Presumptions of advancement are historically coupled with moral obligation. The most obvious examples of moral obligations are the ones which exist in respect of a husband for his wife, and a father for his children.

The operation of a presumption of advancement means that where there is a voluntary transfer, one that is effectively a gift, as a result of no consideration being given, then equitable title *will* follow legal title to the transferee, but that it will do so in order to fulfil a moral obligation. Here the existence of such a moral obligation will transform the transfer effectively to an out-and-out gift.

7.5.1.4 *Gifts, moral obligations, and a context directed by the past*

By looking at the nature and direction of the moral obligations which will give rise to a presumption of advancement, it becomes clear just how old this principle is. It is clear that the presumption that equitable title follows legal title in furtherance of a moral obligation will apply only as between husband and wife (and then only moving in the direction of husband to wife, and not from wife to husband!); and in a transfer from a father to his children (or any other person for whom he stands *in loco parentis*).

Gifts, moral obligations, and limits to the presumption of advancement

The presumption of advancement does not apply between couples who are unmarried, and, as has been indicated, it will not even in the case of a married couple in the direction of wife to husband.

Gifts, moral obligations, and (traditional) male/female parenting roles

Further limitation of the presumption of advancement can be seen within the very powerful obligations flow from parental responsibility in respect of children. The presumption's operation appears to differentiate between the expectations of fathers and mothers. Whilst there is absolutely no doubt that there is such a moral obligation so as to ensure the operation of a presumption of advancement between a father and his children, the exact position and scope of a presumption of a gift in furtherance of an obligation is less clear-cut in relation to the mother of children. In *Bennett* v *Bennett* (1879) 10 Ch D 474, Sir George Jessel MR oriented his judgment around the proposition that the presumption of a gift arises from the moral obligation to give. The judgment reiterated the unquestionable moral obligation that falls upon a father in relation to his children, stating that all that needs to be established is that he is the father of the children concerned. Thereafter, the father's moral obligation is without question.

[T]he father [of a child] is under that obligation from the mere fact of his being the father, and therefore no evidence is necessary to shew the obligation to provide for his child. In the case of a father, you have only to prove that he is the father, and when you have done that the obligation at once arises.

However, in relation to the position of the mother he added that:

In the case of a mother...it is easier to prove a gift than in the case of a stranger: in the case of a mother very little evidence beyond the relationship is wanted, there being very little additional motive required to induce the mother to make a gift to her child.

This is quite a complex passage, but basically Sir George Jessel made the point that a weaker form of the presumption of advancement need apply in the case of the mother of a child. The essence of this passage is that it is far easier to establish that a mother intended to make a gift to her children than it would be to establish that a stranger intended to make a gift, with this convolution reflecting the way in which actually characteristically women had very little economic power during the nineteenth century to which obligations of this nature as envisioned could become attached.

Presumption of advancement founded on intention
The presumption that equitable title should follow legal title can therefore be rebutted. We can see how this intention can be rebutted in two cases; one very old and one more modern case, both of which illustrate the same point:

- In *Marshal* v *Crutwell* (1875) LR 20 Eq 325, a wife was allowed to draw cheques on a joint bank account for the convenience of her husband because he was ill. There was in these circumstances clearly no intention to make a gift to the wife.
- In *Re Figgis* [1969] 1 Ch 123, there was a very similar arrangement to *Marshal* concerning a joint bank account which was not merely for convenience.

It also appears that bank guarantees, for example where a husband guarantees his wife's overdraft, do not attract the operation of the presumption, with *Anson* v *Anson* [1953] 1 QB 636 standing as authority, that instead the ordinary rules of contract apply.

Why do we need the presumption of advancement?
One might reasonably ask *why* there is a need for presumption of advancement especially in light of the view in *Dyer* that the normal rule of common law is one whereby 'where a feoffment [transfer] is made without consideration, the use results to the feoffer [the transferor]'. The need, of course, arises on account of the way in which people do not always make their intentions clear. Indeed, there would be no need whatsoever for such a rebuttable presumption if all intentions were made clear. However, life is not that simple, and if it were there would be a considerably reduced need for lawyers! Indeed, the position whereby intentions are not always clear is particularly pointed as far as evidential problems are concerned, and this arises most acutely where the donor has actually died. It is of course very difficult to second-guess intention in such circumstances, and the presence of a rebuttable presumption is meant to help to clarify such uncertainties surrounding intention.

Modernity, social and economic equality

Given that both the presumption of a resulting trust and the presumption of advancement have a long tradition in history, it might be wondered what application they might have in modern times. Indeed, this is especially so in the case of the presumption of advancement which reflected a society in which there were huge social and especially economic differences between the positions of men and women. The presumption of advancement was constructed around the perceived needs and values of a society in which men were regarded as 'providers' for their families, and this of course included their wives who would not have had any economic independence of their own. The huge social and economic changes which took place, particularly following the Second World War in the second half of the twentieth century, have transformed earning power and capability, and within this the changed position of women is particularly striking. The role of the presumption of a resulting trust and the presumption of advancement in modern times will be considered in chapter 9, which looks at trusts of the family home as illustrations of the operation of resulting and constructive trusts.

The voluntary conveyance resulting trust and sharing homes in the twenty-first century

In illuminating a little further what is said immediately above—concerning the presumptions of a resulting trust and presumption of advancement—it will become very clear in chapter 9 that trusts which are implied have become very important for determining disputed ownership of homes which are shared. This is considered a little further ahead of this within this chapter in section 7.6.2 below, which indicates the significance of the resulting trust in this context, in situations where assets provided in respect of a home have been provided by a person who is not the apparent (legal) owner of the property. Here it is possible to see *Dyer v Dyer* principles at work almost three centuries after the case was decided. There is much more to be considered here, which commences in 7.6.2 and is considered in earnest in chapter 9.

7.5.1.5 *Resulting trusts and rebutting presumed intention*

Although this final word on resulting trusts might have the appearance of a logical continuation of discussion arising from where a resulting trust will be presumed, it also has a wider significance. This is because it can actually be seen as a measure of *how* comprehensively equity *does* actually protect property rights of those who—for lots of different reasons—are not the legal owners of the property concerned. Given that equity recognises resulting trust in circumstances where this is presumed, this raises the possibility that it will not be the case that in all cases where a resulting trust *can* arise one actually *will*: this has already been seen in *Re Osoba* [1979] above. Thus, how comprehensively this mechanism is actually able to protect a donor's potential rights in property which is conferred to another will depend on what exactly is being presumed about the provider's intentions. This can be explored further by introducing *Air Jamaica Ltd v Charlton* [1999] 1 WLR 1399, PC. This case is considered more extensively in chapter 8, but for present purposes, it is the following passage from Lord Millett's judgment that does provide interesting insight into what exactly is being presumed about a donor's intentions:

Like a constructive trust, a resulting trust arises by operation of law, though unlike a constructive trust it gives effect to intention. But it arises whether or not the transferor intended to retain a beneficial interest—he almost always does not—since it responds to the absence of any intention on his part to pass a beneficial interest to the recipient [here, the pension fund trustees].

The presumption of a resulting trust in a situation can be rebutted by evidence that the transferor did not intend to keep equitable interest. Chapter 8 deals with some of the complexities within this apparently simple position, but this is the position in principle.

7.6 An introduction to constructive trusts

The move away from resulting trusts, and a focus now on constructive trusts reiterates one of the important points made at the beginning of this chapter. This suggested that while equity's recognition of trusts which are implied alongside ones which are express can be explained as responses to 'injustice' arising in relation to ownership of property, in doing so equity has also recognized that not all situations (of injustice) will require the same response.

This accounts for the existence of constructive trusts alongside ones which are resulting, but actually explaining what constructive trusts are and what they do is much more complicated.

7.6.1 Introduction

Making a study of constructive trusts is actually very challenging on account of a number of factors. They are not to be found easily defined anywhere, and many discussions of constructive trusts are premised on them not being amenable to easy definition and categorisation. This is one reason why constructive trusts are also considered very flexible, which in turn means they can be found across a number of different 'fact situations', and their perceived inherent flexibility is seen by many as a strength in areas where they are applied, on account of being very adaptable, and extremely capable of meeting the ever-changing needs of society. However, this does make them difficult to pin down in some respects, and there is a vast body of very divided case law and academic commentary in respect of them. However, it was stressed that they are in some respects actually easier to pin down than resulting trusts. This is because, however diversely they may actually be applied, a unifying feature is their imposition in response to a wrong which is committed, and this can be seen across the situations where they have been applied.

7.6.1.1 *In search of definition and illumination of constructive trusts*

As was indicated above, there is broad agreement amongst writers and in the cases that constructive trusts arise in situations where some kind of 'wrong' has arisen, and there is also broad acceptance that constructive trusts arise from imposition rather than from presumed intention. On this reasoning, unlike the position of a resulting trust, a constrictive trust is imposed on the holder of legal title (characteristically in response to a wrong), and operates independently of (and often contrary to) his intentions.

Beyond this however, constructive trusts have not proven easy to define. This is clear from the case *Carl Zeiss Stiftung* v *Herbert Smith (No. 2)* [1969] 2 Ch 276, where (at p. 300), in the words of Edmund Davies LJ, 'English law provides no clear and all-embracing definition of a constructive trust. Its boundaries have been left perhaps deliberately vague, so as not to restrict the court by technicalities in deciding what the justice of a particular case may demand.' Instead, constructive trusts have traditionally been found to exist in a series of disparate and changing situations. This diversity of use and application of constructive trusts is comparable with that pertaining to resulting trusts, but it is also the case that all resulting trusts have the feature of 'settlor-beneficiary'. Over and above the broad association of them with commission of a 'wrong', clarifying the meaning of constructive trust has to be considered much more closely in reference to explaining *where* and *how* they arise.

7.6.1.2 *Issues of intention, and the courts' 'imposition' of a constructive trust*

In working towards this, this passage from Edmund Davies LJ's judgment in *Carl Zeiss Stiftung* v *Herbert Smith* also ties into the notions of flexibility and adaptability which were considered at the outset. The same can be said of the later case, *Sen* v *Hedley* [1991] Ch 425, where (at p. 40) Nourse LJ commented that the constructive trust had been a 'ready means of developing our property law in modern times'.

At the heart of this consideration of what constructive trusts might be and where they can be seen to arise is the way in which, although capable of arising in numerous and diverse circumstances, implied trusts of this nature have a very important fundamental characteristic in common. This is that they are trusts which are imposed by the courts and they operate irrespective of the actual intention of the owner (of what becomes the 'trust property'). This should be borne in mind in what now follows by way of a brief overview of the different situations in which constructive trusts can arise, and the consequences of them doing so.

7.6.1.3 *Consequences where a constructive trust arises*

Immediately below, and by way of an introduction to a more extensive and detailed consideration of constructive trusts (along with resulting trusts) in subsequent chapters, examples will be given of situations in which constructive trusts arise. This does not actually by itself spell out the effect of the court determining that a constructive trust has arisen. For example, it will become clear that strong arguments have been advanced advocating the differences between the constructive trust and the doctrine of proprietary estoppel (as well as more recent ones highlighting their commonality) in situations which have traditionally been the territory of the constructive trust.

7.6.2 **Situations where constructive trusts have been found to exist**

Again like the resulting trust, constructive trusts have come to be applied to numerous and diverse factual situations from which a number of illustrative examples can be drawn.

(i) *Constructive trusts and analysis of constructive and resulting trusts in the applications for implied trusts arising from cohabitation of the family home*

Very brief reference has already been made to the importance of implied trusts in the context of shared family homes in the materials which closed the discussion of resulting trusts in 7.5.1.4. The detail of this was left over until now, to explain that in the case study which looks at determining interests in shared 'family homes' both the constructive and resulting trust are important for this discussion, on account of their function as trusts which are implied in response to injustice. It will become clear that the constructive trust, particularly, has become central in the 'battleground' of difficulties created where a party who is not the legal owner of property can be left disadvantaged, even where resulting trust principles descending from *Dyer* v *Dyer* will allow those who have made financial contributions to a home which does not belong to them in law to 'retain' a proportionate interest in the home. The resulting trust in this respect represents a 'strict property' approach, and what can be recovered is limited by and indeed *to* what is actually contributed.

It is in this context that the constructive trust has become recognised as a more flexible response to injustice which can be caused to a non-legal owner of property in circumstances where the parties have reached an agreement in respect of owning their home which is not reflected in legal ownership, or because representations have been made in relation to the property by the person who is its legal owner. In these circumstances, the constructive trust can be more flexible because it allows a party who is not the legal owner to acquire a share in the property of another which is not determined by (and thus limited to) the contributions made. Here the constructive trust will allow a non-legal owner to acquire a share which reflects the agreement reached *with*, or the representations which have been made *by* the legal owner, by holding the latter to the agreement or representation. In this respect, in the modern law relating to shared beneficial ownership, the constructive trust was at the heart of the landmark decision in *Lloyds Bank* v *Rosset* [1991] 1 AC 10.

However, more recently, *Oxley* v *Hiscock* [2004] 3 All ER 703 became an important indicator of the growing significance of proprietary estoppel in relation to disputed ownership of family homes, and marked a changing emphasis in dispute resolution arising in this context. This case, and a number of earlier Court of Appeal authorities in the broader sphere of 'land law' had sought to emphasise the points of commonality between constructive trust and proprietary estoppel principles, notably that they both represented ways of holding persons to their representations or conduct, and at the same time to suggest that estoppel would give rise to a fairer and more appropriate approach even if the actual outcomes would be the same in a number of cases. And until 2007, the 'case study' on shared homes reflected the 'interplay' between the constructive trust and proprietary estoppel principles.

Stack v Dowden [2007] and the new significance for implied trusts in the context of shared home ownership

In light of events of early 2007 this 'interplay' has had to be reconsidered once again. This was set in motion by the House of Lords' decision in *Stack* v *Dowden* [2007] UKHL 17. The significance of *Stack* will become fully apparent in chapter 9, and for now its discussion is confined to the points which are salient to this introduction to resulting and constructive trusts. The first point to note is that notwithstanding the direction signalled by *Oxley*, *Stack* suggests that an approach based on trusts, rather than one favouring estoppel, is now firmly back at the heart of resolving disputed home ownership. Here the House of Lords appears to hold the view (for reasons which will be explained in due course) that the trusts approach is a better reflection of the valuable property rights which are at stake in these determinations. Where there is less consensus, however, is in respect of which type of implied trust should properly apply in these situations.

In making the case in favour of the resulting trust, Lord Neuberger was clearly impressed with its ability to reflect the actual contributions made by a party. In Lord Neuberger's view the courts should use the resulting trust as a starting point, and depart from it and apply a more flexible constructive trust only where it is evident that (essentially) this was intended.

In this sense, Lord Neuberger was the most conservative judge, and Lady Hale and Lords Hope and Walker were much more in favour of applying a constructive trust approach to reflect the way in which (in Lady Hale's words) the law has 'moved on in response to changing social and economic conditions' from the approach of the resulting trust which (inappropriately) recognises only a limited number of contributions (as capable of counting in these situations).

Stack *v* Dowden *and explaining the significance of the 'ambulatory constructive trust'*

There was also some discussion by their Lordships of the assumptions traditionally built into resolving disputed home ownership, and especially that parties' intentions have been taken to be 'fixed' at the time of acquisition of title (to the property). In this respect, Lords Neuberger and especially Lord Hoffman considered the possibilities of applying a so-called 'ambulatory constructive trust' approach. Although the significance of this and its rationale will only become clear in due course, in terms of explaining what the concept actually is the 'ambulatory constructive trust' is an approach which recognises that the intentions of parties in relation to ownership of the homes which they share often evolve over time in any case, and can be very strongly influenced by the conduct of the parties in relation to the home. According to their Lordships this would help to respond to the situation whereby, for example, the non-legal owner of a home made significant capital improvements to a home owned by another, and which significantly increased the value of the property.

(ii) *Constructive trusts arising in the creation of 'mutual wills'*

The case study which follows on equitable fraud as a context for the imposition of a constructive trust by the courts will include the example provided by mutual wills. Mutual wills arise in situations whereby two people (usually couples) agree by the creation of mutual wills to effect the situation whereby on the death of the first of them, their property shall be enjoyed by the survivor, and thereafter (on the death of the second will-maker) pass to beneficiaries which have been nominated. It shall become apparent that the constructive trust becomes an issue in response to questions of whether, and to what extent, their original 'mutual' agreement does actually control and even dictate the distribution of their property.

(iii) *Constructive trusts arising from the commission of crime*

There are good reasons of policy which suggest that a perpetrator of a crime should be prevented from benefiting from it. At its most extreme, this would operate to ensure that a murderer is not able to benefit from his killing of a testator under whose will he will benefit. The most famous illustration of this principle is the case of Dr Crippen, whose conduct has already been considered within the materials relating to resulting trusts, and will be considered further in the discussion of fraud in chapter 10.

(iv) *Trusteeship and liability following breach of trust*

There are *two broad ways* in which equity's imposition of a constructive trust has become influential in responding to breaches of trust committed by a trustee. They are both premised on the way in which, by acting in breach of trust, a trustee in some way disregards the interests of the beneficiary. They are different because while one actually responds to this in respect of the trustee who is committing the breach of trust himself, the second acknowledges that a trustee's breach of trust can also involve others who are otherwise unconnected with the trust. This latter situation can itself occur in two recognisable ways: first, trust property might actually fall into the hands of a third party unconnected with the trust, and second, it may well be that the trustee had help or 'assistance' in committing the breach of trust. Both these persons are known as 'strangers' to the trust because they are otherwise unconnected with it, but they can nevertheless incur liability where there is a breach of trust by a trustee. The connections between constructive trusts and the liability of strangers for breach of trust will be considered after it is explained how constructive trusts are significant in the position of a trustee who makes an unauthorised profit from his position.

Unauthorised profit by a trustee or other fiduciary

The materials in chapter 15 will explain that any occupant of a fiduciary position (including, but not confined to, the trustee) must act unequivocally in the interests of the person in respect of whom the fiduciary position arises. This means that a fiduciary will not be able to keep for his own use property acquired directly or indirectly from his position. In this respect, chapter 15 will explore the use which is made of the constructive trust in making such a trustee liable 'to account' to the trust for any such 'unauthorised profits' (with further, albeit brief, reference also being made to this in chapter 18).

However, notwithstanding this use of constructive trusteeship in the context of unauthorized profit, and the very clear applications for constructive trusts for the liability of others following a breach of trust (see immediately below), *Foskett* v *McKeown* [2000] 2 WLR 1299 is authority that actually wrongfully appropriating trust property by a trustee should be viewed not as creating a constructive trust for the trustee himself, but as giving rise to the liability which results from the process of tracing (which is discussed fully in chapter 19).

Liability of third party 'strangers' in breach of trust situations: the basic idea

The chapter on remedies, chapter 19, is essentially a consideration of the remedies which are available to a beneficiary where trust property has been applied by a trustee acting in breach of trust. In considering this, it will become clear that an area of particular difficulty is the liability which can be incurred by those other than the trustee himself. It does of course follow that the beneficiary should be able to pursue a remedy in respect of trust property against a trustee acting in breach of trust, but it is also the case that persons other than the trustee may come into possession of misapplied trust property, or may even have assisted the trustee's initial breach.

Where persons who have not been appointed trustees find themselves in receipt of trust property (usually on account of it being 'taken' from the trust in breach of trust), or otherwise 'interfere' with the proper administration of a trust, they may find themselves constituted 'constructive trustees'. Other forms of action available to beneficiaries in such circumstances will be considered later in chapter 19. The purpose of flagging up remedies following a breach of trust at present is to consider very basically the *facilitation* of liability for breach of trust through the machinery of the constructive trust.

Third parties and liability following a trustee's breach of trust

Traditionally, the liability of strangers to a trust has been divided into two categories of 'knowing receipt' (of trust property) and 'knowing assistance' (of a breach of trust). The reason for attaching third-party liability to *receipt of trust property* will be explained fully in chapter 19, but for present purposes, this pertains to the way in which the proprietary remedies available to a beneficiary in these circumstances depend on the continuing existence of identifiable or 'traceable' trust property. Tracing *is* sufficiently flexible that the property need not be *physically* identifiable as such, because it may well have been sold; in these circumstances, it may still be possible to trace the *proceeds* of sale, subject to the rules which apply to tracing trust money which has become 'mixed' with other funds. This is why the significance of recipient liability requires some basic understanding of alternatives to proprietary remedies: here claims which attach to the *receipt* of trust property help to ensure that there is a remedy even where property no longer exists in an identifiable form. For example, trust money which has been spent with nothing identifiable to show for it will not be 'traceable'. In these circumstances, a recipient of trust property can become a constructive trustee of it, on account that he receives trust property with some degree of knowledge of the trust. It will become apparent that there is contention as to the degree of knowledge which is required, with current favour being for a recipient's state of knowledge to be such as to make it 'unconscionable for him to retain the benefit of the receipt' (*per* Nourse LJ in *Bank of Credit and Commerce International (Overseas) Ltd* v *Akindele* [2001] Ch 437). But fundamentally, receipt-based liability is complete *upon* receipt, and does not require property to remain in the recipient's hands in order for him to incur liability. Here, constructive trusteeship will arise upon receipt, and what happens to the property thereafter is immaterial.

In a similar vein, a stranger to a trust is also able to incur liability on the basis of his *assistance of a trustee's breach of trust*. This was traditionally known as 'knowing assistance', but the important Privy Council decision of *Royal Brunei Airlines* v *Tan* [1995] 3 WLR 64 set in motion a new approach in which it is now deemed more accurate and appropriate to characterise the latter category as 'accessory liability'. This is focused on acting as an accessory to a trustee's breach of trust, and has increasingly become associated with an accessory's *dishonesty* rather than his *knowledge*.

In any event, liability as an accessory is distinguishable from recipient liability, because it is only in the latter situation that the stranger concerned actually receives trust property. Strictly speaking, therefore, it may be argued that in the case of knowing assistance or 'accessory liability' there is actually no trusteeship because no property is actually received in respect of which a (constructive) trust could attach. Notwithstanding this obvious difference, and on account of their otherwise similar nature in relation to liability, the two categories—of liability for the receipt of trust property, and that arising from assisting a breach of trust—have generally been treated together, and remain so.

Thus, as already indicated above, there is more detailed consideration of both forms of constructive trusteeship (along with leading cases including *Royal Brunei Airlines* v *Tan; BCCI* v *Akindale, Twinsectra* v *Yardley* [2002] 2 All ER 377; and more recently *Barlow Clowes International Ltd (in liquidation)* v *Eurotrust International Ltd* [2006] 1 All ER 333 and *Adnan Shaaban Abou-Rahmah* v *Al-Haji Abdul Kadir Abacha* [2006] EWCA Civ 1492) in chapter 19.

(v) *Other situations which can give rise to a constructive trust*

These remaining 'other cases' are, like the earlier examples, premised on a common acceptance that constructive trusts all appear to be responses to some kind of 'wrongdoing'. What these two final examples are seeking to do is explore what might actually be meant by 'wrongdoing' and what the limitations of associating constructive trusteeship with imposition of a trust in response to a wrong committed by the legal owner of property might be.

Constructive trusts arising where there is a specifically enforceable contract

A contract is specifically enforceable where (common law contractual) damages would not be an adequate remedy. Although contracts for the sale of personal property are seldom specifically enforceable, because of their 'unique' nature, contracts for the sale of land are. How this translates into the creation of a constructive trust is illustrated in *Lysaght* v *Edwards* (1876) 2 Ch D 499. This case proposes that on account of equity's willingness to enforce such contracts specifically, on the conclusion of the sale the purchaser is considered the owner in equity, and accordingly, the vendor becomes a trustee of the land (property) for the purchaser. The concept of constructive trusteeship arising from specifically enforceable contracts was considered very briefly in chapter 5. Beyond this very broad proposition, theorisation of the way in which specific enforceability engaged a trust situation is not pursued further, save to point out that while there is an element of 'conscience' present there is arguably a lesser exhibition of improper conduct on the part of the purchaser than in other situations in which constructive trusts are seen to arise.

Does a constructive trust arise where a trust is constituted under the 'rule in Re Rose'?

In chapter 3 in the discussion on constitution of trusts generally, and the 'last act' (of the settlor) doctrine more specifically, it was suggested that there are many questions raised by the decision in *Re Rose, Rose* v *IRC* [1952] Ch 499, and that this is so even if it must be seen as correct, and thus as good law (which Court of Appeal endorsement of it in *Mascall* v *Mascall* (1984) 50 P & CR 119 appears to confirm). It was suggested in chapter 3 that the precise mechanism operating in this case is unclear, but one explanation might lie in the imposition of a constructive trust by equity during the period *after* the transfer had occurred in equity, but *before* it could take place in common law. In the course of making this suggestion, concern was expressed about this as a possibility because of the apparent inconsistency between the conferment of a gift, and the more usual manner in which a constructive trust is invoked in order to impose on the conscience of the legal owner of property on account of his conduct. If this is the case then the constructive trust in *Re Rose* must be regarded as anomalous with the other situations listed above in as much as the donor in *Rose* had clearly done nothing wrong, and was actively demonstrating generosity in both his intended outright gift and in the express trust which he did seek.

7.6.3 Is the constructive trust too flexible and too adaptable?

The earlier introduction to constructive trusts pointed to the difficulties entailed in defining them. This was aligned very closely with the flexibility of the constructive trust, and pointed to case law which suggested that it was an extremely useful and adaptable instrument. Although there is much intellectual respect for such views within judicial and academic circles alike, it is not a universal view and certainly not one which is beyond question. Indeed, there is a strong view that during the 1970s and 1980s the constructive trust became too flexible, and Lord Denning's 'new model' constructive trust became (in his Lordship's own words, in his judgment in *Hussey* v *Palmer* [1972] 1 WLR 1338) employed 'wherever justice and good conscience require it'. This use of the constructive trust might be regarded as an approach based on outcomes and result rather than principle or sound theory, as indicated by the statement of Sir Peter Millett (in (1995) *Trust Law International*, 35) that 'the language of constructive trust has become such a fertile source of confusion that it would be better if it were abandoned'. While not all reaction has been so extreme, much academic and judicial commentary has advocated greater employment of the great adversary of flexibility—the need for certainty.

7.6.4 A place in English law for the remedial constructive trust?

The constructive trust in English case law can be seen as a substantive institution which operates to vindicate an existing property right. But this is not the case in many other jurisdictions (including Commonwealth jurisdictions such as Australia, New Zealand, and Canada) which accept also alongside the *substantive* institutional constructive trust, the existence of a different *remedial* type constructive trust which at its most radical may operate to create a new proprietary interest for the claimant, rather than simply to formalise and provide validity for an interest which already exists and which the courts will give recognition to. While the existence of the remedial constructive trust in English law has been left open, it is clearly a principle which is regarded with suspicion in the highest judicial circles. Indeed, the commentary of Lord Millett (1995, above) suggests that it is a device for which there is no room in English law and one which is actually capable of causing much mischief:

In our view it is a counsel of despair which too readily concedes the impossibility of propounding a general rationale for the availability of proprietary remedies. We need to be more ready to categorise wrongdoers as fiduciaries and to extend the situations in which proprietary remedies are made available, but we can still do all this while adhering to established principles.

7.6.5 **Trusts, conscience, and 'overlapping' of resulting and constructive trusts**

There is at present much confusion in the law between resulting trusts and constructive trusts. Consequently, the theoretical differences between them are not clear-cut and it can be difficult, on particular fact situations, to determine which type of implied trust will arise. This will become particularly plain in the later analysis of trusts arising from cohabitation and family arrangements. But for present purposes the way in which confusion is easily reached in an analysis of constructive and resulting trusts is illustrated by reference to an extract from Lord Denning's judgment in *Hussey* v *Palmer* [1972]:

Although the plaintiff alleged that there was a resulting trust, I should have thought that the trust in this case, if there was one, was more in the nature of a constructive trust; but this is a matter of words than anything else. The two run together.

The ways in which this 'blurring' of distinctions can be seen to operate, as well as an assessment of the view that it is a distinction only in rhetoric, shall be carried over into the area in which it can be illustrated most graphically—trusts relating to the family home, considered in chapter 9.

 online resource centre

FURTHER READING

This can be found under substantive consideration of resulting and constructive trusteeship in chapters 8, 9, 10, and 11.

8

Resulting trusts, gifts to
non-charitable unincorporated
associations, and pension funds

A number of the chapters in this book which follow previous chapters' introductions to constructive and resulting trusts, are case studies which require us
to look at constructive and resulting trusts closely alongside each other. All the
'case studies' focus on the features and characteristics of constructive or resulting
trusts which were introduced in the previous chapter. The case studies also try to
communicate how these instruments work in operation, and consider critically
whether, and in what ways, their operation 'in reality' reflects textbook assessments which are made of them. In the same vein, this chapter on unincorporated
associations and pension funds follows one introducing constructive and resulting trusts and as such is a case study on the features and operation of trusts which
are 'resulting'. By way of reminder, although resulting trusts arise in a number of
different contexts, what is common to all is that although legal title is vested in
a trustee, the settlor and the beneficiary are actually the same person. This position will arise on account of two broad situations. It will follow a failed attempt
to create a trust in favour of a third party beneficiary (because equitable interest
which is created upon the transfer of legal title to the trustee never actually leaves
him); or where property is divested from the settlor, but for some reason equitable
interest in it returns to him (e.g., on the occurrence of an event which has not
been provided for because it was unforeseen or the trust instrument was poorly
drafted).

8.1 The question of ownership: who can 'own' property?

Moving into a more substantive consideration of resulting and constructive trusts,
and following on from our earlier discussion of the beneficiary principle and
purpose trusts, this chapter considers difficulties which arise where property is
conveyed to an unincorporated association—for example, to a society, a social
club, or religious group. Such associations will exist to use property for a particular purpose. Un*incorporated* associations cannot own property themselves because
they lack the legal personality to do so. In*corporated* bodies, such as companies, do
have requisite legal personality, and can thus own property in their own right. The
difficulties (and possible solutions) which shall be considered in this chapter will
only arise in situations where the unincorporated body itself is non-charitable.
Indeed, as will become apparent when the position of charities is considered later
in the text, there is no difficulty whereby a gift is made to an unincorporated body

with charitable purposes, because in these circumstances, the association's officers can hold the property as charitable trustees.

Non-lawyers might well be astonished at the legal difficulties to which a transaction as simple as giving property to a club or other unincorporated association gives rise. The problem is that analyses based on trusts do not work very well, whereas a contractual analysis, which can usually be made to work, seems very unfair. In this scenario, the donor of the property has to give up all interest in the gift he is making. In a contractual analysis, the donor cannot make his gift conditional, nor prevent the club members using the property for any purpose they please, whether or not it is for the original purposes of the club.

8.1.1 Advantages of a *Re Denley*-style purpose trust

At first sight, it might be thought that a *Denley*-style purpose trust (considered in chapter 4) might be a good method of allowing property to be conveyed to a non-charitable unincorporated association: the property would be held in trust for the members of the association, for the purposes of the association, and it would be necessary only that the identity of those members was sufficiently certain. This would certainly have advantages for donors, since the property could be constrained to be used for the association's purposes, and members would not be able (for example) to dispose of it for their own benefit. If the purposes of the association were fulfilled (e.g., vivisection abolished where the association in question was the National Anti-Vivisection Association), or became impossible (e.g., where a gun club was prohibited by legislation from carrying out its previously lawful activities), the donor would obtain any property not already used on resulting trust. Unfortunately, however, a gift to members for the time being (i.e. present and future, assuming a fluctuating membership) will usually infringe the perpetuity rules (another difficulty in *Leahy* seen in chapter 4), so the trust solution is not generally appropriate. It should be noted that in *Denley* itself the grant was only effective until 21 years from the death of the last survivor of a number of specified persons (with a gift over to a hospital), so no perpetuity difficulty arose. There are also, of course, no perpetuity difficulties where the association is charitable.

8.1.2 The perpetuity problem

The nature of the perpetuity problem depends on which analysis of *Denley* is correct. If gifts for non-charitable purposes are valid, as long only as persons exist with *locus standi* to enforce the trust, even where they do not have a full beneficial interest, then the applicable rule is the rule against inalienability (see 6.6). In that case the common law rules must be satisfied, and the Perpetuities and Accumulations Act 1964 will (almost certainly) not apply. If *Denley* is just an ordinary trust for beneficiaries then the rule against remoteness applies. The problem arises where there is a fluctuating membership, because of the need to vest beneficial interests in new members as the membership varies; and if this could occur outside the perpetuity period (on which, see chapter 6 generally), then at common law any disposition on this basis will be void, as will any condition re-vesting property in the donor (e.g., achievement of the club's purposes, or their subsequent impossibility). This is subject to three qualifications. First, it is possible for an association, by appropriate drafting of its rules, to avoid the perpetuity problem (see, e.g., Warburton [1985] Conv 318, at 321); but most existing associations have not done this. Second, the donor can constrain a gift so that it satisfies the perpetuity rules; but most donors do not do this (Gardner [1992] Conv 41, especially at pp. 49ff., suggests that donors can choose the manner of their gift, but does not dwell on the perpetuity difficulties). Third, on this analysis the 1964 Act may save the disposition, but 'wait and see' would surely be very difficult to operate in practice, and most of the cases, even now, involve at least some donations made prior to 16 July 1964.

Another limitation on a *Denley* analysis is that the recipients must benefit, directly or indirectly, sufficiently to give them *locus standi*. Warburton observes that there may be difficulties in this regard with altruistic societies, such as an anti-vivisection society, where there is no tangible benefit for the members.

8.1.3 Avoiding perpetuity difficulties

Perpetuity difficulties can be avoided by construing the gift to present members only. The problem is that, if it is construed simply as a gift to them as joint tenants, then retiring members (or indeed any member) are perfectly at liberty to sever and sell their shares. New members could only obtain any benefit from association property by acquiring shares (or part shares) from existing members. No doubt it would be theoretically possible to run an unincorporated association on that basis, but it would be very inconvenient.

Before the contractual solution considered below had become widely adopted, courts strove, in a line of authorities beginning with *Cocks v Manners* (1871) LR 12 Eq 574, to construe a gift as being to the members of the society, and it was often observed that, if all the members of the association could join together to dispose of its property, the rule against inalienability (see 6.6) was not infringed. This is no doubt correct, as long as 'members of the association' means members at the time of the gift. The analysis implied, of course, that conditions could not be attached to the gift. The main problem with the analysis, apart from its artificiality, was that it provided no mechanism for moving beneficial interests as the members of the association changed.

8.1.4 Importance of the contractual analysis

For this reason gifts to non-charitable unincorporated associations are usually construed as being to existing members only, but subject to their contractual duties as members of the society or club. These will be determined by the rules of the association, but usually a member will be prevented from severing his share, and it will accrue to other members on death or resignation. Thus, although present and future members of a fluctuating body will benefit *de facto*, because the gift is construed as one to existing members alone, there is no perpetuity problem.

This was Cross J's analysis in *Neville Estates v Madden* [1962] Ch 832, where (at pp. 849–50) he analysed in detail the methods by which property can be conveyed to a non-charitable unincorporated association:

The question of the construction and effect of gifts to or in trust for unincorporated associations was recently considered by the Privy Council in *Leahy v Attorney-General for New South*

Wales [1959] AC 457. The position, as I understand it, is as follows. Such a gift may take effect in one or other of three quite different ways. In the first place, it may, on its true construction, be a gift to the members of the association at the relevant date as joint tenants, so that any member can sever his share and claim it whether or not he continues to be a member of the association. Secondly, it may be a gift to the existing members not as joint tenants, but subject to their respective contractual rights and liabilities towards one another as members of the association. In such a case a member cannot sever his share. It will accrue to the other members on his death or resignation, even though such members include persons who became members after the gift took effect. If this is the effect of the gift, it will not be open to objection on the score of perpetuity or uncertainty unless there is something in its terms or circumstances or in the rules of the association which precludes the members at any given time from dividing the subject of the gift between them on the footing that they are solely entitled to it in equity.

Thirdly, the terms or circumstances of the gift or the rules of the association may show that the property in question is not to be at the disposal of the members for the time being, but is to be held in trust for or applied for the purposes of the association as a quasi-corporate entity. In this case the gift will fail unless the association is a charitable body.

8.1.5 Trusts for purpose valid only if charitable

This passage is interesting in a number of respects. Cross J (whose views are technically *obiter*, because the property was in the event held on charitable trusts: see chapter 13) first sets out the difficulties of construing a gift to an unincorporated association as a gift to the members of the association at the relevant date as joint tenants. Second, he sets out the usual solution to the problem, that of a gift to the existing members not as joint tenants, but subject to their respective contractual rights and liabilities towards one another as members of the association. In that case, he points out that a member cannot sever his share. Third, he reiterates the orthodox position that a trust for purposes is valid only if charitable.

It is also essential to the analysis that the members at any one time own the entirety of the fund: that they can, if they wish, dissolve the association and divide the property among themselves. Donors can place no conditions on their donation, for fear of infringing the perpetuity rules (and remember that *Neville Estates* was decided prior to the Perpetuities and Accumulations Act 1964). In *Re Lipinski's Will Trusts* [1976] 1 Ch 235, Oliver J gave effect to a gift to the Hull Judeans (Maccabi) Association to be used solely for construction and improvements of the association's buildings, despite having rejected charity arguments, but only by striking out the condition relating to buildings and holding that the present members of the association were absolutely entitled and could use the property in any way they liked. He could thus bring the case within the second *Neville Estates* category.

The limits of the contractual analysis became apparent from Brightman J's judgment in *Re Recher's WT* [1972] Ch 526. The testatrix left some of her residuary estate to a non-charitable unincorporated association which, on the construction of her will, was identified as the London and Provincial Anti-Vivisection Society. By the date of the will, however, that society had ceased to exist, but had amalgamated with the National Anti-Vivisection Society. The question was whether the gift could take effect in favour of the National Anti-Vivisection Society.

Brightman J held that the gift could not be construed as a trust for the purposes of the London and Provincial Anti-Vivisection Society. It would have been possible to construe the gift, on the basis of Cross J's views in *Neville Estates*, as a gift to the members of the London and Provincial Anti-Vivisection Society, subject to the contract towards each other to which they had bound themselves as members, had the Society been in existence at the date of the testatrix's will. By then it had been dissolved, however, and the contract between the members terminated. The gift could not be construed as a gift to the members of a different association (i.e. the National Anti-Vivisection Society) and, accordingly, failed.

8.1.6 *Re Grant*: division between local and national control

A slightly different difficulty arose in *Re Grant's WT* [1980] 1 WLR 360, where a grant to the Chertsey and Walton Constituency Labour Party failed. The difficulty in *Re Grant* was that the members of the Chertsey and Walton Constituency Labour Party (CLP) did not have control over their own property, because they were also bound by the rules of the Labour Party nationally. Thus, a gift to the CLP could not be construed as a gift to the members of the CLP beneficially, since they could not direct that the bequest be divided among themselves as beneficial owners. The gift could take effect, if at all, only as a private purpose trust, in which case it infringed the rule against perpetuities.

This merits further examination, since the relationship between national and local Labour parties was unusual, in that the local association appeared to have virtually no control over its own funds. Indeed, the national party could itself take direct control of the local party's funds, and it is not at all surprising, therefore, that Vinelott J held that the funds were owned by the national rather than the local party. However, it does not follow that gifts can never be made to local branches of federated societies. In *News Group Newspapers Ltd v SOGAT 1982* [1986] ICR 716, the local branch of SOGAT could unilaterally secede from the national union (Society of Graphical and Allied Trades) and was therefore held still to control its own property. Presumably, therefore, it would have been possible to make a donation to the local branch. Many federated societies adopt an intermediate position where, although the local branches cannot unilaterally secede, the national society has no direct control over the local funds, the local society instead paying an annual membership subscription and agreeing to be bound, to a greater or lesser extent, by national rules. It is uncertain whether the reasoning in *Re Grant's WT* applies in this situation.

8.1.7 Limitations of the contractual analysis

It is clear, then, that there are serious limitations on the contractual analysis. Trust analyses were even more fraught with difficulties, as it has been seen, mostly because of the common law rule against perpetuities. Since the 1964 Act, dispositions that would have failed for perpetuity may be saved by 'wait and see' (see chapter 6). The gift in *Recher* predated the Act, but that in *Grant* did not; even so, it might have been difficult to identify beneficiaries had the testator clearly settled the property in trust in *Grant*, especially as the purpose was altruistic, and the case suggests that the courts will not struggle to find a trusts analysis, even where a contractual one does not work, unless the settlor makes the trust explicit.

8.2 **Winding up unincorporated associations**

The correct analysis of a gift to an unincorporated association, such as a club or society, also controls the distribution of its assets when it is wound up, since that question depends on who are the owners of the fund.

8.2.1 **When is a fund wound up?**

It is necessary first to consider when a fund may be wound up. According to Brightman J in *Re William Denby & Sons Ltd Sick & Benevolent Fund* [1971] 1 WLR 973, winding up of a fund is not at the discretion of the treasurer or trustees of the fund, but may occur only when:

(a) the rules allow for dissolution, or

(b) all interested parties agree, or

(c) a court orders dissolution, or

(d) the substratum upon which the fund is founded is gone (e.g., *Re St Andrew's Allotment Association* [1969] 1 WLR 229, where an allotment association was wound up when the land for allotments was sold to developers for £70,000).

Many of the cases arise when the club or association has simply been inactive for a number of years, but no positive moves have been made to wind it up. The courts are reluctant in these circumstances to infer that the substratum has gone. In *William Denby* itself the substratum had not disappeared, although after an industrial dispute many of the company's employees left, and for some time (about four and a half years) nobody had contributed to the fund. But before the dispute the fund was viable, and indeed increasing, and mere inactivity by the members did not necessarily lead to the conclusion that they had acquiesced in the dissolution of the fund, since a less drastic interpretation was possible, namely that they had acquiesced in the temporary suspension of contributions and grants.

A similar dispute arose in *Re GKN Bolts and Nuts Ltd Sports and Social Club* [1982] 2 All ER 855, noted at [1983] Conv 315, where Megarry V-C allowed what he called 'spontaneous dissolution', that is to say, the winding up of a club without any resolution or court order to that effect. He observed, however, that mere inactivity is not enough, unless it is so prolonged that dissolution is the only reasonable inference. A cataleptic trance, he said, may look like death without being death, and suspended animation may be continued life, not death. Here, however, spontaneous dissolution had occurred, but it required a positive act, in this case a resolution to sell the club's only remaining asset, the sports ground.

8.2.2 **Basis on which funds are held**

The types of fund with which this section is concerned are members' clubs or friendly societies, which are unincorporated associations. As it has been suggested, the property of unincorporated associations is not normally held in trust for the members. Instead, the relationship between the members is contractual.

Members' contributions or subscriptions are regarded as out-and-out gifts, each member retaining contractual rights (based on the rules) to use the property of the club or society. On resignation from the club or society, although the gift of the subscriptions remains (otherwise a retiring member could claim back a share of these), the retiring member gives up any contractual claim on the property of the association.

It ought to follow, therefore, that when such an association is wound up, only existing members have a right to claim any part of the fund. The basis of their claim is a contractual right to share in the property, and the method by which the division is calculated is considered in the next subsection.

It is nevertheless possible in theory for funds to be held by trustees on trust for the members, even though this is rare in practice. The main difficulty is the rule against perpetuities (see chapter 6), at any rate if membership is likely to fluctuate, since dispositions in favour of future members might fall outside the perpetuity period. This difficulty will not necessarily apply where the fund is intended only for the benefit of existing members or is of short-term duration (e.g., limited to 21 years from the death of the last survivor of a number of specified persons, like the trust in *Re Denley's Trust Deed* [1969] 1 Ch 373, considered in chapter 4). Otherwise, the normal requirements for constitution of an express trust will apply.

8.2.2.1 *Surplus contributions and the operations of a resulting trust*

If such a fund is dissolved, the *surplus of the contributions themselves* will be held on resulting trust. All contributors, including those who have ceased to contribute, will be entitled to a share, and division will be in proportion to the *total amount* they have contributed. Thus, assuming everyone pays subscriptions at the same rate, a person who has contributed for ten years is entitled to twice as much of the share of the proceeds as someone who has contributed for only five.

This was the basis of division in *Re Hobourn Aero Components Air Raid Distress Fund* [1946] Ch 86, affirmed at [1946] Ch 194. From 1940 to 1944, employees of a company in Coventry made weekly contributions to a fund to assist employees who had suffered damage as a result of air raids. Only contributors to the fund could benefit. The fund was closed in 1944, and the question arose as to what to do with surplus moneys. The Crown did not claim the fund as *bona vacantia*. The contributors wanted the surplus back. The Charity Commissioners wanted to adopt a cy près scheme, which they could do only if the fund was charitable (see chapter 14).

At first instance, Cohen J held that the purposes of the organisation were not charitable, since there was an insufficient element of public benefit. It followed that a cy près scheme could not be directed. That being so, the contributors were entitled to distribute the fund among themselves, in proportion to the total amount each had contributed, on resulting trust principles:

> [The] basis on which the contributions are returned is that each donor retained an interest in the amount of his contributions except so far as they are applied for the purposes for which they were subscribed.

In other words, a proportion of the *total* contribution of each individual contributor is held on resulting trust, the assumption being that he retains an interest in his contribution. On a contractual analysis, however, anyone ceasing to contribute to the scheme loses any benefits they had under the scheme, and also loses any property interest in the fund. All those who are still contributors at the date of closure of the fund are usually entitled to an *equal* share in the surplus, not a share which is based on their past contributions (see further below).

The Crown in *Hobourn Aero* appealed on the issue of the charitable status of the fund alone, and the Court of Appeal upheld Cohen J's decision. On this aspect of the case, see further chapter 13. However, nothing was said in the Court of Appeal about the distribution of the funds.

One of the problems with Cohen J's analysis is that the rule against perpetuities appears to be infringed, unless either the fund is expressly limited in duration, or there are no fluctuations in membership. Arguably the fund in *Hobourn Aero* did not infringe the rule, although there were fluctuations in the identity of the individual contributors, because of its essentially temporary nature. Presumably, however, nobody knew how long the fund would continue at its inception, and no express limit appears to have been put on its duration.

8.2.2.2 Re West Sussex *and the analysis in* Re Bucks

In *Re West Sussex Constabulary's Widows, Children & Benevolent (1930) Fund Trusts* [1971] Ch 1, Goff J thought that it was not part of the *ratio* of the case, but it suggested that it was. He also pointed out that there were no contractual benefits in *Hobourn*, so that the usual contractual analysis may well not be applicable, but that does not in any way answer the perpetuity difficulties inherent in Cohen J's analysis.

It is thus respectfully suggested that Cohen J's analysis set out above is wrong. At any rate, the case cannot be regarded as laying down any principle applicable to the majority of fund cases, since their duration is not limited, and fluctuating membership is assumed.

Walton J's analysis in *Re Bucks Constabulary Widows' & Orphans' Fund Friendly Society (No. 2)* [1979] 1 WLR 936 will usually be more appropriate. The case involved a fund which was made up of voluntary contributions from its members, for the relief of widows and orphans of deceased members of the Bucks Constabulary. In April 1968 the Bucks Constabulary was amalgamated with other constabularies to form the Thames Valley Constabulary, and in October 1968 the society was wound up. The trustee applied to court to determine how the funds were to be distributed. Walton J thought that the members' rights to share in the fund were governed by their contractual rights and duties *inter se* and that, in the absence of evidence to the contrary, members who resigned lost all claim on the fund. Therefore, division should be made among only those who were still members at the time of the dissolution of the fund and, in the absence of evidence to the contrary, they were entitled to an equal share in the fund. Accordingly, he held that the surplus should be held by the trustees for the members at the time of dissolution in equal shares.

8.2.2.3 *Contractual v resulting trust analyses: final resolution?*

It cannot be assumed, however, that the courts have finally resolved the issue in favour of a contractual basis for the holding of funds. In *Re West Sussex Constabulary's Widows, Children and Benevolent (1930) Fund Trusts* [1971] Ch 1, Goff J held that the proportion of the surplus attributable to identifiable donations and legacies was held on resulting trust. He thought these indistinguishable from *Re the Trusts of the Abbott Fund.* Presumably, then, before the dissolution of the constabulary, the donations, and legacies had been given to the association on trust. The problem is that this is not at all like *Re the Trusts of the Abbott Fund* (considered in chapter 4) which concerned a trust for two identifiable ladies, living at the time the trust was set up. There could not possibly be any perpetuity problems with such a trust. It is suggested that nor could there be in *Re Gillingham Bus Disaster Fund* [1958] Ch 3000, where the purposes (or at any rate, the valid purposes) were taken to be defraying the funeral expenses of the identifiable boys who had just died, and caring for those living who in light of the disaster were left disabled. But if there was a trust of donations in *Re West Sussex Constabulary's Widows, Children and Benevolent (1930) Fund Trusts*, the beneficiaries would have been a fluctuating body of present and future members, and exactly the same perpetuity problems would arise as in the *Hobourn Aero Case* (above).

8.2.2.4 *Introduction to pension funds:* Davis *v* Richards and Wallington Industries Ltd

Similar reasoning was adopted by Scott J in *Davis v Richards and Wallington Industries Ltd* [1991] 2 All ER 563, which concerned the winding up of a pension fund. The *ratio* of the case was that distribution of the assets was by a definitive deed which was executed by the trustees, but Scott J went on in his judgment to consider the position if he were wrong. Employers, employees, and money transferred from other funds were the three main sources of contributions to the fund. Scott thought that the employers' contributions should be held on resulting trust for them, on account of their similarity with the *West Sussex* legacies. There was no reason to rebut the conclusion that there was a resulting trust. But the problem is exactly the same as above. What was the trust upon which the funds were held prior to the winding up of the fund? It must have been a trust for a fluctuating body of individuals. Surely similar perpetuity problems arise as before? (Although perhaps in this case the trust could have been saved by the Perpetuities and Accumulations Act 1964 (considered in chapter 6) in a manner which is illustrated below.)

Re Bucks Constabulary Widows' and Orphans' Fund Friendly Society (No. 2) was not mentioned by Scott J, although according to the report the case was cited, and there was some consideration given to a contractual analysis (at pp. 589–90). No obvious reason was given for the rejection of this latter analysis. It is suggested, however, that in such a situation (which is distinct from the more general position of pension funds) a trust analysis simply cannot work. It is greatly hoped therefore that the courts will adopt the analysis of Walton J in *Re Bucks Constabulary Widows' and Orphans' Fund Friendly Society (No. 2)*.

8.3 Conclusion: the general position of unincorporated associations and support for the contractual basis for the calculation of shares

Notwithstanding the alternative approaches considered in relation to the general position of unincorporated associations, it is suggested that a contractual basis for the division of funds is the only tenable mechanism. This is of course the solution provided for by the *Re Bucks Constabulary* case. In this situation, if the rules provide for the contingency of dissolution of the fund, division will be according to the rules, as they will form the basis of the contract.

Often the rules do not so provide, however, and in this event the courts are left to imply terms. In accordance with normal contractual doctrine, this will be on the basis of inferred intention and, since this is largely a question of fact, no rigid rules of law can be stated. Nevertheless, certain presumptions appear to apply:

(1) Only existing members can claim, because it is assumed that past members gave up all claims on the fund on resignation (*Re Bucks Constabulary Widows' & Orphans' Fund Friendly Society (No. 2)* [1979] 1 WLR 936). Sometimes the rules expressly so provide, as in *Re West Sussex Constabulary's Widows, Children & Benevolent (1930) Fund Trusts* [1971] Ch 1.

(2) Generally speaking, in the case of members' clubs, division is equally among existing members. In mutual benefit or friendly society cases, the *prima facie* rule also appears to be equal division (*Bucks Constabulary*), although there have also been cases where division has been proportional to total contributions—this seems appropriate where the benefit contracted for while the fund subsists is also proportional to total contributions. In *Re Sick & Funeral Society of St John's Sunday School, Golcar* [1973] Ch 51, there were two distinct classes of membership, one class of which (adults) paid and received twice the benefit of the other (children). Division was such that adults received twice as much as children. It must be emphasised, however, that inferred intention is a question largely of fact, and that it would be a mistake to deduce rigid principles of law from these cases.

(3) If the assumption can be made that a contributor has made an out-and-out gift of his contributions, retaining no rights in the fund at all, then the property will go to the Crown as *bona vacantia*, because nobody has a claim on it. This conclusion has sometimes been drawn where only third parties could benefit from the fund (e.g., in *Cunnack v Edwards* [1896] 2 Ch 679, where only the widows of contributors were entitled to benefit). The same result was reached in the *West Sussex* case: Goff J thought that the contributors had parted with their property out-and-out, and had retained no interest in the fund since it was held for the benefit of third parties (the widows and dependants of the deceased members), but on this point the case was criticised in the *Bucks Constabulary* case. In the later case, Walton J observed that merely because the members have contracted between themselves to provide benefits for third parties does not mean (in the absence of a valid trust in favour of the third parties) that they have relinquished their property in the fund. They can still, after all, collectively agree to distribute the fund among themselves, or to vary the benefits under the scheme. The position is essentially analogous to *Beswick v Beswick* [1968] AC 58, where although two parties had contracted to provide a benefit for a third party, they could at any time agree to vary the benefit to be provided for the third party, and the third party had no enforceable claim against either of them. If they had set up enforceable trusts in favour of the third parties, of course, the position would be different, but in that case the third parties would have the beneficial interest in the surplus. In neither case should the property go to the Crown as *bona vacantia*.

8.4 **Perpetuities since 1964: general principles**

This section brings together a number of the central issues raised in this chapter, and also positions them alongside the brief study made of perpetuities made earlier. From this earlier study it will have been clear and apparent that the law relating to perpetuities is very, very complicated, and can give rise to some truly bizarre considerations and results. While this was explained as a broad idea in the earlier work, the precise extent of such difficulties and bizarreness is actually very difficult to capture, especially given chapter 6's brevity. Nevertheless, the law is due to change—precisely on account of these considerations, which is why chapter 6 has been very much reduced in extent. This section is designed to bring together the different ways of analysing unincorporated associations, oriented very strongly towards the articulation of a contractual analysis as that which should be preferred. And this brief consideration of perpetuities does explain some of the difficulties of applying a trusts analysis to such bodies. It also provides a working example of just how complicated the perpetuities rules are!

Earlier it was suggested that there are perpetuity difficulties with the trusts cases, such as *Hobourn Aero* and *West Sussex*, because with a fluctuating membership it is necessary to provide for transfers of beneficial interests into the indefinite future, unless a maximum duration is placed on the fund. Where a donation is made to a non-charitable unincorporated association, therefore, and it is not expressed to be by way of trust, in principle the courts ought to adopt the contract analysis in order to validate the gift.

Unfortunately, the contract analysis in *Neville Estates* (considered elsewhere) depends on the members of the society at any time having the entire beneficial interest in the funds, so that they can, if they so wish, dissolve the society and use the assets as they wish. Furthermore, because since 1964 reverters after a condition subsequent are subjected to the rule against perpetuities, by s. 12 of the Perpetuities and Accumulations Act 1964, donors cannot impose any conditions on their donation to prevent dissolution, for example by making a gift for the purposes of the association unless those purposes are charitable. In *Re Hopkins* [1965] Ch 669, a gift was made to the Bacon–Shakespeare Society, not out-and-out but for the purposes of finding the Bacon–Shakespeare manuscripts. In order to validate the gift, Wilberforce J had to hold finding the Bacon–Shakespeare manuscripts to be charitable for the advancement of education (considered below). Otherwise, either the donation will not take effect at all, or the courts will (if they can) validate the gift by striking out the condition. In *Re Lipinski's WT* [1976] 1 Ch 235, Oliver J was able to give effect to a gift to the Hull Judeans (Maccabi) Association to be used solely for the construction and improvements of the association's buildings, but only by striking out the condition relating to buildings, and holding that the present members of the association were absolutely entitled and could use the property in any way they liked.

It is sometimes argued (e.g., *Gardner* [1992] Conv 41) that if donors wish to make gifts on trust, or conditional gifts to unincorporated associations, they should be free to do so, but, at any rate prior to 1964, the law did not allow this (note that both *Hobourn Aero* and *West Sussex* involved pre-1964 dispositions which, if made on trust, ought to have been void). The Perpetuities and Accumulations Act 1964, as explained in the earlier chapter, relaxed the position in two respects, namely by providing for the possibility of stipulating an 80-year perpetuity period and for the 'wait and see' principle. The application of 'wait and see' could lead to considerable difficulties at the end of the period, however, if it became clear that the rule against perpetuities would indeed be infringed. And, although it may be useful to valid-ate temporarily gifts expressed to be made on trust, it is not a satisfactory solution where the gift is silent as to how it is to take effect. Since the contractual analysis clearly works, it should be used in preference to a trust analysis, except where the donor has made it quite clear that a trust is intended.

8.5 Resulting trusts and pension funds

8.5.1 Pension funds and a workable resulting trust analysis

The rise of the pension fund in recent times has ensured that issues of operation and regulation have come sharply into focus on a number of social, economic, and legal fronts. The discourses which have taken place in furtherance of creat-ing a workable legal framework for the operation and safe-guarding of pension assets demonstrate clear favour for the trust as the most appropriate mechanism for ensuring this. The favourable view of the trust was confirmed in the Report of Sir Roy Goode's Pension Law Review Committee (1993, Cmnd 2342). The Committee's recommendations resulted in the passage of the Pensions Act 1995. The 1995 Act sought to reflect the importance of rigorous regulation and supervision of pension schemes, and one of its principal tenets was its accommodation of the reality that the beneficiaries under a pension scheme differed from the normal trust position of volunteers; indeed, the entitlement of beneficiaries under a pension scheme could be seen to arise from contractual origins (provided by their contracts of employment). This aside, the trust was the device which was strongly favoured in the promotion of the expedient and safe use of such schemes. Here, even perpetu-ities difficulties which are usually fatal in other examples of unincorporated associ-ations do not arise thanks to specific consideration made in pensions legislation.

8.5.2 Pensions, trusts, and the future: a clawback to fundamental principles

As a result of this topical interest in pension funds and the primacy of place given to the trust, it is perhaps not surprising that academic commentators are enthusing in the way which is evident in Charles Harpum's [2000] Conv 170 article. Harpum suggests that these are most interesting and even exciting times for trusts lawyers and pensions lawyers alike.

One source of this excitement can be attributed to a theme which runs through-out this text—hailing the trust as one of the most flexible and adaptable, and also most useful, instruments in English law. Much is made of the way in which its application cuts across domestic and commercial contexts, providing cer-tainty and protection in relation to property rights in commercial relationships as much as private familial ones. The use of the trust instrument in the context of pensions operation and pensions law also indicates something in addition to this, and which has up to now been implied rather than made explicit. The issue of pensions and their operation in contemporary society is one of the most important socio-economic issues of today. To recap, with the combination of declining birth-rate, longer life expectancy and a broader global context signalling the dismantling of the welfare state, the focus on privately funded pensions outside state provision have come increasingly to the fore. Today's issues arise very strongly from the need to plan for tomorrow, and private pension schemes (occupational and otherwise) are very much concerned with planned long-term personal asset management.

Indeed, it has already been suggested that while the trust's traditional associations are strongly with wealth and its preservation, it is nevertheless significant that it is these age-old principles which are envisioned as the blueprint for this personal asset management into the twenty-first century. This is a testament to the trust's versatility, adaptability, and also to its endurance. This is so notwithstanding that demonstrating how pension funds are modelled on the trust instrument will reveal some crucial departures from 'ordinary' trust principles.

Clearly the huge shifts in social and economic demography have contributed to the rise of the pension fund, but it is the very characteristics which provided the introduction to this subject right at the outset of this book which form its backbone. It is the fundamental principles of fiduciary responsibility and (from the beneficiaries' perspective) the proprietary rights conferred upon the equitable owners of property which have ensured that the trust has shaped the pension fund, and will remain central to its evolution.

8.5.3 Trust parties and pension situations

The term 'trust' parties in this context is used to illustrate how the parties which are central to the trust—as understood by text—can be applied to the pensions scenario. In this situation, the trust is a pension scheme and trust property arises in the form of contributions made to it, which ultimately become payable under it. In this respect, the term 'trust party' is used to 'locate' the settlor, the trustee and the beneficiary (parties central to the trust's operation) in the pension context. It does not of course refer to parties *to* the trust, because the beneficiary of a properly constituted trust has rights to enforce the trust, but is not party to its creation. But the settlor, the trustee, and the beneficiary are all central to the operation of a private trust, and will now be explained in the operation of the pension trust.

In the case of an occupational pension trust, the employer is the settlor, and the members of the scheme, typically employees and their dependants, occupy the position of beneficiaries. The scheme will have trustees, which may well include the employer and other key organisational figures (e.g., from the board of directors) from the particular occupational culture concerned or appointed from a separate specialist trustee company. The involvement of the employer in the scheme confers even greater (theoretical at least) power than would subsist in the employer–employee relationship alone, in a 'structural' power sense. But in addition to this more abstract sense of power (which *is* regarded as a significant consideration, and is reflected as such in the Pensions Act 1995's provision that a proportion of trustees are to be nominated by members of the scheme), the position of the employer as trustee will vest in him *trust* powers in a real sense under the scheme. A glance back to the work on certainty and the introduction to the nature of trusts in chapter 2 will provide a reminder of the nature of powers— clearly, the powers conferred to trustees of such a scheme will be fiduciary powers, and will include the power to appoint any surplus (in the fund).

8.5.4 Duties and powers of trustees under a pension scheme

Just as in the case of any express private trust, trustees under a pension scheme are duty-bound to protect the trust assets and to administer the trust in accordance with its terms. This is a gross oversimplification, as there are a number of legal considerations reflecting the differences between pension funds and other trust instruments. In terms of protecting the trust assets, the trustees must ensure that settlor contributions falling due under the scheme are paid to it. Duties arising from administration are more complicated, and different issues will arise according to whether the scheme continues to operate and is due to remain operational, or whether it is being wound up. Other factors which will affect the administration of pensions trusts flow from the way in which they are likely to be operational for a long duration of time. On one level, this would ensure important perpetuity implications were it not for the way in which the 1995 Act exempts 'approved schemes' from perpetuities provisions. On another, the long-term management of assets which is required has resulted in pension trustees having powers of investment which are wider and more delegable than would normally be the case. Investment policy is also required to be formalised through the production of a formal statement of investment strategy. Statutory requirements exist requiring trustees to select investments, diversify portfolios, and observe their operations, and to take advice and review them. The trustees of a pension scheme are also under a duty to seek recovery of funds where pension funds become 'lost' (usually on account of a breach of trust), with potential implications flowing from liabilities of fellow trustees and previous ones, and where property applied in breach of trust has come into the hands of third parties.

8.5.5 Members as beneficiaries and key entitlements

It is the members of the pension scheme (along with their relatives and dependants) who are its beneficiaries. And in terms of being 'beneficially entitled' to the fruits of the fund, the members of the pension scheme are no different from the beneficiary under an 'ordinary' private trust. As was noted earlier, the key crucial difference lies in the contributions which comprise the basis of the pension entitlement. Contributions of this nature will include ones made by the beneficiary himself, directly and also indirectly. This is not the position in many ordinary private trusts, and in this respect the beneficiary has provided consideration for the benefit ultimately due under the scheme. However, this does not necessarily give the beneficiaries any additional rights to be informed about decisions taken by trustees (in respect of their own rather considerable obligations arising) regarding the fund, and the 'normal' position on this is considered below in the discussion of trusteeship. It is also the case that the remedies available to the pension fund beneficiary against trustees and 'strangers' (those not parties to the trust) are identical to those arising in any other private express trust—as explained in chapters 18 and 19.

8.5.6 **Workable resulting trusts: *Davis* v *Richards and Wallington***

At this point, it might be wondered how this view of the trust can be squared with the analysis given to *Davis* above, and the important pensions case of *Air Jamaica* v *Charlton* (considered shortly) does distinguish *Davis*. Furthermore, it is especially important to note at this stage that the scheme in *Davis* was unusual in as much as such schemes will normally provide for the allocation of surplus assets on the winding up of such a fund. This was not the case in *Davis*, and this is what triggered the operation of the general law relating to unincorporated associations (and the conclusion offered that the correct analysis to be applied was the one in *Re Bucks Constabulary*).

8.5.7 **The resulting trust in action: *Air Jamaica* v *Charlton***

Air Jamaica v *Charlton* [1999] 1 WLR 1399 (PC) concerned a contributory pension fund which was started in 1969. The fund was wound up following the company's privatisation upon which all the employees were made redundant. Many employees were re-engaged, but under new pension arrangements. The (original) scheme (and subject of the litigation) had been funded from (compulsory) deductions made from employees' salaries, and from matching payments which had been made by the employer. However, whereas each employee became a member of the pension scheme by virtue of his employment, his entitlement to a pension arose under the trusts of the scheme, and not under his contract of employment.

The case concerned two key provisions relating to the scheme. The first was Clause 4 of the trust deed. This provided *inter alia* that: 'No moneys which at any time have been contributed by the Company under the terms thereof shall in any circumstances be repayable to the [airline] company.' The second was s. 13 of the pension plan which authorised the airline to amend the plan or discontinue it, but not in a way which was incompatible with the exclusive use of the fund for the members and families and dependants also entitled under it. The fund was to be used for making annuity purchases for existing and future beneficiaries, and any surplus was to be directed to the provision of additional benefits for dependant beneficiaries following a member's death (to be applied to them at the discretion of the trustees).

8.5.8 *Air Jamaica* **and a familiar problem: disputes arising from distributed funds**

The litigation concerned the issue of the disposition of the large balance in the original fund when the company was privatised in 1994. As a result of new conditions of employment, no further contributions were made to the original fund, nor deductions made from the members of the scheme. The sum remaining was $400 million, and was surplus (i.e. not subject to any liability under the scheme). The members of this pension plan sought declaration that the plan had been discontinued, and, in accordance with s. 13 of the plan, that the balance of the fund should be distributed for the benefit of the intended beneficiaries (the employees and their dependants). Almost immediately, the airline sought to amend the trust deed and plan to try to ensure that the surplus subject of the beneficiaries' claims would return to it, rather than be distributed among the beneficiaries. A royal lives clause was introduced to try to counter claims that the scheme (and its underlying trusts) was void for perpetuity. Meanwhile the Attorney-General alleged that the scheme was void for perpetuity, and that the surplus funds should pass to the Crown *bona vacantia*.

8.5.9 Distribution of the fund and direction of distribution: three parties in dispute

In the Privy Council (following a decision in the Jamaican Court of Appeal that the rule against perpetuities did not apply to the scheme, which arising out of the contract of employment was correctly the province of the law of contract), the Board concluded that the scheme had been established as a trust fund. It was found that membership of the scheme had arisen from the contract of employment, but entitlement to it flowed from the trust nature of the scheme. The scheme was subject to the rule against perpetuities and was found to be in infringement of the common law perpetuity rules. The Perpetuities and Accumulations Act 1964 does not form part of the law of Jamaica, so the common law perpetuity rules applied. This meant that there was no 'wait and see' facility, and the effect of this on the operation of the 'class gift' (in favour of members, their widows, and dependants) was that this would be governed by common law. Under this scheme this meant that some (of the class) were not 'lives in being' at the time of the settlement, and it followed that there was the possibility that the gift might vest outside the perpetuity period (21 years after the death of a member).

8.5.10 Partial failure, distribution, and operation of the resulting trust

As a consequence of the partial failure of the trusts (explained below), determination had to be made about the surplus and to whom it must be directed. It was held that there was a resulting trust in operation in favour of the member contributors and for the airline (on account of its 'matched employer' contributions under the scheme). The share to be returned to the members on resulting trust was to be on a *pro rata* basis, according to the contributions which individual members had made, but without reference to the time (dates) on which contributions had been made, or any benefits received under the scheme.

This case, its decision, and its reasoning can be summarised as follows:

(1) Although the common law perpetuity period applied to this scheme, it did not follow that it was altogether void. The view of the Law Commission (in (1998) Law Com. 251, at para. 353) was adopted. The trusts took effect as separate settlements entered into by each employee. Each separate settlement comprised the contributions made in respect of the employee

either by him or by the employer. This would satisfy the common law rule with the employee as the 'life in being'.

(2) The pension plan was discontinued when the employer ceased to deduct contributions from its employees and to pay matching contributions to the trustees.

(3) The surplus was held on resulting trust, being treated as provided as to one half by the employer and one half by the employees. Clause 4 did not negative the inference of a resulting trust; it is a failure of the company to dispose of the funds similar to *Vanervell* v *IRC* [1967] 2 AC 691. As for the employees' contributions, *Davis* v *Richards and Wallington Ltd* [1991] 2 All ER 563 could be distinguished since here they had not received all they had bargained for, but in any case the inferences as to intention drawn in *Davis* were disproved.

8.5.11 The regulation of pensions trusts: the Pensions Act 2004

The text immediately above has provided a brief introduction to the special features which pertain to pension trusts, and the special rules which apply to them as a reflection of this. Indeed, in due course (in chapter 18) you will come across the reference made by the Law Commission, in its 2006 *Report on Trustee Exemption Clauses*, to pension trusts as ones which are 'to a great extent a law unto themselves'. By way of brief explanation, the Law Commission suggested that such trusts are 'conceptually different from other types of trusts and operate in a distinct manner', and note has already been made of the way in which they are quite unlike other trusts in many respects, including the relationships between the parties, and the way in which beneficiaries thereunder are not volunteers, for example.

In many respects, the Pensions Act 2004 is best understood by reference to the Pensions Act 1995 as legislation enacted to protect the position of beneficiaries in light of the possibilities for maladministration and fraud, and also insolvency. In this respect, requirements that trustees must keep proper records; that contributions received by them must be placed in a separate account within an authorised institution; and that an offence can be committed where an employer fails to pay over contributions which have been deducted from members, are well established in the framework of modern pension trust law. However, this legislation has also sought to 'unpack' still further, and respond to, the rather unusual position of pension trusts and the different 'interests' and relationships which arise between the key parties.

Although many provisions of the 1995 Act remain in force, the 2004 Act has also introduced a number of changes. A detailed discussion of the new Act is beyond the scope of this text, where the consideration given to pensions trusts is very brief and basic. However, it is probably worthy of note that the background to the 2004 Act was one of numerous perceived shortcomings in the 1995 Act, both in terms of its scope and utility, and also in the nature of its operation. Thus, very brief reference will be made to the provisions for new funding requirements under the Act, and also to those relating to enhanced professionalism among the trustees of pension funds. It is also the case that the new Act has created the office of Pensions Regulator.

8.5.11.1 *The 'special nature' of trusteeship under pension funds*

The 'special nature' of pension trusts and the trusteeship which arises from them is recognised in the provisions of the 2004 Act which relate to enhanced expectations of trustees. Under the new provisions, a trustee must (pursuant to s. 249) have the requisite degree of knowledge and understanding to enable him to exercise his functions in accordance with the scheme of which he is a trustee. Accordingly, in *general*, trustees must have knowledge and understanding of the law relating to pensions and trusts, and the principles of scheme funding and investment. In furtherance of s. 247 and s. 248, trustees must also be conversant with a number of key matters relating to their *specific* scheme; namely the trust deed itself, and rules of the scheme in question, the scheme's statements of investment and funding principles, and any documents recording policy adopted by the trustees relating to the scheme.

8.5.11.2 *Pension trusts and their new Regulator*

In the spirit and direction of the 2004 legislation—to continue to emphasise the importance of protecting pension trusts and to recognise shortcomings in the regime provided by the 1995 Act—the new Act has created a new office of Pensions Regulator. The Pensions Regulator now holds all the powers which were originally vested in the Occupational Pensions Regulatory Authority by virtue of the 1995 Act. Accordingly, the new Pensions Regulator has powers under the 1995 Act, many provisions of which remain in force alongside the 2004 Act, as well as the 2004 Act. For example, powers relating to the appointment of 'replacement' trustees originally contained within s. 7 of the 1995 Act have now been vested in the new Regulator. Similarly, provisions which allow the Regulator to prevent a person not considered 'fit and proper' from acting as a trustee (in relation to specific trusts, or more generally), originally located in the 1995 legislation, can now be found in s. 33 of the 2004 Act. Elsewhere, provisions relate to the removal of trustees who become bankrupt or against whom there are proceedings which relate to accusations of dishonesty or deception (pursuant to s. 34). The Pensions Regulator also has the power to impose financial penalties on trustees and others in relation to breaches of their statutory duties (by virtue of s. 256); and to seek injunctions to prevent the misuse or misappropriation of assets, and to apply to the court for restitution in respect of assets misapplied or misappropriated (within s. 15 and s. 16 respectively). Furthermore, although the objective of seeking to prevent losses to pension trusts arising from fraud or maladministration is clear in this very brief overview of some of its key functions and powers, this body—the Pensions Regulator is a corporate body—is intended to be proactive in promoting good practice in pension trust administration, such as, for example, in publishing codes of practice.

Like its predecessor, the Pensions Regulator can order that an occupational scheme is wound up or, where it is appropriate to do so, replace an existing scheme with a different one, but the new winding-up powers include the power (contained within ss. 23–32) to make a freezing order in response to an 'immediate risk' which might be presented to members of the scheme. The Pensions Regulator also has the power (by virtue of s. 17) to recover an employer's contributions to a fund which are unpaid by him, and to issue an 'improvement notice' (under s. 13) to any person where it appears that requirements of pensions legislation are not being complied with, and also to enter and inspect business premises (pursuant to ss. 73–76).

8.5.11.3 *Pension trusts and the need to protect assets from maladministration*

It is also the case that funding requirements have been tightened up by the 2004 Act, with these new provisions also illustrating the role of the Pensions Regulator created under the legislation. The provisions of the 1995 Act relating to scheme funding were, like their successors in the 2004 legislation, designed to try to prevent inadequacies in funding which might otherwise arise in this very complex, and in many respects highly intangible, 'long-term' trust arrangement. The underlying purpose of so-called scheme funding rules was always to try to ensure that any inadequacies could be exposed through regular monitoring, which would allow remedial action (such as increased contributions either from employee or employer) to be taken.

The 1995 Act sought to achieve this by providing a 'minimum funding rule' for occupational pension schemes, which has now been replaced by a more strict scheme of funding rules by virtue of the 2004 legislation. However, while this regime is stricter, it is also more flexible inasmuch as it is one which applies in a 'scheme-specific' manner. Fundamentally, it remains rooted in the most elemental consideration of pensions law: this is of course the need to ensure that each scheme must have sufficient assets to cover its liabilities (2004 Act, s. 222). In furtherance of this strict, but flexible, scheme-specific approach, trustees must (under s. 223) prepare a statement of funding principles setting out their policy for ensuring that these funding objectives are met, and obtain an actuary's valuation of the scheme's assets and liabilities at regular intervals (under s. 224). Trustees must also prepare (under s. 227) and keep under review a schedule of contributions made by employers and also employees, which the actuary must certify.

The significance of the new Pensions Regulator lies in the way in which the Regulator must (by the provisions of ss. 225 and 227) be informed by the actuary if the valuation carried out on the scheme shows that the trustees are failing to meet their funding objectives, or if he is unable—for any reason—to certify the schedule of contributions required under s. 227. If this happens, the Pensions Regulator is also at the heart of the plan for recovery which must then be drawn up (by the provisions of s. 226), detailing the steps which will be taken to meet the statutory funding objective (under ss. 229–231): the Regulator will oversee this, inasmuch as trustees must report any failures in this process, and ultimately the Regulator has the power to wind up the scheme.

 online resource centre

FURTHER READING

Harpum 'Perpetuities, Pensions and Resulting Trusts' (2000) Conveyancer 170.

Gardner 'New Angles on Unincorporated Associations' (1992) Conveyancer 41.

Warburton 'The Holding of Property by Unincorporated Associations' (1985) Conveyancer 318.

9

Beneficial interests in the family
home: a case study

This chapter is an important point of reference for a number of themes covered in this text thus far. Initially, chapter 1 introduced the nature of the trust, and its respective treatment of beneficial interests and legal title, and at that point it was noted that the instrument is widely used across human interactions; increasingly in the commercial sphere, and that it has long been used in relation to family property and financial arrangements. This theme was explained further in chapter 2, which signposted cohabitation of the 'family home' directly. In respect of both these initial chapters, this chapter's discussion of ownership of family homes now brings sharply into focus the everyday significance of trusts and trusts law, and in a context to which almost everyone can relate directly or indirectly. Fundamentally, this is through consideration of central issues flowing from legal ownership of a home, and the ways in which a party who is not the legal owner of a home can nevertheless acquire a proprietary interest in it.

In this respect, the materials in this chapter also resonate with coverage given to the constitution of trusts in chapter 3: this is where consideration was given to the ways in which legal title becomes vested in the trustee, who then holds that property subject to the entitlements of the beneficiaries (and with these considerations shaping his responsibilities in relation to the trust property). This will become very significant for the subject matter which follows, as will closely connected questions of formality requirements considered in chapter 5, which pointed to the differing positions of trusts on account of whether or not they are 'express'.

In many respects this 'case study' chapter follows directly from chapters 7 and 8. Chapter 7 did, of course, introduce non-express trusts, which are classified as constructive and resulting, and which are found under the unifying heading of trusts which are 'implied' by equity in response to some kind of injustice which would otherwise arise in relation to ownership of property. This theme was continued initially in chapter 8 which provided a case study of the operation of resulting trusts, through examining unincorporated associations, and also pension funds. This case study of the family home, and that which immediately follows on equitable fraud examines trusts best described as constructive—at any rate, because the trust is imposed against the will of the trustee—but it will also consider the resulting trust in a way which follows on directly from its introduction in chapter 7.

9.1 A case study in the working of constructive and resulting trusts

Most of the trusts considered in this chapter can, like those in the chapters immediately preceding and immediately following, be categorised as constructive; equally, however, some of the cases are clearly based on resulting trust principles. Furthermore, even where there is a constructive trust, it does not necessarily follow that it has an independent existence, and that better reasoning comes from the way it may well be used solely to avoid the formality provisions of s. 53(1)(b) of the Law of Property Act 1925. It will become clear that in the case of a constructive trust, all the features of an express trust will be present, except for the statutory requirement of formality that the declaration of trust is in writing.

This is a case study of the operation of constructive and resulting trusts, and illustration of their essential features. It also provides a point of reference for considering where they arise; and whether their use in operation always observes the conceptual distinctiveness which 'textbook' accounts of them emphasise. It will become apparent in this chapter that legal disputes surrounding ownership of the family home cluster very strongly around constructive and resulting trusts, and recently this has required extensive consideration of their interplay with proprietary estoppel.

9.2 Appreciating the significance of the family home for exploring resulting and constructive trusts, and finding hypothetical understanding for the model for the case study

The rationale for this case study on the working of trusts which are implied is to explain how the family home has become an important everyday setting for considering their application, on account of the complexities which can be seen to arise from the ownership of property. In this context, the family home can be seen as a setting for appreciating the injustices which can arise from ownership of property, and the ways in which equity responds to such. This was the central theme for the chapter which introduced trusts which are implied, and it is present throughout this case study.

In this setting, the tensions which equity is seeking to respond to reflect the way in which recognising legal title alone in the context of ownership is important for achieving certainty (in relation to valuable property rights), but that doing so can also lead to injustice through the interests of another being overlooked in absence of an express declaration of trust (which according to s. 53(1)(b) must be evidenced in writing and signed to be valid) unless the trust is implied (s. 53(2)). Before progressing any further, this rationale is central to understanding that two key hypothetical models relating to the location of legal title to property dominate the nature of perceived injustice which will arise in relation to the family home. These are:

- Injustices which can arise from situations where a family home is actually owned in law by one of the parties.

  This situation arises where although the property is a shared family home it actually only has one legal owner. Here legal title is vested solely in one party, and this is the most common traditional reason for equity's concern for achieving justice in circumstances where despite this, the non-legal owner should have entitlements to it.

  This has traditionally been the dominant situation in disputes relating to the ownership of shared homes, and indeed it has been the (one) hypothetical model which has been used in previous editions of this text. In this situation, typically, an unmarried couple purchase a home in which they intend to live together, but legal title is conveyed to one party alone for some reason. The issues raised here concern whether the party who is not a legal owner of the property can acquire a proprietary interest in the property nevertheless. Because only one party holds legal title, the nature of any proprietary interest acquired by the other must necessarily be equitable. And it is in these circumstances that equity is concerned with avoiding injustices which are possibly hidden behind sole legal ownership. This raises questions of what conditions must be present for a party seeking an equitable interest in the property to be able to do this, and if this can be shown, there are further questions of size and extent—namely, how large the interest will be.

- A different type of situation? The significance of *Stack* v *Dowden* [2007] UKHL 17.

  As the materials immediately above indicate, traditionally this text has only ever really raised the illustration of the problems arising from 'one party' legal ownership in its main discussion, and the 'problems' arising in the case of a joint legal tenancy were considered a 'postscript' to this main discussion. However, *Stack* v *Dowden* [2007] UKHL 17 is authority that a much more unusual situation also requires attention. In this situation, the shared family home is actually legally owned by both parties, and so here equity's concern is different from avoiding injustices possibly hidden behind sole legal ownership. Here equity must respond to injustices possibly arising from the situation where although both parties are holders of legal title to the property the matter of who actually owns the equity in the home (the valuable part) has not been made clear in the arrangement.

  In this situation *Stack* is authority that having legal title to a property will ensure that a party does have an interest in it in equity. Immediately this makes the situation different from the 'one legal owner' scenario above, because the party seeking an interest is deemed to have established the existence of one for himself, on account of legal ownership. The key issue here is how large this interest will be, and whether the size of the equitable interest will reflect the legal equality between the parties.

9.2.1 Understanding the injustices themselves: how do they arise, and how are they manifested

As has been suggested, the injustices which can be seen to arise in this context, and which equity is seeking to respond to, have traditionally focused on sole legal ownership of one party, and discussion has clustered around injustices which can be caused by recognising the legal owner of property as the only party who has interests in it in circumstances where:

- a non-legal owner has contributed to the purchase of the property which actually belongs in law to another person; or
- because the parties have formed an agreement relating to their home, or the legal owner has made a representation to the effect that ownership of the home is to be shared, and this is not mirrored in legal ownership.

In contrast with equity's concerns (for apportionment) where legal ownership is actually already shared, where there is sole legal ownership, while apportionment is significant, there is fundamentally a question of *whether* an interest should arise at all. Thus questions relating to contributions made by the parties, and any agreement which they might have come to in relation to beneficial ownership—will come to the fore.

However it is important to note at this stage the significance of the wording used above indicating how this chapter is essentially a study of the way in which 'equity is concerned with avoiding injustices which are possibly hidden behind legal ownership'. Reference to the word 'possibly' draws attention to the way in which home ownership, and even disputed home ownership, will not always harbour injustices. And it will become apparent that while this area of law shows equity is willing to respond to injustices which arise, it is equally the case that equity will not read injustice into every case where a home is being 'shared' by parties. It will become apparent that equity's jurisdiction here is strongly based on reflecting the parties' intentions regarding ownership of their property, and in this regard important distinctions are drawn between intention to share actual ownership of property and an intention to share (merely) its occupation and enjoyment.

9.2.1.1 *The context for these disputes, and the significance of formal partnerships*

The context for such considerations of interest in the family home is very much that of relationship breakdown, and it will become apparent that many of the cases examined concern disputes between the parties to the relationship themselves. In this respect, the parties in this hypothetical example are unmarried because, as will become clear at the end of this chapter, by virtue of the Matrimonial Causes Act 1973 (as amended), the courts have the power to alter significantly the property interests of married couples in the event of divorce, a decree of nullity of marriage or a decree of judicial separation. In such an event, the importance of the prior property interests of the spouses is reduced, since they will no longer be conclusive in the face of the court's discretion.

The traditional position has been that it also makes no difference if the hypothetical couple in question is a same-sex couple, or whether a couple is—in the parlance of the Law Commission's recent commentary on home-sharing—a 'non-conventional' couple. This was to make the point that these disputes, and the basic injustices which underpin them, actually occur across a spectrum of personal relationships.

However, the Civil Partnership Act 2004 alters the position of same-sex couples who elect to register their 'civil partnership'. Upon doing so, partners in a registered arrangement will acquire rights to financial interests and relating to property which are broadly similar to those of married couples. The implications of this in relation to property adjustment orders upon the dissolution of a civil partnership are considered below, alongside the position of divorcing couples seeking ancillary relief. What needs to be stressed at this point is that the general hypothetical examples given in this chapter now apply only to same-sex couples who have not registered a civil partnership. For same-sex couples who have not registered a civil partnership, the issues arising around acquiring an interest in property remain the same as for an unmarried heterosexual couple, or a couple in any kind of 'unconventional' relationship.

9.2.1.2 *The reasons underlying the hypothetical model and current policy movements*

It is of course possible for the above position, which at heart concerns the way in which only one party has legal title to a disputed home, to be avoided. Indeed, the courts have frequently expressed the view that it is desirable for transfers of property to contain an express declaration of trust concerning the beneficial interests. It is also worth observing that the law in this area is widely regarded as unsatisfactory, and in 1995 the Law Commission announced that it was to examine the property rights of home-sharers (Item 8, Sixth Programme of Law Reform: Law Com. 234). The Report commented (at 34) that 'the present legal rules are uncertain and difficult to apply and can lead to serious injustice'.

In 2002 the Law Commission published a Discussion paper entitled *Sharing Homes* which suggested the need for new approaches to the issues arising from a variety of personal relationships. Further consideration of this project is made later in this chapter, but it is commonly referred to as a highly disappointing exercise which failed to translate into proposals for reform. What can be added now is that the Law Commission's Cohabitation Project announced in July 2005 has now concluded. By way of brief overview, the project was in many respects a continuation of the findings of *Sharing Homes*, because the Law Commission is continuing to highlight the need for the law to accommodate and respond to a variety of different living arrangements within which relationships of 'intimacy and exclusivity' arise, and to provide fairness to the people concerned which is reflective of the nature of their relationships. The Law Commission published Consultation Paper No. 179, *Cohabitation: The Financial Consequences of Relationship Breakdown*, on 31 May 2006 in light of the Government's instruction to 'examine the options for reforming the law that applies to cohabiting couples on separation or death'. Towards the end of the chapter further reference will be made to the Consultation, and extensive consideration will be given to the Report published in July 2007.

For present purposes the materials in this chapter are now focused on exploring the current law relating to the position of equitable ownership in shared homes, in relation especially to non-legal owners of property. At one level this is intended to provide some explanation of *why* it is the case that this sphere has traditionally been perceived (by a number of academic commentators and by the Law Commission) as 'uncertain and difficult' and capable of leading 'to serious injustice'. Furthermore it looks at the ways in which recent case law has attempted to address these issues, and how they are also being considered in policy spheres. And running throughout will be the proposition that while most earnest encouragement is being given by the courts, and also in policy discourses, for parties to make their intentions relating to ownership of property clear, this chapter is a testament to the way in which equity has sought to respond to the injustices which can arise where parties do not do so, and that this is actually a very common happening.

9.2.2 **An introduction to key issues and concerns arising**

In a direct continuation of the suggestions made above, the importance of this area of study flows from the way in which shared occupation of a home does not necessarily amount to shared ownership of a home. Indeed, *Goodman v Gallant* [1986] Fam 106 is authority that even where legal title to property is vested in both parties, documents of title to land relate to its legal ownership only, and not to the apportionment of the equity in the property. Where there is a declaration of beneficial interests (declaration of trust) contained in the documents of title, this will be conclusive, but it is still very common for legal title in the family home to be vested in the name of one party alone, and there is often no declaration of the parties' interests in the property beyond this.

Goodman v *Gallant* is authority that where there is a written declaration of trust the courts will enforce it, becomes significant in due course, when reference is made to what the parties might feel about the contributions which they actually make to the property. While the Law Commission has recommended that express declarations of trust should be made, and land registry rules now require this where legal title is jointly held, this is prospective and rarely happens beyond this.

Until very recently (and there is a strong sense that *Stack v Dowden*-type situations are rare and exceptional) the most common scenario was one in which legal title of the home is vested in one party only. It is in this light that it becomes very significant that there is no specific property law legislation to determine beneficial interests in this situation and thus it has been left to the judiciary to formulate the relevant equitable principles. It is important to appreciate that this approach has become one focused on equity precisely because the 'other party' has no interest in the property in law. In turn this has become focused on trusts law and especially the *implied trust* as a response to 'injustices' arising from recognising legal title alone in the context of ownership where there is no express declaration of trust. The other points which are noteworthy at the outset include:

- These situations arise because parties in a relationship do not always discuss the beneficial ownership of their home (as in the cases illustrating certainty of intention and also arising in relation to the constitution of trusts, this is an example of people not making intentions clear).
- These issues will often only ever be considered when a relationship is breaking down, or has already done so.

The judge-made property law thus applies to all types of parties sharing a home. However, the courts have a broad ancillary jurisdiction pursuant to the Matrimonial Causes Act 1973 to adjust the property rights of married couples on divorce (or nullity or judicial separation) and this displaces the strict property law rules. This jurisdiction works by giving the courts discretion to vary beneficial shares which would otherwise be determined by ordinary property principles where appropriate, and has now been applied to same-sex couples who register their relationship as a civil partnership under the Civil Partnership Act 2004. Thus, most of these 'ordinary trusts law' cases concern cohabiting unmarried couples.

- Traditionally, the emphasis of this has been ordinary trusts law, but in the last decade there has been a marked trend in the courts taking a distinctive approach based on proprietary estoppel. In common with the trust, proprietary estoppel is an equitable doctrine, and in some respects at least it serves functions which are very similar to implied trusts, but it will become clear that, in other ways, its approach is different from that of the trust.

However, whether the actual approach taken by the courts is one based on ordinary trusts law or proprietary estoppel, there are always two key questions at the heart of every case of disputed home ownership. These are, *first*, can the party who is claiming an interest in the property actually establish that he or she has a beneficial interest in the property? And if so, *second*, how large should that beneficial interest be?

9.3 Uncertainty in the law and the significance of *Lloyds Bank plc* v *Rosset*

In 1995, the Law Commission (Law. Com. No. 234) remarked that 'The present legal rules are uncertain and difficult to apply and can lead to serious injustice', and the Law Commission's concern in this area has continued. In 2002 in a discussion paper entitled *Sharing Homes* it continued to reflect on the inadequacy of the approaches being taken by the courts in this sphere, and the injustices which arise from the law as it has traditionally been formulated. Most recently this can be seen in its Cohabitation Project which, following a Consultation Paper published in 2006, the Law Commission reported on in July 2007.

The Law Commission's contributions in this sphere leave little doubt that the courts have received considerable criticism for the approaches adopted in seeking to prevent injustice arising in the context of disputed home ownership. How this might have been addressed in more recent case law will be considered at several points in this chapter, but in linking the traditional approaches of the courts and the criticism advanced by the Law Commission, it is certainly the case that prior to 1990 this was an area of law which was very difficult to state with any degree of certainty, let alone clarity. Here 1991 is seen as a key point in time because the House of Lords stepped in with a remarkably clear statement on the law by Lord Bridge in *Lloyds Bank plc* v *Rosset* [1991] 1 AC 107.

However, in terms of actually introducing *Lloyds Bank* v *Rosset* as a very clear statement of the law, some background is now given as to why this clear statement of law did actually appear at this point in time. And it was in many respects a response to inconsistencies in the case law which had become apparent through very different responses to the tension between certainty and justice during the 1970s and 1980s.

In this sphere, the tensions between certainty and justice—which provide the setting for implied trusts—had created a body of highly inconsistent case law for a number of reasons. This became very strongly associated with considerable disagreement about the appropriate use and applications for the constructive trust in cases of disputed home ownership. And significantly much of this actually stemmed from the way in which applying the other response to injustice in these circumstances—the resulting trust—was proving to be very limited in scope.

It will be recalled from chapter 7 that the resulting trust is a mechanism for recovering one's own property, with *Dyer* v *Dyer* illustrating how the so-called 'voluntary conveyance' resulting trust would ensure that property belonging to one person could be retained by them even if legal title was then transferred to another. This means in circumstances where a non-legal owner of a property has made no application of his own property to the home, he will be unable to recover any on the basis of a resulting trust. In short the resulting trust will only ever address situations in which money has *actually been provided* in the acquisition of a home at all. And even in this latter situation, the mechanics of recovering 'one's own property' will 'limit' the amount recoverable in respect of this to the amount which has actually been provided, or more accurately the proportion of the *value* of the home which this amount represents.

In these circumstances it is not surprising that the more flexible and adaptable constructive trust has become highly influential. It is not premised on recovering property, and so its remedial properties are not limited in this way. Instead the constructive trust is premised on reasons of imposition on conscience, and in the context of disputed home ownership this has become attached to reasons of conscience as to why the parties *should* share ownership. It will become clear that in turn this has become strongly attached to the way in which the parties appear to have agreed to share ownership, notwithstanding the location of legal title, and that the agreement should accordingly stand. It has also become attached to situations where the legal owner has made some representation to the effect that ownership is to be shared by the parties, and the way in which he should accordingly be held to what has been said.

9.3.1 The application of the constructive trust in disputed home ownership

In seeking to draw together these key elements of the rationale for the constructive trust, it has become recognised as a mechanism to give effect to the parties' 'common intention' that ownership in their home is shared, manifested in a conventional agreement, or an understanding arising from the legal owner's representations. *Both* are linked by the way in which equity imposes a constructive trust because it would be unconscionable for a legal owner of property not to be held to the agreement reached/representation made.

9.3.1.1 *Difficulties arising in the application of constructive trusts to disputed home ownership: divided case law and the context for* Rosset

Although this narrative does explain how the constructive trust has become so influential in determinations of disputed home ownership, it also helps to explain why a number of difficulties have arisen, and why uncertainty came to characterise the approaches adopted by the courts. During the 1970s and 1980s case law reflected the way in which there were inconsistencies in the situations in which constructive trusts were being implied. This occurred along the fault line of finding evidence of a 'common intention' to share ownership in a home, which resulted in two types of response situations where common intention could not be ascertained.

Ascertaining beneficial interests in absence of common intention: strict property principles should apply Where a common intention that the beneficial interest in the home is not to belong solely to the legal owner could not be found strict property principles must be applied. *Burns* v *Burns* [1984] Ch 317 illustrates that mutual intentions regarding the sharing of their lives together and occupying the property together did not amount to mutual intentions to share beneficial ownership in the property. Fox LJ's judgment stated that 'The mere fact that parties live together and do the ordinary domestic tasks is, in my view, no indication at all that they thereby intended to alter the existing property rights of either of them.' *Gissing* v *Gissing* [1971] insisted that a constructive trust could only ever be applied in response to the parties' common intention, and in absence of this strict property principles applied, and at the heart of any interest arising would be financial contributions made by the claimant.

Ascertaining beneficial interests on criteria of fairness and justice Alongside the strict property principles which were being adopted in absence of common intention, an alternative approach based on 'conscience and justice' started to appear. This reflected the belief that too little weight was being attached to indirect contributions, and the courts should be more flexible in looking at the conduct/intentions of the parties after acquiring the property, as well as upon it. Lord Denning pioneered this, and key cases including *Eves* v *Eves* [1975] 1 WLR 1138 and *Hussey* v *Palmer* [1972] 1 WLR 1286 were being based upon a new model constructive trust which could be imposed 'whenever justice and good conscience require it'.

Thus in many respects the 'case study' of disputed home ownership can be seen as a microcosm of the tensions which have subsisted in constructive trust theory which were identified in chapter 7. These cluster differing views on whether in English law the constructive trust is more appropriately viewed as a substantive institution, which formalises an existing proprietary entitlement, or is capable of subsisting as a more radical 'remedial' type, which is capable of actually creating a proprietary entitlement for the claimant.

9.3.1.2 *The context for* Rosset: *clarification and restatement—and finality in law?*

Because of the very divided views on applying constructive trusts coming across in the case law pre-*Rosset*, the law in respect of the position of non-legal owners of property became very difficult to state with any degree of certainty. Cases could easily go 'either way' with very little indication, and in a number of cases a great deal appeared to 'turn' on very little. This was increasingly deemed as being unsatisfactory because property rights are valuable, and the function of equity is to manage the tensions which arise from ownership of property, not to disregard them.

In this respect, Lord Bridge's judgment in *Rosset* was seen as providing a very clear statement of the law, and for this reason it will be the starting point for the substantive consideration given to the law shortly. However, in still having much to say by way of introduction, it is also necessary to point out at this stage that following *Rosset* and since the mid-1990s, notwithstanding its apparent clarity and definitiveness, the law has once again become unsettled and uncertain. This commenced with the Court of Appeal decision in *Midland Bank plc v Cooke* [1995] 4 All ER 562 (noted by Glover and Todd [1995] 4 Web JCLI), which muddied the waters regarding quantification of beneficial interests, and appeared massively to contradict what will become clear has been regarded as *Rosset's* 'strict property' approach.

Although this text has staunchly maintained that it is difficult to reconcile with a correct application of trusts law, the essence of *Cooke* has been followed in a number of cases; has been given very positive affirmation by the Law Commission; and recently received important recognition in the House of Lords in the case of *Stack* v *Dowden* [2007] UKHL.

It is also the case that a number of authorities post-*Rosset* did cast doubt on the continuing operation of trusts law in determining interests in family homes, given that, from the closing years of the 1990s, the courts started to show a preference for an approach based on considerations of fairness and justice associated with a proprietary estoppel analysis. This is in contrast with the period immediately post-*Rosset*, during which the case of *Baker* v *Baker* (1993) 25 HLR 408 stood out against what appeared to be a clear preference for a trusts model. The high watermark of this was the Court of Appeal decision in *Oxley* v *Hiscock* [2004] 3 All ER 703, which the previous edition of this text regarded as the leading case relating to the quantification of beneficial interests in a home where ownership is disputed. It also noted that alongside this, on the policy front, the Law Commission's Cohabitation Project was also focusing on reforming the position of parties within intimate and personal relationships that are not formally recognised legal partnerships. The project was then at Consultation stage, and the Law Commission has now reported.

9.3.1.3 *Beneficial interests and a new leading case*

The discussion which now follows on determinations of the *existence* of and *quantification* of interests in a shared home acknowledges that the leading case for *quantification* of beneficial interests is now actually the House of Lords decision in *Stack* v *Dowden*. It will become clear that while this decision endorses a number of the characteristics of *Oxley* v *Hiscock* it also departs from others. The latter would appear to indicate a reaffirmation of the role of the implied trust—rather than proprietary estoppel—as the most appropriate device for giving effect to interests in equity and for quantifying them.

Notwithstanding, this chapter continues to be written around the touchstone case of *Lloyds Bank* v *Rosset* [1991] 1 AC 107. This is to emphasise the utmost significance which is attached to the presence (or otherwise) of an agreement which subsists between parties as to the ownership of their home, and how the courts determine whether there is such an agreement subsisting. This is something which *Oxley* appeared to suggest remains intact, on account of the apparent distinction being drawn by Chadwick LJ between primary and secondary questions relating to 'common intention'. In this respect, Chadwick LJ's judgment was very much concerned with finding a 'better' reading of Lord Bridge's judgment as it applied to the 'secondary' question of common intention which related to quantification. The judgment suggested very strongly that the primary question of common intention—namely that of 'was there a common intention that each should have a beneficial interest in the property?' remains central. There is much allusion in *Stack* v *Dowden* that the need to establish an interest in property at the heart of *Rosset* remains central in approaches which are in many respects new, and which include strong dicta suggesting that, in his requirements for establishing an interest, Lord Bridge had actually been too strict and not sufficiently flexible to accommodate the 'realities' of modern home ownership. This is so notwithstanding that *Oxley* and now *Stack* are both important authority that the distinctiveness between the two categories of case which were identified by Lord Bridge in *Rosset*—which could be found by reference to ascertaining common intention—is becoming blurred in respect of *how* these interests are *quantified* once they are found actually to exist.

9.3.2 *Lloyds Bank* v *Rosset* [1991]: certainty and restatement articulated through two different types of case

Given the inconsistencies in applying the constructive trust to cases of disputed home ownership, the case law had become very divided and uncertain. *Rosset* was regarded at the time as an important statement of certainty in the law. Interestingly, as Lord Bridge himself saw things, it was actually a restatement of existing law rather than a statement of a new position. It was clearly intended to be an authoritative statement, and even a definitive statement. In Lord Bridge's view, it was a restatement of the way in which the constructive trust subsisted to give effect to the parties' common intentions surrounding ownership of their home, and where a common intention to share ownership could not be found, beneficial interests would be determined by property-based principles (reflecting the parties' contributions of their own assets). Accordingly, the constructive trust was not a device for ensuring 'justice' by reading an injustice into every case of disputed ownership, and if a party actually contributes nothing of his own to the home of another then he will not acquire an interest in it by virtue only of the fact that he has shared its occupation.

In taking this position (and, as he believed, restating the correct position of the law) Lord Bridge identified two types of case in which a common intention to share the ownership of a home could be found, and thus two broad types of situation which were capable of establishing a proprietary interest in a home belonging to another. As will become clear, for Lord Bridge, although both these case types were capable of establishing proprietary interests, they were actually very different types of case. These types of case were to be ascertained from a 'first and fundamental question which must always be resolved' in these cases. For Lord Bridge, this would be central to distinguishing the two types of case, as follows (with emphasis added):

The first and fundamental question which must always be resolved is whether, independently of any inference to be drawn from the conduct of the parties in the course of sharing the house as their home and managing their joint affairs, **there has at any time prior to acquisition, or exceptionally at some later date, been any agreement, arrangement or understanding reached between them that the property is to be shared beneficially.** The finding of an agreement or arrangement to share in this sense can only, we think, be based on evidence of express discussions between the partners, however imperfectly remembered and however imprecise their terms may have been. *Once a finding to this effect is made it will only be necessary for the partner asserting a claim to a beneficial interest against the partner entitled to the legal estate to show that he or she has acted to his or her detriment or significantly altered his or her position in reliance on the agreement* in order to give rise to a constructive trust or proprietary estoppel.

Lord Bridge's judgment continued by explaining that:

In sharp contrast with this situation is the **very different one** where there is **no evidence to support a finding of an agreement or arrangement to share, however reasonable it might have been for the parties to reach such an arrangement if they had applied their minds** to the question, and where the court must rely entirely on the conduct of the parties both as the basis from which to infer a common intention to share the property beneficially and as the conduct relied on to give rise to a constructive trust. In this situation *direct contributions to the purchase price by the partner who is not the legal owner, whether initially or by payment of mortgage instalments, will readily justify the inference necessary to the creation of a constructive trust. But, as we read the authorities, it is at least extremely doubtful whether anything less will do.*

This speech identified *two types of case*, which have since been referred to as:

- *Rosset* **Category 1**: These are cases where there is evidence of agreement to share the property beneficially. In these circumstances the non-legal owner of property can 'claim' an interest in the property in equity by virtue of this agreement. In these circumstances it is the agreement which is central in establishing the beneficial interest, with contributions made being central to invoking this by way of a constructive trust (to avoid s. 53(1)(b) requirements).

- *Rosset* **Category 2**: These are cases where there is no 'independent' evidence of agreement to share the property beneficially and the only means the court has of inferring this is from the contributions which the non-legal owner of property has made to the property. This means that the contributions which are made by the non-legal owner are the only means available to establish that the claimant has a beneficial interest in the home.

9.3.2.1 *Applying constructive trusts to* Rosset's *two categories*

Lord Bridge suggested that the beneficial interest being sought could be 'claimed' by the non-legal owner by virtue of constructive trust or proprietary estoppel. For some time after *Rosset* the courts had a distinct preference for the constructive trust, rather than the estoppel approach, which is also an equitable doctrine (but with a different premise, and a response oriented towards achieving fairness: this is considered further shortly). Given that preference was very strongly shown for the constructive trust route post-*Rosset*, cases in this area became analysed in the following way:

Category 1: *express common intention constructive trust*   This was based on an 'agreement or understanding reached between them that the property is to be shared beneficially' which was reached 'independently of any inference to be drawn from the conduct of the parties in the course of sharing the house as their home and managing their joint affairs'. A constructive trust (or proprietary estoppel) will arise by showing detrimental reliance on this agreement.

Category 2: *inferred common intention constructive trust*   In these circumstances, there is no independently subsisting agreement, and the court must rely '*entirely on the conduct of the parties both as the basis from which to infer a common intention to share the property beneficially and as the conduct relied on to give rise to a constructive trust*'. (NB this latter scenario has also been analysed as an orthodox presumed resulting trust, rather than a constructive trust (see *Oxley* v *Hiscock* [2005] and *Stack* v *Dowden* [2007], and this is given some consideration shortly).

9.3.2.2 *Common intention to share a home beneficially*

At the heart of this is the way in which shared beneficial ownership in a family home will only occur where it is the parties' common intention to share their home in this way. For a long time, the parameters of this area of law have been set by the proposition that *shared occupation* did not amount to **shared ownership**. In circumstances where legal title vested in one party alone, the only option open to the claimant to establish ownership of their home was through being able to establish ownership *in equity*. In this situation equity would imply a trust in response to the injustices arising from having regard to legal title alone (most commonly in the case of a sole legal owner, but, in unusual cases, where legal title is jointly held: see *Stack* v *Dowden* below).

In this passage Lord Bridge clearly distinguished between two types of case. The first type is where there is evidence of an agreement to share the property beneficially. The agreement need not be formal and its terms need not be particularly precise, but it appears that it must be based on evidence of express discussions between the partners (but see further below). More importantly, the evidence of the agreement must be independent of the conduct of the parties in the course of sharing the house as their home (conduct for this category is any detrimental reliance and is wider than that for the second category, considered later). If there is such evidence then, in principle, on this proposition it is not necessary to look at the conduct of the parties in order to establish either the existence of a beneficial interest or its size. On this reasoning, the agreement will reveal both the existence of an interest and also its size. Reference is made to this as a proposition of principle because, as will become clear, this is what the case law prior to *Rosset* had suggested. However it will also become apparent that more recent approaches evidenced in *Oxley* v *Hiscock* [2004] and *Stack* v *Dowden* [2007] have attached significance to what the parties have *actually contributed*.

The second type of case is where there is no evidence subsisting independently of the conduct of the parties (e.g., contributions to the home) of any such agreement. *Rosset* itself was such a case. Here, if any inference is to be drawn of an intention to share the beneficial interests, it can be drawn only on the basis of the contributions themselves. Thus, the contributions are used to establish the existence of the beneficial interest 'owned' by a non-legal owner of property, and because there is no evidence other than this, they also appear to represent the means by which it would actually be quantified. It is important to appreciate at this point that Lord Bridge's opinion was that in this type of situation it was likely that only direct contributions to the purchase price by the partner who is not the legal owner would suffice, and this could be manifested by way of initial deposit money, or subsequently in mortgage repayments, and that nothing else would suffice. More will be said about this shortly, especially given the way in which

Lord Bridge's strict approach to establishing an interest through conduct has been criticized, most recently in *Stack* v *Dowden* [2007] and in the decision of the Privy Council in *Abbot* v *Abbott* [2007] UKPC 53.

For Lord Bridge, the conduct of the parties was also to be relevant in the first type of case, but of far less importance than in the second type, and for the first category it would not be necessary for the conduct to be in the form of direct contributions to the purchase price. This is because the agreement to share is shown independently of the parties' conduct, and for Lord Bridge it appeared that the only function of the conduct is to get around the formalities requirements of s. 53(1)(b) of the Law of Property Act 1925. This allows the inference to be drawn that the legal owner has declared himself trustee for himself and the other party. To be valid, such a declaration would need to be in signed writing (by virtue of s. 53(1)(b)) unless there is an implied, resulting, or constructive trust, in which case, by virtue of s. 53(2), the provisions of s. 53(1)(b) do not apply. There will be a constructive trust if the claimant has acted to their detriment or significantly altered their position in reliance on the agreement. Traditionally, contributions made in these circumstances have thus been regarded as conduct showing detrimental reliance, which will then allow formality requirements to be circumvented, and this function is clear elsewhere in Lord Bridge's speech in *Rosset*:

> Even if there had been the clearest oral agreement between Mr and Mrs Rosset that Mr Rosset was to hold the property in trust for them both as tenants in common, this would, of course, have been ineffective since a valid declaration of trust by way of gift of a beneficial interest in land is required by s. 53(1) of the Law of Property Act 1925 to be in writing. But if Mrs Rosset had, as pleaded, altered her position in reliance on the agreement this could have given rise to an enforceable interest in her favour by way either of a constructive trust or of a proprietary estoppel.

On this analysis it follows that no detrimental reliance is required if the agreement is in writing—for example, where the parties communicate by signed letters—and that it will not be required where the property is not land (e.g., a caravan or houseboat). However, it is also the case that this very functional view of contributions made in the context of category 1 agreements has been challenged by *Oxley* v *Hiscock* and *Stack* v *Dowden* (as intimated above, and will be considered further below).

9.3.2.3 *The modern law and the significance of* Rosset

The decision in *Rosset* was considered a landmark on two counts, which were very closely related to one another. First and foremost, it reasserted that the proper role for the constructive trust was to give effect to the parties' intentions relating to ownership of shared homes. Second, in making this clear, distinction was drawn between two types of case, which, although they were both capable of giving rise to an equitable interest in a home belonging to another, actually operated in very different ways. The decision made a distinction between cases where evidence of agreement between the parties concerning sharing of beneficial interests existed, and cases where there was no independent evidence of this. In making an analysis of the case law, with *Rosset*'s classification at heart, two points of focus are central:

- What must be shown in order for a party who is not a legal owner to establish the existence of a beneficial interest?

- Once a party can establish they have an interest in equity, the courts must decide the extent or quantification of this interest.

9.3.2.4 *Rosset as a definitive statement: introduction to the applications of Rosset's categories*

Rosset was intended to be important clarification of the position of establishing a beneficial interest in property. However, even in respect of the position of a non-legal owner of property who is seeking to establish that shared occupation *does amount to shared ownership* (either on the basis of express agreement, or conduct-based evidence of agreement through making contributions), the position post-*Rosset* has become confused and unsettled in a number of ways. Key reasons for this are explained in brief immediately below but will make much better sense when read alongside the materials relating to applying *Rosset* post-*Rosset*. So for now, just be aware that difficulties in applying *Rosset* post-*Rosset* have emerged from the following occurrences:

- A *blurring of distinction* between category 1 cases and category 2 cases: where (small direct) contributions made in absence of express agreement started to produce very similar results to those Lord Bridge stressed were permitted in the presence of an express agreement to share (category 1). The most striking example of this was *Midland Bank* v *Cooke* in 1995.
- The courts having *regard to indirect financial contributions* in absence of express agreement to share (e.g., in *Le Foe* v *Le Foe* [2001]) contrary to Lord Bridge's statement in *Rosset*.
- The difficulties raised by *any* contributions which arise *after the home is acquired* (acquisition is *Rosset*'s point for ascertaining the parties intentions regarding ownership), including very significant improvements to homes which are capable of adding significant capital value.
- The ***rise and fall*** of the trusts-based analysis of beneficial ownership in the family home. *Oxley* v *Hiscock* [2005] Fam 211 became a high watermark for the courts to apply an estoppel based analysis to quantifying shared interests in family homes where 'each party is entitled to that share which the *court considers fair* having regard to the whole course of dealing between them in relation to the property' (including indirect contributions, and 'later' contributions).
- The *rise and fall* and ***rise again*** of a trusts-based analysis of beneficial ownership evidenced in *Stack* v *Dowden* [2007] UKHL 17. While in favour of *Oxley*'s holistic 'whole dealings' approach, the House of Lords in *Stack* criticised the emphasis on the court's assessment of fairness because the focus should be on what the parties *intended*. References were made to the need for the courts to infer parties' intentions rather than impute them, and that a trusts approach was a better reflection overall of the valuable property rights which were at stake.
- Both *Stack* v *Dowden* and *Oxley* v *Hiscock* appear to leave unchanged a fundamental part of Lord Bridge's requirements in *Rosset*—that any claimant must establish an interest in the home. Thus in the essence of *actually establishing* this agreement to share, the approach adopted in *Rosset* as to how this is shown (through reference to category 1 and category 2 cases) stands.

Here *Oxley* and *Stack* are both best analysed as *quantification* cases with *Rosset* remaining the leading case on establishing the existence of a beneficial interest, although both cases were very critical of the strict approach adopted in *Rosset* concerning 'acceptable contributions'.

- *Stack* v *Dowden* has resolved a number of these difficulties and also the uncertainties which started to emerge/reappear post-*Rosset*. This will be noted as the materials go through the application of *Rosset* in the modern law, at the pertinent times. However, before this happens it is also worth noting that *Stack* v *Dowden* has precipitated recognition that in the absence of an express declaration of trust, even jointly held legal title in a family home does not necessarily reflect the parties' intentions regarding the shared home.

9.4 The significance of *Rosset* in the modern law: applying *Rosset* post-*Rosset*

This next section takes as its starting point what was said above about how analysis of the case law post-*Rosset* gravitates around *Rosset*'s classification in two distinct respects.

- an analysis of *contributions* which are made by a party who is not a legal owner, and who is seeking to establish a beneficial interest.
- the second issue is the *quantification* of this beneficial interest: once an interest in equity is established, the courts must decide its size.

9.4.1 *Rosset* category 1 and independent evidence of common agreement or 'understanding': the express common intention constructive trust

According to Lord Bridge, the essence of such an agreement is of course that it subsists independently of any contributions which are made. What follows now is an examination of the key elements in this formula for establishing an interest, relating to actually forming an agreement, and what is required. And within this, given that Lord Bridge suggested that interests in property arising in this category could do so by virtue of constructive trust or proprietary estoppel, how and in what ways this might actually be signalling different requirements according to which mechanism is actually being used is considered.

9.4.1.1 *Category 1 cases: what actually amounts to an 'agreement'?*

For a case to be a category 1 case, the agreement to share (the basis of the common intention) must be direct, and must actually amount to *express discussion* between the parties. Lord Bridge is more flexible in other respects: this can occur at *any time prior to the* acquisition (note that Lord Bridge did concede that this could in exceptional circumstances arise 'at some later date'). It is also clear from Lord Bridge's speech that the agreement reached does not have to be perfectly remembered or even very precise. Nevertheless, to amount to an agreement, some actual discussion is necessary. Authority for this can be found in *Springette* v *Defoe* [1992] 2 FCR 561 and *Saville* v *Goodall* [1993] 1 FLR 755).

In *Springette* v *Defoe* Miss Springette and Mr Defoe purchased a house, with Miss Springette being able to obtain a 41 per cent discount under a 'right to buy' scheme under Part V of the Housing Act 1985, the discount being based on her 11 years as a tenant. The property was conveyed into joint names, there being no declaration of trust in the transfer, and both were liable to repay the mortgage instalments, and in fact both contributed equally to the repayments. Both Springette and Defoe also provided other moneys, the result being that, taking into account her 41 per cent discount, Miss Springette's financial contributions were about 75 per cent, and Mr Defoe's 25 per cent.

9.4.1.2 *Silences in parties' communications: who benefits?*

The relationship broke down and proceedings were commenced to determine the respective beneficial interests of the parties. Miss Springette claimed a 75 per cent share on the basis of her financial contributions, whereas Mr Defoe claimed 50 per cent on the basis that the couple understood that they were to share the property equally. Mr Defoe claimed that the case should be decided on the basis of the first category in *Lloyds Bank plc* v *Rosset*.

The Court of Appeal held in Miss Springette's favour, applying Lord Bridge's remarks in *Rosset* that the finding of such an agreement, arrangement, or understanding could only be based on evidence of express discussions between the partners. Steyn LJ observed that '[o]ur trust law does not allow property rights to be affected by telepathy. *prima facie*, therefore, the alleged actual common intention was not established' ((1992) 24 HLR 552, at p. 558).

Springette v *Defoe* was distinguished in *Savill* v *Goodall* [1993] 1 FLR 755. Mrs Goodall was entitled to a 42 per cent discount under a 'right to buy' scheme, the entirety of the remainder of the purchase money being raised on a mortgage which Mr Savill accepted liability to repay. As in *Springette* v *Defoe*, the property was transferred into the joint names of the parties. The Court of Appeal held, on the basis of express discussions between the parties, that the beneficial interests should be divided equally, but also accepted that Mr Savill's *quid pro quo* for being granted a beneficial interest was his agreement to repay the mortgage capital and costs of redemption. The net proceeds, after repayment of the mortgage by him, were therefore divided equally.

The only substantive difference between *Springette* v *Defoe* and *Savill* v *Goodall* was the absence of any discussion in the former and its presence in the latter case.

In *Midland Bank plc* v *Cooke* [1995] 4 All ER 562, however, Waite LJ did not regard *Springette* v *Defoe* as laying down any general principle for the following reasons: that Dillon LJ, who had given the leading judgment in *Springette* v *Defoe*, had taken a very different approach in *McHardy & Sons* v *Warren* [1994] 2 FLR 338; that no such requirement for express discussion could be gleaned from *Gissing* v *Gissing* [1971] AC 886 or *Grant* v *Edwards* [1986] 1 Ch 638; and that the couple in *Springette* v *Defoe* were 'a middle aged couple already established in life whose house-purchasing arrangements were clearly regarded by the Court as having the same formality as if they had been the subject of a joint venture or commercial partnership'.

If Waite LJ is correct, it can no longer be assumed that the presence or absence of discussions will be decisive. In principle, however, it is not easy to see how a declaration of trusteeship can occur without at least some form of communication (there was none at all in *Midland Bank* v *Cooke*). In any case, in order to render it fraudulent for Mr A to deny the existence of the trust, Miss B must rely on the declaration, or significantly alter her position. Again, this necessitates communication between the parties, and is again a justification for the requirement for discussion. There are also certainty arguments for requiring communication. Waite J's decision in *Hammond* v *Mitchell* [1991] 1 WLR 1127 shows how much can turn on A's declaration of trusteeship: Vicky Mitchell obtained a half share under the first category in *Lloyds Bank plc* v *Rosset*, having contributed nothing at all to the house itself, solely because of statements that had been made to her by Hammond. Any beneficial interest thereby created will also bind third parties. It should also be borne in mind that a declaration of trusteeship constitutes an irrevocable and onerous commitment. Prior to an act of commitment, it ought to be possible for A to change his mind, however much, at that time, he is determined to become a trustee. It is not unreasonable to require the act of commitment to be in some sense public, or at any rate to be communicated to, the other party.

There is nothing in the *Springette* v *Defoe* line of cases to indicate what needs to be communicated. It follows from the above that Mr A needs to communicate something which leads Miss B to suppose that A is making an immediate and irrevocable commitment, whether or not this is A's actual intention (see Gardner (1993) 109 LQR 263, considered shortly). But in *Re Kayford Ltd* [1975] 1 WLR 279 (considered in chapter 3), Megarry J required only that the intention to declare oneself trustee be manifested. While detrimental reliance requires some form of communication, it may not necessarily require words. If the evidence showed that the parties really were capable of communicating by telepathy, there is no obvious reason why the law should not allow this method of communication to be used to create beneficial interests within this category.

In *Savill* v *Goodall*, the Court of Appeal distinguished *Springette* v *Defoe* on the basis that there were discussions in the later case. The Court did not pay particular regard to the nature of the discussions, and at some levels it *is* surprising that they did lead to the inference of a beneficial interest. The content of the discussions was tenuous, and certainly there was no substantial discussion of beneficial interests in the property. It is thus not obvious that there were actually grounds for distinguishing *Springette* v *Defoe*, and on this reasoning the case appears to have been incorrectly decided.

The requirement in *Lloyds Bank* v *Rosset* (at p. 132F) was for evidence of express discussions, not express evidence of discussions. This suggests that inferred evidence of discussions ought to be sufficient, and indeed, in *Gissing* v *Gissing*, Lord Diplock suggested (at p. 906A) that the parties' intentions could be inferred from their conduct, even in the absence of express words. No doubt is thereby cast on the correctness of *Springette* v *Defoe*, where there was no evidence at all of discussions.

9.4.1.3 *What about communications and proprietary estoppel?*

Everything which has been said in relation to showing the existence of an agreement up to now has been related to a trusts analysis. The commonly accepted formula for proprietary estoppel is that which was adopted by Oliver J in *Taylors Fashions Ltd* v *Liverpool Victoria Trustees Co. Ltd* [1982] QB 133. This requires only that 'it would be unconscionable for a party to be permitted to deny that which, knowingly or unknowingly, he has allowed or encouraged another to assume to his detriment'. There is no express communication requirement in this formula, and there is authority for the proposition that encouragement can be by words or conduct, as illustrated by *Moorgate Mercantile Co. Ltd* v *Twitchings* [1975] QB 225, and indicated in the judgment of Lord Denning MR.

Indeed, it is universally accepted that Oliver J's formulation is intended to broaden the definition of estoppel. More recently it was stated in *Gillett v Holt* [2001] Ch 210 that an estoppel will arise where 'it would be unconscionable for a party to be permitted to deny that which knowingly or unknowingly he has allowed or encouraged another to assume to his detriment'. Thus, there is no express communication requirement for an estoppel to arise, and in theory a party can be estopped from taking a different position (detrimental to the claimant) even in circumstances where no positive acts of communication have been made at all. So although in many cases communication will be necessary to establish an estoppel, this cannot be asserted as being definitive in every case. But it will be necessary in any such case for the party seeking the claim to establish that they have relied on what was being 'encouraged' to their detriment.

9.4.2 *Rosset* and the role of contributions in ascertaining agreement in category 1 cases

What is at the heart of this discussion is the way in which Lord Bridge in *Rosset* envisaged that the contributions actually made by a party seeking to establish an interest in a home belonging to another would serve very different functions in category 1 cases than would be the case in ones under category 2. As Lord Bridge envisaged things, in category 1 cases, the substance of the interest acquired is raised by the existence of an agreement between the parties which exists independently of the contributions which have been made by the claimant. On this reasoning, contributions actually made would matter, on account of the formalities requirements of s. 53(1) (b) of the Law of Property Act 1925. As part of this broad discussion of the role of interests in equity acquired as a result of express agreement, Lord Bridge suggested this could be effected by recourse to either a constructive trust or by way of proprietary estoppel.

What follows on immediately below is a discussion of how the courts have approached this apparent choice between 'trust or estoppel' given by Lord Bridge. In due course under the broad heading of 'quantification' of beneficial interests it will become clear that views on the role played by contributions in category 1 cases have changed. *Rosset* itself is widely accepted as suggesting that their function was to establish the detrimental reliance necessary to both the constructive trust and the estoppel basis, because the express agreement/representation would serve to quantify the size of the interest. The most recent authorities are clearly a retreat from this, and evidence that even in category 1 cases the nature and size of contributions can affect quantification.

9.4.3 Category 1 cases: exploring the question of 'trust or estoppel?'

Lord Bridge's speech focuses on approaches which *could be* applied rather than which *should be*, and the two doctrines do of course enjoy much in common. They are both equitable doctrines concerned with holding people who encourage reliance on the part of others to their promises, and in that regard they can be seen as reliance-based equitable doctrines. However this text has always suggested that it is problematic to equate the two and considerable differences actually subsist beneath their apparent common approach.

In setting out how things could be done, Lord Bridge does not indicate whether the approach should be one of constructive trust or proprietary estoppel, or even whether the concepts are intended to be the same or distinct. Professor Hayton, for example, argues that Lord Bridge is equating these concepts ([1990] *Conv* 370), and this view appears to be shared by Morritt LJ in *Lloyds Bank plc* v *Carrick* [1996] 4 All ER 630 and Lord Oliver of Aylmerton in *Austin* v *Keele* (1987) 61 AJLR 605. However, this is by no means clear from the judgment itself (see P. Ferguson (1993) 109 LQR 114, at p. 118), and even Morritt LJ in *Lloyds Bank plc* v *Carrick* seemed prepared to accept that estoppel might raise different issues, and actually dealt with estoppel separately when considering (and rejecting) the *Rosset* argument advanced by Mrs Carrick, on the ground that her estate contract precluded the co-existence of a *Rosset* interest.

Unfortunately, an investigation of the cases cited by Lord Bridge throws little more light on the issue, and both estoppel and constructive trust reasoning can be found, for example, in *Grant* v *Edwards* [1986] 1 Ch 638 (set out shortly). In the immediate aftermath of *Rosset*, the courts were indicating a clear preference for a trusts analysis and the decision in *Baker* v *Baker* [1993] 25 HLR 408, which appeared to be based purely on estoppel principles, seemed out of place in this context. It is suggested that some cases within the first category are properly categorised as trust cases, while for others estoppel is a more appropriate classification. The traditional view taken in this text has been that facts which give rise to an estoppel will not necessarily suffice for a trust, and the consequences of trusts and estoppel reasoning are different. However this was having to be re-examined in light of a number of cases post-2000, including several Court of Appeal authorities, which indicated the emergence of a clear preference for an estoppel-based approach to disputed home ownership.

In *Yaxley* v *Gotts* [2000] 1 All ER 711, the judgment of Robert Walker LJ emphasised the points of commonality between the constructive trust and proprietary estoppel and defended Lord Bridge's articulation of them as interchangeable:

[T]he species of constructive trust based on 'common intention' is established by what Lord Bridge in *Lloyds Bank plc.* v *Rosset* [1991] 1 AC 107, 132, called an 'agreement, arrangement or understanding' actually reached between the parties, and relied on and acted on by the claimant. A constructive trust of that sort is closely akin to, if not indistinguishable from, proprietary estoppel. Equity enforces it because it would be unconscionable for the other party to disregard the claimant's rights.

Gillett v *Holt* [2000] 2 All ER 289 is authority for the proposition that the detriment which is required to give rise to an estoppel, and forms the basis of the remedy which must follow from this (depending on the nature and extent of the detriment), is not a 'narrow or technical concept'. It is instead part of the 'broader enquiry as to whether repudiation of an assurance is or is not unconscionable in all the circumstances'. Indeed, the detriment pointed to does not need to entail fiscal expenditure, nor be represented by 'quantifiable financial detriment', and 'something substantial' will suffice. What the judgment also makes reference to in relation to calibrating proprietary estoppel alongside constructive trusteeship is the Court of Appeal decision in *Wayling* v *Jones* (1995) 69 P & CR 170, which considered *Re Basham* [1987] 1 All ER 405. The judgment of Balcombe LJ was cited in respect of the principles pertaining to reliance and detriment, which also drew attention to equation between constructive trusteeship and proprietary estoppel (at p. 173):

(1) There must be a sufficient link between the promises relied upon and the conduct which constitutes the detriment—see *Eves* v *Eves* [1975] 1 WLR 1338, in particular per Brightman J; *Grant* v *Edwards* [1986] Ch 638...*per* Nourse LJ and per Browne-Wilkinson V-C and in particular the passage where he equates the principles applicable in cases of constructive trust to those of proprietary estoppel. (2) The promises relied upon do not have to be the sole inducement for the conduct: it is sufficient if they are an inducement—*Amalgamated Property Co.* v *Texas Bank* [1982] QB 84...(3) Once it has been established that promises were made, and that there has been conduct by the plaintiff of such a nature that inducement may be inferred then the burden of proof shifts to the defendants to establish that he did not rely on the promises—*Greasley* v *Cooke* [1980] 1 WLR 1306; *Grant* v *Edwards*...

However, *Yaxley* v *Gotts* also harbours reference to the way in which regard must be had to important differences which nevertheless remain for critical consideration. Such ideas are discussed in reference made to 'those cases in which a supposed bargain has been so fully performed by one side'. The significance of such cases can be found in the way in which 'the general circumstances of the matter are such, that it would be inequitable to disregard the claimant's expectations, and insufficient to grant him no more than a restitutionary remedy'. This points to important differences which are visible in terms of the outcome which the two mechanisms deliver. It reveals that the extent of the equity awarded depends on the circumstances of the case, which will by virtue of estoppel reasoning be the minimum (equity) necessary to achieve justice.

9.4.3.1 *Shared homes, agreement, and* Yaxley *v* Gotts *and* Gillett *v* Holt

While neither of these decisions arose directly in the context of disputed home ownership, both did engage in extensive discussion of the 'shared homes' authorities. The influence that these cases clearly did bring to bear in the sphere of beneficial ownership (as distinct from their authority for consideration of the differences and similarities between the concepts of estoppel and constructive trust) can be found below in the discussion of the Court of Appeal decision in *Oxley v Hiscock*.

The quantification of a beneficial interest acquired in these circumstances will follow shortly, but it is noteworthy that this text has always been concerned that the outcomes of cases decided on these different principles will not always be the same. And thus it has always been a matter of concern that while an estoppel is measured and thus limited by the extent of a detriment suffered, and represents the 'minimum equity to achieve justice', a constructive trust is able to be more generous. The main difference between the two, however, is in the extent to which they can affect third parties. This is especially a problem where a mortgagee is involved since, as Ferguson states (1993, at p. 122), 'the consensus of opinion favours' the view that estoppels do not bind third parties, at any rate until the extent of the interest has been crystallised by a court. The consensus is by no means unchallenged, and Morritt LJ took a different view in *Lloyds Bank plc* v *Carrick* [1996] 4 All ER 630, but this has been considered in greater detail elsewhere: see Glover and Todd [1995] 5 Web JCLI.

Nevertheless, the estoppel approach was applied directly in a case of disputed home ownership in *Oxley* v *Hiscock*, and giving Court of Appeal authority in this context to much of what had been set out in *Yaxley* v *Gotts*. Similarly, at this time interests in property were awarded in both *Campbell* v *Griffin* [2001] WTLR, 981 and *Jennings* v *Rice* [2003] 1 P & CR, 8 with the Court of Appeal reversing the first instance decision in the former and affirming the initial decision in the latter. Both these cases were determined on the basis that some assurances were given, and the claimant in each case relied to their detriment upon this: and in *Jennings*, Aldous LJ suggested the approach which was adopted was discretionary but was made to achieve a proportionate solution with due regard to the nature of expectation.

This approach can also be seen in *Ottey* v *Grundy* [2003] WTLR 1253, with all these cases pointing to achieving justice to the parties and a remedy which is proportionate to the determinant which has been suffered. They all thus point to estoppel as a rounded approach which seeks a remedy that is appropriate in all the circumstances and, to this end, the decision in *Ottey* made reference to the earlier decision in *Re Basham* [1987] in which it was suggested that:

the purpose of proprietary estoppel is not to enforce an obligation which does not amount to a contract nor yet to reverse the detriment which the claimant has suffered but to grant an appropriate remedy in respect of unconscionable conduct.

In this vein it was suggested in *Ottey* v *Grundy* itself that estoppel is a remedy 'in the round' and which does not only have regard to financial detriment and benefit. According to Arden LJ:

It is common ground that proprietary estoppel can arise where an owner of property encourages another to rely to his detriment in the belief that he will obtain an interest in that property. The underlying rationale is that it would be unconscionable for the maker of the assurance not to give effect to his promise. The matter must be looked at in the round.

More shall be said about key decision in *Oxley* in due course, but it is also the case that since then, and in 2007, the competing merits of the constructive trust and proprietary estoppel once again came to the fore notwithstanding *Oxley*'s endorsement of the latter. This was in the House of Lords in *Stack* v *Dowden*. However even prior to *Stack*, but admittedly before *Oxley*, views against the movement in favour of increasing application of proprietary estoppel had been expresssed by Sir Martin Nourse's views in *Hyett* v *Stanley* (2003) EWCA Civ 995 also in the Court of Appeal. Once this issue was considered in the House of Lords in *Stack*, it is interesting that amongst a number of endorsements of the trust as the preferred reflection of the intentions of parties where valuable rights in property are concerned was that of Lord Walker, who recanted quite significantly from his views (as Walker LJ) in *Yaxley* v *Gotts* in favour of assimilation between the two doctrines.

9.4.4 **What must be present for a constructive trust to arise?**

The requirement of detrimental reliance is closely tied in with the agreement which is made between the parties, which can also take the form of representations made by the legal owner of property. Here *Eves* v *Eves* [1975] 1 WLR 1338 and also *Grant v Edwards* [1986] 1 Ch 638 (both Court of Appeal cases) were cited by Lord Bridge in *Rosset* as examples of category 1 cases notwithstanding that they concerned representations made by the legal owner of the property, rather than more conventional examples of agreement and which were actually *untruthful*.

In *Grant* v *Edwards*, a house was purchased in 1969 for the claimant, Mrs Linda Grant, and the defendant, Edwards, to live in as if married (although Grant was actually married to someone else). The house was purchased in the name of Edwards and his brother. Edwards told Grant that her name would not go on the title for the time being because it would cause prejudice in the matrimonial proceedings pending between Grant and her husband. In reality, Edwards had no intention of conveying any legal title to the claimant.

The defendant paid the deposit on the house and most, but not all, of the repayments on the two mortgages. He paid the deposit and all the mortgage instalments on the first mortgage, but Grant paid some repayments under a second mortgage. The claimant also made substantial contributions towards general household expenses, provided housekeeping, and brought up the children. In 1980 the couple separated, and the claimant claimed a beneficial interest in the property. The Court of Appeal held that Edwards' statement that Grant's name would have appeared on the title except that it could cause prejudice in the matrimonial proceedings was evidence of a common intention that Mrs Grant should have a beneficial interest in the property. Grant had relied to her detriment on the common intention, so that she was entitled to a half share on a resulting or constructive trust.

When fuller discussion is made of category 2 cases, it will become manifestly clear that under *Rosset* itself, Grant's actual contributions—which were not particularly significant or extensive—would not have given a half share in absence of Edwards' representation, and this 'reason' why the claimant's name could not be reflected in the legal documentation was the crucial element for the case. The Court of Appeal came to the view that this statement could be explained only on the basis of a common intention that she was to have a half share. At first sight this seems rather a surprising conclusion, since Edwards clearly intended no such thing, but the representation was interpreted (in effect) as meaning 'Your name would go on the title but for the fact that it would prejudice your matrimonial proceedings.' This was because had Edwards intended to say 'the house is to be mine alone', there would have been no need for an excuse. By this somewhat tortuous reasoning, therefore, the Court was able to infer, independently of her contributions, a common intention that Grant was to have a half share, and the case depended on this.

Because there was evidence of a common intention (independent of the contributions themselves), Grant's contributions (unlike those of Valerie Burns) were relevant only in order to get round the formality provisions of s. 53 of the Law of Property Act 1925. It was necessary for Grant to show only that she had relied on the agreement to her detriment, by acting in a manner which was explicable only on the basis that she was to have an interest in the house, for a constructive trust to arise in her favour.

In the paragraph above, the way in which 'excuses' were interpreted effectively as 'express agreements'—or certainly as what Lord Bridge termed an 'understanding' subsisting between the parties in category 1 cases—was described as 'tortuous', and these cases have been criticised on the grounds that the agreement is entirely fictitious, because in each case the man clearly did not intend the woman to have any interest in the property. Thus, Simon Gardner has written ((1993) 109 LQR 263, at p. 265):

But the fact that the men's statements were excuses (i.e. neither objectively valid nor even sincerely uttered) does not mean that the men were thereby acknowledging an agreement whereby the woman should have a share. If I give an excuse for rejecting an invitation to what I expect to be a dull party, it does not mean that I thereby agree to come: on the contrary, it means that I do not agree to come, but for one reason or another find it hard to say so outright. The fallacious quality of the reasoning in *Eves* v *Eves* and *Grant* v *Edwards* is thus clear. It is hard to think that the judges concerned really believed in it...

Gardner contrasted these cases with *Hammond* v *Mitchell* [1991] 1 WLR 1127, where it appears that Hammond really did intend Vicky Mitchell to have a share, and Mitchell did obtain a half share on the basis of statements that had been made to her by Hammond.

Gardner's objection (above) is clearly valid if a subjective view is taken of intention, but the cases considered in chapter 3 on declaration of trusteeship suggest that intention is judged objectively. The courts appear to adopt the position of a reasonable observer. In *Richards* v *Delbridge* (1874) LR Eq 11, Sir George Jessel MR concentrates on the words used, as opposed to the actual intention, observing that 'however anxious the Court may be to carry out a man's intention, it is not at liberty to construe words otherwise than according to their proper meaning'. This suggests that the actual intention is irrelevant. In *Re Kayford Ltd* [1975] 1 WLR 279, Megarry J, at p. 282A, also talks in terms of an intention being manifested, rather than merely held.

9.4.4.1 *Simon Gardner, constructive trusteeship, and objective and subjective intention*

It was for these reasons that Paul Todd and Nicola Glover (Glover and Todd [1995] 5 Web JCLI) felt that Gardner's objection was misplaced. To take *Grant* v *Edwards* as the example, what George Edwards was saying, in effect, was that although legal title must be vested in himself alone, this was for purely formal reasons (so as not to cause prejudice in the matrimonial proceedings pending between Linda Grant and her husband), and the reality was that the property (i.e. equitable title) was to belong to both of them. Once it is accepted that the test is objective, and does not depend on what Edwards actually thought, it is difficult to imagine a clearer declaration of trusteeship than that which was uttered by Edwards.

The approach taken in *Grant* v *Edwards* (and indeed *Eves* v *Eves*) is a far less stringent requirement than that adopted in *Burns* or *Rosset* itself, where there was no outside evidence of any agreement, so that evidence of intention could be inferred only from the contributions themselves. Furthermore, the value of the beneficial interest was determined by the common intention (as evidenced by the defendant's statement) and not by the value of Grant's contributions.

In *Eves* v *Eves* [1975] Lord Denning MR reasoned that equity was still capable of developing, and that the courts had a discretion to depart from strictly property-based criteria in order to achieve what they saw as 'justice'. Although after *Rosset* it is now clear that the case cannot be explained on that basis, and indeed in *Grant* v *Edwards* Lord Denning MR's reasoning in *Eves* v *Eves* was expressly rejected, the decision itself was upheld. Indeed in *Lloyds Bank* v *Rosset*, *Eves* was explained as one of the type where there is evidence of a common intention that beneficial interest in the home should be shared.

Janet Eves was under 21 when she separated from her husband and went to live with a man whose marriage had also broken down. They had a child together and shortly afterwards found a house with the intention that they would live there together. The man told her that if she had been 21 he would have arranged for the house to be conveyed into their joint names, but in reality this was simply an excuse for having the house conveyed into his name alone. The house was in a dilapidated state and Janet did a great deal of heavy building work improving it, including wielding a 14lb sledgehammer to break up the concrete in the front garden so that it could be levelled and turfed. When the relationship broke down, Janet Eves was held to be entitled to a quarter share. As in *Grant* v *Edwards*, the case depended on the representation made by the man: there would have been no need for him to make an excuse had he intended to say 'the house is to be mine alone'. As Brightman J explained (at p. 1345): 'The defendant clearly led the plaintiff to believe that she was to have some undefined interest in the property, and that her name was only omitted from the conveyance because of her age.'

In *Rosset*, *Grant* v *Edwards* and *Eves* v *Eves* were explained as authorities that express that common intention at the heart of category 1 cases could be manifested in representations made, as well as by more conventional agreement, on the basis of the inferences which could be drawn from them by the claimant, and the way in which this was in turn capable of influencing subsequent conduct of the party to whom the representation was being made. Indeed *Eves* and *Grant* were considered 'outstanding examples ... of cases giving rise to situations in the first category'. This was because:

In both these cases, where the parties who had cohabited were unmarried, the female partner had been clearly led by the male partner to believe, when they set up home together, that the property would belong to them jointly. In *Eves* v *Eves* the male partner had told the female partner that the only reason why the property was to be acquired in his name alone was because she was under 21 and that, but for her age, he would have had the house put into their joint names. He admitted in evidence that this was simply an 'excuse'. Similarly, in *Grant* v *Edwards* the female partner was told by the male partner that the only reason for not acquiring the property in joint names was because she was involved in divorce proceedings and that, if the property were acquired jointly, this might operate to her prejudice in those proceedings. As Nourse LJ put it (at p. 649):

Just as in *Eves* v *Eves*, these facts appear to me to raise a clear inference that there was an understanding between the plaintiff and the defendant, or a common intention, that the plaintiff was to have some sort of proprietary interest in the house otherwise no excuse for not putting her name onto the title would have been needed.

The subsequent conduct of the female partner in each of these cases, which the court rightly held sufficient to give rise to a constructive trust or proprietary estoppel supporting her claim to an interest in the property, fell far short of such conduct as would by itself have supported the claim in the absence of an express representation by the male partner that she was to have such an interest. It is significant to note that the share to which the female partners in *Eves v Eves* and *Grant v Edwards* were held entitled were one-quarter and one-half respectively. In no sense could these shares have been regarded as proportionate to what the judge in the instant case described as a 'qualifying contribution' in terms of the indirect contributions to the acquisition or enhancement of the value of the houses made by the female partners.

In *Grant v Edwards*, Nourse LJ drew the following distinction, which essentially summarises the above discussion, between the relevance of the claimant's conduct in *Grant v Edwards* itself, and its relevance in a case like *Burns v Burns*:

In most of these cases the fundamental, and invariably the most difficult, question is to decide whether there was the necessary common intention, being something which can only be inferred from the conduct of the parties, almost always from the expenditure incurred by them respectively. In this regard the court has to look for expenditure which is referable to the acquisition of the house (see...*Burns v Burns* [1984] Ch 317). If it is found to have been incurred, such expenditure will perform the two-fold function of establishing the common intention and showing that the claimant has acted upon it.

There is another and rarer class of case, of which the present may be one, where, although there has been no writing, the parties have orally declared themselves in such a way as to make their common intention plain. Here the court does not have to look for conduct from which the intention can be inferred, but only for conduct which amounts to an acting upon it by the claimant. And although that conduct can undoubtedly be the incurring of expenditure which is referable to the acquisition of the house, it need not necessarily be so.

Elaborating on the question of what conduct would suffice, Nourse LJ referred to *Eves v Eves* and said:

So what sort of conduct is required? In my judgment it must be conduct on which the woman could not reasonably have been expected to embark unless she was to have an interest in the house. If she was not to have such an interest, she could reasonably be expected to go and live with her lover, but not, for example, to wield a 14lb sledge-hammer in the front garden. In adopting the latter kind of conduct she is seen to act to her detriment on the faith of the common intention.

9.4.4.2 *The need to show detrimental reliance*

Both these cases reflect the way in which the equitable interest which arises does so by way of (here a) constructive trust which is imposed on the holder of legal title, as a result of what is said, whatever its precise formulation. However, it is also the case that the agreement/representation itself will not of *itself* give rise to an interest by way of constructive trust, and this must be coupled with detrimental reliance (in order to circumvent s. 53(1)(b) requirements). This is why contributions are important even in the presence of an agreement. In *Grant v Edwards* [1986] Nourse LJ explained this as 'conduct on which the claimant could not reasonably have been expected to embark unless she was to have an interest in the house'. The difficulties which can arise here include establishing conduct actually is detrimental reliance rather than acting 'ordinarily' on account of love and affection. This was considered in *Wayling v Jones* [1993] 69 P & C R 170, and also *Ottey v Grundy* [2003] EWCA Civ 1176.

In *Ottey* v *Grundy* [2003], the test adopted to establish detrimental reliance was according to Arden LJ not to be that 'the claimant would have left the maker of the assurance if the promise had not been made, but only that he would have left the maker of the assurance if the promise had been withdrawn'. This was the test adopted in *Wayling* v *Jones*. Under *Wayling*, once the claimant shows that a promise was made, the burden of proof falls upon the maker to show that the claimant did not, in fact, rely on the promise. Upon determining this, the approach adopted was that taken in *Jennings v Rice* [2003] 1 P & C R, 8. This was an important case prior to *Oxley*, suggesting that questions of relief should be approached with caution, and that they should be determined on what amounts to the minimum equity to do justice, and this must also be proportionate to the detriment.

9.4.4.3 *What are the requirements for an estoppel?*

While a constructive trust is based on irrevocable commitment, an estoppel is premised on a party who has misled another being prevented from going back on his word. It is clear that such 'misleading' can arise through conduct or actual words, with *Gillett* v *Holt* and *Campbell* v *Griffin*, both dating from 2001, standing as authority for this.

A summary of issues arising in relation to whether it will matter whether a trusts or estoppel approach is used

This text has always maintained that there are fundamental differences between a trust and estoppel approach, notwithstanding academic and judicial attempts to equate them, or at least to minimise their differences. Given that the House of Lords has now spoken firmly in favour of a trusts approach in *Stack* v *Dowden*, and in terms of summarising the commonality between trusts and estoppel, it might be helpful to consider the following points:

- While both doctrines appear to be concerned with preventing parties from being able to assert a position which is different from one which they have represented, a trust is premised on an irrevocable commitment, while an estoppel is premised on a party who has misled another not being permitted to go back on his word.
- Estoppels are limited to the extent of 'encouraged reliance' (connection with agreement).
- The 'limited' extent of an estoppel is linked to its remedy which is the 'minimum equity to do justice'.
- Thus the consequences of applying a trusts or estoppel analysis can affect the size of the share received by a party establishing an interest.

9.5 *Rosset* category 2: establishing an equitable interest in property by way of an inferred common intention constructive trust

The case law in this area is very strongly focused around category 2 situations. These cases arise because there is no 'independent' evidence of agreement in these circumstances, and contributions which have been made by the parties provide the only means by which the courts can *infer* the existence of a common intention to share ownership (rather than occupation or enjoyment) of the property, or conclude that such a common intention does not exist. Thus as this category was envisioned and formulated by Lord Bridge, contributions were to have a central role. And in turn, Lord Bridge's determination of which contributions would suffice was very strict, mirroring closely the strict property approaches found in pre-*Rosset* case law, evidenced in cases such as *Gissing* v *Gissing* and *Pettit* v *Pettit*. According to Lord Bridge

- Contributions must be directly referable to the *initial* acquisition of the home: in this category, deposit monies or mortgage repayments will readily justify the inference necessary for creating a constructive trust.
- Contributions which will *not* suffice were all others which did not relate 'directly to the purchase of the home'.

When reference is made to this category of case, it is to cases where agreement to share ownership of a home is inferred from conduct of the parties from contributions which are made to the purchase of the home by the claimant. Although Lord Bridge classified this as an 'inferred common intention constructive trust', reference has already been made to the way in which, for many, this is actually operationally an orthodox presumed intention resulting trust. Most recently this was considered in *Oxley* v *Hiscock* [2004] and by the House of Lords in *Stack* v *Dowden* [2007].

As the materials in chapter 7 explained, a resulting trust arises where the beneficial interest in property results to an original owner of property, and from this it is clear that, for recovery of property on a resulting trusts basis to occur, the claimant must start off by having legal title to some property (under which all rights and entitlements are subsumed). This scenario envisions that legal title to this property is then transferred to another, who in this context will be the person who is or becomes the legal owner of the disputed home. One possible situation would be where the claimant actually has legal title to the home itself and transfers the bare legal title to the new legal owner, such as was the case in *Hodgson* v *Marks* [1971] 1 Ch 892.

This is clearly not the normal *Rosset* situation, but it is nevertheless not difficult to see how a resulting trust can arise from contributions to the purchase money by the party who is not the legal owner. If such a person pays the purchase money (in which she has legal title) over to the other party then in the absence of a presumption of advancement or consideration moving from him, she is presumed to retain equitable ownership in the money. This is a straightforward application of *Dyer* v *Dyer* (1788) 2 Cox Eq Cas 92, on principles explained in that case by Eyre CB. In turn, if the money is referable to the acquisition of property then, on its acquisition by the legal owner, the equitable 'interest' owned in the property by the party who does not have title at law (which remains with him or her) becomes converted into an interest in the property. This latter occurrence arises on principles stated by Sir George Jessel MR in *Re Hallet's Estate* (1880) 13 Ch D 696, a case considered in the context of tracing in the final chapter. Alternatively, if both parties make separate payments to the vendor, then the vendor becomes trustee of the money for him and her in the proportions in which he and she have paid it, until such time as the property is conveyed, when again the equitable interests are converted into interests in the property.

For these purposes the origin of the money advanced by the non-legal owner is irrelevant. If it is obtained by a loan, with the claimant undertaking liability to repay the loan, the position is exactly the same; similarly, if she obtains the money through a mortgage on the property itself, accepting liability to repay the mortgage debt. This explains, for example, *Huntingford* v *Hobbs* [1993] 1 FCR 45, where the entirety of Mr Huntingford's undertaking to repay the mortgage debt was taken into account in calculating his share, although he had not actually paid off any of the capital.

9.5.1 Presumption of advancement cases of disputed home ownership

Reference was made above to what would happen in the case of a voluntary conveyance 'in absence of a presumption of advancement' and at this point there is some discussion of the presumption of advancement which works very closely alongside that of the resulting trust. The materials in chapter 7 indicated that the presumption of advancement was an extremely old principle, and one which was conceived in response to societal conditions which are very different from today's, and so there is some doubt about its continuing role and applicability.

However, if it does still remain applicable in current times, then it can have a bearing on situations where parties are married. Suppose, for example, a matrimonial home is purchased in the name of the husband alone, but his wife has contributed to the purchase price (either the deposit or mortgage repayments). There being no presumption of advancement from wife to husband, on the principles discussed above, the equitable interests remain in proportion to the contributions, and the husband will therefore hold the legal estate on trust for both himself and his wife in proportion to their contributions. The same result obtains, of course, if the parties are living together but not married. However in situations where the purchase money is contributed by the male partner, it *does* matter whether the parties are married, and if they are and a presumption of advancement remains applicable, the wife will obtain both equitable and legal title. If the parties are unmarried, the opposite result obtains, the presumption being that the man retains an equitable title under a resulting trust.

9.5.2 Modernity, changing social conditions, and a continuing role for the presumption of advancement?

All this presupposes that the presumption of advancement has any application in this area of law (there is no doubt that the presumption of resulting trust applies—see *Tinsley* v *Milligan*, below). Obviously, there is scope for it to be regarded as very old fashioned, as illustrated in *Pettitt* v *Pettitt* [1970] AC 777. Here a cottage was purchased in the name of the wife, Mrs Pettitt providing the entirety of the purchase money. The husband significantly improved the property, using his own labour and money, but was unsuccessful in claiming an equitable interest. The reasons for this are considered shortly, but although applying a presumption of advancement would have led to the same result, the House of Lords seemed to be casting considerable doubt on whether the principle had any place in the modern law relating to shared homes. As Lord Diplock observed:

It would, in my view, be an abuse of the legal technique for ascertaining or imputing intention to apply to transactions between the post-war generation of married couples' 'presumptions' which are based on inferences of fact which an earlier generation of judges drew as to the most likely intentions of earlier generations of spouses belonging to the propertied classes of a different social era.

The other judges appeared to favour a weak presumption, with *Gissing* v *Gissing* [1971] AC 886 cited as authority, but in *McGrath* v *Wallis* [1995] 2 FLR 114, Nourse LJ observed that the principle had become a judicial instrument of last resort, and he could not actually recall a modern case where it had been decisive even where one of the parties had died. And it appears that the presumption of advancement will rarely, if ever, be decisive in matrimonial property cases, but whether there is no presumption at all, or a very weak presumption, a matter on which the courts have reached no definite conclusion, can make a difference.

In *Tinsley* v *Milligan* [1994] 1 AC 340, Stella Tinsley and Kathleen Milligan jointly purchased a home which was registered in Tinsley's name alone. On the principles set out above, the beneficial interest would have been shared between Tinsley and Milligan in equal shares, but to both Tinsley and Milligan's knowledge, the home was registered in Tinsley's name alone to enable Milligan to make false claims to the Department of Social Security for benefits. After a quarrel, Tinsley moved out and claimed possession from Milligan. Milligan counterclaimed, seeking a declaration that the house was held by Tinsley on trust for both of them in equal shares. Tinsley argued that Milligan's claim was barred by the common law doctrine *ex turpi causa non oritur actio* and by the principle that he who comes to equity must come with clean hands.

The House of Lords held (Lord Keith and Lord Goff dissenting) that because the presumption of resulting trust applied, Milligan could establish her equitable interest without relying on the illegal transaction, and was therefore entitled to succeed. However, it is also clear that if she had had to rebut a presumption of advancement, however weak, she would have failed, because she would have had to plead the fraud in order to do so. In *Tribe* v *Tribe* [1995] 4 All ER 236, the Court of Appeal allowed evidence to rebut a presumption of advancement where the fraud had not actually been carried out, but this decision will not apply where the fraud has been carried out. Where a husband has conveyed a house to his wife (for example) to perpetrate a capital gains tax fraud, and the fraud has been successfully perpetrated, it does matter whether there is a weak presumption or none at all.

9.5.3 Contributions in category 2 cases: considering the nature of their role and also what is permissible

The discussion up to now has proceeded on the basis that Lord Bridge's statement on contributions is good law, and that the contributions capable of raising an inference of a common intention to share ownership of a home are confined to initial deposit money or mortgage repayments. It will become clear shortly that although Lord Bridge was seeking to make a definitive statement in this respect, his views on permissible contributions have been challenged considerably in recent times.

This will be pursued by reference to the way in which *Oxley* v *Hiscock* and *Stack* v *Dowden* are both very important authorities for the position of financial contributions which might be regarded as 'indirect' on the basis that they relate to the household economy without amounting to mortgage repayments (the payment of bills for example), and also for the position of capital improvements which are made to the property. Both cause problems for *Rosset*'s determination of permissible contributions.

Ahead of this, through reiteration of deposit money and mortgage repayments, it will firstly be explained how reference to these might cast light on why Lord Bridge articulated his categorization of two types of case through reference to trusts which are constructive. This is because it appears from first glance above that these contributions can be analysed on a resulting trusts basis.

Thus, even on Lord Bridge's view, payment of mortgage instalments (and not merely undertaking liability to repay the mortgage) counts, but there are serious difficulties in analysing these in resulting trust terms. For example, where the claimant has paid a mortgage payment over to her partner (who legally owns the property) the claimant might be presumed to retain beneficial title to the money, which will be converted into an interest in the property as each mortgage instalment is actually paid. This would result in the undesirable situation where the extent of a claimant's interest alters every month, but in any event, the explanation works only where the money is paid to the legal owner, rather than made directly to the mortgagee. If both parties pay the instalments directly to the mortgagee, then it is impossible to devise a resulting trust mechanism.

There is also Court of Appeal authority, which nobody has seriously doubted, that an interest can be inferred from contributions in the form of a discount from the purchase price, rather than an actual cash payment. This was the case in *Springette* v *Defoe* [1992] 2 FCR 561, where, in assessing the size of her share, the Court of Appeal took into account Springette's 41 per cent discount, attributable to her council tenancy under a 'right to buy' scheme. Although the Court purported to adopt a resulting trust analysis, it is difficult to see how *Springette* settled anything.

In *Springette* v *Defoe*, her discount arose from a legal chose in action enforceable against the council, and it might be possible to argue that she had transferred the bare legal title to the chose in action; but even this could not explain *Marsh* v *Von Sternberg* [1986] 1 FLR 526, where the discount depended on increased bargaining power as a statutory tenant under the Rent Act 1974, and did not arise from a cause of action at all. It follows that resulting trust reasoning cannot explain the discount cases. This shows that neither mortgage repayments nor discounts from the purchase price can be explained satisfactorily on a resulting trusts basis and it is clear that both are regarded as being acceptable contributions in respect of category 2 cases.

In respect of mortgage repayments themselves, the following example illustrates this further. A and B purchase a house, paying a 10 per cent deposit and obtaining a mortgage advance of 90 per cent, repayable over 25 years. The mortgage is assumed to be an ordinary repayment mortgage, where the monthly repayments are made up partly of income and partly of capital. A and B share the deposit, paying 5 per cent each. The house is conveyed into A's name alone, and A undertakes liability to repay the mortgage, perhaps because A is earning and B is not. For the next five years, the parties live together happily, with A and B sharing the mortgage repayments, half and half. The relationship then terminates, the house is to be sold, and the issue arises as to the extent of B's interest.

Even if a resulting trust mechanism can be made to work at all, certainly no more than a fifth of the mortgage will have been repaid, probably less, since interest always claims a higher proportion of early payments. It is unlikely, in fact, that the total payments, including the deposit, will amount to more than about 20 per cent of the total at this stage; B's contribution therefore amounts to a mere 10 per cent. A resulting trust analysis (if it could be made to work) would give her 10 per cent. Yet all the indications here are that the couple intended to share on a 50:50 basis, and if the house has increased in value, for B to be awarded only 10 per cent would constitute a tremendous windfall for A.

Surely a better analysis is, as Fox LJ observed in *Burns* v *Burns* (at p. 327D), that 'subsequent events may throw light on the initial intention'. Lord Diplock in *Gissing* v *Gissing* also thought that 'what [the parties] said and did after the acquisition was completed is relevant if it is explicable only on the basis of their having manifested to one another at the time of the acquisition some particular common intention as to how the beneficial interests should be held'. This is surely the correct analysis of the situation here. The parties' behaviour is explicable only on the basis that from the start they intended to share 50:50; the mortgage repayments are actually performing exactly the same role as the discussions in first category cases.

A similar analysis of discounts can be found in Staughton LJ's judgment in *Evans* v *Hayward* [1995] 2 FCR 313, at p. 319D: 'I do consider that the facts as to the existence of a discount and the source from which it is derived must be taken into account, and are capable of leading to the inference that the parties have made an agreement as to how the purchase price is provided'.

In other words, the discount leads to the inference that the parties made an agreement, at the time of acquisition, that they are to be treated as having provided the purchase price in proportions which take into account the discount. Conceptually, this is far closer to the analysis we have already seen, in the first category, than it is to the resulting trust. Notice also that in both the mortgage repayment and discount cases, it is the payments themselves which give rise to the inference as to intention; no further evidence of intention is required, since, after all, what other inference could you reasonably draw from payments of this type?

9.5.3.1 Resulting trust: 'discount' cases and repayments on other grounds

Once it is accepted that the true explanation of the discount cases, and of mortgage repayments, is in terms of an inferred agreement, and does not depend on a resulting trust, then we can see that similar reasoning can also apply to the non-financial contributions mentioned in *Burns*. In principle, therefore, it may seem that there is no particular reason to prefer Lord Bridge's views to those of Fox LJ. However, the requirements of the second category are that the claimant's interest can be inferred from the contributions alone, in the absence of other evidence of an agreement to share. Whereas in the discount and mortgage repayment cases this inference can be made automatically, nothing in *Burns* v *Burns* suggests that any automatic inference should be drawn from indirect contributions. They could lead to many different types of inference, depending on the other evidence available. In terms of the categorisation in *Lloyds Bank* v *Rosset*, therefore, indirect financial contributions are not correctly placed in the second category, since the court cannot rely entirely on the conduct of the parties to infer A's intention. Nor do these contributions fit happily into the first category, since there may be no evidence of express discussions between the parties.

If Lord Bridge's categories are exhaustive, therefore, indirect financial contributions cannot create an interest outside the first category. However, there has always been the view in principle that such contributions should nevertheless be capable of being taken into account in inferring the intention of the parties, and that notwithstanding the 'strict property' motivations for suggesting otherwise, to refuse to do so is to place artificial constraints on the evidence that will be accepted. And it will become clear that this position has continued to be articulated, and has in recent times become very prominent in leading case law.

9.5.4 Lord Bridge's views on contributions within category 2 as the definitive statement?

In many ways this section continues the discussion of the previous paragraph, which concluded by suggesting that taking a very strict view on permissible contributions could serve to ignore the realities behind shared ownership, and even generate perverse results in disputed home ownership. The starting point here is to consider a number of cases which do point to Lord Bridge's categories of permissible contributions being exhaustive.

9.5.4.1 *Contributions definitely outside the second category according to* Rosset

The exact scope of the second category in *Lloyds Bank* v *Rosset* is central to this analysis of implied trusts arising in relation to the family home. Here the significance of *Rosset* is focused on the role played by contributions made by the party, in circumstances where there is no independent evidence of their intention. It is therefore not surprising that only contributions which are referable to the property, and indeed to its acquisition, have been taken to count. This was very strongly the message in *Rosset*, and for Lord Bridge contributions amounting to deposit money and mortgage repayments were (with reference in his judgment to the way he understood earlier authorities) likely to be the *only* contributions which were *acceptable*. And such a view is entirely in keeping with *Rosset*'s apparent basis in strict property reasoning.

Rosset *and the significance of capital contributions: exploring the value placed by the law on non-financial contributions*
The cases within category 2 have traditionally stood as authority that other contributions are not valued for the purposes of a claimant acquiring a proprietary interest in a home belonging to another. Ones which are very striking in this latter category are ones associated with what was subsequently termed 'the family economy' in *Le Foe* v *Le Foe* [2001] 2 FLR 970, such as child rearing, payment of the household expenses, or providing furniture and domestic services, and even quite significant DIY and decorating and maintenance services. Generally speaking,

these are contributions more typically made by the woman living in a home, and the law's approach of attaching value only to 'hard cash' contributions such as deposit money and mortgage repayments has long been criticized as operating to the disadvantage of female home-makers.

Traditionally the courts have appeared to attach little weight to non-financial contributions, and this is so notwithstanding the cases dating from the 1970s and 1980s suggesting that the courts should exercise a discretion based on some abstract notion of justice. It was also argued in this line of cases that equity is a flexible instrument. 'Equity', said Lord Denning MR in *Eves* v *Eves* [1975] 1 WLR 1338, at 1340, 'is not past the age of child bearing', and for Lord Denning, this would encourage a more flexible view to be taken of the circumstances, most likely including indirect contributions.

It is now reasonably clear that the courts will not exercise the sort of discretion envisaged by Lord Denning MR in *Eves* v *Eves* (although the actual decision in the case was implicitly approved in *Lloyds Bank* v *Rosset*). Indeed, a rigidly property-based approach was taken by the House of Lords in *Pettitt* v *Pettitt* [1970] AC 777 and *Gissing* v *Gissing* [1971] AC 886 prior to *Rosset*. Mrs Gissing had been married to Mr Gissing for 16 years and had paid a substantial sum towards furniture and the laying of a lawn, but the house had been conveyed into the name of Mr Gissing alone, and Mrs Gissing had made no direct contributions towards its purchase. On their divorce, the House of Lords held that she had no interest (the position would possibly have been different after the enactment of the Matrimonial Causes Act 1973). The main importance of the case is that the House refused to exercise a discretion simply in order to do 'justice'. The interests of the parties were determined on the basis of their intentions at the time of acquisition of the property, and not by their subsequent conduct. It was also clear that normal principles of property law would be applicable.

In *Eves* v *Eves*, Lord Denning MR relied on the following passage from Lord Diplock's speech in *Gissing* v *Gissing* [1971] AC 886, as authority that the courts *did* have a great degree of flexibility. The nature of the interest depended on all the equities of the case, and the law might consider not merely financial contributions at the time of acquisition of the property, but all types of contribution, whether at that time or subsequently:

A resulting, implied or constructive trust—and it is unnecessary for present purposes to distinguish between these three classes of trust—is created by a transaction between the trustee and the *cestui que trust* in connection with the acquisition by the trustee of a legal estate in land, whenever the trustee has so conducted himself that it would be inequitable to allow him to deny to the *cestui que trust* a beneficial interest in the land acquired. And he will be held so to have conducted himself if by his words or conduct he has induced the *cestui que trust* to act to his own detriment in the reasonable belief that by so acting he was acquiring a beneficial interest in the land.

The quotation was taken out of context, since from the previous paragraph in Lord Diplock's speech it is clear that he was referring to the constructive trust here merely as a device to get round s. 53(1)(b) of the Law of Property Act 1925, where all the other requirements of a trust are already present. In other words, this passage merely referred to what has now become detrimental reliance for the purposes of the first category in *Rosset* (set out shortly), and Lord Diplock did not intend this reasoning to be used to create a trust in the first place.

Burns v Burns: *restatement of the conventional view*

The Court of Appeal restated the conventional view in *Burns* v *Burns* [1984] Ch 317, the facts and result of which were similar to *Gissing*, except that though the parties had lived together as husband and wife for many years, they were unmarried. The claimant, Valerie Burns, had been living with the defendant for 19 years, 17 in the house which was the subject of the dispute. She and the defendant, Patrick Burns, had never married. The house had been purchased in the name of the defendant, and he paid the purchase price. The claimant made no contribution to the purchase price or the mortgage repayments, but had brought up their children, performed domestic duties, and recently contributed from her own earnings towards household expenses. She also bought various fittings and a washing machine, and redecorated the interior of the house. The claimant left the defendant and claimed a beneficial interest in the house.

Since the couple had never married the provisions of the Matrimonial Causes Act 1973, sections 24–25 did not apply, and the Court of Appeal held that the claimant's case rested on orthodox property principles. In the absence of a financial contribution which could be related to the acquisition of the property, for example to the mortgage repayments, or a contribution enabling Patrick Burns to pay the mortgage instalments, Valerie Burns was not entitled to a beneficial interest in the house. *Burns* v *Burns* was upheld by the House of Lords in *Winkworth* v *Edward Baron Development Co. Ltd* [1988] 1 WLR 1512. There the House refused to infer that the claimant had an equitable interest in the matrimonial home, which was owned by a company of which she and her husband were sole directors, where she had used the proceeds from her share of her former matrimonial home to pay off the company overdraft, because the payment was not referable to the acquisition of the house (in Hayes Lane).

Lloyds Bank v Rosset: *a landmark decision*

Lastly, there is *Lloyds Bank plc* v *Rosset* [1991] 1 AC 107 itself. Mr and Mrs Rosset decided to purchase a semi-derelict farmhouse for £57,000. Mrs Rosset understood that the entire purchase money was to come out of a family trust fund, the trustees of which insisted that the house be purchased in the husband's sole name (this appears to have been the only reason for the legal title being vested in Mr Rosset alone). The house required renovation, and it was intended that this should be a joint venture. The vendors allowed Mr and Mrs Rosset to enter the property a number of weeks before completion in order to begin repairs and render the house habitable.

During this period, Mrs Rosset spent a lot of time at the house, urging on the builders and attempting to co-ordinate their work (until her husband insisted that he alone should give instructions), going to builders' merchants to obtain material required by the builders, delivering the materials to the site, assisting her husband in planning the renovation and decoration of the house (she was a skilled painter and decorator), wallpapering two bedrooms, arranging the insurance of the house, arranging a crime prevention survey, and assisting in arranging the installation of burglar alarms.

Unbeknown to Mrs Rosset, Mr Rosset was unable to fund the purchase and repairs entirely from the trust fund, and obtained an overdraft of £18,000 from Lloyds Bank, executing a legal charge on the property in their favour on the same day as completion. He later defaulted on the repayments and the bank sought possession. Mrs Rosset claimed a beneficial interest in the property, binding the bank by virtue of her actual occupation as an overriding interest under the Land Registration Act 1925, s. 70(1)(g).

In the Court of Appeal in *Rosset*, most of the discussion revolved around whether Mrs Rosset was in actual occupation when the charge was created, in order to be able to rely upon s. 70(1)(g). The House of Lords were able to avoid all discussion of s. 70(1)(g), simply holding that Mrs Rosset had no beneficial interest. There was no evidence of any agreement between the parties to share the beneficial interest, and the wife's contributions were regarded as *de minimis*. The principles discussed in this section were applied.

The cases culminating in *Rosset* suggest that what is required for beneficial interest to be acquired in this type of case (under category 2), is that the contributions being relied upon must not only be significant (and not *de minimis*) but that they must be referable to the *initial* acquisition of the property. There is no such requirement under the first category in *Rosset*, where there is independent evidence of the intentions of the parties. However, even in relation to category 2 cases, the significance of two recent cases must be considered. These are the Court of Appeal case in *Oxley* v *Hiscock*, and the House of Lords' decision in *Stack* v *Dowden*. Both remain central to the remaining parts of this chapter, but for present purposes they are articulated towards their significance for the nature of contributions which arise in this context, but which fall short of being ones which Lord Bridge would describe as 'direct' and 'financial'. It will be suggested how indirect financial contributions and ones represented by capital improvements can *both* cause difficulties for Lord Bridge's requirements.

In respect of capital improvements it will be suggested that *Oxley* and *Stack* are authority that capital improvements are considered capable of raising the inference of a common intention to share ownership of a home, as well as being a factor which is now taken into consideration when the size of the beneficial interest is being quantified. It will suggest that although both cases are emphasizing a more accommodating approach towards contributions which are indirect (financial and otherwise) than was permissible under *Rosset*, the precise legal status of these remains unclear and controversial. It will become apparent that there is a much wider endorsement of their use in quantifying an interest which has been established on the basis of other contributions than of their capability for actually establishing an interest. However, within this setting it is also the case that even in respect of quantification, attaching value to contributions of this nature remains contentious.

9.5.4.2 *A new approach to 'acceptable' contributions: introducing* Oxley v Hiscock *and* Stack v Dowden

These two cases will remain central for the remainder of this chapter, following their discussion here in the context of contributions which have caused difficulty when being analysed by virtue of *Rosset*. Ahead of this a brief summary of the cases' key facts is now set out.

Oxley v *Hiscock* concerned a home shared by the claimant and her former partner, the defendant. Initially the parties lived in a council house occupied by the claimant and her children from a former marriage, and in September 1987 the claimant exercised her right to buy the council property; the purchase was funded by the defendant from proceeds of the sale of his property. In 1991, a larger house (the disputed property) was purchased using £61,500 represented by the proceeds of sale from the original former council house and by a further contribution of £35,500 from the defendant, and a mortgage loan of £30,000. The new property was registered in the defendant's name, notwithstanding the claimant had been advised by her solicitor to protect her interest through joint registration. Thereafter both parties contributed towards the maintenance and improvement of the property, and pooled resources more generally in the belief that each had a beneficial interest. By 2001, the mortgage had been paid off, but the relationship between the parties had broken down and the home sold. The claimant sought a declaration that the proceeds of sale of the property were held on trust for both parties in equal shares, and at first instance this was upheld. On appeal it was found that in the absence of 'evidence of any discussion between the parties as to the amount of the share each was to have' the fairest outcome would be achieved by a 40 per cent–60 per cent share in favour of the defendant, with the observation made that ordering an equal distribution would actually be unfair to the defendant.

The facts of *Stack v Dowden* are not easy to follow but the litigation arose essentially as follows. Mr Stack and Ms Dowden became a couple as teenagers in 1975, and in 1983 Dowden became the legal owner of a property (10 Purves Road) costing £30,000. The purchase price was paid with £8,000 from Dowden's building society account (it is not clear whether Stack made any contribution to this fund) and £22,000 by way of a mortgage which was executed in Dowden's sole name and for which she took sole responsibility, something she also did in relation to all main outgoings (in the form of utility bills and council tax etc.). Considerable improvements were made to the property by both parties, and in time the couple had four children; throughout Dowden earned almost double that earned by Stack. In 1993 the family purchased a new home which was conveyed into the parties' joint names, but no declaration was made in respect of beneficial ownership. The purchase was made with consideration coming from the following sources: £128,813 from Dowden (from her building society account and from the proceeds of sale of the property in Purves Road) and with £65,025 provided by way of a joint bank loan. Stack paid all mortgage interest payments and joint endowments, and the capital which was repaid on the property was in the following amounts: by Stack £27,000 and by Dowden £38,435. Once again, the utilities arrangements were all made in Dowden's name and the parties kept separate accounts, savings, and investments.

The parties separated in 2002, and at first instance an equal distribution was ordered based on the nature of the partnership underlying the parties' relationship and focusing on their entire course of conduct together. Distribution on this basis would also have split the proceeds of sale from the Purves Road house had the relationship ended at that stage, but the Court of Appeal found that there was no basis on which Stack could show it was intended that he should have an interest at this stage, on the view that he could not be shown to have contributed to the building society account from which the initial payment of the original home was paid. Thus when Dowden appealed, the Court of Appeal upheld her appeal, and beneficial interests were awarded in the proportion of 65 per cent in favour of Dowden and 35 per cent in favour of Stack. Stack appealed to the House of Lords, claiming an additional 15 per cent of proceeds worth approximately £112,000, which would significantly represent a 50 per cent share, where his appeal was dismissed.

9.5.5 *Rosset* and beyond in respect of 'indirect contributions'

Both *Oxley* and *Stack* are important observations on applying *Rosset* post-*Rosset* in respect of contributions which cause difficulty using its analytical framework. This is now pursued through reference to indirect financial contributions, and also substantial ones but which are made 'after acquisition'.

The best-known case for understanding the way in which for Lord Bridge in *Rosset* contributions which are anything less than direct and financial were deemed unacceptable in category 2 cases is of course *Burns* v *Burns* [1984], where contributions associated with 'home-making' were not sufficient for generating an interest in the property. However, a different approach was taken in *Le Foe* v *Le Foe* [2001], which suggested that family economies were complex, and depended upon indirect financial contributions as much as more visible direct ones. These indirect contributions, according to *Le Foe*, could be seen manifested in payment of utilities and council tax and other household bills and expenses, with the complexity of family economies suggesting that at least some of the value to be attached to these necessary contributions stemmed from the way in which they were actually often crucial for freeing up money for the payment of the mortgage. On this reasoning, these contributions were not to be dismissed as not being valuable, and indeed they were capable of having value of utmost importance. This suggested in turn that they should be relevant in the exercise of determining the parties' beneficial interests in a home. Reference will shortly be made to the way in which *Le Foe* was itself strongly influenced by *Midland Bank* v *Cooke* [1995], how in turn the decision in *Le Foe* was praised by the Law Commission in 2002 in its *Sharing Homes* paper, and how the courts were urged to follow its example.

Accordingly, in *Oxley*, indirect contributions were considered part of ascertaining the 'whole course of dealing' between the parties, which it will become clear is at the heart of the new approach to be adopted in relation to quantification. The use of a range of contributions which are indirect and oriented towards the workings of modern families was strongly endorsed in *Stack* v *Dowden*. For most of their Lordships in *Stack* v *Dowden* this was considered closely alongside observations that Lord Bridge's views were out of date. The only Law Lord who appeared to take a different position was Lord Neuberger, whose views on 'day to day living and finances' were that they properly concerned use and enjoyment of a home rather than *ownership* of it.

While regard is now being had to indirect financial contributions—notwithstanding Lord Neuberger's views—in questions of quantification, some ambiguity remains about whether the enthusiasm for them expressed by the House of Lords was meant to apply to establishing an interest or just quantification. There is definitely talk in *Stack* about the law 'moving on', but much of the discussion of indirect contributions is not articulated in a way which would support their capability in giving rise to the existence of a beneficial interest. In this respect, the Privy Council case of *Abbott* v *Abbott* [2007] UKPC 53, which not only followed *Stack* very closely in terms of time, but was actually heard by three of the Lords who had presided over *Stack*, including Lady Hale who had given the leading judgment in the House of Lords, has generated considerable excitement. This is on account of views that the law is now taking a much more flexible view of what is capable of establishing an interest under category 2 cases, in addition to quantifying them (see Martin Dixon in [2007] Conv 456).

However, another view of *Abbott* is that it does not resolve the ambiguity in *Stack* relating to contributions other than deposit money and mortgage repayments (as required by Lord Bridge in *Rosset*). Instead it is suggested that at most *Abbott* widens slightly the category of acceptable contributions, to include alongside these acceptable contributions ones such as undertaking considerable financial liabilities, such as the wife's undertakings in respect of a loan and interest upon it in *Abbott*. But even here Abbott is not clear that undertaking these liabilities would be enough *by itself* to establish an interest in a home belonging to another (and indeed whether a half share would have been awarded on the strength of this alone), and that actually it appeared in any case that the wife was able to do this by virtue of mortgage repayments in a manner which would be acceptable to Lord Bridge under *Rosset*. And while this widening of acceptable contributions is potentially a direction in which the law could evolve in future, this appeared to be the case in the aftermath of *Stack v Dowden* itself.

Moreover, the Court of Appeal decision of *James v Thomas* [2007] EWCA Civ 1212, in May 2007, in the aftermath of *Stack* (and predating even *Abbott* in November 2007), suggests caution in suggesting that *Rosset*'s requirements for establishing an interest have been relaxed. *James* is authority that the courts are continuing to use the *Rosset* formula for these determinations and, especially significantly, that despite recent suggestion (*obiter* in *Stack* and *Abbott*) that Lord Bridge had set an overly restrictive threshold, the courts are reluctant to depart from *Rosset*'s requirements for actually establishing an interest.

9.5.6 **Lord Bridge, contributions, and the difficulties arising in relation to capital 'improvements'**

The problem with improvements is essentially that they are not a direct contribution in a manner which Lord Bridge envisioned in relating to the acquisition of the property. This is so even if they are 'paid for' in capital terms by the claimant (rather than this being represented in the labour undertaken by the claimant) because, by their nature, improvements are likely to arise at some point *after* acquisition. The difficulty with this reasoning is that following it would ensure that even very substantial improvements which can increase a home's capital value do not appear to be capable of establishing an interest in a home.

Rosset does not actually say anything about improvements, but prior to *Rosset* the status of improvements was already problematic, as shown in *Pettitt v Pettitt* [1970] AC 777. Here a cottage was purchased in the name of the wife, Mrs Pettitt providing the entirety of the purchase money. The husband significantly improved the property, using his own labour and money. He claimed an equitable interest, but the House of Lords held that he had no interest in the cottage. However, this was solely on the ground that his improvements were of an ephemeral character and that it would be unreasonable for him to obtain a permanent interest in the house in return for making improvements of this nature, and actually there were marked differences between the views expressed in the individual judgments themselves.

Lord Upjohn was equivocal and certainly Lord Reid expressed some enthusiasm for the position of improvements in principle.

A stronger case is *Thomas* v *Fuller-Brown* [1988] 1 FLR 237, where the Court of Appeal held that a man had no interest in the house in which he lived with a woman (who had legal title), although in the view of Slade LJ (at p. 240):

[The work he did] was obviously quite substantial...*inter alia*, he designed and constructed a two-storey extension, created a through lounge, carried out minor electrical and plumbing works, replastered and redecorated the property throughout, landscaped and reorganised the garden, laid a driveway, carried out repairs to the chimney and the roof and repointed the gable end of the property, constructed an internal entry hall at the property, rebuilt the kitchen and installed a new stairway.

Again, however, the inference must have been that he intended to make a gift of his work, but this was a contentious finding even in the case of *Pettitt* itself. This case actually precipitated enactment of the Matrimonial Proceedings and Property Act 1970 and the Law Reform Miscellaneous Provisions Act 1970, giving the courts discretions to vary beneficial interests in respects of spouses and fiancées on account of 'contributions in money or money's worth to the improvement of real or personal property in which...both of them has or have a beneficial interest'.

In addition to the support in principle in favour of improvements giving rise to an interest in property belonging to another from *Pettitt* and *Thomas* v *Fuller-Brown*, *Cooke* v *Head* [1972] 2 All ER 38 is authority that they are capable of doing so. There are also other authorities pointing to this (couched by reference to 'indirect financial contributions, referable to the acquisition') including passages of Fox LJ's judgment in *Burns* v *Burns*. Although *Rosset* ignored the problems created by improvements, this was not an issue in the case itself, and it could be for this reason that improvements have remained difficult in law, rather than there being any deliberate design on the part of Lord Bridge that they should be so. And indeed long-standing support for them can be seen in statements by Fox and May LJJ in *Burns* v *Burns* [1984] Ch 317:

What is needed, I think, is evidence of a payment or payments by the plaintiff which it can be inferred was referable to the acquisition of the house...If there is a substantial contribution by the woman to the family expenses, and the house was purchased on a mortgage, her contribution is, indirectly, referable to the acquisition of the house since, in one way or another, it enables the family to pay the mortgage instalments. Thus, a payment could be said to be referable to the acquisition of the house if, for example, the payer either (a) pays part of the purchase price or (b) contributes regularly to the mortgage instalments or (c) pays off part of the mortgage or (d) makes a substantial financial contribution to the family expenses so as to enable the mortgage instalments to be paid.

This is obviously wider than Lord Bridge's view, in that Lord Bridge would not recognise category (d) as justifying the inference necessary for the creation of a trust. Lord Bridge does not, however, make clear whether his intention is to alter the law or merely to re-state it, a point made by Patricia Ferguson (1993) 109 LQR 114, at p. 116:

[Lord Bridge's] requirement of 'direct contributions' where there is no express agreement runs contrary to previous authorities which held that indirect financial contributions which were 'referable to the acquisition of the house'—such as F's payment of all household expenses to free M's income for mortgage instalments—were sufficient. It is difficult to know...whether he intends to depart from this view of the law or not.

Although it is conventionally suggested that *Rosset* ignored improvements, it is also the case that Lord Bridge *was* (at least in principle) prepared to acknowledge that an agreement or understanding could arise between the parties at some point *after* the acquisition of the property. Lord Bridge stressed this was likely to be 'exceptional', but he was prepared to consider it as a possibility, and *Oxley* was open to them reflecting the 'whole course of dealings' between the parties.

This position was reinforced by the House of Lords in *Stack* v *Dowden*, still within the framework of the 'whole course of dealings'. Furthermore, *Stack* suggests (albeit *obiter*, and that this could have been more clearly expressed) that significant improvements could extend beyond being treated as 'capital expenditure' in respect of 'an adjustment of apportionment', and are capable of establishing an interest as well as quantifying one established on other grounds. And in terms of addressing the difficulties attaching to reference to contributions 'referable to acquisition', Lords Hoffmann and Neuberger suggested that this could be achieved by adoption of a so-called 'ambulatory' constructive trust. This was premised on responding to the way in which parties' intentions in relation to the ownership of their property will (like their relationship more broadly) often change over time. In turn this could well be influenced by the contributions actually made, including obviously capital improvements, thus resolving the difficulty of requiring contributions establishing an interest to relate to acquisition itself.

9.6 Quantification of beneficial interests

Once it is established that a claimant is to have a share in the property, the question of the *size* of the beneficial interest remains. What the materials up to now have indicated is that in his classification of two types of case, Lord Bridge envisaged considerable differences being drawn between ones where there was evidence of an agreement to share ownership which was independent of the contributions made by the parties, and others where the contributions made by the parties constituted the only evidence of a common intention to share ownership of the home. And it has been suggested that traditionally this has given rise to a very different role played by contributions in the two categories, and until very recently a study of 'quantification' of beneficial interests has traditionally amounted to one of the relative significance of contributions in two quite different categories of case.

- In category 1 cases, the study of quantification has traditionally focused on analysing the relative significance of the declaration of trust (the agreement/ representation) and the contributions made by the party seeking an interest.
- In category 2 cases, the study of quantification has traditionally focused on the dual role played by 'acceptable contributions' in both establishing an interest in a shared home, and also quantifying its extent.

Both these positions have had to be rethought in light of *Oxley* v *Hiscock* and *Stack* v *Dowden*. The facts of these cases have been set out in the previous section on contributions in the context of category 2 cases, and their significance as key developments will accompany an exploration of more traditional approaches.

9.6.1 **Traditional approaches to quantification in** *Rosset* **category 1 cases**

As indicated above, traditionally this has taken the form of an analysis of the relative significance of the declaration of trust (the agreement/representation) and the contributions made by the party seeking an interest.

In a constructive trust analysis as envisioned by Lord Bridge, in category 1 cases, it is the 'independent' *agreement to share* (central to *establishing* the interest) which is also critical for *quantifying the size* of the interest which can be established. The contributions actually made in this situation serve to establish detrimental reliance upon the agreement. Many cases here attest to how parties who have done very little, but have done this in reliance on an agreement, will acquire significant shares in a property, and indeed as much as a half share in the property.

This appears to be the case regardless of the actual contributions which are made by the claimant, and to this end reference at different points has been made to the way in which, as envisioned by Lord Bridge, contributions serve a functional role in category 1 cases, providing evidence of detrimental reliance. In this setting it is the agreement/representation which measures the interest, and (contra category 2) not the contributions.

This can be seen in a number of cases already cited as authority for category 1 cases, where discussion of quantification was incorporated into showing the significance of independent evidence of an agreement to share, albeit that this can take the form of a representation made, as well as a more conventional agreement. Key cases are *Hammond* v *Mitchell* [1991]; *Grant* v *Edwards* [1986]; *Eves* v *Eves* [1975]; and *Ungurian* v *Lesnoff* [1990] Ch 206.

This is the general position, and what appears to be at its heart is a proposition that in circumstances where the declaration of trust (the agreement or representation) is made, but this is actually silent on the size of the share, because of the overall premise of 'common intention', the courts will presume a half share as a starting point. This can be rebutted where there is evidence to the contrary, such as was the case in *Eves* v *Eves*, for example, which resulted in a quarter share in the property, but presumption of a half share appears to be the starting position.

The dominance of pre-*Rosset* case law here reflects the way in which *Rosset* was actually silent on quantification, because it was found that Mrs Rosset could not actually establish an interest. However, there are a number of cases, both pre and post-*Rosset*, which attest to this as a general position by highlighting situations which have been determined on a different basis.

For example, *Stokes* v *Anderson* [1991] 1 FLR 391 and *Passee* v *Passee* [1988] 1 FLR 263 are authority that, even in the traditional approach, contributions can matter for quantification in category 1 cases, but they also indicate that this will only arise in circumstances where the parties have agreed that the contributions they actually make should influence the size of the beneficial interest acquired.

Furthermore, *Drake* v *Whipp* [1996] 1 FLR 826 is authority for the so-called 'broad brush' approach to quantification, in which the courts look at the *contributions actually made* rather than the *presumption of a half share*. In *Drake* v *Whipp* [1996] 1 FLR 826, Mrs Drake was awarded a third share, Peter Gibson LJ observing that 'in constructive trust cases, the court can adopt a 'broad brush' approach to determining the parties' respective shares'. This appears similar to the reasoning in *Midland*

Bank v *Cooke* (considered again shortly) and is subject to the same criticisms on a trusts analysis. In *Drake* v *Whipp*, however, Whipp's intention was not clear from his declaration, and Mrs Drake's share appears to have been determined from all the evidence, including the respective contributions of the parties. Since she had never claimed more than a 40 per cent share, it would clearly have been reasonable to rebut the half share presumption in the light of contrary evidence. The parties' entire course of conduct together was considered relevant, and maybe this can be justified on an analysis similar to that in *Stokes* v *Anderson* above, in which case *Drake* v *Whipp* broke no new ground.

In the preamble to discussion of the modern law, it was suggested that *Stack* v *Dowden* was authority for restating the importance of a trusts approach to resolving disputed home ownership. In this context, issues of quantification arising from an estoppel analysis are likely to have less importance than might have appeared to be so until *Stack*. However, for the sake of completeness, these materials now recap the manner in which this chapter has already made a number of references to the way in which estoppels are quantified as the 'minimum (equity) to do justice'. To this end, cases such as *Gillett* v *Holt* (2001), *Jennings* v *Rice* [2002] EWCA Civ 990 and *Ottey* v *Grundy* (2003) are authority for this position, and in the more immediate aftermath of *Rosset* itself, the decision in *Baker* v *Baker* [1993] attests to the same position.

9.6.2 Traditional approaches to quantification in *Rosset* category 2 cases

The starting point for understanding *how* beneficial interests in *Rosset* category 2 cases *are quantified* is remembering these are situations where there is no evidence of an express agreement between the couple to share ownership of their home. The logic of *Rosset* here is that contributions are not just the only means by which the courts can *infer the existence* of an agreement to share ownership, but that contributions made must also operate to determine *the size* of any interest which can be inferred.

But *how does it work*? Is this through the operation of an implied constructive trust, or retention of equitable interest on resulting trust? Lord Bridge suggested that direct contributions to the purchase price by the partner who is not the legal owner whether initially or by payment of mortgage instalments 'will readily justify the inference necessary to the creation of a *constructive* trust'. This will obviously cover monies paid over as an initial deposit, and mortgage repayments are also permissible according to Lord Bridge, but is this not simply a straightforward application of a resulting trust according to *Dyer* v *Dyer*?

In some respects, this can be analysed as a traditional resulting trust, because applying *Dyer* to the payment of deposit money will enable the provider to retain equitable interest in the monies paid for the house in this way, which can then be converted into 'the house' itself in direct proportion to the contribution. This is because the operation of a resulting trust will prevent equitable title in that proportion following legal title (which is vested in the legal owner).

However, it also became apparent earlier that in other respects, the workings of category 2 were more complex than ones which would arise from a straightforward application of *Dyer*. This could be seen in the complexities surrounding (even if not actually in the basic idea of) mortgage repayments made in furtherance of the obligation of repayment under a debtor/creditor arrangement, and the position became even more complicated in the case of 'discounts'. Nevertheless there is the decision in *Huntingford* v *Hobbs* [1993] to consider, and, more recently, references made to the importance of the resulting trust in this context can be seen in *Oxley* and, most recently, from the House of Lords in *Stack*.

9.6.2.1 *Quantification and* Midland Bank *v* Cooke [1995]

Complications arose in *Cooke*, where, in the absence of any discussion at all, direct contributions amounting to 6.74 per cent of the purchase price of the property resulted in a half share for the non-legal owner. One reading of this is a confusion of resulting and constructive trust principles, but Waite LJ held that once the claimant had established an interest by direct contribution the court was then able to take the conduct of all of the parties into account in determining quantum of interest (this was adopted in *Le Foe*, and then endorsed by the Law Commission in *Sharing Homes*). This became central to *Oxley*'s 'whole course of dealings' approach, and in *Stack* v *Dowden* their Lordships broadly agreed (apart from Lord Neuberger in respect of indirect contributions which are household expenses) that wider approaches to quantification should be endorsed.

9.7 Quantification as it appeared to be in the aftermath of *Oxley* v *Hiscock*

Following on from the facts of *Oxley* as set out earlier, it was found at first instance that, in absence of express agreement, both parties had evinced an intention to share benefits and burdens of the property jointly and equally, and the claimant was awarded a half share. On appeal, the defendant claimed that because there had been no discussion about the parties' respective beneficial interests at the time of the purchase, the presumption of a resulting trust was not displaced and the property was thus held on trust for both parties, but in beneficial shares proportionate to their contributions. In concluding that an agreement to share the property beneficially *could* be found, Chadwick LJ nevertheless insisted that 'it does not follow from the fact that the parties live together in a house they both regard as their home that they share the ownership of that house equally'. In ordering a 40 per cent–60 per cent share in favour of the defendant in absence of 'evidence of any discussion between the parties as to the amount of the share each was to have', Chadwick LJ suggested that declaring that the parties were entitled in equal shares would be 'unfair to Mr Hiscock'. This was so notwithstanding the 'classic pooling of resources' by the couple found by the judge at first instance, and was founded upon Hiscock's contribution of £60,000 being significantly greater than the £36,500 made by Oxley (with the couple being treated as having made roughly equal contributions to the discharge of the mortgage).

9.7.1 The position of the law in the aftermath of *Oxley*

The aftermath of *Oxley* appeared to be characterised by a number of key matters, which must now themselves be reconsidered in the light of the House of Lords' decision in *Stack* v *Dowden*. But in terms of how the law looked in light of *Oxley*, the following points are of note:

- Rosset's significance on agreement to share: the continuing significance of finding 'common intention'.

  The essence of finding between the parties a common intention in relation to the beneficial interests of their home remains, but Chadwick's reading of Lord Bridge's references to it in *Rosset* is that it applies only to the primary question of *whether* there was 'a common intention that each should have a beneficial interest in the property?'. In Chadwick LJ's view, this was a better reading than one which extended to the secondary question—'what was the common intention of the parties as to the extent of their beneficial interests?'.

- A broad acknowledgement remains of the existence of two categories of case from *Rosset*.

  Chadwick LJ makes direct and explicit reference to them in saying that '[i]n many such cases—of which the present is an example—there will have been some discussion between the parties at the time of the purchase which provides the answer to that question. Those are cases within the first of Lord Bridge's categories...', and adding '[i]n other cases—where the evidence is that the matter was not discussed at all—an affirmative answer will readily be inferred from the fact that each has made a financial contribution. Those are cases within Lord Bridge's second category.'

- Broad acknowledgement of two categories remains, but for quantification purposes, it appears that distinction is being made between two different types of category 1 case.

  Oxley is authority for the proposition that, in some category 1 *Rosset* cases, the agreement to share a property beneficially will also determine the size of the parties' respective interests: this is because the couple will agree (prior to the sale of the property or the breakdown of their relationship) that the property will be shared, and will also agree it is to be shared in a particular way (e.g., equally). However, in absence of this, even within category 1 cases, there could be no presumption that the parties intended beneficial interests to be shared equally.

- In the case of category 1 cases where *quantification* is not fixed in advance of the sale of the property or the breakdown of the parties' relationship, and a remedy is sought, it is for the courts to determine the extent of beneficial interests.

  This proposition follows on from the way in which *Oxley* argues that *Rosset*'s 'common intention' does not apply to the secondary question of 'what was the common intention of the parties as to the extent of their beneficial interests?' *unless* the parties have agreed the *size* of their respective interests. Thus, Chadwick LJ suggested that even in category 1 cases there could not be a presumption of equal shares where the parties had themselves left the question open. Pointing explicitly to *Stokes* v *Anderson* (and this text suggests *Passee* v *Passee* appears to be another example), Chadwick LJ suggested that in these circumstances it is up to the court to 'supply' the parties' common intention regarding size of share to be received by both parties. The basis for the court's determination is, according to Chadwick LJ, that which is 'fair having regard to the whole course of dealing between them in relation to the property' (the significance of which is considered below).

- For the purposes of *quantification*, the position of *Rosset* category 2 cases is that it is up to the courts to determine the extent of beneficial interests.

    In cases where there is no agreement to share, under *Rosset* this could be inferred from direct financial contributions made by a non-legal owner. Up to this point *Oxley* is consistent with *Rosset*. However, *Oxley* appears to suggest that where there is no discussion at all (i.e. *Rosset* category 2) but where intention can be inferred by direct contributions, that the contributions establish detrimental reliance, and that each party 'is entitled to a share which the court considers fair having regard to the whole course of dealing between them in relation to the property' (on which see further below). This is a significant departure from that which was envisioned by *Rosset*, which appeared to suggest that contributions in absence of agreement to share not only established reliance but also measured the extent of the interest which arose on the operation of a resulting trust. Chadwick LJ acknowledged that the cases in this area showed that 'the courts have not found it easy to reconcile that final step' (of awarding a share considered to be fair in all the circumstances) 'with a traditional property-based approach'. This is probably on no small account that this 'final step' makes category 2 cases, as envisioned by Lord Bridge, virtually indistinguishable from all but the most clear and unambiguous cases in category 1.

    However, while suggesting that the entitlement of each party to a share which the court considers fair 'must be accepted...at least in this court and below' (thus pointing to an apparent strengthening of authority in absence of a House of Lords' ruling), the displacement of traditional approaches in category 2 cases is technically *obiter* because *Oxley* itself was actually a category 1 case.

- In relation to quantification, the position of category 2 cases would now appear to be the same as all category 1 cases where the parties have not agreed the extent of their share by effectively declaring an express trust to that end.

    In so far as the remedial outcome of disputed homes cases is concerned, by making these observations on category 2 cases, Chadwick LJ effectively aligns them with those which fall into a *sub-category* of category 1 where there *is* common intention that each should have some beneficial interest in the property, but the question of size of share remains open upon the end of the relationship or the sale of the property. In these circumstances, which points to absence of evidence that any thought was given to quantification, 'the necessary inference is that they must have intended that question would be answered later on the basis of what was then seen to be fair'. It is between category 2 cases and this sub-category of category 1 that determination of quantification appears to be becoming merged.

- Continuing 'blurring' of distinction between category 1 and category 2 cases.

    A great deal of criticism can be levied at *Midland Bank* v *Cooke* as a decision of 'trusts law' notwithstanding its apparent connotations of fairness, and also despite the favour it has found in the courts in decisions like *Le Foe* v *Le Foe*, and the manifest support for approaches which emphasise fairness to be found in 'policy' discourses. The objections which can be made in respect of *Cooke* suggest that while providing solutions which are fair and just is a laudable pursuit, that 'broad brush' approaches to quantification also encourage uncertainty and arbitrariness in determinations of valuable property interests. Fundamentally, it can also be argued that *Midland Bank* v *Cooke* undermines *Rosset* and the trusts analysis at the heart of cases where there is no evidence of an agreement between the parties to share a family home beneficially. Equally, as the 'broad brush' approach to quantification has become infiltrated into category 1 cases where there is evidence of agreement, a number of commentators have suggested that the cases of *Midland Bank* v *Cooke* and *Drake* v *Whipp* are difficult to reconcile. Indeed, in these two cases, a smaller contribution in the former gave rise to a larger interest, in absence of independent evidence of an agreement to share property beneficially.

9.7.2 *Stack* v *Dowden*: House of Lords authority for determinations of home ownership

It was suggested in the aftermath of *Oxley* that the apparent position of the law had yet to be considered by the House of Lords. It was so in early 2007 in *Stack* v *Dowden*. And in the House of Lords much of the approach adopted in *Oxley* was endorsed wholeheartedly, and perhaps especially its accommodating views on a range of contributions, which could be applied across category 2 cases and all but the most clear ones in category 1—where the express agreement actually quantifies the interest—certainly in relation to quantification questions (with the position of contributions other than deposits, mortgage repayments, and now capital improvements in giving rise to an inference of common intention not entirely clear not withstanding some support in dicta in *Stack*).

In these latter categories, *Oxley* suggested that a claimant 'is entitled to a share which the court considers fair having regard to the whole course of dealing between them in relation to the property'. And certainly *Stack* endorsed *Oxley*'s assertion of the need to consider 'the whole course of dealings' between the parties on account that it encouraged a holistic and workable approach to these determinations and which reflected a range of contributions which are customarily made in the context of home sharing. However, in departing from some of the 'strict letter' of *Oxley* (whilst leaving much of its spirit intact) the House of Lords in *Stack* signals a renewed enthusiasm for determining this holistic whole dealings approach by way of trusts principles—rather than ones of estoppel. Reference has already been made to *Stack*'s retreat from estoppel earlier, and the views being expressed that a trusts approach was a better reflection overall of the valuable property rights which were at stake in this context.

In this context *Stack*'s significance is such that instead of the 'whole course of dealings' between the parties being determined by what the *court* deems to be fair, the focus should be doing so in light of what the parties themselves intended. Although much of the language surrounding intention of the parties actually used by the House of Lords in *Stack* itself (and subsequently in *Abbott v Abbott*, and particularly in the judgments of Lady Hale in particular) is a bit woolly and imprecise, for Lord Neuberger in *Stack*, this amounted to distinguishing between intention which was inferred and that which was imputed; and while it was permissible for the court to infer the parties' intention from the course of their dealings with one another, it was not appropriate for the court to impute intention on the part of the parties.

9.7.3 Quantification in the case of a jointly held legal title to a shared home

Stack is authority that although once the province of '*sole legal owners v non-legal owners*', disputed home ownership is capable of arising even where couples are joint legal owners of their home: here, the dispute concerns where beneficial ownership lies as a result of this. The point is that legal title is concerned with legal form, and not the equities arising from shared ownership. The view of the House of Lords was that where there is such a legal joint tenancy, it should be assumed that some sharing of beneficial interest is intended by this, *and furthermore that* ordinarily it should be assumed that the beneficial interest should reflect this position through *equal* beneficial sharing. This is an application of the maxim of 'equity follows the law', and that a very high burden should be placed on any party seeking to establish that the legal position is not also the equitable position.

In *Stack* itself the House of Lords also commented that this was a very unusual case, because it was not common for couples who had lived together for so many years and had children together to keep their affairs so rigidly separate. However, on these facts the couple had kept their personal affairs entirely separate, and Stack's contributions overall were much less extensive than those made by Dowden. After *Stack*, *Fowler v Barron* [2008] EWCA is authority that it will be very difficult for joint legal owners to show that this position is not mirrored in equity, and that departure from the presumption of equality will only occur in circumstances that are very exceptional. *Fowler* is authority that this will require more to be shown than simply stark inequalities in contributions made.

There were stark inequalities in contributions made in *Fowler v Barron*, to the extent that the female party (Fowler) had made no direct contributions at all, and very extensive contributions had been made by Barron, ensuring that a significant amount of equity subsisted in the home. However, in finding that Barron had failed to rebut the presumption of equal shares in equity, the Court of Appeal distinguished this case from *Stack v Dowden*. This was because in *Fowler* there were no substantial assets belonging to one party rather than to the other, and because, unlike the parties in *Stack* who—notwithstanding a relationship spanning 20 years and rearing four children together—had kept their financial affairs rigidly separate, all the evidence pointed to Fowler and Barron pooling their assets, derived almost entirely from income. This meant that, unlike the situation in *Stack*, the parties here had not shown any evidence of rejecting an intention to share beneficial interests equally in the face of considerable financial inequalities subsisting between them.

9.8 *Stack* v *Dowden* as a *Rosset* of its time?: its importance and its apparent limitations

Stack v *Dowden* was a very important case in a number of respects, and in a number of ways it has appeared to resolve a number of difficulties which have emerged in **applying** *Rosset* **post-***Rosset*. This includes a number of uncertainties such as questions left open by the 'trusts or estoppel' route option, and the role of capital improvements made subsequently to acquisition. However, it is also the case, somewhat disappointingly, that *Stack*, the key House of Lords decision to emerge post-*Rosset*, in a number of respects fell short of being the '*Rosset* of its time' that it could have been, and the apparent agreement amongst their Lordships does also harbour lesser degrees of consensus. This is perhaps most marked in the context of indirect contributions.

Reference has already been made to the way in which after *Stack* and its successors (notably *Abbott* v *Abbott* and *James* v *Thomas*) it remains unclear whether contributions referred to in this discussion as indirect contributions are capable of giving rise to the inference of common intention to share ownership in category 2 cases. And although *Stack* (like *Oxley* before it, and also *Abbott* in its aftermath) was a quantification case (where existence of an interest was not being ascertained) which would have made any discussion of this nature *obiter*, it is a pity that fuller discussion did not take place around Lord Bridge's requirements in *Rosset*, beyond the opinion of all (apart from Lord Neuberger) that disallowing indirect financial contributions altogether was an approach which was too strict. Fuller discussion could have considered (albeit *obiter*) more clearly the requirements of actually establishing a beneficial interest, and whether or how much the law might have 'moved on' (for better or worse) in that respect since 1990, as well as in relation to quantification. It remains to be seen how the law will develop in this way, but it is significant that *James* v *Thomas* [2007] is the only post-*Stack* authority considering the existence of an interest (as distinct form quantification), and it is Court of Appeal authority for a reluctance on the part of the courts to move (far) from Lord Bridge's requirements.

What follows from this is that it cannot be assumed that (any/all?) indirect contributions are actually capable of giving rise to the inference of a common intention to share ownership in circumstances where the parties have not discussed ownership of the home (in these circumstances contributions are the only way for the court to determine whether there is to be *any share* at all). However, *Stack* has a further limitation which is attached to this. This is because while much discussion did take place around 'indirect financial contributions' (albeit that this could have been more extensive and more focused), very little attention was paid to contributions most commonly associated with *Burns* v *Burns* [1984], i.e. ones relating to home-making, which are indirect, and also non-financial. These are contributions such as child rearing and 'domestic duties' (broadly defined). Because of this, it remains unclear whether any value whatsoever will be attached to indirect contributions which are also non-financial—even in the context of quantification in furtherance of the (flexible and holistic?) 'whole course of dealings' approach. Without some reasoned discussion, it does not appear clear beyond all doubt that such contributions alone would be sufficient even to establish detrimental reliance in a category 1 case where there is independent evidence of agreement to share ownership, and perhaps especially where the interest still remains to be quantified.

9.9 Legislation affecting spouses and property interests under the Civil Partnership Act 2004

The legislature reacted to the House of Lords decisions in *Pettitt* v *Pettitt* [1970] AC 777 and *Gissing* v *Gissing* [1971] AC 886 by enacting legislation which allows the courts to take into account additional considerations when the parties are married.

Section 37 of the Matrimonial Proceedings and Property Act 1970 relating to 'Contributions by spouse in money or money's worth to the improvement of property', was a reaction to *Pettitt* v *Pettitt*. It allows for the beneficial interests of husbands and wives (and by virtue of s. 2(1) of the Law Reform (Miscellaneous Provisions) Act 1970 and fiancées, but not those of other unmarried couples) to be varied by substantial contributions 'in money or money's worth to the improvement of real or personal property in which...both of them has or have a beneficial interest'.

Sections 24 and 25 of the Matrimonial Causes Act 1973 were a reaction to *Gissing* v *Gissing*. The sections allow the courts significantly to alter the property interests of married (but not unmarried) couples in the event of divorce, a decree of nullity of marriage, or a decree of judicial separation. In such an event, the importance of the prior property interests of the spouses is reduced, since they will no longer be conclusive. The Matrimonial Causes Act 1973 applies only on the breakdown of marriages, however, and if the question of the existence or otherwise of a beneficial interest arises during the course of the marriage (as is usually the case, for example, where a third party is involved, as in *Lloyds Bank plc* v *Rosset* itself), the issue will be determined on the basis of the ordinary principles of equity discussed in this chapter.

9.9.1 Property interests and the Civil Partnership Act 2004

In contrast with the uncertainty which continues to prevail in relation to unmarried couples generally—and the scope for injustice which is recognised both judicially and in policy discourses—there has been reform in the position of same-sex couples specifically. The Civil Partnership Act 2004 allows same-sex couples to register their partnership, and upon doing so, rights relating to property are broadly similar to those of married couples. The way in which this impacts on matters of inheritance and survivorship, administration of estates, and pension entitlements is beyond the scope of this text, but there are some important observations to make concerning the family home. It is now possible for persons within a registered civil partnership to acquire an interest, or a greater share, in a shared home (in which one or both has an interest) by making a substantial improvement to the property concerned. In this respect, s. 65 of the Civil Partnerships Act is analogous with s. 37 of the Matrimonial Proceedings Act 1970. In a similar vein, when the partnership is terminated, the court is able to make property adjustment orders with the same discretion as applies to married couples pursuant to the Matrimonial Causes Act 1973, as amended by the Family Law Act 1996.

9.10 Shared homes, beneficial interests, and proposals for reform

In her leading judgment in *Stack* v *Dowden* [2007] Lady Hale noted the long-standing dissatisfaction with the position of cohabitees under the general principles developed by the courts, and the way in which this was taken up by the Law Commission in 2002 in a Discussion Paper entitled *Sharing Homes* (Law Com 278). In this paper, the Law Commission set out a proposed scheme which it devised in an attempt to replace the current system of property entitlement (to promote fairness in a variety of different relationships and in response to a number of differing manifestations of 'contribution' by removing need for common intention and focusing solely on status of the parties). The focal point for the Law Commission was that the huge diversity of domestic living arrangements presented serious challenges for the courts, and created considerable scope for fairness to be evaded and injustices to arise, and that overall 'The emphasis on financial input towards the acquisition of the home fails to recognise the realities of most cohabiting relationships.'

This was noted by this text at the time, along with the way in which the Paper concluded that, notwithstanding that property was such a central aspect of shared living, devising a statutory scheme which accurately captured modern living arrangements was unrealistic, and that it was thus up to the courts to evolve the law to take account of new circumstances. Indeed, at the time, the *Textbook* noted with considerable interest that the Law Commission had strongly encouraged the courts to do this in a way which followed the approach adopted in *Le Foe* v *Le Foe* [2001] 2 FLR 970, which pointed to the 'reality' that family economies depend on indirect financial contributions as much as ones which are 'direct', the latter being the only ones regarded by Lord Bridge in *Rosset* as acceptable in determinations of home ownership.

At the same time, the Law Society also published some proposals for reform in 2002 in *Cohabitation: The Case for Clear Law* (London: Law Society, 2002). These proposals were confined to cohabitees and proposed to give the courts similar powers to those under the Matrimonial Causes Act 1973 (which can now also be found in relation to same-sex couples who register their relationship as a civil partnership under the Civil Partnership Act 2004). Unlike the Law Commission's 2002 proposals which were essentially neutral (retrospective and contributions-based), the Law Society proposals were deliberately instrumental in nature and focused on providing those who care for children with a remedy (court order) on breakdown of the relationship, something designed to help to alleviate the economic disadvantage suffered by persons undertaking that role. This is significant because much of the core thinking in the Law Society's proposals can be seen in the more recent work in this area undertaken by the Law Commission, initially in 2006 in its Consultation Paper No. 179, *Cohabitation: The Financial Consequences of Relationship Breakdown.*

9.10.1 **The Law Commission's Consultation on the financial consequences of cohabitation**

This Consultation Paper was published in May 2006 in light of Government instruction to 'examine the options for reforming the law that applies to cohabiting couples on separation or death'. The detail of this can be found set out in the ORC accompanying this text. And in essence the Consultation Paper set out the parameters for possible reform of personal relationships, designed to give the courts the discretion to make capital/income awards in the event of a breakdown or death within a series of defined relationships. The Law Commission intended to report its findings in summer 2007, and the Report was duly published on 31 July 2007. The key recommendations can be found in the Executive Summary of the Report, which is accessible via <http://www.lawcom.gov.uk>. The Executive Summary is an extremely comprehensive guide to the Law Commission's views on the state of the current law relating to cohabitation and its recommendations for reform, which can be read alongside the reference which was made to the 2006 Consultation Paper in the ORC.

9.10.2 **The Law Commission's Report on the financial consequences of relationship breakdown in the context of cohabitation**

The Law Commission reiterates its concerns that a large number of those who cohabit believe in the 'myth' of common law marriage: namely, that those who live together for an extended period of time are in time treated as if they are married. What can be added to this is the way in which this is often accompanied by the closely related (and equally incorrect) conflation often made in such relationships between 'shared living' and 'occupation' and shared *ownership* of homes. It maintains that while the law does provide unmarried couples with some protection (through property law and contract, and traditionally trusts law) this protection is uncertain, complex, and based on legal rules not developed with family situations 'in mind'. Moreover, for the Law Commission, the application of these rules frequently results in the failure to achieve justice for those who do not own homes, and who occupy homes which belong in law to others. Indeed, as the earlier materials suggest, the Law Commission has been a long-standing critic of the courts' approaches to resolving disputed home ownership.

This Report, like the Consultation before it notes the Law Commission's view that the injustices which can arise in the event of relationship breakdown are particularly acute where the couple concerned have children, and its belief is that the courts need to be vested with powers to make adjustments to property entitlements so as not detrimentally to affect the position of children. And while it agrees that parties should be encouraged to make their intentions relating to ownership (and not simply occupation or enjoyment of) property clear, it also asserts that the law cannot simply abandon responsibility for 'decisions' made by parties to a relationship. This is because parties are not always in a position to protect themselves by ensuring that they get married (or registering their same-sex relationship as a civil partnership), because their partner may not agree to do so. In these circumstances, it is in the interests of all concerned and society generally to achieve the best out-come in the case of a failed relationship.

That having been said, the Law Commission reiterated its belief (expressed in the 2006 Consultation) that cohabitants should not have access to the same remedies as persons who marry (or civil partners) upon the breakup of a relationship because while a core set of assumptions can be made from the public nature of marriage and civil partnership, the same is not true of the numerous and diverse intimate relationships which could be brought under the umbrella term 'cohabitation'.

The Law Commission thus recommended a workable system that responds to separation of parties cohabiting which is to be focused on the financial con-sequences of relationship breakdown (or death). Significantly, as their 2006 Consultation suggested, this would not be available in all cases of cohabitation, and would be confined to particular types of relationship where it is deemed appropri-ate for the court to have the discretion to make adjustments in relation to property rights between the parties. In these circumstances, the availability of such a rem-edy would be available to those couples who, first, are deemed to be *'eligible'* for the application of the scheme (either because they have a child together or because they have lived together for a minimum duration); second, have not agreed to disapply the scheme to their relationship—have *not 'opted out'* of the scheme applicable to their relationship; and, finally, have made what are termed *qualifying contributions to the relationship* which have given rise to *certain enduring consequences*, which will justify the court making an order to adjust property entitlements.

9.10.3 The substance of the recommendations, and those intended to benefit from them

What all this amounts to is that the Law Commission is seeking to ensure that it is only those relationships of cohabitation which might appropriately justify gen-erating financial entitlements (which are distinguishable from 'casual' arrange-ments) that are considered eligible for doing so, and that this is evidenced through having children together, or living together for an extended period of time (the Law Commission suggested in the Report that a period of two to five years might be considered appropriate).

The requirement that the couple does not dis-apply the scheme (by 'opting out') to their relationship is once again seeking to ensure that the recommended scheme applies only to those relationships where it is intended by the parties that their particular partnership should have the kind of financial consequences envisioned by the scheme. The 'opt out' scheme reflects the requirement for this to be based on the parties' 'common belief' and ultimately leaves it to the parties to determine the nature of the relationship which they believe their particular partnership rep-resents. Here the Law Commission favoured an 'opt out' approach rather than an 'opting in', in order hopefully that the scheme will be able to assist more poten-tially vulnerable people than would be the case if the parties effectively had to 'register' their cohabitation, while ultimately respecting the autonomy of parties to choose the nature of their own relationship.

The requirement to make qualifying contributions which result in enduring consequences for the party making an application for an award of capital or income (and later in the Executive Summary illuminated as a retained benefit on the part of 'other' party, or an economic disadvantage experienced by the applicant flowing from making a contribution) is quite clearly designed to distinguish those relationships where breakup does justify making such adjustments to existing financial positions/entitlements from those parties who are 'simply cohabiting'. Here, the Law Commission notes that simply cohabiting even for an extensive period does not give rise to any presumed entitlement to share in any pool of property. It is also the case that the purpose of the scheme is not considered to be based on the needs of a party on separation, and is focused instead on contributions made, and the consequences experienced from making such contributions.

9.10.3.1 *The rationale of reflecting the 'plusses and minuses' of a relationship*

Overall the Law Commission intends that the scheme should work towards ensuring that 'the plusses and minuses of the relationship were shared fairly between the couple', and it is at this point that the courts would be guided by any benefit retained by the other party or a continuing economic disadvantage experienced by the applicant in making qualifying contributions. This in turn would provide a measure of the award made in respect of a successful applicant. Under the Law Commission's recommended scheme, the court would have the discretion to grant such financial relief which ensures fair sharing of a relationship's 'plusses and minuses' through retained benefits/enduring economic disadvantage, and would always give first consideration to the welfare of dependent children.

The Law Commission then explained that it believed that such a scheme would give a principled and sound basis by which to address the economic hardship which frequently arises from the breakdown of a cohabitation. It explains that it believes that such a scheme will respond more comprehensively and more appropriately than the current law (determined by the courts traditionally using trusts principles), and the Executive Summary provides a number of 'case illustrations' of how the scheme is likely to apply in different fact situations, as well as the rationale for this and the outcome of it doing so (see Examples under paras 1.25–1.35).

In terms of reiterating its belief in the need for a new approach, the Law Commission is of course a long-standing critic of the injustices which have been alleged to arise from the courts' traditional approaches to disputed home ownership following relationship breakdown. And the Executive Summary also draws attention to the 'social context' provided by the way in which the 2001 census recorded over two million cohabiting couples in the UK, and that this is predicted to rise to 3.8 million by 2031. In terms of 'what happens next', in the Executive Summary the Law Commission also acknowledges that making recommendations for reform is all that can be done at this stage. The Law Commission notes that it was not asked to draft a Bill when asked to consider this area of law by the Ministry of Justice, and that any change in the law would require legislation.

9.10.3.2 *Ahead of what might happen—a number of interesting questions which arise*

Thus it remains to be seen how much impact the Law Commission's recommendations have, and how quickly they might do so, in generating the requisite political interest which is integral to securing legal change through legislation. In the meantime, these recommendations *as they have been made* do raise interesting questions.

First, there is a very real need to ask whether the scheme which is being proposed will actually, as the Law Commission suggests, provide a more comprehensive response to relationship breakdown than the current law. The current law is what will continue to apply for couples who are not eligible and to those who are eligible but have opted out of the scheme, and while it might be appropriate for couples to choose to regard their relationship as distinct from 'other types' of cohabitation, it does not necessarily follow that the approach provided under the proposed scheme is going to be more satisfactory in outcome than the current law. This is perhaps particularly so given the very flexible and accommodating approaches which exist certainly in relation to quantifying beneficial interests in shared homes following the House of Lords decision in *Stack* v *Dowden*, which is where this discussion commenced. However in having regard to this, it is accepted that *Stack* is not necessarily very helpful for determining the existence of a beneficial interest (as distinct from quantifying one which has been established), and thus this scheme may well be helpful for assisting those who might otherwise find it difficult to establish an interest in property under *Lloyds Bank* v *Rosset* [1991] AC 107.

Second, the Law Commission's emphasis on the differences between marriage and cohabitation might well be intended to 'support the institution of marriage', but it serves another vital function as far as those who cohabit are concerned. This reflects the proposition that those who cohabit rather than marry *often* do so because the parties (or at least one party) deems this to be a more appropriate reflection of their own relationship than the institution of marriage. The Law Commission is keen to preserve the autonomy of parties to determine the appropriate formalisation of their relationship, while appreciating that vulnerabilities can arise in respect of one party where the partners have different views of the nature of their relationship. This is recognised in its hope that requiring parties to opt out of the scheme applying to their relationship can protect more potentially vulnerable persons than if it were left to parties consciously to opt in to the scheme applying to them. This is a logical operation of these two choices—of opting in and opting out—but given that the Law Commission is very conscious that vulnerabilities can be caused by parties having very different ideas of the nature of their relationship, there is still a danger here.

This might be seen to flow from any attempts to formalise informal relationships where one party is in a stronger position than the other (even if this not actually tantamount to exploitation and reflects nothing more than lack of consensus between the parties on aspects of the relationship). Even the 'opting out' option as envisaged will require a written notice from the parties to this effect, and at this point a party in a weaker position might well be pressurised into agreeing. Moreover, being required to opt out may well put pressure on parties to a relationship actually not to cohabit (with the possibility that one party is pressured into this situation) in order to seek to remove themselves from any possible application of the scheme. This situation in which cohabitation may actually be discouraged may generate a number of widely felt negative implications, flowing from the way in which there are a number of social and financial benefits pertaining to a number of forms of shared living. The benefits do of course include important pooling of financial resources which is acquiring increased significance in the climate of rising house prices, or more recently in the context of falling ones, which can also discourage the purchase of new homes. Benefits can also extend to the sharing of practical burdens and responsibilities, and the emotional support that can be found in a large number of 'shared living' arrangements.

9.10.3.3 *An additional significance for the Law Commission's own 'warning'?*

These characteristics of shared living are capable of conferring more general societal benefits in addition to those experienced by those party to the particular relationship (such as promoting greater efficiency in the occupation of dwellings), and thus seeking to formalise informal relationships may threaten this. Within this general 'warning' against formalising informal arrangements, it is not difficult to envisage that this could have particularly harsh impact on children whose parents choose not to share 'living' *at all* for fear of making their relationship 'too formal'. Here it is possible to envision that it is not simply children whose parents split who inevitably 'lose out'—others could well be deprived of many benefits should their parents choose not to cohabit at all. In one respect it is clearly the case that having a child together inevitably creates a relationship between 'parents', but given that such people will likely be given the chance to opt out of the scheme, perhaps a decision might be made by them (or by one of them) not to cohabit at all.

This warning is really intended to accompany the Law Commission's concern with the welfare of children (and also 'vulnerable parties' to a relationship who can 'lose out' financially on the breakdown of relationships) rather than to criticise its endeavours in this area. By its own admission parties who wish to formalise their relationships have the option to marry or to register a civil partnership, and thus there is little harm in suggesting that a great deal of care must be taken in any steps which *might* have the effect of making relationships more formal than the parties to them wish them to be.

online
resource
centre

FURTHER READING

Dixon 'The Never Ending Story: Co-ownership after *Stack* v *Dowden*' (2007) Conveyancer 456.

Ferguson 'Constructive Trusts: A Note of Caution' (1993) Law Quarterly Review 114.

Gardner 'Rethinking Family Property' (1993) Law Quarterly Review 263.

Glover and Todd 'The Myth of Common Intention' (1996) Legal Studies 325 (and (1997) 5 Web JCLI).

Hayton 'Equitable Rights of Cohabitees' (1990) Conveyancer 370.

Mee 'Joint Ownership, Subjective Intention and the Common Intention Constructive Trust (2007) Conveyancer 14.

Pawlowski 'Beneficial Entitlement: Do Indirect Contributions Suffice?' (2002) Family Law 190.

Thompson 'Oral Agreements for the Sale of Land' (2000) Conveyancer 245.

Thompson 'An Holistic Approach to Home Ownership' (2002) Conveyancer 273.

Thompson 'The Obscurity of Common Intention' (2003) Conveyancer 411.

Wells 'The Element of Detriment in Proprietary Estoppel' (2001) Conveyancer 13.

10

....

Secret and half-secret trusts
(and constructive and resulting trusts)

10.1 What are secret and half-secret trusts?

As with *inter vivos* transactions (see chapter 5), there are formality requirements where property is left by will. To be valid, under s. 9 of the Wills Act 1837 (as amended by s. 17 of the Administration of Justice Act 1982), wills have to be made in writing, and properly signed and witnessed. The full text of s. 9, as amended, is as follows:

No will shall be valid unless—

(a) it is in writing, and signed by the testator, or by some other person in his presence and by his direction; and

(b) it appears that the testator intended by his signature to give effect to the will; and

(c) the signature is made or acknowledged by the testator in the presence of two or more witnesses present at the same time; and

(d) each witness either—

    (i) attests and signs the will; or

    (ii) acknowledges his signature, in the presence of the testator (but not necessarily in the presence of any other witness),

but no form of attestation shall be necessary.

If the provisions of s. 9 are not complied with, the will is completely void and any trusts which it purports to create will be invalid also. As will be seen, however, a secret or half-secret trust may take effect on the death of the testator without any need to specify the terms of the trust in the will, or even to reveal its existence.

The purpose of s. 9 (as amended) is to prevent fraud, and formality requirements are meant to prevent this, and to reflect the way in which making a will is a major transaction and the result of deliberate action. As in other areas, however, formalities can sometimes encourage fraud, but 'equity will not permit a statute to be used as a cloak for fraud' and the doctrines of secret and half-secret trusts have evolved in this area to prevent this.

10.1.1 Reasons for testators wishing to avoid formality requirements

There are at least two reasons why a testator may wish to avoid formality provisions (see, for example, Sheridan (1951) 67 LQR 314).

First, he may wish the identity of the beneficiary to remain secret. This was especially common in the nineteenth century, if a gift of land to a charity was intended, when the Statutes of Mortmain (which prevented testamentary gifts of land to charities between 1736 and 1891) were in force. Another common situation was (and still is) where the beneficiary is to be a lover or mistress, or illegitimate child. Possibly the need for secrecy in this situation has diminished since 1969, because until then there was a presumption that a gift to 'children' in a will excluded illegitimate children. Thus, it was necessary to identify them to include them. That presumption was reversed in 1969, so that a gift to 'children' on its own now includes illegitimate children (the relevant provisions can now be found in the Family Law Reform Act 1987). Even so, secrecy may still be desired if the testator wishes to keep their very existence secret.

Second, the testator may simply not have made up his mind at the time of making the will about the details of all the dispositions. It has been argued (e.g., Watkin [1981] Conv 335) that whereas the law should indulge secrecy, it should discourage indecision, and to at least a partial extent, it has taken this line.

10.1.2 Methods of avoiding formality provisions of the Wills Act

There are two methods by which the Wills Act can effectively be avoided. A can leave property by will to B, in a manner which complies with the provisions of the Act, but having come to an (unwritten) understanding with B that he is merely trustee of it in favour of C. The understanding does not, of course, comply with the formality requirements of the Act. This is called a fully secret trust.

Alternatively, A can leave property by a valid will 'to B on trust', but where the beneficial interest under the trust (for example, in favour of C) is undeclared. This is called a half-secret trust because, while the details of the trust are secret, it is made clear that B holds as trustee and not beneficially.

For clarity, A, B, and C will be used in the same fashion throughout the chapter.

In general, the principles for the enforcement of fully secret and half-secret trusts are probably the same (although some argue otherwise). Thus, most of what follows in the next section (on fully secret trusts) applies equally to half-secret trusts. However, because it is necessary to refute arguments that their basis of enforcement is different, and because there are respects in which half-secret trusts are treated differently, there is also a separate section on half-secret trusts.

10.2 Enforcement of fully secret trusts

Subject to the constraints on the doctrine outlined in the remainder of this section, fully secret trusts will be enforced by the courts—C can enforce the trust against B. The question therefore arises: on what basis does equity allow the clear provisions of the Wills Act to be avoided?

10.2.1 Fraud theory

The leading authority on fully secret trusts is the House of Lords decision of *McCormick v Grogan* (1869) LR 4 HL 82 which clearly states that the basis of their enforcement is fraud. The precise nature of the fraud is discussed shortly but, at the very least, if it would be fraudulent for B to take beneficially, he will be required to enforce the trust in favour of C. This would be the case, for example, if the only reason why the property was left to B in the will was because of the unwritten understanding that he would hold it on trust for C.

The facts in *McCormick* v *Grogan* were that in 1851, the testator had left all his property by a three-line will to his friend Mr Grogan. In 1854 he was struck down by cholera. With only a few hours to live he sent for Mr Grogan. He told Mr Grogan in effect that his will and a letter would be found in his desk. The letter named various intended beneficiaries and the intended gifts to them. The letter concluded with the words:

> I do not wish you to act strictly on the foregoing instructions, but leave it entirely to your own good judgment to do as you think I would, if living, and as the parties are deserving.

An intended beneficiary (an illegitimate child) whom Mr Grogan thought it right to exclude sued.

The House of Lords held that although in principle the courts will enforce secret trusts, the terms of the letter in this particular case were not such that equity would impose on the conscience of Mr Grogan, and the secret trust alleged would not be enforced.

10.2.1.1 McCormick *v* Grogan: *different facts and a different result*

Although in *McCormick* v *Grogan* itself it was held that no secret trust was created in favour of C (an illegitimate child), but merely a moral obligation imposed on B, the court made it clear that had the facts been different a fully secret trust would, in principle, have been enforceable by C, in spite of the provisions of the Wills Act. In fact, the principles of enforcement of secret trusts go back at least as far as *Thynn* v *Thynn* (1684) 1 Vern 296.

It is by no means self-evident that equity should uphold a trust despite a clear statutory provision to the contrary. In *McCormick* v *Grogan*, Lord Hatherley LC and Lord Westbury emphasised that the justification for the doctrine is personal fraud. In several places in his speech, Lord Westbury in particular emphasised the need for a '*malus animus*' to be 'proved by the clearest and most indisputable evidence' (at p. 97):

> the jurisdiction which is invoked here...is founded altogether on personal fraud. It is a jurisdiction by which a court of equity, proceeding on the ground of fraud, converts the party who has committed it into a trustee for the party who is injured by that fraud. Now, being a jurisdiction founded on personal fraud, it is incumbent on the court to see that a fraud, a *malus animus*, is proved by the clearest and most indisputable evidence.

10.2.1.2 *Fraud and a deliberate intention to deceive*

On one view, this means that a deliberate intention to deceive must be shown on B's part (for example, where B had deliberately induced the testator to leave the property to him in the will, on the clear representation that he would hold it in trust for C), and it could also be argued that the standard of proof is as in common law fraud; in other words, a very high standard indeed is required. It may well be that this was what Lord Westbury meant. However, the statement has recently been explained in different terms. As will be explained below, *malus animus* may mean no more than the state of mind required for equity to impose a constructive trust on B's conscience, a very different proposition from common law fraud. Further, clearest and most indisputable evidence may mean no more than the standard of proof which the court will require before rectifying a written instrument. This is, at any rate, how the passage was interpreted by Brightman J in *Ottaway* v *Norman* [1972] Ch 698 (see Chapter 11).

10.2.1.3 *How 'fraud enforcement' might work*

The fraud basis of enforcement could operate in one of two ways. Either equity imposes upon the conscience of the secret trustee, B, and forces him to hold the property received under the will on constructive trust for the secret beneficiary, C, or alternatively secret trusts are express trusts to which the Wills Act 1837 does not apply, because equity will not allow a statute intended to prevent fraud to be used as a cloak for fraud (see the equitable maxims in chapter 1). The question whether secret or half-secret trusts are express or constructive is considered shortly.

10.2.2 **Why no resulting trust?**

The principles enunciated in *McCormick* v *Grogan* (1869) LR 4 HL 82 beg an important question. If the only basis of the doctrine is to prevent B from fraudulently keeping the property for himself, why is it necessary to enforce the trust in C's favour? If the defeat of the intended trustee's (B's) fraudulent profit is all that was desired, surely it should be sufficient merely to compel him to hold the property on a resulting trust for the testator's estate? This solution would deprive B of his personal gain and the policy of the Wills Act 1837 would appear to be effected. Why should equity further disregard the requirements of the Wills Act 1837 to the extent of giving effect to the testator's oral instruction that the property should go to someone not named in the will?

Clearly, however, the House of Lords in *McCormick* v *Grogan* would have been prepared to enforce a secret trust on its terms (although on the facts no trust was held to have been created). Indeed, even long before *McCormick* v *Grogan* it was clear that the courts did not favour the resulting trust solution and that equity would enforce the trust in favour of C. There are in fact three answers to the resulting trust argument.

10.2.2.1 *The residuary legatee argument*

A historical reason why a resulting trust would not have provided a satisfactory solution is that, prior to the Executors Act of 1830, an executor was entitled to take as residuary legatee all property not specifically disposed of in the will. If, as might well happen, the intended trustee (B) was also the executor, a resulting trust would merely have the effect of granting him indirectly what the court refused to allow him to take directly.

An early example is *Thynn* v *Thynn* (1684) 1 Vern 296. The testator (A) had made his wife sole executrix. The son (B) persuaded the wife to make him sole executor instead, upon a completely fraudulent pretext. The Lord Keeper held that the property must be held in trust for the wife (C). If the court had not enforced the trust but allowed the property to result to the estate, the fraudulent son B (as executor) would himself have benefited from that as residuary legatee and indeed would have taken beneficially. Clearly, therefore, this solution would have been inappropriate and the only way to prevent personal fraud was to enforce the secret trust.

McCormick *v* Grogan *and the significance of the Executors Act 1830*

By the time *McCormick* v *Grogan* was decided, the Executors Act 1830 had altered the rule. Nowadays, the effect of a resulting trust in favour of the testator's estate will be to pass the property to the person named as residuary legatee, or if there is none, to those persons (usually close relatives of the testator) who are entitled to take in the event of his total or partial intestacy.

Hence, were the same facts to have arisen as in *Thynn* v *Thynn* today, B may not have personally benefited in the same way from a resulting trust. Yet *McCormick* v *Grogan* applied the same principles to a case under the Wills Act 1837. This appears to go further than necessary and to defeat the intention behind the Act. There can still be similar problems today, as in *Re Rees* [1950] Ch 204, where the intended trustee, B (the solicitor who had drafted the will), was also the *named* residuary legatee. Where B is named as residuary legatee the arguments advanced in *Thynn* v *Thynn* retain their full force. Any argument favouring a resulting trust must at any rate make an exception to cover this situation, therefore.

10.2.2.2 *The policy argument*

It is also possible to justify enforcing the secret trust on policy grounds. A common reason for setting up a secret trust is the desire to benefit someone whose existence the testator would prefer to keep hidden from his family, such as a mistress or, as in *McCormick* v *Grogan*, an illegitimate child. A resulting trust in favour of the estate would divert the property to the very last people whom the testator wished to benefit (his legitimate family).

But for the court to give weight to this sort of consideration involves accepting that the testator's wishes are of sufficient importance to justify ignoring the clear terms of a statute in order to enforce the trust. The policy argument alone cannot justify enforcement, as opposed to a resulting trust, although if there are other justifications as well, it is a significant additional factor.

10.2.2.3 *The nature of the fraud*

More importantly, however, we must examine the nature of the fraud upon which the doctrine is based. Just because Lord Westbury insisted on an element of intention to deceive, it does not follow that the nature of that deceit rests only in the personal gain of B.

Hodge [1980] Conv 341 has a different explanation. It should be remembered that the gift to B depended in the first place on B's promise to carry out the wishes of the testator. Hodge argues that the nature of B's fraud lies not simply in keeping the property personally, but in the fact that it was the promise to carry out the testator's wishes *in their exact terms* which induced him to leave his property to the intended trustee. It is the intended trustee's (B's) failure to do this which makes the fraud, not the element of greed.

B's fraud then, in equity, lies in the defeat of the testator's wishes, not necessarily in his own personal gain. He would be just as fraudulent with regard to the testator's confidence if he gave the property to a charity as he would be if he kept it for himself. And the testator would be no less defrauded if the intended trustee were (say) to hand over the gift intended for the testator's mistress to his innocent and long-suffering wife. A deception practised out of high moral principle is still deceit.

Therefore, nothing less than the enforcement of the testator's wishes will suffice to avert a fraud in this situation.

McGormick v Grogan: *the consequences if the circumstances had suggested fraud*

On this argument, had the facts in *McCormick v Grogan* suggested fraud, it could only have been resolved by the enforcement of the trust in C's favour: a resulting trust would not have sufficed.

This line of reasoning is not universally accepted, but is clearly the basis on which at any rate *Blackwell v Blackwell* [1929] AC 318 was decided in the House of Lords (see further below). A similar statement can be found in Lord Sterndale's judgment in *Re Gardner* [1920] 2 Ch 523 (at p. 529): 'The breach of trust or the fraud would arise when [the secret trustee] attempted to deal with the money contrary to the terms on which he took it.' It is not necessary for him to attempt to keep it beneficially, and indeed, in *Re Gardner* itself, he had no intention of so doing.

10.2.3 **Developments since** *McCormick* v *Grogan*

Lord Westbury's requirement in *McCormick* v *Grogan* was for a *malus animus* to be proved by clearest and most indisputable evidence. This seems to suggest that a deliberate intention to deceive must be shown on the legatee's part (for example, where he had deliberately induced the testator to leave the property to him in the will on the clear representation that he would hold it in trust for the secret beneficiary). It also appears that the standard of proof is as in common law fraud: in other words, a very high standard indeed is required.

There is limited authority that since *McCormick* v *Grogan* (1869) LR 4 HL 82, their Lordships' stringent requirements concerning *malus animus* have been relaxed. Before considering the law itself, however, which is not yet clear, it is useful to consider why Lord Westbury was so concerned to limit the doctrine as he did, and what has altered since 1869.

McCormick v *Grogan* concerned an attempt to make a secret gift in favour of an illegitimate child. Secret trusts were also frequently used, however, in providing for charity. Testamentary gifts of land in favour of charities were, at that time, void. The practice therefore grew up whereby A left property to B, who was a trusted friend, on the understanding that he would later give the property to the charity (C).

It must be appreciated that it was not the intended beneficiary (C) in these cases who brought the action. Rather, it was A's family who attempted to show that the secret trust was enforceable. This can be seen from *Wallgrave v Tebbs* (1855) 2 K & J 313, where the secret trust failed, for reasons discussed in the next section.

The reason for this extraordinary state of affairs was this. If the secret trust was unenforceable, B took the property beneficially, and he could be relied upon, as a friend of the testator, to carry out A's wishes. If, however, it was enforceable, then by virtue of the Statutes of Mortmain, it was void. Thus, there would be a resulting trust to the estate (i.e. A's family)! This accounts for the surprising circumstance that it was the very last people who might at first sight be expected to benefit from the secret trust being enforceable who argued that it was. On the other hand, it was in the interests of the charity for it not to be enforceable, because the charity could rely on B carrying out A's wishes.

10.2.3.1 McGormick *v* Grogan: *its strict limitations*

It is likely that the House of Lords in *McCormick* v *Grogan* did not wish to allow gifts to charities to be defeated in this way. On the other hand, if B had procured a bequest dishonestly, they did not wish to see a mistress or illegitimate child deprived of his or her rightful interest because of the provisions of the Wills Act 1837. In the first case B was far from being fraudulent—indeed, he only wished to carry out the trust. In the second case, he was. Hence, the stringent limits placed on the doctrine in that case.

The position changed in 1891, and the last vestiges of the Mortmain legislation disappeared in 1960. Only the second type of secret trust remains today, therefore. Arguably, their Lordships' limits to the doctrine are no longer appropriate. Their status is, of course, *obiter dicta*, albeit from the House of Lords, because in the event C lost on other grounds, and there is some authority that the limitations will no longer be stringently applied.

10.2.3.2 *Equitable fraud and 'other' fraud*

For example, although it seems that the basis of enforcement is still based on fraud, in so far that equity will not allow a statute intended to prevent fraud to be used to perpetrate fraud, it is possible that fraud in equity is nowadays a wider concept than it was in 1869. Today, there is some authority that it bears little relation to the common law or criminal law concept of the same name. It imposes on B's conscience, but may not necessarily demand the same degree of *mens rea* as fraud in the common law or criminal sense. Because of this, it may also demand a lower standard of proof.

Lord Westbury's remarks were not essential to the decision in *McCormick* v *Grogan*, and indeed, seem not to have been adopted in later cases. For example, in the later House of Lords authority, *Blackwell* v *Blackwell* [1929], Lord Buckmaster thought that all that was required to show a fraud was:

(a) the intention of the testator to subject the intended trustee to an obligation in favour of the intended beneficiary;

(b) communication of that intention to the intended trustee; and

(c) the acceptance of that obligation by the intended trustee, either expressly or by acquiescence.

Blackwell v *Blackwell* concerned a half-secret trust, but it is clear that the reasoning was intended to apply equally to fully secret trusts.

10.2.3.3 Ottaway *v* Norman

In *Ottaway* v *Norman* [1972] Ch 698, Brightman J enforced an oral secret trust of land without any suggestion that the intended trustee (B) had procured her prior life interest by deceit. Miss Hodges's (B's) employer, Mr Ottaway (A), left her his bungalow in his will, on terms that she would leave it by her own will to Mr Ottaway's son (C). Brightman J was prepared to enforce that agreement by imposing what he described as a constructive trust upon the bungalow in the hands of Miss Hodges's executor (she having later changed her mind and left her property to a cousin).

At the time of the arrangement between Miss Hodges (B) and the testator Ottaway (A), she clearly intended to carry out her promise to leave the land to

Ottaway's son (C) in her own will. Although she later changed her mind, there was no evidence that she had procured the bequest by deceit: certainly, the evidence was insufficient to surmount the stringent standard of proof required for common law fraud. Her failure in the event to carry out her promise is clearly a fraud in the sense that it defeats the intention of the testator, but no question of *malus animus* arose. Far from requiring fraud in the sense required by Lord Westbury, Brightman J held that enforcement of a secret trust in C's favour depended only on those criteria derived from *Blackwell* v *Blackwell* [1929]. Brightman J also thought that it was immaterial whether these elements precede or succeed the will. This seems correct in principle: if acceptance of an obligation by B persuades A not to revoke an existing will in B's favour, for B to break this obligation is quite as clearly a fraud on A, as it would have been had A been persuaded by B's acceptance of the obligation to make a will in his favour.

Nor did Brightman J see any reason to depart from the ordinary civil standard of proof, i.e. balance of probabilities.

Blackwell v Blackwell *and the imposition of a constructive trust*
Brightman J called the trust which he imposed upon the legatee of the (by then deceased) trustee a 'constructive' trust. This is a description of the mechanism by which secret trusts are enforced, not the basis of their enforcement. The constructive trust is simply a device of equity to protect beneficiaries where trust property has found its way into the hands of someone who, even if personally innocent, cannot assert a better right to that property.

The fact that the trust (of land) was oral was not a bar to its enforcement, despite the Law of Property Act 1925, s. 53(1)(b), because the executor was held to be a constructive trustee of the bungalow. Whether or not this analysis was correct, in principle a fully secret trust of land should be enforceable despite the absence of writing, either on the assumption that such trusts are to be regarded as constructive since they are imposed on the ground of conscience or because equity will not allow a statute intended to prevent fraud to be used as a cloak for fraud.

So much for the trust of land in *Ottaway* v *Norman*. According to the evidence given by the son and his wife, Miss Hodges also undertook to leave them the furniture and other contents, including her money. Brightman J accepted that the secret trust comprised such furnishings and fixtures as Miss Hodges had received under Mr Ottaway's will, but not that it included all Miss Hodges's other property and cash from whatever source.

In respect of the last, it seems that he was not convinced that so far-reaching an obligation had in fact been envisaged in the agreement, but if the intended trustee (B) had clearly accepted such an obligation, it would appear, on analogy with mutual wills (on which, see chapter 11), that this obligation also could be enforced against her estate.

What is the status of the Ottoway trust?
This raises the issue of the status of the trust during Miss Hodges's lifetime. In *Ottaway* v *Norman*, Brightman J employed the concept of a 'floating trust', derived from the Australian case of *Birmingham* v *Renfrew* (1937) 57 CLR 666, which would remain in suspense during the life of the trustee and crystallise on her death, attaching to whatever property was comprised within her estate. This, as the learned judge noted, would seem to preclude Miss Hodges from making even a

small pecuniary legacy in favour of her relatives or friends. This reasoning is similar to that of Nourse J in *Re Cleaver* [1981] 1 WLR 939 in the context of mutual wills.

10.2.3.4 Re Snowden

Sir Robert Megarry V-C partially dissented from Brightman J's view in *Re Snowden* [1979] Ch 528. He thought that a higher standard of proof was required where fraud (which he seemed to view in the narrower Lord Westbury sense) had to be proved, as was necessary for some, but not all, secret trusts. In other words, in his view, there are two classes of secret trusts, some of which require a more stringent burden of proof than others. Unfortunately, he did not go on to elaborate on the distinction, which appears to have been a desperate attempt to reconcile Brightman J's views with the apparently irreconcilable views of Lord Westbury, but perhaps he had in mind that if the only way that a would-be beneficiary can assert the existence of a trust in his favour is to allege facts which necessarily impute fraud to the alleged trustee, then the higher standard of proof applies. If the three elements listed earlier can be shown without proof of fraud, however, presumably he may succeed on the ordinary civil standard of balance of probabilities.

In the event, it was not necessary for Sir Robert Megarry V-C to elaborate, because there was really no evidence at all on which a secret trust could be established. His views are therefore *obiter*. In any case, if the criteria in *Blackwell* v *Blackwell* and *Ottaway* v *Norman* are sufficient, it is difficult to see why it is ever necessary to allege fraud in the Westbury sense, in which case the higher standard ought never to be required. If, on the other hand, Lord Westbury is correct, it is difficult to see why the higher standard is not always required.

10.3 **Limitations on enforcement of secret trusts**

The limitations on the enforcement of half-secret trusts are mainly concerned with the time of communication of the terms of the trust. It appears to be necessary for the existence of the secret trust to be communicated to the trustee before the death of the testator, and there is some authority that the terms also have to be communicated before the testator's *death*. Whether or not these communications precede or succeed the date of the *will* is irrelevant to the enforcement of a fully secret trust (although it is probably different in the case of half-secret trusts). The authorities are *Wallgrave* v *Tebbs* (1855) 2 K & J 313 and *Re Boyes* (1884) 26 Ch D 531.

10.3.1 *Wallgrave* v *Tebbs*

Whether the stringent limitations of *McCormick* v *Grogan* (1869) LR 4 HL 82 still apply, or whether the law was correctly stated by Brightman J in *Ottaway* v *Norman* [1972] Ch 698, it is clear that once B has received a gift absolutely, any subsequently imposed obligations cannot deprive him of that gift. Apart from the principle that gifts are irrevocable, there is no reason, in such a case, to impose on B's conscience.

Thus, in *Wallgrave* v *Tebbs* (1855) 2 K & J 313, the existence of the secret trust, in favour of a charity, was not communicated to B until after A's death. B was entitled to the property absolutely. The testator had left property to close friends (B) without informing them in his lifetime that he wished the land to be used for a religious charitable purpose (i.e. in favour of C). The court held that the friends (B) were entitled to the property beneficially—a decision which, surprisingly enough, was most likely to give effect to the wishes of the testator, since if a secret trust had been found to exist it would have been void under the (now repealed) Statutes of Mortmain.

As it was, the friends were free to carry out the testator's wishes. If, as the testator's relatives had argued, a secret trust had been created, they would have had to hold the property on resulting trust *for those relatives*, the purpose of the trust being unlawful. Hence the surprising situation that the very last people who might be expected to argue for a secret trust (the relatives) did so in that case, and in other cases to which the Statutes of Mortmain applied.

The case is authority for the proposition that for a fully secret trust to be enforced, the intended trustee must be told of the existence of the trust before the testator's death. There is no particular difficulty in justifying the decision in *Wallgrave* v *Tebbs*, since if the intended trustee knew nothing about the trust until after the testator's death, there could have been no fraud in the procuring of the bequest, and thus no reason for the court to compel the intended trustee to do anything in particular with what is now his own property.

Another justification is that any other decision would have permitted the testator (A) to derogate from his grant. A bequest ought not to be 'snatched back' after it has been made, any more than a birthday present could be later reclaimed.

10.3.2 *Re Boyes*

A more difficult case is *Re Boyes* (1884) 26 Ch D 531. Here, the intended trustee (B) was told of the existence of the trust before the testator's death, but was not told its terms until after the death of the testator.

A legacy was given to the testator's solicitor, who was told, before the testator's death, that he was to hold the residuary estate upon trust. However, he was not told its terms until a letter was found, after the death of the testator, which directed him to hold the residuary estate on behalf of a lady who was not the testator's wife. The solicitor wished to carry out the testator's wishes, but the validity of the trust was challenged by the testator's family. Kay J held that the solicitor held the property as trustee, but on resulting trust for the testator's estate.

If *Re Boyes* is correct, then not only the existence, but also the terms of a fully secret trust must be communicated to the trustee before the death of the testator. Kay J said (at p. 536):

If the trust was not declared when the will was made [i.e. fully secret trust], it is essential in order to make it binding, that it should be communicated to the devisee or legatee in the testator's lifetime and that he should accept that particular trust.

This is a difficult case to fit into the general scheme of things, and the result was arguably a fraud on the testator, because A obviously did not intend the property to go to his estate, but it is clear from Kay J's judgment that his understanding of the basis of enforcement was substantially that outlined in the previous sections:

The essence of [the early cases on secret trusts] is that the devisee or legatee accepts a particular trust which thereupon becomes binding upon him, and which it would be a fraud in him not to carry into effect.

10.3.2.1 *Fraud and the knowledge of the intended trustee*

There is nothing in the fraud basis of enforcement, however, which would require that an intended trustee must know the terms of the trust *by the time the will is executed*. There is no real difference between making a bequest on the strength of the intended trustee's promise, and leaving that bequest unrevoked on the strength of his later assurance. So, there is no reason to refuse to enforce the trust where the intended trustee becomes aware of its terms only after the execution of the will. All that is necessary is that he should be aware of them, or where they are to be found, before the bequest takes effect, i.e. *upon the testator's death*.

Further, in *Re Boyes* the intended trustee (B) was willing to carry out those terms. It seems that the case must be explained as one in which the scope of any possible fraud was limited to denying the existence of the trust. The intended trustee could hardly be said to have procured the bequest by a promise to adhere to its terms since he did not know them. All he knew was that the testator wished him to take the property in the capacity of trustee and not beneficially, so by compelling him to hold as trustee the court had done all it needed to in order to make him comply with the terms on which the bequest had been granted.

There may also be sound policy considerations for not enforcing a trust on its terms in a *Re Boyes* situation, sufficient to outweigh that of enforcement of the trust in C's favour. In particular, to enforce the trust would sanction indecision by A, which is arguably bad policy, since to allow a testator to establish a trust whose terms he may change from moment to moment is to permit the very luxury of indecision which the Wills Act 1837 sought to circumscribe. Furthermore, the court has to set a limit on the time for which trustees are required to hold property without knowing who the objects are, and it is a reasonable solution to insist that they know from the outset (although this may be not until the estate has been administered, i.e. later than death, so arguably this rather than death should be the deadline).

10.3.2.2 *Is* Re Boyes *correct?*

Another possibility is that the case is simply wrong: after all, it is a High Court case only, which has not been followed. It is suggested that *Re Boyes is* correct, however, and is explicable on one or both of the bases outlined above.

It is enough, incidentally, for the intended trustee (B) to be aware of where the terms of the trust could be found (for example, if the terms of the trust are to be placed in a sealed letter to be opened only after the testator's death). Then it could be said that he accepted those terms and was bound by them. In this situation, he would hold the property on the terms of the secret trust (*Re Keen* [1937] Ch 236, 242). Further, although B is not informed of them until after A's death (as in *Re Boyes*), the policy reasons discussed above against enforcing the secret trust in C's favour do not apply. A is not being indecisive and B is not being asked to hold property for any length of time as trustee without knowing the identity of the objects of the trust.

10.4 **Half-secret trusts**

Half-secret trusts are also valid in principle and, like secret trusts, can be enforced by the intended beneficiary. The leading House of Lords authority is *Blackwell* v *Blackwell* [1929]. The justification for enforcement of half-secret trusts is exactly the same as that for fully secret trusts: that equity imposes upon the conscience of the secret trustee for the prevention of fraud. This is clear from the speech of Viscount Sumner in *Blackwell* v *Blackwell* (at pp. 335–336):

> For the prevention of fraud equity fastens on the conscience of the legatee a trust, a trust, that is, which otherwise would be inoperative; in other words it makes him do what the will in itself has nothing to do with; it lets him take what the will gives him and then makes him apply it, as the court of conscience directs, and it does so in order to give effect to wishes of the testator, which would not otherwise be effectual.

From the quotation three propositions can be gleaned. First, the reason equity fastens on the conscience of the legatee is for the prevention of fraud. Second, the effect of the trust is to make the legatee 'do what the will in itself has nothing to do with'; in other words, the trust operates independently of the will. Third, in order to prevent fraud, equity directs the legatee to give effect to wishes of the testator. This point is of some importance. The fraud whose commission is being prevented is not the taking of the property beneficially by the legatee, but having taken it, not giving effect to the wishes of the testator.

The facts of *Blackwell* v *Blackwell* were that, by a codicil to his will, a testator transferred £12,000 to five trustees, to apply the income 'for the purposes indicated by me to them', with power to pay over the capital sum of £8,000 'to such person or persons indicated by me to them'. He had given detailed oral instructions on the codicil to one of the trustees, and all five knew the general object of the codicil before its execution. The trustees accordingly proposed to pay the income to a lady who was not the testator's wife. The testator's legitimate family challenged the validity of the half-secret trust. The House of Lords held that the half-secret trust was valid.

10.4.1 **Fraud theory**

It is sometimes argued that the fraud theory ought to draw a distinction between fully and half-secret trusts, on the ground that there is no possibility of an intended trustee of a half-secret trust claiming the property for himself since the fact of the trust is plain from the will. All that is needed to avert fraud, therefore, is to compel him to hold on resulting trust for the testator's estate.

Some writers have argued that fraud cannot be the justification because B cannot in any event take beneficially himself, whereas he could if fully secret trusts were not enforced. This is because half-secret trusts differ from the fully secret variety in that the will makes it clear that B takes as trustee only. So, if half-secret trusts are not enforced, B holds the property, not beneficially, but on resulting trust for the residuary legatee. Therefore, there is no possibility of personal gain by B (unless, of course, B is also residuary legatee).

It is no answer to say that a resulting trust would be a fraud on C, the intended beneficiary. As an argument in favour of enforcement, the reasoning is circular, because if a half-secret trust is not enforceable there is no beneficiary to make the argument work. C is only a beneficiary if the conclusion has already been reached that half-secret trusts are to be enforced.

The answer to the resulting trust argument, however, is exactly the same as that for fully secret trusts. The resulting trust is a fraud on the testator (A), and the property has only been given to B because of an express or implied promise, made by B to A. This is clear from the facts of *Blackwell v Blackwell* itself. A intended to benefit his mistress and illegitimate son. A resulting trust would have given the property to his wife and legitimate child—indeed, it was they who argued for a resulting trust. Clearly, A did not intend that they should benefit. He would not have settled the property on B had he thought that the result would be a gift in favour of his wife and legitimate child. B's acceptance of the property would have been a fraud on A unless the trust was enforced in favour of C. The justification for the enforcement of half-secret trusts, therefore, is exactly the same as that for fully secret trusts.

It is in any case clear from Viscount Sumner's speech that the basis of the enforcement of half-secret trusts is fraud, and that the fraud lies not in the personal gain of the intended trustee (B) but in not giving effect to the promise made to the deceased testator.

The case also contains statements to the effect that the law does not distinguish between enforcement of fully and half-secret trusts.

10.5 **Limitations on enforcement of half-secret trusts**

10.5.1 *Re Keen*

It appears, however, that half-secret trusts differ from their fully secret cousins in one respect. It is necessary for their enforcement for B to have accepted the obligation before the will is made. This distinction is difficult to justify in principle because a will is a revocable instrument having no legal status until death. And if it is argued that the contrary result allows the testator to alter the identity of the beneficiaries every day, at any time up to his death, then why not have the same rule for fully secret trusts?

Nevertheless, there are *dicta* which appear to support the distinction in *Blackwell v Blackwell* itself, where Viscount Sumner observed (at p. 339):

A testator cannot reserve to himself a power of making future unattested dispositions by merely naming a trustee and leaving the purposes of the trust to be supplied afterwards, nor can a legatee given testamentary validity to an unexecuted codicil by accepting an indefinite trust, never communicated to him in the testator's lifetime...

10.5.1.1 *What does the dicta in* Re Blackwell *stand for?*

It is possible that Viscount Sumner meant no more here than to restate the general principle that there must be acceptance by the secret or half-secret trustee and that such acceptance must take place within the lifetime of the testator, but this passage clearly can be taken to support the distinction made in the previous paragraph. *Blackwell* v *Blackwell* was used as authority for that distinction in *Re Keen* [1937] Ch 236. It is arguable that the time of communication was not the true basis of the decision in *Re Keen*, since the alleged communication did not in any way match the description given in the will, but the rule derived from *Re Keen* has since been applied in *Re Bateman's WT* [1970] 1 WLR 1463.

In *Re Keen*, a clause in the testator's will gave £10,000 on trust to two persons, who were directed to dispose of it 'as may be notified by me to them or either of them during my lifetime'. In fact, some months prior to the will, the testator had given one of the two trustees a sealed envelope containing a sheet of paper on which he had written the name and address of the proposed secret beneficiary (a lady to whom the testator was not married).

The Court of Appeal held that no valid half-secret trust had been created, and the £10,000 fell into residue. One reason was that, simply as a matter of construction, the clause in the testator's will referred to a *future* direction, whereas the direction had by then *already* been communicated to one of the two trustees. Therefore, the express terms of the will were inconsistent with the terms of the trust being contained in the sealed envelope. Had that been the only ground for the decision, the case would have created no difficulties, and the position for half-secret trusts would have been identical to that for fully secret trusts.

10.5.1.2 Re Keen *and the timing of the finalisation of the trust*

Lord Wright MR also said, however, that the testator, having declared the existence of the trust in the will, should not be able to reserve to himself the power of making future dispositions without a duly attested codicil simply by notifying them during his lifetime. If that is correct, it follows that the terms of a half-secret trust must be finalised by the date of the will. In *Re Bateman's WT*, the trustees were directed by a clause in the will to pay the income from the testator's estate 'to such persons and in such proportions as shall be stated by me in a sealed letter in my own handwriting and addressed to my trustees'. As in *Keen*, this refers to a *future* direction, but unlike *Keen*, the trustees in *Bateman* received their instructions by means of a sealed letter after the will, but before the death of the testator. Therefore, the express terms of the will were not inconsistent with the timing of the communication.

Nevertheless, the Court of Appeal held that the direction to the trustees was invalid. The only possible explanation for the case, and indeed the one actually adopted by Pennycuick V-C, was that as a general principle, a half-secret trust is enforceable only where its terms are known at the date of the will.

The distinction drawn in *Keen* and *Bateman* has not been adopted in the Republic of Ireland: *Re Prendiville (dec'd)*, Irish High Court, 5 December 1990, noted [1992] Conv 202, where the alternative view of the *Blackwell dictum*, above, was adopted.

10.5.2 **Justifications for *Re Keen***

10.5.2.1 *Analogy with incorporation by reference*

A possible explanation is that there is a second principle at work in addition to the fraud principle already discussed. This is that where reference is made in a will to a document, that document must already be in existence, otherwise the possibility exists of testators creating unattested codicils. It may be that of the two principles, the latter prevails where there is conflict.

With fully secret trusts, the question does not arise because the will is silent. It only applies to half-secret trusts because the existence of a half-secret (but not fully secret) trust is openly declared in a formal testamentary bequest. The argument proceeds that the testator having availed himself of this luxury, later additions or changes to the statement that the property is to be held on trust must also be made in a properly attested will or codicil. Therefore, if the testator chooses to declare the terms of his trust later than the date of executing his will, he is committed to using the correct formalities. Thus the distinction between half and fully secret trusts is justified.

This argument has a superficial attraction, taking account as it does of the fact that the problem of adequate proof is one which bedevils the whole area of secret trusts. If a testator has blandly asserted that property is to be held on trust, it is obviously vital to ensure that any other statements he may have made regarding the precise terms of that trust are indeed referable to that particular trust and no other. B. Perrins [1985] Conv 248 explains the timidity of the courts in accepting evidence which post-dates the will.

In this, they appear to have been influenced by the probate doctrine of incorporation by reference. This, in brief, permits the incorporation into the will of any document which was in existence at the time the will was executed, and was referred to as such in the will itself. It is a useful doctrine in that it saves the bother of copying out lengthy trust documents in the will itself merely for the purpose of adding a fresh sum to those trusts by way of bequest. The testator can instead simply refer to those documents and rely on a short declaration that the bequest is to be held on the terms set out in those documents. He cannot, however, incorporate a document which is not yet in existence at the time of making the will: to allow this would be to tempt fraudulent claims that this or that document was the one to which the testator meant to refer.

Policy for the limitations upon half-secret trusts
It is therefore easy to see why the courts, conscious of the wisdom of these limits to the doctrine of incorporation by reference, may have thought it prudent to import those limits into the enforcement of half-secret trusts. But as a principled justification for the communication rules, the explanation has defects.

For example, it is not necessary to the enforcement of a half-secret trust that any document at all should exist to declare the terms of the trust. So long as he communicates the terms before signing his will, the testator is free to rely on a purely oral communication, which must be even more susceptible to later misrepresentation than a document. If the courts are prepared to accept the existence of fully secret trusts on quite slender evidence, for example *Ottaway* v *Norman*, it would be odd if they refused to accept oral evidence to show the terms of a half-secret trust, where the chance of fraud is, if anything, less.

In any case, to argue that the testator, having once committed himself to formality, remains bound by the need for further formality if he wishes to expound the terms of his trust later than the date of making his will is merely to penalise him for partial compliance with the Wills Act 1837, while allowing the testator who ignores that Act entirely (by creating a fully secret trust) to have his wishes enforced. This seems to fall short of being a rational justification therefore.

10.5.2.2 *Policy against indecision*

Another, related argument which was stated in *Blackwell* v *Blackwell*, and repeated in *Re Keen*, is that to permit a testator simply to state the existence of a trust and communicate its terms at his leisure would be to permit a will to be freely altered by unattested dispositions, thus defeating the policy of the Wills Act 1837.

Thus, for example, Watkin [1981] Conv 335 argues for the *Bateman* position on policy grounds, namely that whereas the law should not and does not object to secrecy, it should not encourage indecision. A testator should have made up his mind by the time the will is made.

The argument reflects a respect for the policy of the Wills Act 1837, and the logic of this reasoning (if correct) applies to fully secret trusts also. Indeed, Watkin argues that they should be brought into line by statute. This, it is argued, would allow the testator who has made up his mind where he wants his property to go, but wishes its destination to be secret, to fulfil his desires by making his communication prior to the will, while defeating the testator who is merely indecisive and wants the luxury of changing his will without the trouble and expense of making fresh testamentary provisions. As Watkin acknowledges, however, the practice of permitting indecisive behaviour via a fully secret trust is so firmly entrenched that a statute would be required to effect the change.

10.5.3 **Codicils**

It has been seen that half-secret trusts must be communicated prior to, or contemporaneously with, the execution of the will. Suppose that the trusts are communicated after the date of the will but before a later codicil. This raises the question of the effect of the codicil. Another issue is whether additional property can be added to an existing secret or half-secret trust by codicil.

In *Blackwell* v *Blackwell* [1929] itself, the gift which was subject to the half-secret trust was contained in a codicil, but in that case the gift was created for the first time by the codicil and the trustees had been duly informed in advance. Suppose, however, that the half-secret trust is originally created earlier, in the will, and the intended trustee (B) has not been informed in advance. There is no direct authority whether the later reference to that trust in the codicil will suffice first to create the trust contained in the will and second to add extra property to this trust.

In favour of allowing the trust, it can be argued that the policy of the *Re Keen* rule ([1937] Ch 236) is merely to ensure that the trust is communicated prior to some properly executed testamentary disposition which indicates its terms, and that therefore the mention of the trust in the codicil should be good enough. A codicil has the effect of republishing a will; in other words it is as though the will itself had been made at the date of the later codicil.

The position is different where additional property is added by the codicil, since the trustees may not have accepted any obligations regarding the additional property. In *Re Colin Cooper* [1939] Ch 811, a testator had left £5,000 to trustees on half-secret trust in his will, having duly informed them in advance and obtained their agreement, and later added a further £10,000 to this trust in a codicil. The Court of Appeal held that only the first amount mentioned in the will could be subject to the half-secret trust, and that the amount added by the codicil fell into residue. In *Re Colin Cooper*, the trustees had agreed to hold £5,000, and that was the limit of their obligation, since they never knew of the further obligation imposed in the codicil. As Sir Wilfred Greene MR said (at p. 818):

it was not with regard to any sum other than the £5,000 that the consciences of the trustees (to use a technical phrase) were burdened.

He seemed to envisage, however, that if the agreement had been that the trustees would hold £5,000 or whatever sum the testator finally chose to bequeath, it would have been enforceable on those terms. This also accords with the view taken by the courts that a sealed envelope may be sufficient communication, despite the fact that the terms are, *ex hypothesi*, unknown to the trustee, who assents to carry them out whatever they might turn out to be.

10.6 Secret and half-secret trusts take effect independently of the will

It is also clear from *Blackwell* v *Blackwell* that secret and half-secret trusts operate independently of the will. It is possible that they operate as express trusts created *inter vivos* by the agreement reached between the testator and the intended trustee, the function or relevance of the will being to vest the property in the intended trustee at the agreed time for the assumption of his office. From the passage in Viscount Sumner's speech, however, to which allusion has already been made (at 10.4), it seems more likely that after the will has transferred legal title to the legatee, the court fastens on the conscience of the legatee by imposing on him a trust. This is probably best analysed as a constructive trust, imposed in order to prevent fraud.

A similar analysis was adopted by Lord Westbury in *McCormick* v *Grogan* (at p. 97):

The court of equity has, from a very early period, decided that even an Act of Parliament shall not be used as an instrument of fraud; and if in the machinery of perpetrating a fraud an Act of Parliament intervenes, the court of equity, it is true, does not set aside the Act of Parliament but it fastens on the individual who gets a title under that Act, and imposes upon him a personal obligation, because he applies the Act as an instrument for accomplishing a fraud.

Whichever analysis is correct, whether secret and half-secret trusts are express *inter vivos* trusts or constructive trusts imposed once the legatee has received the property (on which, see further shortly), the will does no more than constitute the trust, transferring the legal property to the secret trustee. It seems likely that the trust could also be constituted by intestacy, in the absence of any will, if the settlor refrains from making a will in the knowledge that the property will pass to the intended trustee by virtue of the Administration of Estates Act 1925, rather than using a more usual form of transfer for an *inter vivos* trust.

It is sometimes argued that if secret and half-secret trusts are ordinary *inter vivos* trusts, the Wills Act has no application to them. If this is so, then fraud ought not to be strictly necessary for their enforcement. The mere fact of an existing trust should be enough for equity to intervene to enforce it, irrespective of any *'malus animus'* on the part of the trustee.

Yet, while it is undoubtedly correct to say that the *mechanism* by which secret and half-secret trusts are enforced has nothing to do with the will, merely to describe the mechanism is not the same thing as providing a reason for their enforcement. The reason that equity imposes on the conscience of the legatee is fraud, and the mere fact that the mechanism operates independently of the will in no way affects that requirement.

The operation of secret and half-secret trusts independently of this will does have other consequences, however. In *Re Young* [1951] Ch 344 a half-secret trust was enforced despite the fact that the beneficiary had witnessed the will, which, under s. 15 of the Wills Act 1837, would normally have the effect of invalidating the gift to the witnessing beneficiary. Since he took outside the will, however, this rule did not apply. Danckwerts J commented:

> The whole theory of the formation of a secret trust is that the Wills Act has nothing to do with the matter..., since the persons do not take by virtue of the gift in the will, but by virtue of the secret trusts imposed upon the beneficiary, who does in fact take under the will.

In *Re Gardner (No. 2)* [1923] 2 Ch 230, a secret trust in favour of a beneficiary who had predeceased the testator was upheld. It is not possible to leave property to a dead person by will, and it is difficult to justify this decision even on the basis that the will has nothing to do with the matter. The usual analysis is that, at the very least, the will constitutes the trust by transferring legal title to the secret trustee, but Romer J saw no reason why a declaration of trust by the secret trustee should not have occurred at the moment of communication of the trust to him (at p. 233):

> The rights of the parties appear to me to be exactly the same as though the husband [secret trustee], after the memorandum had been communicated to him by the testatrix..., had executed a declaration of trust binding himself to hold any property that should come to him upon his wife's [settlor's] partial intestacy upon trust as specified in the memorandum.

If Romer J's view is correct, then the consequences are not limited to an ability to make a secret or half-secret trust in favour of a beneficiary who predeceases the testator. If the trust comes into force from the moment of communication, then it must also follow that it is irrevocable from that moment, and that neither the testator nor the secret trustee would be able later to change his mind. This would be an unfortunate consequence if the communication was made many years before the testator's death and circumstances had changed radically in the mean-time. Suppose, for example, the secret beneficiary ran off with the secret trustee's wife. Could not the secret trustee inform the testator that he was no longer pre-pared to accept the property on the original terms? Or, if he were no longer able to get in touch with the testator, could he not refuse to take the property under the will? One would have thought that, in principle, he should be able to change his mind, but if Romer J is right, and the trust is created from the moment of commu-nication, then it may well be that he cannot.

Romer J's view is in any case inconsistent with views expressed in the Court of Appeal in *Re Maddock* [1902] 2 Ch 220, to the effect that the trust only becomes binding once the legatee accepts the legacy. For example, Collins MR said (at p. 226):

But the right of the [beneficiary] is wholly dependent on whether the legatee accepts the legacy with knowledge of the mandate, and no right for them arises at all unless and until the legatee has, with notice, accepted the legacy.

Cozens-Hardy LJ took a similar view (at p. 231):

Now, the so-called trust does not affect the property except by reason of a personal obligation binding the individual devisee or legatee. If he renounces and disclaims, or dies in the lifetime of the testator, the persons claiming under the memorandum can take nothing against the heir-at-law or next-of-kin or residuary devisee or legatee.

These statements clearly imply that the trust is not constituted until the testator has died, and the legatee has accepted the trust property.

There is another difficulty with Romer J's analysis. The secret trustee must be declaring himself trustee of after-acquired property, since only on the testator's death is legal title vested in him. The conventional view is that trusts of future property are void, and the orthodox view is that *Gardner (No. 2)* is wrong.

10.7 **Express or constructive trusts: does it matter?**

It has been see that the basis of enforcement of both fully and half-secret trusts is B's fraud, defined in a wide equitable sense. Additionally, both varieties implement the express intentions of the testator, even though those intentions may not be expressed correctly, in writing, signed and attested, etc. Each takes effect outside the will. It is said that it matters whether they are classified as express or constructive trusts because the formality requirements of the Law of Property Act 1925, s. 53(1) (see chapter 5) apply to express, but not (by virtue of s. 53(2)) constructive trusts.

Section 53(1)(b) requires express trusts of land to be declared in writing, yet a fully secret trust of land was enforced in *Ottaway* v *Norman* [1972] Ch 698 despite being oral. Further, that case ostensibly rested on constructive trust principles. This is therefore apparently authority that fully secret trusts at least are constructive. Yet some writers distinguish between the two varieties, and argue that *Ottaway* v *Norman* applies only to fully secret trusts. Indeed, *Re Baillie* (1886) 2 TLR 660 suggests that writing is required for half-secret trusts of land, although perhaps not too much emphasis should be placed on cases prior to *Blackwell* v *Blackwell*, and there can be no justification for the distinction if the basis of enforcement of half and fully secret trusts is the same.

It is suggested that writing is never required for any secret trust of either variety. The mechanism appears to be that B obtains property under the will and that equity, operating outside the will, imposes on his conscience and requires him to hold as constructive trustee for C. On this basis, both fully and half-secret trusts are constructive.

It is also suggested that the issue is wholly academic and of no practical importance whatever. The classification is relevant only to the formality requirements of

s. 53. Yet the validity of half and fully secret trusts depends on a principle of equity, which is not defeated by s. 9 of the Wills Act 1837. Surely it will also not be defeated by s. 53 of the Law of Property Act 1925 or any other statutory formality provision intended to prevent fraud. If equity will not permit a statute intended to prevent fraud to be used as an instrument for fraud, there is no reason why it should distinguish between statutes for these purposes. The principle applies as much to the Law of Property Act 1925, s. 53, as to the Wills Act 1837, s. 9. This will be so however secret trusts are classified because it is not therefore necessary that they fall within the s. 53(2) exception to avoid the requirements of s. 53(1). See further on this point, Perrins [1985] Conv 248, 256–57.

Further support for the view that s. 53(1)(b) is treated in a similar fashion to the Wills Act itself can be found in *Sen* v *Headley* [1991] Ch 425.

The conclusion is, then, that whether secret and semi-secret trusts are express or constructive, they are not affected by any statute requiring formality.

 online resource centre

FURTHER READING

Kincaid 'The Tangled Web: The Relationship Between a Secret Trust and the Will' (2000) Conveyancer 420.

Meager 'Secret Trusts—do they have a future?' (2003) Conveyancer 203.

Perrins 'Secret Trusts: The Key to Dehors' (1985) Conveyancer 248.

Sheridan 'English and Irish Secret Trusts' (1951) Law Quarterly Review 314.

Watkin 'Cloaking a Convention' (1981) Conveyancer 335.

11

....

Equitable fraud and the constructive trust

This chapter is concerned primarily with constructive trusts, differentiating them from other types of trust—namely, express and implied trusts. Previous chapters have described the way in which the express trust and the implied trust will give effect to the express or implied wishes of the settler respectively, with resulting trusts also arising as a consequence (albeit in a less direct sense) of the settlor's intentions. In contrast, constructive trusts are imposed by the courts as a matter of law. They depend on principles of equity and conscience, and are independent of the settlor's intention.

11.1 Constructive trusteeship arising from representations

A number of the cases considered in sections 11.3 to 11.5 involve representations, where equity holds representors to their representation. In 11.4 and most of the cases in 11.5, the representor has either obtained the trust property on the strength of the representation, or at any rate obtained it on terms different from those upon which he or she would have obtained it had the representation not been made. Note that in none of these cases does equity require representors to return the property; the effect of the constructive trust is always to hold them to their representation.

Representations that are relied on by others, to their detriment, can give rise to estoppels as well as constructive trusts, and, as chapter 9 case studying the family home revealed, the consequences of imposing a constructive trust can be greater than the consequences of estoppels (although, recent authorities suggest that the requirements for an estoppel appear to be more stringent than was once thought). This 'consequences' approach suggests that a constructive trust will not necessarily arise in all cases of detrimental reliance. And the reality appears to be that it arises only in a few rigidly defined and discrete categories of case, and that there is no generalised equitable fraud jurisdiction.

Thereafter, in 11.6 a different type of case comes to the fore: a situation for which there is limited but growing authority. These may be (but are not necessarily) cases where the trust is imposed because of unconscionable conduct by the trustee. Here, legal title is obtained by someone who either knows from the outset that she is not entitled to the property, or who does not know from the outset but discovers later. In such situations, where a constructive trust is imposed, the legal owner appears to be required to hold the property on trust for the transferor. It appears that, in contrast to many situations considered within this chapter (where anything beyond holding those who make representations to that which has been represented would be inappropriate), such conduct (knowing that one is not entitled to property, or discovering so later)—will actually have the effect of requiring the return of the property.

In 11.7 consideration is given to whether any generalisations can be made from the categories emerging from progression through the chapter, and as to whether the courts are moving towards a principled jurisdiction based on the defendant's conduct. This will be set against an oppositional proposition that the categories are exhaustive, and that the constructive trust has no wider role in cases of misconduct.

11.2 Defining fraud: the starting point

In this chapter the focal point is fraud which can be classified as *equitable* fraud. The significance of labelling it in this manner lies in the proposition that fraud which is equitable denotes a meaning that is different from, and actually wider than, fraud at common law.

11.2.1 Common law fraud and equitable fraud compared and contrasted

The distinction and difference between common law and equitable fraud was noted in two comparatively recent decisions in *Armitage* v *Nurse* [1998] Ch 241 and *Walker* v *Stones* [2001] QB 902. The significance of *Armitage* v *Nurse* is considered immediately below, but for immediate purposes, the classic definition of fraud at common law hails from Lord Herschell in *Derry* v *Peek* (1889) 14 App Cas 337. At p. 374, Lord Herschell observed that in the context of representations:

fraud is proved when it is shown that a false representation has been made (i) knowingly, or (ii) without belief in its truth, or (iii) recklessly, careless whether it be true or false. Although I have treated the second and third as distinct cases, I think the third is but an instance of the second, for one who makes a statement under such circumstances can have no real belief in the truth of what he states.

The significance of starting with the *common law definition* in this discussion on *equitable fraud* is that in many of the cases considered within this chapter, fraud in the common law sense is not proved. Indeed, for example, in the discussion that will follow concerning *Bannister* v *Bannister*, the claimant may well have believed the representations he made, at the time when they were made, but later he changed his mind. This certainly did not amount to fraud in a common law sense, but as far as equity was concerned, a different set of considerations applied. For equity it was sufficient that the defendant had been induced to rely on the claimant's representations; that she had actually relied on them, and that it was unconscionable for him therefore to renege on his promises. In the discrete sets of circumstances considered in this chapter, equity holds people to the representations they have made, when it would be unconscionable for them to renege. A similar principle operated in *Ottaway* v *Norman* (in chapter 10), where again there was no fraud in the common law sense.

11.2.2 Beyond 'civil fraud' arising from *Derry v Peek*: explaining 'actual' and 'equitable' fraud

This very brief introduction to the significance of identifying and distinguishing fraud at common law and fraud in equity will develop into a much fuller discussion shortly. At this stage attention must be drawn to the important observations made on the interpretation of the meaning of 'fraud' in *Armitage v Nurse* [1998] Ch 241. Crucially, the judgment of Millett LJ distinguished equitable fraud from 'actual fraud'.

This arose in the context of determining the validity of a trustee exemption clause; the significance and operation of trustee exemption clauses will be considered in due course in chapter 18 as part of this text's study of trusteeship. For present purposes, it will suffice to note simply that this is a mechanism designed to protect trustees from liability which can be incurred should they commit a breach of trust. The clause in *Armitage* itself purported to exclude the trustee's ability to incur liability under the trust 'except for losses and damage which is caused by his own actual fraud'. It was in respect of this that Millett LJ explained the meaning of *actual fraud* by distinguishing it from *equitable fraud*. In determining that reference to 'actual fraud' connoted behaviour which was different from equitable fraud, Millett LJ considered that 'actual fraud' required 'proof of dishonesty', and that in this context it:

connotes at the minimum an intention on the part of the trustee to pursue a particular course of action, either knowing that it is contrary to the interests of the beneficiaries or being recklessly indifferent whether it is contrary to their interests or not.

In contrast, the species of 'equitable' fraud:

covers breach of fiduciary duty, undue influence, abuse of confidence, unconscionable bargains and frauds on powers. With the sole exception of the last, which is a technical doctrine in which the word 'fraud' merely connotes excess of views, it involves some dealing by the fiduciary with his principal at the risk that the fiduciary may have exploited his position to his own advantage.

It is with this latter equitable fraud that this chapter is concerned. In this vein, the themes which have been attributed to Millett LJ immediately above will provide the basis for much of the material which will be used in the discussions which follow.

11.3 Equity will not allow a statute to be used as a cloak for fraud

This principle was developed by the courts of equity to prevent people from taking unfair advantage of statutory formality provisions, which are of course intended to prevent rather than encourage fraud. Examples of this have already been seen, for example in fraud certainly being the basis of the part performance doctrine, which has usually been used to prevent reliance on the now-repealed s. 40 of the Law of Property Act 1925. It is probably also the principle that operates to avoid

s. 53(1)(b) of the Law of Property Act in first-category *Rosset* cases. It might be argued that secret trusts are also based on the same principle here preventing reliance on s. 9 of the Wills Act 1837, as subsequently amended. However, for reasons that appear below, this may not explain cases such as *Ottaway* v *Norman*, where the principle operating is that in the following section.

11.3.1 A principle with general application

The principle is also of more general application, applying whenever there is an attempt to use a statute intended to prevent fraud as a means of perpetrating fraud. In *Rochefoucauld* v *Boustead* [1897] 1 Ch 196, the claimant (Comtesse de la Rochefoucauld) owned some estates producing coffee in Ceylon (present-day Sri Lanka), but these properties were subject to a considerable mortgage, which the Comtesse was having difficulty in repaying. In order to stop the mortgagee from foreclosing, an arrangement was made whereby the defendant purchased the estates subject to the mortgage. The precise circumstances of this transfer were disputed, but the Court of Appeal accepted on the basis of both oral evidence and letters that the defendant took the land as trustee for the claimant.

He treated the land as if it were his own, however, and raised more money on it by way of mortgage without the claimant's consent. The claimant later asserted her equitable title, and claimed an account of profits, but the defendant claimed that he was beneficial owner of the property.

Various arguments were advanced by the defendant, all of which were rejected, but the interesting one for our purposes was that the trust claimed by the claimant was not evidenced in writing signed by the defendant, as required by the Statute of Frauds 1677, s. 7, which was the precursor of the Law of Property Act 1925, s. 53 (on which, see chapter 5). This argument was rejected on the principle that equity will not allow a statute to be used as a cloak for fraud.

11.3.2 The principle illustrated

Another case which is probably an example of the same principle, is *Hodgson* v *Marks* [1971] 1 Ch 892 which was considered in the family homes case study (chapter 9). Here, an old lady (Mrs Hodgson) was cajoled into making a voluntary conveyance (i.e. not for value) of her house to her lodger (Evans). Evans told her that the conveyance was just a device to protect him against her nephew, who disapproved of him. Evidence that the transfer to Evans was on express oral trust for Mrs Hodgson (who remained in occupation) was accepted, but there was no writing (and an oral express trust of land is void by virtue of s. 53(1)(b) of the Law of Property Act 1925). Evans then sold the property to a third party (Marks). Two issues arose: first, did Mrs Hodgson have an equitable interest in the property; and, second, did that interest bind Marks? Both issues were decided in favour of Mrs Hodgson in the Court of Appeal. The second issue is of more importance to land law than trusts, because of the application of s. 70(1)(g) of the Land Registration Act 1925. This concerns the first consideration arising from equitable fraud.

In the Court of Appeal Russell LJ, who gave the only substantive judgment, and with whom Buckley and Cairns LJJ agreed, thought that Mrs Hodgson's interest was by way of resulting trust, in which case the decision would be of no help for this discussion, since resulting trusts are expressly exempted from the operation of s. 53 (by virtue of s. 53(2)). A different explanation must, however, be found in the light of Lord Browne-Wilkinson's speech in *Westdeutsche* v *Islington LBC* [1996] AC 669 (which has been noted already in chapters 1, 2, and 7). In any case, Mrs Hodgson did not argue a resulting trust; there was evidence of an express oral trust, and this was the basis of Ungoed-Thomas J's decision in the High Court, who relied on *Rochefoucauld* v *Boustead* to avoid s. 53(1)(b). (Although Ungoed-Thomas J was reversed in the Court of Appeal, the reversal was only as to the interpretation of the Land Registration Act 1925, not on the question of the existence of a trust.)

Russell LJ seemed unsure whether the *Rochefoucauld* v *Boustead* principle could apply to Marks, the third party purchaser. This is why he preferred to base his decision on resulting trust reasoning, but he would have been happy to apply Ungoed-Thomas J's reasoning to Mr Evans, the original lodger: 'Quite plainly Mr Evans could not have placed any reliance on section 53, for that would have been to use the section as an instrument of fraud.'

11.3.2.1 *Equitable fraud: understanding its limits*

Though the doctrine can be generalised beyond secret trusts and the *Rosset* first-category cases considered earlier, it is important to appreciate its limits.

(1) The principle operates only where all the requirements for a trust (or contract) are already present, apart from writing. The part performance doctrine operates only where the contract is in all respects otherwise valid, and would be enforceable if in writing. The case study in chapter 9 provides illustration that all the elements of a trust (apart from writing) must be present in a first-category *Rosset* case. In secret trust cases, all the elements of a valid trust (apart from the formalities) are often present; where they are not (as, for example, in *Ottaway* v *Norman*, where the property was probably not taken by the legatee on trust) the principles in the next section operate.

(2) The doctrine probably applies only to formality provisions, the purpose of which is to prevent fraud.

(3) In all the cases considered, the nature of the fraud is a representation relied on by another party, where it would be unconscionable for the person making the representation to renege upon it. Fraud certainly does not appear to be generalised to include all instances of bad faith. In *Midland Bank Trust Co. Ltd* v *Green* [1981] AC 513 a very important land law case, a sham sale between husband and wife, intended specifically to defeat their son's option to purchase a farm, succeeded in its purpose, solely because the option had not been properly registered under the Land Charges Act 1925. This makes quite a contrast to the cases considered here, but the statute relied on was intended to simplify conveyancing, not to prevent fraud. Moreover, Mrs Green made no representations of any kind to her son, and Lord Wilberforce observed (at p. 531) that in general it is not 'fraud' to rely on legal rights conferred by Act of Parliament.

In the discussion in chapter 10, it was suggested that the mechanism upon which the doctrine operated, at least for secret and half-secret trusts, was the imposition of a constructive trust, and a similar explanation was adopted in chapter 9, in the later case in order to trigger s. 53(2). However, the fact that constructive trusts are not exempted from the Wills Act 1837 suggests that it would have made no difference in chapter 10 had s. 53(2) never been enacted. The mechanism by which the part performance operates may also be the constructive trust; certainly a constructive trust arises, on the principles considered earlier. It is interesting that s. 2 of the Law of Property (Miscellaneous Provisions) Act 1989, which is often said to have abolished the part performance doctrine as far as it related to land, does not apply (by virtue of s. 2(5)) to the creation or operation of resulting, implied or constructive trusts. This strengthens the argument advanced in chapter 10—i.e. to the extent that part performance is a fraud-based doctrine, it survives the enactment of the 1989 Act.

However, it is not clear beyond doubt that the mechanism is always the imposition of a constructive trust; it could, as previously observed, simply be an interpretation of a statute which was intended to prevent fraud—it cannot be used to promote fraud. For similar reasoning to that advanced in chapter 10, it probably does not matter whether the mechanism is one of constructive trust or not, unless it were intended to use these cases to advance a more general principle connecting fraud with constructive trusts.

11.4 Obtaining legal title expressly subject to rights of another

There is now a clear line of authority that where somebody obtains legal title to property by agreeing to take it expressly subject to the rights of another party, equity will require him to hold the property as constructive trustee, to give effect to the rights of the other party.

As in the previous section, equity holds the representor to his representation, where it would be unconscionable to allow the representor to renege. There the unconscionable element was reliance upon a statute the purpose of which was to prevent fraud; here it is the use of the representation to obtain property. It is also an alternative explanation of the secret trusts cases considered in chapter 10.

This development is not particularly startling, and can again be seen as a generalisation of the secret trusts doctrine. It is also not that dissimilar to ordinary express trusteeship, since trustees ordinarily accept legal title subject to the terms of the trust, except of course that in these cases formality provisions are avoided. In so far as these cases cause problems, it is because the trusts which thereby arise are full property interests capable of binding third parties. The problems of life tenancies are considered in chapter 1. Conveyancing problems might also arise where a bare trust is created, since this would not require registration under the Land Charges Act 1972 and, since the beneficiary would often be in occupation, could be an overriding interest under s. 70(1)(g) of the Land Registration Act 1925. That would seem to be an argument for amending the conveyancing provisions, however, rather than curtailing the development of the equitable doctrine.

11.4.1 Fraud and conscionability: case law illustrations

In *Bannister* v *Bannister* [1948] 2 All ER 133, the claimant, who was the defendant's brother-in-law, was able to obtain two cottages from the defendant, at well below their market value, on the understanding that after the sale the defendant would be able to continue to live in one of the cottages rent-free for as long as she wished. She relied on his oral statement—'I do not want to take any rent, but will let you stay [in one of the cottages] as long as you like rent free'—and consequently the claimant obtained the cottages for only £250, as compared with their true market value of around £400. No written agreement to this effect was included in the conveyance. The claimant thereafter occupied the whole cottage save for one room which was occupied by the defendant. Troubles arose between the parties a few years later and the claimant sought possession of the cottage, claiming that the defendant was a mere tenant at will. The Court of Appeal took the view that although the claimant had not actually obtained the property by fraud, since he probably meant what he said at the time, it would now be unconscionable for him to retain it with vacant possession, and therefore decided that he held it as constructive trustee of the defendant for her life.

In *Binions* v *Evans* [1972] 1 Ch 359 Mrs Evans's husband was employed by the Tredegar Estate (near Newport in South Wales) and lived rent-free in a cottage owned by the estate. The husband died when the defendant (Mrs Evans) was 73. The trustees of the estate then entered into a written agreement with the defendant that she could continue to live in the cottage during her lifetime as tenant at will rent-free; she undertook to keep the cottage in good condition and repair. The trustees later sold the cottage to the claimants, Mr and Mrs Binions, expressly subject to Mrs Evans's 'tenancy agreement'. The claimants, having thereby obtained the cottage more cheaply, six months later sought possession from Mrs Evans, claiming that she was a tenant at will. The Court of Appeal held in favour of Mrs Evans but, although the decision was unanimous, the reasoning of the Master of the Rolls was quite different from that of Megaw and Stephenson LJJ.

Lord Denning MR started with the assertion that Mrs Evans had a contractual licence, which bound the purchasers with notice. This is inconsistent with the later Court of Appeal decision in *Ashburn Anstalt* v *Arnold* [1989] 1 Ch 1 (see further below) and is almost certainly incorrect. Indeed, Stephenson LJ doubted whether this line of reasoning was correct in *Binions* v *Evans* itself.

Lord Denning MR's alternative grounds were that because Mr and Mrs Binions had purchased expressly subject to the agreement, equity would impose on their conscience and require them to hold the property on constructive trust for Mrs Evans. This approach, based on *Bannister* v *Bannister*, differs from the views of the other two judges, in that the trust arose not under the original agreement, but only on the sale of the property to the claimants.

11.4.2 Lord Denning: the legacy of a radical judge

Lord Denning MR's constructive trust approach, narrowly interpreted, is probably the *ratio* of *Binions* v *Evans*, and has been followed in subsequent cases. However, parts of Lord Denning's judgment are more radical. He thought that to take property *impliedly* subject to an enforceable agreement would also be enough, and that a constructive trust could be imposed whenever the trustee had conducted himself in an inequitable manner. As with the contractual licence reasoning, this part of the judgment probably cannot survive the criticism in *Ashburn Anstalt* v *Arnold*.

The reasoning of Megaw and Stephenson LJJ was entirely different. In their view, the original agreement between the trustees and the defendant created a life tenancy. Thus, even at this stage the trustees held the property on trust for Mrs Evans for her life, thereafter for the Tredegar Estate in fee simple. Because this was a succession of equitable interests, Mrs Evans had an interest in land coming within the provisions of the Settled Land Act 1925, and the purchasers were therefore bound by an existing trust, on the ordinary principles of the equitable notice doctrine (see chapter 1).

Cases subsequent to *Binions* v *Evans* suggest that the very broad views of Lord Denning MR, that a constructive trust could be imposed whenever the trustee had conducted himself in an inequitable manner, have not gained favour. However, there is now a reasonable body of authority supporting his view that a constructive trust may be imposed on a purchaser (probably of land or chattels: see, for example, Browne-Wilkinson J's judgment *Swiss Bank Corporation* v *Lloyds Bank Ltd* [1979] 1 Ch 548) who purchases expressly subject to a prior agreement.

Lord Denning MR's view was adopted by Dillon J in *Lyus* v *Prowsa Developments Ltd* [1982] 1 WLR 1044, but Dillon J limited *Binions* v *Evans* to the situation where the purchaser took *subject to* a right. It is not enough that he merely knew of it.

The decision of the Court of Appeal in *Ashburn Anstalt* v *Arnold* [1989] 1 Ch 1, comprehensively noted by M. P. Thompson ([1988] Conv 201), is probably more important to students of land law than to those of trusts, but nevertheless it contains important *dicta* which bear on the present discussion. Fox LJ thought that contractual licences are not interests in land and do not bind third party purchasers. The relevance of this point to the present discussion is that if Lord Denning MR's judgment in *Binions* v *Evans* can be justified, it can only be on the basis of constructive trust reasoning, and not on the basis of contractual licence reasoning alternatively advanced.

11.4.3 Ashburn as an illustration of a constructive trust argument

A constructive trust was argued in *Ashburn Anstalt* v *Arnold* on the basis of Lord Denning MR's reasoning in *Binions* v *Evans*. The court, however, took the view that it would be imposed only where it was satisfied that the conscience of the purchaser was affected. This required more than mere notice, even express notice of the contractual licence. Even a purchaser who took 'subject to' a contractual licence would not necessarily be bound. There must be a clear undertaking on the part of the purchaser, and the obligation must be imposed expressly in the conveyance. While Fox LJ supported the decision in *Binions* v *Evans*, he would virtually have limited it to its facts. On his view, a constructive trust will be imposed only where the conveyance to the purchaser is made *expressly* subject to the contractual licence, and he also thought the fact that the purchaser had paid a reduced price in *Binions* v *Evans* was significant. None of these factors was present in *Ashburn Anstalt*, so no constructive trust arose.

The actual decision in *Ashburn Anstalt* has been overruled by the House of Lords in *Prudential Assurance Co.* v *London Residuary Body* [1992] 2 AC 386, but no doubt has been cast on the statements in the previous paragraph, which were *dicta* and not necessary for the decision; the Court of Appeal's decision in *Ashburn Anstalt* was that there was a valid lease, and that aspect of the case can no longer be supported.

11.4.4 **Unconscionable dealings in land; no legally binding agreement**

The case of *Ashburn* regardless of its lack of authority in its own right does provide illustration of a broader principle which is interesting in this examination of constructive trusts. This is a 'chapter setting' which has a very strong orientation towards domestic arrangements. This is so whether the dispute arising is as between the parties themselves, or in respect of a third party who becomes involved (on account of the possibility of having to take property subject to the interests of another): constructive trusts which arise from interests in land are very much dominated by the 'shared homes' scenario. What cases like *Lyus* and *Ashburn* illustrate is the application of a constructive trust in the context of commercial relationships and agreements arising from these relationships. This was also seen in the more recent decision in *Banner Homes Group plc* v *Luff Development* [2000] Ch 372.

Banner Homes v *Luff Development* concerned a proposed joint venture between Luff and Banner, both commercial parties, and in respect of a development of a commercial land site. There had been extensive negotiations between the parties, and there had been much reference within these negotiations to the creation of a joint venture company for undertaking the purchase of the land, and to the idea that each party would have equal shares in the company. On this understanding, a company was purchased by Luff through which the joint venture would be operated, but although these negotiations were kept up ostensibly, Luff started to think about finding a different partner for the venture. Luff decided to keep Banner 'on board' whilst pursuing other partner possibilities, fearing that Banner might act similarly and make an independent bid for the purchase. Banner, meanwhile, unaware of Luff's 'forked tongue' and anticipating that formal agreement would in due course arise in respect of the joint venture, continued to conduct itself with a view to this eventuality. The company made the purchase of the site, and it was only at that point that Luff revealed that the joint venture as between the parties was not going ahead. Banner argued that it was entitled to half shares in the company by virtue of a constructive trust, and at first instance this allegation was rejected. The judge concluded that there was no binding agreement actually reached between the parties. This in turn negated there being requisite common intention to give rise to an equity to which a constructive trust could become attached. It was also found that there was no evidence that Banner had acted to its detriment in reliance on the agreement coming to fruition, because it was not clear it would have made an independent bid if it had been aware of Luff's intention to find a different partner. This was so notwithstanding the judge's view that Luff *had* behaved badly.

In the Court of Appeal a different view was taken, and the conclusion was reached that an equity did arise on account of Luff's conduct. This operated to make it unconscionable for Luff to assert beneficial entitlement to the proceeds of a venture which was pursued on the understanding of a joint venture between the parties concerned. This was so notwithstanding that this understanding arose in the absence of an actual binding contract between them. What *Banner* v *Luff* suggests is that the equity arose from the inequitable conduct of Luff, and that this was itself manifested in the detriment suffered by Banner. This detriment took the form of it not being in a position to secure a new partner, on account of not even realising its proposed venture with Luff was in jeopardy. In other words, Banner's reliance on what it *believed* was an agreement which *would* come to fruition was the key to the detriment it suffered for the constructive trust to operate. Indeed, the judgment suggests that a different finding would have followed had Banner been informed that the venture was being abandoned before the detriment arose.

11.5 Mutual wills and the imposition of constructive trusts

Until fairly recently, the principles behind mutual wills could be viewed as merely another application of those that operated in the previous section, but recent cases have extended the equitable jurisdiction in two major respects. First, there is the notion of the floating trust, which crystallises on the death of the survivor, on all his or her property. Second, unlike the cases in the previous section, it does not appear to be necessary for the trustee to have received any property on the strength of the representation made.

If the principles operating in this section were generalised across the law of trusts, that would amount to a very radical extension of equitable fraud jurisdiction. However, the recent judgments considered here, which have made explicit the existence of a wider jurisdiction than that in the previous section, are merely wide interpretations of previous mutual wills cases; they do not purport to be applicable outside mutual wills. Moreover, mutual wills are in fact a special case, as will be argued more fully below.

11.5.1 What is a 'mutual will'?

Mutual wills are agreements, usually (but not necessarily) between husband and wife. Wills are made (or the parties agree to make them) by each party in (usually) the same terms, and there is a mutual agreement that neither party will revoke, but the essence of the transaction is an agreement that each party will settle his or her property in a particular (usually the same) way.

11.5.2 Mutual wills and the creation of an enforceable contract

Mutual wills create enforceable contracts, the importance of which will be examined further below. The question which arises at this point is how far the analysis in the previous section, which does not of course depend on the existence of enforceable contracts, can be sustained. This is now pursued through imagining an agreement between A and B. B is the survivor. B accordingly receives property under A's will, but he receives it only because he has agreed to settle it in a certain way. If the condition attaches merely to the property received under A's will, then the principles of the previous section, or indeed those discussed in chapter 10, suffice. B has taken property expressly subject to conditions, and equity will, by the device of the constructive trust, require him to carry out those conditions.

Suppose, for example, that as with the land in *Ottaway v Norman* [1972] Ch 698, B has agreed that he will leave the property received to C. B simply obtains a life interest in the property. This is also a possible explanation of *Re Oldham* [1925]

Ch 75, a mutual wills case. A more problematic situation is where A and B agree that each will leave all his property to the survivor on the understanding that the survivor will leave all his property to C. *Re Hagger* [1930] 2 Ch 190 suggests (contrary to *Re Oldham*) that a trust attaches to all the survivor's property, as long as the survivor accepts the legacy under the other's will. This is an extension of the reasoning explained thus far, in that the obligation extends beyond the property actually received by B. It also suggests that unlike express trusts, constructive trusts can cover future as well as existing property.

11.5.3 Constructive trusts covering future property: the 'floating' trust

A similar concept was envisaged in *Ottaway* v *Norman*, in respect of the furniture and other contents, including Miss Hodges' money. In fact, Brightman J thought that the obligation extended only to such furnishings and fixtures as Miss Hodges had received under Mr Ottaway's will, but also thought that if the agreement had included all Miss Hodges' other property and cash from whatever source, this obligation could also be enforced against her estate. He employed the concept of a 'floating trust', derived from the Australian case of *Birmingham* v *Renfrew* (1937) 57 CLR 666, which would remain in suspense during the life of the trustee and crystallise on her death, attaching to whatever property was comprised within her estate. This, as the learned judge noted, would seem to preclude Miss Hodges from making even a small pecuniary legacy in favour of her relatives or friends.

Similar reasoning was adopted, by Nourse J in a mutual wills context, in *Re Cleaver* [1981] 1 WLR 939. However, it is not clear from the report whether the trust imposed actually bound any property not received under Arthur Cleaver's will. If it did not then the *ratio* goes no further than *Re Oldham* [1925] Ch 75 (the widow, who survived her husband, would simply have enjoyed a life interest in the property received under Arthur Cleaver's will). But in *Re Dale* [1994] Ch 31, Morritt J applied the mutual wills doctrine in a situation where the second testator had received no benefit at all under the first testator's will, the mutual agreement having been that their children should share equally. There the trust clearly applied to the whole of the widow's estate, since the widow had received no property to which it could apply.

11.5.4 Fraud and floating trusts: two important extensions

There appear to be two important matters here. The trust can apply to future property, and there is no need for the constructive trustee to have obtained legal title to any property. The issue is, then, the extent to which, if at all, it is legitimate to generalise these extensions beyond mutual wills. It is suggested that this is not legitimate at all, first because the cases themselves reason entirely from earlier mutual wills cases, and second because there are unusual factors operating here. The Court of Appeal in *Re Goodchild* [1997] 3 All ER 63, affirming Carnwath J [1996] 1 All ER 670, accepted the notion of the floating trust, holding also that the floating trust so created was not destroyed by the remarriage of the second testator after the death of the first, but also held that it is not enough for wills to be made in the same terms; there must be a specific agreement that the wills were to be mutually binding (in other words, an enforceable contract between the parties) and there was insufficient evidence of such in the case itself. It also appears (in particular from the judgment in *Re Dale*) that A's refraining from revoking his will prior to his death constitutes consideration in equity, in which case the analysis becomes virtually identical to that in *Pullan* v *Koe* [1913] 1 Ch 9 in chapter 3. The difference between these cases and those discussed in the previous section, therefore, is the existence of the contract enforceable in equity, which can crystallise on future property, just as that in *Pullan* v *Koe* did.

11.5.5 Conclusions

Two conclusions follow from this. First, the floating trust and other developments in this section apply only where there is a contract enforceable in equity. Second, however, in the cases discussed at the start of this section, where the floating trust concept is not needed, and where the trust property is limited to that actually received by B, the principles in the last section suffice, and there is no need for the enforceable contract required by the Court of Appeal in *Re Goodchild*. Note that in *Ottaway* v *Norman*, the trust was imposed only on the property that had devolved to Miss Hodges, and that the floating trust would only have applied if there had been an enforceable agreement relating to other property.

The issues arising in respect of mutual wills have been considered most recently in the decision in *Healey* v *Brown* [2002] EWCH 1405 (Ch). In a typical 'mutual wills scenario', Mr and Mrs Brown made wills which were to be their 'last' and each spouse undertook not to 'revoke or amend', each leaving their estate to the survivor in their relationship. On the death of the surviving spouse, the property under these 'mutual wills' was to pass to Mr Brown's son Paul in part, and also to the claimant, Mrs Brown's niece. Mrs Brown died first, and after her death, her husband transferred the family home, a flat, into the joint names of himself and Paul in consideration of natural love and affection. This ensured that upon Mr Brown's subsequent death Paul became the property's sole owner. This operation of the doctrine of survivorship meant that the property did not pass as Mr and Mrs Brown's original wills had determined. The claimant asserted that through the doctrine of mutual wills, the flat was held by Paul on trust for her. It was found that a constructive trust arose in the claimant's favour, in respect of Mrs Brown's original share of the property. Paul therefore held the flat on trust for himself and the claimant, in equal shares.

The way in which a constructive trust arose only in respect of Mrs Brown's share of the property was explained by the judge as arising from the decision in *Re Goodchild*, which was considered above. This decision had asserted that, in the absence of a binding contract, there was no basis for imposing a constructive trust over property already owned by the survivor. Quoting Morritt LJ in *Re Goodchild* that there was 'a consistent line of authority [requiring] that for the doctrine of mutual wills to apply there must be a contract between the two testators', Donald Davidson QC found in *Healey* v *Brown*, that while some degree of arrangement or understanding short of a binding contract was sufficient for the mutual wills doctrine, the property of the second testator which was not acquired from the first testator (i.e. the survivor's original share) could not be bound by a constructive trust arising in these circumstances. In this case, this outcome appears to have followed precisely the nature of the parties' original intentions. Here, difficulties following from this analysis could conceivably arise where the outcome was not reflected in this way, which would raise issues about the promises made in the original wills, and about how parties to wills made in this way might be able to protect future interests relating to 'mutual' property.

11.6 Returning property to the transferor

In all of the cases considered so far, the effect of a constructive trust has been to hold representors to their representations. In none of the cases in 11.4 or 11.5, where property has been obtained on the strength of the representation, have the courts required that it be returned (indeed, in many of the cases this would have been wholly inappropriate). There is, however, now a line of authority suggesting that this can happen in some cases.

In *Westdeutsche* v *Islington LBC* [1996] AC 669, Lord Browne-Wilkinson thought that a thief of money, who mixed the money with his own, would thereby obtain legal title to the money, but would hold it as constructive trustee for the victim of the theft. Although this statement is not part of the *ratio* of the case, it probably represents good law. However, the reasoning adopted by Lord Browne-Wilkinson in reaching this result is unconvincing. He goes on to say: 'Although it is difficult to find clear authority for the proposition, when property is obtained by fraud equity imposes a constructive trust on the fraudulent recipient...'.

This statement is, in general terms, correct. However, in a way which Lord Browne-Wilkinson himself clearly appreciated, its possible limitations are borne out by the discussions above in 11.4 and 11.5, which showed that where a constructive trust has been imposed, there has been no requirement on the part of the guilty partly actually to return the property. In *McCormick* v *Grogan*, for example, (considered in chapter 10; which Lord Browne-Wilkinson actually cites in *Westdeutsche*), had the facts supported the imposition of a constructive trust, it would have been wholly inappropriate for the trustee to return the property to the estate. This would appear to apply equally to Lord Browne-Wilkinson's thief; but, unlike the thief example, a constructive trust in a 'representation' situation arises from a representation actually made. So what is the basis of Lord Browne-Wilkinson's 'thief conclusion' that property is held on constructive trust for the victim (from which the return of property result follows)?

11.6.1 Justification via a different route

However, it is possible to justify the thief conclusion by a different route. Another case analysed by Lord Browne-Wilkinson is *Chase Manhattan Bank NA* v *Israel-British Bank (London) Ltd* [1981] Ch 105, where a bank which had already been paid was accidentally paid a second time. Although Lord Browne-Wilkinson did not agree with the reasoning in *Chase Manhattan*, he did agree with the result, taking the view that the recipient bank would become a trustee for the transferring bank as soon as it discovered the mistake. The case bears some similarities to *Bankers Trust Co.* v *Shapira* [1980] 1 WLR 1274, cited in *Westdeutsche*, where the

Court of Appeal appears to have assumed that a bank which had been advanced money because of forged cheques presented by its customers became a trustee for the transferring bank when it learned of the mistake. In *Westdeutsche* itself, it was assumed that the local authority would have become trustee had it known that the swap agreement (under which the disputed money had been transferred to it) was void before that money had ceased to exist (having been spent).

There appears, therefore, to be some authority at least for a principle that a recipient of property who discovers that he is not entitled to it becomes trustee for the transferor. Obviously, Lord Browne-Wilkinson's thief is an extreme example of this principle, but note that the general principle has nothing to do with the jurisdiction discussed earlier, and indeed can operate against a recipient who has done nothing wrong.

11.7 A wider conduct-based doctrine?

The cases and the analysis which has been made of them would appear to suggest that the equitable fraud doctrine is probably limited to the cases we have considered. It may be argued that this is unsatisfactory, since there appears to be no clear underlying principle, but the law is perhaps not unlike the law of tort before 1932: the courts do not appear to have taken the step that they took in *Donoghue* v *Stevenson* [1932] AC 562 of bringing together all the strands within a general umbrella. Perhaps they are worried about 'proprietary overkill', since the constructive trust is more than merely a remedy in English law. Perhaps it is simply too difficult to develop a generalised conscience-based doctrine, except by developing specific factors, as in the examples in this chapter.

There have, however, been attempts to extend the jurisdiction beyond that considered so far in this chapter. In two cases the courts have almost gone so far as to hold that whenever a representation is made, certainly where the representation is to the effect that the representee is to have rights in property, that can give rise to a constructive trust. First, in *Re Sharpe (a bankrupt)* [1980] 1 WLR 219, an 82-year old lady, who was in poor health, loaned a large sum of money (£12,000) to her nephew to enable him to purchase a house in which they could both live. The nephew later went bankrupt, and the question arose whether the old lady's money was secured, or whether it formed part of the nephew's assets, to be divided among his general creditors. Browne-Wilkinson J found for the old lady, on the basis that she was a beneficiary under a constructive trust which bound the trustee in bankruptcy. He thought that a constructive trust can be imposed simply because a licensee expends money or otherwise acts to his detriment. If the reasoning in this case is correct, almost any reliance on a promise relating to the occupation of property could give rise to a constructive trust, and the constructive trust could exist in a pure form in the situations discussed earlier.

11.7.1 *Re Sharpe:* confusing constructive trusts and proprietary estoppel

This seems to be confusing the constructive trust with a proprietary estoppel (see Jill Martin (1980) Conv 207), and indeed we argued earlier that trust and estoppel concepts are entirely different. *Re Sharpe* looks wrong as an estoppel case, if the earlier reasoning is correct, since it ought not to be capable of binding a trustee in bankruptcy. Indeed, Sir Nicholas Browne-Wilkinson himself took this view in his Holdsworth Club Address 1991, observing that 'only if the third party's conduct is such as to raise an estoppel against the third party individually will the third party be affected'. If this is correct, the trustee in bankruptcy as the third party could hardly have been affected by an estoppel in *Re Sharpe*.

11.7.2 *Ashburn* and *Re Sharpe* rebuffed?

The constructive trust reasoning in *Re Sharpe* was treated dismissively by Fox LJ in *Ashburn Anstalt* v *Arnold* [1989] 1 Ch 1, but he did not elaborate, since the case before him was sufficiently different not to be affected directly by *Re Sharpe*. Nonetheless, the confusion between trust and estoppel concepts appears wrong in principle, and *Re Sharpe* is unsupported by other authority and is probably wrong.

The second case is *Re Basham (deceased)* [1987] 1 All ER 405, where the claimant was induced to do various things for the deceased, on the understanding that he would obtain the property under the will of the deceased when the deceased died. Edward Nugee QC, purporting to follow *Re Cleaver* [1981] 1 WLR 939 (see 11.4), held that a proprietary estoppel giving rise to a constructive trust arose, the claimant thereby obtaining the conveyance of the estate to her. He said that proprietary estoppel was a form of constructive trust which arose when A acted to his detriment on the faith of a belief known to and encouraged by B that he had or was going to have a right over B's property, so that B was prevented by equity from insisting on his strict legal rights if to do so would be inconsistent with A's belief. If this case is correct, then any act by the claimant, in reliance upon an alleged agreement (or even a mere representation by the defendant), would enable the claimant to succeed on constructive trust reasoning, but the judgment has been criticised recently in *Taylor* v *Dickens* [1998] 1 FLR 806 and *Gillett* v *Holt* [1998] 2 FLR 1 (considered earlier), and like *Re Sharpe*, is probably best regarded as wrong.

11.7.3 Floating trusts outside the context of mutual wills

There have also been cases, such as *Stokes* v *Anderson* [1991] 1 FLR 391 and *Ottaway* v *Norman*, which apply the floating trust concept outside the context of mutual wills. We saw in the previous section that *Ottaway* v *Norman* is probably consistent with the principles in that section. *Stokes* v *Anderson* is a category 1 *Lloyds Bank* v *Rosset* case where the declaration of trust occurred while Stokes was still negotiating to purchase the share that he eventually obtained in the property, and Nourse LJ, founding upon *Birmingham* v *Renfrew*, saw no reason in principle why a constructive trust could not 'attach to an after-acquired estate or interest in property, whether legal or equitable'. Note that unlike the mutual wills cases, there was no enforceable agreement between Stokes and Anderson because of lack of writing (unless interests under a statutory trust for sale could have been regarded as personalty for these purposes: see chapter 1), but it is doubtful whether *Birmingham* v *Renfrew* reasoning was needed in the case, or indeed adopted. All that is needed is to hold (surely quite reasonably?) that Stokes' intention continued until he actually acquired his interest, and that the declaration of trust therefore occurred at that time. *Stokes* v *Anderson* therefore probably does not represent an extension of the equitable jurisdiction considered in this chapter.

FURTHER READING

Davies 'Mutual Wills; Formalities; Constructive Trusts' (2003) Conveyancer 238.

Thompson 'Leases, Licenses and the Doctrine of *Errington*' (1988) Conveyancer 201.

Thompson 'Constructive Trusts and Non-binding Agreements' (2001) Conveyancer 265.

Yondon (1984) 'Formalities for Trusts of Land: The Doctrine of *Rochefoucauld* v *Boustead*' Cambridge Law Journal 306.

12

An introduction to charity

12.1 Charities and the trust

It is usual to deal with charities as an integral part of the law of trusts. It is not necessarily the most appropriate classification, however, because though many charities exist in the form of a trust, this is not universal. Also, historically the law has recognised charities for even longer than the trust itself.

In its earliest institutional form, charity was the province of the medieval Church, and its supervision the responsibility of the ecclesiastical courts. It was the secularisation of charitable donation during the Tudor period and the contemporaneous growth of the jurisdiction of the Court of Chancery by way of the Use which brought the administration of charity under the control of the Chancellor. He began to enforce Uses for 'pious purposes' at around the same time as he began to enforce Uses relating to land. Because of the attractive simplicity of the Use, and later of the trust, for philanthropic donors, coupled with the effectiveness of equitable remedies, the trust rapidly became the commonest method of dedicating property to worthy causes.

12.1.1 The charitable trust as a variety of purpose trust

Charitable trusts are, of course, a variety of purpose trust and, as we have seen, there are difficulties in the enforcement of purpose trusts, especially as in the case of charities there will probably not be easily identifiable human beneficiaries. However, since the early seventeenth century the Attorney-General has undertaken the enforcement of charitable trusts, as representative claimant, and since 1960 the Charity Commissioners have been given supervisory powers over charities. Most recently, the Charities Act 2006 has created a 'body corporate' called the Charity Commission of England and Wales which has assumed this function, and the significance of this development will be considered in due course. Because the Attorney-General has powers of enforcement, there is no need for charitable trusts to be subject to the same certainty of objects requirements as private purpose trusts, and they are not. Indeed, because of the public character of charitable trusts, they are also exempt from other requirements to which private trusts are subject and in addition enjoy certain privileges.

12.1.2 Charities and the trust instrument

Although not all charities exist in the form of a trust, the trust is still the most common medium of charity today, both in terms of the quantity of trusts in existence and in terms of the value of their funds. The trust seems to be most favoured on the one hand by private individuals and on the other by the largest and wealthiest of charitable enterprises, the foundations of which often originate within international commercial corporations.

From the viewpoint of the private donor, the trust form is simple to create and sufficiently flexible to allow for a degree of individuality to be expressed in its provisions. For a large and well-funded organisation, the trust form offers the opportunity to maintain large capital funds producing high levels of income, which can be distributed on a discretionary basis. For these reasons the trust will probably remain the most usual form of charitable enterprise and charity law will continue to take its direction from the doctrines developed in equity. Indeed, the courts have always shown a preference for treating all charities as partaking in the nature of a trust, even where their institutional arrangements are of a quite different sort.

Charitable trusts may take the form of unincorporated associations, companies, or a new form which has been established by the Charities Act 2006 called a charitable incorporated organisation. What all charitable organisations enjoy in common, regardless of their precise form is that responsibility for their governance and administration rests with their trustees, and that in turn this is overseen by the Charity Commission.

12.1.3 Charitable organisations which exist as 'corporations'

An increasing number of charitable ventures nowadays operate within a corporate structure and this form is particularly well suited to collective, active enterprises. A corporate charity will usually be a company limited by guarantee and will usually have a constitution forbidding the distribution of profit among its members. Otherwise, the establishment of a company limited by guarantee is broadly similar in terms of formality to the setting up of an ordinary commercial company. As with a commercial company, the liability of the charity is limited to its assets, thus protecting its members from unlimited personal liability in the event of the charity becoming insolvent.

The advantage of corporate status is that the charity can operate as a legal person. So it has the capacity to make contracts, incur liabilities, and hold property in its own right without the need to involve trustees. Also, it does not need to effect alterations in the documents of title to its property at every change in personnel. Corporate status is therefore well suited to charities which undertake extensive long-term operations. These often have considerable assets, sufficient to make the expense of incorporation worthwhile.

12.1.4 Charitable organisations which exist as bodies which are not incorporated—or 'unincorporated associations'

These are the other most common form, which may convert to corporate status if and when it becomes convenient to do so. The less rigid framework offered by this form makes it attractive to groups of people wishing to undertake active charitable work in accordance with broadly democratic and flexible policies which may change and develop over time. Control of the organisation and its funds, if any, will typically be vested in a committee of managers who will probably be elected in conformity with the wishes of the current membership.

The earlier 'case study' on unincorporated associations (in chapter 8) has already shown that the basis of this form of organisation is usually a contract between the members, formulated as rules which are contained in the constitution of the association. This carries the advantage of extreme flexibility, allowing the terms of the contract to be modified to meet new situations. The main disadvantage is that the managers and members are exposed to unlimited personal liability incurred in the course of the organisation's activities. Nevertheless, the unincorporated association accounts for a moderate proportion of old established charities, as well as some of the newer and most active charitable undertakings.

Other more unusual forms of charitable organization also subsist as follows:

- *Mutual benefit organisations* maintaining funds collected by subscription from members, and being intended to provide benefits during sickness, old age, etc., may be registered under the Friendly Societies Act 1974, and those which qualify as charitable according to the legal definition of that term (see chapter 13) may have the status of 'benevolent societies'. However, their significance appears to be declining in view of the growth in state welfare provision.

- Another form available to charities, and apparently favoured by the growing number of housing associations, is *the industrial and provident society*, a kind of hybrid with some of the features of both the friendly society and the guarantee company, and registrable under the Industrial and Provident Societies Acts 1965 to 1978.

- Long before the newly created charitable incorporated organisation, English law recognised the *charitable corporation*, which is also distinct from the traditional 'incorporated body' charity explained above (where organsiations of this nature are typically 'guarantee companies'). The charitable corporation form has traditionally been illustrated by universities, hospitals, and establishments such as the British Museum, and they are established either by charter from the Crown (known as a 'Royal Charter', as is the case with universities) or else by legislation (e.g., the Charitable Trustees Incorporation Act 1872 and the British Museum Act 1963). The character of these institutions has been diverse with no standard form, and with each endowed with a constitution specific to its own requirements. These charities are generally considered to enjoy high prestige by virtue of their unique character, and represent something of an elite category within the range of charitable organisations.

12.1.5 What is the new 'charitable incorporated organization'?

As information made available by the Charity Commission in May 2008 (and set out in full at <http://www.charity-commission.gov.uk/registration/charcio.asp#1>) explains, this is a new legal form of incorporation which is designed specifically for charities. As the information explains, the CIO (as it is referred to) is designed to streamline procedures for charitable organisations wishing to incorporate, and which are currently subject to two registration procedures—registration as a charity (with the Charity Commission) and with the Registrar of Companies at

Companies House (in furtherance of company law requirements), and providing accounts and returns to both.

The Charity Commission notes that the impetus for this new form has arisen from the way in which much of the framework of the company structure, designed primarily for commercial organisations, may mean that it is not always a suitable vehicle for charities, in which commercial dimensions are actually very restricted. Impetus has also arisen from the way in which, notwithstanding this, corporate status *does* confer advantages, including especially the reduced scope for personal liability for those concerned with the administration of an organisation.

With this in mind, the new structure seeks to combine a single registration procedure (requiring registration only with the Charity Commission), and reporting and accounting requirements which are less onerous than would be required otherwise, and also less rigid ones relating to changes in constitutional and governance arrangements. The combination of all of this with a simpler 'standard form' constitution (which will be produced by the Commission through a series of model forms and which will include fewer fixed governance provisions than is the case with companies) and also exemption from requirements prescribed for *companies* by EC Directives on company law will lead to an overall reduction of administrative costs for charites.

Regulations on how CIOs must be established and must operate will be produced by way of secondary legislation from the Minister for the Third Sector. The Charity Commission has produced 'Choosing and preparing a governing document' which provides information on the current structures open to charities (available at <http://www.charity-commission.gov.uk/publications/cc22.asp>), and the new form is available to those who are setting up charitable organisations *ab initio*. There is also facility for existing charitable companies and charitable industrial and provident societies to convert to the CIO form, and in this latter scenario, the existing corporate body is simply re-registered as a CIO and the conversion process will not affect the legal personality of the organisation or its business relationships.

12.2 **Legal regulation of charities: consequences of charitable status**

Before considering the legal definition of charity in the next chapter some attention needs to be given to the consequences that flow from charitable status. The cases considered in the following chapters have arisen for a diversity of reasons, and this may have led to confusion on the part of the courts as to the policy they should adopt.

For the consequences outlined below to apply it is necessary to show that the property is to be held beneficially for charitable purposes. It is insufficient for the recipient merely to covenant to use the property for purposes which happen to be charitable purposes. In *Liverpool City Council* v *Attorney-General* (unreported), *The Times*, 1 May 1992, Allerton Hall had been conveyed (in 1926) to Liverpool City Council subject to covenants that it would be used only as a public park. It was accepted that the provision of a public park or recreation ground was a charitable purpose (presumably on the principles illustrated below). The Attorney-General nevertheless failed in his contention that the land was held on charitable trusts, so that the City Council were able to treat it as part of its corporate property. No doubt the covenants remained valid, but presumably since the original covenantees had long since died, there was nobody in a position to enforce them.

12.2.1 Tax advantages

Charities enjoy exemption from income tax on all income, rents, dividends, and profits, provided these are applied for charitable purposes, and may reclaim from the Revenue any income tax already paid prior to receipt of the income. Nor is income tax chargeable on the profits of any trade carried out by the charity, so long as these are applied for charitable purposes only and the trade is either exercised in carrying out the primary purposes of the charity or the work is carried out mainly by its beneficiaries (e.g., workshops for the disabled). Charitable corporations are exempt from corporation tax.

Gifts to charity are largely exempt from inheritance tax, and capital gains tax is not payable where gains are applied to charitable purposes. All charities are exempt from half of the rates on premises occupied in connection with the charity, including charity shops, and premises used for religious purposes are entirely exempt from rates. Generally, charities must pay VAT on goods and services, but certain goods, such as some equipment for the disabled, are zero rated.

Some conception of the importance of the taxation consequences of charitable status may be gleaned from the number of cases considered in the next chapter involving the Inland Revenue. In addition, charitable status is often claimed for rates advantages: this can be seen, for example, in *Re South Place Ethical Society* [1980] 1 WLR 1565 and *United Grand Lodge of Ancient Free & Accepted Masons of England and Wales* v *Holborn Borough Council* [1957] 1 WLR 1080, both considered shortly.

The annual cost to the Revenue of these tax concessions is of the order of half a billion pounds or, to put it into perspective, about £50 for every average-sized family in the UK.

12.2.2 Validity

Another common reason for litigation on charitable status is to ascertain whether the gift is valid at all. Probably the commonest situation is where the next of kin challenge the validity of a testamentary bequest (e.g., *Re Shaw* [1957] 1 WLR 729; *Re Pinion* [1965] Ch 85; and *Re Koeppler's WT* [1986] Ch 423). Charitable status has three main consequences for validity.

12.2.2.1 *Charitable trusts in relation to the beneficiary principle*

First, charitable trusts are trusts for purposes, which would often be void if non-charitable. Yet as we have seen, charities are public trusts enforceable at the suit of the Attorney-General, and are supervised by the Charity Commission, so their lack of human beneficiaries is not fatal, as it is to private trusts. Indeed, only the Attorney-General can establish an action against to establish the existence of a charitable trust, which will commonly arise from a challenge to a testamentary gift (purportedly made in favour of a charity) brought by the deceased's next of kin. This is the official position, although the Attorney-General can be substituted as claimant for individuals: *Hauxwell* v *Barton-on-Humber UDC* [1974] Ch 432, where he was substituted as claimant by two individuals. The supervision powers of the Charity Commissioners were traditionally found in the Charities Act 1993, which also give powers to 'the charity trustees, or [to] any person interested in the charity, or [to] any two or more inhabitants of the area of the charity if it is a local charity, but not [to] any other person'. For a discussion of the meaning of 'any person interested' under s. 33(1), see *Scott* v *National Trust* [1998] 2 All ER 705, where local huntsmen and tenant farmers were held to have *locus standi* to challenge a decision of the National Trust to ban deer-hunting with hounds on its estates, because they had an interest materially greater than or different from that possessed by ordinary members of the public in securing due administration of the charity.

Second, it is not necessary for the purposes of a charitable trust to be defined with certainty. A gift on trust 'for charitable purposes' will be valid, and the court and Charity Commission have jurisdiction to create a scheme for the application of the property donated. A gift to charity which is not expressed as a trust will be similarly disposed of by the Crown.

Third, charitable trusts, unlike private trusts, may exist indefinitely. This being so, a gift over from one charity to another may take effect at any time in the future: *Christ's Hospital* v *Grainger* (1849) 1 Mac & G 460. Once property is dedicated to charity, there is no infringement of the perpetuity rules merely because it passes from one charitable body to another. However, the rule against perpetuities applies as usual to prevent a too remote vesting of a gift to a charity in the first instance, and also to a gift over from a charity to a non-charity.

12.2.3 **Registration of charities**

Though the definition of charitable status is at the end of the day a matter for the courts, the process of obtaining recognition as a charity today is primarily administrative, and largely outside the direct control of the courts. Under the provisions of the Charities Act 1993 an organisation seeking charitable status would until very recently have applied for registration to the Charity Commissioners, who have had power under the Act to grant or withhold registration according to their decision as to whether the proposed purposes are, in law, charitable. The modern Charity Commission, charged with supervising charitable endowments, came into being in 1853, although originally it was given only limited powers. Traditionally the Charity Commission has no legal existence as a body, with the functions of the Commission actually being held by the Charity Commissioners themselves personally. However, changes pursuant to the recently enacted Charities Act 2006 inserts into the 1993 Act provisions that create a new body corporate called the Charity Commission for England and Wales: this has the effect of conferring upon the Commission the status of a non-ministerial government department. And while charitable trusts are enforceable by the Attorney-General, in the modern law, the (newly named, but in substance long-established) Charity Commission has taken a larger role in enforcing charitable trusts, alongside its other tasks of registering charitable trusts, monitoring accounts and supervising the running of charities, and advising charitable trustees. A charity must be registered with the

Charity Commission if it has an income of more than £5,000 a year, or has the use or occupation of any land or buildings, or has assets which constitute permanent endowment, unless it is *exempt from* registration (which is the case with universities and most 'educational' establishments such as museums).

12.2.4 The Charity Commission for England and Wales: continuity and change in approaches to the regulation of the governance and administration of charitable organisations

The materials above have explained the way in which persons known as the 'Charity Commissioners' have had a long-standing role in overseeing the regulation of charitable organisations in light of the requirements of charitable status under English law, and which are set out in some detail and at length in the next chapter. Note has also been made of the way in which, pursuant to the recently enacted Charities Act 2006, provisions inserted into ones of the Charities 1993 Act create a new 'body corporate' called the Charity Commission for England and Wales. As the legislation clarifies, this has the effect of conferring upon the Commission the status of a non-Ministerial Government Department. Accordingly, s. 6 of the Charities Act 2006 inserts key provisions into the Charities Act 1993, and as the Explanatory notes accompanying the new law explain, the function of s. 6 (and especially subsections (4) and (5)) is to ensure that, as a non-Ministerial Government Department, the Charity Commission will have a 'significant degree of independence from Ministers and other Government Departments in the performance of its functions'. More about the Commission's functions can be found in s. 7, which sets out its 'objectives, general functions and duties'. Accordingly, s. 7 provides that:

After section 1A of the 1993 Act (inserted by section 6 above) insert—
  '1B The Commission's objectives

  (1) The Commission has the objectives set out in subsection (2).
  (2) The objectives are—
      1. The public confidence objective.
      2. The public benefit objective.
      3. The compliance objective.
      4. The charitable resources objective.
      5. The accountability objective.
  (3) Those objectives are defined as follows—
      1. The public confidence objective is to increase public trust and confidence in charities.
      2. The public benefit objective is to promote awareness and understanding of the operation of the public benefit requirement.
      3. The compliance objective is to promote compliance by charity trustees with their legal obligations in exercising control and management of the administration of their charities.
      4. The charitable resources objective is to promote the effective use of charitable resources.
      5. The accountability objective is to enhance the accountability of charities to donors, beneficiaries and the general public.

(4) In this section 'the public benefit requirement' means the requirement in section 2(1)(b) of the Charities Act 2006 that a purpose falling within section 2(2) of that Act must be for the public benefit if it is to be a charitable purpose.

1C The Commission's general functions

(1) The Commission has the general functions set out in subsection (2).

(2) The general functions are—

1. Determining whether institutions are or are not charities.

2. Encouraging and facilitating the better administration of charities.

3. Identifying and investigating apparent misconduct or mismanagement in the administration of charities and taking remedial or protective action in connection with misconduct or mismanagement therein.

4. Determining whether public collections certificates should be issued, and remain in force, in respect of public charitable collections.

5. Obtaining, evaluating and disseminating information in connection with the performance of any of the Commission's functions or meeting any of its objectives.

6. Giving information or advice, or making proposals, to any Minister of the Crown on matters relating to any of the Commission's functions or meeting any of its objectives.

(3) The Commission's fifth general function includes (among other things) the maintenance of an accurate and up-to-date register of charities under section 3 below.

(4) The Commission's sixth general function includes (among other things) complying, so far as is reasonably practicable, with any request made by a Minister of the Crown for information or advice on any matter relating to any of its functions.

In light of the traditional function and status of the Charity Commissioners explained above, it is significant that traditionally the duty to maintain the register of charities has been placed on the Commissioners themselves by virtue of s. 3(1) of the 1993 Act. In addition to this it is also the case that the Charity Commissioners have a tradition of actually enforcing charitable trusts (alongside the Attorney-General), and this is widely accepted as having resulted in a significant decrease in the number of court decisions which would otherwise subsist in relation to the boundaries of charity; what can be seen instead is a handful of 'test cases' which raise significant issues of law. And it is indeed the case that in reaching their decisions, the Commissioners (and henceforth the Commission itself) may consult with other bodies, such as the Inland Revenue (which has also recently been renamed Her Majesty's Revenue and Customs), whose interest in the validity of claims to be treated as a charity has spawned some of English law's most prominent 'charitable status' litigation.

12.2.4.1 *Refusal by the Charity Commission to register an organisation as charitable*

Refusal by the Commissioners to register an organisation has traditionally given rise to a right of appeal (to the board of Charity Commissioners under s. 4 of the Charities Act 1990), and through the courts (initially through the High Court, and thence to the Court of Appeal and House of Lords). However, the 2006 Act introduces a new mechanism for ensuring critical appraisal of Charity Commission decisions on registration. The new Charity Tribunal, which is due to come into existence in 2008, is regarded by the Act's Explanatory Notes as a 'court of first instance' for decisions relating to appeals and applications made originally to the (new) Charity Commission. The new Tribunal comes into being courtesy of the provisions of s. 8, and the key points in relation to it are as follows:

- Subsection (1) makes reference to the creation of the Tribunal and to its practices and procedures; and also matters relating to appeals *from* the Tribunal *to* the High Court, and the powers of the Attorney-General in relation to matters brought before the Tribunal etc.
- Subsection (2) concerns the Tribunal's composition and membership; its staff and facilities; and matters relating to procedures and practices.
- Subsection (3) has the effect of inserting Schedules 1C and 1D of the *new* Act *into* the Charities Act 1993. Schedule 1C concerns matters such as determining specified rights of appeal against specified decisions of the Commission, and matching these rights of appeal with specified persons with the right to bring such appeals. This is so along with specification of decisions which are reviewable by the Tribunal, and the powers of the Tribunal in relation to said specific matters of appeal. Schedule 1D makes provisions for references which can be made to the Tribunal by the Commission (for example, in matters which involve the operation and application of charity law to its functions) and also the Attorney-General (for matters involving the operation or application of charity law).

The requirement to keep the Register of Charities, and new
functions for the Charity Commission

Under the new regime of the Charities Act 2006, the Charity Commission must continue to keep the register of charities. However, the new provisions located in s. 9 of the Act go further than the provisions of s. 3 of the 1993 Act by prescribing the contents of the register (subsection 3) and the circumstances in which the Commission must or may remove from the register organisations which are no longer considered to be charities (subsections 4 and 5). This is closely connected with what the new legislation envisages as the growing supervisory role of the new Commission. This can in turn be understood from linking the way in which, while charitable status can bring with it considerable advantages for an organisation, it also invites scrutiny relating to curbing abuse of charitable status and maladministration. And, it will become ever more apparent as these materials progress that in the early years of the twenty-first century, this increasingly became associated with perceived declining public confidence in the charitable sector. Politically this became manifested in growing criticism of charities law for some time, and the process of law reform leading to the Charities Act 2006 was formally set in motion in 2002 with the publication by the Prime Minister's Strategy Unit of *Private Action, Public Benefit: A Review of Charities and the Wider Not-For-Profit Sector.*

12.2.4.2 *Registration requirements and the significance of 'exception' and 'exemption'*

More will be said on this shortly, but these issues—clustering political responses to perceived public discomfort about charitable status—are clearly at the heart of a more prescriptive approach to applications for charitable status, the reviewing of charitable status, and ultimately removal of 'unsuitable' organisations from the register of charities. This is also the rationale for another new and distinct policy of the new Act which is evident in the provisions of s. 9, inserting a new section 3A into the 1993 Act. This prescribes a general principle that every charity must be registered (in the register of charities). And while—as under the 1993 Act—certain charities are exempted from requiring registration, these new provisions alter this position by virtue of retaining certain exceptions and exemptions but these are clearly intended to be much narrower and more tightly controlled than has traditionally been the case. A charity can be *exempt* under s. 3A(2)(a) by reference to Schedule 2 of the 1993 Act, and by s. 3A(2) a charity can be *excepted* from requiring registration. The key difference between charities which are exempt and those which are excepted is that in the case of the latter, exception to registration is granted by order of the Charity Commission or by regulations (rather than under statute). According to s. 3A(2)(d), any charity whose gross income does not exceed £5,000 is not required to be registered: this is actually an increase in threshold from a current figure of £1,000 and, as the Explanatory Notes for the 2006 Act suggest, it is designed to 'release the smallest charities...from the registration requirement'. These provisions came into force on 23 April 2007.

12.2.4.3 *The Charities Act 2006 and a new key supervisory function*
A key 'supervisory function' of the Charity Commission under the new Act, and a close companion of registration, is requirements which the new Act has put in place for the Commission relating to 'public benefit'. This can be seen in the general functions and duties provisions of s. 7, emphasised in turn in the 1B objectives (in paragraph (2) as the 'public benefit objective'. Illumination of this is given in paragraph (3) as the promotion of 'awareness and understanding of the operation of the public benefit requirement'; and ultimately paragraph (4) within s. 1B clarifies that for the purposes of this section 'the public benefit requirement' means 'the requirement in section 2(1)(b) of the Charities Act 2006 that a purpose falling within section 2(2) of that Act must be for the public benefit if it is to be a charitable purpose'. The substance of the public benefit requirement is to be found in s. 3 of the Charities Act 2006, which is considered further in the next chapter's examination of the legal definition of charity in English law.

As the materials in the next chapter will also explain, under s. 4 of the Charities Act 2006, the Commission is required (under subsection 1) to issue guidance in furtherance of this objective. Furthermore the Commission is permitted (under subsection 3) to revise this guidance periodically in order to reflect and accommodate societal changes which influence and inform developments 'in the legal concept of public benefit'. Under subsection 5, the Commission is required to publish its guidance under this section (which is of course in furtherance of its 'public benefit' objective within its 'general functions' under s. 7, set out in full above), but the Commission is permitted to elect what it considers to be the most appropriate manner of publication (such as printed word, or through web-based publication). Following consultation commenced in early 2007, the Charity Commission did publish its public benefit Guidance in January 2008, and extensive reference will be made to this in due course, alongside the discussion of the public benefit requirement in the next chapter.

12.2.5 **Cy près**

If a charitable organisation is wound up, any surplus property may be applied cy près. If, on the other hand, the organisation is not charitable, any surplus property will go to the Crown as *bona vacantia*, or to the donors on resulting trust, or in the case of an unincorporated association, to the members of the association, both discussed in chapter 8. In *Re Hobourn Aero Components Ltd's Air Raid Distress Fund* [1946] Ch 194, the sole consequence of the fund being held non-charitable was that a cy près scheme was not directed, and that the surplus was distributed among the contributors.

12.2.6 **Political dimension**

The political dimension to charities has possibly influenced their development and cannot be altogether avoided.

The role adopted by charities a hundred or so years ago has to some extent been superseded by state provision for the least fortunate in society. Some might even go so far as to argue that charities have no value alongside a state-funded system. Most, however, would probably hold that the freedom of individuals to decide whether to distribute any of their property to philanthropic purposes, and if so which purposes, is an important freedom, which is in no way in opposition to the welfare state provision (in which, of course, individuals have very little direct say).

12.2.6.1 *Politics, welfare, and the relief of poverty: a continuing justification for charities?*

At the very least, however, it is more difficult nowadays to justify tax concessions to charities, when at the same time many of the least fortunate are provided for by the welfare state. Also, if the state has decided not to fund a particular purpose through the welfare scheme, it is odd that it should be required to fund it through the back door, by virtue of the tax concessions given to charitable enterprise. Probably such an argument has to some extent been taken on board by the courts and the legislature, the former by laying down more stringent conditions for charitable status, and excluding 'undesirable' forms of altruistic activity, the latter by requiring registration and to some extent supervision by a public body, viz. the Charity Commissioners.

There is also no doubt that the terms of a gift to charity are controlled by the donor, and some might argue that, at any rate where very large sums are concerned, the power that goes with such control is better administered by public bodies than private individuals.

12.3 **The law of charity: conflicting policies adopted by the courts**

12.3.1 **Charities and their operations today**

Courts today are generally unwilling to frustrate the wishes of a settlor and prefer to deem gifts to be valid if they can. This leads to a tendency to expand the legal definition of charity. On the other hand, jealousy of the tax concessions tends towards the opposite result. In other words, there is a tension between two conflicting tendencies, which to some extent explains the haphazard development of the law.

It is not only today that tensions between conflicting policies are felt, and it should be remembered that the legal definition of charity is the result of the development of several centuries, at any rate from the Statute of Charitable Uses 1601 onwards. At certain periods, charity was viewed with extreme suspicion, particularly where, as in the case of the medieval Church, the power of charitable donation could be seen in rivalry to the claims of the then nascent secular state, or where, as in the seventeenth and eighteenth centuries, charity was blamed for taking away the rightful expectations of heirs.

12.3.2 Charity law emerging from Elizabethan times to the eighteenth century

With the decline during this period of the influence of the Roman Catholic Church, and other economic factors, poor relief during Elizabethan times became something of a problem for the state. Statutory provision for the poor, to be administered by the parish and paid for out of local rates, was introduced in 1572, and comprehensive Poor Codes were enacted in 1597 and 1601. However, it was in the interests of the state to encourage charitable donation in order to reduce the burden of poor rates. The development of charity law at this time, therefore, was geared primarily towards relief of the poor, rather than other forms of philanthropic enterprise.

This can clearly be seen by examination of the preamble to the Statute of Charitable Uses 1601, set out in full in the following chapter. The primary purpose of this Act was to provide for commissioners to be appointed to investigate administration of charities, and in particular misappropriation of trust property. This procedure continued in operation for about two hundred years.

Of greater importance for present purposes, however, was that a number of charitable uses (or, in other words, charitable purposes) are listed in the preamble to the Act, and the preamble was later used by the courts to provide the basis for the legal definition of charity. Indeed, this remained so until provisions of the charities Act 2006 came into force.

The preamble in fact contains quite a divergent list of charitable purposes, sufficiently diverse to provide for the expanding definitions of charity in the eighteenth and nineteenth centuries. However, the list as a whole is clearly intended to be confined to provision for the poor, to reduce the burden of the poor rates, and early development of charity was heavily influenced by this bias. The notion of public benefit also appears clearly in the preamble.

12.3.3 Developments in charity law during the eighteenth and nineteenth centuries

This period of development is important because it was then that the legal definition of charity was consolidated. The modern law of charity is based on developments during this period. The two main influences are the decline in importance of genuine poverty charities and the influence of the mortmain legislation (Mortmain and Charitable Uses Act 1736).

The decline in the importance of poverty relief in charitable giving was partly connected with notions of the 'undeserving' poor. At the same time, there was a move towards other types of charitable donation. For example, the NSPCC, Dr Barnardo's Homes, and the National Trust are all creatures of this period.

A major influence on the law of charity at this time was judicial hostility to bequests for charitable purposes which threatened to deprive testators' families from their 'rightful due'. It might be thought that this judicial hostility would lead to a narrowing of the legal definition of charity, but in fact the reverse was often the case. It should not be forgotten that the mortmain legislation made many testamentary gifts of land to charity void during this period (from 1736 to 1891), and this may paradoxically have resulted in a *wider* definition of charity being adopted in order not to frustrate the claims of disappointed relations (if the gift was held void, there was a resulting trust of the property for the estate).

12.3.3.1 *Definition of charity and the emergence of 'public benefit'*

Examples of cases where the adoption of a wide definition of charity led to a gift being struck down under the mortmain legislation were *Townlee* v *Bedwell* (1801) 6 Ves Jr 104, on the establishment of botanical gardens; *Thornton* v *Howe* (1862) 31 Beav 14, on the advancement of religion; and *Tatham* v *Drummond* (1864) 4 De G J & Sm 484, on animal charities.

Also during this period, the original notion of public benefit underwent a change. Originally a benefit to the poor was required, but now almost any public purpose would do. For example, it became clear that a school to educate the sons of gentlemen may be charitable, whereas it had previously been thought that the pre-amble covered only free schools. Also apparent, even at the height of philanthropic activity in the nineteenth century, was that middle-class social values of the time were strongly in evidence in an attempt to limit the distribution of charity to the 'deserving'. Hence, the modern definition of relief of poverty for charitable purposes is by no means limited to the relief of the destitute.

12.3.4 **Charity law developments from the late nineteenth and twentieth centuries**

Two further developments are important during this period: first, the growing tie between tax concessions and charitable status, and second, further changes in the nature of charitable donation, especially with the development of increased welfare provision.

In relation to the first, *Commissioners for Special Purposes of the Income Tax* v *Pemsel* [1891] AC 531, which has formed the basis for the *modern definition* of heads of charity, it became clear for the first time that relief from taxation might be tied in to the definition of charity. The judges themselves do not appear to have appreciated the importance of the connection, however.

In relation to the second, in the twentieth century, relief of poverty has become more clearly a state function, and accordingly charities for the relief of poverty have declined to a greater extent even than in the nineteenth century. On the other hand, gifts to social welfare, disaster appeals, and especially pressure groups have increased. Also, a far greater proportion of charitable income comes from fees and government grants, as opposed to voluntary donations.

It is questionable whether the law has altered significantly to take account of these developments, although Lord Cross clearly faced the taxation issue in

Dingle v *Turner* (considered in chapter 13). On the changing emphasis of charity, the Recreational Charities Act 1958 added a new head of charity, in line with the greater emphasis on social welfare. Also, the fourth head of charity (considered below) appeared to remain actively developing until the charities Act 2006 come into force. As Lord Wilberforce said in *Scottish Burial Reform & Cremation Society Ltd* v *Glasgow Corporation* [1968] AC 138, 154:

But three things may be said about [the *Pemsel* classification], which its author [Lord Macnaughten] would surely not have denied: first that, since it is a classification of convenience, there may well be purposes which do not fit neatly into one or other of the headings; secondly, that the words used must not be given the force of a statute to be construed; and thirdly, that the law of charity is a moving subject which may well have evolved even since 1891.

Similar statements can be found, also in the House of Lords, in *IRC* v *McMullen* [1981] AC 1, a case in which it is clear that the legal concept of charity is not static but changes with ideas about social values.

12.3.5 The validity of non-charitable purposes

Lord Cross's desire to see different tests for validity on the one hand, and tax concessions on the other reflects the way in which the main consequence of charitable status today may well be taxation privileges. And perhaps the law should not be too free in the granting of those privileges, which probably explains the personal nexus rule in *Oppenheim* v *Tobacco Securities Trust Co. Ltd* [1951] AC 297 considered in due course.

In conclusion, it should come as no surprise that the legal definition of charity has fluctuated over the centuries, depending on the prevailing social philosophies of the time, and that this, coupled with the conflicting policies of the modern law, has resulted in the less than logical legal position obtaining when the Charities Act 2006 came into force. It will be interesting to see how the approaches adopted in the new legislation will respond. This is especially so given the new law actually draws much inspiration from traditional approaches.

12.4 The operation of charities: a 'live' issue

Many of the consequences of charitable status considered up to this point, as well as the law relating to charity which has been introduced through brief reference to its evolution in modern times, draw attention to key themes which will dominate the work now being commenced on charitable trusts and their operation. It has been observed that the legal definition of charity has fluctuated over the centuries, very much a consequence of—or at the very least a reflection of—the prevailing social philosophies of the time. Important points of continuity and change have been identified. It is also the case that today's dominant social and cultural interests ensure continuing focus on the consequences of charitable status. Illustration of the 'liveness' of the operation of charity comes in the high levels of activity in this sphere in policy circles. In May 2004 a draft Charities Bill was published, and thereafter a Charities Bill was presented in Parliament in December 2004. After being 'timed out' of the opportunity for progress through Parliament by the General Election of May 2005, it was almost immediately reintroduced. In late October 2006, the Bill then entered the last and very heated phase of its journey through Parliament, and received Royal Assent on 8 November 2006. The Charity Commission website reports that in the 'timetable' for implementing the new Act, some aspects will be implemented within a matter of months, while other aspects will require 'further work before they come into force'. However, even at this point, and in contemplation of implementation of the new provisions, the Charities Bill as it originally appeared in 2004 can be considered an 'end result' of considerable energy which has been given to charities in policy circles. Thus, the following chapter will not only analyse the traditional position of the legal definition of charity, but will also signal important imminent changes. This will require consideration of the new legislation itself alongside 'traditional approaches' for the most part. However, in order to highlight key changes which are being pursued, reference will also be made to the earlier stages of the genesis of the new legislation. This will help to map the significance of the proposed changes within our broader cultural consideration of charity and its position in UK society.

12.4.1 The Charities Bill 2004: introduction and background

The starting point for the examination which will be made of the Charities Bill is recognition of it as *an* 'end' point for an extensive exercise in policy-making and in many respects, this is even the case with the new Act itself on account of the 'timetable' for implementation. But returning initially to the very appearance of the Bill in 2004 as an end point, this is because this did *itself* reflect a wealth of accompanying policy documentation, which, alongside the Bill itself, reveal charities very much as a 'live' issue. There is extensive documentation which will enrich appreciation of this, including the following key works. NCVO (2001) 'For the public benefit? A Consultation Document on Charity Law Reform': the National Council for Voluntary Organisations works with and for the voluntary sector in England by providing information, advice and support and by representing the views of the sector to government and policy-makers. There is also the Report of the Scottish Charity Law Review Commission (the McFadden Report), published in May 2001, making numerous recommendations for the reform of charity law and regulation in Scotland.

Following this, a further two key publications preceded the Bill. The first is the publication of the Strategy Unit of the Cabinet Office, known in government circles as 'the Review'. This publication, entitled 'Private Action and Public Benefit', was presented to the Government in 2002 with a series of recommendations to be considered by the Government. The second is the Government's response to these recommendations, published via the Home Office in 2003 as *Charities and Not-for Profits: A Modern Legal Framework: The Government's Response to 'Private Action, Public Benefit'*. Within the document, the original recommendations of the Strategy Review are presented alongside the Government's response to them, thus providing a comprehensive and convenient 'one-document' representation of much of the key debate in this area. It draws clear and detailed attention to the central tenets of the proposed changes in law: modernisation and effectiveness, transparency, accountability, and regulation. These considerations help to provide the essence of the Charities Bill which actually emerged, explaining its origins and rationale. The result of this—the Charities Act 2006—will be considered extensively in the next chapter.

FURTHER READING

Reading materials relating to charity and trust laws can be found referenced in the following two chapters, which relate to the legal definition of charity and cy près as appropriate.

13

The legal definition of charity

13.1 Introduction

Following on from the previous chapter, this one is focused on the legal definition of charity itself. Although there are many respects in which the Charities Act 2006 is highly significant for the way in which charity is to be defined in English law, the previous chapter also drew attention to the way in which it would be some time before the new provisions across the Act will actually come into force and affect 'existing' law. In this vein, the discussion which is made of the legal definition of charity reflects the way in which as the new Act is implemented, references made to 'traditional law' relate to that which predates the Charities Act 2006. The reference made immediately above to the new law affecting traditional law is also a 'marker' for a theme which is going to become very prominent as the new Act is implemented. This rests on the way in which it will become apparent that as well as inculcating some very important new policy directions in charity law, the new definitions of charity derive much of their direction and authority from traditional law. Thus, at this point, it is not very clear how the new provisions will interact with traditional approaches in many respects. Constraints of space mean it is not possible to explore the full extent of the new regime, even in terms of what is actually known at this point (as distinct from what remains to be fleshed out over time) and so some of the key issues can be found discussed within materials placed on the accompanying ORC website.

13.1.1 Sources of law; identifying the legal definition of charity

In previous editions this section has opened with the statement that 'There is no formal statutory definition of charity, despite occasional proposals'. In this very important respect, the Charities Act 2006 will formally place the legal definition of Charity on a statutory footing, and much of this has actually now come into force, and did so in April 2008. However, it is also highly significant that the statutory definitions of categories of charity do to a large extent represent a legislative consolidation of much of the developments to charity law which have occurred over four centuries.

This development over time has given prominence to the consideration of charity made by the courts, with little statutory intervention at the level of definition (save the Recreational Charities Act 1958 which will be considered in due course). The courts in turn have taken their lead from the Statute of Elizabeth 1601, otherwise known as the Statute of Charitable Uses 1601. It is the preamble to this piece of legislation which the courts have drawn on so extensively as a guideline to simplify their task of determining which purposes could be considered charitable.

The preamble listed purposes which were regarded as charitable at the time, and purposes which fell within the 'spirit and intendment' of the preamble have been accepted by the courts as being charitable. Those which did not would not be so, however much they may have been regarded as beneficial to society. By operation of the doctrine of precedent, what had originally been simply a convenient practice by the courts crystallised into rigid legal doctrine, and thus the preamble came, in effect, to have direct legal force. This was most unusual, because preambles to statutes usually have no legal force. Of course, the authority for the traditional law cannot be the preamble itself, but the cases which subsequently adopted it.

13.1.1.1 *Elizabethan 'spirit' and nineteenth century formalisation:* Pemsel

The Statute of Elizabeth's preamble is set out at a later point in this chapter, but for the present, it is sufficient to say that purposes laid down in it are many and diverse. Fortunately for this consideration of the legal definition of charity, a more modern 'base point' of reference exists by virtue of the decision of the House of Lords in *Commissioners for Special Purposes of the Income Tax* v *Pemsel* [1891] AC 531. In this case, Lord Macnaughten categorised charitable purposes under four main heads which have become known as the *Pemsel* heads'. These are:

(1) Purposes for the relief of poverty
(2) Purposes for the advancement of education
(3) Purposes for the advancement of religion
(4) Other purposes which are beneficial to the community.

Noting the different classification 'heads' at this point is simply a marker for the discussion which is to come. More extensive discussion of each of them will commence shortly, and for present purposes, apart from noting the classification itself, it should also be appreciated that any given charitable purpose may, of course, fall within more than one of these heads.

13.1.1.2 Pemsel: *a statement of modern law; evolution and change*

It has thus become generally accepted that there is no need to go back before 1891 for a judicial definition of charity. But it is also the case, for reasons which will become clear, that in traditional law for purposes under head 4, the test for their validity has continued to remain dependent upon the spirit and intendment of the preamble. An illustration of this can be found in the case of the *Scottish Burial Reform & Cremation Society Ltd* v *Glasgow Corporation* [1968] AC 138. This case also provides authority for the essence of charitable purposes as matters of continuing evolution and development. As an idea this was flagged up in the previous chapter, and in this very case Lord Wilberforce sounded a general note of caution about over-rigorous application of the *Pemsel* heads. He anchored this to his suggestion that the law of charity is a moving subject which may well have evolved even since 1891.

13.1.1.3 *Evolving definition of charity and Charities Bill 2004*

There will be some consideration of the Charities Bill 2004 which formed the basis of the legislation enacted in 2006 throughout this chapter. Alongside the attention which will be drawn to its implications for the 'public nature' of charities, and the activities which charitable trusts engage in during the operation of their purposes, will be explanation of the import of the new Act for the definition and classification charitable purposes themselves. As the very end of the previous chapter suggested, reference will be made to a wealth of policy materials surrounding this particular movement for reform, and in particular the key Home Office publication from 2003. It was explained that in this particular document, the recommendations of the Strategy Review are presented along with the Government's response to them. This and the subsequent Charities Bill 2004 contain important changes to the legal definition of charity, which are going to be key to this latest phase of its evolutionary development.

13.1.1.4 *1601 preamble and its continuing life*

The Statute of Charitable Uses 1601 was *itself* repealed by subsequent legislation, so that for a time only the preamble remained. The preamble itself was repealed by the Charities Act 1960 and was not replaced. This repeal had no legal effect, however, because the cases which used the preamble as a guideline can still be taken to be authoritative. Indeed, Lord Wilberforce in the *Scottish Burial Reform* case, mentioned above, used the spirit and intent of the preamble as a test of charitable status as late as 1968. Because reference has traditionally continued to be made to the preamble, it is here set out in full:

Whereas Lands, Tenements, Rents, Annuities, Profits, Hereditaments, Goods, Chattels, Money and Stocks of Money, have been heretofore given, limited, appointed and assigned, as well as by the Queen's most excellent Majesty, and her most noble Progenitors, as by sundry other well disposed persons; some for Relief of aged, impotent and poor People, some for the Maintenance of sick and maimed Soldiers and Mariners, Schools of Learning, Free Schools, and Scholars in Universities, some for the Repair of Bridges, Ports, Havens, Causeways, Churches, Sea-Banks and Highways, some for the Education and Preferment of Orphans, some for or towards Relief, Stock or Maintenance for Houses of Correction, some for the Marriages of Poor Maids, some for Supportation, Aid and Help of young Tradesmen, Handicraftsmen and Persons decayed, and others for the Relief or Redemption of Prisoners or Captives, and for Aid or Ease of any poor Inhabitants concerning Payments of Fifteens [a tax on moveable property], setting out of Soldiers and other Taxes; which Lands, Tenements, Rents, Annuities, Profits, Hereditaments, Goods, Chattels, Money and Stocks of Money, nevertheless have not been employed according to charitable Intent of the givers and Founders thereof, by reason of Frauds, Breaches of Trust, and Negligence in those that should pay, deliver and employ the same: For Redress and Remedy whereof, Be it enacted...

13.1.1.5 Pemsel *as the source of modern law*

In spite of the caution sounded in *Scottish Burial Reform*, the main source of the modern law can be taken to be Lord Macnaughten's classification in *Pemsel*. In addition to judge-made law, a body of precedent has now been built up by the Charity Commissioners (renamed the Charity Commission by virtue of the Charities Act 2006) in exercising their jurisdiction under what was s. 4 of the Charities Act 1960. This body of precedent is not technically authority but may be assumed to govern the process of registration in practice, unless and until it is successfully challenged in a court.

It will also become clear that prior to the Charities Act 2006, recreational charities have been a special case in traditional law, by virtue of the Recreational Charities Act 1958, which provided a limited extension to the general law.

13.1.2 **Requirement of public benefit**

The previous chapter introduced the public nature of charitable trusts, identifying them as purposes which are publicly enforced and controlled, and which have certain tax concessions. There is also a requirement that to be charitable a purpose must, in addition to falling within the *Pemsel* heads outlined above, involve a public benefit. There are therefore two requirements for a purpose to be charitable. It must confer a benefit upon those who are directly the objects of the charity, and it must also confer an additional benefit upon the public at large.

For example, if a charitable purpose such as education is to be advanced, it must not only confer a benefit on those in direct receipt of the education, but must also be advanced in some way that benefits the public, or at least a substantial section thereof, rather than providing benefits for some artificially limited class of people. However, as will become apparent later, this requirement is not applied with the same rigour to each of the four heads of charity, and in the case of the relief of poverty, its role is minimal. For this reason, the public benefit requirement will be dealt with separately under each head.

13.1.3 **Charitable status and overseas benefits**

There is no rule of law which prevents the benefits of a charity being directed overseas, as opposed to being confined within the UK or primarily directed within the UK. For example, in *Re Niyazi's WT* [1978] 1 WLR 910, a trust to construct a hostel for working men in Cyprus was held charitable as being for the relief of poverty. Missionary societies operating abroad always seem to have been regarded as religious charities, and these will also often involve advancement of education. There are, however, three qualifications concerning overseas benefits:

- Although the Charity Commissioners (Annual Report for 1963, paras 69–76) take the view that trusts to relieve poverty or to advance religion will be charitable wherever found, a trust which falls within the fourth head must involve a benefit, even if indirect, to persons within the UK.
- Charity must not be tainted with political activity, and the large-scale charities which aim at assisting developing nations must avoid this pitfall. It seems that whereas it can be charitable to provide direct relief of observable poverty among a population, it is not charitable to seek to raise the total economy of an overseas country, or to alter its laws in order to alleviate poverty.
- *Gaudiya Mission v Brahmachary* [1998] 2 WLR 175 (CA) is authority that an institution established under the laws of another legal system cannot be charitable under UK law, because the courts cannot administer a foreign charity, or settle a cy près scheme for such a charity. Here the courts have no means of controlling an institution established in another country and administered by trustees there.

13.1.4 **Purposes must be exclusively charitable**

A further point to be noted is that a trust must not merely be capable of application to charitable purposes; it must be exclusively so. If it is possible to benefit an object which is not charitable, then the trust will not be exclusively charitable, and as such will fail unless the courts feel able to sever the offending objects from the main corpus of the otherwise charitable purpose, or to declare that the non-charitable purposes are merely subsidiary.

13.1.4.1 *Charitable exclusiveness and the construction of language*

A great deal therefore depends on whether drafting of the trust is construed conjunctively or disjunctively. For example, if a purpose is described as 'charitable *and* benevolent', it is probable that these will be construed conjunctively: 'benevolent' merely qualifies 'charitable', so only charitable purposes are included. But in *Chichester Diocesan Fund and Board of Finance* v *Simpson* [1944] AC 341, the words 'charitable *or* benevolent' would have permitted the trustees to devote all the funds to benevolent ends which were not also charitable. The trust therefore failed, leading to further litigation because funds had already been distributed by the trustees (*Ministry of Health* v *Simpson* [1951] AC 251). A gift to 'benevolent, charitable and religious' purposes was treated in *Williams* v *Kershaw* (1835) 5 Cl & F 111 as allowing the trustees to select purposes which were benevolent, but not necessarily charitable and religious. In other words, the comma was treated as allowing the trustees to select alternatives (namely, as if it were the word '*or*').

Although each case calls for independent construction, as a general guide it may be said that a comma, or the word 'or', is likely to lead to the listed purposes being interpreted disjunctively (that is, as alternatives), while the word 'and' is usually read conjunctively. Generally this will mean that 'charitable and…' succeeds whilst 'charitable or…' fails.

13.1.4.2 *Towards a uniform rule of construction?*

The reference above made to a 'general' position has been used because this not invariably the case. In *Attorney-General of the Bahamas* v *Royal Trust Co.* [1986] 3 All ER 423, the Privy Council held not charitable a bequest for 'any purposes for and/or connected with the education and welfare of Bahamian children and young people', on the grounds that education and welfare should be interpreted disjunctively, and that a trust for welfare was not charitable. Therefore, although it may be possible to draw up guidelines to construction, categoric statements should be treated with caution.

In *Chichester Diocesan Board of Finance* v *Simpson*, it was impossible to construe the gift as being confined to charitable purposes, rather than benevolent purposes. Sometimes it is possible to construe the gift as a whole as being to charitable purposes, however, and as a matter of construction to exclude all purposes which are not charitable: see, for example, *Re Hetherington* [1990] Ch 1. If so, the trustees will be restrained from using trust property for purposes which are not charitable, even where by so doing they are not contravening the *express* terms of the donation. In *Webb* v *O'Doherty* (unreported), *The Times*, 11 February 1991, the officers of a students' union were restrained from making any payments to the National Student Committee to Stop War in the Gulf, or to the Cambridge Committee to Stop War in the Gulf, whose purposes were not charitable. The union was an educational charity, and the officers were therefore entitled to use its property only for charitable purposes, even though there was nothing in the constitution of the union itself prohibiting such payments.

13.1.5 **Purposes which are charitable must not be profit-seeking**

Generally speaking, it is incompatible with charitable status actively to seek profit as a primary objective, although fees may be charged, and incidental acquisition of profit should not disqualify. In *Scottish Burial Reform & Cremation Society Ltd* v *Glasgow Corporation* [1968] AC 138, the House of Lords held a society charitable for rating purposes (under the fourth *Pemsel* head) whose main object was the promotion of sanitary methods of disposal of the dead, because the society charged fees but was not profit-making.

13.1.6 **Charitable purposes under traditional law**

This general introduction to the legal definition of charity has introduced key sources of law, and provided a reminder that key changes are imminent on account of the Charities Act 2006. It has also identified key features flowing from the nature of charitable status which have influenced the development of the law relating to charities up to this point, and which are essential for appreciating why and how this has occurred in the manner it has. It will also become clear that understanding the introductory matters set out above will enhance appreciation of the proposed future directions which are imminent. What needs to follow now, before consideration is made of the new provisions, is substantive consideration of each of the classifications of charitable purposes laid out in *Pemsel*.

13.2 **Purposes for the relief of poverty**

13.2.1 **What is poverty?**

The courts have not attempted to define poverty in precise terms (which would align this with a particular level of income, for example), but it is clear that this has been influenced by notions of 'the deserving poor'. Hence, poverty is not as extreme a concept as destitution (reflecting that people can be poor who are not destitute) and it varies depending on one's status in life. People who are sufficiently well off to be able to live without state aid can be regarded as being poor for these purposes. Paradoxically, it is nowadays actually very difficult to relieve poverty among the poorest sections of society, because a claimant of state benefit can suffer a reduction in that benefit if he receives more than a small donation from charity.

13.2.1.1 *Relative nature of poverty*

In *Re Coulthurst* [1951] Ch 661, Evershed MR said of poverty (at pp. 665–6):

It is quite clearly established that poverty does not mean destitution: it is a word of wide and somewhat indefinite import; it may not be unfairly paraphrased for present purposes as meaning persons who have to 'go short' in the ordinary acception of that term, due regard being had to their status in life, and so forth.

Poverty, therefore, is a relative matter, depending on one's status in life, and the courts have been willing to allow trusts to assist such categories as 'distressed gentle folk'. In *Re De Cartaret* [1933] Ch 103, a trust for annual allowances of £40 each to widows and spinsters 'whose income otherwise shall not be less than 80 or more than 120 pounds per annum' was held charitable, even though there was a minimum income qualification, and £80 a year was at any rate a moderate income then.

Purposes exclusively for the poor
Subject to the width of the definition of poverty, it is essential that poverty should be imposed as a qualification for benefit and that only the poor can benefit. Whereas a trust under any of the other four heads can be charitable even where affluent people can enjoy its benefits, a trust which may benefit rich persons as well as poor will fail under this head. This is the reason why disaster fund appeals are often not charitable (and considered towards the end of the chapter), but the organisers of recent appeals have sometimes preferred to forgo charitable status, and the consequent tax exemptions, rather than limit compensation expressly to the poor.

The rich must usually be expressly excluded, because the courts have been very reluctant to infer their exclusion even where the nature of the benefit is unlikely to make it attractive except to the destitute. Thus it will become clear that in *Re Gwyon* [1930] 1 Ch 255, a clergyman had provided in his will for the distribution of trousers to the boys in the Farnham area. Though the trousers were described in such a way as to be unlikely to appeal to any but the very needy, because the rich were not expressly excluded, the provision was not charitable, and therefore failed. Another case is *Re Drummond* [1914] 2 Ch 90, where a bequest of shares on trust to provide holidays for employees failed, even though the actual wages received by those employees was very low. In *Re Sanders's WT* [1954] Ch 265, Harman J thought that the provision of dwellings for 'the working classes' in the Pembroke Dock area was not sufficient to limit the benefit to poor persons. Nor will a gift for 'deserving' persons, or 'those in need of financial assistance' suffice, but 'indigent' and 'needy' can be regarded as synonyms for poverty. Poverty can also often be implied in the case of gifts to elderly or disabled recipients.

Construction: the trend against hard-and-fast rules
As with any question of construction, however, no hard-and-fast rules can be laid down. Whereas the courts are reluctant to infer exclusion of the rich in the absence of an express limitation to the poor, it would be wrong to assume that they never do so. For example, in *Powell v Attorney-General* (1817) 3 Mer 48, it was assumed that the widows and children of Liverpool seamen would necessarily be poor, even though the word 'poor' itself was not used. More recently it will be seen that in *Re Niyazi's WT* [1978] 1 WLR 910, Megarry V-C held charitable a bequest of £15,000 'for the construction of or as a contribution towards the cost of a working men's hostel' in Famagusta, Cyprus, although there was no express limitation to the poor. He accepted that persons requiring such accommodation would necessarily be poor. *Re Niyazi's WT* is probably not of general application, however. The amount of money left for the purpose was relatively small, and the word 'hostel', rather than 'dwelling' suggested very inferior accommodation. 'Working men' is more limited than 'working classes', excluding, for example, battered wives and students, and Megarry V-C had regard to the deplorable housing shortage in Famagusta. It follows that it would be inadvisable for settlors to rely too heavily on this decision, and an express limitation to the poor is safer.

13.2.1.2 *Methods of relieving poverty*

The measures must actually relieve poverty, so merely to provide amusement for the poor will not suffice under this head, although it might under the second head, if educational.

It used to be thought that relief of poverty had to be ongoing, rather than by way of an immediate distribution of property. It was thought that an immediate distribution was indistinguishable from an ordinary private bequest. It is now clear from the Court of Appeal decision in *Re Scarisbrick* [1951] Ch 622 that this is no longer the case and that it is possible to relieve poverty by way of one-off payment or distribution. The question of whether or not a trust is perpetual in nature could, in the view of Jenkins LJ in that case, be relevant to the question of public bene-fit (which is set out later) because an immediate gift would be less likely to be in favour of a class of persons, as opposed to individuals. But on the assumption that the public benefit test is satisfied, it is not fatal that the disposition is once and for all rather than perpetual.

Indeed, the growth in state welfare provision has reduced the attractiveness of 'hand-outs', for reasons explained at the beginning of the section. Yet many old trusts to relieve poverty still bind trustees to distribute money or goods. This prob-lem and the solution to it are considered in chapter 14.

Relief need not even necessarily be in the form of direct handouts of money, goods, or services, but could, for example, allow access to necessary amenities at reduced cost. So it was accepted in *Joseph Rowntree Memorial Trust Housing Association Ltd* v *Attorney-General* [1983] Ch 159 that the sale of homes to elderly persons at 70 per cent of cost was charitable.

13.3 Purposes for the 'advancement of education'

13.3.1 What constitutes education?

The scope of charitable educational activities is surprisingly wide. In other areas a wide definition of charitable activity has been motivated by the mortmain legisla-tion but this legislation rarely affected educational charities, many of which were incorporated by royal charter. The preamble to the Act of 1601 speaks only of 'schools of learning, free schools, scholars in universities' and the 'education and preferment of orphans', but in modern times this category has grown to cover a very wide range of educational and cultural activities extending far beyond the administration of formal instruction.

13.3.1.1 *Defining 'education' beyond teaching*

Schools and universities are clearly charitable, and so now are nursery schools, adult education centres and societies dedicated to promoting training and stand-ards within a trade or profession. Education is not limited to teaching, however, and learned societies which bring together experts in a field to share and exchange knowledge may be charitable. Museums, zoos and public libraries may be educa-tional to the public at large, quite apart from their research activities. Even cultural activities such as drama, music, literature and fine arts can come within this head, on the ground that they have a role in the cultivation of knowledge and taste.

As with other heads of charity, it is essential that the organisation should not be profit-seeking and the purposes must be exclusively charitable. Thus, a trust for 'artistic' purposes may be too wide (see *Associated Artists Ltd* v *IRC* [1956] 1 WLR 752).

13.3.1.2 *Education must be advanced*

It is also necessary that education be 'advanced', so that although research can be charitable, probably it will not be if, for example, it is carried on in secret. Scholarship for its own sake is also not charitable, and this is one of the reasons why researching the advantages of a new 40-letter alphabet was held non-charitable by Harman J in *Re Shaw* [1957] 1 WLR 729. The validity of a bequest under George Bernard Shaw's will, which also provided for the transcription of *Androcles and the Lion* into the proposed 40-letter alphabet, was also successfully challenged.

Learned societies are charitable, and professional and vocational bodies which advance education, such as the Royal College of Surgeons, are also charitable, even though one of the ancillary purposes is the protection and assistance of its members. Other examples include the Royal College of Nursing, the Institution of Civil Engineers, and the Incorporated Council of Law Reporting (in *Incorporated Council of Law Reporting for England and Wales* v *Attorney-General* [1972] Ch 73, the Attorney-General tried unsuccessfully to argue that the citation of law reports in court could not be educational because judges are deemed to have complete knowledge of the law). Bodies whose chief purpose is to further the interests of the members and to promote the status of the profession will not, however, be charitable: for example, the General Nursing Council (see *General Nursing Council for England & Wales* v *St Marylebone Borough Council* [1959] AC 540).

13.3.1.3 *Issues arising from physical education*

It will shortly become apparent that physical activity which is of a purely recreational nature will not be charitable unless it falls within the provisions of the Recreational Charities Act 1958. Games and other leisure-time pursuits can be charitable under this head, however, if educational. Thus, in *Re Marriette* [1915] 2 Ch 284, a gift to provide squash courts at a public school was held charitable, Eve J remarking (at p. 288) that the playing of games at boarding schools was as important as learning from books, and that the proper education of young people can include a physical element:

No one of sense could be found to suggest that between those ages [10 to 19] any boy can be properly educated unless at least as much attention is given to the development of his body as is given to the development of his mind.

On the same principle, the provision of toys for small children can be charitable (the National Association of Toy Libraries is a registered charity) as are youth movements, such as the Boy Scout Movement, or trusts to provide school outings. In *Re Dupree's Deed Trusts* [1945] Ch 16, Vaisey J held charitable a chess contest for young men in the Portsmouth area, though leaving the issue open for less intellectually demanding pursuits:

I think that the case before me may be a little near the line, and I decide it without attempting to lay down any general propositions. One feels, perhaps, that one is on a slippery slope. If chess, why not draughts; if draughts, why not bezique, and so on, through to bridge and whist, and, by another route, to stamp collecting and the acquisition of birds' eggs? Those pursuits will have to be dealt with if and when they come up for consideration in connection with the problem whether or no there is in existence an educational charitable trust.

These cases have been approved and followed by the House of Lords in *IRC v McMullen* [1981] AC 1, a case involving the playing of football at schools and universities. The House, holding that the Football Association Youth Trust was charitable, also made it clear that the legal conception of charity was not static but changed with ideas about social values.

All the above cases concerned the education of children or young persons. There is no reason, in principle, why adult education should not also be charitable, but a different approach seems to be taken to adult *physical* education: a police athletic association was held to be a trust for recreational purposes, and therefore not charitable. Nor has it been suggested that driving schools or flying schools should be charitable, although their purposes are undoubtedly, in a sense, educational.

13.3.1.4 *Education for the purpose of defining charity, and the role of 'value judgements'*

Inevitably, with a wide definition of educational purposes, the courts and the Charity Commission may be involved in subjective value judgements as to whether a particular purpose falls within or outwith the definition. There appear to be two separate issues. First, does the activity have any educational value at all? Second, in the case of research, on the assumption that any discoveries made will be of value, to what extent should the courts take account of the likelihood of finding nothing?

Education, research, and value judgements
It is clear that the courts are prepared to embark upon value judgements on the first question. The views of the donor will of course not be conclusive, and expert evidence will be admitted in order to assist in evaluating the merit of artistic and cultural work.

In *Re Pinion* [1965] Ch 85, for example, the testator left his 'studio' for the purposes of a museum to display his collection of what were claimed to be 'fine arts'. However, expert witnesses thought that the paintings were 'atrociously bad', and one 'expresse[d] his surprise that so voracious a collector should not by hazard have picked up even one meritorious object'. The question arose as to the validity of the trust, and this depended on whether it was charitable. Harman LJ described the collection as 'a mass of junk' and, reversing Wilberforce J, the Court of Appeal held the trust void. In *Re Hummeltenberg* [1923] 1 Ch 237, the court held void a trust to train spiritualistic mediums (though perhaps disciplined research into the paranormal, undertaken on scientific principles, could be charitable). On the other hand, in *Re Delius* [1957] Ch 299, a trust for the appreciation of the works of the composer was held charitable, but Roxburgh J made it clear that the undoubted merit of Delius's music was crucial, and the same view would not be taken of a 'manifestly inadequate' composer.

Research and the limitations of an 'outcomes' test
Where research is concerned, the courts will also presumably assess the value of the ultimate aim of the project, but on the assumption that any findings would be of value, it does not seem to be a bar to charitable status that nothing might be

found at all. Of course, it is often difficult to know in advance whether or not the results of research will be useful (after all, if you did know the conclusions, the research would be pointless).

Perhaps this point was in Wilberforce J's mind in *Re Hopkins* [1965] Ch 669, where he upheld as charitable a bequest to the Francis Bacon Society for the purposes of finding the Bacon–Shakespeare manuscripts. Though he observed that, if found, the discovery would be 'of the highest value to history and to literature', the search could equally have been futile, as not only were the manuscripts not known to exist, but Wilberforce J thought their discovery unlikely. Value judgements are very difficult to operate when the outcome of the quest is uncertain, as will usually be the case where genuine research is concerned.

13.3.1.5 *Education and political purposes*

A trust for the advancement of political purposes will not be charitable. Education, however, can undoubtedly cover political theory and philosophy. The borderline appears to fall at the point where partisan propaganda is seen to be masquerading in the guise of instruction. In *Re Hopkinson* [1949] 1 All ER 346, a trust for adult education in socialist principles fell foul of the line. The political angle was another reason why the trust in *Re Shaw* [1957] 1 WLR 729 failed. The Charity Commissioners commented on the problem in their Annual Report for 1967, para. 8, but seem to take a fairly generous view, regarding, for example, the promotion of racial harmony as charitable. Greater attention will be paid later to the problem of political purposes generally.

13.4 Purposes for the 'advancement of religion'

13.4.1 Religion, but what religion?

The law adopts a tolerant stance towards religion, and seems reluctant to enter into value judgements in this area. As Cross J remarked in *Neville Estates* v *Madden* [1962] Ch 832, in which a trust for the members of the Catford Synagogue was held charitable: 'As between different religions the law stands neutral, but it assumes that any religion is at least likely to be better than none.' Another example is *Church of the New Faith* v *Commissioner of Payroll Tax* (Victoria) (1983) 83 AJC 4652, a case concerning Australian Scientology, where the High Court of Australia held that:

There can be no acceptable discrimination between institutions which take their character from religions which the majority of the community recognises as religions and institutions which take their character from religions which lack that general recognition.

13.4.1.1 *Religion and neutrality of the law*

Generally speaking, it seems, the courts are unprepared to engage in value judgements as to the relative worth of different religions.

In *Bowman* v *Secular Society Ltd* [1917] AC 406, Lord Parker of Waddington thought that a trust for the purpose of any kind of monotheistic theism would be a good charitable trust.

The preamble to the Statute of Charitable Uses 1601 gave little support for the tolerant approach the law has taken, the only reference to religion within it concerning the repair of churches. It may be that the explanation lies in the mortmain legislation in force from 1736 to 1891, which as we have seen rendered many gifts to charity void. Religious tolerance in this area, therefore, may have been used simply as a device to strike down testamentary gifts, though the authorities from that period still have validity today.

In *Thornton* v *Howe* (1862) 31 Beav 14, for example, charitable status was extended to a devise of land to promote the writings of Joanna Southcote, the founder of a small but fervent sect in the West of England, who had proclaimed that she was with child by the Holy Ghost and would give birth to a second Messiah. The practical effect of the decision was to bring the trust within the invalidating provisions of the mortmain legislation, but the case is still seen as a landmark in establishing that any theistic belief, however obscure or remote, will fall within the meaning of religion for the purposes of charity law. A recent example to the same effect is *Re Watson* [1973] 1 WLR 1472, where Plowman J held charitable a trust to publish the religious writings of a retired builder who was virtually the sole remaining adherent of a small, fundamentalist group of believers. Expert testimony regarded the theological merits of the works as very small but confirmed the genuineness of the writer's beliefs.

It is not necessary that the religious beliefs in question should be Christian. Certainly, the Jewish, Sikh, Hindu, and Muslim faiths have been accepted. Faith healing was held to be a charitable purpose in *Re Le Cren Clarke* [1996] 1 WLR 288. In *Re South Place Ethical Society* [1980] 1 WLR 1565, however, Dillon J remarked that religion is concerned with man's relations with God, so it seems therefore that one qualification is the need for a belief in some kind of God (or gods). The South Place Ethical Society was held not to be a religious charity, because although its objects included 'the study and dissemination of ethical principles', and 'the cultivation of a rational religious sentiment', its beliefs were non-theistic. Dillon J observed:

Religion, as I see it, is concerned with man's relations with God, and ethics are concerned with man's relations with man. The two are not the same, and are not made the same by sincere inquiry into the question, what is God? If reason leads people not to accept Christianity or any known religion, but they do believe in the excellence of qualities such as truth, beauty and love, or believe in the Platonic concept of the ideal, their beliefs may be to them the equivalent of a religion, but viewed objectively they are not religion.

In an old case in the Privy Council, *Yeap Cheah Neo* v *Ong Cheng Neo* (1875) LR 6 PC 381, a provision for the performance of ancestor worship was held non-charitable. High ethical principles or moral philosophy, being concerned with man's relations with man, cannot amount to a religion, though they may of course be educational and so charitable under that head. Plowman J also thought in *Re Watson*, considered above, that doctrines which were averse to the foundations of all religion, and subversive of all morality, would not be charitable under this head.

It seems that the gift must be exclusively for religious purposes, so that a gift for 'missionary work' or 'parish work' will be too wide, since such work may involve elements not wholly religious. On the other hand, in *Re Simson* [1946] Ch 299, a gift to a named clergyman 'for his work in the parish' was held to be impliedly confined to his religious duties.

Buddhism poses a problem in this context, since although it is generally accepted as being a religion, it is not clear (at any rate to the judiciary) whether or not Buddhists believe in a supernatural or supreme being. It is possible that it should be treated as an exception, since a trust to advance Buddhism is clearly charitable. Difficulties could also presumably arise where a human being sets himself up as a deity, and is worshipped as such—such religions exist, and it is unclear whether or not their advancement is charitable.

13.4.2 Purposes must be for the advancement of religion

It is not enough merely to practise religion, and traditionally in order to satisfy the legal definition relating to religion for the purposes of charity law religion must also be *advanced*. As with education, the means by which religion may be advanced may be many and various. Apart from the provision and maintenance of churches, and provision of or for the benefit of clergymen, such matters as church choirs, Sunday school prizes, and even exorcism, have all been held to advance religion.

The advancement of religion seems also to require some positive action. For example, in *United Grand Lodge of Ancient Free & Accepted Masons of England and Wales* v *Holborn Borough Council* [1957] 1 WLR 1080, Donovan J, in denying charitable status to freemasons (who attempted to claim rates advantages), commented that:

There is no religious instruction, no programme for the persuasion of unbelievers, no religious supervision to see that its members remain active and constant in the various religions they may profess, no holding of religious services, no pastoral or missionary work of any kind.

Religion may have been a necessary qualification for membership of the lodge, as it might be for a church squash club, for example, but the lodge did not advance religion any more than a church squash club would.

13.4.3 Religion, society, and reform of the law?

Some time ago, the Government, in its White Paper *Charities: A Framework for the Future*, HMSO (May 1989), the recommendations of which led to the enactment of the Charities Act 1992, later consolidated in 1993, considered whether the law in this area should be altered. The White Paper noted that:

Anxieties have been expressed, in particular, about a number of organisations whose influence over their followers, especially the young, is seen as destructive of family life and, in some cases, as tantamount to brainwashing.

Nevertheless, although considerable sympathy was expressed for these anxieties, reform of the law was not recommended, mainly because it was considered too difficult to formulate adequate proposals. Removal of charitable status from all trusts established for the advancement of religion was rejected because of the difficulties in which it would leave many existing trusts. Denial of charitable status only to new organisations, established after the legislation came into force, was rejected on the grounds that it would be difficult to justify denying charitable status to new trusts for religious purposes of an existing denomination. Replacing the presumption of public benefit with a positive test of 'worth' considered later which those seeking charitable status would need to satisfy was also rejected, on the grounds that it would be difficult to define any criteria upon which a test of worth could be based. Problems would also occur where there was a single objectionable feature in a complex body of doctrine. The Paper also noted that the public anxieties which have been expressed have generally been addressed to the *conduct* of a movement rather than its *objects*, and that these matters can be dealt with administratively by the Charity Commission.

13.5 'Other purposes beneficial to the community'

The consideration given to this final category which arises from Lord Mcnaughtan's *Pemsel* classification will show that it does, as its 'title' suggests, provide a residual category of charitable purposes. This is where a vast number, and very diverse purposes, can be found 'grouped', and as a reflection of this as much as its imprecise title itself, it is a head and classification which it is almost impossible to define precisely. The first point to note relating to this is that not every purpose which might, by common consensus, be considered beneficial to the community can come within this head. What the law admits as charitable under this head is still governed by the general statement of charitable purposes which was set out in the preamble to the Statute of Charitable Uses 1601, for although this has itself been repealed, the cases which have relied upon its guidance over centuries are still themselves authority. If some wholly novel purpose appears, the question is not whether it is beneficial in some general sense, but whether it falls within the 'spirit and intendment' of the preamble, or can be held to do so by analogy with the principles developed through the cases.

A 'catch-all' category
It should therefore be obvious that it is not always possible to state whether a particular purpose is charitable under this head or not. Some cases are expressly mentioned in the preamble, however, and there are also classes of trust which have been specifically considered by the courts. About these, at least, it is possible to state conclusions.

13.5.1 Purposes specifically included in the preamble

The preamble makes specific mention of the relief of aged, impotent (meaning disabled), and poor people; and it has never been necessary to show that the recipients possess all three characteristics simultaneously. Trusts to assist the elderly are common, as are trusts for the disabled, and no further requirement of poverty in the recipients is imposed. In other words, this head is wider than the relief of poverty head.

It must be the case, however, that the proposed purpose will offer some relief to the recipients. Since many of the disadvantages which accompany age or general disability can in fact be eased by material provision in the form of money or special equipment, this general requirement usually poses no problems. Probably, however, a gift of money which was wholly confined to such elderly or disabled people as are already wealthy could not be charitable, because it would fail to relieve the disadvantage of their condition. It is also likely that the class of recipients would not amount to a section of the public so as to satisfy the additional public benefit requirements.

13.5.1.1 *Trusts for the benefit of the sick*

Trusts to benefit the sick are *prima facie* charitable and before the introduction of the National Health Service in 1946, charitable gifts were the main source of provision for those needing hospital care but unable either to afford it or to insure against illness or injury. Today, gifts to private hospitals will still be charitable, since they help to ease the pressure on public services, as was noted in *Re Resch's WT* [1969] 1 AC 514. It is no objection that such hospitals tend to be of direct benefit to those who are relatively rich, though as under other heads a purely profit-making institution will not be charitable. There is no need to confine the benefits of the trust directly to the patients, and gifts which improve the efficiency of the service by providing homes for nurses, or accommodation for visiting relatives, are included under this head. Even organisations offering help with family planning, and those which seek to promote health by encouraging temperance, have been accepted for registration, but the Commissioners have found difficulty (see their Annual Report for 1975, para. 70) with fringe methods of healing, not generally recognised by the medical profession. Methods which are widely recognised, such as acupuncture, osteopathy, and even faith healing (with *Funnell v Stewart* [1996] 1 WLR 288 as authority for this) are acceptable, but in other cases some evidence of the method's effectiveness will be demanded.

13.5.1.2 *Trusts for the benefit of soldiers*

Another category of benefits mentioned in the preamble was the 'setting out of soldiers', which has been extended to include the wellbeing and morale of the forces, or specific units thereof; charities for ex-servicemen; and the promotion of the efficiency of the police and the maintenance of law and order. Gifts to the Inland Revenue and for 'my country England' have been held charitable (*Re Smith* [1932] Ch 153), but gifts expressed to be for 'public' or 'patriotic' purposes have failed as being too wide and not exclusively charitable.

13.5.2 Anomalies: purposes in the preamble without modern counterparts

Gifts for the 'repair of bridges, ports, havens, causeways, sea-banks and highways' were included in the preamble, and now that the state assumes responsibility for such matters, this category has grown to include such miscellaneous amenities as the National Trust, museums, art galleries, parks, and community centres. In *Scottish Burial Reform & Cremation Society Ltd v Glasgow Corporation* [1968] AC 138, a crematorium was held charitable. And while it is not charitable to erect a monument to oneself, the commemoration of significant people or events (e.g., war memorials) will qualify. The Earl Mountbatten of Burma Statue Appeal Trust has been registered as being 'likely to foster patriotism and good citizenship' (Charity Commissioners' Annual Report 1981, paras 68–70).

13.5.2.1 *Old ideas and modern applications: bringing the preamble up to date*

The 'preferment of orphans' mentioned in the preamble has its modern counterpart in the provision of orphanages and local authority homes, but in *Re Cole* [1958] Ch 888 a majority of the Court of Appeal held non-charitable a trust for the general welfare and benefit of children in such a home out of fear that this might permit the provision of amenities not of an educational nature, such as radios or television sets, and this decision was followed in *Re Sahal* [1958] 1 WLR 1243. In this respect, therefore, purposes are unlikely to succeed under this head unless they will also succeed under the educational head.

Trusts to aid the rehabilitation and reform of prisoners have been accepted as charitable since the nineteenth century. A more interesting example perhaps can be seen in the reference in the preamble to 'ransom of captives'. In one respect it might be easy to dismiss this idea as a relic from the past, and there is certainly the sense that in many respects society has become more safe (and increasingly civilised) and that accordingly it is unlikely to find captives being held for ransom. However it could perhaps be applied in the light of today's heightened concerns about terrorism—here hostages taken by terrorists might in some situations, appropriately be encompassed within the term 'captives'.

A gift for the benefit of a locality such as a town, county or parish, or for its inhabitants, will be charitable although one might have expected it to fail either because of failure to specify exclusively charitable purposes or on the ground that there is an insufficient public benefit. The explanation may lie in an analogy with gifts to local authorities. These have long acted in the capacity of trustees of various charities and so such gifts may be *impliedly* confined to charitable purposes. In any event, gifts to localities were probably within the spirit of the reforms of 1601 historically, as these reforms were largely directed towards easing the burden of local poor rates. The trust must, it seems, be cast in terms of benefit for an area or its residents for the time being (not, for example a trust for expatriate Welshmen, unless the purposes were charitable for some other reason).

13.5.3 **Animal charities**

Animal charities are among the most popular with the public. Their inclusion within this head of charity owes nothing to the preamble to the Statute of Charitable Uses 1601 but rests upon a process of reasoning by analogy. As with religious toleration, the motive may well have lain in the mortmain legislation, but precedents of that period are of course still followed today.

In *London University* v *Yarrow* (1857) 1 De G & J 72, a trust to study the diseases of animals useful to mankind was held charitable, but this would probably have been a valid educational charity anyway. A more general authority is *Tatham* v *Drummond* (1864) 4 De G J & Sm 484, in which a bequest for the relief and protection of animals taken to be slaughtered was held charitable so that the gift failed under the mortmain legislation. Romer J also held a gift to a named lady to aid her work in caring for cats and kittens to be charitable in *Re Moss* [1949] 1 All ER 495.

13.5.3.1 *Animal charities*

It is not, however, the benefit to the animals themselves which has been fastened upon, to provide principled justification for the inclusion of animal charities under this head (although in Ireland, the good of animals requires no further justification). Rather, the assumed benefit is to humans, by encouraging them in 'feelings of humanity and morality generally' (see the judgment of Swinfen Eady LJ in *Re Wedgwood* [1915] 1 Ch 113, at 122).

Homes for lost dogs, needy horses, donkeys, etc., have been accepted as charitable, along with well-known organisations such as the RSPCA and the PDSA. On the other hand, the need to benefit humans leads to the conclusion that the protection of creatures harmful to man could not be charitable under this head, nor, according to the Court of Appeal in *Re Grove-Grady* [1929] 1 Ch 557, would be the creation of a sanctuary where animals would be protected from all human intrusion. No doubt, however, both these could, in the case of trusts appropriately drafted, be valid as educational charities, for example by the inclusion of a provision that the wildlife be studied.

13.5.3.2 *Animal welfare and judgements of competing merits*

Whereas it is usually assumed that a purpose falling under the first three heads of charity is a benefit, no such assumption is made for purposes falling under the fourth head, and indeed, sometimes the courts will be faced with value judgements as to the relative merits of competing benefits. On the issue of whether the abolition of vivisection might be a public benefit, for example, the House of Lords in *National Anti-Vivisection Society* v *IRC* [1948] AC 31 was not prepared to depart from the view of the Special Commissioners for Income Tax, that any assumed public benefit in the suppression of vivisection, in the advancement of morals, was outweighed by a detriment to medical science and research, which was itself of undoubted public benefit. The purposes of the National Anti-Vivisection Society not therefore being charitable, it was not entitled to exemption from income tax. This case in considered in the materials on public benefit.

Private trusts for pet animals are not charitable because there is no public benefit, but they may nevertheless be valid as private purpose trusts as an anomalous category as seen in chapter 4.

13.5.4 **Purposes beneficial to the community;** *Pemsel* **and continuing evolution**

Although one would be wise to give due regard to the views of Lord Wilberforce expressed in the *Scottish Burial Reform* case of the dynamic nature of charity and charity law, it is not surprising that the fourth 'dustbin' *Pemsel* head has been a particular hub of activity. This can be illustrated by a number of examples whereby the Charity Commission has made determinations on such 'topical' issues as unemployment, questions of rural and urban regeneration and conservation, corporate social responsibility, and fair trade. The references made to Charity Commission documents can be followed up on its extremely informative (and even quite straightforward) website (see <http://www.charity-commission.gov.uk>). This is also a reflection of the discussion which will follow about the Charities Act 2006 and the changes it will make to the way in which charity is defined, which are discussed immediately hereafter—following discussion of the Recreational Charities Act 1958. It will become apparent at that point how a number of newer charitable purposes have become embodied in the new statutory definition of charity.

13.5.4.1 *Relief of unemployment*

Trusts for the relief of unemployment (directly, rather than through the traditional routes such as the alleviation of poverty) have recently been considered in the review of the Register of Charities. The Charity Commission ruled that such purposes can be charitable if they are able to establish that they are seeking to address unemployment generally for a community or for a section of it. Examples of addressing or tackling employment which would satisfy the Charity Commissioners would include giving advice or training to those who are unemployed, and initiatives to help business 'start ups' (including, for example, subsidised rents and capital advances, etc.).

13.5.4.2 *Promotion of urban and rural revival*

Under the traditional law, this purpose is one which has been recognized as charitable only very recently. This can occur where it can be shown that the organisation seeking charitable status can demonstrate that it is seeking to improve 'physical, social and economic infrastructure' and assist to alleviate disadvantage which has arisen on account of social and economic circumstances. Such purposes can include the provision of financial assistance or the promotion of improving standards in housing; the provision of education or (re)training; the provision and maintenance of infrastructure (is this perhaps a modern-day counterpart for the Statute of Elizabeth's reference to 'repair of bridges etc.'?); the provision of recreational facilities and public amenities and their maintenance; and the preservation of historic buildings and places of interest.

13.5.4.3 *Preservation of national heritage and conservation of the environment*

Closely related to the promotion of rural and urban revival is the preservation of national heritage and the environment. For example, the National Trust has a long tradition of being charitable, and in 2001 the conservation of the environment was recognised as a charitable purpose in its own right. However, the Charity Commission did make it clear that charitable status shall only follow the provision of public access to the site or habitat or building in question (in order to satisfy the public benefit requirement). If there are good reasons for restricting public access, public benefit can be satisfied with the provision of alternative means of providing the public with information.

13.5.4.4 *Promotion of business ethics and responsibility*

Recently the Charity Commission has determined that organisations which promote the incorporation of ethics into their business practice, and which provide advice or protection for employees faced with ethical difficulties encountered in their work can be recognised as charitable.

13.5.4.5 *Promotion of fair trade*

Trusts for the promotion of fair trade have been recognised as charitable since the 'fair trade mark' received charitable status in 1995. Whilst the motivation for relieving poverty and promoting better standards of living in Third World countries might appear to be a trust for the relief of poverty, it will of course provide benefit for those who are not poor in addition, and thus would not be exclusively for the poor (illuminating the need for charitable status to be sought and conferred by head 4).

13.5.5 **Recreational purposes**

Until the 1950s it was assumed that while some recreational purposes, such as boys' clubs, women's institutes and parish halls, were potentially charitable, sporting facilities were not, unless they were either educational or promoted efficiency in the armed forces. A series of cases in the 1950s, however, suggested that no recreational purpose will be charitable at common law, precipitating the addition by statute of a fifth (limited) head of recreational charities.

13.5.5.1 *Recreation, charity and the 'big three'*

In *IRC* v *Glasgow Police Athletic Association* [1953] AC 380, the encouragement and promotion of athletic sport and general pastimes for officers and ex-officers of the City of Glasgow police force was held non-charitable, although it might have been allowed had the purpose been merely incidental to improving police efficiency. It had been found as a fact that the athletic association played an important part in the maintenance of health, morale, and *esprit de corps* within the police force, and in attracting recruits to the force. The leisure element was considered too prominent however, to be merely incidental to maintaining the efficiency of the police force. Lord Reid said:

I do not doubt that the purpose of increasing or maintaining the efficiency of a police force is a charitable purpose within the technical meaning of those words in English law. It appears to me to be well established that the purpose of increasing the efficiency of the army or a part of it is a charitable purpose. It may be that in some cases the facts hardly justified the conclusion that this was the purpose of the gift in question, but that does not affect the principle. I can see no valid distinction between the importance or character of the public interest of maintaining the efficiency of the army and that of maintaining the efficiency of the police.

But it is not enough that one of the purposes of a body of persons is charitable: the Act requires that it must be established for charitable purposes only. This does not mean that the sole effect of the activities of the body must be to promote charitable purposes, but it does mean that that must be its predominant object and that any benefits to its individual members of a non-charitable character which result from its activities must be of a subsidiary or incidental character.

...I have come to the conclusion that conferring such benefits [leisure and enjoyment] on its members bulks so large in the purposes and activities of this association that it cannot properly be said to be established for charitable purposes only....

In *Williams's Trustees* v *IRC* [1947] AC 447, the London Welsh Association, whose objects were to promote social and recreational purposes among Welsh people living in London had also been held non-charitable, partly on the basis that purely social activities could not be charitable within the spirit of the preamble to the Statute of Charitable Uses 1601. Finally, in *IRC* v *Baddeley* [1955] AC 572, a reduction in stamp duty on a conveyance of land was refused because the purposes of the conveyance were not charitable. The conveyance was to a Methodist mission and the purposes were essentially those of promoting the 'religious, social and physical wellbeing' of residents of an area by providing facilities for 'religious services and instruction; and for the social and physical training and recreation' of such people. The inclusion of purely social purposes prevented these purposes from being exclusively charitable.

13.6 Problems with 'other purposes' and the Recreational Charities Act 1958

The discussion immediately above explains how doubt was cast by a number of decisions in the 1950s on the charitable status of a number of social trusts which had always been assumed to be charitable. The Recreational Charities Act 1958 was enacted to restore what was assumed to be the *status quo ante* in respect of those trusts. The London Welsh Association, for example, was validated by the Charity Commissioners in 1977.

Section 1 states that it shall be, and be deemed always to have been, charitable to provide, or assist in the provision of, facilities for recreation or other leisure-time occupation, if the facilities are provided in the interests of social welfare. A proviso adds that nothing in the section shall be taken to derogate from the principle that to be charitable a trust or institution must be for the public benefit. Under s. 1(2), the requirement that the facilities are provided in the interests of social welfare will not be satisfied unless the facilities are provided with the object of improving the conditions of life for the persons for whom the facilities are primarily intended.

13.6.1 A postscript on the 'other purposes' head

Although the significance of the 'other purposes' head for the evolving nature of charitable purposes envisioned by Lord Wilberforce in the *Scottish Burial Reform* case in 1968 has already been considered, there is one final reference which can be made to illustrate this point. The materials above have shown that a number of purposes which were clearly not within the purview of those who drafted the Statute of Elizabeth in 1601, have been found to be within the 'spirit and intendment' of the preamble. This can be seen with purposes for the protection of the environment, and ones relating to human rights and ones seeking to address world poverty, etc.

The postscript here concerns purposes which necessitated the enactment of the Recreational Charities Act 1958 in order to secure charitable status for recreational purposes for adults. In clear demonstration that things had evolved since the late 1950s, almost half a century later, the promotion of amateur sport for its own sake was recognised as charitable by the Charity Commissioners in 2003.

13.7 The Charities Act 2006 and reform in the definition of charitable purposes

It will quickly become obvious and apparent to anyone who studies the text of the Charities Act 2006 that an exhaustive consideration of it is simply not possible here in terms of space. What *is* provided in this chapter is a basic outline of the way in which the Bill and also the new Act relates to the legal definition of charity. Thus, at this point, attention is paid only to how the Act will impact on the legal definition of charitable purposes. Accordingly, its implications for the 'public benefit' requirement for charitable status are held over to be discussed alongside the traditional provisions relating to public benefit, which follow immediately below.

In looking at proposed changes to traditional approaches to the legal definition of charity (and in due course the provisions relating to public benefit), attention is of course drawn to the relevant sections within the Charities Act 2006. These proposed reforms are themselves positioned alongside the issues which underpinned the policy of *Private Action and Public Benefit*, and the subsequent Home Office Publication from 2003 which contained the Government's response to that Review publication. Reference will also be made as appropriate Parliamentary consideration of the then Charities Bill dating from 2005 and 2006.

And since the Charities Act 2006 received Royal Assent in November 2006, there are already a number of developments which reflect that the framework of the new Act is intended to be 'fleshed out' over time. A number of 'commencement orders' have already brought key provisions into force, including ones relating to defining charitable purposes in the new regime, which place the legal definition of charity on a statutory footing. It is also the case that a number of key consultations and publications have already transpired from the work of the Charity Commission.

At this stage there is one very important element to understanding the provisions of the new Act which give a statutory definition to charity. It is essential to appreciate that in many respects the new provisions represent a consolidation of much of the development of charities law at common law. This is so both in respect of the actual classification of charitable purposes themselves and in the way in which an accompanying framework focused on the general character of charitable operation has been developed alongside this. This latter 'framework' does of course include matters such as that, in order to be charitable, purpose must be 'exclusively charitable'.

13.7.1 The 'starting point' for the new Act: the meaning of charity

The first sections of the Charities Act 2006 attend to what, for the purposes of the proposed new statutory footing for charitable trusts, will be meant by the terms 'charity' and 'charitable purpose'. Two important related considerations flow from the new Act's direction in these matters, and they relate to the significant role played by the courts in the development of charity law over the past 400 years. In defining what is meant by charity, s. 1(1)(a) of the new Act provides that the term 'charity' means an institution '*which is established for charitable purposes only*', and by s. 1(1)(b) one which (accordingly) 'falls *to be subject to the control of the High Court in the exercise of its jurisdiction with respect to charities*'.

The references within s. 1(1)(a) are very clearly to the 'framework' adopted in the development of the traditional law relating to charities which has enabled the courts to develop and refine principles governing charitable purposes themselves. This is thus affirmation that the notion of purposes which are exclusively charitable remain at the heart of English charity law. In this spirit of 'conservation' between traditional approaches and future directions, s. 1(3) provides authority for the continuing operation of the essence of the legal basis of charity law for the past

400 years: '*A reference in any enactment or document to a charity within the meaning of the Charitable Uses Act 1601 or the preamble to it shall be construed as a reference to a charity as defined by this section*'.

An analysis of the Act's new approach, which signals consolidation and confirmation, and importantly clarification, rather than substantive new direction, can be seen in the explanation given to what is meant by charitable purposes as provided by s. 2. Section 2(1) provides that '*For the purposes of the law of England and Wales, a charitable purpose is a purpose which—(a) falls within subsection (2), and (b) is for the public benefit (see section 3).*' Accordingly, a purpose is charitable if it falls within any of the following descriptions of purposes listed there under s. 2(2), **and** it is (a purpose) for the public benefit. The purposes actually listed under s. 2(2) are accordingly:

(a) the prevention and relief of poverty;

(b) the advancement of education;

(c) the advancement of religion;

(d) the advancement of health;

(e) the advancement of citizenship and community development;

(f) the advancement of the arts, heritage or science;

(g) the advancement of amateur sport;

(h) the advancement of human rights, conflict resolution, or reconciliation;

(i) the advancement of environmental protection or improvement;

(j) the relief of those in need, by reason of youth, age, ill-health, disability, financial hardship or other disadvantage;

(k) the advancement of animal welfare;

(l) the promotion of the efficiency of the armed forces of the Crown, or of the efficiency of the police, fire and rescue services or ambulance services;

(m) any other purposes within subsection (4).

The first three categories of purposes within s. 2(2)—purposes (a), (b), and (c)—are instantly recognisable as three of the *Pemsel* heads of charitable purposes. Indeed, the provisions of s. 2(3) even reflect concerns which have arisen in the interpretations given to advancement of religion: according to s. 2(3)(a), '*religion includes (i) religion which involves belief in more than one god; and (ii) a religion which does not involve belief in a god*'. Thus, although in many respects the new Act is an exercise in consolidation and confirmation, it does signal a certain degree of new direction.

However, it is also the case that consolidation and confirmation is particularly strong in analysing the intended direction of the new Act. The remaining 10 heads comprise a mixture of purposes which are recognisable within current understandings of 'charitable purpose' and others which *could* potentially be brought within the scope of the current fourth head in *Pemsel* relating to 'other purposes beneficial for the community', by being in the 'spirit and intendment' of the 1601 Act. Section 2(3) continues to provide clarification of s. 2(2) beyond the position relating to religion in the following ways:

• Section 2(3)(b) provides that in respect of paragraph (d) 'the advancement of health' includes '*the prevention or relief of sickness, disease or human suffering*'.

- Section 2(3)(c) provides that paragraph (e) includes *'(i) rural or urban regeneration, and (ii) the promotion of civic responsibility, volunteering, the voluntary sector or the effectiveness or efficiency of charities'*.
- Section 2(3)(d) provides that for the purposes of paragraph (g) 'sport' means *'sport which involves physical skill or exertion'*.
- Section 2(3)(e) provides that paragraph (j) includes *'relief given by the provision of accommodation or care to the persons mentioned in that paragraph'*.

The spirit of confirmation and consolidation is further indicated in the provisions of s. 2(4)–(8). In this respect, attention has been drawn to the following:

- By the provisions of s. 2(4)(a), purposes which are not included within the statutory categories contained within s. 2(2) can nevertheless still be charitable where they are *inter alia* recognised as purposes under traditional charity law.

By these new provisions they may accordingly be regarded as analogous with any purposes in the new statutory list, or under traditional charity law, referenced in the legislation as 'existing law' (see below). This reference to recognition of purposes which are charitable under 'existing' law will include the purposes made charitable by the Recreational Charities Act 1958.

- By the provisions of s. 2(5) where any term used in the definitions of s. 2(2), or s. 3's provisions for public benefit, has particular meaning under charity law, in the new legislation the term will be taken as having the same meaning where it appears in that provision.
- By the provisions of s. 2(8), references made in s. 2 to 'charity law' denote *'the law relating to charities in England and Wales'* and to reiterate 'existing charity law' means *'charity law as in force immediately before the day on which this* [new] *section comes into force'*.

The provisions relating ot the definition of charitable purposes and companion provisions relating to public benefit are now in force, on account of a commencement order on coming into effect on 1 April 2008.

13.8 Legal definition after classifying purposes: public benefit requirement

In traditional English charity law, in addition to the manner in which purposes must be able to be classified in order to achieve charitable status, as the introduction made clear, there is an additional requirement for all charities that they must confer a 'public benefit'. The spirit of this has been carried through into the new Act which points to *continuity* between traditional and new approaches. However, it will also become clear that the new law marks important points of *departure*, suggesting that the public benefit requirement is to have greater prominence still in new charity law, and promoting increasing robustness in the regulation of charitable organisations. In turn this is believed to be essential for achieving high levels of public confidence in charity, and in the operation of charitable organizations generally. Because once again the new Act can be seen as a project of *continuity* and also *change*, reference is first made to how traditionally the public benefit requirement has been manifested in English charity law.

What follows at this point is a consideration of how public benefit is accommodated in the requirements for traditional approaches, and as a matter of logic which will become apparent, the requirement or 'test' for public benefit will be considered under each traditional charitable 'head', and will be so in the order of heads 2, 4, 1, and 3 respectively. The reason for starting with head 2 is that the test of public benefit for educational charities has been clearly stated, and one of the main issues defining traditional approaches to public benefit is the extent to which that test also applies to the other heads of charity. Most of the cases are on head 4, which is why this head is dealt with immediately after head 2.

Following this consideration of the law as traditionally framed, the discussion will then move to the significance of public benefit in the Charities Act 2006, signalling future direction.

13.8.1 Two key tests for public benefit

As has been noted on a few occasions thus far, in addition to having to be capable of being recognised under one of the *Pemsel* heads of charitable purpose, a purpose seeking charitable status has traditionally in addition had to meet the requirement that it is a purpose for 'public benefit'.

In traditional charity law—that which pre-dates the Charities Act 2006—there must be an identifiable public benefit, capable of having a demonstrable effect, whether tangible or intangible, direct or indirect. And traditionally there has been a presumption that purposes falling within the first three *Pemsel* heads of charity set out above provide public benefit, which is very strongly associated with the historical functions of charity. However as it will transpire shortly, this presumption has been removed by the Charities Act 2006. Although this is a point of clear difference between traditional approaches and new directions envisioned in the Charities Act 2006, the underlying rationale of public benefit is very much one of continuity. This can be seen in two elements based on tests established in case law which must be demonstrated for this test for public benefit to be satisfied.

- The purpose must be, on balance beneficial rather than detrimental to the public; and
- The purpose must benefit a sufficient section of the public.

In relation to the first requirement—for a benefit rather than a detriment to be demonstrated—the *National Anti-Vivisection Society v IRC* [1948] AC 31 is authority that where a purpose would on balance be detrimental to the public the purposes cannot be charitable. In cases where it is accepted or decided that the purposes are, on balance, beneficial to the public, then the second part of this hurdle must still be addressed.

Thus, even where a purpose has fallen within one or more of the four *Pemsel* heads, and is found to be beneficial to the public (rather than detrimental, on balance), it will not achieve charitable status unless the second 'public benefit' requirement is also satisfied. This is that the purpose must benefit a sufficient section of the public. As the materials show, the courts have developed different tests for each of the four traditional heads of charitable purpose.

13.8.2 **Public benefit and educational charities**

In the case of relief of poverty, even benefiting a small number of people may be regarded as conferring a public benefit. Yet whereas education is clearly a benefit to those in immediate receipt of it, it is not self-evident that educating a few people constitutes a benefit to the general public. Indeed, given that many of the cases under this head are in reality disputes over tax relief, it would be quite wrong if the education of a privileged few were to be regarded as charitable. Under this head it is therefore necessary that there is some additional benefit to the general public or some appreciable sector thereof.

That is not to say that a particular form of education has to be capable of being enjoyed by everyone, so long as access to it is reasonably open. Thus public schools may be charitable as long as they are not operated as profit-making ventures, although their fees may place them beyond the means of the majority. Even scholarships or endowed chairs, which can be enjoyed only by one person at a time, present no difficulty. The problems arise where it is sought to limit the potential beneficiaries within a class which is insufficiently wide to constitute a section of the public. It is clear that it may be charitable to provide for instance scholarships, open to:

- persons following a common profession or calling, or their children and dependants, or
- people of common nationality, religion or sex, or
- the inhabitants of a given area, provided this is reasonably large, such as a town or county.

It is also the case that special provisions for disabled people are also permissible, since they are a section of the public in a meaningful sense.

13.8.2.1 *Explaining the* Oppenheim *personal nexus test, in terms of its operation and significance*

However, under this head, and probably under all the *Pemsel* heads except relief of poverty, it will be fatal if the class of potential beneficiaries (however large) is defined in terms of relation to particular individuals or a company. This approach originated in *Re Compton* [1945] Ch 123, where charitable status was denied to a trust to educate the children of three named families. It is understandable that the courts are reluctant to allow an essentially private arrangement to enjoy charitable privileges, especially tax advantages, but it seems that the principle extends to cases where the class of potential beneficiaries is defined in terms of a relationship with an employer, even were the employer is a substantial concern.

The most authoritative statements on this position are those of Lord Simonds in *Oppenheim* v *Tobacco Securities Trust Co. Ltd* [1951] AC 297, where *Re Compton* was approved in the House of Lords. Lord Simonds said that first, the number of possible beneficiaries must not be negligible, and second, that the class must not be defined so as to depend on any relationship to a particular individual or employer:

> Then the question is whether that class of persons can be regarded as such as a 'section of the community' as to satisfy the test of public benefit. The words 'section of the community' have no special sanctity, but they conveniently indicate first, that the possible (I emphasise

the word 'possible') beneficiaries must not be numerically negligible, and secondly, that the quality which distinguishes them from other members of the community, so that they form by themselves a section of it, must be a quality which does not depend on their relationship to a particular individual…A group of persons may be numerous, but, if the nexus between them is their personal relationship to a single *propositus* or to several *propositi*, they are neither the community nor a section of the community for charitable purposes.

In the trust with which the House of Lords was concerned, the number of potential beneficiaries (at least in theory) was certainly not negligible. The income of the trust fund was directed to be applied 'in providing for…the education of children of employees or former employees of the British-American Tobacco Co. Ltd…or any of its subsidiary or allied companies in such manner…as the acting trustees shall in their absolute discretion…think fit'. The number of present employees alone exceeded 110,000, which meant that the number of potential beneficiaries was not an issue, and thus it was only the personal nexus rule which was fatal, and this was because they were all connected with the same company.

As Lord MacDermott pointed out in his dissenting speech, however, the rule is by no means easy to apply, and produces odd results when the *'propositus'* is an employer. For example, a trust to educate the sons of railwaymen, not expressed as limited to a single company, would have been valid before the nationalisation of the railways, and void when British Rail became the sole employer. In any case the test is arguably inappropriate in large companies. Although it is easy to see a rationale for suggesting that the special tax concessions of charitable status should not be given to any arrangement for a private class, the personal link between employees is not as obvious as that between members of a family, among whom considerations of mutual interest might be considered to negate the altruistic status of the trust.

Justifying the Oppenheim approach

Perhaps the real, if unstated, justification for the result in *Oppenheim* was the extent of the trustees' discretion in that case. The benefit to 110,000 or more people may in fact have been entirely theoretical. Indeed if the trustees had used the funds to pay 15 per cent of fees to those employees who sent their sons to boarding school, only the relatively small number who could afford the other 85 per cent would actually have benefited. The problem is that the test in *Oppenheim* may not achieve the desired result in all cases. Perhaps it would have been more appropriate for the House of Lords to have concentrated on the extent of the trustees' discretion to limit the number of people who could in practice have benefited, rather than the nexus which could be found with the company.

The application of the personal nexus test

Nevertheless, the personal nexus rule is law, certainly for trusts under this head. However, there may however be some loopholes, such as the one for example in *Re Koettgen's WT* [1954] Ch 252, in which an educational trust succeeded despite a direction that the trustees should give preference to the families of employees, up to a maximum of 75 per cent of income. On the other hand, doubts have been expressed, and, for example, a preference for the grantor's family rendered a gift non-charitable in *Caffoor* v *Income Tax Commissioner* [1961] AC 584. In *IRC* v *Educational Grants Association Ltd* [1967] Ch 123, affirmed [1967] Ch 993, between 76 per cent and 85 per cent of the income of a fund (varying from year to year) was paid out for the education of persons connected with the Metal Box Co. Ltd. In a dispute with the Inland Revenue, it was held that the money had not been paid exclusively for charitable purposes. Pennycuick J found 'considerable difficulty in the *Koettgen* decision' and thought that a preference for a private class might always be fatal (although he did not actually need to decide that). The problem with laying down a clear rule of this nature would be that extreme cases could be envisaged (e.g., a *preference* up to 5 per cent of income) where its application would further no obvious policy (unless again, of course, an objection is taken in principle to charitable status for an arrangement with any purely private content).

This problem is similar to that which can be said to pertain to *Oppenheim* itself, namely that the rule is arguably too rigid. The real problem in *Oppenheim*, as has been seen, was the extent of the trustees' discretion to limit the number of people who could in practice have benefited rather than the nexus with the company (unless again, objection is taken to *any* private arrangement). It would have been difficult to formulate a clear rule on trustees' discretion, however, where the problem is essentially one of where to draw the line, just as it is difficult to draw the line in the *Koettgen* situation. In both cases, therefore, a rigid rule may well be the only answer.

13.8.2.2 *Class must be a section of the community*

Oppenheim v *Tobacco Securities Trust Co. Ltd* [1951] AC 297 also required that it must be possible to describe the class genuinely as a section of the community, rather than simply a body of private individuals. There are in effect two separate requirements, with one relating to personal nexus and another which states that the class must be capable of being genuinely described as a section of the community, rather than simply a fluctuating body of private individuals. Persons following a common profession or calling, people of common nationality, religion, or sex, or the inhabitants of a town or county can be described as a section of the community. In this respect, special provisions for disabled people are also permissible, since they are a section of the public in a meaningful sense. But in *Davies* v *Perpetual Trustee Co. Ltd* [1959] AC 459, the Privy Council held non-charitable a trust which was confined to Presbyterian youths who were descended from settlors in New South Wales who had originated from the North of Ireland. Although quite large in number, this category of potential beneficiaries was held not to be a section of the public. It was merely a fluctuating body of private individuals.

13.8.3 **Public benefit under the fourth head**

Lord Simonds thought in *Oppenheim* v *Tobacco Securities Trust Co. Ltd* [1951] AC 297 that the test of public benefit may vary between the four heads of charity (in particular he excluded the 'poor relations' cases entirely from consideration). It is clear that the personal nexus test applies to the fourth head, but arguably the requirement that the trust benefits a section of the public is more stringent under the fourth head than under the second.

For example, in *Williams's Trustees* v *IRC* [1947] AC 447, doubt was expressed by Lord Simonds about whether Welsh people living in London could be a section of the public under the fourth head. In *IRC* v *Baddeley* [1955] AC 572, the House of

Lords held that the persons to be benefited must either be the whole community or the inhabitants of a particular area. If some further restriction is imposed, thus creating in effect a class within a class, the test of public benefit will not be satisfied.

Viscount Simonds in *IRC* v *Baddeley* thought 'that a different degree of public benefit is requisite according to the class in which the charity is said to fall', and that public benefit considerations 'have even greater weight [than in the case of educational trusts] in the case of trusts which by their nominal classification depend for their validity upon general public utility'. This suggests that it might be possible that a different degree of public benefit is requisite according to the class in which the charity is said to fall (and this will also become apparent in the discussion below on public benefit in the context of purposes for the relief of property). And it is said that if a charity falls within the fourth class, it must be for the benefit of the whole community or at least of all the inhabitants of a sufficient area.

13.8.3.1 *Baddeley: a different and additional test*

The *Baddeley* test seems therefore to be a different, and additional, test to that adopted in *Davies* v *Perpetual Trustee Co. Ltd* [1959] AC 459 for the second head. Indeed, the very definition of charity under the fourth head (purposes beneficial to the community) would seem to demand a more stringent test of public benefit than under any other head. However, Lord Reid thought otherwise in his dissenting speech in *IRC* v *Baddeley*.

'Section of the public' and the significance of the trust's purposes
It is also likely that what constitutes a section of the public depends on the purposes of the particular trust, and the courts are more likely to strike down arbitrary restrictions which are irrelevant to those purposes, but which simply serve to exclude other sections of the public. For example, in *IRC* v *Baddeley*, the limitation was to Methodists living in West Ham and Leyton, and the trust included the provision of playing-fields. Lord Simonds clearly thought that the restriction to Methodists living in West Ham and Leyton was completely irrelevant to the provision of playing-fields. Referring (at p. 592) to a rhetorical question put in argument that 'Who has ever heard of a bridge to be crossed only by impecunious Methodists?' He went on to say that what is true of a bridge for Methodists is equally true of any other public purpose falling within the fourth head, and of the adherents of any other creed. The limitation merely operated to prevent the purpose from being a public purpose; it could have had no other effect. A purpose which is not a public purpose cannot be charitable within the fourth head.

Variation within the heads of charity as well as between them?
There is some authority that the test of public benefit can vary even within the fourth head itself. In *Re Dunlop* [1984] NI 408 (noted by Norma Dawson [1987] Conv 114), Carswell J upheld as charitable a bequest 'to hold the remainder of my residuary estate for the Presbyterian Residential Trust...to found or to help to found a home for old Presbyterian persons', and a cy près scheme (see chapter 14) was ordered. There was earlier Northern Irish authority that the Presbyterians of Londonderry were not a sufficient section of the public under the fourth head, and it was accepted that there was no difference between Irish and English definitions of charity. Carswell J took the view, however, that public benefit depended on the nature of 'the advantage which the donor intends to provide for the benefit of all

of the public'. A 'bridge to be used only by Methodists should clearly fail to qualify, whereas a gift for the education of the children of members of that church might be a valid charity'. But he was also prepared to distinguish between purposes within the fourth head itself.

It should perhaps finally be observed that neither *IRC* v *Baddeley* nor *Williams's Trustees* v *IRC* actually turned on the issue of public benefit. In the former case the purposes were not exclusively religious, but included social purposes and the provision of playing-fields, and in the latter case purposes were exclusively social and recreational. They would therefore have failed because of the inclusion of a social content, whatever view had been taken on the public benefit issue.

13.8.4 Public benefit and the relief of poverty

It is unquestioned law that to relieve poverty is to confer a benefit upon the public at large, if only by mitigating the burden of support for the poor which would otherwise traditionally (and certainly in a pre-Welfare State society) have fallen upon the community. The House of Lords in *Oppenheim* v *Tobacco Securities Trust Co. Ltd* [1951] AC 297 exempted 'poor relations' cases as anomalous and left open the question whether the personal nexus test applies to them.

The 'poor relations' anomaly stems from the practice of Chancery in the nineteenth century when faced with trusts expressed to be for poor relations; rather than allow these to fail for uncertainty (at a time when the class ascertainability test applied, which was considered in chapter 4) or perpetuity, the courts rescued such trusts by holding them charitable. The 'poor relations' cases have been consistently followed, which is probably why the House of Lords left them alone in *Oppenheim*. The House of Lords has considered them directly in *Dingle* v *Turner* [1972] AC 601, and expressly upheld them. In that case a trust for 'poor employees of E. Dingle & Co.' was held charitable, although it would have failed under the personal nexus test. The same reasoning must apply to 'poor relations', and this is thus authority that the personal nexus test does not apply to this head of charity.

13.8.4.1 *A less strict test, subject to limitations*

In order for a trust to be charitable under this head, it is, however, necessary that the trust should be intended to benefit a class of persons, and not simply to make a gift to an individual, or group of individuals, who happen to be poor. In *Re Scarisbrick* [1951] Ch 622, Jenkins LJ stated the rule thus:

> I think the true question in each case has really been whether the gift was for the relief of poverty amongst a class of persons, or . . . a particular description of poor, or was merely a gift to individuals, albeit with relief of poverty amongst those individuals as the motive of the gift, or with a selective preference for the poor or poorest amongst those individuals.

This statement received the approval of Lord Cross of Chelsea in the leading case of *Dingle* v *Turner*, considered above, and more recently applied in *Re Segelman* [1996] 2 WLR 173. In *Re Scarisbrick* itself the class of potential recipients was sufficiently wide to be incapable of exhaustive ascertainment ('such relations of my said son and daughters as shall be in needy circumstances . . .') so the trust was charitable.

Assuming that Jenkins LJ's test is satisfied, however, the public benefit requirements are less stringent under this head than under the others and the class to be benefited can be quite small.

13.8.5 **Public benefit and the advancement of religion**

There are *dicta* in *Oppenheim* that the public benefit tests advanced in that case
apply to all heads of charity except the relief of poverty. Certainly, for religious
charities, there must also be an element of public contact. Private salvation, however commendable, is not charitable. This is another explanation of *Yeap Cheah
Neo* v *Ong Cheng Neo* (1875) LR 6 PC 381 because a provision for the performance
of ancestor worship could benefit only the family group. The leading case in this
regard is *Gilmour* v *Coats* [1949] AC 426, where the House of Lords had to consider
a gift of £500 towards a Carmelite priory. The priory housed about 20 cloistered
nuns who devoted themselves to intercessory prayer and had no contact at all
with the outside world. This was held non-charitable on the grounds that there
was no contact with the outside world. Arguments based on Catholic doctrine, to
the effect that everyone benefited from the intercessory prayers, were rejected as
being not susceptible to legal proof. Nor could any benefit be found merely in the
example of the piety of the women, as it was too vague and intangible. The House
of Lords also rejected the argument that, entry being open to all women, the priory
should be treated on analogy with an educational institution offering scholarship
entry, holding that an educational establishment which required its members to
withdraw from the world and leave no record of their studies would not be charitable either.

   On the other hand, in *Re Caus* [1934] Ch 162, Catholic masses for the dead were
held charitable. This case was doubted in *Gilmour* v *Coats*, but in principle the case
seems correct, and *Caus* was applied by Browne-Wilkinson V-C in *Re Hetherington*
[1990] Ch 1. The point is that Catholic masses are open to the public at large even
where a private function, such as a funerary rite, is incorporated into the celebration, so in principle *Caus* is distinguishable from *Gilmour* v *Coats*.

13.8.5.1 Re Hetherington, *private masses, and a review of the authorities*

In *Re Hetherington*, Browne-Wilkinson V-C was called upon to consider a gift for
the saying of masses, which did not exclude the possibility that the masses would
be said in private. In practice, however, all or most of the masses would be open to
the public. Reviewing the cases, he said (at pp. 134–35):

   (1) A trust for the…advancement of religion is *prima facie* charitable, and assumed to be
       for the public benefit…This assumption of public benefit can be rebutted by showing
       that in fact the particular trust in question cannot operate so as to confer a legally rec-
       ognised benefit on the public, as in *Gilmour* v *Coats*.

   (2) The celebration of a religious rite in public does confer such a benefit because of the
       edifying and improving effect of such celebration on the members of the public who
       attend. As Lord Reid said in *Gilmour* v *Coats* [1949] AC 426 at 459:

       'A religion can be regarded as beneficial without it being necessary to assume that all its beliefs
       are true, and a religious service can be regarded as beneficial to all those who attend it without
       it being necessary to determine the spiritual efficacy of that service or to accept any particular
       belief about it.'

   (3) The celebration of a religious rite in private does not contain the necessary element of
       public benefit since any benefit by prayer or example is incapable of proof in the legal

sense, and any element of education is limited to a private, not public, class of those present at the celebration: see *Gilmour* v *Coats* itself...

(4) Where there is a gift for a religious purpose which could be carried out in a way which is beneficial to the public (i.e. by public masses) but could also be carried out in a way which would not have sufficient public benefit (i.e. by private masses) the gift is to be construed as a gift to be carried out only by the methods that are charitable, all non-charitable purposes being excluded...

Applying these principles to the case before him, he concluded that:

a gift for the saying of masses is *prima facie* charitable, being for a religious purpose. In practice, those masses will be celebrated in public, which provides a sufficient element of public benefit...The gift is to be construed as a gift for the saying of public masses only...private masses not being permissible since it would not be a charitable application of the fund for a religious purpose.

In other words, he construed the gift in such a way as to exclude purposes which were non-charitable.

13.8.5.2 *Public and private: distinguishing* Gilmour v Coats

It follows that the mere attendance by the public at a prayer service is sufficient to distinguish *Gilmour* v *Coats*. Suppose, on the other hand, the religious organisation conducts all its affairs in private, but unlike *Gilmour* v *Coats* its members have not cut themselves off entirely from the outside world, but mix with it. This also seems sufficient to distinguish *Gilmour* v *Coats*. In *Neville Estates* v *Madden* [1962] Ch 832 (considered in a different context earlier), Cross J held charitable a trust for the members of Catford Synagogue. He thought that the rejection of example as a benefit in *Gilmour* v *Coats* would not apply to a restricted religious group if its members lived in the world and mixed with their fellow citizens, because they could thereby extend their example of religious living to the public at large:

The trust with which I am concerned resembles that in *Gilmour* v *Coats* in this, that the persons immediately benefited by it are not a section of the public but members of a private body. All persons of the Jewish faith living in or about Catford might well constitute a section of the public, but the members for the time being of the Catford Synagogue are no more a section of the public than the members for the time being of a Carmelite Priory. The two cases, however, differ from one another in that the members of the Catford Synagogue spend their lives in the world, whereas the members of a Carmelite Priory live secluded from the world. If once one refuses to pay any regard—as the courts refused to pay any regard—to the influence which these nuns living in seclusion might have on the outside world, then it must follow that no public benefit is involved in a trust to support a Carmelite Priory. As Lord Greene said in the Court of Appeal ([1948] Ch 340, at p. 354): 'Having regard to the way in which the lives of the members are spent, the benefit is a purely private one.' But the court is, I think, entitled to assume that some benefit accrued to the public from the attendance at places of worship of persons who live in this world and mix with their fellow citizens.

On this view, religion can be advanced by example, so long as one mixes in the world in a *physical* sense. *Neville Estates* is authority that no more is required (however, see also *Re Warre* [1953]; but the *Neville Estates* view seems more in accord with recent High Court decisions and the Charity Commissioners).

13.9 **Public benefit: future direction under the Charities Act 2006**

Although the Charities Act 2006 is a lengthy and extensive project relating to charity law, once again, consideration here is directed towards the provisions relating to the legal definition of charity. And following the brief explanation of the new classifications of 'charitable purposes', and the framework for the meaning of the term 'charity', what remains now is for some consideration to be made of what the Act says in respect of the public character of charitable activity, and the requirement of public benefit which has traditionally reflected this. The public benefit requirement is at the heart of the traditional legal definition of charity, and thus of the ability of purposes to acquire charitable status. This spirit continues within the new Act, where it can be found enshrined in s. 3.

It has been suggested that the new Act, in respect of its treatment of the core meaning of charity and the classification of charitable purposes, represents an important project of consolidation and clarification, and one which accords considerable respect to existing charity law. This has already been suggested in relation to the statutory list of charitable purposes, and it is reflected in the retention of a public benefit requirement. Indeed, according to s. 3(1), a purpose must be for the public benefit if it is to be considered charitable. The new section does not actually define what is meant by public benefit, but can be found explicitly connected with traditional charity law in s. 3(3). At one level this can be explained in the language of continuity and with conservation with traditional law in a way that mirrors the approach taken to the statutory definition of charitable purposes: in this respect it should not be too difficult to align what are effectively existing charitable purposes with traditional approaches to public benefit. However, there are important questions surrounding what test (for public benefit) might actually accompany the 'heads' of charitable purpose which are actually new and are not to be found in existing law. This is one important respect in which it is not obvious how new law and existing law might actually map coherently onto one another, and this is likely to result in much more extensive consideration in the foreseeable future for this text.

For now the issue is noted in the text and considered a little further in the accompanying ORC, but how it actually 'shakes out' as the new law is implemented very much remains to be seen. This is all that can be said with certainty at this point in time, notwithstanding that in January 2008, there was a very important development. It is explained very shortly that under s. 4 of the Charities Act 2006, the Charity Commission is under a statutory duty to produce guidance on the requirements of public benefit, and this came into force in February 2007. As ORC materials dating from March 2007 noted, Draft Guidance was published during that month, and the definitive Public Benefit Guidance was published in January 2008. A commencement order brought the new sections relating to the definition of charity into force on 1 April 2008. In this respect, the publication of the Guidance on public benefit represents an important development, but it is part of a suite of developments which remains to be concretised, and as such this discussion must necessarily remain somewhat abstract.

Nevertheless, what is extremely clear from s. 3 of the Charities Act 2006, even if its current discussion might seem a little abstract, is that there is a new and radical direction in the sphere of public benefit as it applies to English charity law. This can be seen on account of the provisions of s. 3(2) which states that there is no longer to be a presumption of public benefit operating in favour of a purpose wishing to secure charitable status. As the Explanatory Notes accompanying the Act explain, '[u]nder existing law there is a presumption that purposes for the relief of poverty, the advancement of education, or the advancement of religion...are for the public benefit...The effect of this presumption is that...[an] organisation's purpose is presumed charitable unless there is evidence that it is not...'. Traditionally all 'other purposes' must demonstrate their public benefit and the effect of the new approach is to remove this presumption by placing all charitable purposes on an equal footing in having to demonstrate their public benefit in order to achieve charitable status. In implementing this new approach—in which *all* purposes falling into *all* categories of the new statutory definitional framework will have to demonstrate the 'public benefit' dimensions of their purposes—as the legislation makes clear, it falls to the Charity Commission to issue guidance on demonstrating this. And as was noted above, the Charity Commission has now published its definitive Guidance. There is thus some 'hard and fast' detail available on how things are likely to work, and this will be considered shortly. What follows now is a brief consideration of how the new approach to public benefit fits the broader framework of the responsibilities of the Charity Commission in the regulation of the activities and governance of charitable organisations.

13.9.1 The continuing significance of public benefit for the legal definition of charity

The task of determining whether or not a particular purpose is charitable, and thus assessing the merits of a purported public benefit is vested now in the Charity Commission by the provisions of s. 4, and both the Strategy Review document and the Government response to it emphasised the desirability that the Charity Commission should carry out ongoing checks on public character. The Government's support of this as desirable rested on its observation of structural weakness in traditional approaches whereby the only time at which systematic check is made on a charity's public character is at the point of its registration. The rationale for this reflected opinion that a move to checks which are ongoing could be used to assess any doubts which might arise in respect of the public character of the purpose during a registered charity's operation. Very interestingly, in addition, the Government suggested that ongoing checks could be instrumentally used to monitor the 'performance' of certain types of charity, which may accrue benefits for 'under-performing' charitable purposes to be aware of their own positions. What this monitoring proposal does not explicitly point to—but the implication is clearly present in the documentation—is the way in which 'performance' is not being directed towards under-performance alone, or even in the main. The import appeared instead to be directed towards concerns that might arise from a charity which is appearing to be *too successful* and might thereby be deemed to be 'performing' in a manner which is difficult to reconcile with charitable status. An obvious point of reference for this might well be the charitable status of independent schools, and this is considered in more detail shortly.

13.9.1.1 *The operation of the public benefit requirement under the Charities Act 2006*

What can be concluded at this point is that, notwithstanding that the term 'public benefit' has not been defined in the statute, and that lack of statutory clarification is capable of being problematic, English charity law as envisioned under the Charities Act 2006 remains grounded in the concept of 'public benefit'. It is set to continue to be central in securing charitable status under the new regime of charity law, in spite of the extensive and often controversial attention which it has attracted at all stages of the Act's genesis. Although the requirement of public benefit is now enshrined in statute, along with the way in which there will be no presumption of charitable status, what potentially charitable purposes actually must establish is not being given a clear legal test within the new Act. The preferred approach appears instead to be framing its meaning in reference to existing, more generalised notions of public benefit, and from the provisions of s. 4 it becomes clear that the Charity Commission will be at the heart of determining this; acting as *regulator* of charitable purposes through being responsible for their *registration*. Accordingly, the provisions of s. 4 are, *inter alia*, as follows:

- Under s. 4(1), the Charity Commission for England and Wales '*must issue guidance in pursuance of its public benefit objective*'.
- Under s. 4(2), the 'public benefit objective' of s. 4(1) is 'to *promote awareness and understanding of the operation of the requirement*' mentioned in s. 3(1) of the Charities Act 1993.
- Under s. 4(3), the Commission may from time to time revise any guidance on the public benefit requirement, but must (under s. 4(4)) carry out public consultation before issuing guidance or making revisions to such guidance, and (under s. 4(5)) must publish any guidance issued or revised as it considers appropriate.
- And, the trustees of a charity must (under s. 4(6)) '*have regard to any such guidance when exercising any powers or duties to which the guidance is relevant*'.

13.9.2 **The Charity Commission and publication of the Guidance on Public Benefit**

As the materials immediately above suggest, under s.4 of the Charities Act 2006 the Charity Commission must issue guidance explaining the requirement for public benefit, and this came into force by virtue of a commencement order in February 2007. The Commission published Draft Guidance in March 2007 and opened up a consultation (as required in the legislation). Following the consultation, the Charity Commission published its definitive Public Benefit Guidance in January 2008. The Draft Public Benefit Guidance stated that 'public benefit' is not defined in the Act, and that it 'remains governed by the existing law', and a brief summary of the Public Benefit Guidance published in January 2008 now follows.

13.9.2.1 *The Public Benefit Guidance published in January 2008*

Full versions of the Public Benefit Guidance are available in PDF and HTML and also a very useful summary of its main thrust can be found on the Charity Commission's website. The structure of the Guidance is essentially as follows:

- The Guidance commences with an Introduction explaining the 'public benefit requirement', and the way in which under the new Act, this is a more stringent and robust requirement than it has previously been.

- The Guidance then progresses by linking the points noted in the introduction with the definition of charity under the new Act, identifying the way in which the new Act sets out 'various descriptions of charitable purposes' representing the 'Meaning of charitable purpose' embodied in s. 2 'and any new charitable purpose that might be recognised in the future'.

- Following this, substantive consideration of public benefit commences in earnest by observing that there are two key principles of public benefit, each embodying a number of factors which must be considered in all cases.

- The section which follows this illuminates the two principles of public benefit and also provides extensive discussion of the factors which must be considered in relation to them. At this point, the text explains that:

  * Principle 1 requires that there must be an identifiable benefit or benefits, and that:
    — by Principle 1a, it must be clear what the benefits are
    — by Principle 1b, the benefits must be related to the actual 'aims' of the purpose
    — by Principle 1c, benefits must be balanced against any detriment or harm.

  * Principle 2 requires that the benefit must be to the public or a section of the public, and that:
    — by Principle 2a, the beneficiaries must be appropriate to the aims of the purpose
    — by Principle 2b, where benefit is to a section of the public, the opportunity to benefit must not be unreasonably restricted either by geographical or other restrictions, or by ability to pay fees charged
    — by Principle 2c, people in poverty must not be excluded from the opportunity to benefit
    — by Principle 2d, any private benefits must be incidental.

- Thereafter the document considers the 'ongoing' nature of demonstrating public benefit for charities, and relates to the way in which trustees are now under a duty to report on this in their annual reports.

  Here, guidance given on reporting (on a) charity's public benefit commences by explaining that the level of detail required in reporting depends on an individual charity's location above or below the so-called 'audit threshold', where an audit is required if a charity's gross annual income exceeds £500,000 or where income exceeds £100,000 *and* the aggregate value of its assets exceeds £2.8m. In their reports, Trustees must indicate how a charity's aims have been carried out for the public benefit, and also confirm that regard has been had to the Charity Commission's guidance where this is appropriate. In respect of the latter, levels of detailed reporting required will depend on whether the charity is a smaller charity (below the audit threshold, where the requirement is for a brief summary of the charity's main activities in light of the requirement of public benefit) or a larger charity, where the reporting requirements are more extensive, and trustees are required to provide 'fuller explanation'.

- In the final section, entitled 'accessing public benefit', the Guidance explains that in the case of all applications for registration as charitable organisations, the Charity Commission will assess whether aims are for the public benefit, and whether bodies already registered continue to meet the public benefit requirement, which they must do under the new law.

It is explained that this is achieved by carrying out generally focused research on the extent to which various types of charity are meeting the requirement and by working closely with representative professional and umbrella bodies. The guidance explains that it may also be necessary to carry out detailed individual assessments of particular charities, and where it is the case that an organisation is not meeting the requirement the Charity Commission will provide clear reason and explanation for this, and also advice for trustees on making changes in order to meet the requirements. Where this happens, reasonable time will be given for changes to be made, and that where there is disagreement with the Charity Commission's assessment, trustees can seek an internal review of a decision made, and will have the right to appeal to the new and independent Charity Tribunal and ultimately to the courts. At this point the Charity Commission suggests that it is seeking to build constructive relationships and dialogue with those whose activities fall within its regulatory jurisdiction.

13.9.2.2 *Public benefit and accountability of the Charity Commission*

And in terms of making the Charity Commission accountable for decisions made in this respect, the significance of a newly created Charity Tribunal under the Act is also apparent in the speech from the Minister for the Third Sector welcoming the publication of this Guidance. As Phil Hope MP stressed: 'The Government has committed to reviewing the success of the public benefit test within three years of it coming into effect, and next month will be launching a new Charity Tribunal to offer all charities an independent and robust mechanism for challenging future rulings by the Charity Commission.'

13.9.3 **Continuing problems for public benefit: the Charities Act 2006 and the position of 'public' schools**

During Parliamentary debates in the House of Commons during June 2006, Minister for the Cabinet Office Hilary Armstrong (as recorded in *Hansard* (26 June 2006), col. 21) proposed that the (then) Charities Bill sought to acknowledge that charities 'play a fundamental role in the fabric of our society', and 'provide a vital service to individuals and communities'. The Government thus wished to 'break down the barriers that face the charitable sector', and to promote their growing importance within society 'by helping to release charities' potential for further public good'. However, it was also stressed that as well as increasing charities' potential in an evolving modern world, it was important to ensure that charities were accountable to 'the public whom they serve' in a way which reflects the 'significant economic and social weight' which the sector wields.

Accordingly, alongside the purposes of providing charities with a legal and regulatory environment which is enabling, and encouraging a vibrant and diverse sector, the Charities Act 2006 is also concerned to sustain 'high levels of public confidence in charities', which is to be achieved through 'effective regulation'. The Minister clarified that the requirement that charitable organisations conferred a public benefit had to remain for these reasons, because (at col. 25) the Act is partly about 'securing public confidence in charitable status' *itself.*

There have been a number of commentaries which have observed that controversy over public benefit is frequently directed at the position of independent schools as charitable purposes. In traditional approaches the operation of a presumption of public benefit (in the first three *Pemsel* heads) has ensured that very exclusive educational establishments—which are in common parlance somewhat ironically described as 'public schools'—have a presumption in favour of them being charitable. This is notwithstanding perceptions that access to many of these establishments is substantially enjoyed by only a very few, and closely related ones that in many ways this position undermines quite fundamentally notions of 'publicness'. Since the first appearance of the Charities Bill in 2004, academics and policy-makers have suggested that the new requirement to demonstrate public benefit is going to be most keenly felt by these establishments, which in many respects eschew accepted understandings of publicness.

In Parliament itself support of the continuing (*presumptively*) charitable status of public schools was expressed by MPs Daniel Kawczynski and Andrew Turner. According to Mr Kawczynski (*Hansard* (26 June 2006), col. 37) the public school in his constituency in Shrewsbury did a great amount of work for charity and was very beneficial to the community generally. And according to Andrew Turner

[w]ho can argue that education is not for public benefit? The principal argument for education being provided at the taxpayers' expense is that it is in everyone's interest that we have a better educated nation...How can it be argued that education that people pay for—those of us who can afford to do so—is of less benefit than other benefits?

In a manner which both acknowledges that this is a critical point in time for such establishments, and also opposes much of the support which was subsequently offered in favour of them in the House of Commons above, in the House of Lords in 2005, Lord Best (*Hansard* (7 June 2005), col. 821) remarked that this might be an appropriate point in time to 'drop the term 'public school'. This is a 'term which so inaccurately describes' educational establishments which are 'clearly distinct from the public sector in their governance and funding'; and in respect of them new charity law is intending to import that 'charitable status means an obligation to reach out to the community outside the school gates, offering bursaries to pupils from less affluent families and joining in partnerships with local education authorities'.

It is uncontentious to suggest that Parliamentary discussion of the new Act was dominated by the highly contentious position of public schools, and in some respects the debates actually became hijacked by the issues arising in contemplation of such establishments having to demonstrate their public benefit. Indeed, in the House of Lords in 2005 it was suggested by Lord Best (*Hansard* (7 June 2005), col. 820) that '[t]he best illustration of the public benefit debate, and the most controversial ingredient of the Bill relates to the treatment of independent schools that charge high fees, but are registered as charities'. It is clear from the commentary immediately above that the continuing 'problem' of (in many ways inappropriately termed) public schools continued to follow the Bill right up until its passage into law, and is likely to continue. However it is also the case that similar issues are raised in respect of private hospitals which have or are keen to secure charitable status.

13.10 **Purposes which create problems under any head of charitable purpose**

Up to now it will have been clear that traditionally English charity law has demanded that for purposes to be charitable, they must fall within purposes which are capable of being recognisable as charitable, and they must be for the public benefit, and also that they must be 'exclusively charitable'. This has remained at the heart of the new law, and locates the Charities Act 2006 as an important project of continuity, as well as one of refinement and new direction. In addition to these questions relating to definition and a nature which is 'exclusively charitable', English law has traditionally demanded one further requirement for purposes seeking charitable status. That is that there are no so-called 'disqualifying factors' which will prevent a potentially charitable organization from acquiring the legal status of such. This has been alluded to in the materials up to now, and, for example, the materials on purposes for the advancement of education pointed to potential difficulties which can arise where a purpose is perceived to have political objectives. It will now become clear how a number of disqualifying factors can interfere with an organisation's ability to acquire charitable status.

13.10.1 **Problems arising from political purposes**

A trust cannot be charitable under any head if its purposes are, directly or indirectly, political. A trust to promote the aims of a particular political party is clearly not capable of being charitable, and attempts to disguise such objectives as educational trusts have generally failed.

13.10.1.1 *What amounts to 'political purposes'?*

The definition of 'political' in this context is somewhat wider than the layman might expect, however. Where the objectives involve attempting to bring about a change in the law, they will be considered political and therefore non-charitable, unless change in the law is merely ancillary to the main purpose of the trust. This was one of the reasons for the failure of the National Anti-Vivisection Society to achieve charitable status in *National Anti-Vivisection Society* v *IRC* [1948] AC 31. Lord Simonds gave as the ostensible rationale that it is for Parliament, not the courts, to decide whether any change would be for the public benefit. He also rejected the contention that alteration in the law was merely ancillary to the purposes of the trust, since in order to abolish vivisection it would have been necessary to repeal the Cruelty to Animals Act 1876 (since replaced by the Animals (Scientific Procedures) Act 1986) and pass an Act prohibiting vivisection altogether. He said at pp. 61–63:

Here, the finding of the Commissioners is itself conclusive. 'We are satisfied', they say, 'that the main object of the society is the total abolition of vivisection ... and (for that purpose) the repeal of the Cruelty to Animals Act 1876 [now replaced by the Animals (Scientific Procedures) Act 1986], and the substitution of a new enactment prohibiting vivisection altogether.' This is a finding that the main purpose of the society is the compulsory abolition of vivisection by Act of Parliament. What else can it mean? And how else can it be supposed that vivisection is to be abolished? Abolition and suppression are words that connote some form of compulsion. It can only be by Act of Parliament that that element can be supplied ...

I would remind your lordships that it is the King as *parens patriae* who is the guardian of charity and that it is the right and duty of his Attorney-General to intervene and inform the court, if the trustees of a charitable trust fall short of their duty. So too it is his duty to assist the court, if need be, in the formulation of a scheme for the execution of a charitable trust. But, my Lords, is it for a moment to be supposed that it is the function of the Attorney-General on behalf of the Crown to intervene and demand that a trust shall be established and administered by the court, the object of which is to alter the law in a manner highly prejudicial, as he and His Majesty's government may think, to the welfare of the State? ... I conclude upon this part of the case that a main object of the society is political and for that reason the society is not established for charitable purposes only.

Purposes which are seeking changes in the law
It follows, therefore, that any trust whose main object includes a change in the law of the UK cannot be charitable. In *Re Bushnell* [1975] 1 WLR 1596, money was left to advance awareness of the benefits of socialised medicine and to show that its realisation was fully possible only in a socialist state. The testator had died in 1941, before the introduction of the National Health Service. One of the grounds upon which the trust was held void was its political bias in favour of socialism. Another ground for the failure of the trust in *Re Bushnell* was that in 1941 legislation would have been needed (and was of course later enacted) to introduce socialised medicine.

This was an additional reason for the failure of Shaw's 40-letter alphabet (see chapter 4), and accounts for the inability of, for example, the Campaign against Racial Discrimination and the National Council for Civil Liberties to be registered. charities may, however, campaign *against* changes in the law, which may enable some political purposes of a generally conservative nature to obtain registration.

Political objects and changes in the law overseas   Lord Simonds's reasoning in *National Anti-Vivisection Society* v *IRC*, above, applies only to changes to the law in the UK, but in *McGovern* v *Attorney-General* [1982] Ch 321, Slade J frustrated Amnesty International's attempt to procure charitable status for some of its activities by creating a trust of those parts which were thought most likely to be accepted as charitable, on the grounds that a main object of the trust was to secure the alteration of the laws of foreign countries. The objects of the trust were a mixture of purposes associated with the alleviation of human suffering abroad, some of which were permissible and others which were political.

The trustees applied to the Charity Commissioners for registration as a charity under s. 4 of the Charities Act 1960, and the Commissioners refused. Amnesty International unsuccessfully appealed to the High Court under s. 5(3). The problem was the inclusion of objects (b) and (c), seeking release of prisoners of conscience and the abolition of torture, which necessarily involved securing changes in the laws of foreign countries.

The decision represents an extension of the principles laid down in the House of Lords in *National Anti-Vivisection Society* v *IRC* [1948] AC 31. The reasoning adopted by Lord Simonds could not be applied directly here, but Slade J thought that to grant charitable status to such purposes might prejudice the relations of the British Government with foreign countries, and this consideration of policy could not be overlooked by the court:

> The point with which I am at present concerned is whether a trust of which a direct and main object is to secure a change in the laws of a foreign country can ever be regarded as charitable under English law. Though I do not think that any authority cited to me precisely covers the point, I have come to the clear conclusion that it cannot.
>
> I accept that the dangers of the court encroaching on the functions of the legislature or of subjecting its political impartiality to question would not be nearly so great as when similar trusts are to be executed in this country. I also accept that on occasions the court will examine and express an opinion on the quality of a foreign law...
>
> Furthermore, before ascribing charitable status to an English trust of which a main object was to secure the alteration of a foreign law, the court would also, I conceive be bound to consider the consequences for this country as a matter of public policy. In a number of such cases there would arise a substantial *prima facie* risk that such a trust, if enforced, could prejudice the relations of this country with the foreign country concerned...

Any political taint will suffice A political taint will in any case be fatal to charitable status, whether or not a trust's direct and main object is to secure a change in the law of the UK or of a foreign country. This can apply even to trusts seeking to promote aims which most civilised nations hold to be high aspirations. In *Re Strakosch* [1949] Ch 529, the promotion of racial harmony between English and Afrikaans communities in South Africa was held non-charitable, and registration of community councils is refused where their principal aims are the promotion of interracial accord. The same will apply where the aims are harmony and peace, if such movements overtly or covertly call upon governments to promote specific policies, such as disarmament. One reason sometimes given for denying charitable status to attempts to promote moral objectives is that they necessarily involve a propagandist element biased in favour of only one side of the argument.

13.10.1.2 *Discussion of political issues, and campaigning*

On the other hand, it is legitimate for an educational charity to discuss political issues, and a political object which is merely incidental will not be fatal. In *Re Koeppler's WT* [1986] Ch 423, a testamentary gift to Wilton Park, whose main function was to organise educational conferences, was upheld by the Court of Appeal as a gift for charitable purposes, although Wilton Park's objects included the promotion of informed international public opinion and the promotion of greater co-operation between East and West. The objects of the trust were:

(1) An enquiry into the 'quality of life'; ecology and the environment; participation in government and industry; tensions in free societies; (2) Europe and the emergent pattern of superpower relationships; (3) the unification of Europe; a balance sheet; (4) the requirements of Western defence and the possibilities of arms control; (5) the European Community and its external relations; (6) the media, public opinion and the decision-making process in government; (7) security issues as a factor in domestic and international politics; (8) labour and capital and the future of industrial society.

In upholding the trust, Slade LJ distinguished *McGovern v Attorney-General* on the grounds that a political purpose which is merely incidental to the objects of a trust will not necessarily be fatal where the purposes are otherwise educational. In *McGovern v Attorney-General*, by contrast, alteration in the law was not incidental to the objects of the trust, but was essential to Amnesty International's aims:

the activities of Wilton Park are not of a party political nature. Nor, so far as the evidence shows, are they designed to procure changes in the laws or governmental policy of this or any other country: even when they touch on political matters, they constitute, so far as I can see, no more than genuine attempts in an objective manner to ascertain and disseminate the truth. In these circumstances I think that no objections to the trust arise on a political score, similar to those which arose in the *McGovern* case.

Another authority that discussion of political issues is not necessarily fatal to charitable status is *Attorney-General v Ross* [1986] 1 WLR 252, where Scott J commented at p. 263 that 'there is nothing the matter with an educational charity in the furtherance of its educational purposes encouraging students to develop their political awareness or to acquire knowledge of and to debate and to form views on political issues'. He also observed that there is no reason why a charitable student organisation should not affiliate to a non-charitable organisation if that enables it to further its own charitable activities for the benefit of students. That is the basis upon which student unions are entitled to affiliate to the National Union of Students, a non-charitable organisation. It is, however, essential that the purpose of the affiliation should be to benefit the student body in their capacity as students.

It may also be that it is legitimate to go beyond discussion and take tentative steps into the arena of persuasion. The following passage is taken from the White Paper, 'Charities: A Framework for the Future', HMSO (May 1989):

Charities can, for example, quite properly respond to invitations from Government to comment on proposed changes in the law. Where a Bill is being debated, they can legitimately supply members of either House with such relevant information and arguments as they believe will assist the attainment of their objects. Where this kind of action is in furtherance of their purposes, charities are free to present to government departments reasoned memoranda advocating changes in the law.

The White Paper continues a few paragraphs further on:

Ministers welcome the advice and the guidance which charities offer to Members of Parliament, to central and local government, and to other public authorities on a wide range of social problems. Charities should feel free to take the initiative in offering advice and opinions and in proposing changes to the law and should not need to wait to be invited to do so.

There is the qualification, however, that such activities must remain ancillary to the charity's primary purposes.

13.10.1.3 *Distinguishing political discussion from campaigning*

There are limits to the extent to which a charity can go in this direction, however. Political discussion may not be fatal to charitable status, but campaigning, in the sense of seeking to influence public opinion on political matters, undoubtedly is. In *Webb* v *O'Doherty* (unreported) *The Times*, 11 February 1991, Hoffmann J, distinguishing *Attorney-General* v *Ross*, granted an injunction restraining the officers of a students' union, which was an educational charity, from making any payments to the National Student Committee to Stop War in the Gulf, or to the Cambridge Committee to Stop War in the Gulf.

In restraining the officers from making the payments, Hoffmann J observed:

> There is...a clear distinction between the discussion of political matters, or the acquisition of information which may have a political content, and a campaign on a political issue. There is no doubt that campaigning, in the sense of seeking to influence public opinion on political matters, is not a charitable activity. It is, of course, something which students are, like the rest of the population, perfectly at liberty to do in their private capacities, but it is not a proper object of the expenditure of charitable money.

The Charity Commissioners exercise supervisory control over charities, and one area is the permissible limits to political involvement by charities. However, as long ago as 1979 and in an excellent contextual work, *Charities, Trusts and Social Welfare*, Chesterman observed that the law was unduly conservative, and that disallowing campaigning activities can actually thwart a charity's purposes and limit the amount of good it is able to achieve, given especially that most charities (illustrated, for example, by Oxfam) actually exist for the very purpose of putting themselves out of business by resolving underlying injustices. In 1989 the Government advanced a very different perspective suggesting in a White Paper, *Charities: A Framework for the Future*, that public generosity towards charity may well wane if charities were permitted for 'some political end'.

13.10.1.4 *Charities and political activities: the current approach of the Charity Commission*

In continuing the theme of a conservative approach, the reasoning behind continuing regard being had to 'political objectives' as a ground for disallowing charitable status was explained in the Court of Appeal decision in *Southwood & Anor* v *Attorney General* [2000] EWCA Civ 204. According to Chadwick LJ:

> I would have no difficulty in accepting the proposition that it promotes public benefit for the public to be educated in the differing means of securing a state of peace and avoiding a state of war. The difficulty comes at the next stage. There are differing views as to how best to secure peace and avoid war. To give two obvious examples: on the one hand it can be contended that war is best avoided by 'bargaining through strength'; on the other hand it can be argued, with equal passion, that peace is best secured by disarmament—if necessary, by unilateral disarmament. The court is in no position to determine that promotion of the one view rather than the other is for the public benefit.

And, as a number of authorities used in these materials suggest, the courts are particularly reluctant to uphold charitable status where an organisation's main purpose is to change the law of the United Kingdom or of foreign countries. The basis which underpins this is that the courts are not the appropriate arbiters of the public benefit of any such change, and in the case of objectives relating to (changing the law in) overseas nations, there is the additional complication arising from possibly jeopardising international relations.

However, alongside this, as the materials above sought to signpost, the Charity Commission takes a more robust approach to encouraging legitimate political activities—crucially campaigning—than the courts. And in response to differing perspectives on what should be permissible, the Charity Commission has sought to acknowledge that some activities fall considerably short of being political purposes, and are actually necessary for achieving the organisation's purposes overall. It also conceded that *Re Keoppler*-type distinctions between encouraging and facilitating proper debate, and political activities which are improper were not always clear-cut. Fuller discussion of the legitimate limits of campaigning can be found on the ORC, and the current guidance published by the Charity Commission in April 2007 which emphasises the benefits of political advocacy by charities, can be found at: <http://www.charity-commission.gov.uk/supportingcharities/campaignqa.asp>.

Finally, it is perfectly legitimate for groups to split up their activities among various distinct organisations with their own separate legal structures. This would allow for the situation whereby some (but not all) of the group's organisations could engage in political activities, which would allow for charitable status to be claimed in respect of those which did not. This is what Amnesty International tried to do in *McGovern* v *Attorney-General* by claiming charitable status only for their Prisoners of Conscience Fund. However, this failed because even the purposes of that sub-group were held to be non-charitable.

13.10.2 Problems with charitable status on account of 'profit seeking'

The discussions immediately preceding have focused on the way in which certain activities have long caused 'compatibility difficulties' with the definition and spirit of charitable activity. These are not confined to but include thorny issues arising from trading activities by charitable trusts. Difficulties also arise when charitable purposes interface with political activism. In respect of campaigning, the Government concluded that there is no evidence that change is warranted, either to allow greater scope for charities to partake in campaigning, or to reduce this scope, and that no change to current permissions and limitations would be pursued. In respect of trading activities by charities, the Government did not agree with recommendations which would have made it easier for charities to trade in a less restricted way than at present, with the benefit of tax considerations and relief from a number of 'burdens' experienced by private business. In this respect, the 2003 publication does reveal the Government's discomfort with the ability of charities to trade outside the context of 'minor' trading activities.

13.11 Charitable status, 'self-help', and disaster appeals

Although self-help organisations may possibly have been regarded as charitable in the nineteenth century when, for example, friendly societies contributed considerably to the then limited provisions for welfare, Hall V-C held in *Re Clark* (1875) 1

Ch D 497 that a friendly society was not charitable because of the absence of any stipulation that benefits should be restricted to those members who were poor as well as old, disabled, or sick.

If they are not poverty charities, self-help organisations clearly fail on the *Oppenheim* personal nexus test. Hall V-C envisaged that they may succeed as poverty charities, where as we have seen public benefit tests are less stringent, but there may be a second principle that the benefits of charity must be provided by bounty and not bargain. Where, as is the case with many friendly societies, the beneficiaries have, in effect, bought their entitlement in a contractual arrangement, the element of altruism essential to charity is lacking.

In *Re Hobourn Aero Components Ltd's Air Raid Distress Fund* [1946] Ch 194, a fund established by employees to relieve members suffering in consequence of air raids on Coventry was held by the Court of Appeal to be non-charitable on the ground that the employees among whom benefit was confined could not be a section of the public. It was not argued as a poverty charity, and the issue was left open whether it could have been charitable had it been so limited. Nevertheless, there are passages in Lord Greene MR's judgment which suggest that it could not have been charitable even as a poverty charity because the Members' entitlement to benefit turned on the fact of their having subscribed to the fund. This was, in his view, a private trust. If this is correct, then no self-help organisation will be charitable.

It should perhaps be observed that the contributors did not want the fund in *Re Hobourn Aero Components Ltd's Air Raid Distress Fund* to be charitable, since if it had been the Charity Commissioners would have applied their contributions cy près (in the next chapter) when the fund was wound up.

13.11.1 **Disaster appeals**

These will be valid if for the relief of poverty; otherwise, like self-help organisations, they will fail on the grounds of public benefit. This leaves the organisers of such funds with two alternatives. One possibility is that they can apply a means test criterion to the receipt of benefit, which they may regard as invidious. For example, in the Aberfan coal-tip disaster of 1966, the majority of victims were children, and far from it being easy to show that their deaths produced material deprivation among the relatives, one could actually argue that the cost of rearing the children was saved. In fact, the Commissioners eventually held that the fund was charitable, when money was paid to enable people to move away from the area altogether. Chesterman, *Charities, Trusts and Social Welfare*, gives an extremely comprehensive coverage of this appeal (pp. 339*ff*) and see also (1982) NLJ 223.

The other possibility, often favoured by fund organisers (e.g., the Penlee lifeboat disaster fund in 1982), is to avoid the means test and draft the appeal in such a way as to avoid charitable status altogether. In that event, of course, the tax concessions will also be forgone. Perhaps more importantly, the cy près doctrine described in chapter 14 will not apply and there may be difficulties over distribution of any surplus left over after the purposes have been achieved (see chapter 8). It may even be that the Crown will take some or all of the surplus as *bona vacantia*, not perhaps the most fitting consequence of the altruism of the donors.

One of the problems with disaster appeals is that they are usually set up very quickly after the disaster has occurred, often before the full legal consequences have been considered. They may well be described as charitable, and donors may believe that their contributions are going to a charitable fund, only for the organisers later to change their minds and draft the purposes so as to avoid charitable status. An interesting question might then arise as to what happens to the money already contributed, in the (probably unlikely) event of a dispute (e.g., if somebody who had contributed on the assumption that the fund was charitable objected when he discovered that it was not).

online resource centre

FURTHER READING

Chesterton *Charities, Trusts and Social Welfare* (London: Weidenfeld and Nicholson).

Dunn 'As 'Cold as Charity'?: Poverty, Equity and the Charitable Trust' (2000) Legal Studies 222.

Morris 'Charities in the Contract Culture: Survival of the Largest' (2000) Legal Studies 409.

14

Cy près

14.1 General principles

The Anglo-Norman phrase cy près (which is sometimes hyphenated) meant something like 'as near as possible', and the doctrine of cy près in charity law lays down that where property given on trust for charitable purposes cannot be used in the precise manner intended by the donor, the court (and since about 130 years ago the Charity Commissioners) may make a scheme for the application of the property to purposes resembling as closely as possible the donor's original intention. The idea, in other words, is not to frustrate the intention of the donor (who cannot be consulted if the gift is testamentary) any more than necessary. The doctrine dates back at least as far as the seventeenth century. It only applies to charities—if private purposes fail, the results are as discussed in chapter 4.

14.1.1 Where the donor's wishes cannot be fulfilled

The question whether cy près can be applied can arise either because it is clear from the outset that the donor's intention cannot be fulfilled, as where the organisation which he has singled out for benefit has already ceased to exist, or because at some later time, during the continuance of the trust, it turns out that the purposes cannot be achieved. Cy près is more easily invoked in the latter case, for once property has been dedicated to charity, there is no possibility of a resulting trust to the donor.

14.1.2 Initial failure and ascertaining the donor's intentions

Where, however, a gift fails from the start, the courts have since the early nineteenth century insisted that before the property can be applied cy près, a general or 'paramount' charitable intention must be shown.

The application of the doctrine has been significantly widened by the Charities Act 1960. This may reflect a difference of emphasis. The equitable doctrine was probably based on the presumed intention of the donor, and could in some circumstances militate against the efficient operation of charitable enterprises. The 1960 Act, on the other hand, is concerned more with the efficient running of charities, even at the expense of the donor's intentions.

14.1.3 Cy près and the Charities Act 2006

Following on from the consideration which has been made of the Charities Act 2006 in the previous two chapters respectively making an introduction to charity and a detailed consideration of the legal definition of charity, very brief reference will now be made to the impact which the new legislation will have for the operation of cy près. It is sufficient to say at this point that apart from some minor amendments being made to the Charities Act 1993 by the Charities Act 2006 (pursuant to sections 15–18), the cy près doctrine will continue to operate in respect of charitable gifts which cannot be applied to the original purposes envisioned by their donor. A number of these changes have been brought into force already with the third Commencement Order relating to the new Act, in March 2008. Accordingly, specific reference will be made to this at a couple of different points during the chapter.

14.2 Initial failure

The question turns on whether the intention of the donor was specific or general. If it was to further some specific purpose which cannot be carried out, or benefit some specific institution no longer in existence, then the gift fails and the property will return to the settlor, or his estate, on a resulting trust, as discussed in chapter 7.

If, however, the intention is a more general one, which might be satisfied by applying the property to a purpose or institution similar to that specified, a cy près scheme may be ordered. The test, then, is whether a general or 'paramount' charitable intention can be found.

14.2.1 Gift to a charity which has never existed at all

14.2.1.1 *Operation of cy près doctrine: general charitable intention*

In *Re Rymer* [1895] 1 Ch 19, a gift for a specific seminary which had ceased to exist failed. This is the general position where no paramount (or general) charitable intention can be found. Whether a general charitable intention can be shown is a question of fact. The cases in this section are illustrations of the factors that can be taken into account but do not lay down general rules.

If the charity specified by the donor has never existed at all, it is usually easier to discover a general charitable intention than where the charity once existed but has since ceased (as in *Re Rymer*), since only a general intention can be attributed to the donor who fails correctly to specify the beneficiary. For example, in *Re Harwood* [1936] Ch 285, a gift was made to the Peace Society in Belfast, which could not be shown ever to have existed. Farwell J found that there was an intention to benefit societies aimed at promoting peace, and the gift was therefore applied cy près. A second gift in the will, in favour of the Wisbech Peace Society, which had once existed but had ceased to do so prior to the testatrix's death, was held, however, to have lapsed. Although the case is a good illustration of the operation of the cy près doctrine, doubt may perhaps be cast on the assumption that the promotion of peace is in fact capable of being charitable.

Finding a general paramount charitable intention: the approach of the courts
In *Re Satterthwaite's WT* [1966] 1 WLR 277, a will listed a number of organisations concerned with animal welfare. The list had been thoughtlessly compiled from the London telephone directory, the testatrix's chief concern being to divert her estate to animal charities, because she hated the whole human race. One of the named institutions, the London Animal Hospital, had never existed as a charity. The Court of Appeal held that the gift to the London Animal Hospital should be applied cy près: a general charitable intention could be inferred from the testatrix's known attitude towards the human race, and from the fact that all but one of the other dispositions were made in favour of genuine animal charities. In the opinion of Russell LJ, therefore, a general intention to benefit animal charities could easily be inferred.

Harman LJ expressed 'the gravest doubts', however, and a better explanation of this case may be that, as with the Peace Society in Belfast in *Re Harwood* [1936] Ch 285, the London Animal Hospital had never existed as a charity. Sir Robert Megarry V-C refused to apply what he described as the doctrine of 'charity by association' in *Re Spence's WT* [1979] Ch 483, on the grounds that *Re Satterthwaite* only applied where the body had never existed. It is also necessary for the other donations to be to charitable organisations of the same type; merely for a non-charitable body to be included among a general list of charities is not evidence of a general charitable intent. In *Re Jenkins's WT* [1966] Ch 249 Buckley J declined to hold that a gift to the British Union for the Abolition of Vivisection (which did exist but was not charitable) could be taken as charitable simply by being included in a list of gifts to unquestionably charitable organisations.

It must be emphasised, however, that the question is ultimately one of fact, and the above cases should not be treated as authorities.

14.2.1.2 *Non-existent body, but no initial failure*
Even where the charity specified does not exist, it may be possible to save the gift if the institution can be said to continue to exist in some other form. In recent years many small charities have amalgamated, and it is sometimes possible to regard the new body thus formed as being the same as the old. In *Re Faraker* [1912] 2 Ch 488, for example, a gift to 'Mrs Bailey's charity, Rotherhithe' (which was taken to mean 'Hannah Bayly's Charity') passed to the new charity formed by an amalgamation of Hannah Bayly's Charity with several others.

Gifts which are made to a charitable purpose and not to a charitable body
Another approach is to find that the gift was made for the *purpose* of the named charity, rather than for the body itself. If the body is unincorporated then by definition the gift cannot be to it but must be to its purposes, and if those purposes can still be fulfilled the gift will not fail. Since there is no failure there is no need to show a general charitable intention. Indeed, this is not an application of cy près as such, but rather an instance of finding a substitute trustee to carry out the purposes of the trust. Where the body is a corporation, however, a gift to it will *prima facie* lapse if the corporation has ceased to exist, just as a gift to a human individual

would lapse if the person concerned had died before the gift was made. The gift may be rescued only on the cy près principles already outlined, i.e. if the court is able to find a general charitable intention going beyond the specific aim of benefiting the named corporate charity.

Distinguishing incorporated and unincorporated bodies: Re Finger's WT

In *Re Finger's WT* [1972] Ch 286, for example, testamentary gifts were made to the National Radium Commission, an unincorporated association, and to the National Council for Maternity and Child Welfare, which was a corporate charity. Both had ceased to exist by the time the testatrix died. Goff J held that the gift to the National Radium Commission was interpreted as a gift to its purposes, and since these still continued, the gift did not fail. The gift to the National Council for Maternity and Child Welfare would have failed, as a gift to a corporate charity, in the absence of a general charitable intention, which in the event it was, however, possible to discern.

Similar principles were applied in *Re Koeppler's WT* [1986] Ch 423 (considered earlier), where Slade LJ construed a gift to a non-existent body as a valid trust for educational purposes. The case concerned the validity of a testamentary gift to the warden of the institution known as Wilton Park. At the time of the testator's death there was no entity called Wilton Park, nor was there a warden of Wilton Park, but there was a Wilton Park project, which organised a series of conferences. The gift was construed as a gift for the purposes of the Wilton Park project, the non-existent body in *Re Koeppler's WT* being treated as analogous to the National Radium Commission in *Re Finger's WT*.

14.2.2 Gifts with conditions attached

Even where the institution to which the donation is made exists there may be an initial failure if there is a condition in the gift which the donee body finds unacceptable. In *Re Lysaght* [1966] Ch 191, the testatrix left £5,000 to the Royal College of Surgeons in order to establish and maintain one or more studentships. There was a condition, however, which would have disqualified Jews and Roman Catholics, and the College declined to accept the gift on these terms. The gift was saved because the court found a general charitable intention on the part of the testatrix, to establish medical studentships. The cy près doctrine therefore operated; the condition could be deleted as not being essential to the fulfilment of the general intention. A scheme was ordered on the terms of the will as it stood without the condition.

Recently, in *Re Woodhams* [1981] 1 WLR 493, a general charitable intention to foster musical education was found, allowing the court to remove the restriction which would have limited scholarships to boys from two named children's homes and would have also prevented the donees from accepting the gift.

14.2.2.1 *Why should a gift fail at all?: Equity will not let a trust fail for want of a trustee*

It may be wondered why the gift fails unless the conditions are deleted. After all, a trust should not fail merely because the trustee refuses to accept the trust property. 'Equity will not allow a trust to fail for want of a trustee', and in principle it might be thought that the court should find a trustee who is prepared to carry out the terms of the trust on the settlor's terms. In other words, it should not be necessary to delete the repugnant condition.

In a case like *Re Lysaght*, however, the identity of the donee is essential to the purposes of the trust, and were the Royal College to decline the gift another trustee simply could not be found to carry out the testatrix's intention. As Buckley J pointed out in the case:

> Obviously a trustee will not normally be permitted to modify the terms of his trust on the ground that his own opinions or convictions conflict with them. If his conscience will not allow him to carry out the trust faithfully in accordance with its terms, he must make way for a trustee who can and will do so. But how, if the identity of the trustee selected by the settlor is essential to his intention? It is of the essence of a trust that the trustees selected by the settlor and no one else shall act as the trustees of it and if those trustees cannot or will not undertake the office, the trust must fail.

14.3 Subsequent failure

Cy près has a much wider application in the event of a subsequent failure, and none of the difficulties which arise in the event of an initial failure arise here.

Once property has been dedicated to charitable purposes, it remains so, and if those purposes cease to be capable of achievement, there can be no resulting trust to the settlor or his estate unless the terms on which the gift was originally made provide for this to happen. It is not necessary to search for a general charitable intention on the part of the settlor. The only relevant consideration is whether there was an outright disposition in favour of charity. Where this is so, funds which cannot be applied to the original purpose, whether because that purpose is impossible, or because there is a surplus left over after the purposes have been achieved, may be applied cy près.

14.3.1 The importance of timing

In *Re Slevin* [1891] 2 Ch 236, a legacy had been left to the Orphanage of St Dominic, Newcastle-upon-Tyne. The orphanage ceased to exist after the date of the donor's death, but before the legacy could be paid over. Since the orphanage had survived its benefactor, by however short a time, the gift was effective in favour of charity and could be applied cy près. In *Re King* [1923] 1 Ch 243, a surplus was left after the purpose (the setting of a stained-glass window in a church) was carried out. Finding that the whole fund, and not just the sum sufficient for the window, had been dedicated to charity, Romer J applied the surplus cy près (to the setting of a second window).

14.3.1.1 *Timing of subsequent failure and gifts which are postponed*

Nor will it matter that the gift to charity was intended to be postponed until some future date under the terms of the will or gift. In other words, the relevant date is that of the original donation, even though the charity may only at that time obtain a future interest in the property. If A dies leaving property to B for his life, thereafter to C (a charity), and C ceases to exist after A's death but before B's, this is regarded as a subsequent, not an initial, failure.

Thus, in *Re Moon* [1948] 1 All ER 300, the testator directed that a legacy should be paid to the trustees of a Methodist church for the purposes of missionary work after the death of his widow. The purposes were no longer practicable by the time of the widow's death and Roxburgh J held that the question of whether the gift had lapsed must be resolved in relation to the time when the gift was made, that is, at the death of the testator. Since the purposes would have been practical then, there was an effective gift to charity at that time, and the failure was subsequent and not initial. A similar result was reached in *Re Wright* [1954] Ch 347, where a testamentary gift for the founding of a convalescent home was to take effect after a life interest, at the end of which time the property was insufficient for this purpose. The date of the testatrix's death was taken to be crucial in determining the question of whether the gift was practicable.

In *Re Welsh Hospital (Netley) Fund* [1921] 1 Ch 655, a surplus of £9,000 remained after the winding up of a (charitable) hospital erected at Netley, and the question arose what to do with the surplus. P.O. Laurence J held that it should be applied cy près, but only after concluding that the donors must be taken to have parted with their donations out and out to charity (much of the money had been derived from anonymous sources, and the issues were essentially those discussed in chapter 8). There was no suggestion, in other words, that a cy près scheme ought to have been automatic, on the basis of subsequent failure. However, in *Re Ulverston and District New Hospital Building Trusts* [1956] Ch 622, Jenkins LJ explained *Re Welsh Hospital (Netley) Fund* as a straightforward case of subsequent failure. The earlier case was distinguished because, in *Re Ulverston*, the hospital had never been built and none of the funds ever expended, so the failure was regarded as an initial failure. There being no evidence of general charitable intention, the fund was not applied cy près.

14.4 Altering charitable objects

14.4.1 At common law

Whereas no difficulties have ever arisen in the case of a clear failure, such as a charitable body ceasing to exist, when the cy près doctrine could operate on the subsequent failure, there could be problems before 1960 where a charitable purpose simply became outdated and obsolete although the original charitable body continued in existence. There was no effective system whereby moribund charities could be modernised and of course the cy près doctrine could not apply if there was no failure.

Until the reforms introduced by the Charities Act 1960, the courts' only jurisdiction was their inherent jurisdiction to apply funds cy près, but the inherent jurisdiction is confined to rather narrow limits, being available only where it is 'impossible' or 'impracticable' to carry out the terms of the trust. Some very peculiar trusts were kept on foot by the limits of the cy près doctrine before 1960, obliging trustees to distribute bread, linen, stockings, boots, etc. among the poor.

One old trust specified the distribution of green waistcoats in memory of the testator's surname. The courts' main concern was not to depart too far from the original wishes of settlors, rather than to promote the efficient administration of charities.

14.4.1.1 *The common law and a restrictive approach to the alteration of charitable purpose*

For example, in *Re Weir Hospital* [1910] 2 Ch 124, a testator left two houses to be used as a hospital. The premises were not suitable, and the Charity Commissioners approved a scheme to use them as a nurses' home instead, perpetuating the testator's name by renaming a hospital in his honour. The Court of Appeal held that the scheme was *ultra vires*, since the original purpose was not impossible to fulfil, merely difficult. Sir Herbert Cozens-Hardy MR's view (at p. 131) was that the court's primary duty was to give effect to the charitable intentions of the donor, rather than to seek the most beneficial application of the property:

The first duty of the Court is to construe the will, and to give effect to the charitable directions of the founder, assuming them not to be open to objection on the ground of public policy. The Court does not consider whether those directions are wise or whether a more generally beneficial application of the testator's property might not be founded.

Similar sentiments were echoed by Kennedy LJ at pp. 140–41:

But neither the Court of Chancery, nor the Board of Charity Commissioners, which has been entrusted by statute, in regard to the application of charitable fund, with similar jurisdiction, is entitled to substitute a different scheme for the scheme which the donor has prescribed in the instrument which creates the charity, merely because a coldly wise intelligence, impervious to the special predilections which inspired his liberality, and untrammelled by his directions, would have dictated a different use of his money...If the charity can be administered according to the directions of founder or testator, the law requires that it should be so administered.

14.4.1.2 *The scope of the courts' inherent jurisdiction*

It is permissible under the courts' inherent jurisdiction, however, to eradicate a condition of the trust which, with the passage of time, has become inimical to its main purpose. In *Re Robinson* [1923] 2 Ch 332, a condition in a gift of an endowment for an evangelical church requiring a preacher to wear a black gown in the pulpit was cut out, since it was thought likely to offend the congregation and reduce attendance: with the passage of time, the condition had become inimical to the main purpose of the gift. Another example is *Re Dominion Students' Hall Trust* [1947] Ch 183, where a colour bar was removed from a trust for the maintenance of a hostel for male students of the overseas dominions of the British Empire, since the main purpose of the trust was to promote community of citizenship among members of the Commonwealth.

Re Robinson was applied by Buckley J in *Re Lysaght* (considered shortly), the same test being used there in an initial failure case to strike out a condition. Unlike *Robinson*, of course, which is a subsequent failure case, in *Lysaght*, it was necessary to find a general charitable intention, in order to invoke the cy près doctrine in the first place.

In *Re J.W. Laing Trust* [1984] Ch 143, Peter Gibson J was prepared to strike out a term requiring trustees to distribute, within 10 years of the settlor's death, a fund which by then had risen significantly in value (from some £15,000 in 1922 when the trust was set up, to over £24 million in 1982). The increase in value had been quite unforeseen when the trust was set up, partly because the settlor had lived much longer than expected (to the age of 98). The recipients of the income from the charity (Christian evangelical bodies) had come to depend upon it, whereas it would have been impossible to distribute such a large amount of capital in such a way as to ensure continuance of the causes which the settlor wished to support. The term was struck out on the basis that it was 'inexpedient in the very altered circumstances of the charity since that requirement was laid down 60 years ago'. It is not entirely clear whether this expediency test is the same as that being applied in the earlier cases, or whether a wider principle is being adopted.

14.4.1.3 *Situations where no cy près scheme is required*

There may also be situations where no scheme is required. In *Oldham Borough Council* v *Attorney-General* [1993] Ch 210, the Clayton Playing Fields in Oldham had been conveyed to the council (or more accurately, to the bodies which preceded it prior to the local government reorganisation in 1974) in 1962, for recreational purposes. The Borough Council proposed to sell the land for development, but also to provide a new site which (it was assumed) would be used for exactly the same charitable purposes. The council expressly disclaimed reliance on the Charities Act 1960, since clearly none of the heads (enumerated below) could apply in this case. Dillon LJ, who gave the only substantive judgment in the Court of Appeal, took the view that the sale of the land would have been approved prior to the Charities Act, since there was no requirement to use *that particular land*. Since the charitable purposes would still be carried out, there was no need for a scheme, and the court was prepared to approve the sale.

14.4.2 **Charities Act 1993, section 13**

Following a recommendation of the Nathan Committee on the Law and Practice Relating to Charitable Trusts (1952, Cmd 8710), para. 365, s. 13 (which replaces a similar provision in the 1960 Act) extends, presumably in the interests of more efficient administration of charities, the circumstances in which property may be applied cy près.

14.4.2.1 *The modernisation of outmoded trusts*

The purpose of this section is to modernise outmoded trusts, and as it has been seen, this can be difficult using only the inherent jurisdiction of the courts. Section 13(5) places a duty upon trustees to seek the application of property cy près if and when appropriate circumstances arise. Much of the work of the Commissioners consists in settling and approving schemes of this kind.

The precise circumstances are set out in s. 13(1). No longer is it necessary to show that it is 'impossible' or 'impracticable' to carry out the terms of the trust. It is enough that the original purpose has been fulfilled as far as possible, or cannot be carried out according to the directions given and the spirit of the gift, or if there is a surplus left over, or if the purposes have been adequately provided for by other means, or become useless or harmful to the community. Cy près may also apply where the original purposes relate to an area, or class of persons, which has ceased to have any relevance, having regard to the spirit of the gift. There are also provisions for the amalgamation of small charities if that is more efficient.

Section 13(1) is in the following terms:

(1) Subject to subsection (2) below, the circumstances in which the original purposes of a charitable gift can be altered to allow the property given or part of it to be applied cy près shall be as follows:—

   (a) where the original purposes, in whole or in part—
      (i) have been as far as may be fulfilled; or
      (ii) cannot be carried out, or not according to the directions given and to the spirit of the gift; or

   (b) where the original purposes provide a use for part only of the property available by virtue of the gift; or

   (c) where the property available by virtue of the gift and other property applicable for similar purposes can be more effectively used in conjunction, and to that end can suitably, regard being had to the spirit of the gift, be made applicable to common purposes; or

   (d) where the original purposes were laid down by reference to an area which then was but has since ceased to be a unit for some other purpose, or by reference to a class of persons or to an area which has for any reason since ceased to be suitable, regard being had to the spirit of the gift, or to be practical in administering the gift; or

   (e) where the original purposes, in whole or in part, have, since they were laid down—
      (i) been adequately provided for by other means; or
      (i) ceased, as being useless or harmful to the community or for other reasons, to be in law charitable; or
      (iii) ceased in any other way to provide a suitable and effective method of using the property available by virtue of the gift, regard being had to the spirit of the gift.

Subheads (a) to (e) of s. 13(1) will generally be wider than the pre-1960 definition of failure, and apparently supersede it. In *Oldham Borough Council* v *Attorney-General* [1993] Ch 210, Dillon LJ took the view that the s. 13 heads were exhaustive, at any rate where alteration of the 'original purposes' is sought (on which, see further below):

Broadly the effect of that section is that an alteration of the 'original purposes' of a charitable gift can only be authorised by a scheme for the cy près application of the trust property and such a scheme can only be made in the circumstances set out in subheads (a) to (e) of subsection (1) of section 13.

14.4.2.2 *The scope of s. 13 and the definition of failure*

Section 13 defines failure and arguably applies to define initial as well as subsequent failure. However, the section begins by talking of 'the original purposes of a charitable gift', which supposes that a charitable gift has taken place. It will not have done so in many cases of initial failure. In that case the question of whether there has been a failure will be determined on the basis of the pre-1960 law.

In any case, s. 13 (by virtue of s. 13(2)) only affects the definition of when failure occurs for cy près purposes, and all the other requirements of the doctrine remain. Thus, for example, it is still necessary to show a paramount charitable intention in the case of an initial failure.

In interpreting the section, the Commissioners attempt, so far as possible, to effect the intentions of the donor, these being understood in the context of modern conditions (see their Annual Report 1970, para. 41).

In *Re Lepton's Charity* [1972] Ch 276, Pennycuick V-C invoked ss. 13(1)(a)(ii) and 13(1)(e)(iii) (above) to increase payment to a church minister from £3 per year to £100 per year. Under the original will of 1715 the testator left land, the profits of which amounted to £5 a year, with a direction to trustees to pay £3 a year to the minister, and the residue to the poor of Pudsey. In 1967 the income from the investments representing the land was £791 14s 6d. Pennycuick V-C approved an application under s. 13 to increase the income of the minister to £100 a year, the residue going, as before, to the poor of Pudsey. The court felt that after the change the relative distribution between the minister and the poor of Pudsey remained as in the spirit of the gift. The main argument in the case was whether s. 13 applied to the trusts in the will as a whole, or to each of the two trusts separately (a trust to pay the £3 a year to the minister, and a separate trust to pay the residue to the poor of Pudsey). Only if (as Pennycuick V-C held) the spirit of the gift related to the will as a whole could the court alter the relative proportions of each part.

Another case falling within s. 13(1)(e)(iii), but where the original purposes were neither impractical nor impossible to achieve, is *Varsani v Jesani* [1998] 3 All ER 273 (CA). The case concerned a charity, established in 1967 by a declaration of trust, the purpose of which was to promote the faith of a Hindu sect. In 1984 the sect split into two factions, with each side accusing the other of having departed from the true faith. As long as either faction in fact adhered to the true faith, it remained possible to achieve the original purposes, but the effect of the schism was that only one of the factions was making use of the main asset of the charity, a temple in London, to the exclusion of the other faction. The Court of Appeal, upholding the decision of Carnworth J, felt that the framework within which the faith was practised in 1967 (i.e. the original purposes) had ceased to provide a suitable and effective method of enabling the property to be used in accordance with 'the spirit of the gift'; therefore the court had jurisdiction to order a cy près scheme. Only the jurisdictional issue was before the court, and it is not reported what was actually done (or will be done) with the property.

14.4.2.3 *Distinguishing substantive purposes from administrative matters*

Section 13 allows only the original purposes of a charitable gift to be altered, and for this reason it could not be used in *Re J.W. Laing Trust* [1984] Ch 143 to delete a provision relating to distribution, which was essentially administrative in nature. Peter Gibson J observed (at p. 153) that 'it cannot be right that any provision, even if only administrative, made applicable by a donor to his gifts should be treated as a condition and hence part of its purpose'. The same view was taken in *Oldham Borough Council v Attorney-General* [1993] Ch 210, above, where Dillon LJ considered that the requirement that the actual land given should be used as playing fields was not part of the 'original purposes' within s. 13. In *J.W. Laing*, the condition was struck out under the inherent jurisdiction, whereas in *Oldham* there was no need for a scheme at all, so these are both cases where the common law applied but the statute did not.

14.4.2.4 *Section 13 and the Charities Act 2006*

The Charities Act 2006 has made some amendment to s. 13 of the Charities Act 1993. This has the effect that property may be applied cy près taking into account not only 'the spirit of the gift' but also the social and economic circumstances prevailing at the time of the proposed alteration of the original purposes. This amendment subsists by virtue of s. 15(3) of the Charities Act 2006 and was brought into force in March 2008, by the third Commencement Order relating to the Act.

14.4.3 Limit to Commissioners' scheme-making powers

One of the problems perceived with the Charities Act 1960 was the inability of the Commissioners to make a scheme of their own volition where no trustees could be found who were able or willing to apply for one. It is true that under s. 18(6), the Commissioners can apply to the Secretary of State to refer to them cases where the trustees have unreasonably refused or neglected to make a scheme, but apparently this provision has never been invoked. The Commissioners have also since 1960 had wide-ranging powers under s. 20 in the event of misconduct or mismanagement in the administration of the charity, for example to suspend trustees and to appoint additional trustees as necessary for the proper administration of the charity, but under the original legislation they had no power to make a cy près scheme themselves. This has now been catered for by the Charities Act 1993, s. 18.

14.5 Charities Act 1993, section 14

Section 14 provides reform to cope with the problems which may arise if property is given for charitable purposes which fail and where it is difficult to find the donors. This is a form of initial failure and often there will be no paramount charitable intention. This most frequently arises in disaster appeal funds.

14.5.1 Position in the case of non-charitable trusts

In the case of private (non-charitable) trusts, the operation of the resulting trust doctrine usually results in a proportion of the funds passing to the Crown as *bona vacantia*. This is because where a donation to such a fund is anonymous (e.g., small change in a street collecting box) and no means of tracing the donor has been left, it is reasonable to construe the contribution as an out-and-out gift. It is difficult to infer that the donor intended any surplus left-over to be held on resulting trust for him since he has left the organisers no means of finding him. That part of the surplus attributable to his donation will therefore have no owner and so goes to the Crown as *bona vacantia*.

It is true that in *Re Gillingham Bus Disaster Fund* [1958] Ch 300, such donations were directed to be held on resulting trust, so that such a result was avoided, but apart from being administratively inconvenient this result is probably wrong. Undoubtedly the usual inference would be that if people give money in an anonymous collection, they intend an out-and-out gift, not to see it back again.

This result (i.e. the out-and-out gift construction) was in fact reached by Goff J in *Re West Sussex Constabulary's Widows, Children & Benevolent (1930) Fund Trusts* [1971] Ch 1. The fund was not a disaster fund but was for widows and dependants, and there were outside contributions in addition to those of the members themselves. It came to an end upon amalgamation with other police forces in 1968, and the court was asked to decide how to distribute the surplus.

So far as identifiable donations and legacies were concerned, the proportion of the surplus attributable to that source was held on resulting trust. But there were also the proceeds of street collecting boxes and in relation to those Goff J declined to follow Harman J's earlier judgment on the ground that the intention to be inferred was also that of an out-and-out gift (see further chapters 7 and 8). Thus, nobody could lay claim to the proportion of the surplus attributable to the last two categories, so it went to the Crown as *bona vacantia*.

14.5.2 Position where purposes charitable

The *West Sussex* result will be the norm not only in the case of non-charitable donations where a surplus is left over after the fund is wound up or its purposes achieved but also where money is given for charitable purposes which initially fail (unless a paramount charitable intention can be found). It does not apply where a charitable fund *subsequently* achieves its purposes because this will be a subsequent failure and there will be no difficulty applying the cy près doctrine. So had the Gillingham Bus Disaster Fund been charitable, cy près would have applied in the normal way on a subsequent failure.

14.5.3 Operation of section 14

Section 14 of the Charities Act 1993, replacing a similar provision from the 1960 Act, is intended to prevent the *West Sussex* result where money is given for charitable purposes which fail. The section has application only in the case of initial failure, as in the case of subsequent failure (as has been seen) no question of returning the gifts to the donors would arise.

Section 14(1) allows the application of such property cy près, regardless of charitable intention, when the property has been given:

(a) by a donor who, after such advertisements and inquiries as are reasonable, cannot be identified or cannot be found (donors may claim within one year of the scheme); or

(b) by a donor who has executed a written disclaimer of his right to have the property returned.

There is a conclusive presumption (in s. 14(3)) that property raised by cash collections by way of collecting boxes or other methods which make it hard to tell one gift from another, or as the proceeds of lotteries, competitions, sales, entertainments, or similar fund-raising activities, belongs to unidentifiable donors without the need for instituting any inquiries:

(3) For the purposes of this section property shall be conclusively presumed (without any advertisement or inquiry) to belong to donors who cannot be identified, in so far as it consists—

(a) of the proceeds of cash collections made by means of collecting boxes or by any other means not adapted for distinguishing one gift from another; or

(b) of the proceeds of any lottery, competition, entertainment, sale or similar money-raising activity, after allowing for property given to provide prizes or articles for sale or otherwise to enable the activity to be undertaken.

Allowance must, however, be made for property given to provide prizes or articles for sale, or otherwise to allow the activity to be undertaken, and the donors of such items are entitled to the return of the property or its proceeds, should they so wish.

In any other case, the court may direct the property to be considered as belonging to unidentifiable donors if it would not be reasonable to return it in view of the amounts involved or the lapse of time since the gift was made.

It would seem then that the law is thus improved to the degree that it is no longer necessary to impute a fictitious general charitable intention to the donors or else attempt the return of the property—a result which, as has been seen, often results in the fund passing to the Crown as *bona vacantia*.

However, David Wilson has argued ([1983] Conv 40) that s. 14 is 'a dead letter of English law', and it is indeed arguable that it made no difference to the pre-1960 law. The argument essentially is that s. 14(1) applies only where the property belongs to a donor. But if Goff J was correct in *Re West Sussex Constabulary's Widows, Children and Benevolent (1930) Fund* [1971] Ch 1, doubting Harman J in *Re Gillingham Bus Disaster Fund* [1958] Ch 300, anonymous contributors do not intend to retain any interest in the property, and hence s. 14 is never triggered. It might be thought that the presumption in s. 14(3) cures the problem, but arguably the presumption goes only to the question of identification, rather than to whether the property also 'belongs to donors'. Indeed, it is natural to read s. 14(3) as applying to identification only. In that case, the property will, as in *West Sussex*, still go to the Crown as *bona vacantia*, and s. 14 will make no difference.

If, on the other hand, any of the fund has actually been applied towards a charitable purpose, then on Jenkins LJ's views in *Re Ulverston and District New Hospital Building Trusts* [1956] Ch 622, the failure would be a subsequent failure, and a cy près scheme would be ordered. In that case, there would be no need for s. 14 anyway. If this argument is correct, in the only situation where s. 14 is needed, it is worded in such a way that it cannot operate.

14.6 Small poverty charities

There are particular problems with old charities for the relief of poverty. Many of these required trustees to distribute money or goods, but the growth of State welfare has reduced the attractiveness of these, and even rendered them counter-productive in some cases, because hand-outs can lead to a reduction in State benefit. As long ago as 1967 the Annual Report of the Charity Commissioners (paras 17–20 and App. B) recognised the problem involved in cash hand-outs by commenting on the undesirability of using charity funds to relieve the burdens of the DHSS and local authorities and, instead, suggested other schemes; for example outings or home decoration.

Yet many old trusts to relieve poverty bound trustees to distribute money or goods. One example required the trustees to spend the income in buying bread and linen for the poor of East Barning—in 1983, the fund available was £5.12p! Obviously, by the 1980s a trust of this type had come to serve little useful purpose.

A possible solution to this problem obviously existed under the provisions of the Charities Act 1960, but the mechanisms for the full scheme-making powers contained therein were arguably too complicated for very small charities. Following a report of a House of Lords Select Committee in 1984, the Charities Act 1985 addressed this problem. Section 2 allowed trustees of charities more than 50 years old, by a simplified procedure, to change the objects to more suitable ones, so long as they were within the spirit of the original donor's intentions. Under s. 3, where the annual income of a charity was less than £200, the trustees could transfer its property to another charity having similar aims, or if its income was less than £5 a year, the trustees under s. 4 could wind it up, by spending the capital as if it were income.

The Government, in its White Paper *Charities: A Framework for the Future* (HMSO, May 1989), proposed to extend the policy of the 1985 Act, by standardising the application of ss. 2 and 3, and applying both these sections to all charities with an income of less than £1,000 a year, without distinction of age, locality, or purpose, the sole exception being those holding land for the purposes of the charity. It was proposed that trustees wishing to modify their objects or amalgamate with another charity need to be satisfied:

> that the original purposes had, since they were laid down, ceased to provide a suitable and effective method of using the property; and
>
> that the new objects specified, or the objects of the charity to which property was being transferred, were as similar as practicable to the charity's original objects having regard to the spirit of the gift.

The Charities Act 1993 did for the most part put these recommendations into effect, but the ss. 2 and 3 financial limits were raised to £5,000 per year (rather than £1,000 as recommended), and the s. 4 limit has been raised to £1,000. Section 74 of the 1993 Act replaces the old ss. 2 and 3, and s. 75 replaces the old s. 4. In turn, the Charities Act 2006 raises the financial threshold for gross income of small charities to £10,000 for the purposes of ss. 74 and 75. This provision was brought into force in March 2008 (see <http://www.charitycommission.gov.uk/supportingcharities/ogs/g001a001.asp>).

Trustees are required to act by unanimous resolution and with the Commissioners' concurrence, and to give reasonable public notice of their intentions. Transfers of property under what used to be s. 3 obviously require the consent of the trustees of receiving charities.

 online resource centre

FURTHER READING

Wilson 'S. 14 of the Charities Act 1960: A Dead Letter?' (1983) Conveyancer 40.

15

The office of trustee: commencement and termination

Up to now, attention paid to private (non-charitable) trusts has been in one of two ways. The first has been to draw attention to the nature of the trust on a general level by looking at its particular features and characteristics, and the way in which core features can be found grouped around different types of trusts and the requirements which must be in place for a trust to be said to be operational. The second has been to try to glean an appreciation of how these more generalised features 'work' through consideration of a number of case studies. What follows now is an examination of how those key characteristics of the trust and its operation are reflected in the responsibilities placed upon those who are involved in their operation. This is a study of how trusts are administered, and as such examines the nature of trusteeship itself, and the duties and responsibilities which must be carried out in furtherance of this. It will also ultimately examine the consequences of a trustee's failure to fulfil his responsibilities to the trust.

What follows in chapters 15, 16, and 18 is an examination of the nature of the office which characterises a trustee's responsibilities and duties; a fairly comprehensive consideration of how the office of trustee arises; and the consequences of it coming to an end. Chapter 16 provides an examination of the actual administration of the trust, and in particular of the nature of trustee duties, and the entitlements of the beneficiaries which flow from this. Chapter 18 looks at the essence of functions which are to be performed by the trustee; the consequences of a trustee not acting in the manner which is demanded of him; and the position in which this leaves the beneficiaries.

In respect of this initial consideration of trusteeship, a few points need to be made by way of introduction.

15.1 Onerous nature of trusteeship

It will soon become clear how onerous the office of trusteeship is. Legal title, without its equitable counterpart is by no means a privilege. It is no wonder that the courts require very clear evidence that in the creation of a trust, a trust was what was actually intended (instead of a gift, for example), as is illustrated by the case law surrounding the settlor's self-declaration of trust (considered in chapter 3). Nor will it come as a surprise that trusteeship is often undertaken on a professional basis and that the charges for such services can be very high.

15.2 **The law and fall-back provisions**

Whereas some of what will follow in these next few chapters is inherent in the nature of any trust, many of the powers and duties which are described represent simply a fall-back or default position where nothing to the contrary is provided in the trust instrument which has given rise to the trust. In reality, the precise scope of such powers and duties will, in the case of most express trusts, be governed by the terms of the trust instrument and not the fall-back legal position. Provision is also frequently made in trust instruments for the remuneration of trustees, and it is usual for examples to include clauses which are designed to limit trustees' liability for breach of trust.

This is not to deny the importance of the general law. As long as people set up trusts without taking proper legal advice the legal fall-back position remains of utmost importance. Also, of course, trust instruments can be considerably shortened to the extent that powers and duties are provided anyway in the absence of provision to the contrary.

15.3 **Constructive trustees of property**

It is less certain how far these legal rules apply to constructive trustees, whose powers and obligations may depend on the circumstances in which the trust arises.

Quite a lot of the material on the administration of trusts is statutory, but usually the provisions only restate the previous law, or re-enact earlier provisions either exactly, or only slightly differently. Thus you will notice that there are on occasions cases which are cited as authority on the interpretation of a section of legislation where the cases actually pre-date the section currently in force.

15.4 **The office of trustee: continuity and change**

It will become clear that much of the law relating to the conduct of trustees in relation to the trust's operation originates from the nineteenth century. You will have noticed throughout this book the way in which the nineteenth century can be seen to represent the origins of many aspects of modern trusts law, and the implicit and more explicit questions which have been raised concerning the appropriateness of continuing application of principles which were forged and refined in a society very different from today's. Along with some of the principles which underpin the determination of shares in shared homes considered earlier in chapter 9, the law relating to trusteeship is itself an excellent illustration of many of these questions and issues. Indeed, there has for some time been considerable dissatisfaction with the persistence of principles of law which clearly date from times long gone. In 1997, and in its Consultation Paper on Trustees' Duties (Law Com. 146) the Law

Commission carried out wholesale consideration of the role of trustees in modern times, against a backdrop of its belief that 'the law governing the powers and duties of trustees has not kept pace with the evolving economic and social nature of trusts—indeed the default powers which trustees have under the present law are generally regarded as seriously restrictive'. In July 1999 its proposals for reform were published. The resulting Trustee Act 2000 was given the Royal Assent on 23 November 2000, containing provisions in respect of investment, the acquisition of land, the appointment of agents nominees and custodians, trustees remuneration, and also a new statutory duty of care for trustees.

15.5 Standard required of trustees

Upon creation of the trust, the trustees become the legal owners of the trust property. Where the trust is created *inter vivos*, they will normally be parties to the deed which creates it, with the effect of vesting in them the trust property. In the case of a testamentary trust, it is usual to appoint the same persons to be executors and trustees, so the acquisition of the legal title to the testator's property is automatic inasmuch as it vests in his personal representatives from the moment of death. Upon completion of the administration of the estate, it may be necessary, depending on the nature of the property, to execute additional formalities signifying that they now hold in the capacity of trustees, or if other persons are to act as trustees, to vest property in them.

In any event, it is the duty of those who take the property as trustees to familiarise themselves with the nature of the property and the terms of the trusts upon which it is held. They must also ensure that all formalities necessary to vest the property have been complied with. As this stage it might also be necessary to consider the conversion and disposal of any unproductive assets, and the settling of any liabilities outstanding against the trust estate. Trustees appointed to an existing trust (replacing a retiring trustee) must satisfy themselves that the affairs of the trust are in order and that no breach of trust has occurred. If it has, steps must be taken as soon as possible to put matters right and recoup any loss.

15.5.1 Duty of care and day-to-day running of the trust

The duty of the trustees in the day-to-day running of the trust is to manage the property so as to preserve the value of the capital and produce an income for the beneficiaries. In effecting administrative functions, they may employ the services of agents such as solicitors, accountants, and stockbrokers, but there are also functions which a trustee must perform personally.

In the Trustee Act 2000 is a statutory duty of care applicable to trustees when carrying out their functions under the Act. Although the idea of a duty of care is not itself new, what *was* new about the 2000 Act's duty is, in the words of the Law Commission, the creation of a 'uniform duty' with the aim of providing 'certainty and consistency to the standard of competence and behaviour expected of trustees'. This works by applying the same standard of care across each of the functions to which the duty applies. In terms of what the legislation should be, it is clear that the Law Commission envisioned a context of increased professionalism and a diverse business environment within which trusteeship can increasingly be seen to operate.

The wording of the new statutory duty of care is as follows:

1. —(1) Whenever the duty under this subsection applies to a trustee, he must exercise such care and skill as is reasonable in the circumstances, having regard in particular—

    (a) to any special knowledge or experience that he has or holds himself out as having, and

    (b) if he acts as trustee in the course of a business or profession, to any special knowledge or experience that it is reasonable to expect of a person acting in the course of that kind of business.

The duty of care applies only in the circumstances listed in Sch. 1, which are the statutory functions of the Act, and thus arise in the following instances:

(a) when exercising the general power of investment (or any other power of investment howsoever conferred), or when exercising statutory duties relating to exercise of a power of investment or to the review of investments;

(b) when exercising the acquiring of land or exercising any power in connection with land so acquired;

(c) when entering into arrangements for the appointment of agents, custodians or nominees or when carrying out the reviewing duties pertaining to such appointments;

(d) when exercising the powers under s. 15 of the Trustee Act 1925, or any similar power to compound liabilities;

(e) when exercising powers of insurance under s. 19 of the Trustee Act 1925 or any similar power;

(f) when exercising the powers under s. 22(1) or (3) of the Trustee Act 1925, or other similar powers relating to reversionary interests, valuations and audit.

Accordingly, where a trustee acts in a way whereby he fails to take reasonable care, but does so in circumstances not covered by the ambit of Sch. 1, his failure is actionable not under the new law but under pre-existing legal provisions. Moreover, the Act provides in Sch. 1, para. 7 that 'The duty of care does not apply if or in so far as it appears from the trust instrument that the duty is not meant to apply.'

15.5.1.1 *Standard of care and the paid professional trustee*

The duty to exercise such care and skill as is reasonable in the circumstances is the basic statutory duty; and the provisions of s. 1 clarify that what amounts to reasonable skill and care in the circumstances will depend on the facts of the case. Indeed, this is the essence of the specific regard which must be given to the factors within s. 1(1)(a) and (b).

The s. 1 criteria give rise to what is often referred to as a combination subjective/objective test. Here, the essence of (a) is directed towards the trustee concerned, and operates in relation to the qualities which he is representing that he possesses. The trustee's own representations are then pitched alongside and against the objective criteria in (b) drawn from the standards which can reasonably be expected from a practitioner within the trustee's own business or profession.

On this model it is clear that a higher standard is expected from a specialist professional, and indeed this principle subsisted at common law. In *Bartlett v Barlcays Bank Trust Co. Ltd (No. 1)* [1980] Ch 515, Brightman J thought that a higher standard of care was required from paid trustees than from unpaid and non-professional trustees, with the former category being judged against the standards of skill and expertise which they claim to possess.

15.5.2 **Duty of care and termination of trusts: distribution among beneficiaries**

Sooner or later a private trust will come to an end and the trustees will be required to distribute the property among the beneficiaries. Needless to say, they must distribute it to those who are properly entitled, and failure in this regard will be a breach for which they may be liable.

The onus is heavy, and trustees have been held liable where they made payment on the strength of a forged marriage certificate (*Eaves* v *Hickson* (1861) 30 Beav 136) or in the erroneous belief that a valid charitable trust was created (*Ministry of Health* v *Simpson* [1951] AC 251). They may even be liable where they acted on legal advice (*National Trustee Co. of Australia Ltd* v *General Finance Co. of Australasia Ltd* [1905] AC 373), although this may be a factor which would induce the court to exercise its discretion under s. 61 of the Trustee Act 1925 to exempt the trustees from liability.

The problems of wrongful payment are dealt with more fully in chapter 18, but it may be noted here that trustees may apply to court for directions in doubtful cases or, in the last resort, protect themselves by paying money into court.

15.6 **Personal nature of trusteeship, delegation, and law reforms**

Throughout this book emphasis is given to the way in which the duty of trustees in the exercise of their discretions is one of a personal nature. Yet although trustees have a hugely onerous job, they will not necessarily be experts in everything which is needed for the safe and profitable running of a trust. Thus, it is obviously very important for trustees to be able to employ others to carry out the more specialised aspects of the management of the trust.

Equity has therefore always allowed the employment of agents in effecting specialised administrative functions, the most common examples of which are solicitors, stockbrokers, and accountants. Prior to the enactment of the Trustee Act 1925 two principles had been established by the House of Lords in *Speight* v *Gaunt* (1883) 9 App Cas 1. First, under *Speight* v *Gaunt* it was permissible to employ an agent where this was reasonably necessary, or in accord with normal business practices. Second, where such an agent was employed, trustees would not be liable for conduct attributable to the agent, so long as proper care was taken in the agent's selection, and the agent was employed within his proper sphere and exercised reasonable general supervision over his work.

This power to delegate has been widened considerably by legislation, and in the following sections we will be considering the Trustee Act 1925, the Trustee Delegation Act 1999, and the Trustee Act 2000. It is fair to say that the position relating to the delegation by a trustee of his functions has long attracted criticism. For example, in 1990 Professor David Hayton argued (in (1990) 106 *LQR* 87) in favour of the necessity of wider powers for the delegation of trustees' functions on account of rapidly changing economic conditions and investment choices. Of particular interest here are Professor Hayton's considerations of wider powers of delegation for investment managers, and also for the accompanying need for trustees not to become vicariously liable for the defaults of the manager. This matter was taken up by the Law Commission in 1997, initially in a Consultation entitled *Trustees' Powers and Duties* (Law Com. 146; and a Report published in 1999); the Law Commission echoed the need for wider powers of delegation. Much of the thrust of the Law Commission's findings was anchored to particularly scathing attacks upon the principle stemming from *Speight* v *Gaunt* distinguishing between so-called ministerial and fiduciary functions, in a social and economic climate which makes personal overseeing of many aspects of running of the trust (and particularly in relation to investment choice and management) impracticable at best and difficult to justify. The Law Commission's recommendations and more recent changes to the law will be considered further under subsequent headings.

15.6.1 **Trustee Act 1925: the statutory right to delegate and pressure for reform**

The 1925 Act retained the distinction between ministerial and fiduciary powers in respect of a trustee's right to delegate, but it did relieve the requirement at common law that delegation must be reasonably necessary or in the ordinary course of business. Sections 23 and 30 of the 1925 Act provided for these wider powers of collective delegation by trustees, the two sections working in tandem (although in a manner which over time became widely regarded as confused and difficult to ascertain). Section 23 (now repealed) allowed for the facility of delegation and provided that there would be no responsibility for the default of an agent 'if employed in good faith' while s. 30 relieved the trustees from potential responsibility for the default of an agent by insisting that a trustee was to be 'accountable only for his own acts…' and not for those of another unless this occurred through the trustee's 'own wilful default'.

The Law Commission's recommendation for 'root and branch' reform can be seen in this extract from their 1997 Consultation Paper.

We consider that there is no longer any continued justification for the existing restrictions on trustees' powers of collective delegation. The principal objection to the present law is that trustees' powers of investment and certain of their powers of management (such as the power to sell, lease or mortgage trust property) are regarded in all respects as fiduciary. As such they must be exercised by the trustees alone and are non-delegable. This position was the product of a time when decisions which trustees had to take were comparatively straightforward and infrequent. However, it is increasingly unrealistic, given that many of these tasks (particularly in relation to investment) now arise regularly and often require speedy professional advice and execution. We consider the 'exigencies of business' now justify the delegation of these discretions because adherence to the present restrictions is likely to frustrate the trustees' paramount duty to act in the best interests of the trust.

15.6.2 **Delegation and the current statutory framework**

The Trustee Act 2000 breathed completely new life into the position of delegation by throwing out an approach concentrated on specifying circumstances in which a trustee can delegate and putting in its place one which conferred a general power to delegate. It combined this with a prescription of functions which cannot be delegated. The relevant provisions are to be found in s. 11 of the 2000 Act, and the general power can be found in s. 11(1): 'Subject to the provisions of this Part, the trustees of a trust may authorise any person to exercise any or all of their delegable functions as their agent.' What amounts to a delegable function is considered in s. 11(2) which states that a delegable function is one which consists:

of any function other than—

    (a) any functions relating to whether or in what ways any assets of the trust should be distributed,

    (b) any power to decide whether any fees or other payment due to be made out of the trust fund should be made out of the income or capital,

    (c) any power to appoint a person to be a trustee of the trust, or

    (d) any power conferred by any other enactment or the trust instrument which permits the trustee to delegate any of their functions or to appoint a person to act as a nominee or custodian.

The Trustee Act 2000 adopts the same approach to the liability of trustees as was present at common law. Here, trustees are obliged to exercise reasonable care in the appointment of agents and also in their supervision. This is achieved through the operation of the new statutory duty of care.

15.6.2.1 *Individual delegation and the Trustee Delegation Act 1999*

Traditionally, individual trustees could delegate all their powers, including fiduciary powers, under s. 25 of the Trustee Act 1925 (as substituted by the Powers of Attorney Act 1971, s. 9). While this must now be seen in light of the Trustee Delegation Act 1999, the traditional position was a reflection of the assumption that the trustee would only want to do this in circumstances where he was actually absent. Indeed, originally, this section only applied where the trustee was away from the UK, and in such a situation it would of course be necessary for the trustees to have the power of the absentee in his absence. This facility was limited to a period of 12 months, and there were other important limitations (including no survivorship of delegation arising from a delegating trustee's mental incapacity (because it was by power of attorney), and a prohibition on delegation to a trustee's only other co-trustee). Of particular significance also is the position in respect of liability for delegation, which, as s. 25(5) of the Trustee Act 1925 illustrates, is in stark contrast to the position in respect of collective delegation. Section 25(5) provides that 'A donor of a power of attorney given under this section shall be liable for the acts or defaults of the donee in the same manner as if they were acts or defaults of the donor.'

    Fuller discussion of the traditional approach, and criticisms of the law can be found considered in more depth on the ORC, and here suffice it to say that an earlier attempt to reform the law was evident in relation to *individual delegation* in the publication by the Law Commission *Delegation by Individual Trustees* (Law Com. 118) in 1991; by 1997, this became conjoined with the main focus of *Trustees' Powers and Duties*.

    The 1997 Consultation Paper in its principal focus on collective delegation was extremely critical of the law as it stood. It made many far-reaching and radical recommendations for reform, seeking amongst other things to establish a relationship between trustees' responsibilities with the nature of various aspects of trusteeship (perhaps especially investment), at the heart of which was abolition of the distinction traditionally drawn between ministerial and fiduciary powers, and introduction of a more general right to delegate, subject to appropriate safeguards. While it was true that all the trustees, by using their powers of individual delegation, could in effect collectively delegate, the Law Commission recommended the enactment of a new and rational system of collective delegation. Their proposal was that, subject to any contrary intention expressed in the trust instrument, trustees should have authority to delegate their powers to administer the trust, including their powers of investment and management, but (except in relation to trust property abroad) should have no authority to delegate their powers to distribute the income or capital of the trust.

In recognition of the considerable width of these proposed powers, the Law Commission also recognised the need for a number of safeguards. At one level this highlighted the need to review the employment of delegation regularly, and especially to consider the appropriateness of any proposed delegation at the outset. There was also the need to draw up and review, at reasonable intervals, a written statement of trustees' policy in relation to the exercise of the powers delegated, reflective of their fiduciary obligations to ensure that the trust is administered in the best interests of its objects, informing the agent(s) of that policy. Particular account was to be taken of the need for such to apply in the delegation of powers relating to the selection of investments, the sale, lease, or charging of trust property; granting of options or rights of pre-emption over trust property; and the acquisition of property for the benefit of the trust.

The Trustee Delegation Act 1999 reformed individual delegation, but did so by tackling some of the specific problems identified in the dual regimes provided for under the 1925 Act (as amended) and the 1985 Act, such as trusts of land—through effective repeal of the Enduring Powers of Attorney Act 1985 and amendments to s. 25 of the Trustee Act 1925.

15.7 Fiduciary nature of trusteeship

At the heart of the 'fiduciary nature of trusteeship' are questions of *which* relationships are fiduciary, and *what* is their nature? The nature of a trustee's duty towards a beneficiary is fiduciary. In this book primary concern is with the duties of trustees, but to understand this, some appreciation that the trustee–beneficiary relationship is one of a number of so-called 'fiduciary relationships' which the law recognises is essential. For example, the relationship between agent and principal in the law of agency is fiduciary, as is the relationship between co-partners in a partnership; another example is the relationship between a company director and his or her company. Indeed, many of the cases considered in this section relate to fiduciary relationships other than trustee–beneficiary, and a number of them are actually 'company–director' illustrations. Nevertheless, all these cases are also authoritative on the position of trustees.

15.7.1 **Trustees, beneficiaries, and the distinguishing feature of all fiduciary relationships**

The exact scope of the fiduciary relationship is also recognised as not necessarily exhaustive, and thus its precise extent is not clear. But for present purposes, what *is* clear and certain and beyond doubt is the way in which all fiduciary relationships are underpinned by one fundamental principle. This principle is that of 'fiduciary integrity' which sets out the expectation that the fiduciary is expected to act impartially in the interests of his principal. Classic expression of this principle of fiduciary integrity is found in Lord Herschell's judgment in *Bray* v *Ford* [1896] AC 44:

It is an inflexible rule of equity that a person in a fiduciary position...is not, unless otherwise expressly provided, entitled to make a profit...It does not appear to me that this rule is...founded upon principles of morality. I regard it rather as based on the consideration that, human nature being what it is, there is danger, in such circumstances, of the person holding a fiduciary position being swayed by interest rather than by duty, and thus prejudicing those whom he is bound to protect. It has, therefore, been deemed expedient to lay down this positive rule.

This can be distinguished from ordinary commercial relationships, where parties act independently in their own interests and are not fiduciary relationships. In *Re Goldcorp Exchange Ltd* [1995] 1 AC 74, the Privy Council refused to recognise the existence of any fiduciary relationship between a company which had sold gold bullion for future delivery, and its customers. Lord Mustill observed that 'the essence of a fiduciary relationship is that it creates obligations of a different character from those deriving from the contract itself' and that that was not the case here. One effect of the lack of a fiduciary relationship between the parties was that the customers were unable to trace the property in equity (see chapter 19).

It is of the essence of any fiduciary relationship that the fiduciary has no personal interest in the way the duty is performed. Thus, where a fiduciary has a discretion, he must not have a personal interest in exercising the discretion in a particular way. A trustee, for example must be motivated to benefit the trust and not himself. That is not to say that fiduciaries are not entitled to receive benefit for their services. Banks, accountants, and lawyers are not accustomed to working for nothing, and trusteeship is clearly an onerous business. What is clear though is that the amount of their reward must not depend on the manner in which their discretion is exercised.

15.7.2 **Trustees, beneficiaries, and a 'core liability with several facets'**

The essence of Lord Herschell's judgment will be found throughout the cases examined in this chapter, and in many throughout this study of trusteeship. This can be seen, for example, in *Bristol and West Building Society* v *Mothew* [1998] Ch 1 CA, arising in the context of breaches of duty committed by professionals working in the broad sphere of commercial activity. In the course of explaining the need to identify and distinguish within these commercial relationships ones which *were* of a fiduciary character and ones which were not, Millett LJ explained that:

A fiduciary is someone who has undertaken to act for or on behalf of another in a particular matter in circumstances which give rise to a relationship of trust or confidence. The distinguishing obligation of a fiduciary is the obligation of loyalty. The principal is entitled to the single-minded loyalty of his fiduciary. This core liability has several facets. A fiduciary must act in good faith; he must not make a profit out of his trust; he must not place himself in a position where his duty and interest may conflict; he may not act for his own benefit or for the benefit of a third person without the informed consent of his principal. This is not intended to be an exhaustive list, but it is sufficient to indicate the nature of fiduciary obligations.

15.7.3 **Payment of trustees**

The remuneration of trustees raises a number of interesting issues flowing from their position as fiduciaries, as introduced and explained above. In many parts of the US statutory rates of payment are established, but in the UK only the Public Trustee and a number of other trustees acting in an official capacity have any statutory entitlement to charge fees. And, in linking the subject of remuneration of trustees to the discussion of appropriate fiduciary conduct above, much flows from the rather tricky starting point that in English law, the general position (which is subject to exceptions) is that trustees are not entitled to benefit from their fiduciary position, and thus have no automatic right to be remunerated at all.

15.7.3.1 *General principle and two justifications*

The general principle (which is subject to the exceptions considered in the following section) that trustees (and other fiduciaries) are not entitled to benefit from their fiduciary position does, as suggested above, lead to the position that trustees have no automatic right to be remunerated for their service in this respect. There are two possible justifications for this position, flowing from the principle of 'no benefit'. First, there is the argument that payment should not be allowed if the prospect of payment affects, or has any possibility of affecting, the manner in which the fiduciary's duties are performed. A fiduciary must act in a manner which is disinterested, and there should be no conflict of interest, or even possibility of conflict of interest with their duties, which are created by the prospect of reward. Second, all money and the property acquired by the trustee when acting in his capacity as trustee rightfully belong to the trust. As we shall see, these two justifications lead to slightly different conclusions, and it is not clear whether the courts have fully adopted the second.

15.7.3.2 *Losses, gains, and liability to account (to the trust)*

It follows from the general principle (subject to the exceptions set out shortly) that trustees are not entitled to claim remuneration for the performance of their duties. Moreover, it is also clear from case law that should it transpire that they do obtain a benefit from their trusteeship, they are required to account for it to the trust. Unlike the situations considered in the chapter dealing with liability arising from breach of trust, many of the cases which stand as authority for this liability to account are cases where there has actually been no loss experienced by the trust, and only gain made by the trustee. While the work on breach of trust below deals with the position whereby an incompetent trustee is required to make good losses which have been experienced by the trust, this chapter is concerned with preventing unauthorised gains by the trustee. In this latter situation, the remedy of account is focused on the defendant's gain rather than the claimant's (the trust's) loss. In this respect a trustee is in a position quite different from an ordinary contract breaker who can generally keep profits which he has gained from the breach so long as he compensates the other party for his losses.

15.7.3.3 *Reform, modernisation, and entitlement to payment: a departure from the general principle?*

Unsurprisingly perhaps in light of the discussions on modernisation and professionalism in trusteeship, the general principle has come under fire. The Law Commission's 1997 Report on 'Trustees' Powers and Duties' insisted that the position set out above was incompatible with the increased professionalisation of trusteeship, and it was accordingly recommended that in the absence of express contrary provision, professional trustees should be entitled to charge as long as the charges are reasonable and do not exceed the amount which trustees would charge in the ordinary course of their business. This entitlement has now been enacted as s. 28 of the Trustee Act 2000, which provides in s. 28(1) that a trustee is entitled to payment (except to the extent that this is inconsistent with the trust instrument) if '(a) there is a provision in the trust instrument entitling him to receive payment out of the trust funds in respect of services provided by him to or on behalf of the trust, and (b) the trustee is a trust corporation or is acting in a professional capacity'. Section 29 provides an entitlement to remuneration for 'certain trustees' where there is no provision elsewhere (i.e. in the trust instrument or by any enactment or secondary legislation), where the trustee is a trust corporation (but not a trustee of a charitable trust), or the trustee is one who acts as a professional trustee. The entitlement which arises is to 'reasonable remuneration out of the trust funds for any services he provides to, or on behalf of, the trust *if each other trustee has agreed in writing that he may be remunerated for the services*'.

This must be regarded as an important addition to the well-established situations in which a trustee is entitled to receive remuneration.

Circumstances in which there is a right to remuneration
These situations, along with the very important entitlement for professional trustees introduced by the 2000 Act, should be regarded as exhaustive.

The right to remuneration is fixed by contract at the outset This will of course be by contract between the settlor and trustee at the outset. Prior to the enactment of s. 28, this will have been the mechanism used by banks and accountants and other professionals which became associated with trust administration. It is also the way in which a director of a company (who stands as a fiduciary in respect of the company) will fix his entitlement to remuneration, by contract at the outset. This mechanism has as its basis the way in which it removes a possible conflict of interest because as his remuneration is fixed *ab initio*, it creates no incentive to act in a particular manner. However, the contract must be one which the company is entitled to make, as was not found to be the case in *Guinness plc* v *Saunders* [1990] 2 AC 663, and the House of Lords held that the directors were not entitled to keep the £5.2 million that they had 'received'.

Section 31 of the Trustee Act 2000 This entitles a trustee to reimbursement for expenses from trust funds. This is wholly restitutionary in nature, and does not allow the trustee any payment for his services as such.

The courts have an inherent jurisdiction to authorise payment, even where no remuneration is provided by the trust instrument   Originally the courts were prepared, if it was in the interests of the beneficiaries and if the trustee felt unable gratuitously to devote his time to trust affairs, to authorise payment of remuneration to him. The authorities and the basis of the jurisdiction were thoroughly reviewed in *Re Duke of Norfolk's ST* [1982] Ch 61, where the Court of Appeal appeared to have accepted as its justification ensuring the efficient administration of trusts. An alternative, implied contract view was expressly rejected by the Court.

In Re Duke of Norfolk's ST (above), the Court of Appeal exercised the jurisdiction to increase the remuneration of a trustee over the amount agreed in the original settlement   The case broke new ground because previously the jurisdiction had been exercised only where no remuneration at all was provided by the trust instrument, and the quantity of work had increased because new property had been added to the settlement, and the tax position had been substantially altered by the introduction of capital transfer tax in 1975 (see further chapter 17). The trustee was held entitled to extra remuneration for the increase in work. The Court saw no difference in principle between increasing an already agreed remuneration and granting remuneration where none was agreed, whereas this would obviously have been difficult had the implied contract justification for the jurisdiction been accepted.

For a trustee who has acted beyond the call of duty   In many of the cases considered in this chapter the trust has suffered no loss, and in many cases it may indeed have gained from the activities of the trustee (or other fiduciary), who may have put in a considerable amount of work, well beyond his normal duties, or taken a substantial financial risk. It is arguable that the trust would be unjustly enriched if the trustee were required to account the entirety of his profits, but the trustee (or other fiduciary) may (assuming he has acted in good faith throughout) claim under a common law jurisdiction based on *quantum meruit*, and an equitable jurisdiction to award an allowance.

In *Boardman* v *Phipps* [1967] 2 AC 46 (considered below), although a solicitor as fiduciary to a family trust was not entitled to keep profits received as a result of his position, he was held at first instance to be entitled to an equitable allowance of remuneration, 'on a liberal scale', for his work and skill, and there was no appeal from this aspect of the decision. The Court of Appeal took a similar view in *O'Sullivan* v *Management Agency and Music Ltd* [1985] QB 428, with Dunn LJ observing:

Although equity looks at the advantage gained by the wrongdoer rather than the loss to the victim, the cases show that in assessing the advantage gained the court will look at the whole situation in the round.

The basis of the jurisdiction therefore appears to be a discretion in calculating the profit made by the defendant, in cases where he has benefited the claimant through hard work. *O'Sullivan* extended the law in two respects: first, the Court of Appeal invoked the equitable jurisdiction even though the defendant was not, as he was in *Boardman* v *Phipps*, morally innocent; second, the remuneration in *O'Sullivan* included even a reasonable profit element (but note that it was not related to the *actual* profits obtained in breach of fiduciary duty, which had to be accounted).

Rewarding trustee zeal; the common law quantum meruit award

There is also a common law jurisdiction, based on *quantum meruit*, where the claimant has been enriched at the defendant's expense. A possible justification for the *quantum meruit* claim is that it is founded on an implied contract, in which case it is simply a variation on the express contractual provision already considered (in (a) above). In that case, it ought not to be possible for a fiduciary to claim on a *quantum meruit* basis where the express contract would be void. The directors in *Guinness plc* v *Saunders* (above) claimed an alternative *quantum meruit* entitlement, because they had after all through their skill brought about a takeover (of Distillers Co.) on favourable terms from which Guinness had undoubtedly benefited. They failed, in Lord Templeman's view, for precisely the same reasons that their claim in contract failed (that the company had no power to authorise payment): Guinness were no more empowered to enter into an implied contract to pay for the services of the two directors, than they were to enter into an express contract for the same.

However, in *Westdeutsche Landesbank Girozentrale* v *Islington London Borough Council* [1996] AC 669, Lord Browne-Wilkinson, disapproving the reasoning in the earlier House of Lords decision in *Sinclair* v *Brougham* [1914] AC 398, doubted whether a personal claim of money 'had and received' (explained in chapter 19), for total failure of consideration, was based on implied contract. Instead, he said, it is based on unjust enrichment, and is therefore entirely independent of the underlying contract. It is difficult to see why similar reasoning should not apply to the *quantum meruit* claim in *Guinness plc* v *Saunders*. An alternative ground for rejecting the *quantum meruit* claim in *Guinness plc* v *Saunders*, particularly in Lord Goff's view, was that it contradicted the long-established principle that a director (or other fiduciary) may not make an unauthorised profit out of his position (see further below).

The problem with this is that Saunders also failed in *Guinness* v *Saunders* to claim an equitable allowance, the criteria for which appear to have been accepted in the case as being similar to those for a *quantum meruit* claim. This aspect of *Guinness* v *Saunders* has to be reconciled with *Boardman* v *Phipps*, and *O'Sullivan* v *Management Agency and Music Ltd*, where a similar restitutionary claim succeeded, although there may have been a conflict of interest. It is not satisfactory to argue that the directors in *Guinness* were dishonest, although the later well-known criminal proceedings cast doubt upon their honesty, because the case proceeded on the assumption that they had acted in good faith. One (not very satisfactory) possibility is that it is a matter of degree: the conflict of interest was much more extreme in *Guinness* than in the other two cases (indeed, it is questionable whether there was really any conflict at all in *Boardman* v *Phipps*). See further generally on this problem, Burrows, *The Law of Restitution* (Butterworths, 1993), p. 308.

Final considerations of payment

It is clear from the previous section that there are a limited number of circumstances where trustees and other fiduciaries are entitled to payment. In none of these cases, however, is the amount of remuneration dependent on the manner in which the discretion (if any) of the trustee is exercised. Thus, there can be no conflict between the interests of the trust and the personal interests of the trustee.

15.7.4 **Trustees and making profit from the trust**

We move on to consider the position where a trustee (or other fiduciary) in fact gains from his position, and the issue now focuses on whether he is entitled to keep his gain. If one starts from the premise that a trustee should not put himself in a position where there is any possibility that his duty and interest might conflict then he should be required to account (i.e. pay over to the trust) his profit when there is any possibility that a conflict of interest may occur. Whether any conflict occurs in fact is not relevant. In other words, it should be immaterial that the trust does not suffer, or even that it gains, from the activities of the trustee. However, if no possibility of a conflict arises, the trustee should not be required to account.

If, on the other hand, the starting point is different and any gains made by a trustee in the course of his duties are the property of the trust, the trustee should be required to account profits even if there is no possibility of a conflict of interest. The trustee should have to go further, and show that there is no causal connection between his position and any profit made by him (outside the payment categories outlined above). It is reasonably clear, but not certain, that the law has adopted this stricter position.

Whichever of these positions the law has adopted, it is at least clear that the law is extremely strict. Some argue that it is too strict and can stifle entrepreneurial spirit; and in some of the cases below such stifling appears indeed to have occurred. This is inevitable if the law insists that a trustee is to exercise truly independent judgement, but it is arguable that the law accords too high a value to the principle of independence, and too little to the encouragement of initiative by trustees. It should be remembered that many equitable principles developed in the days when family settlements were the main variety of trust, and initiative was not therefore an especially valued asset in a trustee. Some would argue that to apply similar principles today is inapposite.

On the other hand, the law has the advantage of certainty. It is fairly clear what trustees may and may not do, and it is possible for prospective trustees to negotiate terms freely before accepting appointment.

The essence of the way in which trustees are not to make profit from the trust in their charge is well entrenched in cases old and new alike (as seen above in the examples provided by *Bray* v *Ford,* and *Bristol and West* v *Mothew*). And, apart from the methods described above whereby a trustee (or other fiduciary) becomes entitled to payment, a trustee will rarely, if ever, be allowed to profit from the office of trusteeship. The words 'rarely, if ever' are used deliberately, because it is not clear whether the law ever allows a trustee to profit from his trusteeship. It is just about arguable that the law prevents only profits being obtained by wrongdoing, or where there is a clear conflict of duty and interest; but it is also arguable that profits made by trustees are never permitted.

Breach of a fiduciary duty is a breach of trust, so where profits are wrongfully obtained all the remedies in chapter 18 also apply here. Often, however, the trust will have suffered little or no loss; but where a trustee has obtained incidental profits from his office, to which he is not entitled on the basis of the principles discussed below, he can be required to 'account' (i.e. pay over to the trust) those profits. In most of the cases discussed in this chapter the remedy sought is account of profits. Moreover, since it is assumed that the fiduciary will have invested the profits made, compound interest is payable on them (see further chapter 19).

15.7.4.1 *Trustees' profit and liability to account to the trust*

Account of profits is, however, a personal remedy, which is of no use if the trustee is bankrupt. Further, although the trustee is assumed to earn compound interest on any profits made, if the trustee invests the profits which have been wrongfully obtained, the account of profits remedy on its own does not allow the trust to claim the investment, which may have increased in value. However, any profits so acquired can be regarded as being trust property, which should have been paid over to the trust. Since equity treats as done that which ought to be done, the profits will therefore also be held on constructive trust by the trustee. The effect of this is that the trust can claim any investment into which the profits can, on the principles discussed in chapter 19, be traced in equity, thereby protecting the trust in the event of the trustee's bankruptcy, and also giving the trust any increase in the value of the investment, as in *Attorney-General for Hong Kong* v *Reid* [1994] 1 AC 324.

15.7.4.2 *Limitations on liability to account?*

Much of the law in this section is very clear, but the precise limits of the requirement to account profits are not. It is clear that a wrongdoing fiduciary must account profits, and there are also two well-defined conflict of interest scenarios: first, a trustee may not purchase trust property (or sell property to a trust); second, he must not set himself up in competition with the trust. It is reasonably clear that these are merely examples of a wider proposition that a trustee must not put himself into a position where his duty and interest might conflict. Less clear is whether a trustee is allowed to make any profit by virtue of his position, even where there is no possibility of a conflict between his duty and his interest. Lastly, there is the question of whether information acquired by a trustee can be regarded as trust property, in which case not only the fiduciary but also third parties who profited from the information might be required to account those profits to the trust.

15.7.4.3 *Profits made by trustees from 'wrongdoing'*

There is at any rate no doubt that where the trustee, or other fiduciary, has acted in bad faith, he will not be allowed to benefit from his wrongdoing. In *Reading* v *Attorney-General* [1951] AC 507, Reading had been a sergeant in the British army and had made at least £19,000 illegally by helping smugglers to transport smuggled goods, by riding in the lorries in his uniform. Unfortunately for Reading, the £19,000 was confiscated and he was forced into the role of claimant, petitioning for its return. He failed because as a fiduciary he was liable to account for his profits to the Crown. An army sergeant would probably not normally be regarded as a fiduciary, but the use in the case of the uniform to deceive the authorities may have been the decisive factor.

Reading v *Attorney-General* was considered and followed in *Attorney-General* v *Guardian (No. 2)* [1990] 1 AC 109 (the *Spycatcher* case, where *The Sunday Times* was required to account the profits that it had received from Peter Wright's deliberate breach of confidence). It was also followed in *Attorney-General for Hong Kong* v *Reid* [1994] 1 AC 324, where a fiduciary who accepted bribes was required to hold them on constructive trust for the Crown (his employer). Because he held them on constructive trust, the Crown's claim was not limited to the value of the bribes, but extended to any property purchased with the secret commissions. Thus the Crown was able to obtain the value of three houses, which had substantially increased. There was old Court of Appeal authority, including in particular *Lister & Co.* v *Stubbs* (1890) 45 Ch D 1, to the contrary, which was disapproved by the Privy Council in *Reid*.

Reid *and the requirement of a fiduciary relationship*

The principles in *Reid* apply only where there is a fiduciary relationship between the parties. In *Halifax Building Society* v *Thomas* [1996] 2 WLR 63, the defendant mortgagor had obtained a 100 per cent mortgage advance from the claimant building society to finance the purchase of a flat, having made fraudulent misrepresentations as to his identity and creditworthiness. He fell into arrears and the building society exercised its power of sale, but because of a rising property market, there was a surplus after discharging the mortgage. The building society claimed this, arguing on the basis of *Attorney-General* v *Reid* that the defendant was constructive trustee for the mortgagee of all the profits made as a result of his fraud. The Court of Appeal held that the remedy of account of profits and the imposition of a constructive trust were not applicable where there was no fiduciary relationship between the parties. Accordingly, the defendant was not required to account to the claimant for the profit he had made from the rising market.

15.7.4.4 *A requirement for bad faith?*

Where there is bad faith there need not be any harm to the claimant. Indeed, in none of the above cases had the Crown suffered any obvious loss. In *Industrial Development Consultants* v *Cooley* [1972] 1 WLR 443, the defendant, a managing director for the claimant company, had been negotiating on its behalf a contract with the Eastern Gas Board (EGB). The negotiations failed and it was apparent from the circumstances that the EGB was not at all happy about entering into dealings with Industrial Development Consultants (IDC) under any circumstances. Thus it appeared that whatever Cooley himself had done, the negotiations between IDC the company and EGB would have broken down. This meant that the claimant company IDC had actually suffered no loss from the personal gain which Cooley ultimately achieved for himself after the original negotiations between IDC and EGB ceased.

After these original negotiations ceased, the EGB began negotiations with the defendant personally, with whom they wanted to work. The end result was that he terminated his contract with the claimant company, obtaining a release on the false representation that he was ill, and contracted with the EGB himself, on terms similar to those originally proposed on behalf of the claimant company. Roskill J held that the defendant was constructive trustee of the benefit of the contract for the benefit of the claimant company.

It is noteworthy that the claimant company had lost nothing, and as a result of the case gained only as a result of the defendant's breach of duty.

15.7.5 **Trustees' profit illustrated by conflict of interest cases**

The wrongdoing cases may be an application of a wider principle that a fiduciary should not put himself into a position where his duty and interest conflict. After all, it is obviously not in the interests of someone accepting bribes or secret commissions to act in an impartial, or fiduciary, manner. A conflict of interest was also assumed to exist in *Industrial Development Consultants* v *Cooley*, since the defendant had negotiated for his own benefit in the claimant's time.

But conflicts of interests can arise even in the absence of *mala fides*. There are two other clear situations where a conflict of interest may arise between the trust and the personal interest of the trustee, which the law therefore prevents from arising. First, a trustee may not purchase trust property (or sell property to a trust). Second, he must not set himself up in competition with the trust.

15.7.5.1 *Trustees may not purchase trust property*

It is possible, particularly in the light of Harman LJ's views at least in *Holder* v *Holder* [1968] Ch 353 (below), to distinguish self-dealing (trustee purchasing trust property for himself) from fair dealing (trustee purchasing from beneficiary). Self-dealing renders the transaction voidable at the option of the beneficiaries. Fair dealing renders the transaction voidable only if the trustee has behaved unfairly.

The distinction is not universally accepted, and both are arguably part of a wider principle that a trustee should not profit from his office as trustee (on which again, see further below).

Conflict of interest: distinguishing 'self' and 'fair' dealing
The rationale for the self-dealing rule is that if a trustee purchases trust property, he can abuse his position and buy at less than the best price obtainable. Similarly, if he sells to the trust, he may be able to demand too high a price.

The self-dealing rule is very strict where trustees are concerned, so that there must be no *possibility* of the trustee taking advantage of his position, whether he does so in fact or not. The lengths to which the law goes are shown by *Wright* v *Morgan* [1926] AC 788, where a trustee who had resigned his trusteeship purchased trust property at a price that had been fixed by independent valuers. One might have thought that not even a possibility of conflict arose here. The arrangements had been made while he was still trustee, however, and the Privy Council held that this sale must be set aside.

It is possible for purchases by trustees to be valid, but only in very exceptional circumstances. It is essential not only that the trustee paid a fair price, as he had in *Wright* v *Morgan*, but also that he took no advantage of his position and made full disclosure of his interest. For example, in *Holder* v *Holder* [1968] Ch 353, an executor (Victor) purchased two farms that were part of an estate at a fair price at auction. The Court of Appeal refused to set aside the sale, although as executor Victor was acting in a fiduciary capacity. It was clear, however, that Victor had not been active in his role as executor, had indeed purported to renounce it, and had acquired no information as a result of it. He took no part in instructing the valuer who fixed the reserves or in the preparations for the auction. Additionally, the claimant beneficiary had accepted his share of the purchase money in full knowledge of the facts, and so was disentitled from taking the action on the grounds of acquiescence.

Limits of self-dealing
Both Sachs and Danckwerts LJJ expressed doubt whether the self-dealing rule should apply today where trust property is sold at public auctions, at least in a case where the sale is arranged by trustees other than the purchasing trustee. However,

Holder v *Holder* was limited almost to its own unusual facts by Vinelott J in *Re Thompson's Settlement* [1986] Ch 99, a case which concerned the purchase of leases of farms owned by a trust, by a company whose director was one of the trustees. Vinelott J explained *Holder* v *Holder* on the narrow ground that the defendant had never acted as executor in a way which could be taken to amount to acceptance of a duty to act in the interests of the beneficiaries under his father's will. He said that the self-dealing rule is an application of the wider principle that a man must not put himself in a position where duty and interest conflict, or where his duty to one conflicts with his duty to another. If Vinelott J is right, *Holder* v *Holder* should not be regarded as laying down more than the narrowest of exceptions to the rule.

The same principles apply to sales of property to trusts by trustees.

15.7.5.2 *Trustees must not set themselves up in competition with the trust*

Similar principles apply here, because the trustee may gain for himself the benefit of any goodwill acquired by the trust, and possibly also useful information. It is not necessary to show that he has in fact done so, however.

In *Re Thomson* [1930] 1 Ch 203, an executor was restrained from carrying out a yacht-broking business in competition with the estate. The substantive issue did not come before Clauson J, because the executor had, as a consequence of an earlier interlocutory injunction granted by the Court of Appeal, transferred the business to the sole beneficiary. The question of costs was still outstanding, however, and depended on whether the original action was justified.

Conflict, competition, and resigning from fiduciary office

The point of interest about *Re Thomson* is that Clauson J, in finding against the executor, did not think it would have made any difference if he had resigned his executorship, as long as he had contemplated starting a competing business while still an executor. There is a logic in this approach, because such contemplation may have affected the manner in which his duties as executor were performed. It has been argued that Clauson J's view depends on the specialist nature of the business, but it is difficult to see why this should make any difference.

15.7.5.3 *Examples of conflict of interest and duty which might be different?*

It is not clear whether the above cases are all part of a wider principle, that a trustee (or other fiduciary) may not make any profit from his position. If so, then all that should be necessary is to establish a causal connection between the profit and the position. It should not be necessary to go further and show either *mala fides* or a conflict of interest.

In *Re Macadam* [1946] Ch 73, trustees who used their position to appoint themselves to directorships of a company were held liable to account to the trust for all the fees they received as directors. This type of situation can commonly arise in private companies, because eligibility for appointment to directorships can depend on the legal ownership of a minimum number of shares, and indeed trustees may be under a duty to procure their representation on the board if it is necessary in order to safeguard the value of the trust shares.

Establishing causation: nothing else required

Arguably, all that is necessary is to establish the causal connection between position and profit. No such connection was established in *Re Dover Coalfield Extension* [1908] 1 Ch 65, a case similar to *Re Macadam*, but where a trustee had already become a director before becoming trustee. *Re Gee* [1948] Ch 284 is similar: here a trustee became a director after refraining from using his vote, which he had by virtue of holding trust shares. He would have been elected anyway, due to the votes of the other shareholders, however he had voted himself; he would even have been elected if he had voted against himself. Harman J held that the remuneration received as director was not accountable to the trust. In neither of these cases could it be said that the trustees had made any profit by virtue of their position.

A closer examination of these cases suggests that they are, in reality, conflict of interest cases, since clearly a trustee who stands to gain from the choice of himself as director cannot advise the trust impartially as to the choice of who to appoint.

Keech v Sandford: *position, profit, and a stronger case*
A stronger case is *Keech* v *Sandford* (1726) Sel Cas Ch 61, where the trustee took over the benefit of a lease which had been devised to the trust when that lease expired. Since the lease had expired, this is not a case of dealing in trust property. The causal connection between position and profit was presumably established, in that he would not have been in a position to take the lease had he not been trustee. The lessor had refused to renew the lease for the trust, on the ground that the beneficiary was an infant against whom it would be difficult to recover rent. The trustee thereupon took the lease for his personal benefit, and profited from it.

There cannot have been any actual conflict of interest, because the trust itself could not have benefited, given the views of the lessor. Nor would Lord King LC say that there was any fraud in the case. Yet he held that the trustee had to assign the benefit of the lease to the infant, and account for profits received. The trustee was the one person in the world who could not take the lease for his own benefit, because by so doing he would be profiting from his position. The same principle may apply where a trustee of a lease purchases for himself the freehold reversion: *Protheroe* v *Protheroe* [1968] 1 WLR 519 (CA) (but there are contrary authorities).

Conflict of interest: absence of bad faith
There was no *mala fides* in *Regal (Hastings) Ltd* v *Gulliver*, originally reported in [1942] 2 All ER 378 and only in the official reports in [1967] 2 AC 134n. Regal were considering applying for shares in a subsidiary company, but were unable to afford them, so the directors subscribed themselves and made a profit. The directors would not have been in a position to profit had they not been directors, but arguably there was no conflict of interest, given that Regal was not in a position to subscribe for itself. Yet the directors were held liable to account. Lord Russell of Killowen said:

> The rule of equity which insists on those, who by use of a fiduciary position make a profit, being liable to account for that profit, in no way depends on fraud, or absence of *bona fides*; or upon such questions or considerations as whether the profit would or should otherwise have gone to the plaintiff, or whether the profiteer was under a duty to obtain the source of the profit for the plaintiff, or whether he took a risk or acted as he did for the benefit of the plaintiff, or whether the plaintiff has in fact been damaged or benefited by his action. The liability arises from the mere fact of a profit having, in the stated circumstances, been made.

This is a fairly clear statement that all that needs to be established is the causal connection between position and profit. Arguably, however, there was in fact a conflict of interest, as the directors themselves must have determined that the company could not afford to subscribe for the shares. It would have been difficult for them to advise impartially where they intended to subscribe for themselves, and hence obtain a profit.

15.7.5.4 *Cornerstone of law or hard case?:* Boardman v Phipps

The leading case is *Boardman* v *Phipps* [1967] 2 AC 46, but it is not clear on what principle it was decided. Boardman was solicitor to a trust, which owned 8,000 of 30,000 shares in a private textile company with whose performance Boardman was dissatisfied. The trust had no wish to buy the remaining shares, and in any case was unable to buy them, although it could have applied to court for power to do so. Boardman decided to purchase them himself, undoubtedly benefiting from information he had received in his fiduciary capacity (in knowing what price to offer), and did not obtain the consent of all beneficiaries (on which see further chapters 16 and 18). The shares later increased in value (partly perhaps because of Boardman's management in selling off some of the assets of the newly acquired company), so Boardman made a large profit for himself. Additionally, however, because the trust still had a large share in the same company, his activities resulted in a large profit for the trust. There was no claim of bad faith, or any obvious conflict of interest, since the trust did not have the power to purchase the shares itself; and in any case, the trust had positively benefited from Boardman's intervention.

By a 3:2 majority, the House of Lords nevertheless held that Boardman held the shares as constructive trustee for the trust, and was therefore liable to account profits. It is not easy to discern the *ratio*, although it seems that whereas the majority thought it enough simply to profit from the trust, Viscount Dilhorne and Lord Upjohn (dissenting) thought that this was insufficient in the absence of a clear conflict of interest. They took the view that there was no conflict or possibility of a conflict between the personal interests of the appellants and those of the trust. Unfortunately, the position is muddied because the majority also took the view that there was a (somewhat theoretical) conflict of interest also: the trust might have changed its mind and sought to buy the shares itself, in which case Boardman as solicitor to the trust would have had to advise on the application to court. It may be, therefore, that the case does not extend existing principles, except in showing how willing the courts are to find even the most theoretical possibility of a conflict of interest.

Is information trust property?

A further difficulty about *Boardman* v *Phipps* is that in the Court of Appeal ([1965] Ch 992), Russell LJ had decided the case on an entirely different ground, that all the information acquired by Boardman in his fiduciary capacity became trust property. Lords Hodson and Guest also seemed to be of this view. Lord Cohen appeared less sure about the trust property point, but was happy to decide the case on causation alone.

The property reasoning raises serious difficulties (see, for example, Gareth Jones (1968) 84 LQR 472), especially where information is obtained by somebody who is trustee to several trusts, or where the information is passed on to other, innocent recipients who also profit from it. Partly for these reasons, Viscount Dilhorne, adopting the views of Lindley LJ in *Aas* v *Benham* [1891] 2 Ch 244, said that information was not the property of the trust, and Lord Upjohn's views were similar. Certainly, the 'information as trust property' reasoning is not part of the *ratio* in the House of Lords.

15.5 **Conflict of interest and duty: conclusion and clarification?**

Although the *ratio* of *Boardman* v *Phipps* is not very clear, the weight of authority probably supports the proposition that all that is required is to find a causal connection between the fiduciary's position and the profit obtained. If Boardman would have purchased the shares anyway, even without the information acquired by virtue of his fiduciary position, there would have been no causal connection between the position and the profit, and the case would have been like *Re Gee*. If not, the case is similar to *Re Macadam*, and Boardman was properly held to account.

It may be objected that the law deters entrepreneurial activity which may well benefit the trust. However, Boardman was liberally rewarded on a *quantum meruit* basis for benefiting the trust, on the principles discussed earlier. What he could not do was to keep any additional profits he made. The law allows private speculators to do so, but takes the view that those who are acting as fiduciaries accept, by taking on fiduciary positions, that their remuneration is limited to the categories described earlier, however much they benefit the other party. Though this view may appear harsh, it at least has the merit of ensuring that their discretion will be exercised in an independent manner.

15.8.1 **Trusteeship, integrity, and entrepreneurialism: new thoughts on *Boardman v Phipps***

The arguments surrounding the continuing operation of the no profit rule as exemplified in the House of Lords' decision in *Boardman* v *Phipps* (in the context of the unauthorised use of property or opportunities rightfully belonging to the trust) fit essentially into two broad interpretations of the result of the case; namely its justifications and its implications. The rule against profiting from a position as fiduciary arises where the justifications in favour of it are strongly outweighed by the opposing position in which it can be seen to unnecessarily stifle entrepreneurial activity. This might have the result of actually depriving the trust of the benefit of business expertise and acumen from which it might otherwise benefit greatly, as was the case in *Boardman* itself. On this reasoning, the operation of the rule against profit will ensure that the potential (and possibly considerable) benefits for the trust will not be forthcoming in light of the fact that trustees have no incentive to act in a manner which is entrepreneurial, as they are not able to benefit personally from doing so. Indeed the rule represents an active disincentive for trustees to act in such a way. The alternative reading of the rule against profiting by virtue of the position of fiduciary is that such a strict 'no profit' rule is required in the interests of certainty and preservation of the principle of fiduciary integrity; or the principle of disinterest.

15.8.1.1 *Entrepreneurialism v integrity: the same arguments?*

The case law in the area of the governance of fiduciary relationships has consistently put at its heart the principle of disinterest. This is promoted as the only position that the law can realistically adopt in order to ensure fiduciary integrity.

Indeed, if it were the case that some profits were regarded as being 'authorised' and others not, it would not only become more difficult on a conceptual level to defend the principle of fiduciary integrity, but it would also become impossible to demark such distinctions appropriately on a practical level. On such a line of argument (against interference with the principle of fiduciary integrity), this impossible middle way of regarding some profits as authorised whilst others remain unauthorised is also actually unjustifiable in light of trustees' ability to fix remuneration in advance, so as to avoid 'disappointment' (this was always possible through provision in the trust instrument, even before the enactment of the express power conferred by s. 28 of the Trustee Act 2000). There are no right answers to the existence of the rule against unauthorised use of trust property, information, and opportunities; what is instead needed is new approaches which can be added to the two well-worn broad and opposing ideas.

15.8.1.2 *Departing from the position of fiduciary integrity*

Making the case for a more entrepreneurial reading of the use of trust information and opportunities would take as its starting point the view that the 'no profit' rule requires reconsideration. Trusteeship is becoming less restrictive as exemplified in the widening powers of investment in the 2000 legislation—for example, in the general power of investment in s. 3(2), on which see chapter 16. The rationale for this arises from recognition of a greatly expanded financial market from which investments can potentially be made and the concomitant increased opportunity that this represents for enhancing the wealth of the trust. Thus, the law relating to trusteeship is becoming generally more entrepreneurial, and discouraging trustees from acting in an entrepreneurial manner is inconsistent with this development. Following this trend towards entrepreneurialism, the policy of the current New Labour Government is the promotion of 'enterprise culture'. Enterprise culture does of course have its roots in the challenges presented by the onset and progression of globalisation, which has itself provided the inspiration of the politics of the Third Way. The broad message of the Third Way, and the way in which it has become attached to New Labour's own reforming zeal, requires all people to be entrepreneurial so as to equip individuals and nation-states to meet the new economic conditions created by globalisation. At this point, it may be asked how the anti-entrepreneurial approach of trusts law as exemplified in the 'no profit' rule can sit comfortably alongside the broad trend towards entrepreneurial behaviour. And while the law of trusts is concerned to safeguard the position of those whose interests the occupants of fiduciary office are bound to protect, can it be readily assumed that trusts and their operation are to remain exempt from this new and never static direction which is sweeping the world? This must surely be a crucial question in view of the Trustee Act 2000 which was itself strongly oriented towards the need to modernise trusts law taking into account twenty-first century reality.

There is also new blood which can be added to the opposing position advocating the preservation of fiduciary integrity. This comes from the work of the American scholar Susan Shapiro. Shapiro works mainly in the field of white collar crime scholarship, and it is through this work that she has actually made some very important points in relation to the law of trustees and fiduciaries. In 1987, Shapiro argued in the *American Journal of Sociology* that scholarly consideration of white collar crime is really a study of the maintenance and abuse of trust in society. This work potentially has important applications for the study of trusts, and here it can be applied to the operation and implications of the 'no profit' rule. As has already been suggested, there is a line of respected authorities which stand as authority for the position of maintaining fiduciary integrity. Shapiro's work means arguments from very old cases can be strengthened by applying to them a new theoretical consideration of integrity, which argues against further empowering fiduciaries (here exemplified in enabling them to profit from their activities).

15.8.1.3 *In defence of the principle of fiduciary integrity*
Power imbalances in the trust relationship

Shapiro argues in a different piece in 1990 that because of the nature of their functions, occupants of fiduciary office operate in circumstances which are integrally highly advantageous to them. Indeed, she describes the relationship between fiduciary and principal (here, the position occupied by the beneficiary under a trust) as 'asymmetrical', and proposes that the huge power imbalances between the parties (which operate in the favour of the fiduciary) arise from the reliance created by inequalities in ability in a particular relevant area. She proposes moreover that the asymmetries which are thus created are further skewed by information which is used by the fiduciary in the performance of his actions, and which is 'hidden' from the beneficiary on grounds of his lack of expertise or other contextual references. This is also exacerbated by the 'moral hazard' which can be translated into behaviour which is committed by the fiduciary in the course of performing his duties, but which is concealed from the beneficiary.

Misconceptions about the 'burden' of trusteeship

Shapiro also argues that the much-vaunted burdens which seemingly attach to the fiduciary's performance of his duties are not only more than compensated for in the remuneration he receives, but that characteristically high levels of remuneration also build in protection against temptation for abuse of position which the fiduciary might otherwise experience (i.e. the 'moral hazard', and how to protect against it). She argues that occupants of fiduciary office are further empowered because the way in which trust and trust relationships are organised in society ensures that abuses of trust are difficult to detect. In this manner, Shapiro's work could be used to assert that the fiduciary position is in many respects advantageous to those who occupy it, and accordingly, that fiduciaries should not be allowed to derive yet further benefit from their positions than they already do. Indeed, although classical statements of the principle of fiduciary integrity (e.g., in *Regal (Hastings)* v *Gulliver*) acknowledge asymmetries in the fiduciary/principal relationship, and the emphasis placed on the duty of protection strongly implies the need not to prejudice the interests of the weaker party, Shapiro adds to this by making direct connection between the occupation of fiduciary office and the active advantages that this confers for the fiduciary.

15.8.1.4 *A more convincing view?*

How persuasive these arguments appear is a matter of personal choice, and simply advancing new ways of considering the tensions created by the relationship between trustee and beneficiary does not necessarily mean that a conclusion in favour of one view or another will necessarily be forthcoming. However, what the advancement of new approaches to the problems which are believed to characterise the trust relationship does provide is scope for its consideration in light of factors other than a line of respected, and also old, authorities. Just as the Trustee Act 2000 finds its *raison d'être* in the need to provide a modern legal regime, its passage must surely signal the need at least *to consider* new approaches to the questions and difficulties which will from time to time arise within it.

15.9 Conflict of interest and duty: a new approach for corporate fiduciaries under the Companies Act 2006

This text is of course directed primarily towards the operation of trusts themselves and is thus focused mainly on the position of beneficiaries under a trust and the responsibilities the trust arrangement creates for those who hold office as trustee. Thus while making the point that fiduciary office subsists in a number of 'relationships', and gives rise to a number of obligations originating in 'utmost loyalty' across these relationships, this chapter has been keen to emphasise this most in the context of the trust arrangement.

That said, a number of the cases which illustrate the responsibility on the part of trustees in relation to the integrity (and indeed utmost loyalty) which they must show in the performance of their functions are actually drawn from fiduciary office more widely, rather than that of trustee alone. Significantly, it is clear that a number of cases encountered in this discussion of conflict of interest have actually arisen from the courts' consideration of the behaviour of fiduciaries operating in the corporate context rather than acting as 'trustees' in a trust scenario. This can be seen in cases such as *Regal (Hastings)* v *Gulliver* [1967] 2 AC 134 and also *IDC* v *Cooley* [1972] 1 WLR 443, and it is also the case that *Keech* v *Sandford* (1726) Sel Cas Ch 61, *Boardman* v *Phipps* [1967] 2 AC 46, etc. are fixtures in leading texts on 'company law'. As suggested, cases like *Gulliver* and *Cooley* are considered authorities for the position of trustees under a trust because they are indicative of how strictly equity will respond to situations *where it is possible* for duty and personal interest to conflict and to persons who personally take up opportunities rightly belonging to the trust.

It is certainly the case that the approaches adopted in company law when it first emerged during the nineteenth century drew heavily on the much older and well-developed positions which had long applied to trusteeship. However, these cases which have arisen, where defendants are company officers (usually directors) and the litigant is a company rather than a beneficiary under a trust, have done so because company directors are said to occupy a fiduciary position which is analogous to that of the trustee in the context of a trust arrangement.

The words 'analogous to' have been used deliberately because although cases involving the misappropriation of funds, and the use of information and opportunities have traditionally seen identical approaches adopted by the courts for corporate fiduciaries and trustees alike, in some instances it is very clear that, as all leading texts on company law note, company law has equated corporate office with trusteeship only up to a point. For example, the very strict rules applying to trustees in relation to setting up a business in competition with a trust (considered above in light of *Re Thomson* [1930] 1 Ch 203 etc.) have never been adopted by company law's 'fiduciary duties' applying to company directors, because doing so would not be consistent with 'commercial reality'.

Most recently, provisions of the Companies Act 2006 (which is coming into force between 2006 and 2008) are signalling further divisions between traditional equitable obligations originating in trusteeship and principles which are being applied to *corporate* fiduciaries. As the Explanatory Notes accompanying the legislation explain, this is so on account of the sense in policy circles that the equitable rules developed around trusteeship can give rise to 'unduly harsh' results when applied to corporate fiduciaries, and can produce outcomes which fetter 'entrepreneurial and business start-up activity' by those who are company directors.

On account of the very strict position taken by equity, company law has evolved to allow for some 'conflict' behaviour on the part of directors to be 'permitted' by the company, and thus to be 'authorized'. The policy of the Companies Act 2006 acknowledges this, and now allows 'most...transactions or arrangements with the company' merely to be declared, and also permits 'board authorisation of most conflicts of interest arising from third party dealings by the director', which includes situations of 'personal exploitation of corporate resources and opportunities'. The key sections of the Companies Act 2006 are ss. 175, 177, and 182, and these changes have occurred in the context of the formulation of a statutory statement of general duties of company directors.

Almost all of this is beyond the scope of this text, but for writers in company law this will necessitate some reappraisal of the traditional 'trusts originated' case law applying to corporate fiduciaries. Reference to this in this text has been included for two reasons, the first of which arises simply because a number of cases cited as authority for the trust arrangement originated in litigation concerning corporate fiduciaries. Secondly, and more significantly, much of the impetus for the new approach in 'company law' has come from 'commercial reality', and the realities of entrepreneurship more broadly. It is of course the case that 'commercial reality' dimensions will have considerably less resonance for trustees than for company officers. However, given what was said about entrepreneurialism more generally in the above discussion of fiduciary integrity and 'entrepreneurial spirit', and the growing professionalisation of trusts services, it remains to be seen to what extent the principle of fiduciary integrity in the context of trusts themselves is able to withstand these external pressures and remain unfaltering in their wake.

15.10 Trusteeship and its commencement: the appointment of trustees

Usually, trustees will be appointed by the document which brings the trust into existence, and this document ought also to make provision for any additional appointments which may be necessary during the continuance of the trust. In addition, however, the Trustee Act 1925 makes provision for any additional appointments which may be necessary, unless the operation of the Act is expressly excluded. The Trustee Act 2000 provisions are necessary if the trust instrument does not make the necessary provision or if there is no trust instrument at all.

The settlor will usually name those whom he wishes to act as trustees, and where the settlement is *inter vivos*, the trustees themselves will normally be parties to the deed of settlement, since the purpose is both to declare the trusts and to vest the property in the trustees. In the uncommon case where the settlor simply declares his intention henceforth to hold some of his property on trust, he will himself be the sole trustee. Alternatively, he may decide to appoint other trustees as well and take steps to vest the property in himself and his co-trustees jointly.

Where trusts are created by will, it is usual to appoint the same persons to be both executors and trustees. The fiduciary duties of executors are very similar to those of trustees, but they are not identical and it may be important to know at what point an executor has ceased to act as such and become a trustee. Generally, this will occur when the executors assent to the vesting of property in themselves as trustees, although in the case of personalty, this assent may be implied since no formalities are necessary. In the case of land, an assent in writing is required, since this is an essential document of title.

15.10.1 Where there is no trustee available

The absence of trustees will not invalidate the trust. If the trust is *inter vivos*, the settlor himself will be the trustee. If it arises by will, the personal representatives of the testator will hold the property on trust. Where an instrument creating the trust names someone as having power to appoint trustees, he may use that power to fill the gap. If all else fails, the court will appoint trustees.

15.10.2 Acceptance is 'once and for all'

No one can be compelled to accept office as a trustee under an express trust, although a person may find himself a trustee against his will by operation of law, by virtue of a constructive trust for example. Once the office is accepted, it cannot later be renounced, although retirement is possible under certain conditions. In theory, the office of trustee is lifelong, and if a trustee dies in office, any liabilities which he has incurred will persist against his estate. Should the trustee wish to disclaim his role as trustee for any reason, he should do so as soon as possible, and preferably by deed, for failure to disclaim may lead to a presumption that he has accepted. Acceptance will also be presumed once the trustee has started to act in relation to the property.

15.10.3 Who may be trustee?

Anyone who has the legal capacity to hold the legal title to property may be appointed a trustee of that property. A corporation may thus be a trustee provided its constitution authorises it so to act. An infant may become a resulting or constructive trustee of personalty (*Re Vinogradoff* [1935] WN 68) although not of land, as s. 20 of the Law of Property Act 1925 declares the express appointment of an infant trustee void (and s. 36(1) of the Trustee Act 1925 permits her replacement by a person of full age). These restrictions apart, the settlor may appoint as he pleases. Traditionally, certain appointments, such as that of a beneficiary or one of his relatives, or the solicitor to the trust, have been regarded as undesirable by the courts, but they are not invalid and are commonly made in practice.

Certain special categories of trustee exist, the most important in practice being the trust corporation, usually but not always the executor and trustee company of a bank. The main advantages of appointing a trust corporation are its longevity, financial stability, and expertise, and the fact that it may act alone in circumstances where two individual trustees would be necessary. The chief disadvantage is that its fees are likely to be high. The qualifications necessary for a company to be a trust corporation are contained in the Public Trustee Rules 1912 (SR&O 1912 No. 348), r. 30, as amended.

Other special trustees include custodian trustees, the public trustee and judicial trustees. They perform specialist functions which in practice are rare.

15.10.4 Appointment of new trustees during the continuance of the trust

If an occasion for the appointment of new trustees arises during the continuance of the trust, rather different considerations apply than those governing the initial appointments. Here the settlor can remain involved if he takes steps to nominate himself in the trust instrument as the person having power to appoint new trustees (this will not arise otherwise by virtue of his being settlor). Alternatively, the settlor will nominate some other person to exercise the power of appointing trustees, and a well-drafted trust instrument will be required for this, because the terms of any power to appoint will be strictly construed.

There are also statutory provisions which can come into play here, found in s. 36 of the Trustee Act 1925, but these will not apply (by virtue of s. 69(2) of the Act) if they have been expressly excluded from applying. In situations where s. 36 does apply, this creates a hierarchy of categories of persons having power to appoint trustees. Further details can be found on the ORC, but essentially in descending order are the following persons (persons falling into the first category have the first right to make the appointment, and this moves downwards only where there is no one in that category able or willing to make an appointment):

- the person(s), if any, nominated in the trust instrument;
- the existing trustees, if any;
- the personal representatives of the last, or only surviving trustee.

If there is no one in any of these categories who is able and willing to act then the power given by s. 36(1) cannot be exercised at all (although the court may have jurisdiction to appoint under s. 41 of the Act). However the circumstances which do give rise to a power under s. 36(1) are specified in the section, and are essentially as follows:

- *Where a trustee has died.*
- *Where a trustee remains outside the UK for more than 12 months.* The absence must be for a continuous period, so that a trustee who occasionally returns for short visits cannot be removed under this head (*Re Walker* [1910] 1 Ch 259).
- *Where a trustee desires to be discharged* from all or any of the trusts or powers reposed in or conferred on him, but does stay partly involved in the trust.
- *Where a trustee refuses to carry out his office*, where it would appear apt to permit an appointment to be made in replacement of a trustee who disclaims his

role (although strictly, of course, such a person never becomes a trustee. Old authorities on the predecessor of s. 36 favour this interpretation).

- *Where a trustee is unfit to act.* This appears to refer to defects of character, and it is generally accepted that the courts will remove a trustee as unfit where he has been convicted of a crime of dishonesty, or has become bankrupt and his continuation in office is opposed by the beneficiaries, or he has been imprudent in the management of his own affairs. However, a bankrupt trustee who is free from moral blame may be permitted to remain in office.

- *Where a trustee is incapable of acting.* This refers to situations where there is unfitness due to mental or physical incapacity, and also where some legal incapacity is imposed, as when wartime regulations forbid certain foreign nationals to hold property in this country.

- *Where the trustee is an infant.* The express appointment of an infant trustee is void, but a trust could be deprived of an active trustee because of the infancy of a person named as a trustee, and the section appears to cover this contingency.

- *Where a corporate body acting as trustee has been dissolved* it is deemed by s. 36(3) to be incapable of acting from the date of dissolution.

In addition to the power of appointing new trustees by way of replacement, there is also power to appoint additional trustees, the existing trustees remaining in office. Where there are currently three trustees or fewer, none of whom is a trust corporation, and it is thought desirable to have more, appointment may be made by the person nominated in the trust instrument for the purposes of appointing new trustees, or by the existing trustee or trustees, in that order. The total number of trustees must not be raised beyond four, although more than one at a time may be appointed. The power is contained in s. 36(6), and is independent of the power to appoint replacement trustees under s. 36(1).

An appointment under s. 36 must be in writing, and in practice it will be made by deed to take advantage of the vesting provisions of s. 40 (as considered below).

15.10.5 Trustee Act 1925, s. 41: trustee appointments by the court

The court has an inherent power to appoint trustees as part of its supervisory jurisdiction over trusts, which is supplemented by s. 41 of the Trustee Act 1925. Under this section, the court may appoint whenever it is expedient that an appointment should be made and it is inexpedient, difficult, or impracticable to bring this about without the assistance of the court. Here an application to the court may be made by a beneficiary or by a trustee, but if it is possible to appoint under a power in the trust instrument or under s. 36, this should be done in preference. Where allegations of misconduct against a trustee are being made, the court may act under its inherent jurisdiction, but the proper course is to begin the action by writ so that the trustee knows what accusations he has to meet. And the court's assistance may properly be sought when no one has power to appoint, or no one is willing and able to exercise it, or where there is some doubt about whether the power has become exercisable (for example in *Re Phelp's ST* (1885) 31 Ch D 351 which concerned a sole trustee aged 85 who was deaf, and failing in intellect); or where the only person having power to appoint is too old or ill, or too young, to be able to exercise it. In practice, application is sometimes made by trustees who wish to avoid later argument over the propriety of a particular appointment. Fuller discussion of this, and the principles governing the court's selection in appointing trustees can be found on the ORC.

15.10.6 **Role of beneficiaries**

Where a sole beneficiary is absolutely entitled to the entirety of the trust property, or where all the beneficiaries are *sui iuris* (i.e. not children or people who are mentally incapacitated) and together so entitled, the rule in *Saunders* v *Vautier* (1841) 10 LJ Ch 354, considered in greater detail in chapter 17, permits the beneficiaries to terminate the trust. They may then, if they so wish, set up a new trust to which they, now as settlors, have the right to appoint the trustees. This course of action, however, will require transfers, which may well give rise to liability for capital transfer or other tax on the dissolution and fresh settlement.

However, although the beneficiaries may make new appointments in this roundabout fashion, equity did not allow them to do so directly. In *Re Brockbank* [1948] Ch 206, a trustee wished to retire and the beneficiaries sought to have a trust corporation appointed in place of the remaining trustees, who opposed the change on the ground of the cost to the trust of the trust corporation's fees. The beneficiaries argued that since they were all *sui iuris* and collectively entitled, the trustees were obliged to appoint in accordance with their wishes. Vaisey J rejected this argument. The beneficiaries might terminate the trust if they so wished but they were not entitled to control the trustees' exercise of their statutory power to appoint while the trust subsisted.

Further, *Re Higginbottom* [1892] 3 Ch 132 is authority that those who have the right to appoint under s. 36 may do so regardless of the wishes of the beneficiaries. The Trusts of Land and Appointment of Trustees Act 1996 gave additional powers to the beneficiaries, effectively overruling *Re Brockbank*, where they are all of full age and capacity, and are together absolutely entitled to the trust property. Section 19 empowers the beneficiaries, by written direction to the trustees, to appoint a person or persons as trustee(s), and to direct the retirement of a trustee. Section 20 allows them to substitute for a trustee who is incapable by virtue of mental disorder of exercising his functions as trustee.

15.11 **Formalities for vesting of trust property in new trustees**

As chapters 1 and 3 have revealed, where a settlement is created *inter vivos*, the trust property will be vested in the trustees as part of the transaction. Equally if the settlor declares himself sole trustee, there is of course nothing more to be done. In a testamentary trust, where the same persons are appointed as executors and trustees, the change of role involves the executors in vesting the property in themselves as trustees, which is notional in the case of most kinds of personalty (personal property, not real property) but requires a formal assent in the case of land. If other persons are to take over as trustees, the property must be vested in them with whatever degree of formality is appropriate to that property. Similarly, when new trustees are appointed to an existing trust, the property must be vested in them so that they hold it jointly with the existing trustees.

The following serves as a reminder of 'transfer formality' requirements which were considered in more depth in chapter 3. Where property is land, the main formalities to be aware of are those arising by virtue of s. 52 of the Law of Property Act 1925 (with texts in land law linking this with considerations relating to land which is registered and that which is unregistered, and also legal estates in land which are freehold and ones which are leasehold). Where the property is personal property, what is required here will hinge, first, on whether the property is a thing in possession or intangible property. Where property is a chattel, it may be physically handed over unless there are specific documents of title to be transferred (such as in the case of a car). Where property is intangible, what is required will vary according to the actual type of intangible property, reflecting a general policy that additional formalities are necessary because what is being transferred is not a physical thing, but a bundle of rights, entitlements, obligations, etc. Some key types include the following:

- *stocks* and *shares*: these must be formally transferred, and the transfer registered in the books of the company or other body issuing the shares;
- *debts*: where the property is a debt, it must be formally assigned and notice given to the debtor, to secure priority over future assignees;
- *negotiable instruments* (e.g., cheques): must be delivered and (unless payable to bearer) endorsed;
- *copyrights and patents*: considerations relating to these are governed by the Copyrights and Patents Act 1988 (s. 90(3)) requiring that transfers must be in writing to pass title.

15.11.1 Consequences of improper vesting

Proper vesting is vital, since the trustees may be held personally liable for any loss arising from failure in this regard. A newly appointed trustee must satisfy himself that all is in order and cannot say that it should have been attended to by the other trustees. However, in the case of a newly appointed trustee, some of the formalities of vesting are obviated by s. 40 of the Trustee Act 1925. The effect of this section is that where he is appointed by deed containing a declaration in appropriate terms, the trust property vests automatically in the new trustee and his co-trustees as joint tenants. But not all property is included within the reach of s. 40, and property which is excluded includes a number of interests and estates in land, flowing from the requirement of writing in transfers. Similarly, stocks and shares are excluded because they must be formally transferred and registered in the company's books. This is because, under the Companies Acts, legal title to stocks and shares depends on registration, and companies can recognise as shareholders only those who appear in their books.

15.12 **Termination of trusteeship**

Materials here concern only the position relating to a trustee's retirement and also death of a trustee. Materials on the ORC consider the circumstances in which a trustee can be forcibly removed from office, with the discussion therein tying this in with discussion which has occurred in this chapter of provisions of s. 36 and s. 41 considered above.

15.12.1 **Retirement**

In principle the office of trustee is lifelong. Nevertheless, a trustee may voluntarily retire in one of several ways. He can, for example, take advantage of any power to retire contained in the trust instrument, although such a power is nowadays uncommon, and if someone can be found to replace him, he may retire under the provisions of s. 36(1) of the Trustee Act 1925. Furthermore, s. 39 allows for retirement even without a replacement being found in the following circumstances: that retirement will not leave the trust with fewer than two individual trustees or a trust corporation to act for it; the remaining trustees must consent to his retirement; and anyone empowered to appoint trustees must consent. Here retirement and necessary consents must be in the form of a deed.

It is also possible for beneficiaries to consent to his retirement, and they will be debarred from holding the trustee accountable for any event arising after the date of such consent. Unless all are *sui iuris* (i.e. suffering from no incapacities, such as infancy or mental incapacity) and collectively entitled to the entire trust property, the trustee will not obtain his discharge from the trust. It will also be prudent to obtain the consents of the other trustees, to avert any claim by them to an indemnity. The only limitation here is that a beneficiary who consents to a breach of trust has no right of action in respect of that breach. And finally, it is possible for the court to discharge without replacement under its inherent jurisdiction, but will not do so if this would leave the trust without a trustee. In such a case it may make an order for administration of the trust by the court, so that the trustee remains in office but is relieved of responsibility.

What these provisions suggest is that although the once-and-for-all nature of trusteeship looks harsh in theory, in practice the statutory provisions for retirement are almost always sufficient.

15.12.2 **Death of a trustee**

Trustees hold their office, and the trust property, jointly. There is a right of survivorship so that upon the death of a trustee, his office and the trust estate devolve on the survivors. Discussion of the Use, the earliest modern trust, showed how estates were able to pass from generation to generation with few conveyances of legal titles. This was achieved in part by vesting the legal title in a number of feoffees to use jointly, and relying on the right of survivorship on the death of any one of them. Trusts today operate in the same way and for essentially similar reasons.

The equitable rule was codified in s. 18(1) of the Trustee Act 1925, which provides:

- Where a power or trust is given to or imposed on two or more trustees jointly, the same may be exercised or performed by the survivors or survivor of them for the time being.
- If one trustee dies, then, the rest may carry on the trust without interruption, subject to the possible need to appoint a replacement if the numbers have been reduced below what is required for effective management.
- Although the trust property vests automatically in the survivors, due steps should be taken to ensure that any register or document of title is brought up to date.
- When a sole surviving trustee dies, the trust property devolves on his personal representatives and is held by them on the terms of the trust. Section 18(2) enables the personal representatives to exercise all the powers of the former trustee, although they are not obliged to do so. The personal representatives can only act until new trustees are appointed. Often, they will themselves be the persons having the power to appoint.

online
resource
centre

FURTHER READING

All reading which relates to the consideration given to trusteeship across chapters 15, 16, and 18 can be found detailed at the end of chapter 18.

16

Powers, discretions, and duties of trustees

16.1 General description and overview

16.1.1 Powers and duties

Equity equips trustees with a number of powers and also imposes a range of duties, most of which may be modified or excluded by the express terms of the particular trust in question. Modern trusts created by deed or settlement or will, and prepared under expert legal advice, generally seek to give the trustee the widest possible powers, being almost invariably drafted with tax saving in mind. It is important to bear in mind that the powers described in this chapter are generally subject to the terms within the trust instrument itself.

The distinction between trusts and powers was considered in chapter 2. This is useful to recall at this point because a similar distinction exists between the duties of the trustee's office on the one hand, and his powers and discretions arising from it on the other. Trustees have a discretion as to whether or not they will exercise a power, and if after proper consideration they decide in good faith not to exercise it, then the beneficiaries have no ground for complaint. Generally speaking, however, there will be a duty to undertake such consideration where it would be appropriate. There is of course no discretion as to whether to fulfil a duty, and the new statutory duty of care in the Trustee Act 2000 will of course apply in the exercise of duties laid down in Sch. 1.

16.1.2 What are the powers and duties?

In view of the different types of situation in which trusts come into being, it is only to be expected that powers and duties will vary according to the character of the trust: for example, whether the trustees are required to accumulate or distribute the income and so on.

However, it will be seen that some kinds of power are in principle widely available to trustees. Most of these are now statutory and they are chiefly concerned with facilitating the management of the trust.

For example, there will be much attention given to the trustees' obligation to invest the funds of the trust according to powers of investment conferred on them by the trust instrument or the newly enacted Trustee Act 2000. They must also ensure the proper payment of tax, and at some stage they may well have to consider matters such as the sale of trust property or making provision for infant beneficiaries. Accounts of trust business must be kept and copies supplied to the beneficiaries, and in this vein, it is usual and desirable for trustees to meet in order to transact trust business; records of such meetings must be minuted in a diary or minute book.

The trust instrument will usually give additional powers appropriate to the trust. In the case of the modern tax-saving trust, these are likely to be extensive, and by and large the statutory powers have more application in older and less profession-ally oriented trusts.

Although the duties of trustees will vary considerably, there are nevertheless certain fundamental duties which are fiduciary in character (for example the duty of loyalty, namely the duty not to profit from the trust) which apply to all trustees. Other common duties will include the safe-keeping of trust property, the proper custody of documents of title, investment, etc. It will also become clear later that trustees also have in addition duties towards the beneficiaries. These include the duty to inform them of their rights and provide information regard-ing the affairs of the trust, and the duty to distribute the property in accordance with entitlements to it. They must also consider the need to maintain fairness between the beneficiaries.

16.1.2.1 *Duties, trust instruments, and the scope for modification*

Some duties can be and indeed are frequently modified by the trust instrument. Others, such as the duty to make proper distribution, are inherent in the nature of any trust, although even here the trust instrument may limit the personal liability of the trustees in the event of breach of trust.

16.1.2.2 *Trusts and the professional context of their operation*

It will be apparent that the administration of all but the simplest of trusts calls for a considerable degree of business competence, and nowadays most trusts of any size will have a professional trustee such as a bank or trust corporation to act for them. The professional may act either as a sole trustee or in conjunction with one or more individuals. This sort of mixture can be useful in family settlements, combining the expertise of the professional with the more intimate knowledge of family circumstances supplied by the private trustee.

16.1.3 **Constructive trustees**

The powers and duties described in this chapter apply to express trusts. Constructive trustees are in a peculiar position because of the fact that they hold property under a trust which has been imposed upon them from the operation of law. The duties of constructive trustees are uncertain, and key in the application of the Trustee Act 2000 and the statutory duty of care which it lays down. The difficulties in ascertaining how and to what extent the new statutory duty can be applied can be seen to flow from the huge variety of circumstances in which constructive trustee-ship arises. One view of this might propose against the application of the duty of care on account of the fact that at the most extreme of the constructive trust's operation, a person can become such a trustee without knowing it and remains ignorant until the matter is determined by the court. In the absence of definitive guidance, it must also be noted that an argument in favour of the duty applying to a constructive trustee can be made from the way in which the legislation expresses the duty of care applying to trustees exercising the powers prescribed 'however conferred'.

16.2 **Sale of trust property**

A power to sell some or all of the trust property is usually given by the trust instrument, either expressly or by implication, and even in the absence of such power, trustees will often be permitted to sell by statute, or as a last resort by order of the court. Some specific cases require consideration.

16.2.1 **Land governed by the Settled Land Act 1925**

Settled land is very rare today and the creation of a statutory trust for sale under the Settled Land Act 1925 is a very unusual type of trust. Here the sole function of the trustees of the settlement is to take the proceeds if the land is sold, so as to protect the (overreached) interests of the beneficiaries under the trusts of the settlement. The legal estate (fee simple absolute in possession) and the powers of sale are not vested in trustees but in the tenant for life. Further, very little limit is placed on the power of the tenant for life to sell the land, who has far more extensive powers than a normal trustee in this regard. Although strict settlements still in existence on 1 January 1997 are unaffected by new powers conferred by s. 8 of the Trustee Act 2000 (see below), the Act has made some changes to the operation of strict settlements. First, under s. 75(2) of the Settled Land Act (as amended by the 2000 Act), the investment or other application of capital monies is no longer the province of the tenant for life and discretion as to how the trust fund should be invested is now vested in the trustees. In addition, a new s. 75(4)(c) provides that anyone authorised to exercise trustees' functions under s. 11 (in respect of the application or investment of capital money) will not be subject to the obligation to consult with the tenant for life and give credence to his wishes.

16.2.2 **Trusts for the sale of land**

Statutory trusts for sale have been abolished by the Trusts of Land and Appointment of Trustees Act 1996. It is still possible (but rarely appropriate) to set up express trusts for the sale of land, in which case the duty to sell will be contained in the trust instrument, and a power to postpone shall be implied.

16.2.3 **Other trusts of land**

Apart from existing strict settlements, all trusts of land are now governed by the Trusts of Land and Appointment of Trustees Act 1996 which gives trustees wide powers of sale, but (unlike the predecessor trust for sale) not duties to sell.

16.2.4 **Personal property**

The Trustee Act 1925 contained a number of provisions for the sale which authorise sale of trust property by trustees (including its s. 16) for situations where no such power was expressly or impliedly given in the trust instrument itself. However, under the new regime, there is no statutory power of sale except in the case of trusts of land, and the Trustee Act 2000 does not include any provision authorising the sale of (personal) property except for the purposes of varying investment.

16.2.5 **Power to give receipts**

The power to sell or otherwise deal with trust property is of little value unless the purchaser can obtain a valid receipt for the transaction. Thus, s. 14 of the Trustee Act 1925 gives a power, notwithstanding anything to the contrary in the trust instrument, to give an effective receipt. The receipt of such a receipt in writing from a trustee operates to exonerate the purchaser from any obligation to ensure that the trustees apply the money received in accordance with the trust. This is very important from the perspective of the purchaser, because his awareness that the property he has purchased was the subject of a trust might otherwise be taken to ensure that he holds it as constructive trustee under the equitable notice doctrine.

16.3 **Power to insure**

Section 34 of the Trustee Act 2000 gives trustees wide powers to insure trust property. The enactment of s. 34 marks the repeal of the previous provisions regarding insurance as laid out in s. 19 of the Trustee Act 1925. The 1925 provisions were regarded as being restrictive in that they gave trustees limited power to insure against loss or damage by fire, but not against other very important insurable risks. This very limited power stemmed from the way in which 1925 predated many forms of insurance which are available to (and increasingly regarded as being indispensable within) commercial dealings. The exercise of this power is now subject to the statutory duty of care.

16.4 **Power to employ nominees or custodians**

Part IV of the Trustee Act 2000 creates a new regime for the appointment of agents, custodians, and nominees. Under this trustees can collectively authorise an agent to carry out 'delegable' functions. The definition of delegable functions can be found in s. 11 of the Act. Furthermore, the 2000 Act confers upon trustees wide powers for the holding of trust property by custodians and nominees. Perhaps most important under this head is the new statutory duty in Sch. 1, para. 3, under which trustees must labour in the appointment of agents, custodians, and nominees, while s. 22 places upon trustees the duty to review the activities of this category of delegatee. Over and above compliance with these duties for the appointment and review of such persons, by the provision of s. 23 of the Trustee Act 2000, trustees incur no liability for any default committed by agents, custodians, or nominees so appointed. Trustees are subject to the statutory duty of care in this respect.

16.5 **Power to compound liabilities**

As the legal owner of the property, a trustee has the right to maintain an action with regard to the trust property. Where the claim itself is a legal claim, it will be the case that it is only the trustee as legal owner who can sue. This is very important, particularly where debts are owed to the trust. Notwithstanding, litigation is still a risky business, perhaps especially so in the pursuit of debts owed, where it is far from clear that there will be recovery of what is owed, and there is expense entailed in the debts pursuit. To this end s. 15 of the Trustee Act 1925 gives discretion to trustees in their dealings with persons who are in contention with the trust (commonly because they owe the trust money). When exercising this power under s. 15 of the Trustee Act 1925 (or any corresponding power, however conferred), trustees are subject to the statutory duty of care as provided by s. 1 of the Trustee Act 2000.

16.6 **Power to acquire land**

The power to acquire land is conferred by provisions within Part III of the Trustee Act 2000. These new powers are extensive and apply to the purchase of leasehold and freehold land. By the provision of s. 8, such purchases can be made for the purposes of investment; for occupation by a beneficiary; or for any other purpose. By the provisions of s. 8(3) the trustee is given all the powers of an absolute owner. The trustee is subject to the duty of care in s. 1 in the exercise of these powers.

16.7 **Powers of maintenance and advancement**

Powers of maintenance and advancement are appropriate to family type settlements, and they have the object of providing for infant beneficiaries who are not as yet entitled to the benefit of any income of capital but who will still require financial support during their minority. In addition to the statutory powers conferred by the Trustee Act 1925, the court has inherent jurisdiction to provide both maintenance and advancement.

16.7.1 **Power of maintenance**

The statutory power of maintenance under s. 31 of the Trustee Act 1925 can only arise where the beneficiary is entitled to receive intermediate income under the trust. This will be the case either where his interest is vested or where it is a contingent interest which carries the intermediate income. If there are prior interests, or if the beneficiary's interest is as a member of a class of discretionary beneficiaries, the power will not be available at all.

16.7.1.1 *The discretion to maintain and the trustees' guiding principle*

Where income is available and the trustees have the discretion as to whether to maintain the beneficiary, s. 31 provides guidance on such matters as the age of the infant and the requirements he may have and the general circumstances of his case. Subject to contrary intention in the trust instrument the power to maintain ceases where the infant obtains majority. This is the 'contingency'. Even if his interest is still contingent, the trustees must pay the whole of the income to him until he obtains a vested interest or dies.

16.7.2 The power of advancement

The power of advancement permits trustees to pay capital sums to, or on behalf of a beneficiary some time before he is entitled to claim the fund. The power may be given by the trust instrument or, subject to a contrary intention, s. 32 of the Trustee Act 1925 may be invoked. The statutory power allows trustees at any time to pay or apply capital money for the 'advancement or benefit' of any person entitled to that capital or a share thereof. Subject to that limitation the powers are wide and apply whether the interest is vested or contingent, or whether it is in possession, in remainder, or in reversion. Up to one half of the beneficiary's share may be advanced.

16.7.2.1 *The significance of the power of advancement and its context*

The trustees' discretion whether to exercise their power of advancement is absolute, so long as it is for the 'advancement or benefit' of the beneficiary. The ambit of the power is very wide, and it is popular in schemes which are designed as tax saving devices. In this context, it can be seen as a device which operates for schemes which are designed to avoid tax on capital transfers. Capital Transfer Tax (or CTT) is due on transfers of capital taking place *inter vivos* as well as ones which occur upon death. It is a tax which was designed to circumvent the avoidance of Estates Duty (by ensuring that gifts were made more than seven years before death), and was designed to tax family capital at least once per generation.

*The power of advancement, CTT, and the significance
of Pilkington v IRC [1964] AC 612*
This case arose from a proposed advancement of part of a contingent share of Penelope Pilkington, who was an infant beneficiary, under the terms of a fund established by her uncle so long as she attained majority (of 21 years). The trustees of the settlement wished to advance to Penelope a sum of £7,600, which was to be settled on other trusts for her and this was for the purpose of avoiding duty payable on death. It was held in the House of Lords that this course of action was a proper exercise of the statutory power of advancement and there was benefit to the infant in the avoidance of tax. In this respect, it did not matter that the purpose of the advancement was for its resettlement on different trusts for the benefit of the infant.

16.7.3 Advancement must be for the benefit of the advancee

However widely expressed the statutory power of advancement might be, it was held by the Court of Appeal in *Re Pauling's ST* [1964] Ch 303 that the trustees must be satisfied that the advancement is for the benefit of the advancee. Further, should trustees decide to make an advance for a particular purpose, they must ask themselves whether the beneficiary is likely actually to carry out the intended purpose. Following this, no payment should be made for such a purpose where the trustees will then leave him free to do with it what he pleases. The question was left open as to whether the trustees can actually recover money which the beneficiary requests for a particular purpose and then applies to something quite different.

16.8 Duty to protect the trust assets: the duty of investment

There is a continuing duty which begins with the collection of the assets upon a trustee's assumption of office and ends only with the final distribution of the property amongst those entitled to it.

16.8.1 Initial duties

From the outset, trustees must acquaint themselves with the terms of the trust and the state of the property they are to hold. They must also ensure that funds are appropriately invested and see that all securities and chattels are in proper custody. If there is property which is outstanding, all proper steps must be taken to gather it in.

16.8.1.1 *Initial duties and trustees' liabilities*

In *Re Brogden* (1888) 38 Ch D 546, trustees were held liable where they refrained from suing to enforce a covenant to pay £10,000 into the settlement. This was so even though their motivation was reluctance at endangering the family business of which the covenantor's estate formed a major part. On the other hand, in *Ward* v *Ward* (1843) 2 HL Cas 777, trustees were not liable for failure to sue a beneficiary who might have been ruined by the action along with his family who were also beneficiaries. However, *Ward* is regarded as an extreme case.

16.8.1.2 *Failure to sue and 'excuses' made*

In *Re Brogden*, the Court of Appeal found that the only excuse for the trustees' failure to sue was that the action was considered to be fruitless. This was not an appropriate reason for failing to enforce payments due to the trust. However, there is now s. 15 of the Trustee Act 1925 which comes to the aid of trustees in weighing up litigation risks. Now, subject to the statutory duty of care, trustees in the exercise of their powers are able to compound liabilities and allow time for the payment of debts and will not incur liability.

16.8.2 The protection of assets by investment

16.8.2.1 *General principles*

Once assets have been 'collected' in this manner by the trustees they must then be protected, and at the heart of this lies the selection by the trustees of proper investments. In this regard two central principles can be seen to operate. First, trustees have a general duty to act fairly as between the beneficiaries, and second the trustees must make investments which are appropriate.

The duty to act with an even hand amongst the beneficiaries
This principle will dictate that, in the selection of investments, the trustee must be mindful of those for whom the property must provide an income and also those who have ultimate entitlement to the property.

The duty to make appropriate investments
In respect of this, the enactment of the Trustee Act 2000 signals the arrival of a new approach to investment which is radically different from the traditional caution of the law relating to investment by trustees in contrast with normal investment culture and practice. The law will provide the fall-back position whereby it will apply in absence of express powers of investment conferred in the trust instrument. It is very common for professionally drafted trusts to contain such express powers, but it might well be that the enactment of a general power to invest by the Trustee Act 2000 might reduce the need for such express provisions.

16.8.2.2 *Departure from the restrictive nature of trustees' powers of investment*
The policy of the law until the recent changes introduced in the 2000 Act was that of restriction and the need for caution. This can be seen exemplified in the 2000 Act's predecessor, the Trustee Investments Act 1961, which demanded that trustees were limited to safe investments in their choice for investment. Extensive criticism of the 1961 regime was made in the Law Commission's 1997 Consultation Paper 'Trustees' Powers and Duties' (Law Com. 261), which described it as 'over cautious and restrictive'. Indeed, the paper argued that such a regime placed huge and unnecessary burdens upon trustees, and that there was evidence of serious under-performance by some trusts on account of it. The Law Commission suggested that instead, trustees should have the same power as individuals in the making of investments, and that the operation of a duty of care would compel them to have regard to the need for diversification and suitability, and that further safeguard would be achieved in the way in which trustees would have to seek proper professional advice in such matters.

16.8.3 **Trustees and investment, and the Trustee Act 2000: the introduction of a more modern regime**

In response to the criticism levelled at the regimes governing trustees' investment activities contained within the Trustee Act 1925 and the Trustee Investment Act 1961, s. 3 of the Trustee Act 2000 provides trustees with new wide statutory powers. The old regime was regarded by the Law Commission as being outmoded and restrictive, and not at all reflective of the tremendous opportunities offered in the diversified investment market of the late twentieth century. The opening of s. 3 of the new Act is illustrative of the new legislation's intent to sweep away much of what is outmoded and replace it with a more appropriate and facilitative legal framework governing investment.

16.8.3.1 *The general power of investment: s. 3*
Section 3(1) states that:

Subject to the provisions of this Part, a trustee may make any kind of investment that he could make if he were absolutely entitled to the assets of the trust.

While the remainder of the discussion of the new legal regime now in place will focus on the limitations of trustees' powers of investment as well as their scope, this statement of intent should remain foremost a matter of context. Indeed s. 3(2) defines this statement of intent as the 'general power of investment'.

Significantly, unlike in the provisions of the Trustee Investment Act 1961, there is no requirement under the new legislation that there should be any division of the trust fund, but the general power of investment is subject to the 'safeguards' prescribed by ss. 4 and 5. These safeguards essentially refer to the duty of trustees to have regard to the 'Standard Investment Criteria', and the obtaining and consideration of proper advice.

16.8.3.2 *Section 4 and the Standard Investment Criteria*
Neither the idea of 'standard investment criteria' nor its precise composition within the Trustee Act 2000 can be regarded as new, and they have in essence been re-enacted from the Trustee Investment Act 1961. According to the provisions of s. 4(1) trustees must have regard to the Standard Investment Criteria when exercising any power of investment whether this is part of the general power of investment conferred by the 2000 legislation or is from a different source (for example, the trust instrument itself, when the power will be an express one provided, rather than a general one available to all trustees). Indeed, in this respect, the general power of investment operates subject to restrictions or exclusions on such activity, which are contained within the instrument which has created the trust. Under s. 4(2), trustees must take into account the Standard Investment Criteria when exercising *any* investment powers. And, as part of this process they should from time to time review whether or not investments made should in any way be varied from their original composition. Again, this need to review is defined in terms of reference to the Standard Investment Criteria, and provides the benchmark against which such an assessment must be made.

The Standard Investment Criteria: a twin set of objectives
The Standard Investment Criteria is composed of two measures of the appropriateness of any given investment, and this is reflected within the legislation. The *suitability* to the needs of the particular trust of the type of investment which is being considered is enshrined in s. 4(3)(a), while the need for *diversification* in so far as this is appropriate to the needs of the individual trust, is signposted within the provisions of s. 4(3)(b).

Trustees' investment choice: explaining suitability and diversification
The requirement that the type of investment chosen should be suitable for the nature of the trust requires that the trustee should look at the type of investment that they are wishing to make to judge its appropriateness for the needs of the particular trust, and for an assessment of suitability to be made. The needs of individual trusts will of course vary considerably, and accordingly so will the factors which will influence questions arising in the assessment of suitability. But it is clear

from authorities such as *Cowan* v *Scargill* [1985] Ch 270 that the calculus of suitability can include within its ambit questions of ethical or moral suitability.

The requirement of diversity is of essence in 'portfolio theorisation' of investment, which takes as its standard of risk assessment the risk level of the *entire portfolio* and not of *individual investments* within it. It is this global consideration of assessing risks taken in investments which articulates that trustees must ensure that investments are appropriately spread, and thus risk is evened out. It would be surprising therefore if the duty to ensure diversification were not applicable to the exercise of all powers of investment (and not simply the general power provided in the 2000 legislation), and indeed it is so applicable to all powers of investment. Whilst this is a duty which cannot be excluded or restricted, and notwithstanding its general policy of promoting the spirit of portfolio in all exercisings of investment power, by the provisions of s. 4(3)(b) the duty to ensure diversification applies (only) 'in so far as is appropriate to the circumstances of the trust'. Thus whilst the import of diversification is within the legislation without dispute, its provisions recognise that there are nevertheless limitations on its appropriateness (for example on grounds of size of the trust and its assets).

16.8.3.3 *Section 5 and the duty to take advice in the exercise of the power of investment*

Under s. 5(1), before exercising power of investment (irrespective of its source) the trustee must (subject to the exception provided in s. 5(3)) obtain and consider proper advice. This proper advice refers to the way in which the power of investment (from whatever source) should be exercised, when regard is had to the Standard Investment Criteria. By the provisions of s. 5(2), when a review is being made of the suitability of investments (by reference to the Standard Investment Criteria, and in furtherance of s. 4(2) of the 2000 Act), the trustee must obtain and consider proper advice as to the way in which the investments should be varied. This requirement marks a considerable point of departure from the 1961 legislation whereby the duty to seek and consider advice was much narrower, while s. 5(3) seeks to deal with the situation whereby the trustee is himself an experienced financial advisor, by providing that 'a trustee need not obtain such advice if he reasonably concludes that in all the circumstances it is unnecessary or inappropriate so to do'.

The question of what amounts to 'proper advice' is provided for in its definition in s. 5(4) as 'the advice of a person who is reasonably believed by the trustee to be qualified to give it by his ability in and practical experience of financial and other matters relating to the proposed investment'. This definition has been lifted from the provisions of the 2000 Act's predecessor, the Trustee Investment Act 1961.

16.8.4 **The 'general power of investment' and its exception**

The important exception to the ability provided by the legislation for a trustee to make any investment as he could do if he were absolutely entitled is the power to invest in land other than loans which are secured on land. However, this will make little difference in practice because the power for purchases of land (including for the purposes of investment) is expressly provided in s. 8 of the 2000 Act.

16.9 The duties of trustees towards beneficiaries

16.9.1 General principles of control by the beneficiaries

Although the ultimate benefit under a trust goes to the beneficiaries the trustees are concerned not only with their wishes, but also with those expressed by the settlor in the creation of the trust. There is therefore no general principle which permits the beneficiaries to control the way in which the trustees exercise their discretions. Were it otherwise, the trustees would be hopelessly handicapped in fulfilling their overriding duty towards the trust as a whole, and the court will never compel the trustees to act under orders from the beneficiaries where a power or discretion has been entrusted to the trustees alone. This will hold as long as the trust continues, although if the beneficiaries collectively wish, they can bring the trust to an end and resettle the property on any terms they wish, under the *Saunders* v *Vautier* doctrine (see further chapter 17).

Tempest v *Lord Camoys* (1882) 21 Ch D 571 shows the position while the trust continues. The beneficiaries desired the trust to purchase an estate but one of the trustees objected. Jessel MR refused to interfere with that trustee's bona fide decision. Strictly, the trustees are under no obligation even to consult with the beneficiaries as to how a power or discretion should be exercised, although of course they will often do so in practice.

An exception arises by virtue of the Trusts of Land and Appointment of Trustees Act 1996, which requires trustees of land under a statutory trust for sale to consult beneficiaries in possession and to give effect to their wishes so far as is consistent with the general intentions of the trust. The reason is, as we saw in chapter 1, that these are really fictitious trusts, whose main purpose is to simplify the conveyancing of shared land, but even in this limited case there is no overriding obligation to follow the beneficiaries' directions.

16.9.2 Disclosure of reasons for decisions

The need to protect trustees from importuning beneficiaries is evident. However, the courts have gone further and established that trustees will not be compelled to disclose the reasons behind the exercise of a discretion. In *Re Beloved Wilkes's Charity* (1851) 3 Mac & G 440, charity trustees were required to select a boy to be educated for the ministry, preference to be given to boys from four named parishes if a fit candidate could be found. The trustees, without giving reasons, selected a boy who did not come from one of the named parishes but whose brother had put forward his merits to the trustees. It was held that in the absence of evidence that the trustees had exercised their discretion unfairly or dishonestly, the court would not interfere.

This poses an obvious problem for any beneficiary wishing to challenge a decision made by trustees. If trustees are not required to give reasons for their decisions, it will generally be impossible to know whether they have exercised their discretions in a proper manner.

16.9.2.1 *Where trustees declare their reasons*

If, on the other hand, the trustees choose to disclose their reasons, then the court may consider their adequacy. In *Klug* v *Klug* [1918] 2 Ch 67, a trustee whose daughter was a beneficiary refused to consider the exercise of a power of appointment in her favour, and from the correspondence it appeared that her reason was annoyance that the daughter had married without her consent. Neville J held that the trustee had not exercised her discretion at all, and that it was the duty of the court to interfere. Where the trustees take steps to keep the basis of their decisions private, however, there appears to be little that a beneficiary can do if the decision is not obviously unreasonable or fraudulent.

This leads to the question of whether the beneficiaries are entitled to have access to any written records of how the trustees have conducted the trust business. It is usual practice for trustees to keep a trust diary or minute book in which decisions affecting the trust are kept, but there is no requirement that the reasons for trustees' decisions should be recorded. The beneficiaries are, however, entitled to access to documents connected with the trust, known as 'trust documents', and indeed have a proprietary interest in such documents. If those documents disclose the reasons for a decision, this would seem to offer the beneficiaries a way round the difficulty that trustees will not be compelled to disclose reasons.

16.9.2.2 *Trust documents and 'closing the door'*

The Court of Appeal, however, in *Re Londonderry's Settlement* [1965] Ch 918, effectively closed this door. In that case a beneficiary, dissatisfied with the sums appointed to her by trustees, pressed them to disclose various documents connected with the settlement. The trustees sought directions from the court. The Court of Appeal found that the category of 'trust documents' had not previously been defined with any degree of clarity, but concluded that all documents held by trustees *qua* trustees are *prima facie* trust documents, but that documents containing confidential matters which a beneficiary is not entitled to know about should not be disclosed, either (in the view of Harman J) because they are protected by analogy with the rule that trustees need not disclose reasons, or (according to Salmon LJ) because a document which a beneficiary is not entitled to see cannot be a trust document.

It would appear, then, that the only way in which a beneficiary can gain sight of documents disclosing the trustees' reasons is to bring a hostile action against the trustees, as a preliminary to which an order for discovery of documents can be sought from the court. Unless the beneficiary already has substantial evidence of misconduct, this course will be fraught with difficulties.

16.9.3 **Trust accounts**

There is no argument here: beneficiaries are entitled to be informed of the condition of the trust property and trustees must be ready at all times to produce trust accounts. Normally, the beneficiaries will be supplied with copies, perhaps in a simplified form, although strictly they are entitled to see the original accounts and to have copies made at their own expense. Income beneficiaries (e.g., life tenants under a family settlement) are entitled to see the accounts relating to the entire property of the trust, but remaindermen are entitled only to those accounts which relate to capital transactions and may therefore affect their interests.

It is not obligatory or even usual to have trust accounts subjected to an audit, but this may be done, at the absolute discretion of the trustees, who may employ an independent accountant and charge the costs to the trust fund. By s. 22(4) of the Trustee Act 1925, an audit is not to be carried out more frequently than once every three years, unless the nature of the property or other special difficulties so require. Any trustee or beneficiary may apply for an investigation and audit of the trust accounts by virtue of s. 13 of the Public Trustee Act 1906. A copy of the auditor's report is supplied to the applicant and to each trustee.

16.9.4 **Apportionment**

The general duty of trustees to act even-handedly as between the beneficiaries entails the necessity, where there are successive interests under a trust, to take certain steps to ensure that a fair balance is maintained between the capital and income of the trust, so that the former is preserved for those entitled in the future while at the same time allowing a reasonable income to those currently entitled. The rules relating to apportionment are an instance of this principle, and although it is nowadays usual practice to exclude their operation where possible, they are by no means without relevance, particularly in their application to accretions to the trust fund. It has been said that in special circumstances the court itself may direct an apportionment (*Re Kleinwort's Settlement* [1951] Ch 860), but this does not appear to have been done in practice.

16.9.5 *Howe v Earl of Dartmouth*

Some types of property are inherently unsuited to being held for successive interests. A wasting asset, which will soon be used up, provides no benefit to the remaindermen, while a reversionary interest which may not accrue for many years will provide no present income for the life tenant. The obvious way to achieve fairness as between the beneficiaries is therefore to sell the property and invest the proceeds so as to produce an income for the life tenant and an addition to capital for the benefit of the remainderman.

Obviously no problem arises if the trust instrument so directs, for example in the case of a trust for sale, but *Howe v Earl of Dartmouth* (1802) 7 Ves Jr 137 compels trustees to sell in other circumstances, even if there is no express direction, in some testamentary trusts of personal property (not land). The principle in the case only applies to settlements of the types of property considered in the previous paragraph, and where there is no contrary intention expressed in the will.

Where a duty to convert (i.e. sell) arises under this principle, the normal date at which the property should be converted is one year from the death of the testator, that is, at the end of the 'executors' year' allowed for the administration of the estate to be carried out. If there is power to postpone the sale and conversion, however, this cannot apply, and the valuation for the purposes of apportionment is taken to be the date of the death.

It will usually not be possible to convert and reinvest on either of these specific dates, so some principle is needed for apportioning the income from the asset until actual conversion. This is unnecessary if there is a clear intention that the tenant for life should have the actual income, or if the property is realty (and so not subject to the rule in *Howe* v *Earl of Dartmouth*) and no contrary intention appears, in which event the life tenant will receive the actual income.

Otherwise complex actuarial calculations are required, which turn on the precise nature of the property. For property which produces no present income, such as a reversionary interest, the principles deriving from the decision in *Re Earl of Chesterfield's Trusts* (1883) 24 Ch D 643 apply, and apportionment between capital and income is calculated by a formula. In effect, an assumption is made of 4 per cent interest, compounded annually. Thus, suppose the property produces £1,000 at sale. The capital element will be the amount which if invested at 4 per cent compound interest would have produced £1,000. This will be less than £1,000, and the income will be the rest.

Where the asset produces income, the life tenant is entitled to 4 per cent of its value as interest, and if extra income is actually produced, it accrues to capital.

There is also a formula, based on an assumption of 4 per cent compound interest, for apportioning the payments of liabilities out of the fund (e.g., funeral expenses, debts of the testator) to capital and income. This formula derives from *Allhusen* v *Whittell* (1887) LR 4 Eq 295.

It seems likely that none of these formulae could easily be applied without employing the services of an accountant, to the obvious detriment of the fund. Perhaps for this reason, they are in fact frequently ignored. Another difficulty is that 4 per cent is a very low rate of return today, and it is possible that if the issue were to come again before a court, a higher rate would be considered appropriate, on the principles discussed in chapter 18. This in turn gives rise to a third problem, which is that until that occurs, trustees do not know which interest rate to apply.

It is no surprise, therefore, that the Law Reform Committee, reviewing these principles in its 23rd Report (1982), advocated their replacement with a statutory duty of a more general nature, to hold a fair balance between beneficiaries, with express power to trustees to convert capital to income and vice versa, and a duty to have overall regard to the investments of the trust. The effect of this if enacted would simplify the actuarial calculations required in these situations.

16.9.6 Duty to distribute

This has already been mentioned, and the remedies available to those who suffer as a result of wrongful distribution are considered in chapter 18.

16.10 Trustees' powers and duties in investment: proposals for law reform

In 2004 the Law Commission published Consultation Paper No. 175 on *Capital and Income in Trusts: Classification and Apportionment*. This is a very important project in light of this study of trustees' powers and duties relating to investment.

It is described by the Law Commission as a project to reform the complicated rules governing (1) classification of trust receipts and outgoings as 'capital' or 'income', and (2) the requirement that trustees apportion capital and income in order to keep a fair balance between different beneficiaries.

16.10.1 **The Consultation's remit and underlying context**

The Consultation's remit in this respect has arisen from the reappraisal of trustee-ship which arose from the Trustee Act 2000. This book has already made many references to this far-reaching modernisation of the office of trustee, which did of course include provisions relating to investment of trust assets. However, the Law Commission noted in Consultation Paper No. 175 (at para. 1.5) that at the time when the (then) Trustee Bill was heading towards becoming law, concerns were expressed as to whether the Act would 'tackle the difficulties caused in the management of trust estates by the distinction which trust law draws between income and capital'.

In the Consultation Paper, the Law Commission identified the principal issues arising from its consideration of how income and capital are classified in trusts law as follows. First, in relation to private trusts:

- appraisal of the rules which govern trusts receipts as income or capital; and
- consideration of the statutory and equitable rules which require conversion of the original trust property or apportionment between the capital and income accounts.

And thereafter, the impact of these rules on charities.

16.10.2 **Appraisal of existing rules and proposals for reform**

Following publication of the Consultation Paper (No. 175) the Law Commission stressed that work on this project would be suspended until 2007, to allow the completion of the Cohabitation Project to take place. At the time this announcement was made, the provisional recommendations made in the Consultation Paper which relate to *private* trusts were as follows:

- in absence of any contrary provision in the terms of the trust, that the current rules relating to the classification of corporate receipts by trustee-shareholders as income or capital should be replaced by *a simpler alternative based on the form of receipts* (with the rules relating to the classification for other receipts and expenses remaining unaltered);
- to make available to trustees a new *'power of allocation'* in respect of investment returns and trust expenses *as income or capital in so far as is necessary to maintain a balance between income and capital*;
- to *abrogate* all existing *equitable rules of apportionment* (namely, the rules in *Howe* v *Earl of Dartmouth* etc.);
- to *replace* the provisions of the Apportionment Act 1870 in so far as they relate to trusts *with a discretion to apportion periodic payments which accrue from day to day*, when it is just and expedient to do so (and there is no contrary intention shown in the terms of the trust).

As the materials in chapter 9 suggest, the Cohabitation Project has now been completed, and accordingly the Law Commission website has now reported that work on the Capital and Income in Trusts project recommenced in January 2008.

16.11 Judicial control over trustees' discretions: the rule in Re Hastings-Bass

As a brief postscript to this consideration of the powers and duties of trustees in the context of exercising discretion, reference is made to *Re Hastings-Bass* [1975] Ch 25. This case is authority that where a trustee has not exercised a power or has exercised a power inappropriately, this can be overturned by the courts, with the effect that the power will be considered to have been exercised in the former situation and its exercise will be considered void in the latter. This 'rule in *Re Hastings-Bass*' will be applied in situations where it is found that the trustee would have acted differently if he had taken into account factors which should have been taken into consideration, or had he not taken into consideration factors which should not have been considered.

16.11.1 The significance of relevant and inappropriate factors in trustees' decision-making

Where this rule is invoked, as it is suggested above, this will have the effect that the course of action which should have been taken actually has been. The rule can be seen applied in *Abacus Trust Co. (Isle of Man)* v *NSPCC* [2001] STC 1344, where the premature exercise of a power of appointment had resulted in exposing the beneficiaries to tax liability which could have been avoided had the power been exercised at the proper time, which was a matter of days later. In this case, the premature exercise of the power was declared void by the court. Shortly after this two cases considered the requirements of the rule, in terms of what must be present for it to be invoked, with *Abacus Trust Co. (Isle of Man)* v *Barr* [2003] ChD 409, suggesting that in an erroneous exercise of or failure to exercise a power there must be some breach committed by a trustee, but this position was doubted in *Sieff* v *Fox*.[2005] 3 All ER 693.

16.11.2 What is required: that a different decision would have been reached or that a different one could have been reached?

Sieff also considered whether the rule required that a trustee *would* have acted differently had he taken into consideration pertinent factors and/or disregarded ones which were not appropriate, or whether it was sufficient that a different decision could have been reached. *Seiff* appears to suggest that in most situations the appropriate question was one of whether a trustee *would* actually have decided differently, but it also indicates that the rule might be invoked in circumstances falling short of this 'would actually' standard where a trustee *could* have acted differently. In turn, the relevant standard—whether this is would have done, or could have done—appears to be related to the position of pension trust funds, where beneficiaries thereunder have actually provided consideration for their rights enjoyed under the trust, rather than being the 'windfall' recipients of a settlor's generosity.

In seeking to understand this distinction apparently at work, it is worth remembering that pension trust funds are considered to be a species of trust which is quite distinct, and, as the materials in chapter 8 suggest, this has given rise to a body of distinctive rules, and increasingly an emergent body of 'pensions law' designed to reflect the entitlements of beneficiaries under such arrangement.

FURTHER READING

All reading which relates to the consideration given to trusteeship across chapters 15, 16, and 18 can be found detailed at the end of chapter 18.

17

....

Variation of trusts

17.1 Inherent equitable jurisdiction

As a general rule, as we have seen throughout this book, trustees are bound to carry out the settlor's wishes, and any deviation from the terms of the trust will amount to a breach of trust. Nonetheless, circumstances may arise in which an extension of the trustees' powers, or even a substantial alteration in the beneficial interests of the trust, would be desirable in the interests of efficient administration, or for the sake of preserving the value of the beneficiaries' entitlements.

The main reason for wishing to vary trusts is to reduce liability to taxation, and that is what this chapter is really about. Yet although it has become apparent that equity permits trustees to have discretion in many aspects of performing the trust, it has also become apparent that equity does not generally allow them to recast its terms. Until recent statutory reforms, therefore, powers to vary have been extremely limited, especially where tax planning is the motive.

There are nevertheless circumstances apart from those provided for by statute where variation is possible.

17.1.1 Express powers to vary

Obviously the trust instrument itself may have been drafted so as to confer upon the trustees powers far wider than those contemplated by the general law. Modern trust instruments generally contrive to allow the trustees considerable discretionary powers, and not uncommonly provide for variation of the beneficial interests themselves, by means of suitably drafted powers of appointment. The terms of such powers must, of course, be strictly observed, but it is often possible through careful drafting to obviate the need for recourse to more complex variation procedures. Reliance upon express powers contained in the trust instrument, needless to say, creates no exception to the duty not to deviate from the terms of the trust, for such powers are themselves among the terms of the trust.

17.1.2 *Saunders* v *Vautier*

In the absence of express powers, it may be possible to effect a variation in the trust by taking advantage of the rule in *Saunders* v *Vautier* (1841) 10 LJ Ch 354. Collectively, the beneficiaries, so long as they are all adult, *sui iuris*, and between them entitled to the entirety of the trust property, can bring the trust to an end and resettle the property on any terms they wish. Thus, in a simple settlement of property upon a life interest for X with remainder for Y, X and Y may agree to end the trust and divide the capital between them immediately. More complex settlements may require more sophisticated measures, involving perhaps the actuarial valuation of future entitlements, and possibly the need for insurance against any risk of loss, but the principles are basically the same.

17.1.2.1 *Variation with the collective consent of the beneficiaries*

The beneficiaries can also collectively consent to any act by the trustees which has the effect of varying the terms of the trust, without going through the process of dissolving and resettling the property which may involve a number of separate conveyances, all attracting stamp duty. It is very important, however, to appreciate the limits of the *Saunders* v *Vautier* doctrine.

First, it depends on the beneficiaries all being collectively entitled. Thus, donees under a power cannot use it, and though beneficiaries under a discretionary trust usually can, they will not be able to unless the entire class of objects is ascertainable. Second, it turns upon all the beneficiaries being able to consent to dissolve the trust, or to what would otherwise be a breach of trust by the trustees. If some of the beneficiaries are infants, or if the settlement creates any interests in favour of persons who are not yet born or ascertained, variation of the trust upon this basis will not be possible. This is a serious limitation when dealing with family settlements of the usual type, which almost invariably give interests to non *sui iuris* persons. As will appear below, this is the difficulty tackled by the Variation of Trusts Act 1958.

Third, unless the trustees also agree, the beneficiaries cannot vary an existing trust, and keep it on foot, instead of dissolving it and resettling the property, *Re Brockbank* [1948] Ch 206 has already been discussed in 15.10.6. Although the *ratio* of the case (which does not survive the enactment of the Trusts of Land and Appointment of Trustees Act 1996) is confined to the appointment of new trustees under s. 36 of the Trustee Act 1925, there are remarks by Vaisey J of a much wider scope:

> It seems to me that the beneficiaries must choose between two alternatives: either they must keep the trusts of the will on foot, in which case those trusts must continue to be executed by trustees...not...arbitrarily selected by themselves; or they must, by mutual agreement, extinguish and put an end to the trusts...

Walton J expressed similar views in *Stephenson* v *Barclays Bank Trust Co. Ltd* [1975] 1 WLR 88. One of the reasons he gave was that otherwise the beneficiaries could force upon the trustees duties quite different from those they had originally accepted. This reasoning would seem to survive the 1996 Act.

17.1.3 **Limited inherent jurisdiction of courts to vary trusts**

The problem arises with persons unable to give consent, especially children and unborn persons. As will shortly be explained, the Variation of Trusts Act 1958 confers upon the court a discretion to give its approval to a proposed variation on behalf of such persons if the court is satisfied that such a variation would be for their benefit. Before considering the effect of that Act and other statutory provisions, however, it is necessary to outline the extent to which the courts have traditionally been willing to permit a variation of trust under their inherent jurisdiction, where not all beneficiaries are adult and *sui iuris*.

It has long been recognised that the court may, in the case of necessity, permit the trustees to take measures not authorised by the trust instrument. In *Chapman* v *Chapman* [1954] AC 429, the House of Lords indicated that this inherent jurisdiction is narrow, encompassing for the most part only emergency and salvage. Originally, this seems to have been confined to cases where some act of salvage was urgently required, such as the mortgage of an infant's property in order to raise money for vital repairs. Gradually, it was widened to cover other contingencies not foreseen and provided for by the settlor, but the House of Lords reaffirmed in *Chapman* v *Chapman*, unanimously approving the formulation of Romer LJ in *Re New* [1901] 2 Ch 534, that some element of emergency still needs to be shown.

Chapman v *Chapman* applies only to variations in the *beneficial interests* as such. There is a wider inherent jurisdiction regarding the administration of the trust fund. For example, as seen earlier, in *Re Duke of Norfolk's ST* [1982] Ch 61, the court authorised payment of remuneration to a trustee under its inherent jurisdiction (considered in chapter 15).

The courts may also approve compromises of disputes regarding the beneficial entitlements on behalf of infant or future beneficiaries. Arguably, this is not a matter of genuine variation of the trust, since by definition its terms are not clear: hence the dispute. The courts, however, showed a willingness to extend the term 'compromise' to cover situations where no real dispute had arisen, and approval was sometimes granted to what were, in reality, mere variations worked out between the beneficiaries. This broad conception of the inherent jurisdiction was firmly disapproved by the House of Lords in *Chapman* v *Chapman*, and held to be confined to instances where a genuine element of dispute exists.

Thus, in *Re Powell-Cotton's Resettlement* [1956] 1 All ER 60, the Court of Appeal decided that there were no disputed rights where an investment clause was ambiguous and it would have been advantageous to the beneficiaries to replace it with a new clause. In *Mason* v *Farbrother* [1983] 2 All ER 1078, genuine points of difference were found to have arisen where two contending interpretations of an investment clause had widely different implications for the permitted range of investments. The court, however, was reluctant to approve the substitution of a new clause under its inherent jurisdiction, preferring to rely upon s. 57 of the Trustee Act 1925. In *Allen* v *Distillers Co. (Biochemicals) Ltd* [1974] QB 384, the court was asked to approve a settlement of the claims of the child victims of the drug thalidomide, and the question arose as to whether the court could postpone the vesting of capital in the children to an age greater than 18. Eveleigh J, on the basis of the rule in *Saunders* v *Vautier*, held there was no inherent jurisdiction to order such a postponement, but found it to be authorised by the terms of the settlement itself.

Clearly, therefore, the inherent equitable jurisdiction is of limited value to those whose main motive for variation is to reduce liability for taxation.

17.2 Statutory powers to vary trusts apart from the Variation of Trusts Act 1958

17.2.1 Matrimonial Causes Act 1973

The narrowness of the court's inherent jurisdiction to give approval to variations in the terms of trust is offset by several statutory provisions. A particularly useful and important addition to the jurisdiction was made by the Matrimonial Causes Act 1973, which, by ss. 24 and 25, gives a wide power to make orders affecting the property of parties to matrimonial proceedings, so as to avoid the unfairness which sometimes arose where the property of a married couple, in particular the matrimonial home, came under the rules governing resulting trusts (see chapter 9). The court may order provision for either spouse to be made by payments in cash, by transfers of property, or by the creation of a settlement for the benefit of a spouse and children.

More important in the context of variation, s. 24(1)(c) and (d) allow for variation of an ante or post-nuptial settlement, including settlements made by will or codicil, and also permit the making of an order extinguishing or reducing the interest of either of the spouses under such a settlement. The term 'settlement' has been widely interpreted to include any provision (other than outright gifts) made for the benefit of the parties to a marriage, whether by themselves or by a third party, and the acquisition of a matrimonial home has been held to be a settlement (*Ulrich* v *Ulrich* [1968] 1 WLR 180). Further, the court has the power to vary or discharge any order for a settlement or variation under s. 24(1) made on or after a decree of judicial separation if the separation order is rescinded or the marriage subsequently dissolved.

17.2.2 Mental Health Act 1983

The power given by s. 96(1)(d) of the Mental Health Act 1983 to the Court of Protection to make a settlement of a patient's property also allows the judge to vary the settlement as he thinks fit if it transpires that some material fact was not disclosed when the settlement was made, or if substantial changes in circumstances arise.

17.2.3 General powers in the 1925 legislation

The above provisions are designed to meet rather special situations. More general powers may be made available to trustees by virtue of provisions contained in the Trustee Act 1925 and the Settled Land Act 1925. Section 57(1) of the Trustee Act 1925 in effect widens the inherent jurisdiction with regard to 'emergency' by making the jurisdiction available in any case where it is 'expedient':

(1) Where in the management or administration of any property vested in trustees, any sale, lease, mortgage, surrender, release or other disposition, or any purchase, investment, acquisition, expenditure, or other transaction, is in the opinion of the court expedient, but the same cannot be effected by reason of the absence of any power for that purpose vested in the

trustees by the trust instrument, if any, or by law, the court may by order confer upon the trustees, either generally or in any particular instance, the necessary power for the purpose, on such terms, and subject to such provisions and conditions, if any, as the court may think fit and may direct in what manner any money authorised to be expended, and the costs of any transaction, are to be paid or borne as between capital and income.

The section operates as though its provisions were to be read into every settlement, but it is clearly limited to matters falling within the management or administration of the trust property and does not permit the alteration of beneficial interests under the trust.

Applications under the section are usually heard in chambers and so are not generally reported, but the few reported cases show that it has been used to authorise a sale of settled chattels, to partition or sell land where necessary consents had been refused, to purchase a residence for the tenant for life, and to sell prematurely a reversionary interest.

Settlements of land do not fall within s. 57(1) of the Trustee Act 1925, but they may be varied by recourse to s. 64(1) of the Settled Land Act 1925, which allows the court to make an order authorising the tenant for life to effect any transaction affecting or concerning the settled land or any part of it, if the court is of the opinion that the transaction would be for the benefit of the settled land or any part of it, or of the persons interested under the settlement. The transaction must be one which could have been effected by an absolute owner. The section is not confined to cases of management or administration alone, although it includes such purposes and allows alteration of the beneficial interests with a view to reducing tax liability. In the days of estate duty, the especial vulnerability of the strict settlement to onerous charges might be mitigated by rearrangement of the beneficial interests under this section.

This section was invoked by Morritt J in *Hambro* v *Duke of Marlborough* [1994] Ch 158, to allow the eleventh Duke of Marlborough (as tenant for life) to execute a conveyance the effect of which was to disinherit the Marquis of Blandford, who (the trustees had concluded) displayed unbusinesslike habits and lack of responsibility.

The Settled Land and Trustee Acts (Court's General Powers) Act 1943, as amended by the Emergency Laws (Miscellaneous Provisions) Act 1953, permanently extends the court's jurisdiction to authorise the expense of any action taken in the management of settled land or land held on trust for sale in the context of ss. 57 and 64 to be treated as a capital outgoing where the action is beneficial and the income insufficient to bear the expense.

The inherent jurisdiction to make provision for infants is somewhat extended by s. 53 of the Trustee Act 1925, which allows the court to authorise dealings with the infant's property with a view to application of the capital or income for the infant's maintenance, education, or benefit. 'Benefit' has been interpreted to cover dealings having the effect of reducing estate duty for the benefit of the infant (*Re Meux* [1958] Ch 154).

In that case, the proceeds of sale of property were to be resettled upon the infant, and so could be regarded as an 'application' for the infant's benefit. However, in *Re Hayworth's Contingent Reversionary Interest* [1956] Ch 364, a proposal to sell an infant's contingent reversionary interest to the life tenant for cash, thus ending the trusts, was thought not to be for the 'benefit' of the infant. Other types of dealing approved under the section have included the barring of entails to exclude remote beneficiaries (*Re Gower's Settlement* [1934] Ch 365) or to simplify a proposed application to the court for approval of a further variation under the Variation of Trusts Act 1958 (*Re Bristol's Settled Estates* [1965] 1 WLR 469).

17.3 Variation of Trusts Act 1958

The decision of the House of Lords in *Chapman* v *Chapman* [1954] AC 429 curtailed, as explained above, the broad approach previously developed by the courts in the exercise of the inherent jurisdiction to approve compromises or 'disputes', and the Law Reform Committee was asked to consider the question of the court's powers to sanction variations (see Law Reform Committee, *Court's Power to Sanction Variation of Trusts* (Cmnd 310, 1957)). The Variation of Trusts Act 1958 was based on these recommendations and provides a new statutory jurisdiction independent of the Trustee Act 1925 or the Settled Land Act 1925.

Under s. 1(1) of the 1958 Act, the court has discretion to approve, on behalf of the following categories of person, any arrangement varying or revoking all or any of the trusts, or enlarging the trustees' powers of management and administration over the property subject to the trusts. The categories are as follows:

(a) infants or people who are mentally incapacitated; or

(b) people who have a mere expectation of benefiting under the trusts, but those with interests, whether vested or contingent, should consent on their own behalf (see further below); or

(c) any person unborn; or

(d) any person with a discretionary interest under a protective trust.

Proposals to vary the beneficial interests under a trust may be approved, provided (except in the case of para. (d) persons) that the court is satisfied that such variation will be for the benefit of the persons on behalf of whom approval is given. In deciding whether to approve a proposed settlement, the court will consider the arrangement as a whole since it is the arrangement which has to be approved and not just those aspects of it which happen to affect a person on whose behalf the court is being asked to consent.

17.3.1 Use of the 1958 Act

Where an extension of the trustee's powers of management is sought, the jurisdiction of the Act is invoked in preference to s. 57 of the Trustee Act 1925 wherever possible. The courts have shown themselves willing to approve the insertion of powers of advancement or a period of accumulation, or to terminate an accumulation, among other matters.

So far as investment is concerned, in *Trustees of the British Museum* v *Attorney-General* [1984] 1 WLR 418, Sir Robert Megarry V-C took the view that the powers conferred by the (then in force) Trustee Investments Act 1961 were becoming outdated, and that the effects of inflation and the character of the trust may amount to special circumstances in which it would be proper to give approval under the 1958 Act. The decision was based on the changes of investment pattern, including the movement from fixed interest investments to investments in equities and property, that had occurred between 1961 and 1983.

The reasoning is by no means of universal application, however, and indeed, Sir Robert Megarry V-C's judgment is in quite restricted terms. At the time of the case, investing in equities was relatively risk-free, and there had been a more or less continuous bull market for some eight years. That is not the case today. Sir Robert Megarry V-C also said:

The size of the fund may be very material. A fund that is very large may well justify a latitude of investment that would be denied to a more modest fund; for the spread of investments possible for a larger fund may justify the greater risks that wider powers will permit to be taken.

The main application of the Variation of Trusts Act 1958 has been to vary the beneficial interests for tax-saving purposes, and this has been assumed to be its natural sphere of operation. Some would argue that those, for example infants and the unborn, who cannot give a valid consent to schemes which would be for their benefit should not be deprived of the advantages which their consensual counterparts could obtain on *Saunders* v *Vautier* principles; nor should their incapacity prevent the opportunity of gain to the trust as a whole.

17.3.2 **Persons on whose behalf the court may give its approval**

The way in which the statute works is to allow the court to give consent on behalf of *non sui iuris* beneficiaries, but the principles underlying the rule in *Saunders* v *Vautier* were preserved by the Act inasmuch as the court will not provide a consent which ought properly to be sought from an ascertainable adult, *sui iuris* beneficiary. Hence, the limits placed on para. (b) of s. 1(1).

The difficulty with para. (b) arises with interests which are very remote, such as interests in default of appointment, or in the event of a failure of the trust. The subsection allows the court to consent on behalf of:

any person (whether ascertained or not) who may become entitled, directly or indirectly, to an interest under the trusts as being at a future date or on the happening of a future event a person of any specified description or a member of any specified class of persons, so however that this paragraph shall not include any person who would be of that description, or a member of that class, as the case may be, if the said date had fallen or the said event had happened at the date of the application to the court.

It is the words after 'so however' which cause the problem since those persons have to consent on their own behalf: the court cannot consent for them. There is no problem over, for example, potential future spouses, since they clearly have a mere expectation of succeeding. They clearly come within the first part of para. (b) and the court can consent on their behalf. But if somebody is named in the instrument as having a contingent interest, however unlikely that contingency is to arise, the court cannot consent on his or her behalf. They must consent themselves to any variation.

17.3.2.1 *The scope and limitation of the 1958 Act*

This can seriously limit the scope of the 1958 Act. For example, in *Re Suffert's Settlement* [1961] Ch 1, the court could not consent on behalf of a cousin who benefited only if Miss Suffert died without issue, and even then subject to a general testamentary power of appointment. Other examples are *Re Moncrieff's ST* [1962] 1 WLR 1344, and *Knocker* v *Youle* [1986] 1 WLR 934. In the latter case the court could not consent on behalf of sisters who would benefit only in the event of failure or determination of the trust, and Warner J felt constrained to adopt a fairly literal interpretation of the Act.

The application should be made by a beneficiary, preferably by the person currently receiving the income, but the settlor may also apply, and as a last resort the trustees may apply if no one else will apply and the variation is in the interests of the beneficiaries. Otherwise, it is undesirable for trustees to apply, as their position as applicants may conflict with their duty impartially to guard the interests of the beneficiaries. The settlor, if living, and all the beneficiaries, including minors, should be made parties, special attention being paid to ensure proper representation for minors and the unborn.

17.3.3 What is benefit?

The general scheme of the 1958 Act is to give a wide discretion to the courts, but the one limit on the discretion is that, except for persons within para. (d), the court may not approve a variation unless it is satisfied that such variation will be for the benefit of those persons on behalf of whom approval for the variation is given. Stamp J took the view in *Re Cohen's ST* [1965] 1 WLR 1229 that the benefit must be to those persons considered as individuals and not merely as members of a class.

The benefit requirement does not extend expressly to a variation proposed on behalf of a beneficiary under a discretionary protective trust (para. (d)) but the court has an unfettered discretion as to the exercise of its powers under the Act, and in *Re Steed's WT* [1960] Ch 407 the Court of Appeal refused its consent in such a case where it thought no benefit was shown (see further below).

17.3.3.1 *Nature of benefit*

It is not possible to state categorically what the court will regard as benefit, except that it will adopt the test of what a reasonable *sui iuris* adult beneficiary would have done in the circumstances.

Financial benefit is clearly included, and most tax-saving schemes will satisfy the requirement since such saving preserves the total quantum of property available for distribution among the beneficiaries.

Assessing financial benefit: long-term considerations v short-term considerations
In assessing financial benefit, the court may have to balance short-term against long-term factors, and take account of the character of the persons on whose behalf approval is sought. In *Re Towler's ST* [1964] Ch 158, Wilberforce J was prepared to postpone the vesting of capital to which a beneficiary was soon to become entitled, upon evidence that she was likely to deal with it imprudently. In *Re Steed's WT* [1960] Ch 407, the proposed scheme was for the elimination of the protective element in a trust relating to land. The principal beneficiary, who was a life tenant (but not *sui iuris* because of the protective element), wanted a variation such that the trustees held the property on trust for herself absolutely. Clearly, this was in theory to her financial advantage, but evidence suggested that advantage would

in fact be taken of the life tenant's good nature by the very persons against whose importuning the settlor had meant to protect her, and the Court of Appeal refused its consent (considered shortly).

Though it will be rare for the court to look beyond the financial advantages contained in the proposed arrangement, the unfettered discretion given by the Act to the courts can lead them to refuse a variation where there is a clear financial benefit. In *Re Weston's Settlements* [1969] 1 Ch 223, the Court of Appeal refused to approve a scheme which would have removed the trusts to a tax haven (Jersey), where the family had moved three months previously, on the ground that the moral and social benefits of an English upbringing were not outweighed by the tax savings to be enjoyed by the infant beneficiaries. Harman LJ said that 'this is an essay in tax avoidance naked and unashamed', and Lord Denning MR noted (at p. 245) that:

There are many things in life more worthwhile than money. One of these things is to be brought up in this our England, which is still 'the envy of less happier lands'. I do not believe it is for the benefit of children to be uprooted from England and transported to another country simply to avoid tax... Many a child has been ruined by being given too much. The avoidance of tax may be lawful, but it is not yet a virtue.

Re Weston is perhaps atypical, and the court will not always refuse approval to the removal of a trust from the jurisdiction. It will depend on the circumstances. In *Re Windeatt's WT* [1969] 1 WLR 692, a similar scheme was approved by Pennycuick J, but there the family had already been in Jersey for 19 years and the children had been born there: there was no question of uprooting them. Similarly, in *Re Seale's Marriage Settlement* [1961] Ch 574, Buckley J approved a scheme removing the trusts to Canada, to which country again the family had moved many years previously, with no thought of tax avoidance, and had brought up the children as Canadians.

In reality, the use of the 1958 Act to export trusts is quite common, but *Re Weston* shows that all circumstances will be taken into account, and that the existence of a clear financial benefit will not necessarily be conclusive.

Another possibility, included for the sake of completeness, is that some beneficiaries will benefit at the expense of others. An example is *Re Remnant's ST* [1970] Ch 560, where Pennycuick J approved the deletion of a forfeiture clause in respect of children who became Roman Catholics. Some of the children were Protestant and others Roman Catholic, but the court approved the deletion of the clause on policy grounds (as being liable to cause serious dissension within the family) although this was clearly to the disadvantage of the Protestant children. The settlor's intentions were also not considered conclusive (indeed, they were overridden).

The courts may go further and approve schemes where there is a positive disadvantage in material terms. In *Re CL* [1969] 1 Ch 587, the Court of Protection held that there was a benefit to an elderly mental patient in giving up, in return for no consideration, her life interests for the benefit of adopted daughters. This was, in effect, giving approval to a straightforward gift by the beneficiary, from which in strictly material terms she could not possibly benefit. The lady's needs were otherwise amply provided for, however, and the court, in approving the arrangement, took the view that it was acting as she herself would have done, had she been able to appreciate her family responsibilities.

These cases should not be regarded as typical, however. Assuming that a proposed arrangement is otherwise unobjectionable, it will be rare for the court to look beyond the financial advantages contained therein.

17.3.3.2 *Extent of court's discretion*

The only constraint on the court's discretion under the Act is the requirement that it must be satisfied of a benefit, except in the case of para. (d) persons. However, even if it is clear that the court has *jurisdiction* to consent to a variation, it has an unfettered discretion to exercise its powers under the Act *'if it thinks fit'*. Thus, whereas the court cannot approve a variation except where the Act so provides, it has an unlimited discretion to refuse its approval where it is given jurisdiction under the Act.

It follows that, even where a benefit is clearly shown for the persons on whose behalf approval is sought, the court is not required to approve. For para. (d) persons, it is not even required that a benefit be shown, yet the court, in its discretion, refused to approve a variation in *Re Steed's WT* [1960] Ch 407.

17.3.3.3 *Relevance of settlor's views*

In *Re Steed's WT* [1960] Ch 407, the Court of Appeal was undoubtedly influenced by the views of the settlor, who in his will had clearly expressed his concern about the welfare of the beneficiary under the protective trust, for whom approval was sought. Yet though the settlor's views can be relevant, they are rarely paramount: they were overridden in *Re Remnant's ST* [1970] Ch 560, and it was the settlor who applied for the variation in *Re Weston's Settlements* [1969] 1 Ch 223 (see above). Moreover, the Court of Appeal held in *Goulding* v *James* [1997] 2 All ER 239 that they have no relevance at all unless they relate to someone on whose behalf the court's approval is required. In *Goulding* v *James*, the proposed variation (which was clearly for the benefit of the testatrix's unborn great grandchildren for whom approval was sought) would have frustrated her desire to restrict the ability of two adult, *sui iuris* beneficiaries to touch the capital of the estate. Since the court's approval was not required for the adult beneficiaries, however, who were able to consent for themselves, the settlor's views were entirely irrelevant.

17.3.3.4 *Risks*

Sometimes, a proposed arrangement may involve some element of risk to the beneficiary for whom the court is asked to consent. An element of risk will not prevent the court from approving the arrangement if the risk is one which an adult beneficiary would be prepared to take. Such a test was applied by Danckwerts J in *Re Cohen's WT* [1959] 1 WLR 865.

In *Re Robinson's ST* [1976] 1 WLR 806, the fund was held on trust for the claimant for her life, with remainders over to her children, one of whom was under 21 (the age of majority at the time). The claimant was 55 and expected to live for many years. The variation proposed was to divide up the fund, giving the claimant an immediate capital share of 52 per cent (the actuarial capitalised value of her share), the children dividing the balance in equal shares. The children who got their share immediately and those who were over 21 consented to the variation. The court was asked to approve variation on behalf of Nicola (who was 17).

Before the introduction of capital transfer tax in 1975, division of the fund in this way, by giving the children their interests immediately rather than on the death of the life tenant, was almost certain to reduce liability to estate duty, because at that time there was no liability to estate duty on any advance made more than seven years before the death of the life tenant. The same is true today under inheritance tax. However, for a short period following the Finance Act 1975, which introduced capital transfer tax, all *inter vivos* gifts were also taxable, albeit that liability was lower so long as the transfer was made more than three years before the death of the life tenant.

At the time of *Re Robinson's ST*, therefore, the division would not necessarily have favoured Nicola. The transfer would have been taxed immediately so that the value of the fund would be reduced. On the other hand, Nicola would get her share immediately and not have to wait for the death of her mother. Whether this would be to her benefit or not would depend entirely on how long her mother was likely to live. If she died immediately, Nicola's share would be less than she would have received under the unvaried trust since tax would have been paid on it. It was calculated, however, that, given the mother's life expectancy, the deficiency would be made up in income on her share between the date of the variation and her mother's death.

Templeman J took the view that the court should require evidence that the infant would at least not be materially worse off as a result of the variation. He adopted as the test whether an adult beneficiary would have been prepared to take the risk: a 'broad' view might be taken, but not a 'galloping, gambling view'. The arrangement was approved subject to a policy of insurance to protect the infant's interests, but Templeman J did not require the entirety of the possible loss to be covered, the view being taken that the saving in premium on a lesser cover was worth the small risk.

A diagramatic representation of *Re Robinson's ST* can be found in figure 17.1.

A different type of case was *Re Holt's Settlement* [1969] 1 Ch 100. The trust provided for a life interest of personal property for Mrs Wilson, and then to her children at 21 in equal shares. The variation proposed was that Mrs Wilson should

		Mrs Robinson	Children
Before proposed variation	Capital	Life interest on 100%	Remainder on all, but subject to CTT
	Income	Income on all until death	Income on all, but only after Mrs R's death
After proposed variation	Capital	52% immediately	48% immediately, maybe lower CTT
	Income	Immediate income on 52%	Immediate income on 48%

Figure 17.1 *Re Robinson's ST* [1976] 1 WLR 806

surrender the income of one-half of her life interest to the fund, but another effect of the proposed variation was to postpone the vesting of the children's interests until 30. The court was asked to approve the variation on behalf of Mrs Wilson's three children who were 10, 7, and 6.

The surrender of the income (whose real purpose was to reduce Mrs Wilson's liability to surtax) was also clearly to the advantage of the children, since the value of the trust property would be increased. However, the postponement to 30 (on the grounds that it would be undesirable for Mrs Wilson's children to receive a large income from 21) was clearly to their disadvantage. Megarry J approved the variation on the same test adopted in *Re Robinson*.

17.3.3.5 *Benefit must be to individuals, not just class as a whole*

In *Re Cohen's ST* [1965] 1 WLR 1229, Stamp J held that in considering questions of benefit under the 1958 Act, the court was being asked to consent on behalf of *non sui iuris* beneficiaries considered as individuals, and not merely as members of a class. It follows that if only one member of the class can be envisaged who cannot possibly benefit from the proposed variation, even if the class as a whole will benefit, the court will refuse its consent.

In *Re Cohen's ST*, the variation sought, with a view to saving estate duty, was to substitute for the death of the life tenant (who was an elderly lady) a specified date (30 June 1973) for the vesting of her grandchildren's interests. It was very unlikely that the life tenant would survive beyond 30 June 1973, although of course it was a theoretical possibility. Consent was sought on behalf of infant and unborn beneficiaries.

There was no problem regarding the infant beneficiaries, although even here, an element of risk was involved. They all stood to gain from the tax advantages of the proposed variation. If, however, the life tenant died before 30 June 1973, any infant grandchild who died between her death and the specified date would inevitably lose out (the grandchild would have taken under the unvaried, but not under the varied settlement). Also, the share of all the infant beneficiaries would be reduced if further grandchildren were born between her death and the specified date. On balance, however, these risks would be worth taking given the likely saving in estate duty (the principles applicable being those considered in the previous section).

Risks beneficiaries and unborn grandchildren
The difficulty concerned unborn grandchildren. Although it was unlikely, it was theoretically possible for the life tenant to live beyond the specified date. Had she done so, it was also theoretically possible for an unborn grandchild to be born after 30 June 1973, but before the life tenant's death. Any such grandchild would take under the unvaried settlement, but not under the proposed variation, and therefore could not possibly benefit from the variation. Of course, the chances of *both* these events occurring were very low, and it may well be thought that the class of unborn grandchildren, as a whole, might be prepared to take the risk of the life tenant living beyond the specified date, and having further grandchildren before she died. Weighed against the tax advantages of the proposed variation, it might be thought that any reasonable unborn grandchild would be prepared to take this risk.

Stamp J held that it is not permissible only to consider the position of the class as a whole. If any individual grandchild was born after the specified date, but before the life tenant's death, then under the proposed variation, he or she would lose his or her entire interest. That individual would clearly not consent, since he or she would have no conceivable benefit. Since it was therefore possible to envisage unborn persons who could not possibly benefit, this was fatal to the proposed variation, and Stamp J refused his consent. It was not enough that the proposed variation would benefit the class as a whole, if it were possible to envisage *a single individual* who could not possibly benefit.

The argument that any unborn individual would have a greater chance of being born before 30 June 1973, because (since the life tenant was unlikely to live that long) more time would probably be available in which to be born, was also rejected on the ground that the court would not ascribe chances to a disembodied spirit. Stamp J observed:

Now it is of course perfectly true that as a result of this variation there would be a greater chance of there being some person or persons now unborn becoming beneficially interested in the trust fund [by being born], but to say that some particular unborn person will, immediately on the variation taking effect, have a better chance of being born within the qualifying period or a better chance of satisfying the necessary conditions seems to me to involve an excursion into metaphysics, on which I am unwilling to embark. Such a proposition seems to me to involve the logical conclusion that the court must regard one whose body may come into the existence in the future as having nevertheless such a present imaginary existence as to enable the court to ascribe to him a present chance of coming into existence at some specific time or during some specified period. My mind recoils at the idea of the unborn having prior to his birth such an identity as to enable the court to ascribe to him any such chance, or to enable one to say that he can more or less easily satisfy a condition of coming into existence during some particular period.

Only once birth (albeit in the future) had occurred could chances of benefit be ascribed to any individual.

Re Cohen's ST was distinguished in *Re Holt's Settlement* [1969] 1 Ch 100. There, the settlement was in essence that Mrs Wilson gave up part of her income from the fund (so increasing the size of the fund), but vesting of the children's interest in possession would be postponed. If a child was born the year after the variation, and his or her mother died very soon afterwards, that child could not possibly benefit. The benefit from Mrs Wilson surrendering part of her income under the trust would be minimal if Mrs Wilson died soon after the birth, whereas the postponement would operate entirely to his or her disadvantage. *Re Cohen's ST* was distinguished, however, because here two chances had to occur: first, that of the unborn person being born next year and, second, that child having been born (and thus become a legal entity), his or her mother dying shortly afterwards. The first chance could be disregarded on *Cohen* principles, but not the second. Both were independently unlikely possibilities, so approval for the scheme was given. Even once the theoretical unborn child had been born, he or she would still have been well advised to agree to the variation, and accept the slight risk of his or her mother dying shortly afterwards.

It follows that the reasoning in *Cohen* applies only when the date of *vesting in interest* (or in other words the date on closing the class) is altered, and does not apply merely to alterations in *vesting in possession* (see further on this distinction, chapter 6).

It might be objected that two independent chances also had to occur in *Cohen* before an unborn beneficiary was certain to lose: first, the hypothetical beneficiary being born after 30 June 1973 and, second, the life tenant living beyond the date of his or her birth. However, no unborn beneficiary born after 30 June 1973 could possibly gain from the variation, and might lose, so there could be no advantage in the hypothetical beneficiary consenting to the variation. In this regard, the proposed variation in *Re Cohen's ST* differed from that in *Re Holt's Settlement*, where the hypothetical beneficiary had a good chance of benefiting from the variation.

17.3.4 Variation or resettlement?

According to Megarry J in *Re Ball's Settlement* [1968] 1 WLR 899, the courts will not approve a proposal for a total resettlement which alters completely the substratum of the trust. This is a question of substance not form.

17.3.5 Juristic basis of variation

In *Re Holmden's ST* [1968] AC 685, Lord Reid took the view that a variation under the 1958 Act must be regarded as one made by the beneficiaries themselves, rather than by the court, with the court acting merely on behalf of those beneficiaries who are unable to give their own consent and approval. His view did not form part of the *ratio* of the case, nor was it explicitly shared by his Brethren, but it was accepted as being good law by the Court of Appeal in *Goulding* v *James* [1997] 2 All ER 239, probably as part of the *ratio*, since it followed that the adult *sui iuris* beneficiaries could consent to the variation for themselves, and that any reservations the settlor might have had were irrelevant. Since, however, as was shown earlier, even where all beneficiaries are *sui iuris* and consenting they may not be able to vary the trusts in all circumstances, it must follow that the jurisdiction under the Act takes the form of a *Saunders* v *Vautier* revocation, followed by a re-settlement (this presumably requires the consent of the trustees, since the re-settlement cannot be forced on them against their will).

On this view of the matter, however, it arguably follows that the adult beneficiaries at least ought to give their consents in writing so as to comply with s. 53(1)(c) of the Law of Property Act 1925. In fact, however, variations are seldom in writing. In *Re Viscount Hambleden's WT* [1960] 1 WLR 82, it had been stated that the court's approval was effective for all purposes to vary the trusts, and this has been relied upon in countless subsequent instances. The problem was posed directly in *Re Holt's Settlement*, considered above, where Megarry J, aware that possibly thousands of variations had been acted upon without writing conforming with s. 53(1)(c), accepted, though without enthusiasm, two grounds put forward by counsel in favour of the view that no writing was necessary.

First, it might be said that in conferring express power upon the court to make an order, Parliament had impliedly created an exception to s. 53. Second, and alternatively, the arrangement might be regarded as one in which the beneficial interests passed to their respective purchasers upon the making of the agreement, that agreement itself being specifically enforceable. The original interests under the (unvaried) trusts would thus be held, from the moment of the agreement, upon constructive trusts identical to the new (varied) trusts and, as constructive trusts, would be exempt from writing under s. 53(2). Whether or not these reasons are regarded as adequate, the assumption that no writing is required has continued to prevail.

The point was also important in *Re Holt's Settlement* because the order of the court took effect after 15 July 1964, whereas the original trust had been set up in 1959, and Megarry J thought that the provisions of the Perpetuities and Accumulations Act 1964 (see chapter 6) could apply. If all the court had done had been to provide consent then the perpetuity period would have been that applicable to a 1959 instrument (i.e. the common law period).

 online resource centre

FURTHER READING

Riddall 'Does it or doesn't it?—contingent interests and the Variation of Trusts Act 1958' (1987) Conv 144.

18

Breach of trust

18.1 A question of liability: what is breach of trust?

This chapter follows the consideration given to the nature of trusteeship in chapter 15, and the nature of duties which arise from this, examined in some detail in chapter 16. In terms of 'locating' breach of trust within this text's overall coverage of trusteeship, generally speaking, any failure to comply with the duties laid upon the trustee will amount to breach of trust. This is so whether the duties arise from the trust instrument itself, where there is one, or whether they arise from obligations imposed by equity. Such failure may take the form of some positive action, such as investing in unauthorised securities, or an omission, such as neglecting to have the trust property placed in the name of the trustee. Even a merely technical act of maladministration may result in liability if in fact it causes a loss to the trust estate. This can be illustrated by reference to *Armitage* v *Nurse* [1998] Ch 241, in which according to Millett LJ (at 251):

Breaches of trust are of many different kinds. A breach of trust may be deliberate or inadvertent; it may consist of an actual misappropriation or misapplication of the trust property or merely of an investment or other dealing which is outside the trustees' powers; it may consist of a failure to carry out a positive obligation of the trustees or merely of a want of skill and care on their part in the management of the trust property; it may be injurious to the interests of the beneficiaries or be actually to their benefit.

In addition, at least in the case of an express trust, it does not matter how the trust was created (although the duties imposed on constructive trustees, as we have seen, may be less). Volunteer beneficiaries are entitled to have their interests protected to the same extent as those who have given consideration, and it is of no relevance either that the trust was created voluntarily by the same person who, in his capacity as trustee, is now charged with breach of trust. In other words, a settlor-trustee is liable to the same extent as any other trustee.

18.1.1 Basis of liability

The basis of a trustee's liability is compensation to the beneficiaries for whatever loss may have resulted from the breach, or, if an unauthorised profit has been made, the restoration to the beneficiaries of property rightfully belonging to the trust. The objective is not to punish the trustee, so his personal fault is immaterial once a breach is established. Of course, fault in an objective sense may be relevant to the question as to whether there has in fact been a breach, there being, as we have seen, a general standard of care based on normal business practice.

In many of the cases considered earlier, the trust had generally not suffered a large loss, and the remedy sought against the defendant was actually account of profits. In most of the cases considered in this chapter, the remedy sought is compensation for breach. In *Target Holdings Ltd* v *Redferns* [1995] 3 WLR 352, the House of Lords held that this is governed by principles similar to damages at common law. The claimants Target Holdings Ltd, were persuaded to advance approximately £1.5 million on a mortgage, on the assumption that the selling price of the property was to be £2 million. In fact the property was sold for £775,000. The defendant solicitors acted for both vendor and purchaser. They had taken the money advanced and paid it over to the purchaser and associated companies before the purchase and mortgage were executed, and in this respect (because they had paid the money away before being authorised to release it) were clearly in breach of trust with the claimants.

The purchasers later became insolvent, and the claimants sold the property, but for only £500,000 (so that they had lost around £1m), and sued the defendants for breach of trust. The defendants argued that the claimants had suffered no loss, because the defendants had obtained for the claimants exactly the mortgages to which they were entitled. The claimants would have suffered exactly the same loss, whether or not the defendants had paid out the money in breach of trust. The House of Lords held in principle in favour of the defendants, that a trustee who committed a breach of trust was not liable to compensate the beneficiary for losses which the beneficiary would, in any event, have suffered if there had been no such breach. The defendants would therefore not be liable on the assumed facts, that the transaction would have gone through anyway, even in the absence of Target's advance. If the assumed facts were wrong, and Target's advance was necessary for the transaction to go through at all, then Target would be entitled to be compensated for the entire loss that they had suffered, since in that event, but for the breach of trust, nothing would have been paid over.

There are no degrees of breach, however. Liability can attach to a trustee who has acted honestly in the beneficiaries' interests, just as it can to a trustee who has acted fraudulently for his own ends. Further, since the standard of care is objective (i.e. measured against the level of competence of a notional reasonable man, rather than that of the particular trustee), liability can attach to a trustee who lacks the knowledge or skills to avoid the breach and is doing his incompetent best, if that best is not up to the objective standard required. Protection of the beneficiaries, and not the nature of the wrongdoing, is the crucial element.

The court may, however, take into account degrees of culpability in exercising its discretion to grant relief from liability, or in fixing the amount of interest which the trustee may be liable to pay on the sum lost to the trust estate, both of which are considered shortly.

18.1.2 Personal nature of trustee's liability

A trustee is liable personally for his own breach of trust, and not vicariously for breaches committed by fellow trustees. In *Re Lucking's WT* [1968] 1 WLR 866, Lucking had committed a breach of trust in entrusting large sums of money to a manager, without adequately supervising him. His fellow trustee, Block, was not liable for Lucking's breach of trust, but was entitled to rely on what Lucking had told him about the company's affairs, unless he had a positive reason to disbelieve him.

However, a trustee who passively permits a breach to occur may thereby put himself in breach of his own duties because, though trustees are not required to police each other's conduct, they are expected, as we have seen, to be active in the administration of the trust. Thus, a trustee who leaves funds under the control of a fellow trustee without enquiry, or fails to take steps to obtain redress if he discovers a breach, will be in dereliction of his own duty to the beneficiaries.

The personal nature of trusteeship can be appreciated through examining case law under the 1925 Act. By virtue of s. 30:

A trustee... shall be answerable and accountable only for his own acts, receipts, neglects, or defaults, and not those of any other trustee... nor for any other loss, unless the same happens through his own wilful default.

In *Re Vickery* [1931] 1 Ch 572, Maugham J assumed that s. 30 had altered the law, at least in relation to liability for agents, for he interpreted the phrase 'wilful default' as meaning 'a consciousness of negligence or breach of duty, or recklessness in the performance of duty'. If this meaning is applied in relation to co-trustees, the section clearly confers extra protection.

Apart from *Re Vickery*, it is generally accepted that s. 30 did not alter the previous law: the section does not alter the principle that a trustee remains liable for his own acts, upon which the liability in the extract set out above is based. Under the previous law liability was incurred where a trustee handed over money without securing its proper application, or permitted a fellow trustee to recover money without enquiring what he did with it, or refrained from taking steps to obtain redress for a breach of which he was aware. It has yet to be decided whether, in these circumstances also, it will be necessary to prove that a passive trustee was guilty of 'wilful default' as defined in *Re Vickery*, but we would suggest that this is unlikely. This position must now be seen in light of the repeal of s. 30(1) by the 2000 Act. The current position appears to be that a trustee now labours under the requirement to establish that he acted properly.

A trustee will not, upon accepting office, become liable for breaches committed prior to his appointment. His first steps on taking office, however, should be to examine the documents and accounts of the trust, and if he discovers that a breach has occurred, he should take action against the former trustee to recover the loss. Failure to do so may itself amount to a breach for which he will be liable, save perhaps in the rare case where he can show that action would have been futile (because there would then be no causal relationship between the breach and the loss).

A trustee cannot escape liability for his own breach of trust by retiring from office, for even after his retirement he remains liable for breaches committed while he was in office, and his estate remains liable after his death. He will not be liable for breaches committed after the date of his retirement, unless it can be shown that he retired in order to facilitate a breach of trust (*Head* v *Gould* [1898] 2 Ch 250).

18.1.3 Liability as between trustees

The liability of trustees is said to be joint and several, which means that if two or more trustees are liable, a beneficiary may choose to sue some or all of them, or perhaps only one, and recoup the entire loss from those against whom he chooses to proceed. Similarly, he may levy execution against any one of them for the whole amount.

As between themselves, however, the trustees were until 1978 regarded by equity as being equally liable, so that a trustee who was compelled to pay more than his fair share of the loss could in turn enforce a contribution from the others. In enforcing equal contribution, equity disregarded any differing degrees of involvement in the breach. Thus, in *Bahin* v *Hughes* (1886) 31 Ch D 390, a passive trustee was liable to the same extent as an active one.

There were exceptions to the principle of equal contribution, which were unaffected by the 1978 legislation (considered below):

(a) Where there has been fraud. A fraudulent trustee is solely liable, and can claim no contribution from the honest trustees.

(b) Where a trustee has got money into his hands and made use of it, he will be liable to indemnify a co-trustee who is obliged to replace the funds.

(c) Where one trustee was a solicitor and the rest relied on his judgement (*Re Partington* (1887) 57 LT 654). The mere fact that a trustee happens also to be a solicitor will not make him liable to indemnify the other trustees, for it is necessary also that the others rely on his judgement. Thus, he will not be liable if it is shown that the other trustees were active participators in the breach, and did not participate merely in consequence of the advice and control of the solicitor (*Head* v *Gould* [1898] 2 Ch 250).

(d) Where a trustee is also a beneficiary he will be required to indemnify his co-trustees to the extent of his beneficial interest, and not merely to the extent that he has personally received some benefit from the breach (*Chillingworth* v *Chambers* [1896] 1 Ch 685). Only after that interest is exhausted will further liability be shared equally. The principle seems to be that a beneficiary may not claim any share of the trust estate until he has discharged his liabilities towards it.

18.1.3.1 *Departing from the principle of equal responsibility*

The equitable position has been affected by the Civil Liability (Contribution) Act 1978. Under this Act, any person liable in respect of damage suffered by another person, including damage arising from breach of trust, may recover a contribution from any other person in respect of the same damage. By s. 2(1) the amount of the contribution is:

such as may be found by the court to be just and equitable having regard to the extent of that person's responsibility for the damage in question

—and may by virtue of s. 2(2) amount to a total indemnity. The Act therefore gives the court a discretion (but not a mandatory duty) to depart from the rule of equal distribution and have regard to degrees of fault.

The Act does not apply to the limited number of exceptions to the general equitable principle described above, and may indeed not affect the equitable position at all, since it is left to the court to determine what is 'just and equitable'. One other situation is clearly unaffected by the 1978 Act. If all the trustees were involved in a fraud, equity would not allow those who paid the damages to claim any contribution from the rest, on the ground that a claimant could not base a claim upon his own wrongdoing. The 1978 Act makes no special provision for such a case, but though the court is theoretically free to exercise its discretion in allocating liability to contribute, it is inconceivable that a fraudulent trustee would be allowed to sue.

Where some but not all of the trustees are excused from liability under s. 61 of the Trustee Act 1925, it would seem to follow that those who are not excused can claim no contribution from them. Under the 1978 Act, the excused trustees would seem not to be persons who are liable in respect of any damage, so presumably the court cannot direct them to contribute.

18.1.4 **Trustees and criminal liability**

In the course of a breach of trust criminal offences may be committed, but breach of trust is not of itself a criminal offence. There used to be a difficulty about theft, because the trustee as legal owner of the trust property could not be guilty of stealing it, and a special offence of conversion by a trustee had to be created in order to make him punishable. However, by virtue of the provisions of the Theft Act 1968, a trustee may be guilty of ordinary theft. This is possible through the statutory definition of theft found in sections 1(1) and 5(2) of the 1968 Act. Section 1(1) provides that 'A person is guilty of theft if he dishonestly appropriates property belonging to another with the intention of permanently depriving the other of it.'

The significance of s. 5(2) rests on the 'problem' that the trustee is actually the legal owner of trust property. Section 5(2) contains provisions for the meaning of property 'belonging to another' for the purposes of the s. 1(1) definition. By virtue of s. 5(2), 'property belonging to another' includes property held on trust so that 'where property is subject to a trust, the person to whom it belongs shall be regarded as including any person having a right to enforce the trust, and an intention to defeat the trust shall be regarded accordingly as an intention to deprive of that property any person having that right'.

This chapter is primarily a consideration of how breach of trust arises and the key dimensions of how the personal remedies against a trustee who has committed a breach of trust will operate. Previous editions reflected this position and, accordingly, attention paid to trustees' criminal liability was brief and confined to the above references to sections 1(1) and 5(2) of the Theft Act 1968, to draw attention to the way in which a trustee who misappropriates trust funds can also be guilty of theft and thus incur criminal liability. Although it was always deemed necessary to point to the way in which, according to the criminal law, a legal owner of property can nevertheless be guilty of its theft, this was also deemed sufficient.

There was always scope for considering the way in which the criminal law dimension formed part of a 'bigger picture' of questions of trustee liability and accountability for the property which is entrusted to him for the beneficiaries. In this vein, it may well be the case that the threat of *criminal* liability serves important functions in deterring misappropriations of trust property, because of the *stigma* which is believed by many to attach to exposure to criminal culpability. However, at this point it is now necessary to give criminal liability arising from the office of trustee much fuller consideration on account of the Fraud Act 2006.

Notwithstanding, this chapter remains a consideration of the consequences in equity which attach to a trustee's breach of his duties: this progresses from looking at what amounts to a breach, and how this becomes a 'measure' of the liability which can be incurred upon being found in breach. To preserve this emphasis, at this point only very brief reference is made to indicate that trustees *can* incur criminal liability in addition to that arising in equity. The more extensive consideration of the criminal consequences of trusteeship which is necessary in light of this recent change to English criminal law will close this chapter on breach of trust.

18.1.5 Bankruptcy of a defaulting trustee

If a trustee who is liable for a breach becomes bankrupt, the claim in respect of the breach is provable in his bankruptcy. His duties towards the trust are not affected by his bankruptcy, so the odd situation arises whereby he has a duty (as trustee) to prove in his own bankruptcy (as debtor to the trust). If he fails to do this, he commits a further breach of trust which is not affected by any subsequent discharge from bankruptcy and he will be liable to the trust for the resulting loss (i.e. dividend that he would have received in the bankruptcy).

18.2 Qualifications and defences to liability

English law's position on trustee liability is that where there is a breach of a duty this gives rise to breach of trust. The numerous ways in which breach of trust can arise are explained above, with illustrative reference made to Millett LJ's judgment in *Armitage* v *Nurse*. In terms of what breach of trust means across the spectrum of its possible manifestations is that a trustee is liable to account, to the beneficiary, for losses experienced by the trust and its assets. This is the position in principle, and it is, like liability across legal regimes, liability which operates within certain limitations. In trusts law, these limits are defined in reference to defences which a trustee accused of breach of trust may be able to invoke.

18.2.1 Consent or participation by beneficiaries

A beneficiary who consents to or participates in a breach of trust will not usually be able to succeed in a claim against the trustees, even if he has obtained no personal benefit from the breach. The consent or participation of one beneficiary will not, of course, prevent those who did not consent from claiming, and if it is uncertain which beneficiaries have consented, the court may order an inquiry. No particular form of consent is required.

To be effective, consent must be that of an adult who is *sui iuris* and not acting under an undue influence which prevents him from making an independent judgement. In *Re Pauling's ST* [1964] Ch 303, trustees of a marriage settlement had made a series of advances in breach of trust because the trustees did not ensure that the moneys advanced were used for their proper purpose. A wide range of defences was argued, both before Wilberforce J and in the Court of Appeal, but on this issue several of the payments which went to benefit the parents were presumed to have been the result of undue influence over the children. Whether undue influence has been exercised is a question of fact, depending on circumstances. The trustees will not be liable if it cannot be shown that they knew, or ought to have known, that the beneficiary was acting under such influence.

In *Re Pauling's ST* itself, the Court of Appeal held that where a presumption of undue influence existed, as between a parent and child who was still subject to parental influence (albeit a child who had reached her majority), an advance to the child which was given to her parents, could not be retained by the parent unless it was clear that:

(a) the gift was the spontaneous act of the child; and

(b) the child knew what her rights were. It was also desirable that the child had obtained independent and, if possible, professional advice.

In this regard, the courts treat with suspicion gifts from children to their parents, whereas the reverse is true of gifts the other way round (see, for example, the presumption of advancement in chapter 7).

18.2.1.1 *Acquiescence and the requirement of 'consent'*

Consent involves more than mere awareness of what the trustees are proposing to do. Otherwise, trustees could protect themselves by simply telling the beneficiaries, beforehand. In *Re Pauling's ST* [1962] 1 WLR 86, Wilberforce J (at p. 108) explained that:

> [T]he court has to consider all the circumstances in which the concurrence of the *cestui que trust* was given with a view to seeing whether it is fair and equitable that, having given his concurrence, he should afterwards turn round and sue the trustees.

He went on to say that it is not necessary that the beneficiary should know that what he is concurring in is a breach of trust, provided that he fully understands what he is concurring in. Nor is it necessary that he should personally benefit from the breach. This statement of the law was neither approved nor disapproved by the Court of Appeal in *Re Pauling's ST* itself [1964] Ch 303, but was approved by the Court of Appeal in *Holder v Holder* [1968] Ch 353, in which a beneficiary was held unable to set aside a sale after affirming it and accepting part of the purchase money.

18.2.2 **Release or acquiescence by beneficiaries**

A beneficiary will also be unable to succeed in his claim if, on becoming aware of the breach, he acquiesced in the breach or released the trustee from liability arising therefrom. A partial defence succeeded on the basis of the acquiescence doctrine in *Re Pauling's ST* [1964] Ch 303.

Release suggests some active waiver by the beneficiary of his rights. A waiver requires a positive act which is intended to be irrevocable. It is like making a gift and, as with gifts, no consideration need move from the donee (in this case the trustee). As with consent, there need not be any particular formalities and release may even be inferred from conduct.

If a release cannot be shown, it may still be possible to show that the beneficiary acquiesced in the breach. It is usually accepted that the acquiescence doctrine is based on an implied contract, whereby the beneficiary is taken to have agreed not to rely on his rights. The evidence required for this intention to be inferred is less than in the case of release, and the doctrine is often applied where a beneficiary has done nothing to pursue his claim.

Delay in making the claim is not in itself evidence of acquiescence, but where the length of time between the breach and the claim is very great, slight additional evidence will suffice. As in the case of consent, the release or acquiescence must be that of an adult who is *sui iuris*.

Undue influence or lack of full knowledge will prevent the trustee from relying on these defences, the test being as in the consent doctrine, above.

18.2.3 **Impounding beneficiary's interest**

The court has an inherent power to impound the interest of a beneficiary, thus providing the trustee with an indemnity to the extent that the beneficiary's interest will suffice to replace the loss to the trust.

The power can arise where a beneficiary has merely consented to the breach, but only if some benefit to him can be proved, and then only to the extent of that benefit. If the beneficiary has gone further, and actually requested or instigated a breach, the power can be exercised whether or not he has received a personal benefit from the breach.

Needless to say, the trustee has to show that the beneficiary acted in full knowledge of the facts, but it is not necessary to show that he knew that the acts he was instigating or consenting to amounted to a breach.

There is also a statutory discretion to impound. Section 62(1) of the Trustee Act 1925 (replacing an earlier enactment) provides:

Where a trustee commits a breach of trust at the instigation or request or with the consent in writing of a beneficiary, the court may, if it thinks fit, make such order as to the court seems just, for impounding all or any part of the interest of the beneficiary in the trust estate by way of indemnity to the trustee or persons claiming through him.

The courts seem to have treated this largely as a consolidating section, rather than extending their powers, except that Wilberforce J in *Re Pauling's ST (No. 2)* [1963] Ch 576 thought that it gave an additional right, among other things, to deal with a married woman beneficiary. This additional right is no longer necessary, because of changes in legislation on family property, and that part of the section was repealed in 1949.

The effect of the court making an order impounding a beneficiary's interest is that the beneficiary is not only debarred from pursuing his own claim against the trustee, but also liable to replace the losses suffered by the other beneficiaries, to the extent ordered by the court, and perhaps up to the full value of his own interest. To this extent, the trustee is protected at the beneficiary's expense.

The discretion is a judicial discretion, and though the section appears to extend the inherent power of the court by giving a discretion to impound a beneficiary's interest regardless of whether he obtained a benefit, it has received a restrictive interpretation. It seems that the court will make an impounding order in any case where it would have done so before the Act; generally speaking, in any case where the beneficiary has actively induced the breach (for which it has never been necessary to show benefit).

18.2.3.1 *Requirement of full awareness by beneficiary*

It must, of course, be shown that the beneficiary was fully aware of what was being done. In *Re Somerset* [1894] 1 Ch 231, a beneficiary had urged the trustees to invest in a mortgage of a particular property, but had left them to decide how much money they were prepared to invest. Lindley MR said (at p. 265):

> In order to bring a case within this section the *cestui que trust* must instigate, or request, or consent in writing to some act or omission which is itself a breach of trust, and not to some act or omission which only becomes a breach of trust by reason of want of care on the part of the trustees.

The words 'in writing' have been held to apply only to consent, and not to instigation or request (*Griffith* v *Hughes* [1892] 3 Ch 105). So a request or instigation need only be oral.

The power to impound will not be lost on an assignment of the beneficial interest. Nor is it lost when the court replaces the trustees in consequence of the breach. In *Re Pauling's ST* [1962] 1 WLR 86, the trustees resisted removal because they were claiming an indemnity out of the interests of the parents. Wilberforce J held that they were entitled to such indemnity and that this would be unaffected by their replacement. They were therefore unable to use this as a ground for continuing in office: see *Re Pauling's ST (No. 2)* [1963] Ch 576.

Apart from statute, it is the practice, where trustees have under an honest mistake overpaid a beneficiary, for the court to make allowance for the mistake in order to allow the trustee to recoup as far as possible (*Re Musgrave* [1916] 2 Ch 417). An over-paid beneficiary is not compelled to return the excess but further payment may be withheld until the accounts are adjusted.

If a payment is made by mistake to someone who is not entitled, the trustee may recover on an action for money had and received if the mistake was one of fact, but not if it was a mistake of law (*Re Diplock* [1947] Ch 716). It is also certain that the error must be corrected where trustee-beneficiaries overpay themselves.

18.2.4 **Trustee liability and lapse of time**

Lapse of time may protect a trustee in one of two ways. By the Limitation Act 1980, limits are set upon the time within which certain actions for recovery may be brought, while in cases not covered by statutory limitation, a defendant may rely on the doctrine of laches.

18.2.4.1 *Limitation Act 1980*

By s. 21(3) of the Limitation Act 1980, any action by a beneficiary to recover trust property or in respect of any breach of trust (other than situations covered by the self-dealing and fair dealing rules) must be brought within six years from the date on which the right of action accrued.

A right of action in respect of future interests is not treated as having accrued until the interest falls into possession: this was also part of the *ratio* in *Re Pauling's ST* [1964] Ch 303 (discussed in this chapter).

Under s. 21(1), no period of limitation applies where the action is in respect of any fraud to which the trustee was a party, or privy, or where (in summary) it is sought to recover from the trustee trust property still in his possession or the proceeds of sale of such property. Protection is also lost where the trustee converts trust property to his own use. Conversion to the trustee's own use, however, implies application in his own favour, so that if the funds have been used to maintain an infant beneficiary, or dissipated by a fellow trustee, the protection of limitation remains available.

Where fraud is the issue, this must be fraud by the trustee himself. In *Thorne* v *Heard* [1894] 1 Ch 599, a trustee was protected by a section in similar terms of an earlier Act, where he had left trust funds with a solicitor who had embezzled them, the trustee himself being no more than negligent. Where the trustee is in possession of trust property or its proceeds, however, no dishonesty need be shown. Fraud for these purposes is wider than common law fraud or deceit, but nevertheless requires unconscionable conduct on the part of the trustee, something in the nature of a deliberate cover-up: in *Bartlett* v *Barclays Bank Trust Co. Ltd (No. 1)* [1980] Ch 515, the bank was held able to rely on what is now s. 21(1) of the 1980 Act, in respect of income lost outside the limitation period, since, being unaware that it was acting in breach of trust, it could not be guilty of fraud for these purposes.

Section 22 prescribes a limitation period of 12 years for actions in respect of any claim to the personal estate of a deceased person. It is often hard to determine at what point executors have completed the administration of an estate and become trustees, but it is thought that the 12-year period will apply though for all other purposes the executors would be regarded as trustees.

Claimants 'under disability' are permitted an extended period in which to bring an action by s. 28, and by s. 32; where fraud, concealment, or mistake is alleged, time runs only from the point when the claimant discovers the fraud or mistake, or could with reasonable diligence have discovered it.

It should be noted that a person other than a *bona fide* purchaser for value without notice who receives property from a trustee also falls within these rules.

18.2.4.2 *Equitable doctrine of laches*

Where no statutory limitation period applies, the defendant may rely on the equitable doctrine of laches, that is he may show that it would be unjust to allow the claimant to pursue his claim in view of the time that has elapsed since it accrued. The court has a discretion to allow or refuse the defence, and mere delay may suffice, but, where possible, the courts have preferred to regard delay as furnishing evidence of acquiescence by the claimant.

18.2.5 **Trustee Act 1925, section 61**

This section gives the court a wide discretion to excuse honest and reasonable trustees from liability for breach of trust. It applies also to executors. The section provides:

> If it appears to the court that a trustee ... is or may be personally liable for any breach of trust, whether the transaction alleged to be a breach of trust occurred before or after the commencement of this Act, but has acted honestly and reasonably, and ought fairly to be excused for the breach of trust and for omitting to obtain the directions of the court in the matter in which he committed such breach, then the court may relieve him either wholly or partly from personal liability for the same.

Dishonesty will obviously disqualify a trustee from obtaining relief, but a trustee is also required to act 'reasonably'. The standard applied appears to be the same as that for breach of trust itself, that of the prudent man of business in relation to his own affairs, and the bank failed on this test in *Bartlett* v *Barclays Bank Trust Co. Ltd (No. 1)* [1980] Ch 515. Failure to obtain directions might be thought to fall below this standard, but the section implies that relief may nonetheless be granted.

Unauthorised investments appear to be the most common circumstances in which applications are made, and it may not be easy to show that this sort of risk-taking meets with the standard of the prudent business person. Reasonable conduct may be more easily shown where the breach consists in some error made in the course of a complex administration. Professional trustees may claim the protection of the section, but the courts have been less ready to excuse failure where a high standard of expertise is professed by the trustee. See again *Bartlett* v *Barclays Bank Trust Co. Ltd (No. 1)* [1980] Ch 515.

It may be that, even if the trustee is shown to have acted honestly and reasonably, the question of whether he ought fairly to be excused will be separately considered.

18.3 Trustee exemption clauses

The position traditionally taken in this text in relation to exemption clauses has always been that '[t]here is no reason why an appropriately drafted exemption clause in the trust instrument should not protect a trustee who would otherwise be liable for breach of trust'. However, beyond this (and identifying the authority provided by *Armitage* v *Nurse* [1998] Ch 241 for this position), this represented the extent of coverage of the topic.

The essence of the trustee exemption clause is much like it sounds. Like exemption clauses found in contract law, the trustee exemption clause is a mechanism to restrict or exclude liability which may otherwise be incurred in the course of trusteeship. The context for such clauses is the occurrence of breach of trust, which flows from the duties trustees are subject to in their administration of the trust, or from the trust instrument, or duties imposed by law: it is any failure to comply with these duties which will amount to a breach of trust. And, as was made clear earlier, there are no 'degrees' of breach of trust; a breach can be innocent as well as fraudulent, and the law does not even distinguish flagrant incompetence from incompetence arising from misfortune. It is even the case that liability for breach of trust is not confined to situations which have detrimentally affected the trust—liability will arise equally where the breach has actually brought beneficial consequences for the trust. In short, all incidences of breach of trust leave the trustee open to incur liability for it.

This scope of breach of trust should therefore explain trustees' attempts to limit or exclude the liability which it is possible for them to incur—even trustees who are competent and *bona fide* might with very good reason elect to try to protect themselves in such a manner. This also serves as a reminder of the very close relationship between performance of the trust and its breach; itself a further illustration of the very close interrelationship between all these chapters on trusteeship, and the way in which the essence of trusteeship is actually very difficult to 'parcel' into more discrete aspects for study. Indeed, just as exemption clauses can be seen as a mechanism to protect trustees against breach of trust, they can also be seen as a measure of trustees' duties: this latter analysis emphasises them as devices to 'manage' expectations of trustees in the performance of their duties. In light of this 'dual perspective', this consideration of exemption clauses would therefore be equally at home in chapter 16 as it is in the present one.

18.3.1 Context for current discussion

A very narrow technical reading of exemption clauses would explain them as one of the 'guards' which can be used by trustees to exclude or to restrict their liability to beneficiaries arising from breach of trust. It will become clear in due course that there are a number of such mechanisms that have this effect, and so there is need to explain the significance of anchoring attempts of trustees to limit the liabilities which can flow from the performance of their duties to exemption clauses specifically. This is attributable to the current 'policy direction' for considering the liabilities arising from trusteeship, whereby the Law Commission has been asked specifically to consider the position of exemption clauses.

In 2002 the Law Commission published Consultation Paper No. 171 entitled *Trustee Exemption Clauses*. This was an extremely interesting and highly readable document, which provided an excellent point of reference for much of the coverage on trusteeship in this text in earlier chapters. In this more general sense, it provides an excellent opportunity to review understanding of many of the core issues, as well as an opportunity to examine them more critically. In July 2006 the Law Commission published its *Report on Trustee Exemption Clauses* No. 301 (Cm. 6874) following this Consultation. Before looking at the recommendations for reform which have been made, there will be a more general discussion about the issues arising in relation to exemption clauses, which will be pursued through an examination of leading case law and its historical development. Thereafter, reference is made to the lengthy attention given in the Consultation Paper to the 'economic dimensions' at stake, before moving on to considering whether the recommendations of the *Report* published in July 2006 point to an appropriate future direction to be taken in this area.

18.3.1.1 *Meaning and significance of 'exemption clause'*

In 2002 the Law Commission introduced its involvement in the consideration of trustee liability by identifying the 'unrestricted nature' of liability for breach of trust as explanation for the appearance in trust instruments of various mechanisms employed to try to provide some limitation on this, and some concomitant protection for trustees. There were a number of other mechanisms which the Law Commission identified as achieving this outcome by alternative means. First, reference was made to the *duty modification* clause as a potential means to limit or exclude exposure of trustees to legal accountability. This operates by restricting the scope of a trustee's duties at the outset (rather than restricting his liability *after* a breach has occurred) and has the effect of making a breach of duty harder to establish. Also identified was the *'extended powers'* or *'authorisation'* clause, capable of conferring wider powers on trustees expressly through the trust instrument, and even vesting them with authority in respect of acts which would otherwise be prohibited. A further mechanism which could achieve the protection of trustees against liability was the use of an *indemnity* clause. This would operate by attacking the traditional entitlement of beneficiaries in respect of 'any losses' to the trust arising from a trustee's failure to carry out his duties. Here, an indemnity could add to the way in which a trustee is currently entitled to be reimbursed for expenses legitimately incurred in his administration of the trust, extending this to any liability which he incurred for breach of trust (except perhaps that which was attributable to his own individual fraud).

The exclusion or *exemption* clause became the axis for the Law Commission's Consultation on account that it is the most widely used mechanism for limiting exposure to legal accountability, both within trust instruments themselves, and within a broader cultural setting of trusteeship in English law. And, it is this current state of affairs which thus provided the key point of reference for a broader consideration of the extent to which trustees should be able to protect themselves from legal accountability. On one level, the Law Commission appreciated that this would involve confronting the essence of the trust, as an institution in private law which derives its direction from the settlor of trust property. It is also the case that the exemption clause raises important issues of compatibility flowing from the way in which liability for breach of trust is actually intended to protect the beneficiaries under a trust, who are not owners of the trust property at law. Such difficulties were recognised by the Law Commission at many points in the Consultation. There is, for example, the insistence that any conclusion that the exemption clause can be accommodated alongside the need to protect beneficiaries' interests would have to involve extensive consideration of questions of scope: scope of the operation of such clauses, and the extent to which trustees should be able to limit their legal accountability in this manner.

18.3.1.2 *An exclusion clause compatible with the institution of the private trust*

In respect of the first consideration, arising from the need to confront the exemption clause in light of the institution of the trust, the Law Commission accepted that exemption clauses had arrived, and that they are here to stay. No small part of this assessment was attributable to the changing culture of trusteeship and the ever-growing professionalisation in the provision of trust services which has been occurring. However, the Law Commission's 2002 publication also noted in the document's early stages that the use of clauses either to limit or exclude liability flowing from breach of trust on account of the 'unrestricted' nature of this liability is not itself new, and that trustees have long appreciated the need to try to protect themselves through such provisions. In providing a useful reminder of how modern trusteeship grew up, in the nineteenth century, very much in the context of family-type settlement trusts, the Law Commission made a number of useful points relating to the historical formulation of the exemption clause and also the nature of its interpretation.

18.3.2 Exemption clauses commonplace within modern trusts

The Law Commission made note of the way in which earliest attempts at exemption clauses were drafted 'narrowly', denoting greater 'containment' of the notion of trusteeship than is the case today. Here, it pointed to the authority of *Seton* v *Dawson* (1841) 4 D 310, relating to the timelessness of the idea of limiting trustees' legal exposure for breach of trust, and its traditional application through early ideas on interpreting such attempts. Such early explorations into restricting and excluding liability were construed strictly against trustees, which is of course consistent with traditional ideas on the onerous nature of trusteeship and its location within a broader fiduciary context. What has brought the exemption clause so sharply into focus can, according to the Law Commission, be explained on account of the changing conditions in which trusteeship now operates. The rise of the professional trustee is itself a reflection of the way in which the nature of trust assets has considerably changed; and the way in which the trust is now being used extensively for novel purposes has provided the context for extended powers being given to trustees in their management of trust assets and trust estates more broadly.

18.3.2.1 *Professionalisation, the changing nature of trusteeship, and approaches to exemption*

Attention has been drawn to the changing nature of trusteeship throughout these chapters. Particularly prominent illustration of this can be found by reference to the powers trustees now have in relation to making investments, and the way in which they are able to make appointments which result in certain delegation of their duties in recognition of their growing need to enlist 'expert' services in the successful management of trust assets and estates. Greater powers and increasing dimensions to management of trusts do of course give rise to increasing expectations in 'delivery' and satisfaction, something that is recognised in the Consultation as a potential source of increasing litigiousness among beneficiaries. It is to these reasons that the Law Commission attributed the common presence in trust instruments of clauses which purport to protect trustees from incurring liability in respect of acts and omissions which would normally be regarded as breach of trust. It noted also that, on reasoning outlined above, '[a]s the powers of trustees have increased as a result both of express provisions in trust instruments and by legislation, so has the breadth of trustee exemption clauses'.

By the Law Commission's own admission in the 2002 Consultation Paper, while the Trustee Act 2000 (which was itself underpinned by extensive Law Commission consideration) had done much to liberalise trusteeship, and to better equip it for an entirely new context (provided by huge changes in the nature of trust assets, and even in the use made of the trust arrangement itself), this legislation which was responsible for the 'expansion of trustee powers' did not make any attempt to regulate the use made in trust instruments of exemption clauses. The Law Commission also emphasised that in many respects this was deliberate, and operated to maintain a crucial tenet of trusts law to provide a 'fall-back' position for situations where specific instructions are absent. This is a position which gives primacy of place to the trust instrument and to the settlor as the right and proper source of directions on the trust's operations. The Law Commission cited as authority for this the pronouncement from Sch. 1, para. 7 that the statutory duty of care under the Trustee Act 2000 does not apply 'if or in so far as it appears from the trust instrument that the duty is not meant to apply'.

18.3.3 **The key problem of exemption clauses in modern trusts**

It is within this setting that in 2002 the Law Commission identified the nature of the problem at the heart of its remit in relation to the position of trustees and liability for breach of trust. Given that the way in which the rise of the professional trustee combined with the changing nature of trust assets and even trust usage has already been explained, these considerations can now be combined with the approach which it appears is being taken by the courts in relation to exclusion clauses. This is explained below in some detail, but for present purposes, it is sufficient to introduce what the Law Commission identified in 2002 as the central problem for its inquiries. The Law Commission explained (at para. 1.5) that:

English law does not at present provide a readily available means for beneficiaries to claim that a trustee exemption clause should not be invoked by a trustee and, as a result, trustees have considerable scope to protect themselves from liability for breach of trust. The question arises whether reliance on trustee exemption clauses is seriously endangering the interests of those whom the trust relationship is directed to promote.

18.3.3.1 *Managing expectations, and the interpretation of exemption clauses in English law*

Affirmation of the exemption clause

How and why this position is believed to have arisen in English law then becomes apparent within the Law Commission's own narrative. This adds to the discussion of the ever-changing scope of attempted restrictions on liability, and the influence brought to bear on this by managing beneficiary expectations, by setting out a typical clause now to be found in trust instruments:

No Trustee shall be liable for any loss or damage which may happen to the Trust fund...at any time or from any cause whatsoever unless such loss or damage shall be caused by his own actual fraud.

This illustration of a typical exemption clause is followed by the identification of, within recent judicial approaches, a particular pattern to interpretation. The courts are now clearly adopting an approach to exemption clauses which is 'less restrictive' (than older formulations, for which a number of other authorities are cited and considered). Explanation for this is then illustrated by reference to the decision in *Armitage* v *Nurse* [1998]. The Law Commission explained that from *Armitage*, there could be no doubt that such clauses are valid, and that they will be interpreted in a way by which liability for losses caused to the trust arising from negligence, and even gross negligence, can validly be excluded. And the position of the law in England and Wales is that trustees are currently able validly to protect themselves across the sphere of breach of trust through use of exemption clauses, except for losses which are caused by fraud. *Armitage* v *Nurse* expressed this through reference to the ability of a trustee to protect himself 'no matter how indolent, imprudent, lacking in diligence, negligent or wilful he might have been, so long as he has not acted dishonestly'.

Striking the best balance

This endorsement of the authenticity of the exemption clause by the courts, and the limits of its application—apparently only stopping at actual fraud—and the way in which this in turn provides affirmation that exemption clauses are very strongly entrenched in trustee law and culture in English law, led the Law Commission to the not terribly startling conclusion that 'the protection offered to beneficiaries...is weaker than in the past'. And, it conceded that within this setting, the task of the law was thus to strive to achieve the best possible protection for beneficiaries. This meant that for the Law Commission there was no possibility of absolute protection of beneficiaries, and for the purposes of the study made of trusteeship throughout *this* text (both direct and also less direct) this position has to be squared with the way in which beneficiary protection is the *raison d'être* of the way in which trusts are accommodated within the law. This is clearly a point of tension, which the Law Commission itself appreciated through its reference to the protection of beneficiaries as 'one of the prime concerns of trust law'. How the best balance in the law can be struck given these limitations thereafter provides the guiding framework through which discussions on the shape of future policy could take place. The discussion pursued throughout the first parts of the Consultation Paper makes very interesting reading, in terms of setting out the parameters for consideration, through an examination of leading case law and historical development.

18.3.4 Managing inevitability: empirical study of the economic dimensions to greater regulation of exemption clauses

The discussion gathers particular momentum after this initial 'setting the scene' which identified the problem, and also raised the question of whether the case could be made for some formal regulation of exemption clauses (which are currently considered only in the courts, case-by-case as a matter of construction and an assessment of merits). At this point, the Law Commission acknowledged that in considering the introduction of any legal regulation of exemption clauses, the economic impact that this might have was a central consideration. And in order to make an assessment of this, independent research had been commissioned from Trusts scholar Dr Alison Dunn. The Consultation reported that the empirical research confirmed wide usage of exemption clauses in trust instruments, and in a broader cultural sense this was particularly so in relation to professional trustees, where reliance upon them 'as a means of protection from liability for breach of trust' was particularly prevalent. Unsurprisingly, among professional trustees there was also strong feeling that such clauses are a necessary component in modern trust practice, that regulation would lead to a decline of the availability of trust services, increases in their cost, and even that it would result in a relocation of the industry as a whole to a different jurisdiction which did not seek to restrict such practices. It was suggested in the previous edition of this text that this formed part of a larger 'regulatory balance' argument which is ever more pertinent in an increasingly globalised society, in which both financial capital and also social capital (human beings) are highly mobile.

In 2002 the Law Commission clearly regarded these considerations very seriously, and accordingly identified its major concerns (at para. 1.13) as:

- the way in which increased regulation might lead to significant increases in charges made for providing trust services;

- that lay trustees may be deterred from undertaking trustee responsibilities on account that they might feel unable to protect themselves; and
- the risk that professional trustees may move their operations to less regulatory burdensome jurisdictions.

Equally, the Law Commission was also able to point to a lack of universality of opinion about the necessity of exemption clauses. This was because the commissioned research had revealed, even among professional trustees, credence that those who charge for their services should be properly accountable to the beneficiaries under a trust in the event of a breach of that trust.

18.3.4.1 *Law Commission's initial position: limits of exemption within its broader acceptance*

In the penultimate section of the 2002 publication which set out the case for the direction of future policy and the manner in which this might be pursued, the Law Commission set out the parameters of possibility. This placed outright prohibition of the use of exemption clauses at one end of the spectrum and allowed completely unrestricted use of them at the other, with a number of positions lying within these extremes. The Law Commission at this point revealed its initial feeling that an absolute prohibition was not at this point in time justifiable. What is particularly interesting about its views in favour of allowing (rather than dis-allowing) exemption clauses in English law is the way in which this was explained. This position of favour 'in principle' was expressed with reference to the way in which it would not be in the interests of the parties concerned to prohibit such restrictions: this would undermine the settlor's capacity to determine appropriate administration of the trust, and to direct trustees accordingly. It was even proposed that there were persuasive arguments that a complete ban on exemption clauses might actually impact negatively on the nature of the trust arrangement itself, by interfering with its flexibility.

18.3.4.2 *Striking a balance and moving forward: Law Commission's provisional proposals*

The Law Commission's qualification of this lay in the way in which it believed that some regulation of trustee exemption clauses must be achieved, itself founded in its view that the present law does not strike the best balance between the points of interest and tension operating within the trust. The current law under *Armitage* v *Nurse* did, in the Law Commission's view, allow too much accommodation of trustees at the expense of other interested parties. The main body of the document's text explains how *Armitage* v *Nurse* allows trustees validly to exempt themselves from liability for breach of trust, except that attributable to fraud. And within this, on the construction of the clause in *Armitage* itself, this extended beyond 'equitable' notions of fraud (as explained and considered in chapter 11 of this text) and that establishing 'actual fraud' required dishonesty to be shown ([1998] Ch 241, 251): in this regard, the Law Commission made reference to the decision in *Walker* v *Stones* [2001] QB 902, where the test for dishonesty was where 'no reasonable trustee' would have considered the action in the interests of the beneficiaries. The scope of protection which *Armitage* affords to trustees seeking to resist liability for breach of trust was a matter of considerable concern to the

Law Commission. Its view was firmly that the balance had swung too far away from the interest of beneficiaries, and that the law had become 'too deferential to trustees'.

18.3.4.3 *Law Commission's initial proposals: a blueprint for reform and a store of problems to resolve?*

To complement this, in its initial outline of reform, on which responses were invited for consultation, the Law Commission recommended a number of proposals which would improve the current position of exemption clauses in English law. There were a number of proposals which would require legislation. In addition, the Law Commission suggested that, as a matter of good practice, at the outset of any trust arrangement, those responsible for drafting the instrument should bring to the settlor's attention the presence of any such clause. This should be accompanied by clear explanation of its implications and a discussion of the alternatives which might be available as protection for those acting as trustees thereunder.

The Law Commission summarised the directions requiring legislation as:

- All trustees should be given power to make payments out of the trust fund to purchase indemnity insurance to cover liability for breach of trust.
- Professional trustees should not be able to rely on clauses which exclude their liability for breach of trust arising from negligence.
- In so far as professional trustees may not exclude liability for breach of trust, they should not be permitted to claim indemnity from the trust fund.
- In determining negligence in the professional trustee, the court should have the power to disapply duty modification clauses or extended power clauses, where reliance on these mechanisms would be inconsistent with the overall purposes of the trust, and it would be unreasonable in the circumstances for the trustee to escape liability.
- Any regulation of trustee exemption clauses should be made applicable not only to trusts governed by English law but also to persons carrying on a trust business in England and Wales.
- Any legislation should apply to any breaches of trust which occur on or after the date when the legislation comes into force, but it should not act retrospectively.

The Law Commission also invited views on other possible directions for reform, including:

- Possible introduction of a 'reasonableness' requirement for exemption clauses: the question for discussion asked whether a requirement of reasonableness should be applied where a trustee seeks to rely on an exemption clause to exclude or restrict his liability for breach of trust.
- Possible role for reasonableness within the context of the professional trustee: the question for discussion asked whether professional trustees should (or should not) be able to rely upon a trustee exemption clause where it is not reasonable to do so by reference to all the circumstances (including the nature and extent of the breach of trust itself).

18.3.5 **After the Consultation: the Law Commission's** *Report on Trustee Exemption Clauses*

In earlier editions of this text, and in response to the 2002 Consultation Paper, it was suggested that the Law Commission's initial recommendations indicated a very strong orientation towards reform, emphasising 'reasonable' use of exemption clauses, and the desirability of distinguishing between trustees who are profession-als who charge for their services and others who do not. It was noted that such a reasoning was entirely consistent with the approach taken by the law to expecta-tions of professional trustees as enumerated in *Bartlett* v *Barclays Bank* [1980] Ch 515, and reflected also more recent ways in which the 'professional trustee' had informed legislative changes arising in the Trustee Act 2000. However, it was also suggested that the Law Commission's initial findings needed in several respects to be squared with many 'fundamentals' of the trust.

In the Consultation, the Law Commission suggested that in respect of trustees, and especially professional trustees, other interests in the trust have become much more obscured than they ought to be through the use of exemption clauses. At this time, this concern appeared to provide the rationale for reform, and the Law Commission stressed that it certainly was not an exercise designed to place obsta-cles in the way of efficient and cost-effective administration of trusts. It appeared that the exercise in reform would aim to restore some much-needed balance in the overall calculus of interests. The analysis which was offered in this text at the time was that, in principle, this approach had strong justifications: as long as it really were the case that the hypothesis of 'imbalance' is the most appropriate basis for analysing the current state of trustees' liability for breach of trust, and the role of exemption clauses in limiting this. It was thus proposed by this text that *if* this were the case, this was a sensible and measured approach to take to reconsider-ing the position of exemption clauses, distinguishing the professional and the lay trustee, and emphasising that there are interests other than those of the trustee to be considered.

It was suggested that this was particularly important for the beneficiary who lies at the absolute heart of trust law's interests. The settlor may be the person who actually settles trust property, but he does this for the benefit of another, and through use of a mechanism which removes from that party all burden and responsibility arising from the trust property. To do otherwise could be achieved through an out-and-out gift: in the trust scenario the settlor intends the bene-ficiary's enjoyment of the property to be unburdened with responsibility, and to achieve this, responsibility is placed upon the trustee (and in the case of the professional trustee, charges will be made for such an undertaking). Thus, it was suggested that the interests which are currently balanced must be reconsidered, but that alongside this there must be a critical appraisal of whether following a rebalancing of interests a beneficiary will once again receive sufficient protection in respect of trustee-caused losses to the trust estate and its assets. This was so on account of the Law Commission's own admission that beneficiary protection is 'much weaker' than it once was, and that it was the law's responsibility to ensure that any recommended accommodation of exemption clauses will confer *suffi-cient* protection. It was in respect of this latter observation that this text's analysis asked whether the Law Commission was right to accept so readily the presence of such mechanisms as 'inevitable', and whether greater consideration should actually be given as to whether, fundamentally, exclusion clauses are actually compatible with a trust and its purposes.

Previous editions of this text suggested that the Law Commission's proposals did try to address the 'economic implications' of regulation, and welcomed its appreciation that these considerations had to be balanced alongside the centrality of beneficiary protection. In this vein the text concurred with the Law Commission's concern that the actual provision of trust services would not be compromised as a result of regulation, either in decline in availability or through steep increases in costs. As part of its response to the Law Commission's consideration of the possible 'migration' of trusts services—if recommendations made encountered resistance from the providers of professional trusts services—this text suggested that too much accommodation of the providers of such services might have the effect of empowering these well-resourced businesses to an extent that regulatory 'reach' into their activities would be ever harder to achieve.

18.3.6 **The Law Commission's** *Report on Trustee Exemption Clauses*

In 2006 the Law Commission reported on the responses it received following publication of the 2002 Consultation Paper. It reported that the responses clustered a number of key points which could be summarised as follows:

- There was strong concern about the way in which exemption clauses are used widely and even indiscriminately in trust instruments, and especially the way in which settlors are often unaware of their import, or even their existence. Accordingly, there was support for some degree of regulation, but there were also concerns about the impact of any regulatory regime upon settlor autonomy and the protection of trustees in the performance of their duties.

- Although there was support for the Law Commission's proposals for legislation, there was concern about the recommendations made in respect of duty modification clauses on grounds that this could lead to uncertainty as to whether trustees could actually rely on the 'apparent terms of the trust'.

- The proposed distinction between professional and lay trustees was considered difficult to apply and capable of causing unfairness (especially in the case of professional trustees who acted in a *pro bono* capacity on behalf of certain trusts).

- Questions were raised about the practicality and financial implications of the proposal that all trustees should have the power to purchase indemnity insurance using trust funds.

- Although there was support for the Law Commission's proposals, concerns were also expressed about a number of adverse implications which could flow from legislation that sought to restrict reliance which can be placed on exemption clauses. These clustered:

- the increasing costs of indemnity insurance and the possibility that this might become prohibitive for trustees, and could even lead to insurance becoming unavailable if high levels of claims result in insurers no longer being prepared to insure the 'risk' of potential liability.

- the operation of 'defensive trusteeship' which can lead to increased expense incurred by the trust: this is especially a consideration in respect of exercising *discretionary* powers, where trustees might be especially vigilant in seeking legal advice ahead of their proposed actions.
- 'defensive trusteeship' also has the capacity to undermine a trustee's effective administration of the trust; and again that especial caution in respect of discretionary powers may result in dis-benefits both for the trust estate itself and its beneficiaries.
- an increase in speculative litigation for breach of trust might well result from law which either reduces the protection of trustees, or makes their level of protection unclear and uncertain.
- a decline in willingness to accept trusteeship on account of either perceived insufficient protection or uncertainty as to its extent (which might well occur in concert with increasingly costly indemnity insurance or even its unavailability).

At one level this summary of responses is clear and concise, and the Law Commission was able to glean from the exercise a range of views and concerns on a number of key issues. In this respect the Law Commission was able to ascertain that there was 'instinctive support for reform of some sort'. However, in other respects, it is clear that the Law Commission found the responses difficult to process, and it accepted that the Consultation had not translated into 'unambiguous support for any particular regulatory regime'.

18.3.6.1 *Following Consultation: 'obstacles' to proposals for legislation*

In light of this, the Law Commission has accepted that there are a 'number of obstacles' to the statutory intervention which was initially proposed in opening the Consultation. It accepted that attention needed to be paid to the following.

The impact on the operation of the trusts system as a whole
The Law Commission accepted that exemption clauses operate to control risks which arise from trusteeship, and to keep costs incurred down, which encourages a 'sufficient number of trustees to operate in the market'. In proposing that there was no clear alternative protection available to trustees, the Law Commission accepted that the Consultation had revealed that indemnity insurance would not be capable of providing an alternative model for achieving protection for trustees.

The possibility of adverse consequences and the position of beneficiaries
Although the Law Commission suggested it was impossible to assess what the precise impact of regulating the reliance placed upon exclusion clauses in this manner would be, it had concluded from the Consultation exercise that there was a 'significant risk that any such legislation could lead to adverse consequences', and these might be 'more damaging' than originally envisaged in the Consultation. Especially worryingly, given the impetus for the original Consultation, the Law Commission was concerned that any adverse consequences arising—such as trustees' reluctance to administer the estate if any part of this is deemed 'too risky'—would be felt most keenly by beneficiaries.

The impact of original proposals for legislation on the trust mechanism itself
Attempts to restrict reliance on exclusion clauses in this manner would restrict the autonomy of settlors to determine the terms on which they settle assets. The Law Commission suggested that in turn, this would limit the flexibility of the trust 'and in doing so detract from one of its greatest attractions'.

18.3.6.2 *After the Consultation: considerations on clauses restricting the liability of trustees which remain unresolved*

In the 2006 *Report*, the Law Commission reiterated that serious concerns continue to pertain to the use of exemption clauses: this is because they are able—at their most extreme—actually to exclude liability, and this also renders them capable of undermining attempts which may be made to regulate them. But it sought to balance this with its assertion that '[s]uch clauses are often included in trust instruments for perfectly good and practical reasons not motivated by an intention to avoid liability for breach of trust'. In so doing, the Law Commission conceded that it had been 'unable to frame legislative regulation in a way which would effectively distinguish between these two types of use, other than by creating a complicated system with even greater potential adverse impact'. Thus, in the *Report* the Law Commission shifted its focus to an alternative strategy which reflected a core set of issues on which it did remain convinced following the Consultation, but which would pursue them through a system of 'rule of practice' rather than legislation.

A reiteration of core concerns

In making its alternative proposals for regulation, the Law Commission indicated that it shared very strongly concerns held by 'reputable trustees' that trustee exemption clauses should not be included in a trust instrument 'without the full knowledge and consent of the settlor' (see *Report*, para. 3.40). This was so in light of an apparently common situation currently pertaining in which many settlors 'appear to be unaware of the existence or the effect of' such provisions. The Law Commission stated this was completely unacceptable because it undermines settlor autonomy in determining the protection which they wish to give to trustees, and because it challenges the view that exemption clauses operate in a properly functioning market in which protection given to trustees is appreciated by settlors.

Accordingly, the Law Commission stated that its view was that trustees should be required to ensure settlors are aware of any exemption clauses within their trust deeds. In doing so it made two key points on the inculcation of this into the practice of those who provided trusts services. The *first* was the belief that many providers of trusts services would share this view and support its inculcation; and the *second* concerned whether this should be achieved through legislation 'or some other means'.

In this respect, the Law Commission reiterated that it had already considered the possibility of introducing a statutory requirement that trustees must disclose to the settlor 'any exemption clause on which they wish to be able to rely', but had rejected this during the Consultation on two grounds. *First*, because it would be likely to cause delay and additional cost when setting up a trust, and could create uncertainty as to the validity of the clause thereafter. *Second*, the Law Commission suggested it was unclear how such a statutory requirement could adequately frame the regulation of duty modification clauses at all (see *Report*, paras 6.16–6.21, and 6.28–6.32, and especially 6.34–6.40).

18.3.6.3 *Beyond proposals for legislation: a new approach*

In light of its continuing concerns about introducing legislation to regulate the use and operation of trustee exemption clauses, the Law Commission concluded that a better means for achieving reform is for a 'rule of practice' to be adopted by 'regulated persons'. The Law Commission suggested that such a 'rule of practice' would be the most 'appropriate and effective means of influencing and informing trustees so as to secure the proper disclosure of exemption clauses' because '[r]egulated persons would be required to adhere to defined good practice'. The Law Commission believes that such a scheme would not suffer the same defects which could undermine one based in statute because '[c]ompliance with the rule would be a matter of professional conduct for the trustee'. Being in breach of good practice in this manner will not invalidate the clause or affect a trustee's reliance upon it but it will 'render the trustee open to professional disciplinary measures' (*Report*, para. 6.43). In turn, this amounted to a 'proportionate response' to any failure by a trustee to ensure adequate settlor awareness of any exemption provisions within the trust instrument.

The *Report* thus recommended the following 'rule of practice':

> Any paid trustee who causes a settlor to include a clause in a trust instrument which has the effect of excluding or limiting liability for negligence must before the creation of the trust take such steps as are reasonable to ensure that the settlor is aware of the meaning and effect of the clause.

Reporting on its communication with regulatory and professional bodies on the matter, the Law Commission stated that a number, including the Law Society and the Institute of Chartered Accountants in England and Wales, are currently in the process of developing regulation to this effect which is appropriate to their disciplinary structures (*Report*, paras 6.58–6.60). Accordingly, the Law Commission recommended that Government should 'promote the recommended rule of practice as widely as possible across the trust industry'. The Law Commission added that:

> [w]e encourage relevant regulatory authorities to adopt a version of the rule appropriate to the particular circumstances of their membership, and to enforce such regulation in accordance with their existing codes of conduct.

18.3.7 **The Law Commission's *Report on Trustee Exemption Clauses*: a postscript**

As we await to see how the Government might promote the application of the rule across the trust industry, and the trust industry's response in adopting the rule and enforcing it in accordance with existing disciplinary structures, the Law Commission appears very optimistic that the 'rule of practice' route will 'overcome the technical difficulties presented by the use of duty modification provisions' where legislation would not be able to (*Report*, paras 6.45–6.50). Indeed, the Law Commission's confidence is evident in its statement that:

We anticipate that the successful adoption of the rule across the trust industry will significantly ameliorate the problems associated with trustee exemption clauses. It will ensure that such provisions represent a proper and fully informed expression of the terms on which settlors are willing to dispose of their property on trust.

In terms of the intended scope of the rule of practice, the Law Commission explains that such a rule should apply to most commonly created trusts, except where the settlor has been independently advised, and in which case 'it is reasonable for a prospective trustee to assume that the adviser will draw the settlor's attention to any exemption provisions' and it is not necessary for the trustee to do so (*Report*, para. 6.79).

Other circumstances where the Law Commission deems that no action is necessary on the part of the trustee to ensure that the settlor is aware of the existence and effect of exemption clauses are:

- In the case of *Commercial trusts* on the basis that 'the settlors of such trusts tend to be market equals of the trustee and so are in less need of protection' (*Report*, para. 6.80), and in any case it is 'already standard practice in many commercial trust situations for information to be provided to settlors about exemption and similar provisions' (para. 6.81).

In respect of 'commercial trusts' the Law Commission also wished to confirm that the rule would have no application in circumstances where *the trustee is subject to statutory regulation of exemption provisions*, such as in the case of unit trust schemes and trustees of debentures where 'an exemption clause can be rendered void by statute'; and where *the settlor acts in the course of a business* (which would cover the majority of corporate settlors and some individuals) unless it ought to be 'reasonably apparent to the trustee that the transaction is an unusual one for the settlor to enter into' (*Report*, para. 6.82).

- In the case of *Pension trusts* because '[p]ensions are to a great extent a law unto themselves'. Such trusts are 'conceptually different from other types of trusts and operate in a distinct manner' and they are already subject to the pensions regulator, created by the Pensions Act 2004 (*Report*, para. 6.83).

- In the case of *Charitable trusts* the draft rule will be largely inapplicable because such instruments do not include exemption clauses and/or have trustees who are remunerated. However, in charitable trusts where there is such a clause, and a paid trustee, making the rule applicable is complicated by the proposition that 'every donor to charity should be viewed as a settlor' for its purposes, and being required to provide explanation to all donors would be 'wholly impractical' (*Report*, para. 6.87). In these circumstances, the Law Commission recommended that the rule should only be engaged in relation to the original settlor who is involved in establishing the terms of the trust (para. 6.88), and reported (in para. 6.89) that the Charity Commission has indicated that it will be considering an appropriate response to the Report's recommendations.

18.3.7.1 *Ensuring settlor awareness in everyday trusts*

These 'everyday' situations are ones in which 'asymmetries' between the person settling property on trust and those who are to be responsible for its administration will be most pronounced. In this vein, and through its ubiquitous and direct references to 'asymmetries', the Law Commission's *Report* does appear to attach considerable significance to the importance of 'settlor awareness', and is concerned that currently settlors frequently fail to 'understand a key component of the bargain negotiated with paid trustees for their professional services'; namely, limitations or exclusions on the liability which can be incurred in relation to these professional services (*Report*, para. 6.3). The Law Commission believes that settlor autonomy is actually a powerful justification for upholding exemption clauses, to encourage effective and competitively priced trusts services. However, it insists equally that while in these circumstances steps should be taken to ensure that the inclusion of such clauses is a manifestation of settlor autonomy 'and not something which has happened by accident rather than design', this does not require the settlor to be furnished with 'a detailed understanding of all the trust's terms'. Accordingly, the rule of practice is seeking to strike a balance between a settlor's entitlement to appreciate the basis on which trusts services are provided, and what is reasonable and practicable for a trustee to communicate.

As the Law Commission itself accepts (see *Report*, para. 3.20), it is perhaps easy to 'overplay' a settlor's capacity to influence the terms on which he engages trusts services, because of the conditions which *actually* operate in the market: this is so on account of 'take-it-or-leave-it' packages commonly on offer, and because such provisions can be buried in 'boilerplate' administrative provisions which the settlor is unlikely to read. However, the Law Commission is right at least to emphasise the *rhetoric* of settlor autonomy and choice because, although it is the beneficiary who will ultimately enforce the trust, settlors are at the heart of trusts created. Thus, settlors' intentions and wishes must remain at the rhetorical centre of trusts, and be paramount in the professional administration of trusts as far as this can be reflected in market provision and practice.

18.3.7.2 *Balancing settlor awareness with the need to give trustees sufficient protection in performance of their duties*

It was noted above that in the *Report*, the Law Commission accepted that provisions which seek to 'manage' the risks which arise from trusteeship serve important functions in controlling the cost of trust services and ensuring a 'sufficient number of trustees to operate in the market'; and furthermore that there was no clear alternative protection available to trustees, because the Consultation had revealed that indemnity insurance would not be capable of providing an alternative model for achieving protection for trustees. This is an important acknowledgement of the 'trustee dimension' in seeking to justify the continuing operation of clauses seeking to restrict a trustee's exposure to liability because '[s]uch clauses are often included in trust instruments for perfectly good and practical reasons not motivated by an intention to avoid liability for breach of trust' (*Executive Summary*, para. 1.11). In seeking to confer appropriate protection, the Law Commission's view was that 'any regulation should focus on trustees who receive payment in respect of their services as trustees'. Drawing distinction on the basis of payment has occurred in response to concerns about situations in which an otherwise professional trustee acts in a *pro bono* capacity in respect of a particular trust, but 'payment' is intended to be interpreted flexibly to accommodate indirect financial benefits (*Report*, para. 6.67). Although it is argued by some that trusteeship is 'structurally duplicitous' and an 'asymmetrical' office which is open to easy abuse (see Shapiro (1990) 55 *American Sociological Review*), it is also the case that the office is a highly burdensome one. In its proposals the Law Commission is seeking to reflect this by drawing a distinction between those who are paid for undertaking this onerous office and those who are not.

18.3.7.3 *Compliance with the rule of practice and the interests of beneficiaries*

The Law Commission appears to be very convinced that the rule of practice route will provide a flexible and workable route to informing settlors, which is also 'proportionate' in the onus it places upon trustees to draw attention to clauses which affect their exposure to liability. And in drawing attention to 'reputable trustees' who support settlor awareness, the Law Commission must be hopeful that the providers of trusts services will be more open to a route which allows a rule to be accommodated within their own regulatory framework rather than being imposed by statute. And in terms of how compliance can be evidenced, the Law Commission envisions that because (as a result of the consequences of non-compliance) the rule does not require onerous formalities, making disclosure of a clause will not be unduly difficult, and accordingly establishing observance will be relatively straightforward and un-burdensome (*Report*, para. 6.101).

There is good cause for this optimism at one level from the responses it has received from organisations such as the Law Society and the Institute of Chartered Accountants, but the Law Commission does accept that decisions 'whether to invoke disciplinary sanctions would be in the hands of the relevant regulatory body' (*Report*, para. 6.44). In so doing it appreciates that '[t]he regulator's concern would be to promote compliance with the spirit of the rule and the wider aims of regulation'. This, according to the Law Commission, was an entirely different situation from that in which a court 'is asked to rule on whether or not a trustee could rely on a particular protection to escape liability' and in this vein that a regulator is thus 'unlikely to be concerned with unintentional, minor or technical breaches, provided the trustee had acted with reasonable care and in good faith'.

Fundamentally, it remains to be seen whether the Law Commission is correct in its prediction that '[w]e do not believe that the introduction of a rule of practice is likely to provoke great efforts at avoidance' (*Report*, para. 6.96), and to assume with confidence that in the enforcement of the rule, it will be 'applied sensitively with a view to ensuring compliance with the aims of regulation' (para. 6.101). In circumstances where the 'most severe remedies would be likely to be applied only where there was sharp practice or repeated breach' (para. 6.44), it remains to be seen how settlor awareness interacts with a trustee's incentive to take care in the performance of his duties, and whether sufficient protection will be afforded to beneficiaries accordingly.

In this vein the Law Commission also notes that regulatory bodies have a number of mechanisms for policing compliance with their rules, and that it would be open to 'interested parties', which included the settlor and also beneficiaries, to bring breaches to the attention of the relevant governing body. It added that although the consequences of a regulated person's non-compliance would depend on the penalties available to that body, and it accepts that few will have the power to order compensation to beneficiaries, it attached utmost significance to the way in which failure to comply can expose trustees to 'public censure, fines and even expulsion from membership and removal of authorisation to act' (*Report*, para. 6.55).

It is in this light that the issue of beneficiary protection requires further thought because while many trustees *do*, according to the Law Commission, belong to such industry associations (in order to take advantages of 'restricted access' opportunities for marketing, networking, and education) there are varying degrees of regulation operating between such bodies: while some have rules of conduct, others operate under the 'general principle that membership can be refused or withdrawn where appropriate'. The Law Commission suggested that these latter organisations 'should also promote the proposed rule of practice' (*Report*, para. 6.56), while expressing confidence that its discussions with several professional and regulatory bodies suggest that 'a number would be willing and able to introduce regulation on the basis of the recommendations in the *Report*'.

18.3.7.4 *The 'rule of practice' and the implications of (self)-regulation of exemption clauses by trusts service providers*

In many respects, this *Report* represents a balanced appraisal of current use and operation of exclusion clauses, and it is difficult not to be convinced that the Law Commission believes it has found a workable way forward in its recommendations for a rule of practice. This is premised on its belief that there are good reasons for upholding the use of such clauses, beyond providing protection for trustees. These pertain to the way in which 'interfering' with their use could impact considerably upon the cost of trusts services, and even their availability. In addition to the attention which has been paid to promoting 'settlor awareness', the Law Commission has continued to emphasise that upholding exclusion clauses also remains a delicate 'balancing act' of the interests of trustees and beneficiaries which are, it accepts, in many respects actually 'wholly opposed' (*Report*, para. 3.22). Thus, it is suggested that the Law Commission has made a convincing case in favour of the rule of practice to redress the widespread and indiscriminate use of exclusion clauses which is currently also too often undisclosed to settlors.

It is also the case that while enhancing good practice among trustees in respect of disclosing the limits of their liability will help to redress some imbalances between trustees and other interested parties, fundamentally fiduciary office remains one which in the opinion of some is intrinsically and structurally unequal. Those who take this view also propose that asymmetries which are stacked in favour of its occupants can be deployed at the expense of (if not actually against) those whose interests a trust scenario is intended to safeguard. What the rule of practice is in danger of adding to this are the possibilities for cushioning against liability which are commonly associated with the self-regulation of professional practice.

Mary Seneviratne's study of the legal profession (Sweet and Maxwell, 1999) has a number of useful applications in this discussion of trustees' liability and compliance with disclosure of limitations which are placed on this. This work points to the powerful positions enjoyed by professional sectors in society, and the way in which this is connected with deeply rooted perceptions of professionals and professional activity. Seneviratne points to the way in which, in contrast to the concept of a 'trade' or a 'business' (alongside and against which the idea of a 'profession' is often compared) that is a 'commercial enterprise designed for profit', a profession is commonly regarded as being based on 'complex and sometimes arcane learning, and a discipline capable of study which has to be mastered before professional membership becomes available'.

Seneviratne's work also uses theories of professionalism drawn from the work of Durkheim and Weber to make a critical assessment of whether professions really are embodiments of 'selflessness, service of the community and the common good' and 'making necessary sacrifices to obtain the relevant qualifications'. And in the context of this immediate discussion, it is the case that the 'professional' or at least *aspirational* professional dimension of trusts services provision was noted in the 2006 *Report* by the Law Commission's reference to the attractions of belonging to 'regulated bodies', attaching to networking and marketing opportunities, and 'access' to educational opportunities.

What is especially significant for this discussion is the emphasis Seneviratne gives to the close associations of professions with 'ascription to training, ethics, disciplinary action and self-regulation', because these occupational sectors perceive that they place clients' interests before their own, have the highest standards of training and integrity, and accept (as far as is reasonably possible) responsibility for members' failures. In this respect, the rule of practice shows a number of key features of Seneviratne's assessment of self-regulation, in which relevant occupational bodies will 'lay down quality standards for practice'. However, although the proposed self-regulation of the rule of practice for trusts services providers is envisioned as being encouraged through 'government backing', the Law Commission's tenor in the 2006 *Report* is very much that of 'encouragement' and 'recommendations' of adoption. This is of utmost significance given that a number of discourses within 'regulation literatures' point to the way in which 'self-regulation' can be seen to amount to 'self-interest'.

In this light, Seneviratne's observations on self-regulation as a means for achieving consumer protection are highly relevant to this discussion of the proposed rule of practice and the *consumers* of *trusts services*. Illustrating her contentions with the legal profession, she has suggested that self-regulation can be criticised because rules of conduct can be 'drafted in vague and ambiguous terms', and significantly that they can appear to reflect aspects of 'market control', or even the need to 'present an image of geniality', rather than consumer or even societal protection. And in the case of solicitors, her work points to the way in which increasing self-regulation does not necessarily translate into 'a tougher regime for professional discipline and conduct', and she also expresses concerns about lack of 'independence' because rules of conduct, along with any required licence to practice, will be controlled by bodies 'drawn exclusively or predominantly from the profession'.

Following on from this, Seneviratne suggests that 'conflicts' in regulation can arise from the way in which a 'governing body' seeks to *promote* as well as *regulate* its members. This means there are 'doubts as to whether one body can effectively both protect the public and serve [its members], as well as carrying out the necessary disciplinary functions'. Thus, it remains to be seen whether the rule of practice and its envisioned regulation will empower this already powerful office still further—an office which even the Law Commission readily admits can harbour 'asymmetries', one which more extreme views propose is fundamentally 'structurally duplicitous', and one perhaps which needs more regulation rather than less.

18.3.8 **A further postscript? What happens now?**

The current reference to its work on exemption clauses on the Law Commission's website indicates its recommendation that the trust industry should adopt a non-statutory rule of practice and that this should be enforced by the regulatory and professional bodies who govern and influence trustees and the drafters of trusts. It also documents the way in which a number of professional bodies are working towards introducing regulations for their members which are intended to be binding, and which reflect the key proposition at the heart of the (Law Commission's) recommendations. This is that the use of clauses in trust instruments which have the effect of limiting or excluding liability for negligence is disclosed and explained, and that paid trustees must take reasonable steps to ensure that settlors understand the meaning and effect of such clauses before including them in trust instruments, with the recommendation that those who actually draft trusts should also be subject to the rule. Given the concerns which have been set out as the Law Commissions findings and recommendations have been examined, it is interesting that the Law Commission notes that its approach has been 'welcomed by the Better Regulation Executive'. This was with the affirmation that 'With complex and important issues such as trustee exemption clauses it is all too easy to play it safe and legislate,' and that it was good to see that 'the Law Commission has listened to people on all sides of the debate and developed a proportionate risk-based approach to the issue'. Whether this optimism is well placed remains to be seen.

18.4 **Personal remedies against trustees**

The materials here concern the issues arising where a break of trust *has* occured, and where a financial remedy in sought on account that losses have been incurred as a result of this.

18.4.1 **Measure of liability**

This is the actual loss to the trust estate which arises, directly or indirectly, from the breach, usually with interest. Where an unauthorised profit has been made, the trustees must account for this profit, but this will be the limit of their liability. It should also be noted that the trustees are liable only for losses which arise causally from a breach of trust. They are not required to act as insurers for the beneficiaries, and any losses which arise despite the exercise of due diligence on the part of the trustees must be borne by the trust estate.

Subject to the above limitations, assuming the claimant can establish a causal connection between the breach and the loss, there are no rules governing remoteness of damage such as apply in tort or contract. Inquiries as to what a reasonable trustee ought to have foreseen or contemplated are not relevant in this context. This may not matter as much as in, for example, a tort action, because the spectre of virtually unlimited liability, such as could occur in a negligence action, for example, if a cigarette end negligently thrown away causes a large ship to explode, is unlikely to arise. The value of the trust property, and profits from its use, provide a natural limit to liability without the need for additional remoteness rules, but trustees could find themselves in difficulties where, for example, the property unexpectedly increases in value. Nor, incidentally, can a trustee set off against the amount which he is obliged to restore to the trust funds the tax which would have been payable on that amount, had he not lost it through his breach (*Re Bell's Indenture* [1980] 1 WLR 1217).

Further, a trustee cannot set off a profit made in one transaction against a loss made in another. The reason is that any profits made out of the trust property belong to the beneficiaries, so the trustees have no claim against those profits to lessen their own liability for loss caused by a breach. A frequently quoted authority is the old case of *Dimes* v *Scott* (1828) 4 Russ 195.

If the profit and loss can be seen to be part of the same transaction, however, the principle of *Dimes* v *Scott* will not apply. In *Bartlett* v *Barclays Bank Trust Co. Ltd (No. 1)* [1980] Ch 515, loss had resulted from a disastrous development, but another development had produced a profit. Although acknowledging the general rule, Brightman J allowed that gain to be set off against the loss, remarking that it would be unjust to deprive the bank of an element of salvage in the disaster. The explanation was that the loss and gain arose from the same policy of speculation in the *Bartlett* case, and that, where gains and losses arise in a single dealing or course of dealing, the trustees will be liable only to the extent that a net loss results.

18.4.2 Investments

Many of the cases concern losses arising from improper use by the trustees of their powers of investment, and some specific points should be noted:

(1) If trustees make an unauthorised investment, they will be liable for any loss which is incurred when that investment is realised. There are, however, qualifications to this principle.

   (i) If the beneficiaries are all *sui iuris* and collectively entitled to the entire trust property, they may adopt the unauthorised investment as part of the trust property. It is not clear whether, if they do this, they may nonetheless call upon the trustees to make good any loss which arises from that investment: *Re Lake* [1903] 1 KB 439 seems to suggest that they may, but this result appears contrary to principle. If the beneficiaries do not unanimously agree to adopt the investment, the trustee's duty is to sell it and to make good any loss.

   (ii) The trustee is alternatively entitled to take over the investment for himself, subject to refunding the trust estate, the beneficiaries having a lien on the investment until the refund is made.

   (iii) If an unauthorised investment brings in a greater income than an authorised one would have done, and this income has already been paid over to a beneficiary, the trustees cannot, it seems, require him to repay the excess above what he should have received, or set off this excess against future income.

(iv) In *Nestlé* v *National Westminster Bank plc* [1993] 1 WLR 1260, Staughton LJ observed that trustees will not be liable if, although they applied the wrong criteria in their choice of investments, their decision is nonetheless justifiable on objective grounds, since then there will be no loss to the trust.

(2) Where unauthorised investments are improperly retained, the measure of liability is the difference between the present value of the investment and the price it would have raised if sold at the proper time: for example, in *Fry* v *Fry* (1859) 28 LJ Ch 591, the trustees were liable for the difference between the offer of £900 and the sum eventually obtained.

(3) If the trustees are directed by the trust instrument to make a specific investment, and either they make no investment at all or else they invest the fund in something else, their liability is to supply the same amount of the specific investment as they could have acquired with the trust funds had they purchased it at the proper time. Account will, however, be taken of any payments which the trustees would have had to make regarding the investment if they had acquired it at the correct time.

Where the trustees are given a choice of investments but make no investment at all, they will only be liable to replace any deficit in the trust fund, with interest. This is simply because it cannot be assumed that any particular investment would have been chosen by the trustees if they had acted properly, and it is therefore impossible to base their liability on the value of any particular investment.

(4) A trustee who uses trust money in his own business will be liable to hold any profit which he makes as a constructive trustee for the beneficiaries, or to account for the money with interest, whichever happens to be the greater. If he mixes trust money with his own, the beneficiaries may demand the return of the trust money with interest, or else claim a share in the profits proportionate to the amount of the trust money employed in the venture. Any loss must, of course, be borne by the trustee, and where he has become insolvent, the beneficiaries may have a proprietary claim for the return of the trust fund, in preference to his creditors (see chapter 19).

18.4.3 Interest

Normally, a trustee will be required to replace a loss with interest. Traditionally, the rate of interest was 4 per cent, which was in line with the rate produced on old-style trustee securities, but this is now recognised as unrealistic, and the proper rate at present appears to be that allowed from time to time on the court's short-term investment account established under s. 6(1) of the Administration of Justice Act 1965 (*Bartlett* v *Barclays Bank Trust Co. Ltd (No. 1)* [1980] Ch 515).

A trustee may be liable for a higher rate, at the discretion of the court. If he has actually received more than the standard rate, he will be liable for what he has actually received. Similarly, if it can be shown that he ought to have received more than he did, he will be liable for what he should have received, for example where proper investment producing a higher rate has been wrongfully terminated. Traditionally, if the trustee was guilty of fraud or other active misconduct, the rate was raised from 4 per cent to 5 per cent, on the presumption that this represented what he had actually received. On the same presumption, compound interest may nowadays be charged, and it seems that this will be a matter of course if the trustee was under a duty to accumulate. Despite the frequent reiteration that higher rates are charged merely as reflecting the actual gain made by the defaulting trustee and not by way of penalty, the extent of the trustee's misconduct may be a relevant factor in the court's exercise of its discretion (see *Wallersteiner* v *Moir (No. 2)* [1975] QB 373).

18.5 Trustees and criminal liability: examining the implications of the Fraud Act 2006

18.5.1 The significance of the criminal law and its limitations

It was noted above (in 18.1.4) that the criminal law may be a very important mechanism for protecting trust property and promoting compliance with lawful behaviour on the part of trustees. However, this notwithstanding, it is also the case that the function of criminal law is different from civil wrongs such as breach of trust (along with commission of a tort or breach of contract) because in today's society it represents the state's concern to protect citizens from harm by making some harms liable to criminal punishment. Thus for a beneficiary, the criminalisation of misappropriations of trust property might have a deterrent effect, and could help to assuage anger against a trustee who has misappropriated property, but unlike remedies found in the civil law, the criminal law does not engage in financial recompense to victims. This is highly significant because in the context of misappropriation of trust funds, a beneficiary is most likely to be concerned with restoration of the trust property.

18.5.1.1 *Fiduciary conduct and the limitations of the Theft Act provisions*

Another factor which can severely limit the use of criminal law in the context of trustees' conduct is that it is clear from the commencement of this chapter that not all breaches will involve misappropriations of property by a trustee. This is very important because the legal definition of theft hinges on 'appropriation' of property belonging to another. So while some trustees might simply misappropriate trust property, chapter 15 pointed to numerous examples of trustees' behaviour which, in different ways, illustrated trustees profiting from their fiduciary positions which did not involve this. There was reference, for example, to trustees' 'interested' transactions with the trust's business or its property, and of course unauthorised profit-making. All these examples pointed to equity adopting a very strict approach to making trustees accountable where they have in any way compromised their fiduciary responsibilities, and under newly enacted provisions of the Fraud Act 2006, these activities have the potential to become criminal offences alongside actual misappropriation of trust property. Fuller discussion of the new provisions, their likely reach into fiduciary activity, and the possible implications can be found on the ORC.

FURTHER READING

Dal Pont 'Wilful Default Revisited—Liability for a Co-trustee's Defaults' (2001) Conveyancer 376.

Giddens *The Third Way and its Critics* (Cambridge: Polity, 2000).

Hayton 'Developing the Law of Trusts for the Twenty-first Century' (1990) Law Quarterly Review 87.

Jones 'Unjust Enrichment and a Fiduciary's Duty of Loyalty' (1969) Law Quarterly Review 472.

Seneviratne *The Legal Profession; Regulation and the Consumer* (London: Sweet & Maxwell, 1999).

Shapiro 'The social control of interpersonal trust' (1987) American Journal of Sociology 623.

Shapiro 'Collaring the Crime, not the Criminal: Reconsidering the Concept of a White-collar Crime' (1990) American Sociological Review 346.

Sullivan 'Framing an Acceptable General Offence of Fraud' (1989) Journal of Criminal Law 92.

Sutherland 'Is "white collar crime" crime?' (1945) American Sociological Review 132.

Wilson 'Collaring' the Crime *and* the Criminal?: "Jury Psychology" and Some Criminological Perspectives on Fraud and the Criminal Law' (2006) Journal of Criminal Law 75.

Wilson and Wilson 'Can the General Fraud Offence 'Get the Law Right'?: Some Perspectives on the 'Problem' of Financial Crime' (2007) Journal of Criminal Law, 38.

19

Remedies

19.1 Structure of this chapter

The general principles applicable to equitable remedies have already been covered in chapter 1. Here personal remedies are now examined in greater detail, but an in-depth consideration of specific performance, injunctions, rectification, and recission, etc. is beyond the scope of this text and can be found in works more generally focused on the English legal process (such as Terence Ingman's *The English Legal Process*), as well as in more specialized student texts in substantive areas of contract and tort.

The second part of this chapter pays considerably more attention to proprietary remedies, with which (unlike the most common personal equitable remedies) students are far less likely to be acquainted. The essential difference between the two (personal and proprietary) rests on the way in which a personal remedy is exercised against a 'wrongdoer'. This may be for example a trustee who has acted in breach of trust, where a proprietary remedy amounts to an assertion to a right over trust property. The action will not necessarily be brought against the person responsible for the original wrong (in this example, the trustee), but against a third party who has come into possession of the property. The remedy is proprietary in the sense that it goes with the property, and the liability of the third party depends on his possession of that property.

We then move on to consider the liabilities of third parties who may no longer be in possession of (for example) trust property, or where that property is no longer identifiable. The remedies here are again personal remedies, with the third party being liable in his own right for breach of trust as a constructive trustee.

Throughout there will be considerable emphasis placed on the huge complexities and uncertainties which characterise this difficult and at present highly dynamic area of law, within which a number of very different principles are very influential.

Finally, the latest developments will be set out so that some understanding of them can be achieved at a basic level. This is meant to ensure that, at the very least, students will be able to appreciate the nature of the complexities which are characteristic of the remedies that are potentially available, their requirements, and their relationships with others.

19.2 **Personal remedies**

19.2.1 **Introducing the range of equitable remedies**

The primary remedy at common law is damages, which are available as of right, whereas equity developed its own range of remedies, which were discretionary. The focus here will be on specific performance and the injunction, but there are other personal equitable remedies, for example account of profits and rescission (see the misrepresentation section of any textbook on the law of contract). And the function of this attention paid to specific performance and injunctions is strongly focused on regarding them as illustrations of how equity works and what the scope and limitations of its applications might be.

The materials now reflect the way in which specific performance and injunctions are the most important general equitable remedies known as 'personal' equitable remedies. Equity *does* actually provide a *number* of remedies, and a *variety* of remedies distinguished according to whether they are personal remedies or what are known as 'proprietary' remedies. The study of specific performance and injunctions illustrates two personal equitable remedies—remedies granted against the defendant *personally* most commonly encountered. In due course, attention will be paid to remedies developed by equity which are attached to the aftermath of breach of trust, and specifically the recovery of trust property.

19.2.1.1 *Wider perspectives on equity's development of its own remedies: the significance of the common law*

The focus on the personal equitable remedies of specific performance and injunctions reflects the maxim equity acts *in personam*. Ahead of this there is a brief reminder of the way in which chapter 1 sought to explain why it is that equity has developed its own remedies, and also the nature of the relationship of these remedies with ones subsisting at common law.

It was suggested in chapter 1 that in many respects equity's development can be understood by reference to appreciating the nature of the common law and its own development. At a number of points this book has touched on rights which are legal rights, and which give rise to remedies which are available as of right. Equity works differently, and a fundamental tenet is that its operation is discretionary. In the context of remedies, this means that equitable remedies are not available as of right and will only be available in certain circumstances. There will be a number of illustrations of this throughout, but it is this notion that equity's jurisdiction is discretionary which provides the basis for the maxim that a claimant seeking equity must have 'clean hands'. It is also the case that equity's operation can be seen by differences in the nature of the outcomes of remedies at law and in equity. Indeed, while it is the case that the most common remedy which is awarded at law is that of damages (which will be clear in any study which is made of the laws of contract and tort), equity has a variety of outcomes which try to reflect the position that damages will not always be an 'adequate remedy'.

However, notwithstanding equity's distinctive nature, it is important to appreciate that equity's jurisdiction is premised on the existence of the common law.

For example, studying the family home provided an illustration of the maxim that 'equity follows the law' (in examining *Stack* v *Dowden* [2007] UKHL 17), and one of equity's functions is to assist the enforcement of legal rights. However, equity is perhaps best known for mitigating the inflexibility of the common law, and on occasions also the harshness which is sometimes evident from strict approaches to rights which are ones at law, and responses to breaches of them.

19.2.2 Specific performance and contracts

For breaches of most contracts the only available remedies are at common law, but sometimes injunctions can be granted to restrain breaches of contract, and some contracts are enforceable by decree of specific performance.

Where the remedy of specific performance is granted, the court orders the party in breach to carry out his obligations under the contract. If he fails to do so, he will be guilty of contempt of court. Traditionally, the remedy has been granted only very sparingly in breach of contract cases, but today the rigid requirements for specific performance seem to have been abandoned in favour of the simpler requirement that specific performance must be the most appropriate remedy. So first we consider some of the more rigid requirements, and then look at whether they have indeed been relaxed.

19.2.2.1 *Damages not adequate remedy*

The traditional position is that if damages are an adequate remedy then an equitable remedy will not be available. Damages will generally be adequate in sale of goods contracts, because the buyer ought to be able to buy equivalent goods elsewhere, and indeed should do so in order to mitigate her loss (if specific performance were generally available then that would significantly weaken the contractual mitigation doctrine). However, *Walsh* v *Lonsdale* (1882) 20 Ch D 9 is authority that it has long been recognised that contracts for estates and interests in land are enforceable in equity. It is even the case that contractual licences are specifically enforceable, as illustrated in *Verrall* v *Great Yarmouth Borough Council* [1981] QB 202. The Great Yarmouth council had agreed to hire out the Wellington Pier pavilion to the National Front, but there were elections before the date agreed for the hire. The Labour Party took control from the Conservatives and purported to repudiate the contract. The Court of Appeal held this contract to be specifically enforceable, and though it came as no surprise that contractual licences were specifically enforceable, this was the first case where that was actually part of the *ratio*.

Difficulties arising from making 'bright line' distinctions
between real and personal property

Specific performance is not usually available to enforce contracts for the sale of goods, and in this respect contrasting real and personal property is a helpful general starting point in determining the availability of this remedy. However, it may be possible to obtain specific performance for contracts for personalty where the goods are unique (e.g., a Van Gogh painting), or in other cases where the claimant could not reasonably be expected to find a substitute. Indeed, the courts are expressly empowered by the Sale of Goods Act 1979, courtesy of s. 52 (which actually re-enacts a similar provision in the Sale of Goods Act 1893), to grant specific performance of certain contracts for the sale of goods. The courts are, in general, reluctant to conclude that the goods in question are sufficiently unique. For example, in *Cohen* v *Roche* [1927] 1 KB 169, McCardie J refused to decree specific performance of a contract for the sale of a set of eight Hepplewhite chairs, on the ground that such chairs were merely ordinary items of commerce. Ordinary damages for breach of contract were awarded instead.

The relaxation of 'uniqueness': a new test emerges

Arguably, there have been relaxations in recent years, where uniqueness of the goods has been held to be not the only criterion in establishing whether the claimant could reasonably be expected to find a substitute. For example, in *Sky Petroleum Ltd* v *VIP Petroleum Ltd* [1974] 1 WLR 576, Goulding J granted an injunction restraining the defendant from withholding supplies of petrol, in breach of his contract with the claimant. Although the actual remedy was an injunction, it was accepted that it amounted to a decree of specific performance. Although petrol is hardly unique, the case arose during a worldwide petrol shortage, when the claimant could not easily obtain supplies elsewhere. Were the remedy not granted, the claimant might have been forced out of business, so that it could not be said that damages were an adequate remedy. Goulding J observed:

Now I come to the most serious hurdle in the way of the plaintiff company which is the well-known doctrine that the court refuses specific performance of a contract to sell and purchase chattels not specific or ascertained. That is a well-established and salutary rule and I am entirely unconvinced by counsel for the plaintiff company when he tells me that an injunction in the form sought by him would not be specific enforcement at all. The matter is one of substance and not of form and it is, in my judgment, quite plain that I am for the time being specifically enforcing the contract if I grant an injunction. However the *ratio* behind the rule is, as I believe, that under the ordinary contract for the sale of non-specific goods, damages are a sufficient remedy. That, to my mind, is lacking in the circumstances of the present case. The evidence suggests, and indeed it is common knowledge, that the petroleum market is in an unusual state in which a would-be buyer cannot go out into the market and contract with another seller, possibly at some sacrifice as to price. Here, the defendant company appears for practical purposes to be the plaintiff company's sole means of keeping its business going, and I am prepared so far to depart from the general rule as to try to preserve the position under the contract until a later date. I therefore propose to grant an injunction.

Beswick v *Beswick* [1968] AC 58 is another case where damages were considered inadequate, and specific performance granted to the estate, even though the obligation was only to pay money (an annuity). The problem was that the annuity was to be paid to a third party, and damages to the contracting party would therefore have been nominal only (because he personally had suffered no loss). There are, however, other justifications for the remedy in *Beswick* v *Beswick*. Lord Pearce thought that damages would not have been an adequate remedy even had it been an ordinary two-party contract, because a single award of lump sum damages is not appropriate where the contractual obligation had been to provide a continuing annuity. Further, the contract satisfied the mutuality requirement (considered shortly), since the obligation of the innocent party (whose personal representative was suing) was to transfer the goodwill of a business, and if he had failed to do so, specific performance could have been awarded against him.

If, however, the courts regard the fact that a contract is intended to benefit a third party *per se* as a strong ground for the grant of the equitable remedy, then that provides support for the view that the requirements for specific performance have been relaxed.

19.2.2.2 *A remedy which is discretionary*

Specific performance will not be awarded where it is not the most appropriate remedy, and this may follow from the discretionary nature of the remedy. The remedy of specific performance is, in principle, available to enforce a contract for the sale of land, but it will not be granted, for example, where due to some special circumstance granting specific performance would be grossly unfair to the defendant. *Wroth* v *Tyler* [1974] Ch 30 concerned a contract to sell a bungalow, for which specific performance would normally be available. As far as both parties to the contract knew, the only encumbrance on the title was the vendor's mortgage, which would ordinarily not matter as the vendor would use the purchase price to pay it off. Unfortunately, the vendor's wife objected to moving, and subsequently tried to stop the sale by entering a notice of her right of occupation under the Matrimonial Homes Act 1967. This put the vendor into an impossible position, since in order to fulfil his contract he would have had to sue his own wife in order to get the notice removed, and he withdrew from the sale. Megarry J refused to grant specific performance, and awarded the purchaser damages instead, which were based on the difference between the market value of the bungalow at the date of the contract and its value at the date of the judgment (and since house prices had risen considerably in the meantime, the award was substantial).

19.2.2.3 *The implications of contracts which require constant supervision to ensure performance*

The cases show that as far as specific performance is concerned, contracts concerning a one-off sale of property are regarded as perfectly permissible where the test for appropriateness is met, but that seeking an order which would require the defendant to perform a series of acts over a period of time is quite another matter. This is because the courts have no machinery for exercising continuous supervision to make sure that the defendant carries out an order, and rather than risk the law being undermined, they will refuse to grant an order in such circumstances.

In *Ryan* v *Mutual Tontine Westminster Chambers Association* [1893] 1 Ch 116, the lessor of a flat agreed in the lease that he would appoint a porter who would be constantly in attendance to clean the passages, deliver mail, etc. In fact, he appointed a porter who also worked as a chef in a nearby club, and who was constantly absent. The claimant sought specific performance, but the Court of Appeal held that his only remedy was damages for breach of contract: the court would not attempt to supervise the daily goings-on in a block of flats.

Specific performance and contracts for building and repair

Contracts to build or repair will not normally be specifically enforced. This is partly because the courts will not supervise resolutions which are 'ongoing', but also because the wronged party can normally find another builder to do the work (in other words, damages are an adequate remedy, on the principles discussed in the previous section). Nevertheless, there are exceptional cases where specific performance has been awarded. One such case was the Court of Appeal decision in *Wolverhampton Corporation* v *Emmons* [1901] 1 KB 515, where the claimant corporation had actually sold the land to the defendant, who had contracted to erect a number of buildings on the land, in pursuance of a scheme of street improvement. The defendant had defaulted on his obligations regarding the buildings, but as purchaser had gone into possession of the land; the corporation could not have sent in a different firm of builders without committing a trespass. In this case, the court held that the corporation could not be adequately compensated by damages, and ordered the defendant actually to carry out the work. Another material factor was that the building obligations had been defined in detail in the contract, so the court could see the exact nature of the work required.

There are also a number of old cases involving railway companies. If the company had built a railway through a farmer's land, having undertaken to build a bridge to allow the farmer to go from one part of his farm to another, the courts used to regard damages as an inadequate remedy, and decreed specific performance. The most important single factor in these cases is that the defendant is in possession of the land, so that it is impossible for the injured party to provide for the work to be done by other means.

19.2.2.4 *The requirement of 'mutuality'*

In any case involving land the contract is specifically enforceable by *both* parties (vendor as well as purchaser), and generally speaking any contract which is specifically enforceable by one party is also specifically enforceable by the other. This is termed the 'mutuality requirement', and though there are exceptions, a common ground for specific performance of a contract being refused is that the contract could not be similarly enforced by the other party.

In *Flight* v *Bolland* (1828) 4 Russ 298, for example, a minor failed to obtain a decree of specific performance, since specific performance will not normally be ordered *against* a minor. A contract is specifically enforceable, however, as long as there is mutuality at the date of trial—it does not matter if mutuality did not exist at the time the contract was made. In *Price* v *Strange* [1978] Ch 337, the defendant had agreed to grant to the claimant a lease, which contained a provision that the claimant should carry out internal and external repairs. The courts will not normally enforce a contract to repair, so there was no mutuality at the time the contract was made. However, by the time of the trial, the claimant had carried out the internal repairs and although the external repairs had been carried out by the defendant, the claimant had expressed willingness to pay for them. By the time of the trial, therefore, repairs were no longer an issue, and the only question was whether the agreement to grant the lease should be enforced. The Court of Appeal held that mutuality was now satisfied, and that specific performance could be granted.

An exception to the mutuality requirement is that a victim of misrepresentation may enforce a contract, even though the contract could not be enforced against him because the misrepresentation would entitle him to avoid the contract.

19.3 **Equity's jurisdiction illustrated by injunctions**

The materials up to now have sought to explain the *origins* as well as the *operation* of equity's remedies, and have drawn attention to equity's support and protection of legal rights and equitable rights (as well as its role in bringing flexibility and just-ice in circumstances where rights and remedies at law are unable to achieve this). Moreover, the study of specific performance itself can also provide insight into what lies ahead in looking at injunctions. This is because if specific performance is considered a mechanism whereby a person is actually compelled to perform his legal obligations (rather than simply providing monetary compensation for failing to do so) then the function of an injunction in many respects contrasts with this, but is also capable of mirroring it closely.

That is because ordinarily an injunction is the means by which the court can prevent a person from acting in a particular way by ordering him to refrain from particular activity or conduct. But like specific performance, failure to comply with the court's order will amount to being in contempt of court. It is also the case that (albeit rarely) like specific performance, injunctions are capable of compelling a defendant to act in a particular way.

The materials which follow will look at a number of different types of injunction which can be found in English law, illustrating the range of situations in which injunctions can be found, and also the key features which are associated with equitable remedies which are remedies 'in personam'. However, because looking at these remedies is intended to show the nature and features of equity's jurisdiction, the following discussion is intended to be an outline treatment only, and a detailed examination of the various types of injunction is beyond the scope of this book.

19.3.1 **Introducing different injunctions through key terminology**

Within this brief study of injunctions there are a number of distinctions of termin-ology which will arise. There will be emphasis upon explaining and distinguishing injunctions in a number of respects:

(1) *Distinguishing injunctions which are prohibitory from those which are mandatory*
Injunctions can broadly be classified as those which are *prohibitory* (the commonest type), which are used to order the defendant to refrain or desist from doing some-thing, and those which are *mandatory*, which order the defendant to carry out a pos-itive act or conduct. A mandatory injunction is very like specific performance, but whereas specific performance usually arises out of contract, a mandatory injunction usually arises out of an action in tort (subject to comparable considerations such as the adequacy of damages and the need for supervision—and it could be used to force the defendant to 'correct' something which he has done in breach of contract).

(2) *Distinguishing injunctions which are perpetual*
and interlocutory (or interim) injunctions
A *perpetual* injunction is granted in final settlement of the dispute in question, while an injunction which is considered *interlocutory* (or interim) is an interim

measure seeking to control the parties' behaviour or conduct prior to the court hearing. This acknowledges that irreparable damage might otherwise be done to a claimant if he were always forced to wait for final judgment following an action in order to obtain an injunction.

(3) *Quia timet injunctions*

This remedy (translated as 'because he fears') can arise if the claimant can show that there is a very real danger of substantial damage being done to his interests. It can be perpetual or interim, and prohibitory or mandatory, but because it relates to threatened rather than actual breach of the claimant's interests (and the defendant has not actually done anything wrong) it is rarely granted, and is subject to the claimant having to show what was described in *Attorney-General* v *Nottingham Corporation* [1904] 1 Ch 673 as 'a strong probability almost amounting to moral certainty' of the threatened or apprehended infringement of the claimant's rights.

19.3.1.1 *Perpetual injunctions: explaining their significance and requirements*

The general jurisdiction of the High Court for granting injunctions is set out in s. 37(1) of the Supreme Court Act 1981. Accordingly, the High Court may grant an injunction (whether interlocutory or final) 'in all cases in which it appears to the court to be just and convenient to do so'. The actual wording of s. 37, subsections 1 and 2 is as follows:

> (1) The High Court may by order (whether interlocutory or final) grant an injunction or appoint a receiver in all cases in which it appears just and convenient to do so.
>
> Any such order may be made either unconditionally or on such terms and conditions as the Court thinks just.

However, alongside this, there are a number of requirements which must be shown by the claimant for the court to be prepared to exercise this discretion and grant an injunction. These are now considered in brief.

(1) *The claimant must have a cause of action*

Paton v *British Pregnancy Advisory Service* [1979] QB 276 provides illustration of the requirement that the claimant must have a right which is enforceable in law or equity in order for an injunction to be obtained. This applies generally, but not in the case of a *Quia timet* injunction which is premised on *threatened harm* rather than an *actual breach* of right, and which because of this is governed by the more stringent requirements set out in *Attorney-General* v *Nottingham Corporation* [1904].

(2) *The requirements which pertain to an injunction must be complied with*

The nature of the rights which can be protected by grant of an injunction is extensive, and they can be found covering substantive areas of legal and equitable rights arising from a number of areas within the broad scope of tort (including trespass, nuisance, waste, and libel); contract; 'land law' (including restrictive covenants); breach of trust; commercial matters including intellectual property rights; and also ones arising in relation to 'family matters'. However, the grant of an injunction is *discretionary* (there is the possibility that damages may be awarded in lieu, which is considered shortly under heading 19.3.1.1).

Once again, as in the case of specific performance, *damages must not be an adequate* remedy for an injunction to be awarded, and this jurisdiction is (like specific performance) *in personam*. Moreover, cases like *Miller* v *Jackson* [1977] QB 966 and *Kennaway* v *Thompson* [1981] QB 88 are authority that public interest should not be permitted to prevail over a claimant's rights.

(3) *Requirements and key features attaching to perpetual injunctions which are prohibitory*

The circumstances must be such that damages would not be an adequate remedy (and in respect of this, it does not appear to be important that damages could easily be quantified or that it would involve only a small sum). It is not necessary for the defendant to show grave damage or inconvenience for an injunction to be granted (see *Kelsen* v *Imperial Tobacco Co Ltd* [1957] 2 QB 334, noting that an injunction might be refused where trespass is trivial, or infringement temporary or infrequent).

(4) *Requirements and key features attaching to perpetual injunctions which are mandatory*

Given that *prohibitory* injunctions are more usually granted, in many respects what is being stressed here is that mandatory injunctions are more unusual. The reason for this is that a mandatory injunction requires a defendant to carry out a positive act (which can include 'undoing' a wrongful act). Because the implications of this go beyond merely seeking to prevent wrongful action, mandatory injunctions are much harder to obtain than prohibitory ones, and the requirements attaching to mandatory injunctions reflect that fact.

When an injunction is being granted in order to *require conduct* on the part of the defendant, this raises issues already considered in relation to the courts' general approach to 'supervision' difficulties. If it is otherwise appropriate to compel the defendant to act in a particular way, *Redland Bricks* v *Morris* [1970] AC 652 explains that this will be subject to considerations of the potential hardship experienced by the defendant. There are a number of cases which cast light on the way in which for a mandatory injunction to be awarded, the terms must be certain because court must be able to supervise the defendant's conduct (see *Gravesham Borough Council* v *British Railways Board* [1978] Ch 379). Moreover, *Redland Bricks* v *Morris* [1970] is authority for two key propositions related to this: first, the court's view of the defendant's conduct as showing 'disregard to his neighbour's rights and [that he] has tried to steal a march on him or has tried to evade the jurisdiction of the court or...has acted wantonly and quite unreasonably in relation to his neighbour'; and second, that where an injunction requires a series of acts and the continuous employment of people over years, it will only be granted in exceptional circumstances.

19.3.1.2 *Interlocutory injunctions: explaining their significance and requirements*

The availability of interim injunctions reflects the way in which High Court cases can take many months to come to court. Thus the courts are able to grant so-called 'interlocutory injunctions' pending trial, which have the same effect as any other injunction, except that they last only until the full hearing. The purpose of such an injunction is to influence the defendant's behaviour until the case can come to trial, so that the claimant's case will not be prejudiced by the defendant's conduct. However, the implication of this 'pre-trial' determination of the court is that if an injunction is not eventually granted to the claimant at the final trial, then the defendant may have been restrained from doing something he was perfectly entitled to do. This explains the nature of the requirements which must be met by the claimant for an interim injunction to be awarded.

Traditionally, on account of the way in which there was inevitably some 'prejudging' of the parties' conduct ahead of the full trial and thus before all evidence could be heard, the requirements which had to be met before an interlocutory injunction would be awarded were very stringent. Indeed, before 1975 it appeared that an applicant for an interlocutory injunction would have to prove that there was a serious question to be tried, that he had a strong *prima facie* case, and that the so-called 'balance of convenience' was in favour of the grant of the remedy. The last point was likely to be satisfied if, for example, the claimant was likely to suffer irreparable damage, which could not be adequately compensated by an award of damages, were the defendant's actions allowed to continue until the full hearing. For example, any action which seriously affected a claimant's ability to trade would qualify on balance of convenience.

American Cyanamid Co. v Ethicon Ltd [1975] AC 396 and the liberalisation of requirements for interim injunctions

As the materials above suggest, the significance of this case rests on the way in which prior to this House of Lords' decision, securing an interlocutory injunction depended upon the claimant being able to show not only that there was a serious question to be tried but that there was also a strong *prima facie* case—essentially, it was more likely than not that he would succeed in obtaining an injunction at trial. However, in *American Cyanamid* itself, Lord Diplock noted that the whole point of the procedure was to allow a remedy to be granted *before* the full trial of the main issues. Thus, while it would be clear at interlocutory stage that there would be important issues to be determined at trial itself, the purpose of this stage was not to resolve the underlying substantive issues, and that it instead served to maintain a *'status quo'* until that time came. Thus, in granting an interlocutory injunction the following so-called *American Cyanamid* requirements must be satisfied:

- The claimant needs only to establish that there is a 'serious question to be tried' (and that his case is not 'frivolous or vexatious').
- The courts must consider the 'balance of convenience' (or the 'balance of the risk of doing an injustice') between granting the injunction and refusing it, and the consequences for each party if the case was decided in favour of that party at trial. Where the factors are evenly balanced, 'it is a counsel of prudence to take such measures as preserve the status quo'.

It is also clear that there may be other 'special factors to be taken into consideration in the particular circumstances of individual cases' (see, for example, the consideration given to loss of business in *American Cyanamid* itself, as well as to *Hubbard* v *Pitt* [1976] QB 142 and *Series 5 Software Ltd* v *Clarke* [1996] 1 All ER 853).

American Cyanamid as the general position: special cases where American Cyanamid principles are either not applied or are modified

Having made the point that the requirements for obtaining an interlocutory injunction have generally been liberalised by *American Cyanamid*, it is also the case that these more flexible principles are not applicable to all situations where interlocutory injunctions are sought. Indeed, there are a number of examples in case law which illustrate that there are circumstances in which this more claimant-friendly approach is not considered to be appropriate.

(1) In respect of trade disputes Section 221(2) of the Trade Union and Labour Relations Act 1992 shows how *American Cyanamid* principles have been modified to reflect the position that applications for injunctions in this context rarely went beyond the interlocutory stage. The balance of convenience test would operate in favour the claimant (the employer) and deny trade unions their power to pressurise employers.

(2) American Cyanamid is applied only where the case is actually likely to come to trial *Cambridge Nutrition* v *BBC* [1990] 3 All ER 523 is authority that *American Cyanamid* principles do not apply in situations where a matter is unlikely to come to trial at all, on account that it is designed to regulate the relationship between the parities *pending trial*, and that other factors must be applicable where this is unlikely to transpire.

(3) Additional requirements where the issue concerns the fundamental freedom of freedom of expression Freedom of expression is protected by Article 10 of the European Convention on Human Rights. Here s. 12 of the Human Rights Act 1998 Act applies in situations where the court is considering whether to grant any relief that is capable of affecting the Article 10 right. Section 12(3) of the Act provides that no such relief is to be granted (with the effect of restraining publication) before trial unless the court is 'satisfied the applicant is likely to establish that publication should not be allowed' having regard (by s. 12(4)) to the Convention's protection of freedom of expression. The court must look at the strength of the case rather than apply *American Cyanamid*, with the term 'likely' pointing to the likelihood of being successful at trial. However *Douglas* v *Hello Ltd* [2001] OB 967 is authority that even where this test is resolved in favour of the claimant, an injunction will not necessarily be granted, as factors such as the balance of convenience must still be satisfied.

Freedom of expression and the rise of the 'cult of celebrity'
The justification for these additional requirements can be seen in light of the nature of the right of freedom of expression and the protection which it is perceived to deserve. This must also be considered alongside the way in which in the UK, unlike in a number of other jurisdictions, the approach has traditionally been that there is no right to privacy. There are, however, continuing tensions here, and notably so given the rise of the 'culture of celebrity' characteristic of recent times. This is an age in which celebrities actively court publicity, and particularly media publicity, in pursuit of professional goals, but are then often less happy when aspects of their lives which are not 'media choreographed' are exposed and then published. It is in this context that the notion of a 'right to privacy' becomes newsworthy. In this light it will be interesting to observe developments which will no doubt follow from the recent case of *Moseley* v *News Group Newspapers Ltd* [2008] EWHC 1777 (QB). In this case the President of Formula One motor sport was able to argue successfully that his privacy had been infringed by unfounded allegations made by the *News of the World* newspaper (however, it is also the case

that Mosely failed to get an injunction preventing the paper from uploading material onto its website).

19.3.1.3 *A case study of 'special types' of interlocutory injunction: Freezing injunctions and Search Orders*

In a number of respects these types of interlocutory injunction fit the broad pattern of the observations made in relation to injunctions generally, and interlocutory ones more specifically. But in other respects, these injunctions also have characteristics which are quite different from other interlocutory injunctions.

The Civil Procedure Rules 1999: Freezing injunctions and Search Orders explained
Until 1999 interlocutory injunctions now known as Freezing injunctions and Search Orders were known as *Mareva* injunctions and *Anton Piller* orders respectively. They were renamed in April 1999 by the Civil Procedure Rules as part of the Lord Chancellor's Department's drive to make the law and its language, and indeed the whole legal process, more simple, more user friendly and more generally accessible. This direction has its origins in the famous Woolf Report which identified three central tenets in the (civil) law's failure to meet the needs of 'ordinary' people. This would impact on a number of traditional legal terms that were given new names in 'plain English' which also sought to explain their function: this included the replacement of terms such as plaintiff (now 'claimant') and *ex parte* (now 'without notice'). These two interlocutory measures thus ceased to be named after key cases relating to their origins, and were renamed accordingly.

(1) Freezing injunctions previously termed Mareva Injunctions The Freezing injunction is a form of interlocutory relief designed to prevent a defendant from moving his assets out of the jurisdiction, or otherwise dealing with them, until the action pending against him has been tried by a court. The courts' jurisdiction in this respect now has a clear statutory footing, under the Supreme Court Act 1981. Once again, under s. 37(1) and (2), this is where the High Court may by order (whether interlocutory or final) grant an injunction or appoint a receiver 'in all cases in which it appears just and convenient to do so', and (under subsection (2)) 'Any such order may be made either unconditionally or on such terms and conditions as the Court thinks just'.

General features and considerations of Freezing injunctions The original name *Mareva* comes from the case of *Mareva Compañia Naviera SA* v *International Bulk Carriers SA* [1975] 2 Lloyd's Rep 509 (although this was not actually the first reported case in which the order appears), where the claimants were afraid that the defendants would remove their assets from the jurisdiction before the claimants' claim could be heard. Because this is a form of interlocutory relief, the courts are reluctant to be drawn into lengthy and detailed assessments of the strengths and weaknesses of the applicant's case at trial. These concerns were evident in *Derby & Co. Ltd* v *Weldon (No. 1)* [1990] Ch 48, and Parker LJ insisted that there must be no attempt made to persuade the court to resolve the dispute by looking at the merits of the underlying claim or any detailed arguments 'on difficult points of law on which the claim of either party may ultimately depend'.

In addition, the 'test' which must be satisfied by the claimant before a Freezing injunction can be granted is much more stringent than under *American Cyanamid* tests and can be found in *Re BCCI (No. 9)* [1994] 3 All ER 764 (in the judgment of Rattee J and upheld in the Court of Appeal) as follows: that the applicant has a *good arguable case*; the applicant has satisfied the court that there are *assets within* (and, where an extra-territorial order is sought, without) *the jurisdiction*; and that there is a *real risk of dissipation or secretion* of assets so as to render any judgment which the applicant may obtain nugatory.

In terms of what property can be made subject to a Freezing injunction, it can be applied to any property belonging to the defendant. Orders may relate to cars, jewels, and even aeroplanes. However, it is also the case that the court will not order delivery of the defendant's clothes, bedding, household goods, or tools of his trade, livestock, equipment, etc., and the court should take care not to put the defendant out of business or prevent him earning his living. The remedy is also personal against the defendant, and is not intended to confer to the claimant a preferential position in the event of the defendant's bankruptcy.

Freezing injunctions in light of the growth of international fraud   The increasing concern about 'international' frauds has brought the Freezing injunction sharply into focus on account of the significance accorded to preventing the removal of assets 'from within the jurisdiction'. *Babanaft International Co. SA* v *Basantine* [1990] Ch 13 and *Derby & Co. Ltd* v *Weldon (Nos 3 & 4)* [1990] Ch 65) are authority that Freezing injunctions can be granted on a worldwide basis. However, because anybody with notice of the injunction can be affected by it, it is granted only in exceptional circumstances, and the courts are careful to frame the order so as to protect the position of third parties. According to Parker LJ in *Derby* v *Weldon (No. 1)* [1990] Ch 48 (at p. 58):

It is to be hoped that in future the observations of Lord Diplock and Lord Templeman [in *American Cyanamid*] will be borne in mind in applications for a *Mareva* injunction, that they will take hours not days and that appeals will be rare. I do not mean by the foregoing to indicate that argument as to the principles applying to the grant of a *Mareva* injunction should not be fully argued. With a developing jurisdiction it is inevitable and desirable that they should be. What, however, should not be allowed is (1) any attempt to persuade a court to resolve disputed questions of fact whether relating to the merits of the underlying claim in respect of which a *Mareva* is sought or relating to the elements of the *Mareva* jurisdiction such as that of dissipation or (2) detailed arguments on difficult points of law on which the claim of either party may ultimately depend.

(2) Search orders (previously Anton Piller orders)   This is a type of interlocutory mandatory injunction which (like the Freezing injunction) now derives its jurisdiction from the general power of the High Court, found within s. 37 of the Supreme Court Act 1981, to grant an injunction when it appears 'just and convenient' to do so. Before being renamed in 1999, the order was named after the case which gave it judicial recognition by the Court of Appeal, *Anton Piller KG* v *Manufacturing Processes Ltd* [1976] 2 WLR 162, and it received House of Lords' approval in *Rank Film Distributors Ltd* v *Video Information Centre* [1982] AC 380.

General features and considerations of Search orders   A Search order is obtained what used to be known as *ex parte*, which means in the defendant's absence, and has now been renamed 'without notice'. It is used where the court believes there is a danger that the defendant will remove or destroy documents or other property 'evidence' relating to the claimant's case (e.g., money, papers, or illegal copies of music or films), which may or may not actually be the subject matter of the dispute. In addition to ordering the defendant not to move or destroy evidence, the court may require him to allow the claimant to inspect the relevant evidence or property at the defendant's premises. This is not tantamount to a search warrant, and the defendant is required only to allow the claimant to carry out an inspection of the property.

The order is very powerful, and the courts are concerned to protect the interests of defendants, as Lord Wilberforce observed in *Rank Film Distributors Ltd*:

> Because they operate drastically and because they are made, necessarily, *ex parte*—i.e., before the persons affected have been heard, they are closely controlled by the court: see the judgment of Lord Denning MR in *Anton Piller* [1976] Ch 55, 61. They are only granted upon clear and compelling evidence, and a number of safeguards in the interest of preserving essential rights are introduced. They are an illustration of the adaptability of equitable remedies to new situations.

This is manifested in safeguards which are built into the requirements which must be met before such an order is made. The key ones are that the applicant (for the order) must show: a *strong prima facie case*; that the *damage* (potential or actual) must be very *serious* for the applicant; there is a *real possibility* that the *evidence will be destroyed; and* that the *injunction would do no real harm* to the defendant or the defendant's case.

(3) Issues remaining in current use of Freezing injunctions and Search orders   The Civil Procedure Rules 1999 under which these special interlocutory injunctions were renamed were concerned with increasing simplicity promoting accessibility to law and legal processes. There are interesting issues arising from the renaming exercise itself, but these remaining materials are concerned with the underlying function of these 'special' instruments, *beyond* their new names, which remain unchanged. These issues relate to the way in which the requirements governing their use can be seen to reflect the way in which they are seeking to strike a balance between, on the one hand, potentially safeguarding claimants' abilities to bring actions; and, on the other, pre-judging defendants and their activities at a time before trial through discussions of the criteria which must be met before such an order can be granted.

These instruments remain very powerful ones, and are capable of having considerable impact upon a defendant and his interests notwithstanding the safeguards in place which reflect mindfulness of this—because the 'pre-trial' location for these discussions makes this inevitable to some degree. However, it is not difficult to appreciate their potential use and application in the age of international fraud, in which property rights (relating to films and music, for example) are increasingly under threat from increasingly digitised technologies and global 'access' made possible by the internet (which is also an important point of reference for a number of concerns about the increasingly international reach of fraud), and from ever more sophisticated displays of deliberately self-interested behaviour. These challenges suggest that the need continually to assess and *reassess* interests and consequences which are at best competing (and more often actively in conflict) is likely to remain, and is more than likely set to increase.

19.4 **Outcomes in equity's discretion, specific performance, injunctions, and 'damages in lieu'**

The background 'story' which explains equity's emergence and its relationship with the common law can be found throughout leading texts and key readings in equity and trusts, and reference has already been made to the rationale for equity's origins and developments, and the nature of these in relation to those of the common law. The introduction made to this in this chapter also included very brief reference to the way in which this can be seen in the nature of the administration of civil justice, with the common law courts and court of equity being administered separately until their fusion by the Judicature Acts 1873–75. This meant that historically the remedies of common law and equity were administered separately.

This in turn meant that a claimant was in a very difficult position in terms of deciding whether to seek equity's assistance, and thus gain access to its more flexible remedies, or play safe in the event of a breach of his legal rights and seek relief from the common law. This was a very stark choice because prior to 1858 when the Chancery Amendment Act (Lord Cairns' Act) was passed, the Court of Chancery had no power to grant damages instead of (or in lieu of) specific performance where it was felt that in the particular circumstances equitable relief should not be granted.

19.4.1 **The power to award damages in lieu of specific performance**

This power to award damages in lieu of or in addition to specific performance is now found in s. 50 of the Supreme Court Act 1981. Accordingly:

Where the Court of Appeal or the High Court has jurisdiction to entertain an application for an injunction or specific performance, it may award damages in addition to, or in substitution for, an injunction or specific performance.

In this context, much has been made of the way in which the remedy of specific performance, in common with grant of an injunction is discretionary, and by no means a *fait accompli* for a litigant. In times when the courts of common law and equity were administered separately, a claimant who failed to secure a decree of specific performance would then be in the position whereby he had to start his action all over again in the common law courts to recover damages. In this respect, ahead of the fusion of jurisdiction brought about by the Judicature Acts 1873–75, the 1858 Act gave the Chancery courts power to award damages in lieu, or even in addition to, specific performance.

Like specific performance itself, damages granted in lieu of specific performance are discretionary, and the claimant will only be able to obtain 'equitable damages' where the court could have granted him specific performance at the date when the action was begun. Moreover, additional damages will only be awarded if there has been some special damage to the claimant.

19.4.2 **The power to award damages in lieu of injunctions**

As can be seen in the section above setting out s. 50 of the Supreme Court Act 1981, this also provides the basis for the courts' power to award damages in lieu of injunction. In this respect, the jurisdiction and its source within the same provisions within the 1981 Act reflect the similarities between specific performance and injunctions which have been emphasised in this book up to now.

However, it is also the case that alongside these similarities, there are also some distinct issues which arise from damages in lieu of injunction. These relate to the way in which injunctions are commonly a response to some kind of wrongdoing (whether this requires the defendant to be restrained or compelled to 'right' a wrong), and thus indicative of situations in which damages are much less likely to be adequate than is the case in breaches of contract where the possibility of specific performance arises.

What the court must be sure of in considering whether to award damages *instead of* an injunction is that this does not amount to a 'licence' permitting the defendant to 'carry on' as before—subject only to the financial inconvenience of having to pay damages to the claimant. These issues were considered in *Shelfer* v *City of London Lighting Co.* [1895] 1 Ch 287, which is now considered a good working rule in response to the issues raised by awarding damages instead of actually seeking to control the defendant's behaviour.

19.4.2.1 *The significance of Shelfer v City of London Lighting Co. [1895] 1 Ch 287: shedding further light on the implications of granting and not granting an injunction*

Given the potential impact of awarding damages rather than actually restraining behaviour, *Shelfer* is authority that damages should be awarded in lieu only where the injury to the claimant was *small*; and where the injury is actually capable of being *estimated in monetary terms*, and is of a kind which would be *adequately compensated* by a small payment; and where it would be *oppressive* to grant an injunction.

The *Shelfer* principles are obviously open to interpretation, as illustrated in the case of *Redlands Bricks* v *Morris* [1967], which was considered earlier. But it is the case that the courts are generally reluctant to grant damages in lieu, especially where a continuing trespass, or a continuing nuisance is complained of. In *Kennnaway* v *Thompson* [1980] 3 WLR 361, the Court of Appeal set aside the trial judge's refusal to grant an injunction against power-boat racing, where damages of £16,000 were awarded in lieu, and substituted an order restricting the racing to certain times and limited noise levels. The significance of 'oppression' can be seen in *Gafford* v *Graham* (1999) 77 P & CR 73.

Significantly also, *Daniells* v *Mendonca* (1999) 78 P & CR is authority that even if the *Shelfer* criteria are satisfied (thus suggesting damages in lieu) an injunction will still be granted if the defendant has acted in bad faith, has recklessly disregarded the claimant's rights, etc.

19.4.3 'Measuring' damages arising in lieu of specific performance and injunctions

In exercising this power to award damages in lieu of (or in appropriate cases in addition to) specific performance or injunctions, one question which remains is that of how this will be calculated. *Johnson* v *Agnew* [1980] AC 367 is a decision of the House of Lords which is authority that damages can only be awarded on the same compensatory basis as the common law. This does of course support the assertion that the very origins of equity can be understood in relation to the common law and its own operation (noting the references made in chapter 1, and at other points in this text as well as earlier in this chapter, considering how equity can be seen to provide support for the law, for legal rights, etc.), and there is of course the equitable maxim that 'equity follows the law'.

19.4.3.1 *The significance of so-called 'equitable damages'*

Here we work from the premise of *Johnson* v *Agnew*, and take a closer look at how *differently* from the common law equity might measure damages. An illustration of how this might be different can be seen in *Wrotham Park Estate Ltd* v *Parkside Homes* [1974] 1 WLR 798, where damages awarded were regarded as amounting to a 'just substitute', which reflected the amount which might reasonably reflect the 'cost' to the claimant of 'relaxing' the restrictive covenant to which the defendant was subject (and acting in breach of), and moreover that the defendant 'should not be left in possession of the fruits of their wrongdoing'. Significantly, at common law the claimant would only have been able to recover nominal damages because he had suffered no loss. However, *Surrey County Council* v *Bredero Homes Ltd* [1993] 1 WLR 1361 questioned whether the *Wrotham Park* measure of compensation was consistent with *Johnson* v *Agnew*.

In *Jaggard* v *Sawyer* [1995] 1 WLR 269, an application for an injunction was refused because granting an injunction would be oppressive, and so the claimant was awarded damages in lieu. In this case, damages were measured as compensation for 'continuing invasion' of the claimant's rights, which were calculated 'not at a ransom price, but at the price which might reasonably be demanded by the plaintiff for relaxing the covenant and for right of way'. Moreover Lord Bingham MR observed that 'I can see no reason why a judge should not assess damages on the *Wrotham Park* basis when he declines to prevent commission of a future wrong'.

19.5 Remedies and third parties: tracing, receipt of trust property, and breach of trust

This section concerns remedies developed by equity to assist a beneficiary 'recover' trust property which has 'gone missing' when a trustee commits a break of trust. What a beneficiary can *actually* do will depend on the circumstances, and particularly what has happened to the property. But in principle there is a range of personal and propertiary remedies available.

19.5.1 The need to consider persons other than the original wrongdoer

Although the liability of a trustee acting in breach of trust is considered to be personal, the necessity for proprietary remedies and the ability to pursue persons other than the original wrongdoer lie in the reality that property that is stolen (and this will of course include property applied in breach of trust) is likely to change hands many times because stolen property is 'hot property'. This may involve the same property changing hands several times, and even ending up in the hands of someone unaware of its dubious origins. Equally, it may well be the case that what ends up in the hands of someone entirely unconnected with the original wrongdoing is actually not the original property itself but either its (monetary) proceeds or a completely different article. This latter instance of the appearance of different property is another reality of stolen property as 'hot property', but whether the property is the original subject of the theft or replacement property, its original 'thief' is likely to want to off-load it at the earliest possible opportunity.

19.5.2 Remedies: range and application

The remedies which are potentially available in the circumstances can be fairly clearly set out. However, their treatment here does not in any way capture the complexity of their operation in practice, or even at a theoretical or conceptual level. This is a very complex area, because of its dynamism and the incredible pace at which the law is developing—to such an extent that any clear statement about the law as it stands in this area is virtually impossible. The current position of many of these remedies and their relationship and interactions with others is the subject of much complexity and even confusion. In a climate where the principles of restitution and proprietary entitlement have both been very influential, students will need to have a grasp of the requirements of the applicable remedies, and the factors which operate to distinguish them.

19.5.3 Making a clear statement on the remedies which are available

While the paragraph above suggests that it is possible to set the remedies which are actually available, it also stresses that the current climate in which they are subsisting renders making any clear statement of the present law in this area virtually impossible due to its current complexity and confusion. It is an area which is undergoing significant change, with many of the traditionally applicable requirements and distinctions constantly being considered and reconsidered, and this is also the case for the principles themselves and also the relationships subsisting between them.

19.5.4 Remedies following breach of trust and key terminology encountered

Given that there is much confusion and lack of clarity in the sphere of remedies, while it is also the case that this is a very dynamic area of law because it is actually very important, the best place to start is perhaps explaining the broad parameters for consideration, and this will be articulated through reference to the key terminology which will be encountered.

19.5.4.1 *Actions against the participants in a breach of trust: distinguishing personal and proprietary actions*

From earlier materials, two key factors which are central to understanding this area are apparent. The first relates to the materials more immediately above, drawing attention to the way in which in responding to a breach of trust involving missing property, a beneficiary will often need to consider action not only against the recalcitrant trustee who has caused the breach, but the other parties who may have been involved, either because they received property wrongly applied to them (with the incentives for the original trustee to dispose of the property often being considerable) or because they actually assisted the breach. This also paves the way for appreciating that there are actually a number of actions which are potentially available to the beneficiary, which explains the second factor, and which in some way takes the discussion back to the very outset of this chapter. This second factor is that what is potentially available to the beneficiary is a range of remedies which are both personal and proprietary.

To recap, personal remedies are ones which attach to the defendant himself, while proprietary ones will relate to the property itself. It will become apparent in the course of this chapter that there are a number of advantages which attach to remedies which are proprietary rather than purely personal against the defendant. For example, the facility for proprietary remedies allows for specific recovery of an asset, and also for recovering increases in value which might accrue to the property. Crucially also, proprietary remedies allow a beneficiary's interests to be protected in circumstances where the defendant is insolvent, where the former's interests lie in priority to the general creditors of the latter.

19.5.4.2 *The study of remedies is a (further) case study in the features and operations of the constructive trust.*

In the introduction made in chapter 7 to trusts which are private non-express trusts, it was noted that the constructive trust is considered a very flexible device for giving effect to entitlements relating to property (for the purpose of vindicating existing property rights, rather than a remedial type capable of creating new ones). This was illustrated by reference to materials which 'listed' some of the common applications of the constructive trust today. At that point it was suggested that constructive trusts arose in the context of trusteeship, and that, beyond their application to hold trustees themselves to account to the trust for unauthorized profits, constructive trusts were also being used to 'fix' strangers to a trust with liability following a breach of trust. It was suggested that constructive trusteeship was at the heart of the liability which a stranger to a trust could incur as a recipient of trust property, and also as an accessory to a trustee's breach of trust. More will be said about recipient liability and also accessory liability in due course, including reference to the way in which these species of liability can give rise to personal and also proprietary claims.

The limits of the use of the constructive trust in this context can be seen in distinctions which are drawn between the liability of the trustee acting in breach himself, and those who are strangers to the trust. In relation to the former, *Foskett* v *McKeown* [2000] 2 WLR 1299 is authority that the wrongful appropriation of trust property by a trustee should be viewed as giving rise to liability resulting from the process of tracing, rather than creating a constructive trust. Lord Millett's speech in *Foskett* v *McKeown* [2000] 2 WLR 1299 will resonate with the materials from chapter 18 which make reference to the way in which a trustee's liability to a beneficiary for a breach of trust is in principle a personal claim for 'equitable compensation'.

It does not entitle him to priority over the trustee's general creditors unless he can trace the trust property into its product and establish a proprietary interest in the proceeds. If the beneficiary is unable to trace the trust property into its proceeds, he still has a personal claim against the trustee, but his claim will be unsecured.

19.5.4.3 *Explaining the meaning and significance of 'tracing'*

Traditionally, discussion of tracing has been divided into a discussion of the rules applicable in equity and those applicable at common law. Although such a division has been challenged by *dicta* of the House of Lords in *Foskett* v *McKeown*, this introduction and also much of the chapter has remained structured in this way, and because of the general uncertainty and lack of clarity subsisting, the materials as traditionally understood are then annotated with discussion of the apparent challenges to them.

As an initial point, it may be noted that, in principle, tracing is available irrespective of whether the property is in the hands of persons actually at fault in some way for the improper application of the property, or in the hands of innocent volunteers who might have received it.

Tracing and the identification of property wrongfully applied

'Tracing' is a term from art traditionally given to processes which are essentially a means of 'following' property into the hands of others. As the materials immediately above suggest, traditionally there have been two systems of tracing available to a claimant wishing to 'follow' into the hands of others property rightly belonging to him. The differences between these two systems of 'following' are reflected in their traditional characteristics and requirements.

For *tracing in equity* three conditions have traditionally subsisted. These reflect the requirement of an initial fiduciary relationship (although this has recently been challenged, it has in practice proven relatively straightforward to establish), and that the claimant must own an equitable proprietary interest (easily satisfied by a beneficiary under a trust). Finally, the right to trace must not have been lost, and it is capable of being so where property has ceased to be identifiable, where it has been transferred to a *bona fide* purchaser for value, and significantly where allowing tracing a claim would be inequitable on account of the defendant's use of the property.

Traditionally, an important distinction between tracing in equity and at common law has been that in equity it was possible to trace money into mixed accounts, and the significance of this, and its requirements, will be explained shortly

Tracing at common law is in principle similar to tracing in equity, but because it is the legal title which is being followed into the hands of another, it is not an action available to a beneficiary, who does not own the legal title. However, it can be used by a trustee, and in some respects its 'requirements' are not as stringent as ones relating to tracing in equity—for example, there has never been an initial fiduciary relationship requirement. Traditionally it has been more limited in scope than equity, because it has not been possible to trace money into a mixed fund.

Recent developments affecting the nature and classification of tracing

Tracing has traditionally been regarded as a proprietary remedy, and as such it would permit the beneficiary to proceed against a particular asset in the defendant's hands, but it is increasingly becoming associated with being an exercise in identification of inherent value (rather than of the property itself). This was suggested in *Foskett* v *McKeown*, in which Lord Millett also proffered that:

Tracing is thus neither a claim nor a remedy. It is merely the process by which a claimant demonstrates what has happened to his property, identifies its proceeds and the persons who handled or received them, and justifies his claim that the proceeds can properly be regarded as representing his property.

This view of tracing does raise questions for a continuing need to distinguish between tracing in equity and tracing in common law. More will be said about this in due course, including some reference to what more recent cases are currently stressing.

19.5.5 Personal actions arising in the recovery of property belonging to another

Bearing in mind the distinction drawn between remedies which are personal and ones which are proprietary, although much of the focus below is on a proprietary approach to recovering property belonging to another (with an emphasis on that which follows a breach of trust specifically), there will also be reference to a number of personal actions which can arise in these situations. At this introductory point they can be found to arise at common law, in the action for money 'had and received'. There are actions in equity which are personal in nature, which for the purposes of this introduction can be summarized as follows:

19.5.5.1 *Personal action for breach of trust against a trustee*

It was suggested above that a beneficiary under a trust will have a personal action against a trustee where property is disposed of in breach of trust. This is explained immediately below in relation to the constructive trustee, but in relation to the express trustee, reference has already been made to the way in which *Foskett* v *McKeown* [2000] is support for the proposition that 'A beneficiary's claim against a trustee for breach of trust is a personal claim'—and this is of course liability to provide 'equitable compensation.'

19.5.5.2 *Personal actions arising from 'stranger' liability for breach of trust*

Reference was made above to the way in which liability which can be incurred under the banner of constructive trusteeship can be proprietary and personal. As will become apparent, a recipient of trust property may or may not retain it: if property is retained then the beneficiary's action will be a proprietary one, and if not, it will be a personal action relating to actual receipt of the property. The position of an accessory to a breach of trust is distinctive because such a person does not actually receive trust property. So while regarded as a species of constructive trusteeship, so-called 'accessory liability' is joint and several for any losses which the beneficiary suffers as a result of the breach of trust, and the requirement is that the accessory must account for any personal profit which he has made from this. Fuller discussions of both recipient liability and accessory liability will follow, where reference will be made to a number of recent cases including *Ultraframe (UK) Ltd* v *Fielding* [2005] EWHC 1638 (Ch).

19.5.5.3 *Re Diplock and the 'personal action in equity'*

The introductory descriptions of personal liability given above all have in common their reference to personal actions against those who are culpable parties in the wrongful application of trust property. Accordingly, this has related to the trustee (or trustees) who has responsibility for the trust property, and who holds legal title to the property on account of this, and who actually acts in breach in the first instance. It has also introduced the personal liability which can be incurred by those who are strangers to a trust, but who have somehow participated in its breach, either being the recipients of trust property 'available' because of the breach committed, or because they have somehow assisted in the breach committed by the trustee. The personal action in *Re Diplock* is different. *Re Diplock* [1951] AC 251 is authority that a personal action in equity can be directed against those who are said to receive trust property innocently because they have no knowledge of the breach but who are *not bona fide* purchasers for value and so cannot take the property unencumbered. However, it will become apparent that, because of the absence of blameworthiness, what can be recovered by a beneficiary in these circumstances is limited, and it appears it might only to be available in the administration of estates. Here, the law is seeking to strike a balance between competing claims in which (at least two) innocent parties have become caught up as a result of wrongdoing by another.

19.6 **Tracing**

In this section distinction is drawn between common law and equitable tracing, and also between personal and proprietary claims. A proprietary tracing claim involves the claimant in seeking to locate his property in the hands of the defendant. It is necessary here for the defendant not only to have received the claimant's property, but also to *retain* it. Hence, if the defendant no longer has the property, a proprietary tracing claim will not be available. However, a proprietary claim is essential if the defendant is bankrupt, and is also useful if the property has increased in value, since the claimant by identifying the property can benefit from its increase in value.

At common law, there is also the restitutionary action for money had and received. This is a personal claim, which requires the claimant to show only (subject to the complete and partial defences described below) that the defendant received the claimant's property, and not necessarily that he still retains it. Though it is conceptually entirely different from a proprietary tracing action, it is nevertheless usually described as a form of common law tracing, and so is being considered in this section. There is also a personal form of equitable tracing, which is more conveniently dealt with subsequently, along with the other personal claims in equity.

By way of a recap, personal claim arises from the receipt by the defendant of the claimant's property, and the defendant remains liable even if she later divests herself of it, or indeed if the property is destroyed or is no longer identifiable. It is no use if the defendant is bankrupt, and unlike a proprietary claim, a personal claim will not allow the claimant to recover increases in the value of the property.

19.6.1 **Traditional approaches to tracing at common law**

Traditionally tracing at common law has been considered an exercise in 'following' property into the hands of another. And as might be expected given the titular reference to 'common law', what is being followed into the hands of another is property to which the claimant has *legal* title. Given that what is being followed is *legal* title, it must be pointed out—considering the emphasis which is being placed on remedies following breach of trust—that this is not an action which is available to beneficiaries. This is because a beneficiary under a trust does not have legal title to the property, and instead owns an equitable interest in it. However, this type of 'following' property into the hands of another can be used by a trustee.

Because there are in fact two regimes of tracing to be considered—tracing at common law and tracing in equity—finding an appropriate starting point for any discussion is difficult. This is because although the two are very similar in underlying objective and principl—because both have traditionally been concerned with 'following' property into the hands of others—the manner in which each approaches this is quite different. Explaining the significance, features, and limitations of one will to some degree involve comparison with the other.

On balance it is possibly easier to make tracing at common law the starting point. This is because it is concerned with following 'legal title', and in many respects has traditionally operated without a number of the 'complexities' associated with tracing in equity. However, this has led to a system which is not only quite different from 'following' in equity, but one which is more limited in scope and less sophisticated. For example, traditionally the key limitation associated with tracing at common law—over and above the fact that it is only available to legal owners of property—is that it cannot be used to recover property which has become mixed with other property.

This is most notably so in relation to money in mixed accounts. The reasons for this, and its implications for using the common law to trace property will be discussed shortly, along with the way in which more recent approaches might influence this. Key cases here are *Lipkin Gorman* v *Karpnale* [1991] 3 WLR 10 and *Foskett* v *McKeown*. In *Lipkin Gorman* v *Karpnale Ltd* it was held that the claimant firm could trace at common law where money was improperly withdrawn from the client account and paid over to a casino. The identifiable asset which could be followed was the chose in action represented by the debt of the bank to the firm, and the same approach was adopted in *Foskett* v *McKeown* which is a central case throughout this chapter. Indeed it will become apparent that *Foskett* is at the heart of a current belief which is emerging that the distinctions traditionally drawn between tracing at common law and in equity are becoming both less significant and less appropriate, and even that there is (per Lord Millett) 'no sense in maintaining different rules for tracing at law and in equity' when 'One set of tracing rules is enough...'.

However, first, the traditional approaches to tracing at common law (and then in turn tracing in equity) will provide a 'roadmap' for gaining initial insight into what tracing actually is and how it might work; and for signalling the most appropriate points at which to indicate recent developments.

19.6.1.2 *Explaining Tracing at Common Law*

Reference was first made to the significance of legal title in English law in chapter 1 in the course of introducing the trust. It was suggested at that point, and on occasions subsequently, that legal title provides the basis for the almost unfettered ways in which the owner of property can deal with it, and it was suggested that in turn this was premised on the way in which in principle, legal title 'binds the world', and is thus enforceable against anybody in the world. Because of this, it follows that if a claimant can establish that the defendant has his property in circumstances where title has not passed from the former to the latter—because the property was not sold to him or given to him—then the claimant should be able to recover the property in question.

This works as a point of logic, but in fact while the common law has developed an action for the recovery of a specific piece of land, it has never extended this 'real' remedy to allow a claimant to recover a specific chattel. Although the common law acknowledged the claimant's ownership of the chattel, his action in the face of being aggrieved in this way was a personal action in detinue, the remedy for which was damages. The defendant could therefore choose whether to return the claimant's chattel or pay him its full value as damages.

The Common Law Procedure Act 1854, s. 78, gave the court a discretion to order specific delivery of the chattel, and this power is retained by s. 3 of the Torts (Interference with Goods) Act 1977. But there is no absolute right to the return of the chattel. The importance of the proprietary claim lies rather in the fact that it entitles the claimant to the full value of the chattel, in preference to the claims of the defendant's other creditors.

The common law also concluded that the claimant's right should continue even if the defendant had exchanged the claimant's property for some other property, or sold it and purchased other property with the proceeds. And accordingly, as long as it continued to be possible to 'trace' or 'follow' his original property—i.e. to show that what the defendant now holds can be regarded as simply a substitute—his claim was unaffected. In *Re Diplock's Estate* [1948] Ch 465, Lord Greene MR explained the doctrine in terms of the claimant ratifying the wrongful sale of purchase, to enable the legal owner to claim the substitute.

In *Taylor* v *Plumer* (1815) 3 M & S 562, Sir Thomas Plumer had handed over money to a stockbroker with instructions to purchase exchequer bonds, but the stockbroker instead purchased American investments and bullion, and attempted to abscond with these. He was caught before he could leave England, and the investments and bullion were seized by Plumer. The assignees of the stockbroker then brought an action to recover them from Sir Thomas, but failed. The investments and bullion were held to be Sir Thomas's own property. In effect, Plumer's money was traced into the investments and bullion because, according to Lord Ellenborough, at p. 575 'the product of or substitute for the original thing still follows the nature of the thing itself, as long as it can be ascertained as such'.

Millett LJ suggested in *Trustees of the Property of F.C. Jones & Sons* v *Anne Jones* [1996] 3 WLR 703 that *Taylor* v *Plumer* was actually decided on equitable principles (see also Lionel Smith [1995] LMCLQ 240), but claims to substitute assets were upheld in *Banque Belge* v *Hambrouck* [1921] 1 KB 321 and *Lipkin Gorman* v *Karpnale Ltd* [1991] 2 AC 548 (below), and indeed in *Trustee of the Property of F.C. Jones &*

Sons v *Anne Jones* itself. So it is clear that a substitution doctrine is recognised by the common law.

Two other points need to be made about the substitution doctrine. First, if it depends on ratification, the claimant is equally entitled not to ratify the transaction and instead to claim the original property. Second, where (for example) money is paid into a bank account, at any rate where it is unmixed with other money, it is exchanged for a cause of action against the bank. In *Diplock*, Lord Greene MR thought that there was no reason why the common law would not allow the substitution of the money into the cause of action, and vice versa. Accordingly:

> If it is possible to identify a principal's money with an asset purchased exclusively by means of it, we see no reason for drawing a distinction between a chose in action such as a banker's debt to his customer and any other asset. If the principal can ratify the acquisition of the one, we see no reason for supposing that he cannot ratify the acquisition of the other.

This passage was approved by Millett J in *Agip (Africa) Ltd* v *Jackson* [1990] 1 Ch 265, but he thought that it was limited to following an asset into a changed form in the same hands, rather than following the same asset from one recipient to another. Millett J did not think that it necessarily followed that the common law allowed free tracing of causes of action from one person to another.

19.6.1.3 *Proprietary tracing at common law and the significance of 'money 'had and received'*

The proprietary tracing claim considered above depends on the claimant being able to trace or follow his actual property, or as in *Taylor* v *Plumer* its product or substitute, into the defendant's hands. Difficulties arise with this in the case of currency where title passes to the recipient upon receipt, but here the law imposes on the recipient of money stolen from the claimant an obligation to reimburse the claimant with an equivalent sum. From the House of Lords decision in *Lipkin Gorman* v *Karpnale Ltd* [1991] 2 AC 548, and in particular the speech of Lord Goff, the basis of the action appears to be that the defendant has been unjustly enriched at the expense of the claimant.

The claim is established merely by showing that the defendant has received the claimant's property. The defendant's knowledge (or lack of it) is irrelevant. On this reasoning, the claimant's action will not be defeated where the recipient subsequently disposes of the money or mixes it with his own money, and this is because the claim is not a proprietary one (attaching to the property) and is instead a personal one against the defendant. It is defeated, however, if the recipient has not been unjustly enriched. Innocently to receive stolen money in return for full consideration is not to be unjustly enriched at all, so that, for example, a shop which has innocently taken stolen money to pay for its goods is not liable to the victim of the theft.

In these circumstances, if the recipient of property belonging to the claimant is wishing to defeat the claim—by arguing that he has not been unjustly enriched—then he must establish that he provided consideration, and that this is consideration recognised as such by the common law. This can be illustrated by In *Lipkin Gorman* v *Karpnale Ltd* itself, which concerned a solicitor, Cass, who was a partner in the appellant firm of solicitors, and a regular client of the casino in question. Cass was cashing cheques of which he was an authorised signatory to fund his gambling habits, and he stole a large sum of money from the firm's clients' account. He took the cash to the Playboy Club, which was owned by the respondents, whereupon he gambled it away. The appellants successfully claimed the club's winnings from Cass. This was so notwithstanding that the property in the money had undoubtedly passed to the respondents, and they no longer had the money. The owners of the club were unable to claim that they had provided consideration for the money, since contracts by way of gaming and wagering were rendered null and void by virtue of s. 18 Gaming Act 1845: gambling contracts are not in law contracts for consideration.

Lipkin Gorman: two further points

Two further points arise from *Lipkin Gorman*. First, the claimants (the firm of solicitors) never had legal title to the money in the clients' account, only a debt (i.e. a cause of action) against the bank. The House of Lords held that they were entitled to trace the cause of action, however, since that was a species of legal property (but see the criticism of this by Halliwell [1992] Conv 124). On the tracing of causes of action see further below. There is a further possible explanation of the cause of action in *Lipkin Gorman*. There was nothing apparently wrong with the cheques that Cass presented to the bank, and the bank was entitled to pay him the money, as it did. But there is no reason to suppose that title to the money, which had, after all, been obtained by virtue of his position in the claimants' firm, passed to Cass. The correct analysis must surely be that he drew out the claimants' money, which he used to gamble at the Playboy Club.

Second, the case establishes a change of position defence to the restitutionary common law claim, where the defendant has altered his position in good faith, so that it would be inequitable to require him to make restitution or restitution in full. This defence was used in *Lipkin Gorman* to limit the claimants' right to recover the net winnings taken by the casino, rather than all the money gambled by the thief. Paying out money as winnings constituted a change of position by the club.

Subsequent adoption of the change of position defence

The change of position defence was applied by Tuckey J in *Bank Tejarat v Hong Kong and Shanghai Banking Corporation (Ci) Ltd and Hong Kong and Shanghai Bank Trustee (Jersey) Ltd* [1995] 1 Lloyd's Rep 239. Bank Tejarat had been induced, by a fraudulent transaction, to advance money (under a bankers' documentary credit) to the account of the fraudsters (CAK) at Hong Kong and Shanghai Banking Corporation (Ci) Ltd. Hong Kong later paid the money, in pursuance of an apparently legitimate instruction, to one Madame Parvin Farzaneh, a lady in Paris. When the fraud was discovered, Bank Tejarat sued Hong Kong for money had and received. They failed because they were unable to establish that Hong Kong had ever received any of their money, but also because Hong Kong had a change of position defence, having paid the money away, in good faith, before receiving any notice of Tejarat's claim.

It is not yet clear whether the change of position defence applies only to money had and received, or to any of the restitutionary claims considered in this and the following section, but there is some suggestion that it applies in tracing claims in equity. However, as the recent case *Campden Hill Ltd v Chakrani* [2005] EWHC 911 (Ch) suggests, this is controversial.

It is also not clear what happens when money is paid to a second recipient, but Millett argues in (1991) 107 LQR 71 (at p. 79) that since the action is personal and not proprietary, what happens to the money after it has been received by the first recipient is irrelevant. It becomes the property of the first recipient, and any subsequent recipient will be receiving the first recipient's money, rather than that of the claimant. It ought also to follow that the first recipient will be liable to reimburse only the value of what was received, and if he makes a favourable investment with it, he should be able to keep the benefit of that. Authority to the contrary can be found in Nourse LJ's judgment in *Trustee of the Property of F.C. Jones and Sons (a firm)* v *Anne Jones* [1996] 3 WLR 703, [1996] 4 All ER 721, but this looks incorrect in principle, and it is in any case weak authority as Millett and Beldam LJJ reasoned on the basis of a proprietary tracing claim.

19.6.1.4 *Identification of property as the claimant's property at common law*

The main constraint on common law tracing is establishing that what the defendant has, or, in the case of the money had and received claim, what he received, was in fact the claimant's property. While *Taylor* v *Plumer* shows that tracing is available where a straightforward exchange of the property has occurred, the position is more complicated where the property or its proceeds have been placed into a bank account, and it is in this area that equitable rules appear to be more generous. However, in *Re Diplock's Estate*, Lord Greene MR saw no reason in principle why money should not be substituted for a chose in action, or vice versa, at any rate where the entirety of the money was substituted for a chose in action, for example where it was used to open a bank account in which there was no other money.

The leading case on identifying the claimant's property
The leading authority is *Banque Belge pour L'Etranger* v *Hambrouck* [1921] 1 KB 321. Hambrouck, who was a cashier, stole cheques from his employer, altered them so as to make it appear that they were drawn by his employer on the claimant bank to Hambrouck's order, and used them to pay money into a new account (at Farrow's Bank) which he opened specifically for the purpose. Farrow's Bank collected the proceeds from the claimant bank and credited them to Hambrouck's account. Hambrouck then paid various sums, by cheque, from this account to Mlle Spanoghe, with whom he was living, either for no consideration, or in consideration for her future cohabitation, a consideration which would not be recognised at common law. She paid the cheques (and no other money) into a deposit account of her own at a different bank (London Joint City and Midland Bank). Mlle Spanoghe later spent most of the money in this account, but £315 remained, and the Court of Appeal held that the claimant bank was entitled to trace this money.

It is difficult precisely to ascertain the *ratio* of *Banque Belge* since the three judgments differ considerably. Scrutton LJ apparently took the view that the money could not be traced at common law, since it changed its identity when paid into the account at Farrow's Bank, but could be traced in equity (as is undoubtedly the case). Bankes LJ felt that tracing at common law was permissible, but only because the proceeds of Hambrouck's fraud had never been mixed with any other money, either at Farrow's or Mlle Spanoghe's bank. Atkin LJ appeared to take the view that the question of the property's identification was the same in common law and equity, in which case common law tracing would be possible even into mixed funds.

The orthodox view (but see Goode (1979) 95 LQR 360) is probably that of Bankes LJ, and it is impossible to support Atkin LJ's view in the light of the Court of Appeal decision in *Agip (Africa) Ltd* v *Jackson* [1991] Ch 547, considered further below. Bankes LJ appeared to treat the claim as a proprietary claim at common law. Clearly, the claimant bank started with legal title to the money, and since Bankes LJ rejected the proposition that the money passed between the banks as currency, the money would have remained the property of the claimants when it was transferred to Hambrouck's account at Farrow. It is not clear that any cash was transferred from Farrow to London Joint City and Midland Bank (Mlle Spanoghe's bank), so presumably the claimants could not continue to follow the money itself. However, since there was no other money in Hambrouck's account, they could presumably convert the money into the causes of action represented by the cheques, and convert back again into the money in Mlle Spanoghe's account (where again, there were no other funds). Bankes LJ did not accept that title ever passed to Mlle Spanoghe, so this must have been a proprietary common law tracing claim (since title passes with a money had and received claim—in any case, there would have been no reason to limit a personal claim to the £315 remaining in the account).

Identification, orthodoxy, and restrictions in analysis
There are, however, serious restrictions on this analysis, which limit the value of common law tracing of money. There is the requirement in *Re Diplock* that the money must be exclusively converted into the cause of action, and vice versa. This implies (as Bankes LJ accepted) that if, at any stage, the claimant's money had become mixed with other funds belonging to Hambrouck or the defendant, it would have been impossible to trace it at common law. The common law will not trace into mixed bank accounts. Since mixing will often occur where funds are misappropriated, this severely curtails the usefulness of tracing at common law.

An unusual recent case, where a proprietary tracing claim succeeded at common law, is *Trustee of the Property of F.C. Jones and Sons (a Firm)* v *Anne Jones* [1996] 3 WLR 703. Mrs Anne Jones opened an account with a firm of commodity brokers in order to deal on the London Potato Futures Market, and paid into it three cheques totalling £11,700, drawn on the firm's partners' account; the money in which (it was held) belonged to the claimant. Mrs Jones's dealings in potato futures proved to be highly profitable. She received two cheques totalling £50,760 from the commodity brokers and paid them into a call deposit account (at Raphaels), in which there was remaining a balance of £49,860. This money was claimed by the claimant, on the grounds that the legal title was vested in him, and the Court of Appeal held that he was entitled to the entirety of the £49,860 remaining in the call deposit account, and hence the profit element. In Millett LJ's view, this was a proprietary claim, none of the money having been mixed with other money, and no property having passed to Mrs Jones. He thought that, in contrast, a money had and received action would have been limited to the amount of the money received, or £11,700, but that the trustee had made a proprietary rather than a personal claim. Indeed, a money had and received claim was not available here because title to the money had not passed to Mrs Jones. Nourse LJ agreed with Millett LJ, but also (apparently) took the view that the same result could be reached on the basis of a money had and received claim.

Receipt of money and the reasoning in F.C. Jones

Note that the reasoning in *F.C. Jones* can apply only where the money is not mixed. If Anne Jones had mixed the money with her own before investing it, legal title would have passed to her, in which case the only action at common law would have been for money had and received (for £11,700). Only if she had the requisite knowledge for a knowing receipt claim (which is considered shortly) would the claimant then have been able to claim the profit element, in equity rather than at common law. It might be thought that since Mrs Jones was a volunteer, the claimant would also have been able to trace in equity, whatever the state of her knowledge, on the principles in *Re Diplock*, considered below, but this is not correct because the claimant originally had only legal but not equitable title to the money.

Apart from the problem that the common law cannot follow money once it has become mixed, another limitation was suggested by Millett J in *Agip (Africa) Ltd v Jackson* [1990] 1 Ch 265, that whereas the common law will substitute causes of action for tangible property, and vice versa, as long as the property remains in the same hands, it can only follow a physical asset, such as a cheque or its proceeds, from one person to another. Without the cheque, in other words, it would have been impossible to follow the chose in action it represented into Mlle Spanoghe's account. The inability to trace money into and out of mixed bank accounts, and to follow causes of action except where they are represented by a physical asset, such as a cheque, was fatal to the (common law) claim for money had and received in *Agip (Africa)* itself.

Misappropriation and mixing: Agip (Africa) v Jackson

In *Agip (Africa)*, the claimant company's chief accountant fraudulently altered payment orders which had been signed by an authorised signatory of the claimant, altering the name of the payee to that of a company (Baker Oil) of which the defendants were directors and shareholders. The forged payment order (for over US$ half a million) was taken to the Banque du Sud in Tunis, which debited the claimant's account and sent telexed instructions to a London bank (Lloyds) to credit the account which Baker Oil had there. The Banque du Sud also instructed its correspondent bank (Citibank) in New York to reimburse Lloyds with an equivalent sum. Lloyds duly credited Baker Oil with US$518,000, of which about US$45,000 remained in the account. The claimants sued Baker Oil at common law for the full amount received by them. Had the claim succeeded it would have been irrelevant that Baker Oil had subsequently disposed of all but about US$45,000 of the money, but the claimants failed to show that the money received by Baker Oil was the same money that had left the Banque du Sud. Both Millett J and Fox LJ in the Court of Appeal (which upheld Millett J's decision) held that the money could not be traced through the New York clearing bank system, since there it clearly became mixed with other money.

Since Lloyds must surely have had a contractual claim against the Banque du Sud at the latest when they had received and acted on the telexed payment order, and Baker Oil a cause of action against Lloyds, the alternative would have been to trace the causes of action from Agip to Baker Oil, but at first instance Millett J distinguished between a payment order and a cheque, commenting that the payment order never moved from Tunisia, and that nothing passed between Tunisia and London but a stream of electrons. The common law can only follow a physical asset, such as a cheque.

Fox LJ did not adopt Millett J's distinction, relying instead on the fact that Lloyds had credited the money to Baker Oil before it was reimbursed with the claimant's money. They thereby took a delivery risk, Fox LJ commenting that whereas the Banque du Sud could be regarded as having paid with the claimant's money, Lloyds must be regarded as having paid Baker Oil with its own (Lloyds') money, since at the time of payment it had no other money with which to pay. The money in Baker Oil's account could not therefore be identified as the claimant's money. This, however, would seem to be merely an additional reason why the *money* could not be traced through the New York banks. It does not explain why Agip could not follow the causes of action, and it is necessary to adopt Millett J's distinction to do that.

Millett J's reasoning was applied by Tuckey J in *Bank Tejarat v Hong Kong and Shanghai Banking Corporation (Ci) Ltd and Hong Kong and Shanghai Bank Trustee (Jersey) Ltd* [1995] 1 Lloyd's Rep 239, the facts of which have been set out above. As in *Agip (Africa)*, the money was paid by telegraphic transfer, through clearing banks, and for the same reason a common law tracing claim failed. Bank Tejarat also failed successfully to argue that since (as is common in documentary credit transactions) they had paid against presentation of a draft (i.e. a bill of exchange) that operated similarly to a cheque. The draft was not being used, as a cheque would be, as the method of making the payment. Its presentation to the claimant bank was merely the trigger for payment, so the analogy with the cheque failed. Tuckey J observed that:

> The simple answer to this submission is that the drafts were not the means by which Tejarat paid their money to CAK. The payment out of Tejarat's account…was probably made by telex instructions…(a stream of electrons). It was certainly not made by the drafts, so there is nothing from which Tejarat can trace.

Note, incidentally, that, since the common law does not recognise equitable interests in property, a beneficiary under a trust cannot follow trust property in the hands of a trustee, although he can in equity compel the trustee to trace the property at common law, where it has fallen into the hands of a third party.

19.6.2 Traditional approaches to tracing in equity

Bearing in mind what has been said about a number of recent developments questioning the distinctions traditionally drawn between tracing at common law and in equity, and given the emerging views on the nature and meaning of tracing itself, the structure of this chapter broadly follows the traditional approach. This is not only for the purposes of explaining this traditional distinctiveness but it is also considered the best way in which actually to highlight recent developments in light of continuing debate and uncertainty. What follows initially is an examination of the traditional requirements for tracing in equity, and an indication of how more recent approaches might be seen as influential.

19.6.2.1 *There must be an initial fiduciary relationship*

Traditionally, this has been a requirement for tracing in equity, based on the need to give rise to an equitable proprietary right in the claimant. In the context of this text's interest in trusteeship and breach of trust, this can clearly be established in the case of the relationship between trustee and beneficiary, but it is also the case that this allows for tracing to operate across a range of fiduciary positions accounting for extensive litigation around fiduciary relationships in professional/ commercial arrangements. Although the requirement has been in question for some time, as evident in the case of *El Ajou* v *Dollar Land Holdings plc* [1993] 3 All ER 717, the traditional view was reaffirmed in *Westdeutsche Landesbank* v *Islington LBC* [1996].

It will become apparent shortly that this requirement was the subject of further criticism from the House of Lords in *Foskett* v *McKeown*. And this textbook has traditionally expressed the view that the requirement of a fiduciary relationship for tracing in equity is not easy to justify in principle. This is because it means that a (mere) equitable owner may have a better action than someone who owns property outright (according to *Westdeutsche*, in this situation legal title is where all rights and entitlements to property are manifested) because there will always be a fiduciary relationship in the former case, with the trustee. Thus a beneficiary can always trace in equity—but someone who is an outright owner of property can do so only if he can find an additional fiduciary relationship—hence the litigation point above.

At this point, some attention is paid to how the requirement actually became established as such, and the case law indicates it did actually appear to emerge from historical accident rather than conscious attempt to create a necessary pre-condition for tracing in equity.

19.6.2.2 *Fundamental principle or no more than historical accident?*

The way in which *Foskett* v *McKeown* casts serious doubt on the need for a fiduciary relationship has been signposted above, and it will be considered more substantially shortly. What this part suggests is that prior to this, the authorities in the area strongly suggested that this requirement did in any case appear to arise as a result of historical accident, rather than bound principle.

As the materials introducing the general features and significance of tracing suggest, one of the traditional benefits of tracing in equity has become attached to being able to trace into mixed funds, and the original authority for this is found in *Re Hallett's Estate* (1880) 13 Ch D 696, which is considered further shortly. *Re Hallett's Estate* involved a trustee mixing money rightfully belonging to the trust with his personal assets. And the principle of tracing into mixed funds was extended in *Sinclair* v *Brougham* [1914] AC 398, from which it has always been difficult to determine a clear *ratio* for the case, because the speeches given in the House of Lords where characterized by much difference and little agreement. Although *Sinclair* has now been overruled, and was so in *Westdeutsche*, its complexity arises from how it was interpreted in *Re Diplock's Estate*. In Re *Diplock*, the mixing was done by a fiduciary, and the case was itself interpreted as authority that an initial fiduciary relationship was required. The precise import of *Re Diplock's Estate* is complicated still further because the claimants also succeeded on a personal claim, so it might be thought arguable that remarks on the proprietary tracing claim were *obiter*, except that the proprietary remedy was necessary for the interest claim.

In *Agip (Africa)* v *Jackson* [1990] 1 Ch 265, Millett J accepted *Re Diplock* as Court of Appeal authority for the requirement, and ahead of its reaffirmation from the House of Lords in *Westdeutsche* v *Islington LBC* it was reiterated in the Privy Council in *Re Goldcorp Exchange* [1995] 1 AC 74, and by the Court of Appeal in *Trustee of the Property of F.C. Jones and Sons (a Firm)* v *Jones* [1996] 3 WLR 703.

19.6.2.3 *Initial fiduciary relationships and the affirmation in Westdeutsche*

As explained in chapter 1, in *Westdeutsche*, Lord Browne-Wilkinson doubted the very concept of someone being both legal and equitable owner, on the ground that the equitable ownership would have no existence in the absence of separation of legal and equitable titles (e.g., on the creation of a trust). Further support for the *Diplock* approach can also be read into his opinion that where a trust arises, there will inevitably be a fiduciary relationship; this may also justify the *Re Diplock* conclusion in principle, since it will be difficult to conceive of an equitable title existing in the absence of a fiduciary relationship. In the case where legal title is transferred to someone who is not a *bona fide* purchaser for value without notice, and where there is therefore separation of legal and equitable title but not necessarily a trust, this proposition is not negated, since it depends on the initial creation of a trust, albeit that it is not between the parties to the action. There is no need for the fiduciary relationship to exist between the parties to the action, as long as it originally existed; this follows from *Re Diplock* [1948] Ch 465, above, where an action was successful against a volunteer.

19.6.2.4 *Tracing in equity and the presence—not necessarily initial presence—of a fiduciary relationship*

Some time before this in *Chase Manhattan Bank NA* v *Israel-British Bank (London) Ltd* [1981] Ch 105, the claimant mistakenly paid a sum of money twice to the defendant, and on the defendant's liquidation was able to trace the money mistakenly paid into the hands of the liquidators. There was no fiduciary relationship initially between claimant and defendant, but Goulding J held it sufficient that a fiduciary relationship arose as a result of the mistaken payment. Goulding J's reasoning was heavily criticised in *Westdeutsche* (see further the 1998 or 2000 editions of this text), but the proposition that the fiduciary relationship need not have arisen initially appears to be good law. In *Agip (Africa)*, Millett J observed that:

> In [*Chase Manhattan*] however, equity's assistance was not needed in order to trace the plaintiff's money into the hands of the defendant; it was needed in order to ascertain whether it had any of the plaintiff's money left. The case cannot, therefore, be used to circumvent the requirement that there should be an initial fiduciary relationship in order to start the tracing process in equity.

The general proposition, then, is that it is necessary for the fiduciary relationship to exist before the tracing process starts. In *Agip* itself, therefore, it was necessary to show a fiduciary relationship before the money got into the New York clearing system.

Unfortunately, before Goulding J's reasoning in *Chase Manhattan* was criticised into oblivion in *Westdeutsche*, it led Tuckey J into error in *Bank Tejarat* v *Hong Kong and Shanghai Banking Corporation (Ci) Ltd and Hong Kong and Shanghai Bank Trustee (Jersey) Ltd* [1995] 1 Lloyd's Rep 239. He observed that Millett J's analysis of *Chase Manhattan* was wrong, since the money became mixed (in another bank account) before it reached the defendant. Tuckey J therefore concluded that where a pay-ment is made under a mistake of fact (in *Bank Tejarat* itself the bank had been deceived into thinking that the shipping documents tendered to it represented goods that had been shipped, whereas in fact they were simply forgeries), a fiduci-ary relationship arises as soon as the money has been paid out; it is not delayed until it has been actually received by the recipient. In the light of *Westdeutsche*, this must now clearly be regarded as wrong; in any case, in *Westdeutsche*, Lord Browne-Wilkinson observed that Goulding J had been asked to assume that the money was traceable into the hands of the defendant, the only issue being whether the claim-ants had a proprietary claim.

19.6.2.5 *A fiduciary relationship: more problematic in principle than in practice?*

Not long after *Agip (Africa)* v *Jackson* Millett argued (extra-judicially, in (1991) 107 LQR 71, at pp. 75–76) that the fiduciary requirement is not particularly problematic in fraud cases, because 'the embezzlement of a company's funds almost inevit-ably involves a breach of fiduciary on the part of one of the company's employees or agents' as was the case in *Agip* itself. Fraud by a stranger, such as that which occurred in *Bank Tejarat*, and such as would be typical in maritime frauds, presents greater difficulties in this regard, but if it can be established that the fraudster has induced the victim to convey property to him, then the fraudster may become a constructive trustee on the principles in *Bannister* v *Bannister* (see chapter 10). That would have the effect of establishing the fiduciary relationship for subsequent tracing purposes, but it would not help if, for example, it was necessary to trace through a mixed bank account to establish that the fraudster had received the victim's money in the first place. Victims of theft by a stranger will not normally be able to trace in equity, since the thief will not acquire legal title and therefore cannot become a trustee, whether constructive or otherwise. That is the main limi-tation of proprietary tracing in equity.

19.6.2.6 *The fiduciary relationship requirement, judicial criticism, and the position post Foskett v McKeowen*

Discussion of the facts of *Foskett* is probably best held over for the time being, until this exploration of tracing in equity progresses further. For present purposes it is sufficient to note the way in which it is clear that in *Foskett* the House of Lords was very critical of the fiduciary relationship requirement, and even the cases which are cited as authority for it indicated it is a principle with a questionable pedigree. However, it was reaffirmed by the House of Lords in *Westdeutsche* and also has strong Court of Appeal authority, which was recognised by Lord Millett himself—albeit at earlier stages of his judicial career.

Although the views in *Foskett* are very clear and definite, the approach which will be adopted by the courts for the future does still remain unclear. To this end, it is interesting that the authoritative nature of *Foskett* was questioned in two subsequent decisions, albeit at first instance. *Shalson* v *Onofrio Russo* [2003] EWHC 1637 (Ch) affirmed that *Foskett* v *McKeown* had not decided that it was no longer necessary to identify a fiduciary relationship as a precondition to tracing in equity, and the same approach was adopted in *Campden Hill Ltd* v *Chakrani* [2005] EWHC 911 (Ch).

The claimant must own an equitable proprietary interest
While it is the case that whether or not the presence of a fiduciary relationship is a necessary pre-condition is not clear after *Foskett* v *McKeown*, the traditional requirement that the claimant must own an equitable interest in the property being traced remains. This is premised on the need to give rise to an equitable proprietary right for the claimant. As the materials above explained, this can clearly be established in the case of the relationship between trustee and beneficiary, and this book is concerned primarily with how tracing can be applied in the aftermath of breach of trust.

The right to trace must not have been lost
For a person who owns an equitable interest in property, whether or not the presence of a fiduciary relationship is a continuing requirement, the right to trace then depends on the right to trace not having been lost. The way in which the right to trace can be lost can be illustrated with reference to examples, with *Re Diplock* [1948] Ch 465 serving as a key illustration of both the principle and the manner in which it can arise.

Re Diplock was mentioned briefly above in relation to understanding how the requirement of a fiduciary relationship for equitable tracing might have arisen. It will be mentioned again throughout this chapter, so at this point an explanation of its background will be given. The testator, Caleb Diplock, gave the residue of his property 'to such charitable institutions or other charitable or benevolent object or objects in England' as his executors should, in their absolute discretion, select. In the belief that this created a valid charitable trust, the executors distributed some £203,000 among 139 different charities. Then the next of kin successfully challenged its validity in *Chichester Diocesan Fund and Board of Finance* v *Simpson* [1994] AC 341. The next of kin, having exhausted their remedy against the executors, successfully recovered money from the various charities. The personal claim is considered later, but a proprietary claim also succeeded against some of the charities. The advantage of the proprietary claim was that it allowed the next of kin to claim interest.

On the proprietary claim, the Court of Appeal, extending the principles derived from *Re Hallett's Estate* and *Sinclair* v *Brougham*, held that the right to trace into a mixed fund is not limited to cases where the defendant is the person who has mixed the funds. Nor does there need to be a fiduciary relationship as between the parties to the action. The right to trace is available against an innocent volunteer. This is an application of the *bona fide* purchaser rule: a volunteer is not a purchaser, and provides no value. Here, the volunteer charities had mixed Diplock money with their own, and hence the question of apportionment arose.

Returning to the right to trace, and the way in which it is capable of being lost in a variety of circumstances, these arise where:

The property ceases to be identifiable   This is most easily illustrated where property is destroyed, but it also applies where property is dissipated, or where its identity has been lost by being mixed in a manufacturing process. This is because the nature of the claim is proprietary, and will not be available if the property has ceased to be identifiable. This will account for example for the way in which *Bishopsgate Investment Management Ltd (in Liquidation)* v *Homan* [1994] 3 WLR 1270 and more recently *Ultraframe (UK) Ltd v Fielding* [2005] EWHC 1638 (Ch) are authority that there may be no tracing into an overdrawn bank account (however, there is contrary *dicta* in the Court of Appeal judgment in *Foskett* v *McKeown*: see [1998] 2 WLR 298 (CA)).

The property is transferred to a bona fide purchaser for value   While *Diplock* illustrates that the right to trace is available against an innocent volunteer, by so being it is also authority that an equitable tracing claim can be defeated by transfers to third parties who give value and do not have the requisite knowledge to be bound (on which, see further below). This is not a limitation of common law tracing, but its application for tracing in equity is clear from *Agip (Africa) Ltd v Jackson* [1990] 1 Ch 265. Millett J held that the claimant's funds could be traced in equity into the hands of anyone still in possession of the funds, except for a *bona fide* purchaser for value without notice of the trust. This is an application of the *bona fide* purchaser rule, and a volunteer is not a purchaser and provides no value, and its application was reaffirmed in *Foskett* v *McKeown*.

Tracing would be inequitable (e.g., where the mixed fund is applied to make improvements to real property or has been used in the payment of debts).   Because tracing in equity works by the declaration of a charge on the property, *Re Diplock* [1948] Ch 465 is authority that the remedy will not be granted where a charge on the property would be inequitable. This was illustrated in *Diplock* itself by the situation where an innocent volunteer has spent the money on alterations or improvements on his land, and also applies where there has been payment of mortgages or other loans on the property. In such cases, the imposition of a charge enforceable by sale would be unreasonable; it would also be impracticable where the land concerned was an active institution such as a school or a hospital.

Where the defendant has bona fide changed his position   It is suggested that applying the common law change of position defence to equitable tracing claims would provide an alternative way of achieving the same result, and there is authority in *Boscawen v Bajwa* [1996] 1 WLR 328 that it should also be available in a tracing action. However recently, *Campden Hill Ltd v Chakrani* [2005] EWHC 911 (Ch) is authority that there is a great deal of controversy about the application of change of position in relation to (and affecting) the right to trace in equity. Indeed, if this were generally available, it would undermine 'proprietary entitlement' significantly.

19.6.3 Tracing and the issues raised by mixed assets

Traditionally, an important distinction between tracing in equity and at common law has been that in equity it was possible to trace money into mixed accounts. And once it is accepted that equity can trace into mixed funds, it is necessary to consider the basis on which the fund is apportioned between rival claimants. Usually, the problem is that payments have been made out of the fund, leaving insufficient to satisfy all the claimants. But another possibility is that the payments out have been wisely invested, in which case claimants may prefer to claim a share of the payments out, rather than what remains in the fund.

  The principle that equity can trace into mixed bank accounts, and also that this raises issues of apportionment amongst those entitled to trace in this way can be illustrated by reference to *Re Hallett's Estate* (1890) 13 ChD 696. This case was referenced briefly earlier, as authority for the fiduciary relationship requirement. It was noted then that this case involved a claim by a beneficiary over mixed funds, where the trustee had mixed trust money with that of his own.

19.6.3.1 *Mixing of funds by a fiduciary: the rule in Re Hallett's Estate (1880) 13 Ch D 696*

Where a trustee wrongly mixes trust money with his own, the principles in *Hallett's Estate* apply, essentially to ensure that a trustee is disadvantaged by this kind of conduct. In such circumstances the general rule seems to be that where money is withdrawn, the trustee is deemed to be spending his own money first, with the result that the beneficiary can trace against any balance remaining.

This case arose when Hallett, a solicitor, a trustee of his own marriage settlement, paid some of the money from that trust into his own bank account, into which he also paid money which had been entrusted to him for investment by a client. He made various payments into and out of the account, which at his death contained sufficient funds to meet the claims of the trust and his client, but not those of his personal creditors as well. The estate tried to argue (using the rule in *Clayton's case* considered below) that the payments out had been of the trust money, and that what was left was his own. However the Court of Appeal held (Thesiger LJ dissenting) that both the trust and the client were entitled to a charge in priority to Hallett's general creditors, and that the various payments out of the account must be treated as payments of Hallett's own money. The principle is that *where an act can be done rightly, the trustee is not allowed to say that he did it wrongfully*. Hallett had the right to spend his own money, but not that of the trust or the client, and his estate was therefore unable to claim that he had done so. Therefore, he must have spent his own money, leaving that of the trust and the client in the account.

19.6.3.2 *The scope of the rule in Re Hallett's Estate: Re Oatway [1903] 2 Ch 356*

Re Oatway is authority that this does not prevent the beneficiary from enjoying a charge (or lien) over any property purchased from the mixed account. In this case the trustee had withdrawn money from the mixed account and invested it in shares, leaving a balance which at that time was ample to meet the claims of the beneficiaries. Subsequently, however, he dissipated the balance further. The argument (based on *Hallett*) that he must be treated as withdrawing his own money first (so that his shares would be treated as his own property) was rejected. The beneficiaries' claim must be satisfied out of any identifiable part of the fund before the trustee could set up his own claim. They were entitled to the shares in priority to the general creditors. The principle is the same as before. The trustee was entitled to dissipate his own but not the trust money, so it could not be claimed that what had been left in the account, and subsequently dissipated, was trust money, rather than his own.

19.6.3.3 *Are there limits to the choices available to beneficiaries?*

However, there are limits to the rights of beneficiaries. Once it is clear that all money belonging to the trustee has been withdrawn, so that any further withdrawals must have been from trust money, they cannot claim that any subsequent payments in must be taken as intended to replace the trust money, unless the trustee shows an intention to make such repayment. In such a case, the right to trace will apply up to the lowest balance of the account in the period between the trust fund being paid into the account and the time when the remedy is sought. For example, if the trustee mixes £1,000 of his own money with £3,000 of trust money and later withdraws £2,000, the right to trace will not extend beyond the £2,000 which is thereby left in the account, even if the trustee later pays in further sums of his own. In such a case, of course, the beneficiaries will have a personal claim against the trustee for any outstanding sum.

Another limit on the beneficiaries' right to trace is that there may not be any principle of proportionate entitlement. In situations where the trustee has used the mixed fund to purchase property which has increased in value, this raises the question of whether the beneficiary can claim any part of the increase? *Re Hallett's Estate* and *Sinclair v Brougham* suggested this was not possible, and that the beneficiary's remedy was limited to a charge on the property for the amount of trust money expended in its purchase. This is a surprising result given the strict rule against profits by trustees, and some doubt was cast on this in *Re Tilley's WT*, albeit that this was *obiter* and a decision at first instance. In this case a sole trustee who was also a life tenant had mixed a small amount of trust money in her own bank account before embarking on a series of property speculations which were so successful that on her death her estate was worth £94,000. The beneficiaries entitled in remainder claimed a share of this wealth in the proportion which the trust money in the account bore to the balance of the account at that time. Ungoed-Thomas J held them entitled only to the return of the trust money with interest.

It is significant that this decision was based on a finding of fact that Ms Tilley had not invested the trust money in property but merely used it to reduce her overdraft. In different circumstance, for example where a trustee has in fact laid out trust money towards a purchase, Ungoed-Thomas J thought that the beneficiaries would then be entitled to the property and any profit to the extent that it had been paid for with trust money.

The reasoning is that if the trustee draws on a mixed fund to purchase property but leaves enough in the account to cover the trust funds, the rule in *Re Hallett's Estate* requires that the purchase be treated as made entirely with his own money, in which case, should no further dissipations to the mixed fund occur, the property, and any profit, belong to him. But should he then go further and dissipate the remaining balance, the beneficiaries will have a charge on the property (*Re Oatway*), and this, according to Ungoed-Thomas J, may be for the proportionate part of the increased value and not merely for the original amount of the trust fund.

Most recently support for this position—whereby beneficiaries have the choice of a charge for an amount of the trust money, which will be to their advantage where the funds are depleted, or a share in the property where its value has risen—has come from *Foskett v McKowen*. In making clear the position taken in *Re Hallett's Estate* and *Sinclair v Brougham*, that in the case of a *mixed* fund the beneficiary could not choose to assert beneficial ownership over the asset in proportion to the amount of trust monies, Lord Millett suggested:

In my view the time has come to state unequivocally that English law has no such rule. It conflicts with the rule that a trustee must not benefit from his trust. I agree...that the beneficiary's right to elect to have a proportionate share of a mixed substitution necessarily follows once one accepts, as English law does, (i) that a claimant can trace in equity into a mixed fund and (ii) that he can trace unmixed money into its proceeds and assert ownership of the proceeds. Accordingly, I would state the basic rule as follows. *Where a trustee wrongfully uses trust money to provide part of the cost of acquiring an asset, the beneficiary is entitled at his* option *either to claim a proportionate share of the asset or to enforce a lien upon it to secure his personal claim against the trustee for the amount of the misapplied money* [our emphasis]. It does not matter whether the trustee mixed the trust money with his own in a single fund before using it to acquire the asset, or made separate payments (whether simultaneously or sequentially) out of the differently owned funds to acquire a single asset.

19.6.3.4 *Apportionment amongst competing innocent claims to mixed funds*

While there are justifications for preventing trustees profiting from wrongdoing, there will also be a number of claims in cases where trust property has wrongfully been mixed with that belonging to others, all of whom one innocent, rather than that of the trustee. Some will be more easy to resolve than others, and particularly difficult issues are raised where there is in fact more than one innocent claimant. Within this there is a further additional likely reality—that the amounts which are available are not going to be sufficient to satisfy all claims which are made against the fund in question. This can be seen in cases such as *Re Diplock*, where the volunteer charities were innocent and they were not in any way apparently less deserving than the next of kin seeking to trace money paid out in breach of trust. Thus the volunteers in *Diplock* were treated just like any other innocent claimant to a share in a mixed fund. As a result this case is regarded as authority that an innocent volunteer's duty of conscience is regarded as akin to that of a person having an equitable interest in a mixed fund towards the other equitable owners. Thus, where Diplock money was used to purchase stocks, where the charity already had similar stocks, the charity ranked *pari passu* with the next of kin (i.e. in proportion to the amount each has contributed to the amalgam). This is clearly the fairest method of apportionment in such a case, but there are others.

19.6.3.5 *The rule in Clayton's case*
Mixing and current bank accounts

For current bank accounts, however, the Court of Appeal in *Diplock* applied the rule developed in *Clayton's case* (1816) 1 Mer 572, which enshrines the principle of 'first in, first out': the first payment in is appropriated to satisfy the earliest debt. The basis of the rule is said to be the presumed intention of the person operating the account. A preferable solution, in the opinion of the authors of the Report of the Review Committee on Insolvency Law and Practice (Cork Report 1982, Cmnd 8558), paras 1076–80, would be to divide the mixed fund rateably (i.e. in *pari passu*). However, in *Barlow Clowes International Ltd* v *Vaughan* [1992] 4 All ER 22, noted [1993] Conv 370, the Court of Appeal held that *Clayton's case* normally applied, the court being bound by the *ratio* of *Diplock*. Actually, in *Barlow Clowes* itself, the presumption in *Clayton's case* was rebutted, but it would normally be very difficult to operate *pari passu* distribution with a running bank account, because *pari passu* distribution assumes a starting date for the fund (otherwise how can you determine how much each has contributed to the amalgam?).

19.6.3.6 *Dissatisfaction with Clayton's case and an entreaty to the House of Lords*

However, notwithstanding, it is clear from at least two judgments in *Barlow Clowes* that judicial support for the rule in *Clayton's case* is not altogether unequivocal. While Clayton's presumed authority was not being denied, Leggatt LJ offered that 'During the 175 years since the rule in *Clayton's case* was devised, neither its acclaim nor its application has been universal.' Even Woolf LJ's insistence that the rule was 'settled law' was unenthusiastic, claiming that this was so 'short of [intervention from] the House of Lords'. In the *Denning Law Journal* (1997, pp. 43–62), Lowrie and Todd argued that rather than being a restatement of the supremacy of the rule in *Clayton's case*, *Barlow Clowes* instead amounted to a strong entreaty to the House of Lords to consider the rule and its continuing application in the law.

This article considers the operation both of the rule in *Clayton's case* and *pari passu* methods of distribution in some depth, and did so at least in part of our larger articulation of the appropriateness of the adoption by the English courts of the so-called North American rolling charge (NARC). Just by way of background, the NARC works not by looking at the time at which contributions were made, but instead at the relationship which contributions bear to one another at the moment before a withdrawal takes place. In the words of Woolf LJ again in *Barlow Clowes* the NARC:

involves treating credits to a bank account made at different times and from different sources as a blend or cocktail with the result that when a withdrawal is made from the account it is treated as a withdrawal in the same proportions as the different interests in the account (here the investors) bear to each other at the moment before the withdrawal is made.

The 1997 *Denning Law Journal* article considered the relative strengths and weaknesses of *pari passu* and *Clayton* alike through use of examples which illustrated both dissipations and investments. This was done alongside detailed accounts of how and in what ways adoption by the English courts of the NARC might transcend current difficulties, offering a brief description of the charge, its judicial basis, and its justifications in principle. The article contends the NARC has a number of advantages, and will normally amount to the fairest method of distribution. Perhaps its greatest virtue, and one which arises from its consideration of the relationship existing between all contributions immediately prior to all withdrawals, is that it ensures that pre-existing property rights are never disturbed by subsequent transactions. Here later payments do not diminish existing interests in the remaining fund, nor will they obtain the advantage of earlier investments, and there is no distortion of existing beneficial interests in property purchased using proceeds from the fund. It points to the way in which the Canadian case *Re Ontario Securities Commission v Greymac Credit Corporation* (1986) 55 OR (2d) 673 is important authority in favour of the NARC, and it has features which suggest it would work in the context of English law: significantly, for example, that it does not interfere with prior property interests. On a practical level, in a number of situations it will adopt a middle approach (between that arising from use of *Clayton* and *pari passu* distribution) and outcome. However, the piece also suggests that in practice it will seldom be any party's preferred option (and notes that it will never be the cheapest method of distribution).

Most recently, *Foskett* v *McKowen* is now authority in favour of *pari passu* distribution reflecting the beneficiaries' proprietary interest in the fund, on the basis of a *pro rata* entitlement: this is clear in the passages from the judgment which accompany a brief narrative of *Foskett* immediately below, which acts as a summary for the considerable significance of the case in the modern law.

19.7 *Foskett* v *McKowen* and a 'new type' of tracing?

Tracing has traditionally been regarded as a proprietary remedy, which works on allowing the pursuer (and in equitable tracing the beneficiary) to proceed against a particular asset which is in the hands of the defendant. However, as part of the huge reconsideration of the whole remedies question, there is a body of opinion gaining considerable strength which is linking tracing most appropriately to an exercise in identification. The central case law here is *Boscawen* v *Bajwa* [1996] 1 WLR 328, and particularly *Foskett* v *McKeown*. The latter case is a very important pointer of key directions and developments which are most likely in the area of remedies, and of particular relevance here is Lord Millett's consideration of the nature of tracing.

The case arose from trust funds which had been collected in respect of holiday properties in the Algarve, and which were used by the trustee to pay some of the premiums on a life policy which had been executed in favour of his wife and children. When the trustee committed suicide, the beneficiaries (also referred to as the purchasers) of the trust fund claimed that they were entitled to a proportionate share of the proceeds of the policy which were paid at the time of the suicide. In 1998, this case reached the Court of Appeal, and in a majority decision the beneficiaries were held only to be entitled to a charge on the proceeds to secure their restitutionary claim for the value of their money that went to pay the premiums. However, in May 2000 in the House of Lords ([2000] 2 WLR 1299) it was held that the beneficiaries under the trust were entitled to trace in equity into the policy proceeds, and to do so in proportion to their contributions to the premium payments. Indeed, it was held that the beneficiaries' claim was simply an assertion of an equitable proprietary interest arising from the mixing of the value of the premiums with the value of the policy, which was analogous with the mixing of moneys in a bank account. It followed thus that the beneficiaries were entitled to a *pro rata* share of the policy moneys.

Whilst the majority view was that this was a vindication of the beneficiaries' proprietary interest in the fund, and their entitlement to a *pro rata* share, Lord Hope of Craighill and Lord Steyn dissented. The minority concurred with the Court of Appeal majority view which was founded on the basis of opinion that such a misapplication of trust moneys (to pay for insurance policy premiums) did not entitle the purchaser beneficiaries (not to be confused with the named beneficiaries under the deceased man's life policy) to a *pro rata* share in the property. It was suggested instead that this situation was more akin to use by a trustee of moneys held on trust for maintenance of his own property (thus invoking the principle that a trustee cannot profit from his own breach of trust) rather than mixing money in bank accounts. This was discussed at length in the Court of Appeal by Sir Richard Scott V-C, and the essence of his reasoning was that it followed that unless it could be demonstrated that he obtained a profit as a result of the expenditure, a trustee's liability to repay extended only to the money misapplied, thus invoking *Re Tilley's WT* principles. Here, the purchasers would be entitled to no more than the return of their contributions plus interest.

There have been many references to *Foskett* v *McKeown* at different points in this discussion of tracing in equity up to now. What happens now is that references to the case are directed towards the considerable time which was spent in the House of Lords considering the very nature of tracing. Given that Lord Millett's views are likely to be highly influential, it is worth taking some time here to consider what was being said about tracing and its general nature.

Most importantly Lord Millett talks about the appropriateness of tracing's alignment with the traditional concept of 'following' property, and insists that:

> The claimant claims the new asset because it was acquired in whole or in part with the original asset. What he traces is therefore not the physical asset itself but the value inherent in it. Tracing is thus neither a claim nor a remedy. It is merely the process by which a claimant demonstrates what has happened to his property, identifies its proceeds in the persons who handled or received them and justifies his claim that the proceeds can properly be regarded as representing his property. Tracing is also distinct from claiming. It identifies the traceable proceeds of the claimant's property. It enables the claimant to substitute the traceable proceeds for the original asset as the subject matter of his claim but it does not affect or establish his claim. That will depend on a number of factors including the nature of his interest in the original asset. He will normally be able to maintain the same claim to the substantial asset as he could have maintained to the original asset.

What this is suggesting is that tracing is a process of identification of property, and is a process rather than a claim or even a remedy. There are a number of implications for this analysis, the most significant of which is clearly that if this rationale is accepted, then the traditional distinction between equitable and common law tracing becomes moribund. Realization of this and recognition of its significance can be seen explained in the parts of Lord Millett's judgment in *Foskett* which point to powerful arguments that there is no need for two distinctive regimes of tracing, and indeed that injustices can arise from the current pursuers which are attached to tracing in equity. According to Lord Millett:

> There is no sense in maintaining different rules for tracing at law and in equity. One set of tracing rules is enough...There is certainly no logical justification for allowing any distinction between them to produce capricious results in cases of mixed substitutions by insisting on the existence of a fiduciary relationship as a pre-condition for applying equity's tracing rule.

Although earlier introductions to tracing explained it as a mechanism for 'following' property, and while Lord Millett in *Foskett* v *McKeown* noted that both common law and equitable rules are 'exercises in locating assets which are, or may be taken to represent, an asset belonging to the plaintiffs and to which they assert ownership', his judgment added yet further weight to his insistence that tracing is best considered as a process of *identification*. This is of course the identification of property. Significantly this judgment suggested that there were actually important distinctions to be recognised between tracing and following (with emphasis added):

The processes of tracing and following are, however, distinct. *Following* is a process of *following the same asset as it moves* from hand to hand. Tracing is a *process of identifying* a new asset as a substitute for the old. Where one asset is exchanged for another, a claimant can elect whether to follow the original asset into the hands of the new owner or to trace its value into the new asset in the hands of the same owner.

19.8 Constructive trusteeship and the liability of strangers to a trust following breach of trust

The introduction to this discussion on the liability of strangers for breach of trust has in many respects already been made in the materials introducing tracing and constructive trusteeship. What is fundamentally to be understood for this part of the chapter, and indeed for any discussion of the liability of 'strangers' to a trust where breach of trust occurs and trust property 'goes missing' is that a trustee who acts in breach of trust will often not act alone. If necessary, it might be a good idea to return briefly to the discussion of breach of trust in the previous chapter, to be reminded of the kind of conduct which is treated as amounting to breach of trust. The liability of 'strangers' to a trust for its breach acknowledges that those other than the original trustee acting in breach can incur liability where this happens.

And in making the connection of this with 'constructive trusteeship' what must now be noted is the way in which persons other than those who have been appointed as trustees can nevertheless find themselves constituted as trustees if they interfere with the funds of a trust, or otherwise with its administration. At this level this might appear simple enough, and even to be a sensible approach to accommodating the realities—and indeed the complexities—of the way in which trusts law seeks to protect the interests of beneficial owners of property. However, this is actually a highly complex area of activity, and one which has been very dynamic in recent times. This makes it very difficult to set out a comprehensive 'map' of stranger liability, let alone to make a definite statement about the state of the law.

Because of these difficulties, it is probably best to commence by setting out traditional approaches to the difficulties created when those other than holders of legal title to trust property are in some way drawn into a breach of trust where trust property is misapplied. Traditionally, the liability of strangers to a trust has been divided into two categories: 'knowing assistance' and 'knowing receipt' (with the latter often including reference to 'dealing'). *Barnes* v *Addy* (1874) 9 Ch App 244 is authority for this traditional approach while the important Privy Council decision of *Royal Brunei Airlines* v *Tan* [1995] 3 WLR 64 suggested that a more accurate way to characterise the former category would be as the liability of an accessory to a trustee's breach of trust. This was followed by the majority in *Twinsectra Ltd* v *Yardley* [2002] 2 WLR 802 and it will become apparent that the term 'dishonest assistance' is now widely employed, but a strong equation of the traditional terminology with the new appears to be continuing, as evident in *Adnan Shaaban*

Abou-Rahmah v *Al-Haji Abdul Kadir Abacha* [2006] EWCA Civ 1492. It will also become apparent that more recent approaches to 'knowing receipt' are increasingly including the descriptor of 'recipient liability'.

19.8.1 The traditional framework for analysing 'stranger liability' for breach of trust

The paragraph above drawing attention to the language which has been central to the traditional analysis of stranger liability provides the first clue to understanding *how* strangers can incur liability for breach of trust. This is because this species of liability does not arise automatically from the circumstances (of receiving property which is being applied in breach of trust, or assisting a breach), and it is liability which instead arises from a party in some way appreciating or 'knowing' that this is being committed.

This raises questions of *what* precisely must be known, or *how much* must be known for liability to arise. The traditional 'starting point' for this has been the case *Baden Delvaux* [1983] BCLC 325 (more recently reported at [1992] 4 All ER 161) which identified five categories of knowledge. According to the so-called *Baden Delvaux* classification, there are five 'degrees' of knowledge which can be classified accordingly as:

(i) actual knowledge

(ii) wilfully shutting one's eyes to the obvious

(iii) wilfully and recklessly failing to make such inquiries as an honest and reasonable person would make

(iv) knowledge of circumstances which would indicate the facts to an honest and reasonable person and

(v) knowledge of circumstances which would put an honest and reasonable person on inquiry.

We will now discuss current approaches to both species of stranger liability, but first we will explain how these classifications of knowledge have traditionally been mapped on to liability for what will now be referred to respectively as 'accessory liability' and 'recipient liability'.

For liability which has traditionally been termed 'knowing assistance' a number of key cases—notably *Belmont Finance Corporation* v *Williams Furniture Ltd (No.1)* [1979] Ch 250—have indicated a relatively strict requirement for 'actual knowledge', which has appeared to embrace *Baden Delvaux* categories (i), (ii), and (iii). Others, including *Agip (Africa) Ltd* v *Jackson* [1991] 3 WLR 116 (CA), have suggested a different approach whereby a defendant can be found liable by virtue of having either 'actual knowledge' or 'constructive knowledge', ensuring that any of the *Baden Delvaux* categories are capable of giving rise to such liability.

As the materials in chapter 7 referenced briefly, the case of *Royal Brunei Airlines* v *Tan* [1995] marked the arrival of a new approach. Here the Privy Council suggested that the correct test was not one of knowledge but one of dishonesty; and this test was followed in *Houghton* v *Fayers* (*The Times* 9 February 2000) and *Al-Sabah* v *Grupo Torras* (unreported 2 November 2000). This has signalled movement away from the *Baden Delvaux* tests, and much remains to be considered in terms of current approaches and their implications, which will follow shortly.

The position of even traditional approaches for liability termed 'knowing receipt' has been far less certain. While some authorities have suggested that constructive knowledge or constructive notice will suffice (respectively *Belmont Finance Corporation Ltd* v *Williams Furniture Ltd (No.2)* [1980] 1 All ER 393 and *Agip (Africa) Ltd* v *Jackson* [1990] Ch 265), others have suggested that this is not sufficient, but without being very clear on the point, with a number of cases—notably *Eagle Trust plc* v *SBC Securities Ltd* [1993] 1 WLR 484 and *Polly Peck International plc* v *Nadir (No.2)* [1992] 4 All ER 769—suggesting that this is especially problematic in the context of commercial dealings. It will become apparent that—unlike in the case of accessory liability—this uncertainty has not altogether been resolved for recipients of trust property.

19.8.2 Current approaches to stranger liability arising for those who assist a breach of trust

In terms of linking liability for assisting a breach of trust with constructive trusteeship, it was suggested earlier that where a stranger *receives* trust property and *retains* it, that the beneficiary has a proprietary claim against a person who has become constituted a constructive trustee by virtue of receiving misapplied trust property. This claim is of course lost and becomes a personal one if the property leaves the hand of the constructive trustee. But in the case of the person who *assists* a breach of trust, without receiving trust property, constructive trusteeship works differently. Earlier it was noted that in the case of accessory liability, although this is sometimes said to give rise to a constructive trust, there is no proprietary claim as the accessory has not received any of the beneficiary's property. The liability of an accessory to a breach of trust is always a personal liability to account for the loss suffered by the trust.

The purpose of our discussion now is to build on what was said above in relation to what is required for constructive trusteeship of this nature to arise. This builds on earlier reference to the way in which this liability will not arise automatically where a trustee is assisted in his breach, and a 'state of mind' that must exist for a stranger to be liable as an accessory to a breach of trust. We have said that this 'state of mind' had traditionally been attached to degrees of knowledge required for liability to arise, but that *Royal Brunei Airlines* v *Tan* had marked the arrival of a new approach which would relate to whether or not the stranger had acted dishonestly in assisting a trustee's breach of trust—hence the appearance of the language of 'dishonest assistance'. We now examine the movement away from knowledge (as classified by *Baden Delvaux*), looking at the nature of these developments, their chronology, and also their implications.

In the early days following *Royal Brunei Airlines* v *Tan*, its approach was followed in 2000 in *Houghton* v *Fayers* and *Al-Sabah* v *Grupo Torras*. This approach was premised on how for determining accessory liability it was necessary to ascertain the state of mind of the third party, rather than the trustee, because otherwise it would be too easy for an unscrupulous third party to take advantage of an initial breach of trust which (as the materials in the previous chapter explain) is capable of occurring innocently. Indeed, it might even be the third party who actually procures the breach of trust on the part of the trustee. In focusing on the motivations of the third party, honesty was to be judged objectively. It was further made clear that acting dishonestly (or with a lack of probity, which was synonymous) meant not acting as an honest person would have acted in the circumstances and could usually be equated with conscious impropriety. However, it would also be the case that a third party might be considered to have acted dishonestly if he recklessly disregarded the rights of others. The conduct of the third party was to be assessed on the basis of his actual knowledge at the time, not on the basis of what a reasonable person would have known or appreciated. However, regard would be had to the third party's personal attributes, such as his experience, intelligence, and reason for so acting. In *Al-Sabah* v *Grupo Torras* 'blind eye' dishonesty rendered the defendant liable.

The issue was considered again by the House of Lords in *Twinsectra Ltd* v *Yardley* [2002] 2 WLR 802, which has already had some extensive consideration in respect of *Quistclose* trusts. We now embark on a detailed consideration of how it appeared to affect the position of accessory liability in the wake of the acknowledged high watermark provided by *Royal Brunei Airlines*.

The case involved two solicitors and a loan transaction, and raised questions as to the status of the loan transaction: was it subject to a (*Quistclose*) trust or otherwise? The existence or otherwise of a *Quistclose* trust hinged on whether or not the (second) solicitor, Sims, held the loan subject to a trust (arising from its mandated application towards a purpose specified by the lender, through his instructions), and the question of accessorial liability involved the other (first) solicitor, Leach. This followed the way in which the loan was in the event not applied in accordance with the lender's instructions, and then was not repaid. Twinsectra sued three parties: the two solicitors and the client Yardley. Sims was sued because his release of the money to the client amounted to breach of trust. The money was released to the client through Leach, and it was alleged that Leach's failure to take any steps to ensure the correct application of the money amounted to dishonest assistance of a breach of trust: this occurred when Leach paid out the money in contravention of the lender's instructions, acting on Yardley's behalf.

In respect of liability as an accessory, it was found at first instance that the first solicitor had not been dishonest although he had deliberately shut his eyes to the implications of the undertaking. The Court of Appeal reversed this finding and gave judgment against Leach for the proportion of the loan which had not been applied in the acquisition of property. The House of Lords' consideration arose following an appeal by Leach, whether or not he had assisted in the breach of trust which had been committed by Sims (the Court of Appeal finding that the loan was subject to a trust was upheld on *Quistclose* principles) and could incur personal liability on account of doing so.

Following the decision in *Royal Brunei Airlines* v *Tan*, the liability of a stranger to a trust who assists its breach (as distinct from being a recipient of trust property) is now referred to as 'accessory liability' rather than 'knowing assistance'. This revision of terminology appears to be very welcome to commentators (e.g., Thompson [2002] Conv 387), and it does appear to address a number of difficulties evident in the law prior to *Royal Brunei Airlines* v *Tan*. Given that *Royal Brunei Airlines* v *Tan* had swept away the requirement of an initial fraudulent breach of trust, *Twinsectra* provided the opportunity to consider what new accessory-focused basis might be applied in order for personal liability as an accessory to a breach of trust to be incurred. The House of Lords focused this new vein of enquiry on the presence or otherwise of dishonesty in the assistant's actions, and the imposition of liability accordingly. However, actually finding a meaning to be given to dishonesty which would be appropriate for this species of liability was a complex and divisive exercise for their Lordships.

In considering what meaning might appropriately be given to the term 'dishonesty' in this context, it was held that for an accessory to be liable (1) he had to have acted dishonestly by the ordinary standards of reasonable and honest people *and* (2) have himself been aware that by those standards he was acting dishonestly.

19.8.2.1 *Accessory liability and three approaches to dishonesty*

In considering what meaning might appropriately be given to the term 'dishonesty' in this context, greatest issue was taken with whether the test should be objective or a combination of objective and subjective elements. As Lord Hutton's judgment makes clear, a completely subjective approach to dishonesty—the 'Robin Hood' test (whereby a person is only regarded as dishonest if he transgresses his own standard of honesty, even if that standard is contrary to that of reasonable and honest people)—is not accepted in the courts. The difference between an objective test and one which combines objective/subjective criteria was explained as follows. The former will involve the court determining that the defendant's conduct is dishonest as judged against the 'ordinary standards of reasonable and honest people, even if he does not realise this', while the latter makes reference to the defendant *himself* within a broad setting of objectivity. This latter combination test rests on whether the defendant's conduct was dishonest by the ordinary standards of reasonable and honest people, and that he *himself* realised that by those standards his conduct was dishonest. The majority appeared to prefer the combination test, with Lord Millett dissenting in favour of an objective test.

What is extremely interesting about this refocusing of accessorial liability on the honesty (or lack of honesty) of the potential accessory is the way in which, by extensive reference to Lord Nicholls' judgment in *Royal Brunei Airlines* v *Tan*, Lord Hutton concluded that the test for accessory liability was substantially the same as the test in criminal law for dishonesty, as laid down in *R* v *Ghosh* [1982] QB 1053. Indeed, in *Royal Brunei Airlines* itself, Lord Nicholls explained how the law determines dishonesty with reference to standards which are objective, but will assess the defendant's position in light of this by reference to what he actually knew, and not what a reasonable person would have known, having regard to his experiences and intelligence and reasons for acting in the way he did:

Whatever may be the position in some criminal or other contexts...in the context of the accessory liability principle acting dishonestly, or with lack of probity, which is synonymous, means simply not acting as an honest person would in the circumstances. This is an objective standard.

But, notwithstanding this, Lord Nicholls continued that:

Ultimately, in most cases, an honest person should have little difficulty in knowing whether a proposed transaction, or his participation in it, would offend the normally accepted standards of honest conduct. Likewise, when called upon to decide whether a person was acting honestly, a court will look at all the circumstances known to the third party at the time. The court will also have regard to personal attributes of the third party, such as his experience and intelligence, and the reason why he acted as he did.

From the application of this proposition by the majority of the House of Lords, the outcome of *Twinsectra* appeared to be that incurring liability as an accessory to a breach of trust required the defendant to have acted dishonestly by the ordinary standards of reasonable and honest people, and have been himself aware that by those standards he was acting dishonestly. In this vein, the judgment of Lord Hutton explained that:

> There is, in my opinion, a further consideration which supports the view that for liability as an accessory to arise the defendant must himself appreciate that what he was doing was dishonest by the standards of honest and reasonable men. A finding by a judge that a defendant has been dishonest is a grave finding, and it is particularly grave against a professional man, such as a solicitor. Notwithstanding that the issue arises in equity law and not in a criminal context, I think that it would be less than just for the law to permit a finding that a defendant had been 'dishonest' in assisting in a breach of trust where he knew of the facts which created the trust and its breach but had not been aware that what he was doing would be regarded by honest men as being dishonest.
>
> It would be open to your Lordships to depart from the principle stated by Lord Nicholls that dishonesty is a necessary ingredient of accessory liability and to hold that knowledge is a sufficient ingredient. But the statement of that principle by Lord Nicholls has been widely regarded as clarifying this area of the law and, as he observed, the tide of authority in England has flowed strongly in favour of the test of dishonesty. Therefore I consider that the courts should continue to apply that test and that your Lordships should state that dishonesty requires knowledge by the defendant that what he was doing would be regarded as dishonest by honest people.

This was of course a direct reference to Lord Hutton's understanding that *Royal Brunei Airlines* is widely considered the leading case on accessory liability, and one which is regarded as providing the law in this area with important (and much-needed) clarity. In making these observations, Lord Hutton attached much import to the defendant's awareness that his conduct would be regarded as dishonest by ordinary standards. However, his *Twinsectra* judgment also shows—rather incongruously—Lord Hutton being concerned that the *Royal Brunei Airlines* position should not allow a defendant to escape 'a finding of dishonesty because he sets his own standards of honesty and does not regard as dishonest what he knows would offend the normally accepted standards of honest conduct'. This reasoning was one of the concerns which is evident in Lord Millett's dissenting judgments.

19.8.2.2 *Accessory liability flowing from Twinsectra, and Lord Millett's dissent*

Lord Hoffmann's concurrence with Lord Hutton was manifested in his view that dishonesty requires a dishonest state of mind which amounts to 'consciousness that one is transgressing ordinary standards of honest behaviour', and that wrongful conduct of this species requires more than mere 'knowledge of the facts'.

Lord Millett disagreed with this assessment. In his view, the appropriate approach to accessory liability should be formulated around the defendant's awareness that he was doing something he should not have been doing (rather than his perception of whether this was 'honest' or otherwise). He did not approve of the use of a criminal standard in the context of liability arising under the civil law. Lord Millett argued that the civil law was not concerned with whether the defendant has a 'guilty mind' (the *mens rea* in criminal law), and the issue was instead one of whether the conduct should be regarded as dishonest because the defendant knew (or ought to have been aware) that it was something he was not supposed to be doing. According to Lord Millett, the combination test found in criminal law:

[i]s not generally an appropriate condition of civil liability, which does not ordinarily require a guilty mind. Civil liability is usually predicated on the defendant's conduct rather than his state of mind; it results from his negligent or unreasonable behaviour or, where this is not sufficient, from intentional wrongdoing.

And furthermore (in Lord Millett's view) the law itself (in the form of *Royal Brunei Airlines* v *Tan*) appeared actually to reject this highly inappropriate position:

A dishonest state of mind might logically have been required when it was thought that the accessory was liable only if the principal was guilty of a fraudulent breach of trust, for then the claim could have been regarded as the equitable counterpart of the common law conspiracy to defraud. But this requirement was discarded in *Royal Brunei Airlines Sdn Bhd* v *Tan* [1995] 2 AC 378.

Lord Millett's view was that liability as an accessory to a breach of trust does not depend upon dishonesty in the normal sense of that expression. It is sufficient that the defendant knew all the facts which made it wrongful for him to participate in the way in which he did. Indeed, His Lordship contended that the only subjective elements allowed by *Royal Brunei Airlines* were the defendant's experience, his intelligence, and actual state of knowledge, and there was no requirement that he must have realised he was acting dishonestly.

Lord Millett's preferred test was an objective one, in which liability was not dependent upon the defendant's appreciation that he was acting dishonestly, or even his detailed knowledge about the details of the trust and its breach:

The question here is whether it is sufficient that the accessory should have actual knowledge of the facts which created the trust, or must he also have appreciated that they did so? It is obviously not necessary that he should know the details of the trust or the identity of the beneficiary. It is sufficient that he knows that the money is not at the free disposal of the principal. In some circumstances it may not even be necessary that his knowledge should extend this far. It may be sufficient that he knows that he is assisting in a dishonest scheme.

Lord Hoffmann's view of Lord Millett's judgment was that it was not open for the House to concur with a view other than that 'consciousness that one is transgressing ordinary standards of honest behaviour' was required for conduct to be wrongful and capable of incurring liability. In this vein, the previous edition of this text concluded that majority support for a combination objective/subjective test—which requires that conduct is dishonest by ordinary standards and that the defendant realised that by those standards his conduct was dishonest in order to incur liability—must be considered authoritative. This was so notwithstanding that it was in many respects difficult to square with the spirit and intendment of *Royal Brunei Airlines* v *Tan*, which sought to liberalise accessory liability by transferring focus away from the trustee (and whether his initial breach of trust was dishonest or not) and placing it firmly upon the accessory himself. In this vein it was asked whether the very welcome decision in *Royal Brunei Airlines* would be able to achieve its full potential in the sphere of accessory liability in the wake of *Twinsectra*.

Predictably, following *Twinsectra*, suggestions were made in some quarters that the position it appeared to adopt—in what had to be present for accessory liability to be incurred—was too 'pro defendant' (see Ryan (2006) 70 Conv, 188). However, *Twinsectra* itself must now be considered in light of the recent decision of the Privy Council in *Barlow Clowes International Ltd (in liquidation)* v *Eurotrust International Ltd* [2006] 1 All ER 333, and developments beyond this still.

19.8.2.3 After Twinsectra v Yardley: accessory liability in the wake of Barlow Clowes International Ltd (in liquidation) v Eurotrust International

This case has very important implications for the discussion which has just taken place, which suggested that the majority in *Twinsectra Ltd* v *Yardley* appeared to attach '*Royal Brunei species*' of dishonesty to an individual's awareness that what he was doing would be regarded as dishonest by ordinary standards, to determine whether liability for assisting a breach of trust can be incurred.

The background to the decision in *Barlow Clowes* can be gleaned from earlier references to it in this chapter (and also to its discussion in Lowrie and Todd [1997] *Denning Law Journal*), which explain how during the 1980s a fraudulent scheme which purported to offer high returns on UK gilt-edged securities was run by Clowes, and operated through a company called Barlow Clowes International. Thereafter, it was into Isle of Man-based bank accounts maintained by Eurotrust International that investors' funds were paid during 1987. The three defendants in this action were Eurotrust International itself and also two principal directors, and in the High Court of the Isle of Man, Barlow Clowes International claimed that the two defendants and, through them, Eurotrust International had dishonestly assisted Clowes and an associate in misappropriating investors' funds.

The High Court found all three defendants liable for dishonest assistance, and all three appealed, whereupon the appeals of the first and third defendant (the company and one principal director respectively) were dismissed. However, the appeal of the second defendant—Henwood—was allowed, on account that it was not supported by evidence. It was at this point that Barlow Clowes International appealed to the Privy Council.

Originally, in the High Court of the Isle of Man, it had been found that Henwood could incur liability for dishonestly assisting the misappropriation of sums paid into bank accounts during 1987. This was on the basis that the Court had found that the defendant had strongly suspected that the funds passing through his hands were funds received by Barlow Clowes International from members of the public believing they were making gilt-edged securities investments. With these suspicions it was found that no honest person could have assisted the subsequent disposal of the assets for the personal use of Clowes and his associate. In respect of this defendant, it was found that his decision not to make enquiries amounted to a conscious strategy to avoid running the risk that he would encounter the truth.

On appeal to the Privy Council, counsel for Henwood argued that on *Twinsectra* principles, the defendant's state of mind was not dishonest unless he was aware that by ordinary standards it would be regarded as dishonest: it was only in such circumstances that he could be said to be 'consciously dishonest' (as emphasised by Lord Hoffmann). Counsel argued that in the original ruling, finding was made only to the way in which by normal standards he had been dishonest, and that his own standard was different. It was thus agued that because there had been no finding about Henwood's understandings of normal standards of honesty, the High Court's findings in respect of Henwood did not satisfy the *Royal Brunei Airlines* test for dishonesty as this appeared in light of *Twinsectra*.

19.8.2.4 *The Privy Council and reappraisal of Twinsectra*

The Privy Council was unanimous in its rejection of the defendant's argument, and upheld the original findings in respect of Henwood. What is significant is the way in which the Judicial Committee reflected on the majority approach in *Twinsectra*, which had been relied upon by the defendant's counsel. Especially significantly in light of the nature of these reflections, this Judicial Committee included Lords Nicholls and Hoffmann.

The Privy Council's judgment was delivered by Lord Hoffmann, who sought to clarify the position of dishonesty under *Royal Brunei Airlines* in light of the apparent effect of *Twinsectra*. Especially, His Lordship sought to clarify that in *Twinsectra* in 2002 the House of Lords did not seek to alter or refine the *Royal Brunei Airlines* test, and their Lordships accepted that:

There is an element of ambiguity in these remarks which may have encouraged a belief, expressed in academic writing, that *Twinsectra* had departed from the law as previously understood and invited inquiry not merely into the defendant's mental state about the nature of the transaction in which he was participating but also into his views about generally acceptable standards of honesty.

Indicating that this was not the intended import of Lord Hutton's judgment, Lord Hoffmann continued by explaining that:

The reference to 'what he knows would offend normally acceptable standards of honest conduct' meant only that his knowledge of the transaction had to be such as to render his participation contrary to normally acceptable standards of honest conduct. It did not require that he should have had reflections about what those normally acceptable standards were.

In the course of proposing that the Privy Council has 'restored what appears to be the better interpretation of the *Royal Brunei* test' and has thus also 'clarified' *Twinsectra*, Desmond Ryan (in (2006) above) suggests that Lord Hoffmann's allusion to 'an element of ambiguity' which might have been created by *Twinsectra* is rather an understatement. It is difficult not to agree with this, or with his observation that *Barlow Clowes'* reading of *Twinsectra* is not 'a particularly obvious interpretation' of the implication that the defendant should know his actions 'would offend normally accepted standards of honest conduct'. In this vein, it is our view that it certainly is not the most obvious reading of it. Indeed, Ryan also points to the Court of Appeal decision in *Harrison v Teton Valley Trading Company* [2004] 1 WLR to propose that interpretations of *Twinsectra*, which Lord Hoffmann suggests were not intended, are not even confined to academic opinion, and have been adopted by judges.

The way in which this appears more as a retreat from the House of Lords' 2002 direction becomes difficult to avoid from examining Lord Hoffmann's reflections in *Barlow Clowes* of his own judgment in *Twinsectra*, in which he proposed that a dishonest state of mind required 'consciousness that one is transgressing ordinary standards of honest behaviour'. In *Barlow Clowes*, his Lordship explained that this was to denote the significance of 'consciousness of those elements of the transaction which make participation transgress ordinary standards of honest behaviour. It does not also require him to have thought about what those standards were.'

In this decision the Privy Council clarified that it is 'consciousness of the elements of transaction' which make participation in it transgressory, and this does not require the defendant to be aware at the material time that a trust was being breached, or even that it actually existed, and that suspicion that this might be the case was sufficient.

It was suggested at the time that *Barlow Clowes'* confirmation that for accessory liability to arise a dishonest state of mind was required was somewhat different from how things appeared from *Twinsectra*. Indeed, although the *Barlow Clowes* mental state is a subjective one (based on factors such as knowledge, or in absence of knowledge suspicion, which leads to deliberate failure to make enquiries which might reveal the truth; along with intelligence and reasons for the defendant's conduct), the standards by which the law determines *whether* a state of mind is actually dishonest is that of 'ordinary standards of honesty'. According to this approach, it was not relevant that a defendant ascribed to a different moral code, or that he was unaware that by ordinary standards that his conduct would be considered dishonest. The decision appeared to be welcome clarification of *Royal Brunei Airlines* and a welcome reappraisal of the very severe limitations for accessory liability potentially flowing from adopting the position that the defendant must know his actions 'would offend normally accepted standards of honest conduct', but it also appeared to be a considerable retreat from *Twinsectra* without very much acknowledgement of this from Their Lordships. However, as Desmond Ryan (in (2006) above) suggests, while there is a very attractive simplicity in Lord Nicholls' *Royal Brunei Airlines* proposition that '[i]n most situations there is little difficulty in identifying how an honest person would behave', a consideration of both *Twinsectra* and *Barlow Clowes* provided a salutary reminder of the 'formidable difficulties' confronting judges who must *apply* the test.

In turn, more recent case law provides a salutary reminder of the way in which it can very quickly become apparent that decisions which appear to clarify the law do not in fact do so. This is because just over a year after *Barlow Clowes* the issue came to the fore again in the Court of Appeal in *Adnan Shaaban Abou-Rahmah* v *Al-Haji Abdul Kadir Abacha* [2006] EWCA Civ 1492. And while two Lord Justices of Appeal (Rix and Pill LJJ) both took the view that the case could be determined without engaging with the controversies left open by *Barlow Clowes'* implications for *Twinsectra*, Arden LJ enthusiastically engaged with the case as the first opportunity for the Appellate Court to engage with *Barlow Clowes*. It was her view that *Barlow Clowes* should be followed, but she has also surely ensured that the controversies with continue on account of suggesting that 'the *Barlow Clowes* decision does not involve a departure from, or refusal to follow, the *Twinsectra* case'. Her view was that *Barlow Clowes* gives guidance as to the proper interpretation to be placed on it as a matter of English law, showing how 'the *Royal Brunei* case and the *Twinsectra* case can be read together to form a consistent corpus of law'.

Arden LJ's reading of the cases was that the widely held interpretation that *Twinsectra Ltd* v *Yardley* required both an objective and subjective test was a wrong interpretation, with the accurate position being clarified in *Barlow Clowes*. According to Arden LJ it was not a requirement of the standard of dishonesty that the defendant should be conscious of his wrongdoing, and that instead the test was 'predominantly objective' but with subjective aspects. On this reasoning the position was that taken by Lord Nicholls in *Royal Brunei v Tan*, with an assessment (of dishonesty) being made on the basis of what the defendant actually knew at the time (thus accounting for the *subjective* elements) rather than what a reasonable person would have known or appreciated. On the facts it was found that although a bank manager had a general suspicion that two individuals might possibly be involved in money-laundering, he did not have any particular suspicions about the two transactions which were being litigated. This meant that the judge at first instance was correct in finding that this did not amount to dishonesty.

19.8.3 Current approaches to stranger liability for those who receive property applied in breach of trust

The introduction which was made to the two species of stranger liability for breach of trust suggested that there was considerable uncertainty in English law relating to what is required for a stranger who receives trust property to be a 'knowing receiver' and in current parlance capable of incurring liability as such. The materials which follow consider the current position, and the way in which the key Court of Appeal decision in *BCCI (Overseas) Ltd v Akindele* [2000] 3 WLR 1423 has helped to shape the current parameters for this species of liability.

Clearly influenced by the approach taken in *Royal Brunei Airlines v Tan*, *Akindele* did provide good cause for some optimism in 2000 when it was suggested by Nourse LJ that a 'single test of dishonesty for knowing assistance'did now subsist', and thus there ought 'to be a single test of knowledge for knowing receipt'. While the Court of Appeal in 2000 was clearly blissfully unaware of the issues which would be raised in applying *Royal Brunei Airlines v Tan* in *Twinsectra* and then *Barlow Clowes*—and indeed subsequently, *Akindele* did seek to provide some resolution. By finding reference in the case of *Re Montagu's ST* [1987] Ch 264 (described as the 'seminal judgment') to its test of 'want of probity', it was held that dishonesty was not a requirement for incurring liability for knowing receipt. Instead what is required is that '[t]he recipient's state of knowledge must be such as to make it unconscionable for him to retain the benefit of the receipt'. This was considered to avoid difficulties of definition and allocation found in earlier categorisations, such as those in *Baden Delvaux* (which was in any event a case concerning knowing assistance).

What remained unclear after *Akindele* was what the difference between dishonesty and unconscionability actually amounted to, and some clarification was provided by the Court of Appeal in *Criterion Properties plc v Stratford UK Properties LLC* [2003] 1 WLR 2108. According to this decision from the Court of Appeal, the question of unconscionability could not simply be answered by considering whether or not there was actual knowledge of the circumstances giving rise to the breach of duty. However, when that case was heard by the House of Lords, it was decided that neither it, nor *Akindele* itself, were truly concerned with knowing receipt, and although this suggested that there would once again be considerable uncertainty, in *City Index Ltd v Gawler* [2007] EWCA Civ 1382, it was accepted *Akindele* 'represents the present law'.

In between these happenings, *Twinsectra* v *Yardley* was heard in the House of Lords, and parts of this judgment concerned a discussion of knowing receipt, notwithstanding that the case was most prominently concerned with accessory liability. Indeed, the consideration given to knowing receipt arose in many ways because of the significance of accessory liability. This was because in framing the claim in question as one of assistance, Lord Millett explained why knowing receipt was not the appropriate basis for recovering sums from payments made to him in costs:

Mr Leach received sums totalling £22,000 in payment of his costs for his own use and benefit...But he did not receive the rest of the money for his own benefit at all. He never regarded himself as beneficially entitled to the money. He held it to Mr Yardley's order and paid it out to Mr Yardley or his companies. Twinsectra cannot and does not base its claim in respect of these moneys in knowing receipt, not for want of knowledge, but for want of the necessary receipt. It sues in respect of knowing (or dishonest) assistance.

The majority view insisted that for liability as constructive trustee in respect of trust property to arise, there must be fault on the part of the recipient. Indeed, this position of a requirement of fault is consistent with the authority provided by Lord Browne-Wilkinson in the House of Lords' landmark judgment in *Westdeutsche* that 'unless [the recipient of the trust property in question] has the requisite degree of knowledge he is not personally liable to account as trustee'. And, cases such as *Re Montagu's ST* and *Baden* as well as *Westdeutsche* stand as authority that what has occupied the courts' time is not discussion over the presence or absence of fault, but instead compositions of appropriate degrees of fault.

However, in his dissenting judgment in *Twinsectra*, Lord Millett took a very different approach, and his submission was based on making the case for 'no-fault strict liability' constructive trusteeship. This was because, in his Lordship's view:

Liability for 'knowing receipt' is receipt-based. It does not depend on fault. The cause of action is restitutionary and is available only where the defendant received or applied the money in breach of trust for his own use and benefit. There is no basis for requiring actual knowledge of the breach of trust, let alone dishonesty, as a condition of liability. Constructive notice is sufficient, and may not even be necessary. There is powerful academic support for the proposition that the liability of the recipient is the same as in other cases of restitution, that is to say strict but subject to a change of position defence.

19.8.3.1 *A continuing role for the requirement of 'fault'*

Notwithstanding the considerable academic support which Lord Millett claims exists in respect of his position, the decision of his Brethren in *Twinsectra* illustrates that English law does not at present accept that a stranger can incur 'strict liability' as a recipient of trust property, and fault-based liability (in equity) founded in the principles of constructive trusteeship remains central to the area of stranger liability. The way in which there remains contention as to the degree of knowledge which is required before a stranger to a trust can incur liability for the receipt of trust property is also evident in the approach taken by Nourse LJ in *Akindele* [2001] Ch 437, which is where this discussion actually started. Nourse LJ proposed that a recipient's state of knowledge must be such as to make it 'unconscionable for him to retain the benefit of the receipt'. The recent affirmation in *City Index Ltd* v *Gawler* that *Akindele* is good law is a powerful argument against the greater utilisation of no-fault restitutionary claims. This is because in *Akindele* itself, Nourse LJ explained that it was doubtful whether strict liability coupled with a change of position defence 'would be preferable to fault-based liability in many commercial transactions'.

However, it is also the case that liability for knowing receipt and dealing is based on unjust enrichment in some jurisdictions (such as New Zealand), and thus the state of mind of the recipient is not relevant for securing liability. In addition to this, and as the closing sections of this chapter will support, there is considerable academic opinion in support of recipient liability being receipt-based rather than fault-based. Certainly Lord Millett's views in *Twinsectra* have limited support in the leading case law, and *Akindele*—the case where this discussion on recipient liability started—suggests strongly against it. However, in *Charter plc* v *City Index Ltd* [2007] 1 WLR 26, while it was accepted that *Akindele* was good law, there was also the suggestion that 'knowing receipt' may also be described as 'restitutionary'.

19.9 **The personal action in *Diplock***

Reference has already been made to *Re Diplock's Estate* [1948] Ch 465, which concerned actions brought by the next of kin of testator Caleb Diplock in respect of money paid out by mistake of law (this created a valid charitable gift, for the reasons considered in chapter 13, to various charities; see reference to *Chichester Diocesan Fund and Board of Finance* v *Simpson* [1944] AC 341). The next of kin, having exhausted their remedy against the executors, successfully recovered money from the various charities. As well as the proprietary claim which succeeded, the next of kin also succeeded by way of a personal claim against the charities to which the money had been paid out.

In common with the common law action for money had and received, this personal claim against the charities arose upon their receipt of the property applied mistakenly. Unlike knowing receipt, however, liability was strict, evidenced by the way in which the defendants were innocent volunteers who took in good faith with no notice of the next of kin's title. This personal equitable action affirmed in *Re Diplock* appears to apply only to volunteers, but according to *Re Montagu's ST* [1987] Ch 264 it does not appear to apply to all volunteers. If this is correct then this raises issues about both its scope and its limits.

In *Diplock*, the executors had made the payments to the charities under a mistake of law. The charities unsuccessfully argued that the personal action was limited to payments made under a mistake of fact (on analogy with the common law money had and received action) where the administration of the estate had been made by the direction of the court. It is arguable that the action applies only to the administration of estates, but it seems more probable that it applies generally against volunteers. There is a requirement, however, that remedies against the wrongdoers (in this case the executors) should be exhausted first, which is presumably why no *Diplock*-based personal action was brought in *Montagu*. It is also possible (but not certain) that the change of position defence in *Lipkin Gorman* v *Karpnale Ltd*

[1991] 2 AC 548 applies also to this equitable action. However, as indicated earlier, *Campden Hill Ltd* v *Chakrani* [2005] EWHC 911 (Ch) is authority that this proposition is contentious and uncertain.

19.10 Proprietary entitlement, restitution, and the current 'state of play'

Given the context that where trust property 'goes missing', it will often end up in the 'wrong hands,' much of considering the actions available to a beneficiary concerns how a person who *receives* the property can be liable to the beneficiary. Property wrongfully received in this way may either be retained by the recipient, or passed onto another, and from the mid 1990s onwards questions of liability became dominated by considerable disagreement as to whether the basis for the beneficiary's recovery of (wrongfully applied trust) property should be restitutionary (and thus based on 'unjust enrichment principles'), or based on 'proprietary entitlement'. By way of reiteration:

• Where liability is restitutionary, it is said that liability arises because the recipient is unjustly enriched at the rightful owner's expense (in this case the rightful owner is the beneficiary).

• Where liability is based on 'proprietary entitlement' it is said to arise because the recipient of wrongfully applied property has interfered with the owner's (the beneficiary's) property rights attaching to the property.

Most recently *Foskett v McKowen* is authority for a triumph of 'proprietary entitlement' principles in 'tracing' cases. This is a central development on account that applying these different approaches can lead to very different outcomes in terms of what can be recovered by the beneficiary, and the way in which these can be seen as representing different degrees of fairness and appropriateness from the perspective of a liable recipient and also an owner wrongfully parted from his property. Here the favour shown by the courts for principles of 'proprietary entitlement' does in many ways mark a full circle back to where this text commenced—the importance of property, and particularly the *ownership* of property in English law.

A very good analysis of the triumph of proprietary entitlement in the context of tracing can be found in Tang Hang Wu [2001], Melbourne University Law Review, 8, but it is also the case that these issues of the basis of liability can be seen in recent developments in the personal remedies which attach to the receipt of trust property, and particularly considerations of whether equity's remedy for 'knowing receipt' should evolve to be more like the common law action for money had and received which is very effective. Indeed, in *Adnan Shaaban Abou Rahmah v Al-Haji Abdul Kadir Abacha* [2006] Rix LJ suggested the courts (still) consider that this area of law is 'in flux or at any rate subject to a process of analytical change'.

In assessing whether the law should develop in such a way, it *is* the case that the precise scope of the change of position defence in the common law action is unclear. However some clarity is evident form recent decisions in *Niru Battery Manufacturing Co v Milestone Trading Ltd* [2004] 2 WLR 1415, *Barros Mattos Junior* v *MacDaniels Ltd* [2005] 1 WLR 247, and *Adnan Shaaban Abou Rahmah* v *Al-Haji Abdul Kadir Abacha* clustering around change in position defence. In *Niru Battery*, it was held that in order to defeat the defence of change of position, it did not have to be shown that the recipient had been dishonest, rather that what needed to be shown was that he had not acted in good faith; and that a person who had or thought that he had good reason to believe that a payment had been made to him by mistake failed to act in good faith if he paid the money away without making enquiries of the payer. It was held in *Barros Mattos Junior* that an innocent recipient of stolen money could not rely upon the defence of change of position where the circumstances in which this arose were considered to be wrongful: this meant that in the case the defendants were not able to rely on foreign exchange transactions which were illegal under Nigerian law, and accordingly the defence failed. In *Adnan Shaaban Abou Rahmah* v *Al-Haji Abdul Kadir Abacha*, attention was drawn to the significance of whether the conduct was considered to be 'commercially acceptable', but it was also considered (by the majority) that a general suspicion of involvement in a money-laundering scheme was not sufficient, and that there must have been particular suspicions about the two payments in question.

In terms of the significance of this for the effectiveness of common law, it has been argued (see Martin, 'Recipient Liability after *Westdeutsche*' (1998) Conveyancer 13) that equity too should provide a personal action based on the same principles. Furthermore, it is clear from *Kleinwort Benson Ltd* v *Lincoln City Council* [1998] 3 WLR 1095 that the scope of restitutionary actions has also now been extended to cover situations in which money is paid over under a mistake of law, as well as to those in which money is paid over under a mistake of fact, where it has traditionally been recognised.

 online resource centre

FURTHER READING

Andrews 'The Redundancy of Dishonest Assistance' (2003) Conveyancer 399.

Birks 'Property and Unjust Enrichment: Categorical Truths' (1997) New Zealand Law Review 623.

Ingman and Wakefield 'Equitable Damages and Lord Cairns' Act' (1981) Coveyancer 286.

Lowrie and Todd 'In Defence of the North American Rolling Charge' (1997) Denning Law Journal 43.

Martin 'Recipient Liability after *Westdeutsche*' (1998) Conveyancer 13.

Millett 'Tracing the Proceeds of Fraud' (1991) Law Quarterly Review 77.

Millett 'Restitution and Constructive Trusts' in Cornish et al (eds) *Restitution Past, Present and Future: Essays in Honour of Gareth Jones* (Oxford: Hart Publishing, 1998).

Ryan '*Royal Brunei* Dishonesty: Clarity at Last' (2006) Conveyancer 188.

Stevens 'Vindicating the proprietary nature of tracing' (2001) Conveyancer 94.

Tang Hang Wu (2001) '*Fosketl* v *McKeown*: Hardnosed property rights or impisit enrichment?' Melbourne University Law Review, 8.

Thompson 'Criminal Law and Property Law: An Unhappy Combination' (2002) Conveyancer 387.

INDEX